Real-World Decision
with DMN

"This comprehensive and incredibly useful book offers a wealth of practical advice to anyone interested in decision management and its potential to improve enterprise applications. Using a blend of user case studies, patterns, best practices and pragmatic techniques, "Real-World Decision Modeling with DMN" shows you how to discover, model, analyze and design the critical decisions that drive your business!"
—**David Herring**, Manager of BPM & ODM Delivery at Kaiser Permanente.

"Well written and very impressive in its scope."
—**Alan Fish**, Principal Consultant, Decision Solutions, FICO and author of "Knowledge Automation: How to Implement Decision Management in Business Processes".

"If you are looking for a complete treatise on decisions, look no further. Even though you end up in decision modeling and Decision Modeling Notation (DMN), you are treated to all the aspects of decisions explained with great care and clarity. This is a greatly needed book that will be studied by decision managers and practitioners for the next decade or more. It will end up on my physical and logical bookshelves."
—**Jim Sinur**, Vice President and Research Fellow, Aragon Research.

"Written by two of the foremost experts in decision management, this book provides an extensive exploration of business decisions and how they are used in modern digital organizations. Taylor and Purchase distill for us the why, how, when and where to apply decision modeling in order to specify business decisions that are effective. Going beyond just an introduction to the Decision Model and Notation (DMN), the authors position this standard with respect to other well established standard notations such as BPMN. This is truly a first comprehensive handbook of decision management."
—**Denis Gagne**, Chair of BPMN MIWG, CEO & CTO at Trisotech.

"This book contains a wealth of knowledge and brings together the expertise of two decision management & modeling authorities. It is written by and for professionals, and I particularly like the numerous real-world experiences, best practices, misconceptions, patterns and business examples.
At the same time, because the Decision Model and Notation (DMN) standard is used throughout the book, it is also a full and readable description of all aspects of the standard, from the business value, the business context, the decision requirements level, all the way to FEEL and decision tables (a part which I read with specific care). All well elaborated and clearly explained. A must read."
—**Jan Vanthienen**, Professor of Information Management, Business Information Systems Group, KU Leuven (Belgium), Pioneer of Decision Table Theory and Long Term Contributor to Business Rules, Decisions, Validation and Verification Research.

Real-World Decision Modeling with DMN

James Taylor
&
Jan Purchase

Meghan-Kiffer Press
Tampa, Florida, USA, www.mkpress.com
Visit our Web site to see all our specialty books focused on
Innovation at the Intersection of Business and Technology
www.mkpress.com

ISBN 0-929652-59-2 ISBN 13: 978-0-929652-59-7
Published by Meghan-Kiffer Press
310 East Fern Street — Suite G
Tampa, FL 33604 USA

Company and product names mentioned herein are the trademarks or registered trademarks of their respective owners.

Meghan-Kiffer books are available at special quantity discounts for corporate education and training use. For more information write Special Sales, Meghan-Kiffer Press, 310 East Fern Street, Tampa, Florida 33604 or (813) 251-5531 or email info@mkpress.com

Meghan-Kiffer Press
Tampa, Florida, USA
Innovation at the Intersection of Business and Technology

Printed in the United States of America.   SAN 249-7980
MK Printing 10 9 8 7 6 5 4 3 2 1

Contents

Detailed Contents

Index of Best Practices

Two chapters, 14 and 15, contain a set of best practices. To make it easier to find these best practices when using this book as a reference the table below categorizes them.

Best Practice	Decision Requirements	Decision Logic Design	Decision Model	Decision Logic Format	Data and Glossary	Decision	Business Context	Section #
Make decision models self-contained	▓		▓		▓			14.8.5
Consider refactoring when you make changes	▓		▓					15.3.5
Do not assign multiple jobs to a single Decision Table	▓		▓					14.5.3
Eliminate sequence	▓							14.8.4
Seek out reuse within and across models	▓							14.8.1
Use Business Knowledge Models only when necessary		▓						15.2.2
Maintain the integrity of Information Requirements	▓		▓		▓			14.8.3
Decompose decisions until they rely on separate Input Data and Knowledge Sources			▓					14.3.1
Use order to aid readability				▓				15.3.1
Consider Knowledge Sources that have Input Data as authorities					▓			15.2.5
Associate Knowledge Sources with the lowest level decision						▓		14.3.4
Use business oriented names for decision model components						▓		14.2.4
Decompose decisions before deciding on automation							▓	14.2.6
Document constraints and authorities with Knowledge Sources							▓	14.3.3
Assess decision models for analytic authorities	▓							15.2.4
Assess Input Data to see if it is really a decision outcome	▓							15.2.3
Clarify Decision Requirement Diagrams with annotations	▓							14.3.6
Clarify meaning with spatial layout	▓							14.3.5
Document hierarchical Knowledge Sources	▓							15.2.1
Model decision feedback loops	▓							15.2.6
Represent multiple perspectives using multiple diagrams	▓							14.3.2

Best Practice	Decision Requirements	Decision Logic Design	Decision Model	Decision Logic Format	Data and Glossary	Decision	Business Context	Section #
Remember not all decisions have decision logic		■	■			■		14.4.1
Only use boxed expressions as a last resort		■		■				14.6.2
Refactor Decision Tables to keep them as small as possible		■						14.5.6
Select an appropriate format for logic		■						14.4.4
Only classify data with property flags when they are independent		■			■			14.7.6
Use enumerations not strings		■			■			14.7.1
Avoid redundant inputs		■						14.4.2
Be explicit about failure modes		■						14.5.5
Ensure Decision Tables cover all logical possibilities		■						14.5.4
Keep inputs logically independent		■						15.3.2
Keep multiple conclusions cohesive but independent		■						15.3.4
Only use rule order dependent hit policies in appropriate situations		■						15.3.3
Use only Unique, Any and Collect hit policies		■						14.5.2
Separate preparation, validation and business decisions			■		■		■	14.8.2
Consider the boundary conditions of data			■		■			14.7.4
Don't neglect unstructured Input Data			■					14.7.2
Split up large Input Data objects			■					14.7.5
Adopt a consistent Decision Table format				■				14.5.1
Avoid confusion with ranges				■				14.6.1
Express decision logic in a format inspired by existing business policy statements				■				14.4.3
Use rule level annotation of rationale				■				14.5.7
Carefully consider placement of business data constraints					■			14.7.3
Align models to business goals and KPIs						■	■	14.2.3
Specify a main owner for all decisions						■	■	14.2.2
Capture decision properties						■		14.2.5
When designing decisions, focus on questions and answers						■		14.2.1

Foreword

Decisions, decisions. Do I buy this book, or move down the line to some other tome on decision-making, or just chuck it all and go get a latte? Every decision is a trade-off of resources—time, space, cost—and return—time, space, money. Many decisions are trivial (e.g., the aforementioned latte!), but the other end of the spectrum harbors life and death decisions. Even those, however, are tradeoffs, though generally with rather nonlinear results. The "seat of the pants" are far too often the center of the decision-making process, but as more data becomes available and processing power enables dealing with the available flow of data, managers' excuses for ad hoc decision-making are less and less viable.

And a flood of data is in fact infecting the world. Turning that flood of data into information, and that information into informed decisions -- in real-time -- is becoming harder and harder, and more and more important. The advent of the Internet of Things means not only a better-metered world, but an inundation of content the likes of which the world has never seen before. Estimates of connected devices on the worldwide Internet range into the hundreds of billions by the year 2025 (consider that the number of people on planet Earth in the same time range will still only be in the billions); each of those little devices pumping out data will certainly amount to more than even Noah could handle.

The only viable approach to solving this problem—the dove bearing an olive leaf—will be automation. The good news is that modern computing infrastructure is up to the task. An unheard-of convergence of forces implies that viability: computing speeds literally four orders of magnitude greater than in the 1960's, a level of connectivity ubiquity no-one foresaw in even 1990 due to the popularity of the World-Wide Web (and the attendant growth of the Internet beneath it), and plummeting costs for all that compute power, connectivity, and even storage. The move to cloud computing, along with widely available open source software, even allows an approach to computing that tears away initial cost and allows data manipulation to be within reach to anyone, everywhere.

The missing link connecting that dove to that ark is, of course, a consistent and pragmatic approach to defining and carrying out that decision-making automation. That link is an international standard for defining operational decision processes, the Object Management Group's Decision Management Notation (DMN). DMN is not so much a process for defining decisions, but rather a modeling language for capturing the design of decision processes. Operational decisions can always be defined in terms of inputs (the current operational situation) and outputs (the wished-for outcome), and the DMN language allows non-programmers to capture that model in a well-defined—and automatable—notation.

The power of shared and standardized notation is frequently not fully appreciated, but consider the role of shared world languages (the lingua franca of medieval Europe, a French/Latin amalgam; or even the Bad English of the modern world). Shared notations knit together organizations, companies, peoples, communities and countries; they decrease costs (consistent and shared tools; lower training costs; portable and reusable designs). They bring about higher productivity and lower costs, and standards of practice in the automation field even decrease switching costs (often to zero), allowing a choice of implementations based on price, support and feature lists.

That's what you hold in your hand -- a disciplined approach to decision-making based around the DMN. That is, not a book just about the technology of DMN, but a way to think about decision-making as a management discipline, preparing for automation of decisions in the face of the data onslaught. Decisions, decisions. This book is an important step forward to moving decision making away from the seat of the pants.

Richard Mark Soley, Ph.D.
Chairman and Chief Executive Officer
Object Management Group, Inc.
27 September 2016

Preface

It has been 14 or more years since I first used the phrase "Decision Management" to describe the use of technology for the systematic identification, automation and improvement of operational business decisions. At the heart of any successful Decision Management project is a clear and thorough understanding of the decisions involved. The advent of the Decision Model and Notation (DMN) standard has given us an industry standard way to model decisions using proven techniques and approaches. Decision modeling with DMN is a powerful, real-world approach to unambiguously describe decision-making, specify analytic requirements and develop decision logic—business rules.

This book is not just a description of the standard and the notation, but a distillation of many hard-earned lessons from real projects. Jan and I bring different perspectives having worked on different kind of projects. As we brought this experience together it became clear that we shared a common approach and agreed on a wide ranging set of best practices. This book is the result.

James Taylor
Palo Alto, California
james@decisionmanagementsolutions.com

All elegant and empowering innovations—for example, the wheel, the jet-engine, the printing press and the internet—have one thing in common: after they are adopted, it becomes hard to imagine what the world would be like without them. We make no lesser claim for Decision Management and Decision Modeling. Once organizations routinely and consciously capture, manage, improve and are able to justify their key decisions, they will wonder how automated systems ever evolved without this facility. Furthermore, as laws such as the European General Data Protection Regulation (GDPR) and industry compliance legislation insist with increasing force that all automated systems must be capable of comprehensively explaining their behavior after the fact, there will be an ever increasing legal requirement for a more rigorous approach to automated decision-making. The increasing use of machine learning in automation will also increase the need for regimented governance of decisions and the ability to explain counterintuitive decision outcomes—both use cases for decision modeling.

Like James, I have seen Decision Modeling transform the way organizations run their businesses and give their subject matter experts a truly effective means of communicating their ideas. Our goal for this book has been to present the case for decision modeling and bring the benefits of this simple idea to new organizations.

Jan Purchase
London, United Kingdom
purchase@luxmagi.com

Acknowledgements

The authors would like to acknowledge the assistance of many in the industry who shared their experiences with us, provided inspiration, answered questions, reviewed the manuscript or otherwise allowed us to stand on their shoulders as we wrote the book. Any remaining errors are, of course, our own. Some of those acknowledged below have published books and papers that are listed in Appendix A.

Many thanks to Dan Binney, Nick Broom, Scott Broomfield, Geoff Chapman, Jolyon Cox, Nigel Crowther, Jacob Feldman, Alan Fish, Denis Gagne, Gary Hallmark, David Herring, Jean-Christophe Jardinier, Henk Jonkers, Olena Karazieieva, Robert von Kaufmann, Siamak Masnavi, Don Perkins, Justin Phillips, Juergen Pitschke, Andrew Ray, Gil Ronen, Sjoerd Ronner, Gil Segal, Odd Stein and Jan Vanthienen.

Our special thanks to David Petchey and Gagan Saxena for substantial contributions to early versions of the manuscript and their diligent contributions to the review process.

To my family, as always
(James Taylor)

To Diane and Miranda for laughter, love, constancy and perspective.
(Jan Purchase)

1 Why Write This Book?

Because it's there
— George Mallory, British Mountaineer, when asked why he wanted to climb Mount Everest.

It's interesting to consider one's motivation when writing a book. Mallory's quote resonates because, by the time you have written over 100,000 words it seems somehow impossible not to have done so. Nevertheless, some justification seems in order along with some transparency as to our intent, our motivation and our goals.

The title of this book is "Real-World Decision Modeling with DMN". This title reveals three key things about the book:

- It is about decision modeling and intended to help readers master this powerful technique and understand where it is most appropriate.
- It uses the Decision Model and Notation (DMN) standard as a vehicle to illustrate best practices in decision modeling.
- It is based on real-world experience of applying decision modeling to business problems.

Each element of the title illustrates a part of why we wrote this book.

1.1 Unleashing the Power of Decision Modeling

Decision Modeling is a way of unambiguously expressing the decisions organizations make every day. These decisions involve making a choice or determination as part of business operations. These decisions may be repeated many times a day, a hour or a second, determining how an organization will conduct its business, interact with its customers, manage its supply chain, meet regulatory demands and much more. It might be deciding if a loan application should be accepted, directing a web query to the right content, working out the most appropriate set of products for each customer or determining how to process an insurance claim: whether to accept, reject or refer it to a claims assessor. Each such decision selects from a number of possible outcomes based on a set of inputs. These decisions are repeatable, have business value and impact how an organization is perceived by its clients and business partners. They may be made by people, by a system or by some combination.

Decision modeling captures the questions these decisions pose and the answers that are possible. It documents the information they rely on and how they are influenced by company policies, external regulations and local expertise. Decision modeling focuses on the structure of decisions and the dependencies between decisions, sub-decisions, data and knowledge. This results in a thorough and precise definition of decision-making and one that allows the impact of any proposed change to be quickly assessed. It can also capture the business logic that underpins these decisions so you can completely represent their structure and meaning.

Decision Modeling offers a common language for describing decisions so that organizations can systematically document how they intend to make decisions, understand them better and continuously improve them.

Decision Modeling can be used to quickly determine the requirements of a decision and reveal gaps or flaws in an organization's approach or understanding. The technique brings clarity and transparency, shining a spotlight on business decisions by making decision-making more explicit, more thoroughly documented and more streamlined.

Decision modeling separates decision-making from business processes and information systems. This separation improves business processes and systems by ensuring they are kept free from the bloat of decision logic.

Decision Modeling is a powerful technique that has yet to be widely adopted. By writing a book aimed at practitioners we hope to increase adoption and bring this technique into the mainstream of business analysis, requirements modeling and business architecture.

1.2 Expressing Decision Modeling Best Practices Using Decision Model and Notation (DMN)

There are many ways to model decisions but a standard notation promotes collaboration, reduces misunderstandings and helps eliminate ambiguities. A standard approach to decision modeling improves consistency and allows the results to be effectively shared with others.

DMN—Decision Model and Notation—is a standard, precise means of representing and communicating how to make a business decision. DMN is the best approach to Decision Modeling available today.

- It has been developed by a group of companies with a great deal of expertise. The vendor team behind the DMN specification includes Decision Management Solutions, Fair Isaac Corporation (FICO), IBM, Knowledge Partners International, Oracle and TIBCO Software Inc. among others. As a result, the standard is forged from a tremendous amount of industry experience.

- It is an open standard, not one owned by a specific vendor or subject to restricted distribution. This makes it easier to learn from other organizations as open standards tend to get broader adoption. The support available from tools, published materials and the practitioner community is often higher for open standards. Openness also promotes innovation.

- DMN is defined, ratified and freely published by the Object Management Group (OMG). The OMG is an international, not-for-profit, technology standards consortium specializing in standard notations used by businesses. They are responsible for standards like the Unified Modeling Language (UML) and the Business Process Model and Notation (BPMN) that are very widely used.

- DMN is the richest standard available: it documents the dependencies decisions have on supplied data, external regulations and local expertise. In addition to defining the logic of decisions using Decision Tables, it supports analytic models and many other representations.

However, DMN is not a complete approach. It's a notation: a way of representing and exchanging decision models. It describes formal and precise ways that certain things can and should be represented. It does not explain *how* you should develop decision models. It does not document a methodology or best practices; it does not describe patterns or provide many examples and it does not describe how to integrate decision models with other models you are developing. This book is designed to fill these needs.

Basing the book on DMN future-proofs the advice in it and ensures that the models it describes can be read by anyone familiar with the standard. By presenting a discussion of DMN aimed at business analysts and business subject matter experts, the book can replace the OMG DMN Specification Document for these audiences. The DMN specification is, by its nature, a formal and precise document aimed at those who might implement software to support DMN. It contains a lot of technical detail about metamodels, compliance and a formal grammar and is ill suited to a business audience. In contrast, this book focuses on how to use DMN to build effective decision models and is aimed at practitioners.

1.3 Conveying Real-World Experience of Decision Modeling

This book is about decision modeling in the real-world. It's not a book about the DMN standard, although you can learn most of DMN by reading it. It's not a comparison of the DMN standard to other decision modeling approaches, although it offers best practices to practitioners of other standards transitioning to DMN. It's not a theoretical guide to how you might build a decision model. It's a practical guide to using decision modeling based on dozens of real-world projects and training hundreds of people how to model decisions and use DMN.

To this end it combines several elements:

- It provides a definition of DMN, and decision modeling as an approach, based on experience with teaching and working with business analysts and business subject matter experts on real projects. As a result, technical details and clever tricks are always secondary to effective communication through simplicity.
- It shows how decision modeling interfaces with business process, architecture, data and motivation in real organizations.
- It explains why and when to use decision modeling, illustrating the practical value of the approach and best practices through multiple examples based on the authors' experience as well as that of many others.
- It includes recommended techniques for decision discovery and analysis and a proven framework for integrating decision modeling into an overall Decision Management effort.
- It documents details of DMN patterns: combinations of techniques for problems that frequently appear in projects

By focusing on the overall approach and the use of the approach on real projects, not narrowly on the standard, the book can help practitioners maximize the benefit of using the standard and avoid common pitfalls.

2 This Book In Context

Always design a thing by considering it in its next larger context
— Eliel Saarinen.

This book focuses on decision modeling as a core technique for success in Decision Management and the effective use of business rules and Business Rules Management Systems (BRMSs) in specifying decision-making systems. It has examples and best practices pertinent to this focus. The Decision Management market is estimated by IDC to have a value exceeding $10bn[1]. This market builds on long established technologies (business rules, business analytics, business processes, business events), several of which are rapid growth markets. The number of vendors explicitly participating in the market is growing every month and research analyst firms such as Gartner Group have identified Decision Management and optimization as the key elements of moving from predictive analytics to the more effective and higher ROI prescriptive analytics that are now the objective of organizations adopting analytics.

The goal of this book is to illustrate how a decision modeler can build consistent and effective models of business decisions using the Decision Model and Notation (DMN) standard. It is especially aimed at business subject matter experts with little knowledge of IT and a need to capture and communicate business decisions and their logic—a very important group of people because they are the real users of DMN.

The DMN specification, in contrast, is a technical document released by the OMG for the benefit of tool vendors and implementers. With its focus on formal grammar and metamodels, it is of limited use to non-technical decision modelers. This book aims to replace the DMN specification as the primary DMN reference for business decision modelers. It provides best practices, advice, patterns, examples and discussions of additional modeling considerations which have been (rightly) omitted from the specification.

This book is no substitute for the specification when seeking definitive answers to technical questions concerning the grammar, compliance levels, metamodel and interchange format of DMN (see Appendix A). Readers should always consult the latest version of the DMN specification when these are required. Wherever possible we have kept the content of this book consistent with the standard and indicated clearly any material that is outside or contrary to it.

In order to explain some concepts of decision modeling more effectively to those unfamiliar with IT terms, this book has replaced some of the more idiosyncratic DMN terminology with more business friendly terms. This substitution has only been used where the authors felt that terms used in the DMN specification might be obscure or misleading to the target audience. This is intended to aid effective communication of the standard and how it

---

[1] IDC MarketScape Worldwide Decision Management Software Platform 2014 Vendor Assessment (doc #250351, September 2014).

is used. A complete mapping of this book's terminology to the DMN standard terms can be found in Appendix A.

Decision Modeling is also rapidly establishing itself in adjacent markets. In the data mining and predictive analytic markets, the need for more effective requirements and for additional ways to bring non data-scientists into analytic projects is increasingly clear. Widely used methodologies such as CRISP-DM identify the need for "business understanding" but don't really explain how to develop this. Several organizations have recognized decision modeling as an ideal approach for this and one of the authors is publishing work on this for the International Institute for Analytics, led by Tom Davenport.

Beyond data mining and advanced analytics, all business analytics whether reporting, dashboards or visualization are focused on improving decision-making. Despite the huge amount of money spent on these technologies many companies find that their decision-making is no better. Some more rigorous way to model the decision-making itself is increasingly required.

In the business process and case management markets there is a growing recognition that identifying and modeling the decisions required by business processes and case management environments makes them simpler, easier to manage and change, while also improving their effectiveness in terms of straight through processing. Leading experts in the process management space, as well as several software vendors, are identifying decision modeling with the new DMN standard as a critical need for process management.

To effectively target all these markets with a single book would be unrealistic as, while the underlying techniques are the same, the way the driving business problems are stated is quite different and different examples would be called for. This book is focused on business logic and business rules because this is the most mature use case and the one in which there is significant prior art.

This book touches on some of these adjacencies, providing some guidance on using decision modeling as part of an overall business architecture as well as discussing the role of decision modeling in analytics and its integration with process modeling. A detailed description of using decision modeling to frame and specify business analytics is beyond its scope; as is a detailed description of decision modeling as part of an overall business architecture approach that links DMN to BPMN, UML, TOGAF, Zachman and more. These areas require additional books.

3 Who Should Read This Book

Tis the good reader that makes the good book
—Ralph Waldo Emerson

This book is designed to help everyone who wants to understand and improve how their organization makes business decisions. However, these aims are multi-faceted and important to many different audiences for varied reasons. To guide readers, this chapter:

- Explains the intended audiences through a discussion of the challenges addressed by the book;
- Distinguishes different readerships based on the questions they have and illustrates which subsets of the work are most relevant to each;
- Includes a visual representation of the chapters and their relevance to various project roles *and*
- Describes the assumptions the authors have made about readers' experience and background.

3.1 Intended Audience

3.1.1 The Challenge

Many businesses today are engaged in a struggle to improve the agility, transparency, consistency and effectiveness of their most important and differentiating asset—their business decisions. Decisions are determinations made repeatedly by organizations during their business operations; some are made thousands of times per minute. They are important: they have business value; they require expertise to make and this expertise must not be lost; they must be made consistently; they must be transparent and they may need 'after-the-fact' justification. Many professionals are striving to understand, articulate and improve the complex business decisions that steer their organization's main processes. They are finding it hard to mine this valuable insight from various sources ranging from the heads of expert staff members who may leave at any moment to the opaque code of legacy systems, the verbosity and complexity of policy documents to the confusion of ad-hoc, incomprehensible spreadsheets. The livelihoods of many people and the success of most organizations depend on how thoroughly these decisions are understood and to what extent they can be continuously improved.

3.1.2 How This Book Can Help

This book will equip you, and the people you work with, to meet this challenge and do your job more effectively by showing you how to describe business decisions precisely and unambiguously. This book can show you how to reliably and accurately communicate decision-making strategies with colleagues across a global enterprise or bridge the gap between business experts and IT.

This book can help you eliminate ambiguity in your organization's policies, understand complex written documentation and resolve the inconsistencies resulting from how policy is applied to your company's manual and automated processes.

3.1.3   The Target Audience

This book is aimed at everyone engaged in this challenge. It will teach you how to do all of the things discussed above more effectively. The wealth of practical advice in this text will make you more effective, whether you are:

- A business analyst or business subject matter expert who needs to capture, describe, review and consolidate this decision-making;
- A program or project manager responsible for efforts to automate and improve decisions;
- An architect or developer working to implement these decisions and integrate the resulting decision services into existing service based architectures *or*
- A business strategist looking to understand and innovate decision-making to outperform a competitor or satisfy a regulatory mandate.

This book intends to help both the business and IT communities and aims to improve their collaboration through unambiguous representation of decisions. How well and how consistently decisions are made contributes to the profitability, client reputation and competitiveness of the organization that makes them. Decisions can also be an obligation as companies may have their decisions audited or have to demonstrate that they comply with externally defined, regulations. Competitive and regulatory pressures mean decisions need to be implemented accurately and regularly challenged and improved, requiring that they be widely understood. For these reasons, and others, decisions need to be explicitly captured and managed. This important task cannot be left to IT alone; it must be a joint effort between IT and the business.

3.2   How to Read This Book

This book can be loosely broken into four main sections:

- **Why**, explaining the rationale for decision modeling (chapters 4, 5, 6);
- **What**, explaining the mechanics of decision modeling (chapters 8, 9, 11);
- **Where**, explaining the context of decision modeling within an organization and its architecture (chapters 7, 10) *and*
- **How**, explaining the best approach to decision modeling (chapters 12-18).

Therefore, any reader already convinced by the value proposition of decision modeling and desiring to learn the mechanics should proceed directly to Chapter 8.

Readers with insufficient time to read the whole book can also be guided by the questions they have concerning decision modeling. The following sections outline a set of complementary, and overlapping, reading plans based on questions.

3.2.1 What are decisions and why should my company model them?

Those seeking an understanding of decision management and modeling as well as the value proposition they have for any business—that is virtually every reader of this book—should consult Chapters 4 and 5. These chapters are also relevant for those trying to motivate others (perhaps their boss) to use the technique.

Chapter 4 covers a brief definition of decisions, Decision Modeling and its relationship with Decision Management and Decision Management Systems, before focusing on the business benefit of these approaches. This is aimed at readers unfamiliar with these concepts and their business benefits.

Chapter 5 describes the anatomy of a business decision, including how they are defined and the context in which they are made. It then analyzes when decision modeling is most effective, how to select business decisions that will benefit most from the technique and how to initiate a decision modeling pilot in your organization. This is aimed at readers who need to kick-start the use of decision modeling within their organization.

3.2.2 How can my team get started with decision modeling on a project?

Managers and practitioners who wish to understand how to get started with decision modeling, how decisions fit within their organization and how decision modeling projects should be run should read chapters 5, 6, 7, 9, 12 and 18.

Chapter 5 describes the conditions in which decision modeling is most effective—this will help readers to target their application of this powerful technique. Chapter 6 explains why you should adopt a standard notation for decision modeling and summarizes the structure of the Decision Model and Notation (DMN) standard. A more detailed explanation of DMN is pursued in other chapters (see below).

Decisions don't occur in a vacuum and Chapter 7 focuses on how decision modeling contributes to the business and technical architecture of an organization and the contexts in which it is used. It examines application usage, business value and technical deployment of decisions.

Chapter 12 discusses an iterative, decision modeling methodology and how this fits within an agile or waterfall software development lifecycle—whether you are modeling manual decision-making or need to automate part or all of your operation decisions. It provides a step by step guide for using decision modeling from initiation to implementation.

Chapter 13 outlines some common misconceptions about decision modeling that the authors have encountered in projects, discussed in decision modeling training sessions, seen on internet forums, experienced in conversations with colleagues and even read in articles. The flaws of each misconception are thoroughly explained. Many of these notions arise from confusion between decision modeling and other related techniques like business rules and business processes. This chapter helps to clarify the distinctions between them and is essential reading for anyone who has one of the viewpoints listed within.

Section 2 of Chapter 18 describes how to select and set up an appropriate pilot project for decision modeling.

3.2.3   How can a beginner start modeling decisions in DMN?

Readers with no previous experience who want to start learning the Decision Model and Notation (DMN) standard for decision modeling should consult chapters 6, 8, 14 and the first example of Chapter 17 initially.

Chapters 6 and 8 define the core DMN standard. The former is an overview and introduction, the latter covers what we consider to be the essential elements of the modeling notation: the most useful parts that will suffice for initial projects. These chapters are designed to teach readers how to understand and use the notation and illustrate its application in simple examples. Note that they document the standard faithfully and without our opinions. One goal in this book has been to segregate the details of the standard in the earlier chapters from our views about them that follow in later chapters.

Chapter 14 includes a wealth of best practices suited to newcomers to decision modeling and these should be read as soon as a basic mastery of the notation is achieved. Every best practice is illustrated with practical examples. Soon after this chapter has been read, the skills learnt should be applied in real projects. As experience is gained, readers should occasionally return to this chapter. Chapter 14 and appendix C contains our thoughts, opinions and experiences of the standard.

Chapter 17 contains three examples of which the first is especially relevant to newcomers because it explains, step-by-step, how a decision model is built from the beginning. Readers will gain an appreciation of what larger decision models look like, how they are built and how they inform the organization that makes them.

Appendices A and B are also designed to be a valuable reference for all decision modelers working on projects. Appendix A defines all the terminology used in the book and Appendix B is a formal reference for DMN.

3.2.4   I've used TDM; how can I transition to DMN?

Decision modelers with experience of Sapiens' The Decision Model (TDM) should consult Appendix D and then follow the chapter recommendations in Section 3.2.3.

Appendix D includes a comparison of DMN and TDM and helps readers to leverage their knowledge of TDM to learn DMN more quickly. It also describes a set of pitfalls that experienced TDM users might encounter when they migrate to DMN. These are usually established practices, relevant to TDM, that are inappropriate or ineffective when using DMN.

3.2.5   How can I improve my decision modeling skills?

Decision modelers, with existing experience of DMN, seeking more insight and best practices, should consult chapters 11, 14, 15, 16 and 17. Readers interested in exploring the boundaries of DMN should consult appendix C.

Chapter 11 covers advanced DMN techniques: unusual or uncommon decision model structures and additional detail not normally required by newcomers. The mechanics of DMN, including its expression, language, FEEL, is described here. Again, this chapter documents the standard faithfully and without our opinions.

Chapter 14 contains best practices that assume little previous experience with DMN. In contrast, Chapter 15 is designed for practitioners already familiar with decision modeling as it addresses issues and associated best practices that might not be apparent without practical experience. It also includes some advanced techniques.

Chapter 16 contains a set of decision modeling patterns illustrated using DMN. Patterns are frequently occurring challenges and combinations of approaches that have proven effective at resolving them. This chapter illustrates each pattern by example, explaining how to recognize the problem, how to address it and the benefits of resolving the problem in this manner.

Chapter 17 contains decision model examples. Experienced modelers should look at the second two examples which resolve complex challenges and demonstrate the value of decision modeling in large projects.

Appendix C includes our view of what elements of the standard require more work and some potential additions.

3.2.6   How can we scale up our success with decision modeling?

Readers who have achieved some small, localized successes with decision modeling projects but need to scale the approach to handle larger problems, spanning organizational units, should consult chapters 9, 10 and 18.

Chapter 9 addresses the concept of a glossary, a dictionary of business terms, which is essential to support decision models that need to be shared effectively between different project teams or across multi-site groups. The chapter describes what glossaries are, why they are important and how to build them.

Chapter 10 describes how decision models in DMN integrate with other enterprise models, specifically: business process (BPMN), data (UML/ERD), architecture (ArchiMate) and motivation (the business motivation elements of ArchiMate) models. This integration is an important means of connecting decision models to a broader business context. Section 10.2 is especially important as it explains the synergy between BPMN and DMN.

Chapter 18 discusses the creation of a broad decision modeling practice within an organization. It outlines some pre-requisites to accelerate corporate acceptance and a step-by-step guide to drive adoption across multiple projects. It also discusses various approaches to selecting and adopting tools to support decision modeling.

3.3   Suggested Roadmap By Project Role

Laying out a prescriptive road map through this book based on a reader's role or job description ignores the context-specific and fluid nature of work assignment in modern organizations. However, Table 3-1 shows the relevance of sections of the book to roles in a business organization and serves as a rough guide for the reader. Those cells with a dark color represent chapters of direct importance to the role. The authors strongly advise that practitioners in this role read these chapters. A light color indicates a chapter of moderate importance that may be omitted on a first reading. An empty cell indicates that the chapter concerned is not essential for this role.

Chapter Number and Content	Reader Role									
	Bus/App Architect	Business Analyst	Business SME	Data Architect	Decision Modeler	Decision Practice Lead	Program Manager	Project Manager	Process Modeler	Infrastructure Architect
4 Value of Decision Management and Modeling										
5 What is Decision Modeling and when to use it										
6 Introduction to DMN Standard										
7 Business Context										
8 The DMN Standard										
9 Dispelling Some Common Misconceptions										
10 Business Glossary										
11 Integration with Other Notations										
12 Advanced Decision Modeling in DMN										
13 Methodology Overview										
14 Best Practices for New Modelers										
15 Best Practices for the Experienced										
16 Patterns										
17 Examples										
18 Establishing a Decision Modeling Practice										
Appendices										
A Definitions and Terms										
B FEEL Reference										
C Proposals for Changes to DMN										
D The Decision Model (TDM)										

Table 3-1 Book Chapters by Reader Role

3.4 Prerequisites

This book assumes no prior knowledge of decision management, decision management systems, decision modeling, DMN or any specific tools or technologies. However, we have assumed that readers are in some way engaged in the world of business operational decision-making and are most likely working to improve the business performance of one or more semi-automated business processes. Readers should have elementary understanding or exposure to the following concepts:

- Business Process and Event Architecture
- Service Oriented Architecture (SOA)
- Basic Data Modeling

4 The Value of Decision Management and Decision Modeling

There is one thing worse than managing your decisions and that is not managing your decisions
—After Oscar Wilde

Decisions are important to organizations, determining how customers are treated, how risk is managed, how supply chains are controlled and ultimately determining the profitability and effectiveness of the organization. Understanding, modeling, managing and automating decisions is an increasingly important element of many organizations' business strategy. Modeling these decisions is pivotal to using them as a focus to improve business outcomes.

Before delving into the practicalities of decision modeling, it is necessary to build a baseline understanding of decisions and of what we mean by four very similar terms:

- Decision
- Decision Modeling
- Decision Management
- Decision Management System

While these phrases share a focus on decisions, there are distinct differences between them and the value they have for organizations.

4.1 Definitions and Introductions

4.1.1 Decision

> *A decision is a determination that businesses make on a regular basis, a selection or calculation of an outcome that depends on a number of prevailing circumstances (inputs) and which, ultimately, has an observable impact on the behavior of the organization.*

In this book, the term *decision* means <u>operational</u> business decision. An operational decision is one made repeatedly, during regular business activity, that controls or influences the organization's business behavior.

Operational decisions do not include ad-hoc strategic or tactical resolutions devised by CEOs in board meetings: *should our company merge with XYZ Inc? Should we enter the Taiwanese bond market? Should we diversify into an adjacent vertical?* Because decisions of this type occur infrequently, are unique in character and require considerable human intuition, they are harder to model and benefit less from such analysis. Instead, operational decisions refer to the smaller, frequently repeated and often automated decisions companies need to make many times every day, like the examples in Table 4-1.

These decisions may not seem as important as more strategic ones. Individually they certainly don't involve the same large sums of money, publicity or personnel. However, operational decisions are more voluminous and are collectively very significant. Make a small mistake a thousand times and it's a big mistake. Make a little more money a thousand times and it's a lot of money. Treat every customer as an individual and you retain more of them. Moreover, for many of your customers or internal departments these decision outcomes come to define your company and will be interpreted as your company's deliberate policy—whether they are or not. Something of this importance warrants considered management.

Decision	Outcome	Inputs
Should we accept this client's loan request?	Yes, No	Client income, credit rating, age, other debt, requested loan amount.
What category of risk should I assign to this asset?	Rating AAA…D	Asset type, issuer, country of jurisdiction, currency, volatility.
In which other products would this customer be interested?	List of Products	Products customer already has, customer age, marital status, previous customer spending, available products.
Should this claim be paid?	Fast-track, Pay, Investigate for Fraud, Reject	Claim details, policy, customer history, provider history
Can a permit be issued for this building proposal?	Yes, No	Proposal definition, location, citizen information

Table 4-1 Operational Decision Examples

4.1.2   Decision Modeling

Decision modeling expresses how a decision should be made as a rigorous, verifiable model. It formalizes decision-making so it can be clearly and widely understood, managed and used effectively. Decision modeling supports the documentation of an organization's decisions such that they can be made consistently, improved over time and automated where appropriate.

Decision modeling involves decomposing a decision into its component pieces or sub-decisions. It involves modeling the requirements for each such decision in terms of the information that must be available to make the decision and the knowledge required to know how the decision should be made. Because decision-making is part of the core of an organization's business operations, it also involves modeling the business context for a decision.

Not every decision benefits equally from being modeled. The more often a decision must be made and the more value there is to consistency of decision-making, the more value decision modeling will offer (how to select decisions for modeling is described in more detail in Chapter 5).

Documenting decisions using decision modeling is important because a company's operational business decisions are a tangible asset—worthy of careful documentation, communication and review.

4.1.3 Decision Management

The Decision Management Manifesto (Taylor, The Decision Management Manifesto, 2013) states:

Decision Management is an approach that improves day-to-day business operations. It increases an organization's business agility and adaptability by making its systems easier to monitor and change. It puts Big Data to work improving the effectiveness and profitability of every action. It is a proven framework for effectively applying innovative technologies such as business rules, predictive analytics and optimization.

Decision Management is thus based on the general premise that decisions are first class objects, they should be part of a business architecture (see Chapter 7) and they should be managed for continuous improvement. The first section of the Manifesto clearly identifies this under the heading "Decisions First" where it lists several key statements:

- Decisions, especially operational decisions, link an organization's performance metrics and objectives to its operational systems.
- Decisions are first class objects, just like business processes or data, and should be identified, described, modeled, reviewed and managed in business terms as part of a business architecture.
- Decisions should be modeled first before considering how business rules and or analytics will be used[2].
- Decisions support business processes and help organizations respond to events, simplifying their expression and management. However, decisions are not subsumed by either processes or events.
- Business, IT, and analytic professionals all have a role in identifying, describing, modeling, reviewing and managing decisions.

Decision Management in this sense is therefore much more than just the adoption of Decision Management technologies such as a Business Rule Management System (BRMS). While Decision Management can and should be used to effectively automate and manage decisions, it can also be used to manage and improve decisions that are still being made largely or wholly manually. What matters is that an organization focuses explicitly on the creation, active measurement and continuous improvement of decision-making assets and

---

[2] See also the section on the decision/business rules myth in section 4.2.3

that it creates a framework for managing and governing these assets through a lifecycle of definition, verification, deployment, monitoring, change and ultimately retirement.

Decision Management impacts the way organizations approach business and systems management in three broad areas:

- Techniques and tasks to explicitly identify and model the decisions of a business must be added to the requirements and modeling tasks already undertaken by the organization. This is known as Decision Discovery and Modeling.

- When all or part of a decision is identified for automation, it must be deployed explicitly as a decision-making component—a Decision Service. It should not be considered just one more piece of an application or a business process. The existing Software Development Life Cycle or SDLC must therefore be extended and revised to handle both the Decision Services Definition and Implementation and the ongoing change and updates that these services require.

- The performance management and monitoring approach used in the organization needs to be extended to include formal Decision Measurement and Improvement. This means tracking decision outcomes as well as business results and associating the two. It also means tracking how decisions were made so that this information can be analyzed and having the reporting and analysis tools necessary to conduct decision-making experiments and compare their results.

This approach is further described in the chapter on methodology (see Chapter 12).

4.1.4   Decision Management Systems

Decision Management Systems are different from typical information systems in three ways—they are more agile, more analytic and more adaptive. (Taylor, Decision Management Systems: A Practical Guide to Using Business Rules and Predictive Analytics, 2012)

Organizations that are applying Decision Management are often going to find themselves automating some, perhaps most, of the decisions they are managing. The reality of a modern business is that the need for rapid, even real-time response combined with a need to scale cost-effectively means that automation of decision-making is as critical to success as automation of workflow or data management. Automating decisions in this way is best achieved by creating Decision Management Systems that are agile, analytic, adaptive and that contrast with more traditional decision support systems.

4.1.4.1   Decision Management Systems are agile

Because decision-making changes all the time, any system that implements it must be **agile** in that it must be cheap and easy to make accurate changes to its behavior. This requires the use of technologies such as Business Rules Management Systems to manage the logic required to make decisions. This technology in turn requires the use of decision modeling to ensure that the rules are being effectively written and managed.

This combination of decision modeling and business rules creates a system that is easy to change and also delivers systematic traceability. A decision model backed by decision logic, managed in a BRMS offers design transparency: it is precisely clear, even to non-technical participants, how decisions will be made. Any change to this design is likewise transparent, allowing such changes to be traced and managed. A BRMS also offers execution transparency: tracking exactly how each decision was made by logging all the rules that were fired to make it. This enables business results to be traced back to the decisions made both for compliance and for ongoing improvement and adaption.

4.1.4.2 Decision Management Systems are analytic

Decision-making is increasingly data-driven in many organizations as the era of Big Data results in greater use of analytics in decision-making. It is increasingly unacceptable to make decisions based on gut feelings or historical policies alone. Organizations want to use analysis of both their own data and external data to drive analytic decision-making. Applying these trends to automated decision-making means making the systems themselves more analytic. It is not enough that systems support analytics for their users—they must also be consumers of analytics so that their own behavior is analytically enhanced. Embedding predictive analytics and the results of data mining into Decision Management Systems allows the decisions these systems make to be more analytic. Decision models allow these analytics to be applied effectively and mixed appropriately with any policies and regulations that constrain the decisions.

4.1.4.3 Decision Management Systems are adaptive

Decision Management Systems are designed to be adaptive. They assume that an organization will want to learn, experiment and adapt. Historically the trend has been to deliver scale in applications by applying a ruthlessly cookie-cutter mindset—only if every transaction is handled in the same way can there be scale. This prevents learning because only one approach is ever tried. In contrast, a Decision Management System assumes that experimentation and learning will be built in from the beginning. Decision modeling is used to determine which pieces of the decision should be experimented on and how.

4.1.4.4 Decision Management Systems are not Decision Support Systems

Decision Management Systems share some characteristics with Decision Support Systems. Because Decision Management Systems focus on automating decisions, rather than presenting information to a human decision-maker, they also differ from this more traditional approach to building decision-making systems in some important ways.

There are four areas of similarity between Decision Support and Decision Management:

1. The results of the decision being made must be measured. Neither kind of system can be used effectively if the value of a decision is not known, not measurable or not actually measured.
2. Human judgment and experience matter a great deal. While it is obvious that human judgment is applied by the user of a Decision Support System, Decision Management Systems involve the embedding of this judgment into the system and its continual controlled evolution.
3. The basis for better decisions is data and that data must be analyzed, aggregated and interpreted in both Decision Support Systems and Decision Management Systems.
4. The end result should always be action. Decision support systems are designed to

help people take a more appropriate or profitable action, while Decision Management Systems are designed to take those actions in a more automated fashion.

There are also four areas of critical difference:

1. How human experience and judgment are applied is very different. Decision support systems rely on the user to have the experience and judgment to use the information provided correctly, while Decision Management Systems rely on this experience having been correctly modeled, embedded and maintained in the system itself.
2. While both kinds of system rely on data analysis and often use the same underlying mathematical techniques, the presentation of this analysis is different. Decision support systems must present the analysis so that a person can use it, while Decision Management Systems must be able to apply the analysis programmatically.
3. Policies and regulations are modeled and embedded into Decision Management Systems so that the decisions they make are inherently compliant. The users of Decision Support Systems are often responsible for reading and applying policies and regulations themselves.
4. In a Decision Management System, the same decision-making approach is applied every time—programmatically and repeatedly. In a Decision Support System each user has some amount of freedom to use the system as he or she likes. The process may be constrained by policy but there is generally more flexibility and more degrees of freedom.

Regardless of the kind of decision-making system being developed, however, decision modeling has tremendous value because it allows the decision-making to be explicitly documented and designed independently of the implementation.

4.2   A Decision-Centric Approach

Adopting Decision Management and decision modeling, as well as building Decision Management Systems, brings a new focus to the way organizations make decisions. In particular, it corrects the historical omission of decision-making from the way business processes and systems have been designed. These concepts are interrelated and should be considered together to deliver a truly decision-centric approach.

4.2.1   A focus on decision corrects a historical omission

Automation of business operations began with a focus on basic functions and data management, before transitioning to automating workflow and ultimately the business processes of the organization. Basic decisions such as validation, calculation or routing decisions might be automated, though the use of inline code limited the ability of organizations to maintain and update them. In general, automation included few business decisions as they were considered too complex. This meant decisions were left to human users and the role of automated systems was simply to bring the right human into the process at the right time.

Broad adoption of Business Process Management (BPM) has brought a level of transparency and flexibility to these business systems. A BPM approach allows rapid change to automated processes as the business environment changes. As the frontiers for automation have advanced further, the decision logic being embedded within automated processes in this way has become progressively more complex, harder to understand and challenging to maintain. Changes to this embedded decision logic increasingly require too much effort to be feasible, especially as the pace of change continues to increase. The agility of the process is thus compromised (See Section 7.2.1).

The limitations of early automation approaches and the singular focus on processes has resulted in an historical lack of focus on decisions. Most organizations do not identify, model, automate or manage the operational decisions that are critical to their business. As such, they often lack the requirements approach (decision modeling) as well as the architectural vision (Decision Management Systems) to really improve the decision-making power of their application portfolio. A decision-centric approach addresses the challenges resulting from this unfortunate history.

Adopting decision modeling as a requirements technique raises the visibility of decisions across the board. Adopting Decision Management as a framework ensures these newly visible decisions can be managed. Building Decision Management Systems safely and effectively pushes the boundary of automation to include more and more complex decision-making.

4.2.2 There are relationships between these concepts

While separate, these four concepts (Decisions, Decision Modeling, Decision Management and Decision Management Systems) are all part of a decision-centric approach and related as shown in Figure 4-1. They all relate to decisions and to the systematic analysis, management and automation of decisions. They are also connected because succeeding at each of them requires some degree of success at the others. Decision Management relies on the accurate identification and description of an organization's decisions. It is possible to identify, describe and even specify decisions with a degree of precision without using decision modeling. Realistically, however, it is hard to succeed at Decision Management without adopting and likewise succeeding at decision modeling. Decision modeling brings a degree of precision, of specificity and transparency, to decisions that are central to an organization's ability to manage them.

Similarly, it is unlikely that an organization will attempt to manage decisions, to adopt and benefit from Decision Management, without also attempting to develop some Decision Management Systems. The scale of most organizations makes completely manual decision-making impractical, while continuously improving decisions generally requires some degree of automation to create the data needed for analysis and improvement. Many uses of Decision Management as an approach specifically focus on the automation of decisions in Decision Management Systems and the phrases are sometimes used almost synonymously.

Decision modeling could be adopted as a standalone modeling technique or as part of an Enterprise Architecture or Business Process Management practice. For instance, an organization might identify the need to model its decisions but fail to consider them as first class elements of their business architecture and simply automate or describe them as part of an overall process. Decision modeling with DMN would work in these circumstances, allowing for an accurate and transparent description of the decisions. Without a matching focus on Decision Management, however, the value of those models would be limited and likely to degrade over time. This would also be limiting from a technology perspective. Experience with Business Rules Management Systems, for instance, is that they work best not as part of a business process or as part of a large system, but as a platform for developing and managing distinct Decision Services. This requires a focus on Decision Management Systems, not just a decision model.

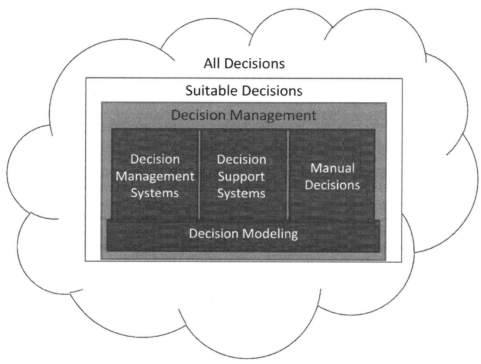

Figure 4-1 Relationships between the concepts

From a practical point of the view the connections between them are threefold:

1. Decision Discovery and Modeling is the first step in Decision Management. Beginning to develop a decision model for decisions that are discovered is a powerful tool for identifying the best candidates for automation as well as for providing the description needed for ongoing management.

2. When defining and implementing the Decision Services at the heart of a Decision Management System, a decision model scopes and drives the design in a way that works for both waterfall and more agile methodologies.

3. Decision Monitoring and Improvement, as well as maintenance of decision-making, use decision models to track impact of change and manage experimentation.

Decision modeling can thus both drive and orchestrate the use of technology to develop and sustain Decision Management Systems as shown in Figure 4-2.

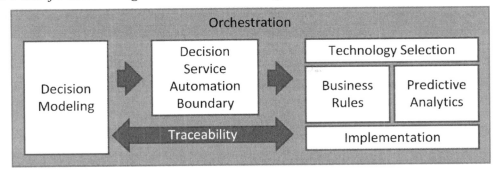

Figure 4-2 The role of Decision Modeling

4.2.3   Myth: decisions are just scaled up rules

Before leaving the topic of definitions it is worth putting down one persistent myth. Because the definition of a decision is often best accomplished using business rules, there are those who see decisions simply as "scaled up" business rules. This, it is argued, means that a new decision-centric approach to modeling and managing decisions is not required—the use of existing techniques developed for business rules will work well.

The authors have been using business rules and BRMSs for decades. We have seen projects using virtually every combination of business rules analysis and design techniques. This experience makes it clear that there are real and distinct differences between business rules and decisions that make it essential to focus on decisions **first** and to use decision-centric techniques, such as decision modeling:

- Decisions are tangible to the business, do things the business cares about and are delivered directly to them (usually via a service oriented architecture). While Subject Matter Experts (SMEs) and sponsors will have strong opinions on decisions, they may never have heard of some individual rules.

- Decision modeling focuses on the forest not the trees. By modeling decisions first and decomposing initial, high-level decisions into more focused and granular sub-decisions, a clear picture of a project emerges. Collecting all the business rules first, in contrast, provides a mass of detail with no such organizing principle.

- Decisions directly steer business processes (by producing a significant outcome or event). If the outcomes of business rules are to have a direct impact on a business process they will need to be packaged as a decision for embedding in the process. There may be "process rules"—rules about the process itself, such as rules governing escalation or routing—but these should not be confused with the critical business rules that drive decision-making.

- Decisions have a clearly defined business value and a set of associated performance metrics that they impact. Business rules often do not have such a defined impact because their scope is too narrow.

- Decisions manage their own business exceptions internally, always returning an answer, even if serious errors arise, whereas individual business rules frequently do not address exceptional circumstances because their scope is too narrow. This makes decisions a much more self-contained, packaged element of a business architecture.

- Decisions are reused by service invocation while business rules are most often reused by integrating them directly into applications or components.
- Business rules cannot be applied except when a decision is being made.

Decisions are more than just scaled-up business rules and should be identified, modeled and managed as the first class objects that they are.

4.3 The Value of Decision Management

The value of Decision Management can be seen in the different ways decisions can be improved when it is applied. Automation projects generally focus on increasing speed, improving consistency and reducing costs. Business rules projects are often focused on improving the agility of information systems. Analytic efforts, meanwhile, often focus on the accuracy of decisions being made. The value of Decision Management should thus be considered holistically across five dimensions: accuracy of decision, consistency of decision, agility of decision, latency of decision-making and cost of decision-making[3].

Experience in multiple industries is that Decision Management efforts that recognize that value can be added across all these dimensions are broader-based and have a stronger foundation than those more narrowly focused only on speed and cost of decision-making. Organizations that also consider the potential value of improving accuracy, agility and consistency in decision-making will find more (and increasingly beneficial) opportunities for Decision Management technologies. Even where the initial ROI is based on improvements in speed and cost, a broader based approach will make the value of ongoing analysis and continuous improvement clearer.

Comparing existing decision-making approaches with those possible with Decision Management can use radar charts to show where the improvement might come from.

Figure 4-3 for instance, plots an initial assessment of a manual insurance claims adjudication decision against a planned Decision Management system. Accuracy of the current manual decision is considered reasonable in this example and agility is reasonably good also, because there are not too many claims adjustors who need to be kept up to date. Consistency, cost and latency are all challenges, however, that the automation is designed to address.

It is also worth noting that Decision Management, by automating previously manual decisions, can often "up-level" jobs. Rather than making a largely repetitive manual decision, employees are responsible for managing the decision-making approach and using their judgment to handle exceptional cases. Such up-leveled jobs are significantly more rewarding.

---

[3] This is based on a similar set of five dimensions first described by FICO in 2006 as part of their "Decision Yield" concept.

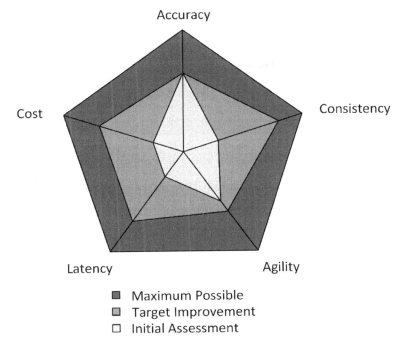

Figure 4-3 Aspects of Decision Management Value

4.3.1 Accuracy

Improved accuracy in decision-making often comes from applying analytics to make more data-driven decisions. Such decisions are often more fine-grained, focusing on individual customers or transactions. This allows for more accurate and specific risk management and more targeted customer treatment. More generally a focus on modeling and managing decisions results in fewer errors and less rework.

4.3.2 Consistency

Decision Management ensures that policies are applied consistently across different channels, different business processes and over time. This results in fewer fines as well as lower audit and legal costs. Consistency is also a driver for improved customer satisfaction as customers strongly dislike inconsistency in their interactions. This consistency can be extended across channels, regions and product lines to maximize the value of Decision Management.

4.3.3 Agility

Decision Management allows for more rapid response to business threats and means fewer missed opportunities. It also helps organizations cope with change imposed from outside such as changes in regulatory mandates. By facilitating quicker change of existing decisions and a faster time to market for new ones, Decision Management materially increases agility. The time and cost to make changes is reduced, opening up opportunities for change. The traceability of change makes for more accurate changes and increases the likelihood that an organization will "risk" a change because they are more confident in its outcome and in their ability to reverse it should this prove necessary.

4.3.4   Latency

Reducing the time it takes to make a decision, its latency, can offer an immediate and direct value to the decision (as described in the section on Decision Latency 5.4.7) because the worth of its outcome may decay rapidly with time. It can also be more efficient, allowing greater throughput of transactions through a particular process by reducing the time required for critical decisions.

4.3.5   Cost

Decision Management allows for more effective automation of decisions and this automation drives down costs by eliminating the need for manual decision-making. This cost benefit is multiplied by the volume of the decision. Automation can also facilitate processing at volumes that are impractical for manual processes. Even where completely automated Decision Management Systems are not being developed, partial automation in the form of Decision Support Systems allows for human decision-makers to make accurate decisions more rapidly and cheaply.

4.3.6   Continuous improvement

One final note on the value of Decision Management. Regardless of how many of these dimensions are being improved, organizations can get additional value from Decision Management thanks to its focus on continuous improvement. Organizations can improve the quality of their decision-making assets through a process of effective internal review and performance monitoring. Decision Management allows them to identify poorly performing, redundant, inconsistent and missing decisions. It permits the effective 'stock taking' of decision assets so that the responsibility for the future stewardship of these assets can be consciously assigned.

4.3.7   Quantitative studies of the benefit of Decision Management

Adopting Decision Management has measurable benefit for organizations as the following examples taken from the authors' experience, illustrate.

4.3.7.1   Accuracy

A European provider of cable TV and broadband services used Decision Management and a Decision Management System to improve customer loyalty and reduce churn through more accurate decision-making. Churn is a constant problem in the cable TV business and a key factor preventing it is the ownership of multiple products—customers with multiple products are far more loyal than those with only one. This makes the decision of which cross-sell to offer and when to do so critical in driving increased customer retention.

This provider used predictive analytics to identify those customers most at risk of churn and to identify which of its products would be most appealing to each such customer. They identified that it was not just the decision about the most appropriate cross-sell and the best time that had to be right. Critically, the decision as to what script should be displayed to the call center representative to help them close this cross-sell had to be accurate—the script had to perfectly fit the product being sold, the customer and the customer's prior experience with the provider.

Using business rules, the provider implemented a decision to generate a specific script for each transaction, targeting the customer very accurately using customer data, the predictive models developed and the customer's prior use of the provider's products. This extremely accurate script had an average success rate of between 13% and 18% across all the representatives with individual representatives achieving up to 40% success. Teams that used the script saw three times the cross-sell success of those that did not. This case demonstrates a dramatic increase in accuracy through a clear and detailed focus on the critical decision and its automation.

4.3.7.2   Consistency

A US government agency needed to calculate vehicle licensing fees accurately and consistently across multiple channels (batch mailings, over 150 offices and a new online channel). The difficulty was heightened as the regulations governing these fees were changed on a regular basis by elected officials. The fees amounted to several billion dollars a year in revenue from about 50 million registered drivers and vehicles. This was a challenge because the batch system that processed the fees was 30 years old and a completely separate system was used to support the offices.

Decision Management was applied to separate out the fee calculation decision itself from the rest of the process. The process was very stable and so could be left on the legacy platform while the decision was moved to a business rules-based Decision Service. This service supported both the batch and office systems, ensuring consistency across these channels. The use of business rules to manage and automate the decision enabled the thousands of rules involved to be easily updated by non-technical users, ensuring they were accurate and consistent. The Decision Service handled hundreds of thousands of transactions a day. The same rules were then used to support a new online form allowing consumers to accurately calculate their fees in advance of receiving their bill. All three channels were implemented in different technologies and ran different processes but the shared Decision Service ensured that the fees were identical regardless of which channel was used.

4.3.7.3   Agility

The scenario outlined in Section 4.3.7.2 illustrated a dramatic improvement in agility. The use of a Decision Management approach enabled non-technical users to comprehend, maintain and update the decision logic deployed in the Decision Service. They were able to investigate problems, determine and test solutions and even prepare rules for final deployment. An external study identified 13,000 hours of maintenance work that was saved in the first year alone. As an example: a problem identified when the system went live was identified, fixed, re-tested and re-deployed into production in about 15 minutes by a business analyst. Previously even the most minor change had required between two hours and a day of technical development time so; this represented a saving of between 87% and 97%.

As an aside, the new approach also allowed some capabilities to be added to the system that had never been added to the legacy system because the cost-benefit was too poor. These lower transaction volume decisions would have taken too much effort to implement in the old system and so were handled manually. Decision Management lowered the cost of development sufficiently to make it worth adding them to the system, expanding its capabilities in addition to making it easier to maintain and change.

4.3.7.4   Latency

One of the most obvious ways in which Decision Management can reduce latency (improve speed) is through increased straight through processing. Not delaying a process for manual approval has an obvious and immediate impact on speed. Automated approvals are not the only way to increase speed, however.

A large telecommunications company received orders for complex products and services to run on the network. These orders had to be validated to ensure that the network could be configured to deliver them. Existing equipment had then to be configured to deliver the service before the client could use it and be billed for it.

A Decision Management system was developed to accept orders and enable them to be processed straight through, all the way to live services. Rules maintained by the product teams validated the orders to ensure they were workable. Additional decisions used rules developed by the engineers to take these valid orders and correctly configure the network to deliver those services for that client. All of this was handled automatically, reducing a task that had previously taken days to one taking only minutes. This provided better service for the customer and faster time to market for the company.

In addition, this approach allowed them to develop a more flexible and powerful network because they were confident they could configure and sell more complex products and services. They could offer a broader and more rapidly changing portfolio of services and the system enabled engineers to be assigned to higher value tasks rather than configuring standard services.

4.3.7.5   Cost

Cost savings are often the focus for Decision Management and the ability to replace staff with an automated decision-making service can drive dramatic reductions in cost. One European bank, for instance, adopted Decision Management to automate loan approval decisions across its individual, commercial and private banking businesses. The automation of these decisions resulted in much faster decision-making of course, eliminating the need to wait for an available loan officer. More impressive, however, was the reduction in cost. This bank was able to reduce its loan handling headcount by 90%—this was critical as it was simultaneously transitioning to a much more competitive local market as foreign banks entered its market. This change represented an increase in employee productivity of over 800% and reduced their cost per loan to just 23% of what it had been before. Case histories like this are not uncommon with companies seeing massive changes in their staffing and cost ratios.

4.4   The Value of Decision Modeling

Decision modeling adds value by bringing the organizations' decision-making approach "out of the shadows". Creating an explicit, managed and business-accessible definition of decision-making allows for validation, management, automation and more.

4.4.1 Transparent, traceable, business oriented representation

When decision models are based on an approved business vocabulary, they visualize decision-making exclusively in business terms and make it tangible to non-technical staff. The visual representation is not tainted by implementation detail and is entirely separate from code. Decision modeling therefore supports the capture of decisions so that they can be effectively communicated to a wide audience, including business subject matter experts. It allows specialists to review, validate, refute and optimize decision-making in the organization. This transparency of decision models brings clarity to the business and improves quality by facilitating effective peer review. This effect is improved further if a standard notation for decision modeling is used.

Decision modeling also permits the direct linking of the decision-making approach with external mandates such as regulations and laws. This makes it possible to justify each part of a decision by reference to an authority (be it legal or regulatory), helps confirm that the decision-making approach is compliant (improving the audit process) and facilitates targeted, 'keyhole surgery' to the decision-making when a specific external mandate changes. As new rules such as the European General Data Protection Regulation (GDPR) insist with increasing legal force that all automated systems must be capable of comprehensively explaining their behavior after the fact, there will be an ever increasing legal requirement for a more rigorous approach to automated decision-making. Furthermore the more frequent use of machine-learning in decision-making will require an enhanced explanatory facility to support the counterintuitive outcomes that can often result.

4.4.2 Precise and executable representation of requirements

Decision models express decision-making requirements formally and precisely. This allows modelers to detect inconsistencies, ambiguities, omissions and other logical flaws. The rigor of decision modeling also helps to maintain the integrity of large models; reduces the size of complex models; facilitates reuse of logic across the model and allows for strong verification to ensure the model's internal consistency can be enforced.

Decision modeling enables the capture, analysis, organization, management and communication of business logic in the form of declarative statements that focus on 'what' is to be done, not 'how' it should be done. Decision models offer such a precise definition of business logic that they can be made executable. This allows some tools to simulate decision-making using test data to improve an SME's understanding of the behavior of their decision-making under specified conditions. This not only 'brings to life' the decision model but is a superb training aid for new business employees.

Some tools also allow this precise definition of logic to be directly 'deployed' into production infrastructure, such as a Business Rule Management System, avoiding the usual need for 'translation' by developers. Whilst this in no way eliminates the need for developers in the creation of Decision Management Systems, it does reduce the error associated with the translation from specification to implementation and reduces time to market.

A useful side effect of this precision is that it drives the early discovery of the real data and knowledge requirements of decision-making. Frequently this eliminates the late discovery of data requirements that is a significant source of delay in projects that are based on untestable, paper specifications.

4.4.3   Enterprise consistency and compliance

Explicit packaging of decisions allows for the reapplication of the same decisions across multiple business processes. This in turn enables consistent behavior across an enterprise. A clear separation of business process and decisions simplifies the management and evolution of both process models and decisions and enables the safe reuse of decisions across many business processes.

Decision models allow organizations to effectively manage their regulatory compliance by using a decision model to represent their interpretations of these regulations. When auditable compliance is required, decision models can replace separate textual interpretations of these specifications and associated code with a single executable model that is fully traceable to the regulations and to the results of its execution. This helps guarantee consistent, demonstrable compliance.

4.4.4   Support for any balance of manual and automated decision-making

Decision models can be developed for manual decisions, automated decisions and blended decisions. Each element of a decision model can be identified as one to be automated in a BRMS as part of a Decision Service or one to be left as a manual decision. Manual decisions can be defined in great detail, down to the logic that is meant to be applied by the decision-maker, or left at a more conceptual level. Decisions documented in this way can be used for training and to help ensure consistency of approach among decision-makers.

A single decision model may contain any mix of decisions defined to any level of detail. This flexibility has a number of benefits:

- Decision models can be developed before choices are made about how much of the decision should be automated. This allows these automation decisions to be made after the decision is well understood rather than before. Decision models can even inform the choice of where the automation boundary should lie.

- Decision models can be used as the level of automation evolves. As an organization gains comfort and prowess with decision automation technology or as its understanding of the decision logic in a particular part of a decision increases, previously manual decisions can be automated.

- Because the same notation and properties are captured for manual and automated decisions, it is possible to integrate the results of manual decision-making into an otherwise automated decision-making system using a single decision model.

4.4.5   Managed complexity

The clear specification of dependencies between business decisions structures decision logic and supports the separation of distinct business concerns for easier management and understanding. This separation allows a decision model to handle very complex problems without compromising its transparency by decomposing them into independent pieces. It also allows layers of the model to be insulated from changes in other layers—allowing each layer to be simpler than it would otherwise be. Consider, for example, the separation of data validation decisions from business decisions (considered in Section 14.8.2). The ability of decisions to provide a structuring principle for business logic makes them more potent than business rules alone.

Layering and structuring also enables agile and iterative development of models while speeding analysis, design and implementation of the model. The separation of decision analysis and infrastructure development means that SMEs can mine, analyze, formulate and test decision logic independently of development efforts. SMEs can often perform early testing of complex logic against real and synthetic data in their *own* environment and therefore benefit from better and earlier consistency checking of their decisions.

4.4.6 Integration of analytic technologies

As organizations adopt an increasingly data-driven approach to decision-making, they are turning to analytic technologies. Initially most organizations will begin with reporting and visualization technology designed to support human decision-making. Over time many will adopt data mining and predictive analytic technology and seek to embed the results of this technology into more automated decision-making. Decision models support all such analytic approaches effectively.

When analytics are being defined to support manual decision-making, a decision model offers an effective frame for the analytic. By understanding the decision-making that must be improved, it is possible to design and build a more suitable analytic and use it more effectively.

When more advanced analytics are developed these will often replace specific decision logic within a decision model. For instance, a decision may change from being defined with decision logic developed by a SME to one defined using decision logic that results from a formal, mathematical data mining exercise or a combination of the two. The logic in a specific decision may be enhanced to use the result of an analytic decision such as "how much risk is there that this claim is a fraudulent claim?". These analytic decisions are implemented not with decision logic but with a mathematical model. A decision model orchestrates and specifies requirements for both.

4.4.7 Measurable performance and continuous improvement

A key tenet of Decision Management is that decision-making must be continually revisited and analyzed so it can be continuously improved. This is especially true if the decision has been automated as the organization will begin to "forget" how to make the decision manually as soon as it is automated. A decision model provides a valuable framework for this kind of ongoing measurement and improvement.

While the overall decision may be easy to track and monitor using the basic information architecture of the organization, this is not sufficiently granular for real analysis. Improvements in decision-making as well as potential problems with decision-making are likely to be focused in specific parts of the decision. A decision model helps clarify where decisions might need to be improved and allows for higher resolution tracking of results. In addition, any changes made to the decision-making can be tracked using the decision model and any changes in the results observed can more easily be mapped back to these changes.

4.4.8   How adopters have benefited from decision modeling

Experience of decision modeling adoption over tens of projects has been extremely favorable, not least in the passion it inspires in some business analysts but also in the way it facilitates meaningful discussion of business ideas and the way in which it avoids many of the problems encountered with previous techniques. Projects have seen the following benefits:

4.4.8.1   Lower time to market

Many projects have experienced a greater parallelism of team effort between business and IT. Typically, decision modeling tools have permitted the identification, analysis, modeling, simulation, testing and refinement of decision logic to progress in the absence of implementation infrastructure. This meant that business analysts could start to devise models from specifications and test them against real data from the outset—there was no need for them to await a candidate implementation in order to test their understanding of the specification. Freed from the dependency on development infrastructure, business analysts have devised viable and testable decision models after only 2-3 days of effort. This meant they could thoroughly analyze the specification and build an executable model of it while architects and developers were still devising an implementation. The time saving was considerable because:

- The issues with, or misunderstandings of, the specification were resolved before the implementation was ready. This meant that once the implementation environment was built, the logic of the decision model could be deployed to it without delay. The conventional period of debugging that normally occurs when logic is first deployed into an implementation was almost completely avoided.

- The structure of the decision model informed the infrastructure build effort by defining the interfaces of the Decision Services early.

One of the biggest reasons for wasted time in projects is data provisioning. The rapidity and precision of decision model development has, for several projects, resulted in early determination of the real (rather than the supposed) data requirements. This has led to the realization that data was required that had been overlooked by the provisioning process. Fortunately, as this unwelcome discovery was made early, time remained to acquire the missing data before it became a bottleneck to the implementation itself. Indeed, in one scenario, the decision model forced the clarification of the relationship between missing and available data items, actually informing the procurement effort.

Very often the intuition of business subject matter experts (especially those that have experienced data provisioning oversights) is to request more data than is required and at a higher quality level than is warranted. This is especially true of projects requiring reference data (e.g., counterparty, product and industry subscriptions) because decision modeling forces the data inputs to be constrained by real need, paring down the provisioning to the essentials and saving both time and money.

Finally, because the use of a standard decision modeling notation helps teams collaborate more effectively and efficiently, it reduces the opportunities for misunderstandings and saves time that might otherwise be wasted resolving them. Many business analysts have been surprised at the rapid assimilation of their decision models by trained colleagues and how this has 'increased the bandwidth' of their communication. They report that less time has been wasted quibbling about the meaning of their paper specifications, freeing more time for productive discussion about the business impact of specific parts of the model. Models have been completed in review meetings lasting only a few hours, whereas previous approaches based on reviewing business rules would have required days.

4.4.8.2 Lower development cost

All of the time savings listed in the previous section translated directly to cost savings. But other potential cost savings are enabled by decision modeling.

Flaws, omissions and inconsistencies with a specification can often result in a large amount of expensive rework. The rigor and precision of decision modeling is an enormous help here. Very often, the mere act of expressing requirements within a decision model is enough to detect ambiguities, contradictions and gaps in a specification, without even executing it. Decision Tables are particularly good at drawing attention to this problem. In addition, decision modeling facilitates the detailed peer review of decision-making. Both factors are especially true of projects involving regulatory compliance specifications. Very often the regulatory bodies charged with producing these specifications are new to the task and the specifications documents they draft are produced under extreme time pressure. As a result, they are frequently riddled with inconsistency and subtle omissions. Several projects have discovered flaws within the first ten hours of analysis and confirm these issues by peer review. The questions these discoveries raised could be quickly directed at the appropriate regulatory bodies and the answers used to save development time that might otherwise be wasted on implementing incorrect solutions. In two other projects involving the modernization of legacy systems, the rigor of decision modeling helped to detect and eliminate redundancies in existing rule sets; in one case the rule set was reduced in size by over 65%.

Decision modeling also prevents needless investment in paper specifications that are: quickly rendered obsolete by change, challenging to read and understand, difficult to verify and in need of translation by IT into executable code. Instead, a fraction of this time is spent building an executable representation of decisions that is easier to maintain, easier to reference, verifiable by execution and capable of direct deployment into a production system. The cost associated with the error-prone step of translation to code is substantially reduced.

In fact, this reduction in paper specifications also has a pay-off in terms of increased agility, improved business engagement and greater scalability as noted below.

4.4.8.3 More agility

One of the advantages of rigorously documenting, in fine detail, the dependencies that decisions have on input data and authorities is that it enables impact assessment. It is possible to answer questions like: "What would happen if we incorporated another rating agency into our risk management process?", "What if clause X of the regulations was abolished?" and "What are consequences of our business partners no longer providing reliable hurricane statistics by zip code?". Decision modeling tools have made this impact analysis very straightforward, making it possible to make a very quick assessment of the consequences of a change. This has greatly improved the speed and safety of change control on many projects and increased the level of confidence and ability clients have to make accurate 'surgical changes' to their decision-making. Their growth in confidence was due in part to the knowledge that their changes would not have unintended side effects.

One of the many benefits of decision modeling over a traditional BRMS solution is that, especially in complex decision models, specific decisions are easier to find quickly, change, simulate and compare without any need for a deployment or release process. This empowers subject matter experts to propose more considered change solutions more quickly. This increase in agility brings new business opportunities as it can be used as a competitive edge. One organization has used this, for example, to continuously improve the funding efficiency of their equities trading activities.

4.4.8.4   Improved business engagement

Although some business analysts have warmed to business rules and exploited them to regain some control over the business behavior of their systems, the majority still perceive them as the domain of IT. The same is not true of decision models for a number of reasons. Firstly, in many projects it's clear that subject matter experts are much more comfortable with the ideas of decision modeling than business rule design. Many more discussions about business requirements break out over a decision model 'drawn on a napkin' than over a collection of business rules. Analysts like to see the relationship between key decisions, and business rules have no means to show this.

Secondly, there is the support decision modeling tools offer for simulation and champion/challenger testing without deployment. This is appealing to many analysts because it allows them to experiment and test their ideas without large, up-front commitments. Many find this immediacy very liberating.

Often business analysts are more comfortable with business processes than business rules and the decision model's direct connectivity with the former, supported by many modeling tools, is a strong attractor for analysts who need to see the 'big picture'. The ability to tie a decision model to the organization and business context builds on this, allowing business analysts to see who needs to be involved in changes, how to measure successful changes and much more.

This engagement is more likely to go beyond 'go-live' too. This is especially true in business domains like regulatory compliance, healthcare and insurance where constant ongoing change is expected and embraced.

4.4.8.5   Greater scalability

One repeated finding over the past ten years is that business rule approaches have no 'higher concept' to help them scale to embrace large, complex problems. As a result, they can become unwieldy to manage and difficult to understand at scale. Many decision management engagements have had the specific goal of rescuing business rules projects that have foundered in a mire of hasty rule edits and ill-considered unplanned expansion. Decision modeling introduces a new structuring concept that separates concerns and allows decisions to be hierarchically broken down into independent parts without losing sight of the whole. This single innovation, the Decision Requirements Level (see Section 6.4.3), means that decision models are effective at a far higher scale than business rules alone. This structure allows them to be apportioned to specific analysts, perhaps by business specialty, whilst maintaining the coordination of the whole.

Projects successfully approached using decision modeling have been an order of magnitude larger than many of their forebears based on business rule repositories. These projects would have been substantially more difficult, if not impossible, had they been attempted using conventional business rule technology.

5 How and When to Apply Decision Modeling

Timing in life is everything
—John Sculley

Decision modeling is a powerful technique that is broadly applicable. Many different business problems can be addressed, wholly or in part, by decision modeling. Like any technique, however, there are some problems to which decision modeling is well suited and others where it is not.

This chapter introduces the basics of decision modeling and considers the situations where it will work well and those where it is less likely to do so. It discusses how to target decision modeling, including the specific characteristics of decisions that make them benefit most from the approach. Finally, it puts decision modeling in context, by outlining a Decision Management approach and showing where decision modeling fits in that approach.

5.1 How Decisions Are Modeled

5.1.1 Decision modeling basics

Later chapters discuss decision modeling in detail, covering the notation, basic and advanced concepts, best practices and the integration of a standards-based approach to decision modeling into an overall business architecture. This section introduces the basics of decision modeling to facilitate a discussion of when and where to adopt it.

Decision modeling is fundamentally about expressing decision-making as a rigorous, structured, verifiable model rather than as unstructured, informal and potentially ambiguous text. Instead of simply writing out long-hand what decision-making an organization wants, needs or wishes to conduct, decision modeling formalizes it so it can be clearly and widely understood, managed and used effectively.

Any decision modeling approach must support the definition of decisions, allow for the specification of the information and know-how required to make the decision, express the business value of a decision and put that decision in context.

5.1.2 Defining decisions

A decision is primarily defined by:

- Its **outcome**: what it is trying to determine, its conclusion(s);
- Its **inputs**: the information it uses to make this determination and on which it is dependent;
- Its **structure**: the elements involved in making it *and*
- Its **logic**: the means of selecting or calculating a specific outcome value in each scenario to which the decision is applied by using its inputs.

A repeatable decision's outcome is knowable in advance. It can be one of a number of discrete values (e.g., should we accept a client's loan request—yes or no? What credit rating should we assign a customer—AAA, AA, A, B...?) or a continuous value within a range (e.g., the price of this insurance policy, the interest rate to charge). It can be a simple value or a complex document containing multiple elements, for instance a proposal for restructuring a debt. A decision's outcome has a direct impact on the business, often directing a business process between alternative paths or creating a critical piece of information. Each one also has a measurable business value.

Like decision outcomes, each input also has a range of expected values. The logic of a decision shows how an outcome is derived from its inputs. One way to do this is to describe how its conclusions are determined according to sets of conditions tested on its inputs. As this logic represents business policy it is important that decision definitions focus on the business meaning and intent of this logic rather than the technical details of how it is implemented. Logic should be expressed clearly and concisely to support review and, where necessary, challenges to its accuracy.

This logic is divided up and managed by the decision's structure (see Section 5.1.4). The structure breaks a decision down into more granular pieces, each of which can have its own outcome, inputs, structure and logic.

5.1.3   Question and allowed answers

The pivotal property of a decision is its business rationale. Failure to define this early can lead to misidentified or unclear decisions. The purpose of any decision being modeled should be carefully considered. The most effective way to capture a decision's purpose and to establish its outcome is to identify:

- What business question is answered by the decision?
- What are the possible or allowed answers? Is there a default?

Every decision should have a crisp and succinct description for each of these, expressed in standard business terms. The business purpose of a decision is to answer this question using one (or more) of the allowed answers.

5.1.4   The structure of decisions

Most business decisions are non-trivial and many are extremely complex. Decision modeling addresses this by breaking down decisions into smaller, more granular decisions. Through this decomposition even the most complex decisions can be understood. This creates a hierarchical structure for a decision that can be effectively linked to the information inputs with which each piece of the decision is made and to the knowledge that will allow it to be made legally, accurately and effectively. For each decision being modeled the structure defines:

- Which other decisions are dependent on this decision or are required by it?
- What inputs do these decisions have and how does each decision in the model consume the available inputs?
- Is there any supporting knowledge that might constrain or guide how the decision reaches its conclusion such as external mandates or regulations, internal policies, expertise or best practices?

This information is collected and refined iteratively to model the decision in increasing detail.

5.1.5   Business value of decisions

It is important to know the business value of a decision and precisely how it is measured or determined for all decisions (automated or manual). This clarifies their definition and assists in monitoring their business performance. Business value defines what makes a good (or bad) decision and shows what trade-offs might be required when the decision is being made. The definitions of different types of business value are discussed in Section 5.4.5.

5.1.6   The context of a decision

The context of a decision frames and surrounds it. This context is separate from the decision and adds clarity to its definition. A definition specifies what decision is being made whereas a context describes how it is used. Specifically, the context defines:

- **Business process**: which business processes use or are controlled by the decision? Which events trigger (or are triggered by) it? How are decisions coordinated?

- **Business organization**: which parts of the business, or even individuals, own (i.e., are accountable for) the decision? Which parts of the business maintain and execute it (i.e., perform it operationally)? Which parts of the organization are interested in the decision and need to be informed of changes?

- **Business motivation**: the value the business derives from the decision and how this is measured as a Key Performance Indicator. What is the business importance and priority of each decision?

- **Architecture**: which existing systems or components use (or are used by) the decision?

- **Business data**: what business data is required by or available for decision-making? How are distinct data sources related and what timeliness and data quality do they provide?

5.2   Where Decision Modeling Works Best

One of the challenges in identifying that decision modeling will be an effective technique in a given scenario is that, by definition, the decisions in question will not necessarily be well understood until decision modeling is applied to them. This means that the characteristics that make a decision a good target (discussed below in Section 5.4) may not be known when the choice to adopt decision modeling must be made.

To resolve this, it is possible to assess existing systems, business processes or business areas with a view to adopting decision modeling without first identifying the decisions within them. Three key elements indicate that decision modeling will be beneficial: value, scale and transparency. Figure 5-1 shows how these three characteristics intersect to create both a sweet spot where value, transparency and scale overlap as well as some clear areas of additional opportunity.

Processes that have high value and need to be transparent are good targets as decision modeling makes it clear how and why value is being created or lost.

Processes that have high value and operate at scale are generally excellent targets as decision modeling drives automation and the effective use of analytics in decision-making.

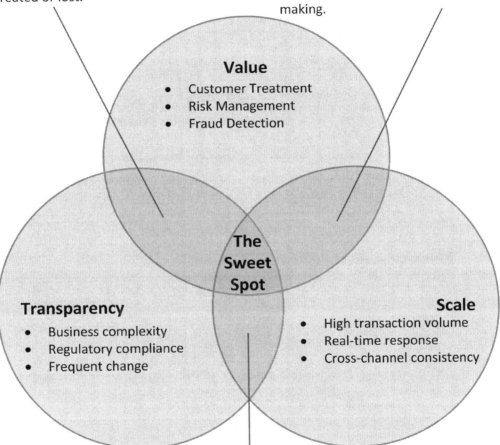

Value
- Customer Treatment
- Risk Management
- Fraud Detection

The Sweet Spot

Transparency
- Business complexity
- Regulatory compliance
- Frequent change

Scale
- High transaction volume
- Real-time response
- Cross-channel consistency

Any process that must operate at scale and with a degree of transparency has likely been modeled. The decisions within such a process will likewise benefit from being modeled so they can be reliably automated and the overall process simplified.

Figure 5-1 Three dimensions of suitability

Regardless of the business area's characteristics, however, there is value to an organization of understanding and modeling decisions. Organizations often find it easier to manage risk if all the decisions involved in risk are clearly modeled and managed, even those decisions and business areas that don't "pass" the tests in this chapter. When personnel are retiring, when organizations are undergoing a significant reorganization or for a myriad of other reasons, decision modeling can create and capture organizational value well outside these boundaries.

5.2.1   High value operations

The way in which a business process, system or business area adds value makes a difference to the potential for decision modeling. Those areas focused on customer treatment, on risk management and on fraud prevention and detection are particularly likely to show a return on decision modeling. These are all decision-centric problems where the decisions made determine business outcomes directly. For instance, it does not really matter how efficiently an insurance organization can process a claim if it decides to process a fraudulent claim as though it were legitimate—bad decision-making has a far larger negative impact than efficient processing has a positive one.

5.2.1.1   Customer treatment

Most organizations want or need to treat customers in accordance with their corporate policies. At the same time, they want to treat good customers better than poor ones, reflecting the value of a customer in the value of the treatment offered to that customer. They may also want to target new and existing customers effectively to drive future growth. This combination of a need for consistency and for targeted customer treatment puts a premium on well-defined and well managed decision-making and creates an opportunity for decision modeling to add value.

5.2.1.2   Risk management

All organizations need to manage risk. They need to impose controls on their business activities to ensure safe operations and to correctly account for risks they accept. They may need to accept or reject transactions based on their impact to the organization's overall risk profile and, potentially, disclose this impact to a third party (e.g., a regulatory authority). In parts of the business where managing risk is a day to day activity, decisions must be made in the context of the organization's risk portfolio and risk policies. A clear understanding of decision-making is essential in these circumstances because the decisions made must uphold the risk policies and be demonstrably compliant with industry mandates and regulations. In addition, decisions can articulate tradeoffs between risk and customer growth.

5.2.1.3   Fraud detection and prevention

Organizations at risk of fraud, those where the identity of those they interact with may be falsified or where false transactions may need to be processed, are engaged in a running battle with those who seek to defraud them. For example, trying to manage fraud through a "pay and chase" approach that seeks to detect payments that should not have been made has a very poor success rate. This puts a premium on preventing fraudulent transactions from entering the system in the first place. Ensuring that decisions to detect, report and prevent fraud are made quickly and effectively is critical. Decision modeling is a powerful tool in ensuring that they are.

5.2.2   High scale operations

Decision modeling is a way of defining, in advance, how decisions should and will be made. As such, the scale at which decisions need to be made acts as a powerful multiplier for its value. Decision-making is going to require scale and repay an investment in decision modeling when there is: high transaction volume, a need for real-time response or a desire for consistency across different channels.

5.2.2.1 High transaction volume

Any transactions that must be processed in large numbers require an organization to think about how it is going to handle these transactions. Business process and other models can help define how a transaction will flow through an organization and its systems. Most transactions, however, will also require an organization to make decisions. When transaction volumes are high the value of modeling these decisions to ensure they can be made repeatedly, correctly and consistently will be likewise high.

High transaction volumes also motivate organizations to optimize the cost of making decisions—by reducing or eliminating the need for manual intervention or minimizing use of expensive resources. Decision modeling's support for automation directly facilitates this.

5.2.2.2 Real-time response

If a transaction must be handled in real-time then it will not be practical to have manual handling of that transaction—some form of automation is going to be required. Without time to escalate or refer a transaction, decisions about transactions will need to be made automatically. Because decision modeling allows a precise, automatable definition of decision-making, it is extremely valuable as part of designing a real-time response to a transaction or event.

5.2.2.3 Cross-channel consistency

As organizations become more complex they must handle interactions across multiple channels. Web, mobile, in person and automated channels must be coordinated and must behave consistently. While the systems and processes involved in each channel are often different, decision-making must be consistent or at least integrated across the channels. Decision modeling allows this coordination to be managed effectively.

When a business area includes many business processes across which consistency is desirable or demanded, this area is likely to be a good candidate regardless of the motivation for consistency. While delivering consistency across channels is the most common, it is the need for consistency that is the driver here. Because decision modeling enables the reuse of shared decision services across many parts of the organization, it is essential for this consistency.

5.2.3 Operations requiring transparency

The final aspect of a business domain that identifies it as one where decision modeling may offer great value is a need for SMEs, business owners and external parties (e.g. regulators or auditors) to clearly see and understand what is happening in the business—for transparency. Where a business domain has a great deal of business complexity, where regulatory compliance is critical or where change is constant the transparency of decision modeling is required.

5.2.3.1 Business complexity

Most organizations have some aspects of their business that are fundamentally more complex than others. Where the business is complex, there is value in enabling business experts to understand and control the behavior of information systems. There is also value in being able to capture best practices and tribal knowledge so that the expertise of experienced staff is not lost when they move on or retire. Decision modeling is an effective tool in both situations.

5.2.3.2   Regulatory compliance

Some organizations have the luxury of operating without detailed regulatory oversight, but many must constantly focus on following, and being seen to follow, detailed regulations. Because ensuring compliance with regulations is complex, demonstrating compliance is often even harder and punishments for non-compliance can be severe, effective tools are required for managing the impact of regulations on the business. Decision modeling is one such tool which also enables the use of other tools such as BRMSs that can likewise help.

5.2.3.3   Frequent change

Regardless of the complexity of a business area or its regulatory framework, it is always a challenge to manage a business domain that is subject to constant change. If the way the business operates must constantly be adjusted, it is essential that there is transparency and clarity as to how it is operating now. It's only safe to change something if you understand it. Decision modeling is a powerful tool for making it clear how the business is (or should be) operating such that it can be rapidly, and safely, changed as business needs change.

5.3   When Decision Modeling is Less Useful

Decision modeling can be less useful simply when none of the above conditions are true. In addition, when decision logic is being discussed and decision modeling considered, there are a few red flags that identify the domain as one in which decision modeling is likely to be less useful:

- If the domain of discussion is a technical one rather than a business one. Decision modeling is fundamentally a way to model *business* decisions.
- More specifically, if the decisions are implementation specific rather than business focused; for example, logic aimed at cleaning up data quality issues across systems.
- If the decisions concerned are trivial and have no inherent business value such as those required for purely technical data format translation.
- If the decisions are highly localized, tactical, short-lived and their value is not transferable such as the logic involved in one-off system integration.

Even if the area is one that appears to meet the criteria for decision modeling, it may also be the case that the logic involved is not consciously understood or that it cannot be readily analyzed. In these circumstances decision modeling may not be useful. Care is warranted, however, as some areas are considered poorly understood only because no-one has really attempted to understand them or to use a suitable approach. Developing an initial decision model, or attempting to, may reveal that some of the area can be usefully modeled. Do not write off any area too quickly.

5.4 Characteristics of a Suitable Decision

If a business domain is suitable then the next step will be to identify candidate decisions within that business domain. How to discover decisions within an area of the business is described later (see the Section on methodology in 12.2). Many organizations conduct initial decision discovery workshops and quickly generate many candidate decisions. Decision discovery is also an ongoing activity, however, best managed in tandem with an evolving set of business processes. As the business evolves and changes, as new business processes are considered or new systems implemented, new decisions will be discovered.

As decisions are identified it is possible to consider each to see how suitable it is for decision modeling—how much benefit will accrue from modeling the decision. Each decision can be considered in turn for suitability. This too should also be an ongoing activity, subject to periodic reevaluation. Some decisions may be initially ruled out of scope—perhaps they were not the focus of the project during which they were discovered—and later need to be reassessed. For instance:

- If the regulatory environment tightens or court rulings make it imperative that decision-making be compliant then a decision may become a better candidate for modeling.
- New competitors or changed behavior on the part of existing competitors, especially a competitor that is now changing and adapting more rapidly, may likewise increase the value of modeling specific decisions such as those related to pricing or promotion.
- The business of the organization may evolve to make a decision more important (e.g., the volume or cost of manual processing may increase), driving up the value of modeling it.

It is also important to periodically re-assess decisions already modeled to see if they still need to be maintained and updated. While few regulations are withdrawn, it does occasionally happen and this will cause some decisions to be retired. Similarly, changes to business models and the competitive environment may sideline decisions or even make them irrelevant. It is important that redundant models are retired otherwise governance and modeling teams can be overwhelmed with work on old decisions, leaving no capacity for new ones. It is important to maintain the relevance and leanness of decision repositories.

A set of characteristics can be described for a decision that allow it to be characterized as suitable for decision modeling. No one characteristic or group of characteristics is definitive. These characteristics are better thought of as ways to prioritize and order decisions in terms of the likely value that decision modeling will bring. The characteristics, in descending order of priority, are:

5.4.1 Is made frequently

Perhaps the most basic characteristic of a suitable decision is how often that decision must be made. The more often a decision must be made the more value there is likely to be from understanding and being able to systematically improve that decision. The value of a decision can be considered to be the impact of that decision multiplied by its frequency. Thus a decision made more frequently is going to be more valuable than it might at first appear. Even a relatively simple, low value decision that is made frequently may have a significant cumulative value making it a better target for decision modeling. Decisions made many times an hour or more are ideal.

For instance, one large retail bank considering a Next Best Action initiative identified 140M touch points a month with customers. This means that the decision as to the most suitable action or offer to make to a customer must be made approximately 200,000 times an hour.

While most decisions that are modeled are made frequently, there are some good use cases for modeling low volume decisions, sometimes even those that will only be made once. Where the value of knowing how a decision will be made in advance is high, or the impact of making it is substantial, it can be worth modeling a decision even if it is not made very often.

5.4.2   Needs to be applied consistently

In parallel with the frequency of the decision, it is worth considering how consistently it must be made. Generally, a decision that is made frequently should also be made consistently and decision modeling is particularly effective when this combination is seen. Especially when a decision must be made consistently across many parts of an organization or across many channels or multiple processes, decision modeling will be a powerful tool for consistency.

Note that this does not mean that the decision will have the same outcome each time, only that the approach used to make the decision should be consistent. A decision to determine the correct content to display to a website visitor based on their profile, interests and behavior, for instance, may result in different content every time but is likely to be based on a consistent decision-making approach and so be a good fit for decision modeling.

Sometimes a decision is not currently being made consistently but there is a desire to make it consistent and repeatable. For instance, different claims adjustors might be reserving against claims in a different way at present. An organization may decide that this is unacceptable and use decision modeling to drive to a consistent, repeatable approach.

5.4.3   Has real business impact

The business impact of a decision may be assessed in terms of direct financial consequences (e.g., profit increase or cost reduction) as well as non-financial benefits such as risk reduction, preservation of reputation or legal compliance. To be quantifiable, such measures of business value should be linked to metrics that are monitored on an ongoing basis such as customer retention rate or fraudulent claims paid. The impact of a decision can be seen in the metrics or measures that it alters.

The value of a decision might be obvious and immediately calculable such as the revenue from an automated cross-sell or the amount of money saved by not unnecessarily referring a policy to an underwriter. Alternatively, the value might be such that it can only be measured after-the-fact with analysis, such as by measuring how many loyal customers were retained by offering a strategic discount. Value may also come from the cost and probability of error in a decision, for instance if a non-compliant decision can result in a fine that could be avoided.

5.4.4 Is measurable

Strongly related to the business impact of the decision is the ease with which that business impact can be accurately measured. Bitter experience suggests that a decision that has a real business impact but one that cannot easily be measured is a poor candidate for modeling. If the impact of improving a decision cannot be proven, then improving it can seem like an expense without a return.

Decisions may be poorly measurable because the required data cannot be captured, because it cannot be captured at a sufficiently granular level to notice the improvement or because it cannot be captured often enough. Solving a measurement problem like this can be addressed as part of a decision-centric project, and will need to be if the decision in question is going to be targeted effectively. It may also be that other impacts exist that are poorly understood, obscuring any improvement caused by better decision-making.

5.4.5 Has inherent business value

Distinct from the previous two considerations, this characteristic concerns the value of the business logic *itself*. Does the business logic have an inherent and lasting value or convey an explicit benefit or advantage? This value may be proprietary, representing an interpretation or a specification into which much analysis time has been invested or a resource that would be expensive to replace. For instance, the logic might currently reside in the heads of SMEs who may leave the company. Decisions can also have value if their definition is, or could be, contested. For instance, if multiple versions of policy exist and the organization needs to select one and justify it in each case.

Modeling such a decision creates value in various ways:

- It creates durable documentation that is concrete and easily understood. This is available to employees and won't be lost when the experts who created it leave the company.
- It eliminates confusion when a decision is subject to many competing forces by expressing the current policy or regulatory 'interpretation' clearly.
- It provides the ability to review and optimize decisions based on an accessible definition.
- It can be used as an effective training resource.
- It allows implicit business knowledge and requirements to be explicitly formulated and captured by subject matter experts.

5.4.6 Changes frequently

Some decisions are stable and the way they are made need not be changed very often. In contrast, other decisions must be constantly adjusted and refined to reflect new regulations, court rulings, policies, competitive behavior, business partner practices or similar. The more frequently the decision-making approach must change, the more value there is from a formal, manageable model of the decision-making. A model of the decision-making is easier to assess to see how it might need to change, easier to change and it is easier to verify that it has been changed appropriately.

Just as some decisions have regular change imposed upon them, others require frequent business-led change from within an organization. Triggers for change in such decisions are likely to be business triggers: an update to the business domain or an innovation to optimize profit or reduce costs. The need for this kind of change is generally first observed, and better understood, by business personnel rather than members of the technical team. The best approach is to allow management of these decisions by the business themselves so they can determine when and how the decision-making approach must be changed. Modeling this kind of decision allows greater control by business professionals.

5.4.7   Must be made very quickly

Some decisions must be made very quickly. If a decision is required as part of a real-time interaction, then it cannot be deferred to a person and must be completely automated. Modeling decisions that must be automated in this way has high value.

Similarly, some decisions that need not be made in real-time have more value if they are made quickly. There is a concept in decision-making of **Decision Latency**. This concept, first articulated by Richard Hackathorn of Boulder Technology Inc., in articles published in 2002[4], states that the value of a decision generally declines the longer it takes to make it unless a delay can improve the accuracy of the decision.

Figure 5-2 shows some of the ways in which value can decay with time and the matching ways in which value increases when time to decide is reduced:

- Sometimes it displays a classic decay curve: decaying quickly initially and then slowing.
- Sometimes this decline is gradual, with each small delay in decision-making reducing the value of the decision linearly.
- Sometimes this decline is more of a step function, with delays longer than a certain threshold (a regulatory deadline for instance) causing a significant reduction in value.
- Sometimes the value stays flat for an extended period during which a change in the time taken to make the decision has no impact on the value of that decision.

The decision latency of the decision can impact the value of modeling and automating the decision. If significant value can be created by making the decision more rapidly, then a more rigorous understanding of the decision—a decision model—is likely to be valuable.

5.4.8   Is expensive to make

If a decision has a high processing cost in terms of manual work (e.g., personnel time), relative to the cost of automation, then it is likely to be worthwhile to automate it. When decisions are made manually, there is often a great deal of variation, even inconsistency, in decision-making. It is also common that much of the domain expertise required to make the decision well is not documented or managed effectively. This means that the retirement or departure of critical personnel can significantly degrade the accuracy and timeliness of decision-making. Modeling and managing these decisions captures this domain expertise so it can be reviewed, shared, and automated where this is cost effective.

---

[4] *Minimizing Action Distance* in DM Review, September 2002

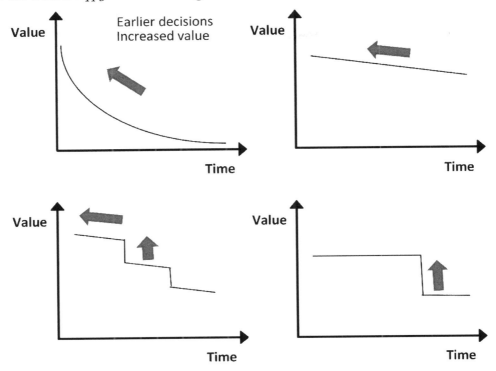

Figure 5-2 Decision Latency and the Rate of Value Increase in Different Scenarios

5.4.9   Can be audited or reviewed

Many decisions are driven by external regulations. Organizations making these decisions often have to demonstrate that their decisions are compliant with these regulations. In addition, decisions based on policies or a mix of regulations and policy are often subject to audit and must be explicable to an external or internal reviewer, sometimes under time pressure. In these circumstances the decision needs to be traceable to supporting documentation and it must be possible to justify its behavior. Decision modeling helps with both of these.

5.4.10 Has a high cost or risk of error

Sometimes making a poor decision has a serious consequence in terms of business outage, loss of reputation or fines. In some scenarios the consequence is more modest but it is easy to make a poor decision. In either case, the potential losses from poor decision-making (the product of the maximum loss and its probability) are significant. Decisions that have these kinds of risks need to be well understood so that the risk can be minimized and mitigated. Decision modeling provides the clarity and transparency necessary for risk mitigation efforts while also helping to identify exactly where in the decision-making errors are most likely and allowing this decision-making to be improved.

5.5   Decision Modeling in Context

Decision modeling is a key technique in the successful adoption of Decision Management and the construction of Decision Management Systems. Decision Management has a basic structure consisting of three main phases: Decision Discovery and Modeling, Decision Service Definition and Implementation and Decision Measurement and Improvement[5]. These phases progress iteratively while decision modeling has a role in all three phases as shown in Figure 5-3 Phases of Decision Management.

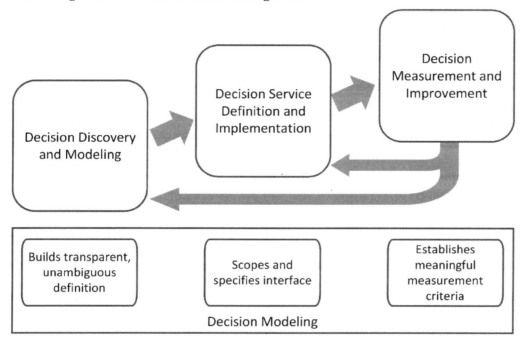

Figure 5-3 Phases of Decision Management

5.5.1   Decision Discovery and Modeling

The first step in Decision Management is Decision Discovery and Modeling. Decision Discovery and Modeling identifies and describes the repeatable decisions that matter to a business—the ones that drive operational results. It separates these operational decisions from business processes and systems, externalizing them and allowing them to be managed and evolved independently.

Decision Discovery and Modeling is first and foremost about capturing a transparent, unambiguous definition of the decisions that are to be managed. This involves the use of a decision modeling approach such as that described in Chapter 12. Identifying a broad set of

---

[5] In previous publications these have been referred to as Decision Discovery, Decision Service Definition and Implementation and Decision Measurement and Improvement. The names have changed but the meaning has not.

candidate decisions allows Decision Management efforts to find the most effective focus points. These decisions are modeled for clarity and specificity using DMN. A decision model ensures there is enough precision to draw automation boundaries and to drive towards a successful implementation. The use of DMN, a standard and business-friendly notation, allows these decisions to be understood and owned by the business. Decision modeling using DMN also provides common language between business analysts, architects, business owners, IT professionals and analytic teams so these models can orchestrate the Decision Management technology required by each business problem.

This combination of process separation and modeling allows decision-making to be linked explicitly to performance measures and KPIs (Key Performance Indicators), so that it is clear what changes to decision-making will be required to improve any given measure. This linkage helps drive effective models—ones that will have a positive business outcome in terms of these measures and KPIs—and establishes the framework for monitoring decision effectiveness.

The use of DMN also exposes decision logic to earlier and more thorough expert review by bringing it earlier in the development cycle, into Decision Discovery and Modeling. This allows for rapid identification of vague definitions, contradictions and misunderstandings.

Decision Discovery and Modeling extends an organization's requirements and architectural approach to explicitly focus on operational business decisions. This is where the core activities of decision modeling should be performed.

5.5.2 Decision Service Definition and Implementation

The second step in Decision Management is the creation of Decision Services to automate some or all of the decisions identified and modeled in Decision Discovery and Modeling.

Decision Service Definition and Implementation uses decision modeling to scope and specify the interface for these Decision Services. Decision Services replace hard-coded decision logic in processes and systems to make those processes and systems simpler, smarter and more agile. Decision Services are stand-alone components, generally built using Business Rules Management Systems. They can be enhanced with the results of data mining and predictive analytics, at the time of their original creation or anytime thereafter.

Decision Services implement all or part of a decision model. They are business services in a Service Oriented Architecture (SOA) that deliver an answer to a specific business question—the one defined for the decision. These services do not update information or have other side effects. They just answer questions such as "how should we handle this claim?" or "what is the right discount for this order?" They are how systems and processes find out what the best or most appropriate decision outcome—answer—is for a particular customer or transaction. Because they don't make any permanent changes and they have no memory, they can be used to answer questions whenever they arise without worrying about potential side effects, making the decision reusable and widely applicable.

Most organizations have developed an SOA infrastructure for deploying and managing services. This infrastructure is used to access a Decision Service just like any other service. In addition, it allows the Decision Service to access enterprise resources and other services (using the same SOA infrastructure) and can make various business-level interfaces available for other services to use.

Decision models play a critical role in Decision Service Definition and Implementation. As noted in section 8.1.6, a Decision Service is defined in terms of the decisions that are included in the service, the data and decision results required as inputs to the service and the decision(s) that can be invoked in the service. Decision models also provide a framework for agile and iterative development of Decision Services, allowing each phase or iteration to be scoped, modeled and implemented in a controlled way without forcing a waterfall development approach. Because decision models also make the interactions and dependencies within and between Decision Services explicit, they help organizations scale to dozens or hundreds of Decision Services while avoiding complexity issues such as the management of dependencies.

Most importantly, decision models show how the various technologies used in a Decision Service are being orchestrated to deliver the overall answer. Currently, Decision Services are built primarily using decision logic—business rules—specified as part of the decision model and often managed using a BRMS. Many Decision Services implement decisions based entirely on policy, regulation and best practices—all of which can be represented using business rules. Other Decision Services also require analytic insight from data mining and predictive analytics to be integrated into the service to deliver the required decision-making. Some may even require constraint-based or other kinds of optimization. All the required technologies should be encapsulated within the Decision Service and orchestrated according to a defined decision model.

5.5.3   Decision Measurement and Improvement

The final step is to close the loop with Decision Measurement and Improvement. Decision Measurement and Improvement ensures that decision-making is monitored and constantly improved to cope with a changing environment and deliver increasing value over time.

Decision Measurement and Improvement—the application of performance management techniques and technologies to the monitoring of decisions—is critical. With a Decision Management approach, the business understands how specific decisions create value. These decisions are linked to the performance metrics being tracked for individuals as well as for the business as a whole. To continuously improve business performance, decision-centric organizations monitor decision performance, throughput and basic statistics. For example, how many times a decision is made to approve, reject or refer a customer case is a measure of decision effectiveness. Too many referrals will increase the burden on staff doing manual reviews. Too many rejections, thanks to false negatives for instance, will impact customer service or sales. Similarly, decisions that take too long or that cost too much (because they use data that must be purchased, for instance) may have a negative overall impact. Tracking and reporting this information will help the business owners understand and thus manage their decisions more effectively by targeting improvements.

Decision models provide meaningful measurement criteria and crucial connective tissue for this phase. Connecting decisions to both the KPIs and metrics they impact and to the decision logic that implements them, decision models glue a decision monitoring environment together. Decision models support impact analysis and other investigative techniques as they can be used to see which higher-level decisions are impacted by a specific proposed change and how those decisions impact the business and its systems and processes. By connecting a local change to its broader business context, decision models support more sophisticated analysis and more systematic improvement.

6 Introduction to the DMN Decision Modeling Standard

We could, of course, use any notation we want; do not laugh at notations; invent them, they are powerful.
—Richard P. Feynman

This chapter explains what a decision modeling notation is and why a standard notation is needed. It describes how enterprises benefit from using a notation to model their decisions, what drives the need to standardize decision modeling and the typical content of such a model. The purpose and rationale of the Decision Model and Notation (DMN) standard is described before summarizing its specific advantages and providing simple examples of its internal structure. The chapter concludes with an examination of DMN's most important feature: its declarative nature. Subsequent chapters include a more detailed examination of DMN.

6.1 Why Use a Standard Notation?

Compose and perform a concerto to challenge the world's most accomplished orchestras and soloists. Produce a commercial aircraft with a larger range and better fuel economy than all your rivals. Devise a revised set of Atlantic shipping lane routes based on new tidal patterns and exclusion zones. These activities are examples of large-scale ventures requiring the participation of many people with diverse goals, backgrounds and locations. There may be a small number of authorities in the creative process, but the realization of their work will require collaboration with many others. Projects like these need to be able to effectively and unambiguously communicate complex ideas. They need to convey intent accurately and engage many participants. Such efforts are also more effective when they can avoid mistakes and benefit from the experience of previous, similar endeavors. This leads many such projects to adopt a proven, standard notation and vocabulary that all participants can share.

6.1.1 Use notation not prose to be unambiguous

The need to be precisely understood means involved parties cannot rely exclusively on natural language prose. This is too ambiguous and lacks sufficient structure to represent complex ideas. A formal notation with precisely defined meaning enables experts to build a model of their ideas, not simply write a document. It also encourages a more methodical approach. A notation that defines the elements that must be described, identifies the information that should be captured about these elements, ensures that elements can only be combined in meaningful ways and formalizes how all these elements are presented can eliminate ambiguity, reduce inconsistency and avoid incompleteness. Complex projects need a shared terminology and standard notation—be it music, aeronautic design or marine cartography—so that all the participants can communicate reliably and precisely. This allows teams to collaborate more effectively and prevent errors and wasted time due to miscommunication of ideas.

Furthermore, a standard means of communicating business decisions allows organizations to:

- provide a vehicle for experts to share, review, compare, refute, experiment with and improve business decisions;

- develop a widely-shared understanding of the business logic embodied by decisions;

- communicate company and industry best practices;

- clarify the requirements of business decisions early so that the appropriate resources (e.g., data and knowledge) can be provisioned; *and*

- provide a mechanism to audit the use of business decisions and traceability to tie specific outcomes to defined policy.

6.1.2   Engage and develop a community

Collaborators in complex projects benefit from using an appropriate, widely-accepted standard notation to represent their ideas, even if it is not perfect. Using an industry standard notation to convey key facts and design intent allows experts to be understood unambiguously by other professionals in their domain (e.g., the community of musicians, aeronautical engineers or sea pilots) and share ideas and best practices. The alternative, using an ad-hoc notation of their own invention, would be unsatisfactory as all collaborators would be obliged to learn it before any work could begin.

The use of an accepted and widely used standard means cooperation requires less advance planning and preparation. There is no need to select or invent a new, project-specific notation and train collaborators in its use. Instead, everyone can assume a shared understanding of a common, professional 'language' that facilitates meaningful dialog on the subject matter from the outset. Collaborators can focus on their work rather than the notation.

Standard notations also help to commoditize the skills required to produce good designs or compositions. This allows projects to get help from the marketplace in reviewing, refining, sharing and realizing ideas. Mature industries are characterized, in part, by the extent to which they use standard notations.

6.1.3   Leverage the experience of others to avoid mistakes

These kinds of industry standards are generally created by groups of experts and refined over many years of use. Users of standards can leverage this experience and industry best practice to avoid repeating the mistakes of their predecessors. Some examples of the benefits of using a standard notation are provided below:

- Good notations encourage brevity, structure, integrity and even elegance in what they express.

- Many highlight or prevent common mistakes and internal contradictions. Music notation, for example, provides temporal structure to a piece and supports the rules of music theory.

- Proven notations emphasize the important abstractions they are trying to convey.

For example, marine and aerial charts use specific projections to ensure they remain a good analogue of what they represent (e.g., by preserving scale or bearing angles) to simplify navigation and prevent error.

- The form of a notation highlights structures that require attention (e.g., sensitive international borders, navigational beacons or hazardous tides) while omitting irrelevant features (e.g., mean sea temperature and oceanic species migration paths). Good notations support the compact representation of complex, relevant ideas.
- Industry notations often represent a visual analog of the underlying information. For example, one can see, in the visual depiction of a sea route, if it has too many intersections or ventures too close to sensitive areas.

Tried and trusted industry notations are more likely to have these benefits, and less likely to have flaws, than home-grown ones. Industry standards also change at a much slower rate since shortcomings are more likely to have already been resolved. Because they have been refined by collective use and are owned by an authority, they are also less likely to be burdened by needless, ad-hoc extras added by 'creative' users. The lack of such extras promotes brevity and elegance in the notation.

6.1.4 Plug in to a software market

Finally, the most pragmatic advantage of using industry, rather than home-grown, notations is the availability of software support. More specifically, access to tools that can empower the use of the notation while removing much of the error-prone drudgery of manually maintaining internal consistency. While organizations can and do develop software to support their own notations, this is an expensive proposition and the software often "ages" as user interface and platform norms change. In contrast, a widely used industry notation will be supported by an array of commercial and open source software.

6.2 Documenting Business Decisions with a Standard Notation

The benefits of using a standard notation apply to the problem of describing complex business decisions. Decisions such as determining which rental vehicle best meets each client's requirements, deriving the optimum price of an insurance policy or assessing the likelihood that a transaction is fraudulent are among many that are complex enough to justify modeling. Whether the ultimate goal is to automate these decisions, provide definitive documentation and improve consistency of manual decisions or a combination of both, a standards-based approach is the best means of enabling effective collaboration, leveraging industry expertise and facilitating tool support.

6.2.1 What is a Decision Modeling notation?

A decision modeling notation is a graphical representation expressing the structure, requirements and logic of repeatable business decisions. For each decision, the notation documents:

- the purpose of the decision;
- the information that is needed to make it;

- the possible outcomes;

- how an outcome is generated or selected in any given scenario based on the information provided;

- what decisions and sub-decisions collaborate to determine the outcome and their interdependencies;

- how external business knowledge (i.e., know-how, mandates or policies) influences decision-making and the location of these references (authorities); *and*

- why the decision is made: its business value and rationale.

To be most useful, a decision modeling notation should:

- be unambiguous, concise and complete;

- be business rather than implementation oriented;

- provide an organizing principle that allows models to scale arbitrarily; *and*

- offer sufficient structure and formality to allow business subject matter experts (SMEs) to understand decisions entirely and yet avoid intimidating them with irrelevant complexity.

6.2.2   The DMN standard

The Decision Model and Notation (DMN) standard meets the needs described above. It is an open standard defined, ratified and published by a team of vendors under the auspices of the Object Management Group Inc. (OMG). The OMG is an international, not-for-profit, technology standards consortium specializing in the development and custodianship of standard notations used by businesses in over twenty market verticals.

DMN provides a notation and formal grammar for representing decision models and business logic. It has a simple, extensible and easy to learn structure that captures much of the essential information required to define decisions. It is designed for use by business analysts and business subject matter experts as well as IT professionals.

6.2.3   Why use the DMN standard?

DMN is a standard that is integrated with many other established industry standards (see Chapter 10). It has been created by experienced practitioners and ratified by a prominent standards authority. It is flexible and extensible. It is already supported by many software tools (see the DMN Tools Catalog in A.2.2); indeed, DMN represents the most complete and best supported means of modeling business decisions that is currently available or likely to become available in the near future.

6.2.3.1   An open standard

DMN is not the only decision modeling notation in use, but it is the first *open*[6] standard for decision modeling. It was created and is maintained by a group of industry practitioners

---

[6] It is not owned by any specific vendor, specific to a given product or subject to restricted distribution. Users may propose amendments to the OMG.

with decades of cumulative experience in decision and business rule management (including Decision Management Solutions, Escape Velocity LLC, Fair Isaac Corporation—FICO, IBM, Knowledge Partners International, Oracle and TIBCO Software Inc.). DMN was ratified in 2014 by the OMG. So it is administered and supported by one of the most effective open standards consortia with a track record of creating, enduring and pragmatic modeling techniques that are of genuine use to thousands of companies.

This industry support, combined with the innovations that DMN garnered from earlier decision modeling techniques such as The Decision Model (or TDM, see Appendix D) and broad academic research into the effective use of tabular decision logic[7], ensures it is fully featured and fit for purpose.

Open standards often achieve a broader adoption and better support from tools, published materials and the practitioner community. Openness also promotes innovation.

6.2.3.2 Integrated with existing standards

The OMG already administers many of the most successful integration standards in the world, including: BPMN, for modeling business processes; UML, for modeling application structure, behavior and architecture; and the Model Driven Architecture standard (MDA). Further, DMN is designed to integrate with many of these existing OMG standards, e.g., BPMN, UML and BMM[8] (see Chapter 10). This places business decisions among the other first class citizens of effective business change (alongside data, process, events and business rationale) and cements its place at the heart of business architecture (see Chapter 7).

6.2.3.3 An extensible standard

DMN uses established means of representing business logic, such as decision tables, for which there are already many published best practices. It also supports analytic models and is open to extension to other logic representations. It remains under active review and development, with the 1.1 revision, for instance, adding formal support for the definition of Decision Services.

6.2.3.4 Effective tool support

DMN is supported by considerably more vendor products than any other decision notation and this number is growing. It allows tools to support different approaches to decision modeling while using a standard model and notation. DMN's support for multiple diagrams acting as views on an underlying model allows it to benefit significantly from repository-based tooling while the model offers sufficient precision that fully formed decision models can be simulated or even generated as working code by some software tools. DMN offers a level of precision that provides a basis for tools to perform verification checks for logical integrity (i.e., the checking of consistency, gaps and redundancies). Most importantly, many tools support collaborative building of decision models, effective communication and sharing of ideas across large distributed teams.

---

[7] "The History of Modeling Decisions Using Tables (Part 3), Standardardizing Decision Table Modeling", 2012, http://www.brcommunity.com/b652.php

[8] The Business Motivation Model, Business Rules Group and the Object Management Group (OMG), http://www.businessrulesgroup.org/bmm.shtml

6.3 Overview of DMN

6.3.1 Goals of DMN

The primary goal of DMN is to communicate the meaning of business decisions precisely and clearly to a wide audience using a standard visual and textual notation. More specifically, it has the goals outlined in Sections 6.2.1 and 6.2.2. In addition, DMN aims to:

- Express business logic precisely, in sufficient detail to support verification and execution, while still retaining ease of comprehension for business subject matter experts by excluding technical implementation details.

- Integrate with business process models (usually expressed in BPMN) to establish the context of a decision within a business process. This defines when it is used, what events trigger it, which parts of the organization are involved and how its outcome influences the remainder of the process.

6.3.2 Decision models integrate process and business logic

To illustrate the layers of DMN and how they integrate with the business process model, a fragment of a decision model is introduced in Figure 6-1. The goal of the business process in this example is to determine the quality of a financial instrument and, from this, whether or not it can be used as collateral—its *collateral eligibility*. One important decision made as part of this process is to determine what kind of financial asset the instrument represents. This example will be developed and explored in Chapter 8 and it is not essential to understand the details at this point.

All decisions occur in the context of a business process, whether or not that process is explicitly modeled. A process is a sequence of business tasks orchestrated across one or more business actors. A special type of task—**a decision task**[9]—is used to denote the invocation of a decision at a certain point in the process (for example, see the ringed task with a business rule icon at the top of Figure 6-1).

Every decision task is associated with one or more associated decisions (as showed by the upper large arrow in Figure 6-1). These decisions may be modeled in, and thereby have their logic defined by DMN. DMN definitions occur at two levels: The **Requirements Level** (in the middle of Figure 6-1) shows how each top-level decision depends on sub-decisions, data and sources of knowledge; and the **Logic Level** (at the bottom of Figure 6-1) specifies the detailed logic, inputs and outcomes of each decision and sub-decision in the model. These two views are summarized in Table 6-1.

It might appear that the Decision Requirements Level provides an 'executive summary' suitable for management whereas the Decision Logic level allows subject matter experts to communicate details. However, in our experience both parties benefit from both views.

---

[9] Named 'Business Rule Task' in the current BPMN terminology.

View	Goal	Content
Decision Requirements Level	Expresses the dependencies of decisions on subordinate decisions, data inputs and knowledge artifacts. Allows decisions to be decomposed into a hierarchy of simpler sub-decisions. Shows collaboration of decisions to achieve a goal.	A drawing of shapes representing decisions, linked by lines to other shapes representing the artifacts on which they depend. A scalable, explicit statement of dependencies for each decision.
Decision Logic Level	Lists the inputs and the outputs (outcome) for each decision. Defines the possible outcome values of a decision. Expresses the logic by which the outcome value is determined based on conditions satisfied by the inputs.	Precise definition of logic in a wide variety of formats (e.g., decision table, analytic model, decision tree, expression or function in a purpose built language). For each combination of input values, defines the outcome.

Table 6-1 The Two Levels of DMN Models

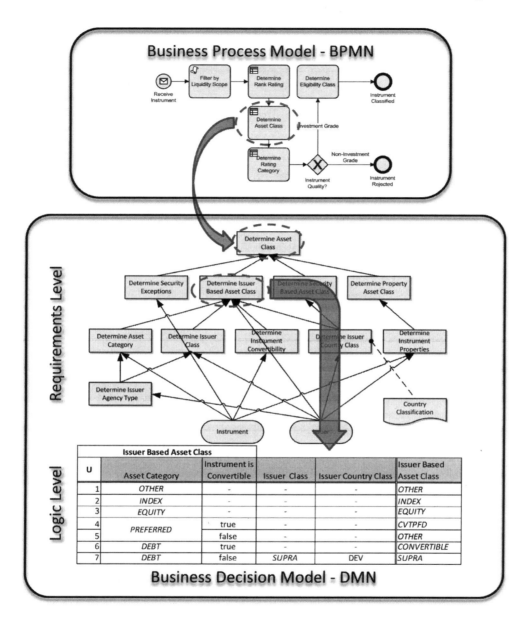

Figure 6-1 Linked BPMN and DMN Models showing Business Process, Decision Tasks, a Decision Requirements Diagram and Decision Logic in a Decision Table

6.3.3 Decision Requirements Level

The **Decision Requirements Level** provides a visual overview of the decisions and their inter-dependencies, including their reliance on more fundamental information like input data and knowledge (business policy, constraints, external mandates or know-how).

The visual view is simple and elegant; it only features four types of symbols and three types of relationships. This simplicity belies considerable expressive power but allows decision requirements to be communicated effectively to personnel without a technical background.

The Decision Requirements Level supports scalability by allowing complex decisions to have a hierarchy of dependencies on other, simpler, subordinate decisions—*sub-decisions*. The outcomes of each sub-decision acts as inputs to its 'parent' decision, permitting the assembly of complex logic from simple (potentially reusable) pieces. This encourages a separation of different parts of the decision logic and supports arbitrary complexity while retaining ease of understanding. This ability to assemble many simple sub-decisions into a complex decision is why business decisions scale much more effectively than conventional business rules that lack such a mechanism.

The Decision Requirements Level is explicit about all the dependencies between decisions and sub-decisions. It also expresses their dependencies on the other components of decision-making:

- **Knowledge Sources**: an internal or external reference to business policy, mandate, law or know-how that acts as an authority for a decision (see section 8.1.3).
- **Input Data**: information items used by decisions.
- **Business Knowledge Models**: a reference to a reusable fragment of business logic or know-how. Business Knowledge Models represent commonly required logic that is invoked in many different contexts and therefore cannot be associated with fixed Input Data (see section 11.1.1).

The visual representations of the Decision Requirement Level are called **Decision Requirement Diagrams**. Each diagram is a 'view' of part of the network of dependencies between named decision, Knowledge Source and Input Data components. Different diagrams may overlap with each other provided they are mutually consistent. Each type of component in a Decision Requirements Diagram is represented with a unique symbol and is linked by a set of lines representing the dependencies between them. There are different types of dependencies and each dependency type has a different symbol.

In such a diagram, the decisions appear as rectangles enclosing their name. A subject (top-level) decision is often shown, by convention, at the top of the diagram. However, this is not mandated by the standard[10]. The subject of a Decision Requirements Diagram is defined as the decision on which no other component depends (i.e., it has no parents). A diagram may have more than one subject, but should have only one for clarity. Consider the example Decision Requirement Diagram in Figure 6-2. The single subject decision of this diagram is *Determine Instrument Asset Class*. It depends on subordinate sub-decisions: *Determine Overriding Asset Class*, *Determine Issuer Based Asset Class* and *Determine Fallback Asset Class*. It requires two Input Data components (*Instrument* and *Issuer*) and two Knowledge Source components (*Conduit Know How* and *SEC[11] Asset Classification Guide*). These components and their relationships are examined further in the sections that follow.

---

[10] Some modelers find a depiction showing the subject in the center of the decision requirements diagram, with dependencies inbound from all sides, more natural.

[11] U.S. Securities and Exchange Commission.

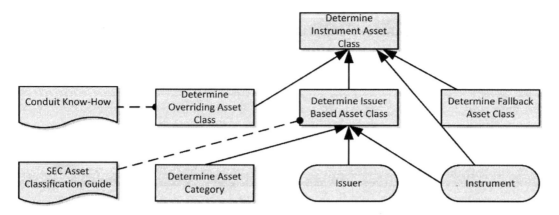

Figure 6-2 Example Decision Requirement Diagram (DRD)

The solid arrows depict the fact that *Determine Instrument Asset Class* depends on information either received from a data source (i.e., *Instrument*) or resulting from a sub-decision (e.g., *Determine Issuer Based Asset Class*). The dotted line depicts the knowledge requirement of a decision (e.g., *Determine Issuer Based Asset Class*) on an authority (e.g., *SEC Asset Classification Guide*) to support its definition. This is discussed further in Chapter 8.

The Decision Requirements Level also captures many properties of decisions that are not visually represented in a Decision Requirements diagram, such as the purpose of a decision (the question it answers) and its business value.

6.3.4   Decision Logic Level

The Decision Logic Level defines, for each decision in the Decision Requirements Level, the detailed logic that derives the outcome of the decision from the values of its inputs (also shown in the requirements level). This view can express detailed business logic in many ways. One of the skills of an experienced decision modeler is the ability to select the most appropriate logic representation based on the style of logic being documented. Many factors influence this selection, for example: the degree of complexity, the uniformity of conditions used and the pace of expected change. Several DMN representations are demonstrated in Chapter 8 and some non-standard ones are discussed as best practices in Sections 11.3 and 14.4.2 with advice on how to select the most appropriate.

It is a strength of DMN that it does not mandate the use of a single representation of logic. However, at the time of writing, only the decision table and analytic model formats are defined as part of the standard. Nevertheless, the range of representations is open to future extension.

The format, grammar and internal consistency of each logic representation is strictly controlled. Modelers are free to choose which representation of logic they use, be it formal or informal. However, if they select a formal representation they must abide by its rules.

At the Decision Logic Level, each decision is defined more formally, as an expression showing how each combination of input values is mapped to a decision outcome (one or more conclusions). A common representation of this is the **Decision Table**. Figure 6-3 shows a Decision Table expressing the logic of the *Determine Issuer Based Asset Class* decision. In this example, a single conclusion (the column to the right of the double vertical divider) depends on three conditions (the headed columns to the left of that divider): *Asset Category*, *Instrument is Convertible* and *Issuer Class*.

Issuer Based Asset Class				
U	Asset Category	Instrument is Convertible	Issuer Class	Issuer Based Asset Class
1	OTHER	-	-	OTHER
2	INDEX	-	-	INDEX
3	EQUITY	-	-	EQUITY
4	PREFERRED	true	-	CVTPFD
5	PREFERRED	false	-	OTHER
6	DEBT	true	-	CONVERTIBLE
7	DEBT	false	SUPRA	SUPRA

Figure 6-3 Example Decision Table

Decision Tables are a popular and intuitive means of expressing conditional logic and an intuitive means for subject matter experts to represent their knowledge. In Figure 6-3, every numbered row is a separate rule. This is referred to as the 'rules as rows' format, which is arguably the most familiar and accessible layout for business subject matter experts when denoting simple 'truth table' logic, especially those who have any experience of Business Rule Management Systems (BRMSs). This decision table determines the core class of an *Asset* based on its *Category, Convertibility* and *Issuer Class*. For brevity, not all rows are depicted in this example. Each rule defines the outcome of the decision based on conditions expressed on the input values. For example, row 4 asserts: 'if the *Asset Category* is PREFERRED and the *Instrument is Convertible*, then the *Core Asset Class* is *CVTPFD'*. The details of this representation are covered in more detail in Chapter 8.

6.4 The Importance of a Declarative Standard

DMN is a declarative approach to modeling decision-making. This is important as it ensures that DMN decision models stay focused on statements of fact about the desired or intended decision-making requirement and are not contaminated by implementation detail. Specification and implementation must be kept separate.

6.4.1 Precision is not implementation

As covered earlier, DMN's main goal is the precise representation and communication of business decisions. Automation is not the main goal, although it is supported and is frequently highly desirable. Unfortunately, there is often a tendency for business analysts and subject matter experts to confuse 'precision' with implementation. Ask a business analyst for a detailed definition of a decision and they may begin to describe how it is currently implemented. Worse, they might describe how it was implemented historically. This confusion is understandable as, until now, the only commonly used, precise and shared representation of business logic that many analysts had was its implementation—in Java, SQL or some other implementation vehicle. All other representations (e.g., English prose or spreadsheets) are more open to interpretation and, because they are not testable, can have hidden, internal inconsistencies.

This has led some analysts to use implementation as a means of expressing requirements, becoming fluent in a programming or database language as a means of expressing themselves. A few others exploit the innate ambiguity of textual documentation in order to conceal their incomplete analysis and, thereby, defer detailed requirements investigation to implementers. Their specifications have hidden gaps in areas where they lacked the time, willingness or ability to perform a thorough investigation of the requirements. It is part of the grand tradition of software development that some of the thorniest issues of business requirements are often left to be resolved by developers with limited business knowledge.

6.4.2 Decision models are statements of fact about what is required of a decision.

DMN seeks to address the confusion between precision and implementation by expressing requirements in a declarative manner—one which focuses exclusively on need and that is entirely free from implementation concepts. Consider this analogy: a business requirement can be compared to the need to travel from one place to another. In this analogy, a statement of requirement based on implementation would be an exhaustive, step-by-step set of instructions for how to start up and drive a specific model of car from one's current location to the destination—one of many potential means of achieving the journey. It would focus on how to steer the car, when to change gear and so on. A declarative statement of the same requirements would be equivalent to a map showing the origin and destination with an approximation of the route between them. The latter omits the specific technical means by which the journey is achieved (implementation detail), focusing instead on the precise definition of what is needed and the intermediate steps to achieve it.

DMN is primarily a means of unambiguously modeling requirements. It is not a means of implementation, nor is it a mandate to automate decision logic. Indeed, it is perfectly satisfactory to model logic in DMN that is not automated and that will remain manual. DMN specifies what decisions are to be made, what information is needed and the logic that will determine the outcome—not *how* this logic is implemented. Good decision models do not contain implementation hints; instead, they focus on an exact definition of what is needed and the relationship of a decision with its process and data context.

DMN is precise enough to produce executable decision models. However, this precision is primarily valuable for facilitating testing of decision logic, allowing experimentation with different approaches, supporting the impact analysis of a proposed change and improving the transparency of the model by showing analysts how it behaves when presented with certain data.

6.4.3 Why enforce this separation between specification and implementation?

What is required of a business decision and how it is implemented are entirely separate concerns addressed by different areas of expertise. If these concerns are mixed, this risks:

- **Polluting requirements with extraneous detail.** Implementation languages introduce many details and idiosyncrasies that are irrelevant to specification, making them poorly adapted to the task of representing requirements. For example, depicting an aggregation in Java requires temporary variables and the selection of an iteration technique. Both are irrelevant to the definition of the aggregation requirement.

- **Making requirements less accessible.** A representation of requirements steeped in implementation references will be much harder for a business subject matter expert with no technical expertise to understand.

- **Preserving outmoded historical concepts.** Basing a decision model on historical implementation concepts increases the risk of perpetuating old ways of doing things, which are entirely ill-suited to the current requirement and that introduce unnecessary and unhelpful additional detail. It gives the modeled implementation approach a degree of undeserved authority that makes it harder to challenge, even when it should be.

- **Making premature implementation choices.** Early use of an implementation language for expressing requirements may lead to hasty and inappropriate selection of implementation technique before the requirements are fully understood. Early stipulation of decision sequence may limit implementation options; instead, one should focus on decision interdependencies.

7 Business Context

Form follows function
—Louis Sullivan

Success with decision management involves integrating decisions with your overall business architecture. Decisions don't occur in a vacuum and it is useful to lay out the overall decision context so that decisions can be designed, executed, managed and improved systematically. As organizations become increasingly focused on the knowledge economy, the need for a decision architecture in this context is clear. A decision architecture is a decision-centric view of your business that puts real value on understanding and managing your decision-making.

Managing decisions as part of an overall business architecture requires that those decisions fit into the context formed by your applications, your organization and your infrastructure.

Decisions use data to select appropriate actions that enable an organization to respond correctly to events and drive business processes to desired outcomes. Clearly defining the relationships between decisions, business processes, events and data establishes this operational context.

Decisions are the responsibility of people and organizations and have an impact on their behavior. How well decisions are made determines if the organization meets its targets and objectives. The relationships between decisions, KPIs, objectives and organizational structure represent the organizational context of decisions.

Finally, many decisions are automated, in whole or in part, and must therefore be deployed to the organization's infrastructure. As needs and situations change, these deployed decision-making components must also change. This is the infrastructure context of decisions.

7.1 Decisions and Business Architecture

7.1.1 Business Architecture

An architecture consists of components, their relationships and their behaviors. Different architecture views address different concerns of different stakeholders. Although there is currently no single definition of the list of exact components that make up a business architecture, most would acknowledge business motivation, capabilities and processes. The particular architecture view selected is based on current business priorities and concerns. Business architectures do evolve over time, but most continue to reflect their original perspective.

The perspective of a business architecture serves as the organizing principle for its components. This perspective generally defines the business architectures as one of the following types:

- process centric;

- data centric; *and*
- strategy-map centric.

Regardless of its type, a business architecture contains other related views to support what is generally a diverse set of business initiatives and solutions. For instance, a process-driven architecture is appropriate for streamlining workflows and an organization's value chain. A focus on process necessarily involves the data used within the processes. In addition, process efficiency and effectiveness can only be evaluated in the context of business goals and performance metrics that are part of a strategy map.

7.1.2   Business Architecture in the Knowledge Economy

Many enterprises are evolving from an industrial assembly line structure to a more knowledge driven, networked and collaborative structure. Decision-making is becoming more distributed, sophisticated and automated. To support this, a business architecture should align processes, events and data—the operational context—with decisions and track how these decisions impact business strategy and the strategy's key performance indicators, i.e., the organizational context.

Figure 7-1 shows how an overall business architecture needs to encompass decisions and their context. How an organization makes decisions drives the behavior of the rest of the business environment, i.e., processes, events, data and the organization's structure. Decisions are linked to the operational context as strongly articulated decisions are increasingly the means by which business processes and systems are steered. Decisions are also made in the context of a specific enterprise and must take account of the organizational realities of the enterprise. Organization structure (the division of responsibilities among organizational entities) and culture (their behavior and goals) dictate the formality with which the enterprise considers decision-making and can result in multiple, sometimes conflicting, points of view.

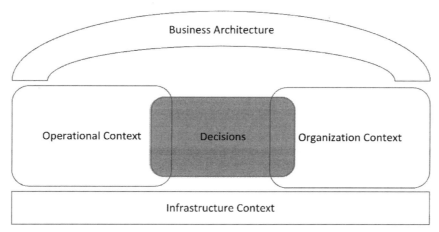

Figure 7-1 Decisions Are Part of a Broader Architectural Context

7.1.3   Decision Architecture

A decision-centric view of business architecture is an essential organizing principle to deal with a data-driven, knowledge-based economy. Without an understanding of decision-making and of how decision-making fits into the broader context of an enterprise, data and knowledge cannot be effectively applied to the day to day operations of the enterprise. The knowledge economy, boosted by the growth in Big Data and analytics, is leading more enterprises to consider a decision centric business architecture—a decision architecture if you will.

A decision architecture relies on a repository of decision models cross-referenced with other architectural components and an associated governance mechanism for building and managing these decision models. A decision architecture is a decision-based view of a holistic business architecture, one that links decisions to processes, events, data, organizations and effectiveness measures. While the focus is on the decision-making elements at the heart of a decision model—decisions, Knowledge Sources and Input Data—these elements are placed in a broader context.

In a decision architecture the decision models are linked to other components of the business architecture such that navigation to other architectural views is seamlessly possible as shown in Figure 7-2.

The general goals of a good architecture apply to a decision architecture. It should be possible to use simplifying models to manage complex behavior, increase transparency, enable consensus, promote reuse and manage change. These models should be based on established notations. The specifics of how such models can be integrated are discussed in Chapter 10.

7.2 Operational Context

Decisions do not stand alone but are part of how an organization performs its work, i.e., its operational context. The application usage context of decisions involves business process, business event and business data contexts.

7.2.1 Business process context

As discussed in Section 4.2, most business systems only automate simple decisions, such as validation, calculation or routing. Adopting the BPM approach allows more rapid change to automated processes, especially when process models are developed using BPMN to bring clarity and transparency. However, decisions remain neglected even in BPM. As the frontiers of automation have advanced, the need to identify, model and manage decisions has grown.

Once decisions are identified, it becomes clear that many business processes are executed as a consequence of a decision having been made. Other processes describe the preparation needed to make a decision. Many processes are executed in response to transactional stimuli and rely on decisions being made to steer them as they execute. In all these cases, decision logic describes how the decision needs to be made and the conclusion of that decision drives the process. A process definition is, therefore, not complete without describing both the process goals and the decision-making logic used to achieve them.

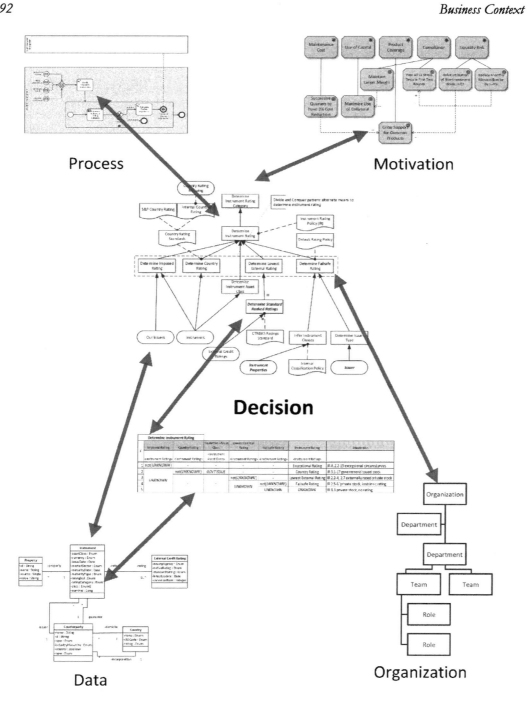

Figure 7-2 Decision Models Connect to Other Models for a Complete Business Architecture

For instance, a claims process is triggered by the receipt of a claim, but the critical path choice is whether (or not) the claim is valid and will be paid. This decision drives the process, and the goal of the process—to pay all valid claims quickly and efficiently—cannot be met unless the decision is made correctly.

Because the outcomes of decisions often steer business processes, it is beneficial to model decisions within a strong business process context, whether or not this process context is itself explicitly modeled. To ensure transparency and flexibility, a decision model should be built in parallel with any process model being developed. Process models are not necessary for decision modeling but when process models are being developed, all business decisions that would otherwise be embedded within the process should be explicitly pulled out into a decision model. This enables a clear focus on decisions and supports the implementation of specialized technology stacks for both decision management and business process management. The process context for the decisions is most fully described by linking process and decision models. How DMN decision models and BPMN process models can be integrated is the subject of Section 10.2.

7.2.2 Event context

Events are an integral part of how business processes are defined, especially when BPMN is used to model the process. Some organizations prefer to model events more independently of their processes thereby developing an event-decision-action architecture. CMMN—the Case Management Model and Notation—is emerging as a standard for representing processes in this way, as it establishes a context (a case) and then defines how events in that context are responded to. Generally, there are multiple responses possible, therefore requiring a decision to be made about the 'best' warranted response in a given situation. This ensures that the events affecting an enterprise are responded to appropriately, even if the response is *do nothing*. For instance, in a credit card fraud monitoring system, a pattern of events indicative of fraud may be detected and yet ignored because there is an existing dispensation legitimizing the events.

The event context can be thought of as a different architectural lens, focusing on events and their responses rather than on events as part of business processes. If such a lens is applied, then it is important that the decisions made about how to respond to these events are described formally and completely. Such a lens is commonly combined with Complex Event Processing (CEP), where many low-level technical events are assessed to see if a business-relevant event has occurred so that it can be responded to. Deciding if a pattern of low-level technical events represents such a business event is sometimes modeled as a decision also.

Whether the event is external or internal to the enterprise, and whether it is planned or unplanned, a decision architecture allows the enterprise to plan the decisions that should be taken for each such event. Each decision uses the best available data and the most relevant knowledge and expertise to pick the most advantageous and appropriate response to that event. That response is executed through pre-defined processes and workflows. Decision models allow explicit consideration of information and knowledge in picking the best possible response.

Decisions designed to handle high volume events can be automated, whereas contingency planning for occasional, but high impact, events can rely on manual decision-making.

Alerts from sensors on an assembly line need to be evaluated through automated decisions because of the high volume and because the bulk of responses will be automated corrections in any case. In contrast, most disaster recovery plans anticipate various catastrophic events and build out a suitable response plan. This includes manual decision-making criteria for which responses will be triggered by which combination of events.

The pervasive set of sensors spawned by the Internet of Things (IoT) is generating a flood of signals that can be harnessed for a variety of preventive and opportunistic actions. CEP technologies are evolving rapidly to deal with this onslaught. These technologies can be used to determine that a specific business event of note has occurred and the correct decision triggered to determine an appropriate response. In this way, well designed, automated decisions can be applied to these event streams to highlight the best response to these events.

Being explicit about which events trigger which decisions provides an event context for decision models. These events might be modeled as part of a process, marking the beginning of a process or an error condition in a process. If the event is local or central to a specific process, then the process context will dominate and should be used for the context of the decision. In those organizations that move to increasingly pure event-decision-action architectures, however, the event context may come to dominate.

7.2.3   Data context

The data required to be created, stored and managed by an enterprise should depend on how that data will be consumed in making decisions—whether the decision is embedded in an automated process or is made manually by subject matter experts with the aid of reports and dashboards. Data that is never used in decision-making has little or no business value. Data management efforts can be both inefficient and ineffective, without a description of the decisions that are going to consume the data being managed.

Data Management has become complex and costly with the various recent trends collectively and conveniently bundled under the moniker 'Big Data'. There were always many flavors of data, but now there are many more, starting with the need to consider both structured and unstructured data. It is easy to get sidetracked into building costly and complex data management infrastructure, if there is no logical framework for picking and prioritizing which data needs more attention than others. This can, and does, cause organizations to overestimate their data requirements.

Even more insidious than the temptation to collect and store all possible data is the impulse to ensure the highest possible data quality for every piece of data. Obviously data quality is critical in certain decision-making scenarios, but in some others approximated data or targeted data quality may be sufficient. There is a cost associated with ensuring data quality and investments should be made consistent with returns expected from that investment.

A decision architecture ensures decisions are described along with their data requirements. This decision-oriented view of data helps plan data infrastructure based on real need and guides prudent investments in that area. The decision models and data models involved should be integrated as described in Section 10.3.

There are situations where organizations have consciously decided to store all the data available in the belief that the data may be valuable and can be monetized through data mining and advanced analytics. This has some merit, provided there is a considered strategy for applying advanced analytics. Something more than ad-hoc analyses for answering ad-hoc questions is required, however. An analytics strategy based on a robust decision architecture describes the network of interdependent operational decisions that can be improved by applying data analytically and will ensure this data value is realized.

The data context for decisions is thus bi-directional. The data architecture ensures that the decisions being modeled and managed in the decision architecture will have the data they need, with a level of quality and timeliness that will support effective decision-making. At the same time, the decision architecture provides targets and objectives for the data architecture to help ensure the data adds value and that investments in data quality, integration and availability will actually result in improved decision-making.

7.3 Organizational Context

While the operational context for decisions describes the mechanical context for decision-making, the business impact of decision-making is described through motivation and organization contexts. The motivation context defines the goal and success criteria for decisions. It defines the purpose of decision-making and how to tell a good decision outcome from a bad one. The motivation context provides a purpose for managing and improving decision-making. The organization context ensures that decision-making responsibilities have been effectively assigned across the organization. Understanding this context is essential if decision-making is to be managed, measured and improved systematically. It is also important in determining who is responsible for decision governance.

7.3.1 Motivation context

All enterprises are organized to achieve a set of goals, governed by a vision and described in terms of objectives. There are generally a number of quantitative metrics and other indicators to measure the performance of each and every aspect of the enterprise in the achievement of these objectives. Sometimes, these are formalized under the umbrella of Enterprise Performance Management. Some enterprises are modeling their motivation and measurement approach formally and such models can be integrated with decision models as described in Section 10.5. All decisions need to be made in a way that will maximize the overall performance of the enterprise given this motivation context.

To motivate and manage an organization, the performance of people and business units within that organization should be measured using metrics that they can influence. Because high-level metrics generally cannot be directly influenced by operational staff, a 'hierarchy' of metrics are used by some to show how lower level operational metrics roll-up into higher level enterprise performance metrics. Even when this is done well, operational staff and those building operational systems cannot generally see how they can influence these metrics day to day.

Good performance is a result of making appropriate decision every time an opportunity arises. One of the best ways to improve performance is to describe and manage all the decisions that can affect a given goal or objective. Given a metric, a list of decisions that directly influence that metric can be readily defined. These decisions can be modeled and linked to other contexts as described in this chapter. The way in which each decision contributes to a metric or an objective can be documented and measured.

The linked metrics and objectives—the motivation context—allows the success criteria for each decision to be defined. Good decisions move metrics in a positive direction or make progress toward goals. Where multiple objectives are impacted by a single decision, as is often the case, trade-offs are clearly identified. As a result, the action plan to improve performance becomes very evident, since each metric is mapped to one or more decisions. Make those decisions better, and performance will improve.

7.3.2 Organization context

The quality, currency and consistency of decisions made by an organization has a direct impact on its performance and viability. It is important to have a responsible owner for each decision and, equally important, that the organization structures discourage fragmented or outmoded decision-making. All variations of responsibility, accountability and reward structures in organizations are related to the values and risk-impact of enterprise decisions. To be effective, an organization needs to map reliably to a decision architecture.

It is important decisions have an organizational context. Organizations need to define who is responsible for how decisions are made, which is often the organizational unit that owns the metrics that are influenced by the decision. This unit will expect to define and maintain the decision-making algorithm or be directly responsible for others who do this.

Other organizational units, or roles within them, will have to execute the decision if it is not automated. The way the decision-making is described and supported needs to be aligned with this organization's incentives and work style. Those making the decision need the capability to provide feedback from decision-making into the decision design for constant improvement.

Besides owners and makers, other organizational entities may take an interest in decision-making, for instance, for risk or compliance reasons. They will need to be kept informed as the decision-making changes.

An organizational context should assign responsibilities to specific organizational units and managers. Decisions should be owned by designated parties, even though some decisions may be executed by other parties under guidelines established by the owners. For instance, promotional pricing decisions are owned by the marketing group, even though the actual decision may be made by a call center agent.

Organization structure should minimize fragmentation of decision-making. It is important to detect and resolve any conflict of interest among the parties associated with a decision. A decision architecture shows decision dependencies across the entire organization and so supports smart partitioning of decision-making responsibilities across it. In some cases, it may be better to adjust the organization structure to accommodate natural boundaries in decision-making highlighted in the decision models (see the example in Section 17.2).

7.4 Infrastructure Context

Many decisions in an organization are automated. These decisions must be packaged and deployed into a technical infrastructure. Increasingly, this means a service-oriented environment and one that supports agile, iterative development.

7.4.1 Deployment context

Once decisions have been identified, modeled and put in context, they still need to be deployed. The most effective way to do this is to give every process or system the ability to contact a separate Decision Service with a question in order to receive a considered answer back.

A Decision Service is a service that encapsulates an automated decision so that it can be invoked from any system or process. If planned and designed correctly, a Decision Service is a standalone piece of decision-making that answers a specific question and that can be called from any system that needs a considered answer to this question to continue processing. This considered answer is based on all relevant and applicable business data and knowledge, defined in the decision model for that decision and provided by the questioner.

For simplicity and reliability, the Decision Service itself should be stateless and side-effect free so that it does not need to be aware of previous or subsequent processing. The process or system can then focus on handling the possible outcomes. The decision made may be simple or complex, but the process is not impacted, as it can always get the answer it needs.

For implementation and live execution of a decision, a standalone Decision Service can fit most modern system architectures. The concept of Web Services and a Service Oriented Architecture (SOA) is now mainstream and most modern systems support some form of services integration.

A well-designed Decision Service is self-contained in terms of business logic and depends on the external environment only for access to information that needs to be evaluated for generating a conclusion. The relatively independent nature of Decision Services allows rapid implementation because decision logic development work can be performed independently of, and in parallel with, technology integration, once a 'data-handshake' has been defined. Decision models and a decision architecture ensure that this handshake—the information requirements of the decision—is explicit, reducing the risk of late discovery of onerous requirements.

Since Decision Services are fully compatible with a Service Oriented Architecture (SOA), all benefits of an agile, iterative development and of a distributed, maintainable systems architecture translate seamlessly over to a decision architecture.

While a formal assessment of deployment context is critical for automating decision-making, the same principles are equally useful in describing manual decisions. Manual decisions are made every day by subject matter experts. Documenting them with decision models and putting these decision models in context helps share best practices, train new team members and minimize business expertise loss when personnel leave. In addition, explicit documentation often uncovers gaps and improvement opportunities in the decision-making and can prepare the way for partial or complete automation in the future.

7.4.2 Change control context

A business architecture allows organizations to cope with planned and unplanned changes—from assessing the impact of changes, to planning for and implementing required alterations. A good architecture lowers overall risk during change since most of the planning, scoping and experimenting can be done with this virtual representation of all relevant organizational elements. Mutual dependencies between architectural components are minimized, thereby lowering the impact and change cost.

Planned changes are either the result of a continuous improvement program or a specific infrastructure or capability upgrade. Most continuous improvement programs rely on measuring operational performance and making operational adjustments for better results. In many situations, perhaps even most, processes are less likely to be the focus of a proposed change than the decisions they invoke. The most common improvements are, therefore, likely to come from improvements to decision-making. Defining and managing decisions formally in a decision architecture means a continuous improvement cycle can be controlled much more effectively and transparently. Such closed-loop decision improvement also supports a focus on experimentation and champion/challenger testing where continuous improvement is built right into the decision design.

The other type of planned changes are large projects initiated to upgrade or install new infrastructure and related capabilities. Many of these new capabilities relate to data—especially 'Big Data'—and analytics. The value of these technologies comes from improved decision-making, i.e., from improving the precision, profitability and speed of decision-making. A decision architecture effectively injects these forms of automated knowledge into processes and systems. A formal decision architecture helps ensure that these knowledge-based capabilities are not left out.

Unplanned changes can also be managed more effectively with a decision architecture. Unplanned changes often result from the behavior of competitors, court rulings, amended compliance regulations or unexpected changes in consumer behavior. The best immediate response to these kinds of sudden change is to adjust decision-making before considering more fundamental changes to process or infrastructure. A decision architecture is a good place to start impact analysis, since it describes all decisions within the appropriate business context and their dependencies.

8 The Decision Modeling and Notation (DMN) Standard

To create a new standard, it takes something that's not just a little bit different; it takes something that's really new and really captures people's imagination
—Bill Gates

This chapter describes the Decision Model and Notation (DMN) standard for decision modeling and illustrates how it is used. No prior knowledge of decision modeling is assumed, although readers new to decision modeling should consult Chapter 6 before reading this. This chapter is designed for ease of reference: concepts are introduced in ascending order of sophistication, each one within its own sub-section. Following the introduction of each principle, it is applied to a simple, on-going example.

A series of sections describe the structure of decision models and how models are separated into two levels: one depicting their requirements and the dependencies between decisions; and the other, the detailed logic that defines a decision's meaning. The chapter establishes a practical core understanding for new decision modelers rather than covering all of DMN's features. After reading this chapter, readers should attempt decision modeling in multiple projects before consulting the more advanced DMN material in chapter 11.

8.1 Decision Requirements Level

Section 6.3 identified the two main aspects of all decision models: decision requirements and logic. The Decision Requirements Level of DMN documents decisions and their dependencies. This level is represented by a set of Decision Requirements Diagrams, each of which shows the relationships between decision model components, as described in the following sections.

To illustrate decision modeling notation, the text that follows will introduce one modeling concept at a time and use it to incrementally build a decision model based on a simple finance example. For readers not familiar with financial jargon, a highly simplified introduction can be found in the following sidebar. Important concepts are shown in bold and these will be used in many of the examples that follow.

> Investment banks trade in a diverse set of **assets** each with a changing value. Some of these assets represent tangible products with inherent value, for example: commodities (e.g., gold, oil); debt issued by a government, corporation or municipal body; or shares issued by a corporation. Others are more abstract and derive their value from some underlying asset, for example: an option to buy or sell something at a set price, or a share in an index like the Dow Jones. **Instrument** is a collective term for these assets. Instruments are provided or issued by a company known as the **issuer**. Some instruments are secured (underwritten) by a third party: the **guarantor**.

When an organization trades in instruments, it is interested not only in the current and potential value but in the **risks** of trading (e.g., the chances that the trade may default for any reason). Risk can come from a number of factors including: the country issuing the instrument (it may be politically unstable); the currency being traded (it may have a volatile exchange rate); the issuer (it may be financially unsound or have a poor credit history) and the risk of the asset itself (it may have a volatile value). To offset the risk, the organization must understand the net short-term exposure of every trading portfolio and ensure it is covered by **collateral** (underlying, high quality liquid assets that address the risk of a deleterious events).

Deciding the inherent risk of every instrument traded is, therefore, a key decision for any financial organization. The risk level is needed to determine: whether or not to trade, how much margin to charge to offset the risk and what collateral will be required. Risk classification usually occurs in at least three stages: inferring the type of asset represented by the instrument—the **asset class**; finding the standard credit risk rating of an instrument by using external rating agencies which rank the risk using a standard scale (the CTRISKS scale in our example) and determining the company's own view of the investment rating category which is informed by their own policies and attitudes to risk (e.g. *ABC Bank Counterparty Risk Guidelines*). From this, a categorization of risk (the *Instrument Rating Category*) can be determined.

8.1.1 Decisions

8.1.1.1 Definition

A decision represents the act of determining the answer to a business question by applying business knowledge to a specified set of input values (see Section 4.1.1) for a fuller definition). Inputs can come from an external data feed or be determined by other (sub) decisions. Often the answer (or outcome) of a decision is determined by checking these input values against a series of conditions. A decision outcome is made of one or more distinct conclusion values.

Be aware that, colloquially, the terms decision and outcome are used interchangeably. The phrase "that was a bad decision" usually refers to a poor outcome in a specific case. When decision modeling, be careful to distinguish the definition of a decision-making approach (the decision) from its result in a given case (the outcome).

8.1.1.2 Diagrammatic representation

Decisions are depicted in a Decision Requirements Diagram as a rectangle labelled with the name of the decision (see Figure 8-1).

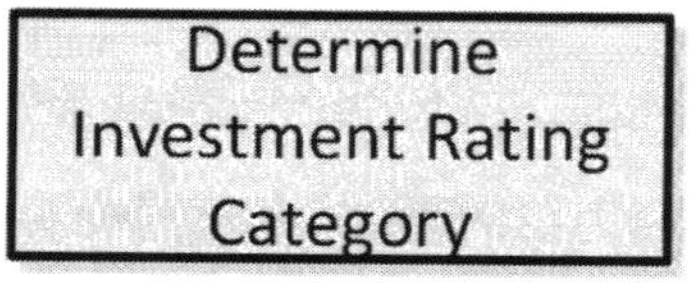

```
┌─────────────────────┐
│     Determine        │
│  Investment Rating   │
│     Category         │
└─────────────────────┘
```

Figure 8-1 Representation of Decision in a Decision Requirement Diagram

This name should meaningfully represent the decision's outcome and it is good practice to build it from well-defined business terms (see Section 9.1). Decisions may have many properties (see Section 14.2.4.1), but only the name must appear on the Decision Requirements Diagram component. Decisions can be associated with logic (e.g., a Decision Table or analytic model) defined at the Decision Logic Level (see Section 8.2).

8.1.1.3 Dependencies between decisions

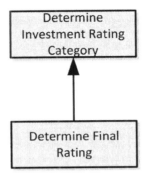

Figure 8-2 Decision's Dependency on a Sub-Decision

Decisions can use the outcomes of 'child' or 'sub' decisions as inputs. In Figure 8-2, for example, *Determine Investment Rating Category* requires (is dependent on) the outcome of the decision *Determine Final Rating* to produce its own outcome. In order to determine the *Investment Rating Category* one must know the *Final Rating,* which must be separately decided. The arrow between the decisions is a data dependency (called an **Information Requirement**) representing this need. Note that the arrow points towards the dependent decision: the one that requires the information. The information conveyed from one decision to the other, the *Final Rating* in this case, is referred to as an **Information Item**.

The subject(s) of a Decision Requirements Diagram are those decisions at the top of the chain of dependencies, i.e., those that no other decisions require. These have no outbound arrows. Each diagram may have more than one subject, but it is often more readable if it has only one. *Determine Investment Rating Category* is the subject of Figure 8-2.

Any decision component in a diagram can be directly linked to one or more business processes through a decision task (6.4.2), not just subject decisions. This supports the modular reuse of decisions and enhances consistency across business processes.

8.1.1.4 Standard properties of decision components

Additional, essential[12] properties of decisions, defined by the standard, include:

- a description or explanation;
- a question—a natural language question that precisely frames the decision; *and*
- the allowed answers to this question.

Properties of decisions that should always be defined if they are different from those of their 'parents' include:

---

12 Although these are considered optional (by the DMN standard) for the purpose of data interchange, we consider them mandatary for the models themselves. See the best practices chapters (specifically Section 14.2.4.1>) for more specific advice.

- Any business objectives supported by the decision (perhaps defined in a business motivation model, see Section 10.5).
- Any key performance indicators by which this decision can be measured. These may be a measure of how effective it is in meeting the objectives defined above or a more general measure of business effectiveness impacted by the decision.
- The organizational units within a company that:
  - o   make the decision;
  - o   own the decision (i.e., that determine how it should be made; *or*
  - o   have a vested interest in the decision.

In addition, decision components share standard properties with all other Decision Requirement Diagram components:

- a unique identifier *and*
- an extended set of user defined attributes.

8.1.2   Input Data

8.1.2.1   Definition

Input Data components represent specific Information Items required by, and supplied to, the decision-making process that are not the outcomes of decisions. Instead, Input Data comes from outside the model—from users, source systems and datastores.

Input Data may be: attributes with a single, simple value (e.g., the value of an asset or the name of a company); a complex data structure with many attributes of its own (e.g., an issuer, asset or shopping cart); or a collection of either (e.g., a portfolio of assets or list of asset values). Each should be named after a well-defined business term. DMN does not dictate the form of this business term or its association with a corporate data model or business glossary (but see chapter 9 regarding the importance of a glossary to decision modeling).

8.1.2.2   Diagrammatic representation

Input Data components are represented on a Decision Requirements Diagram as rounded rectangles labelled with the name of the data being supplied.

Figure 8-3 Example Input Data Instrument

In Figure 8-3, the decision *Determine Final Rating* has an Information Requirement for the complex Input Data *Instrument*. This suggests that the *Instrument* data structure has one or more attributes that are being used to determine the final rating for each one.

Note that, in this view, the Input Data is represented as a separate component in the diagram. An alternative representation of the same model, referred to as the **Listed Input Data** option, is demonstrated in Figure 8-4. In this diagram, which is equivalent to Figure 8-3, the *Instrument* Input Data (and any other data dependencies this decision may have) is listed in the lower compartment of the *Determine Final Rating* decision itself.

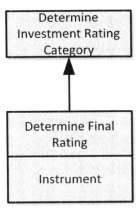

Figure 8-4 Input Listed Mode Equivalent of Figure 8-3

Both layouts are acceptable in diagrams, although mixing them is not recommended. The representation of Figure 8-3 allows the dependencies of multiple decisions on the same Input Data to be clearly represented (e.g., see *Instrument* in Figure 8-8) and clarifies the separation between decision and data. This style is generally preferred for these reasons and it will be used exclusively from here on.

8.1.2.3   Standard properties of Input Data components

Standard properties of Input Data components include:

- a description *and*
- a data type that describes the values the data can hold. See Section 9.7 in the glossary chapter for further information.

8.1.3 Knowledge Sources

8.1.3.1   Definition

A Knowledge Source component is a reference to information outside the decision model that influences or controls some aspects of how a decision is made. They are sometimes called 'authorities'. Knowledge Sources vary in three key ways: their content, their degree of influence, and their form.

A Knowledge Source might refer to a mandate, law, policy, standard or regulation that must be obeyed. It might refer to some information that controls, guides or informs the decision by providing departmental boundaries, helpful know-how or best practices accrued from experience. The referenced knowledge can be represented in any form, including: web pages, files, books, legal documents, audio or video content. Knowledge Sources may also refer to expertise held by organizational entities, groups or even individuals. The handling of Knowledge Sources in DMN is independent of their representation.

Knowledge Sources have different levels of influence over decision-making. Some sources dictate and control decision-making fully (e.g., policy definitions). Others constrain it (e.g., regulatory or legal standards), inform it (e.g., best practices or know-how) or justify it (e.g., policy rationale). The level of influence of a Knowledge Source cannot always be determined from its content, as it might exert different amounts of influence over different decisions. For instance, some decisions may be dictated by a particular regulatory standard, while others may only be influenced by it.

Knowledge Sources act as 'authorities' for decisions. The knowledge to which they refer exists outside the model and may be defined by the organization owning the model or an external governing body (e.g., a standards organization or regulatory authority). It is important to be clear if a Knowledge Source is a specific document, such as a cited authoritative reference, or one of the entities that produces or owns these references, i.e., the origin of the reference such as a governing body or expert. The latter may sometimes confusingly be referred to as the 'source of knowledge' or 'the authority'.

Knowledge Sources are primarily for documentation, but they can also be used to resolve questions that arise during the analysis and maintenance of decision logic by acting as a final arbiter in the event of confusion or conflict. They can also be used to justify the outcome of decisions after the fact and for impact analysis ('what would be the impact of changing this policy').

When a Knowledge Source represents a regulation or legal stipulation, a modeler may need to prove consistency between the logic of a decision and its Knowledge Sources.

8.1.3.2 Diagrammatic representation

In Decision Requirements Diagrams, Knowledge Sources are represented by rectangles with wavy undersides—a 'document' shape (see Figure 8-5). DMN dictates that the Knowledge Source must be given a name reflective of the knowledge content. A Knowledge Source must have properties that locate the document (allowing readers of a model to access it themselves) or describe the originating entity.

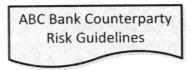

Figure 8-5 Example Knowledge Source

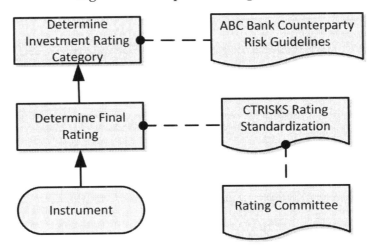

Figure 8-6 Example Use of Knowledge Source

Figure 8-6 shows that the logic embedded in the *Determine Investment Rating Category* and *Determine Final Rating* decisions are both influenced by authorities. The first must comply with standard local guidelines on categorization of risk (*ABC Bank Counterparty Risk Guidelines*). The name implies this Knowledge Source is defined by the company that owns the model. However, the *Determine Final Rating* decision must comply with the global CTRISKS definition of credit rating equivalences (*CTRISKS Rating Standardization*) and this is an externally defined, regulatory standard. In the latter case, this Knowledge Source is itself authorized and controlled by the *Rating Committee* (a Knowledge Source representing an organization) that controls the application of these standards. In either case, it may be necessary to prove that the definition of each of these decisions is compliant with the constraints defined in these Knowledge Sources.

8.1.3.3 Standard properties of Knowledge Source components

Additional standard properties of a Knowledge Source include:

- a description of the content;
- the form;

- the owner; *and*
- a unique URI (the location of the authority if it is embodied as an external document).

If the Knowledge Source is versioned (i.e., subject to periodic revision and re-issue under a new version number or data label), it is also best practice to supply version information in order to be explicit about the revision of the authority with which the decision logic complies. Lack of version information implies that the decisions are actively kept up to date with the evolution of the Knowledge Sources.

8.1.4 Annotations

Annotations act as text comments in a Decision Requirements Diagram. They have no formal meaning, but allow the diagram to be adorned with additional text blocks to explain or embellish some aspect of the model. They may appear in isolation or they may be an anchored to an existing DMN component with an association relationship (both forms are shown in Figure 8-7).

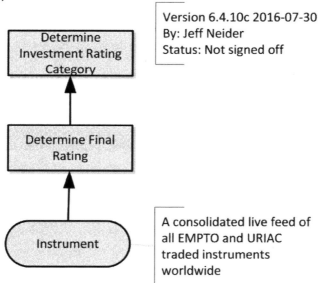

Figure 8-7 Example Annotations Documenting an Input Data Component

The annotation is depicted as a bracketed text block and the association relation as a finely dotted line without end markers. Other than their text block, they have no additional properties.

8.1.5 Relationships

DMN defines two semantic relationships between components. In each case, the relationship is directional or asymmetric and it represents a dependency of one component on another. Every relationship can simultaneously be interpreted in two ways:

- Information Requirements
    - o Towards the arrow, the relationship depicts the availability of information

from a provider to a consumer.
   o From the arrow to the root, the relationship depicts the dependency (or requirement) that a consumer has for information.
 • Authority Requirements
   o Towards the circle, the relationship depicts the availability of knowledge from a provider to a consumer.
   o From the circle to the root, the relationship depicts a requirement that a consumer has for knowledge.

The two core relationship types and the nodes they can connect are depicted in Table 8-1.

Relationship	Symbol	Meaning (Arrow to Root)
Information Requirement	⟶	A Decision requires information from another Decision or an Input Data.
Authority Requirement	· — — — ●	A Decision requires the authority of a Knowledge Source. This relationship also has more advanced uses that are covered later. (see Section 15.2).

Table 8-1 DRD Relationship Types

Section 11.1.1 introduces Business Knowledge Models and its associated Knowledge Requirement Relationship.

8.1.6   Decision Services

8.1.6.1   Decision Service definition

A decision service is an executable, architectural component: a means of packaging the logic of one or more decisions and delivering it as part of a component based architecture (for example a service oriented architecture, SOA). This is the most common means of integrating automated decisions into an architecture. Decision Services typically encapsulate implementations of the decisions in a Decision Requirements Diagram and get deployed from a Business Rules Management Systems (BRMSs) into a production service oriented architecture. They can then be used as needed by other architectural components, such as Business Process Management Systems (BPMSs).

A Decision Service defines an interface by which it may be 'invoked'. This interface, like a contract, specifies all the data required by the decision (its data inputs) and what it provides in return (its outcome). When invoked with all the required information, the decision service returns the relevant outcome. In accordance with modern architectural principles, the decision service retains no state and has no side effects[13]. It determines the out-

---

[13] When a Decision Service is invoked it determines and yields a result but has no other lasting impact on its environment. The service has no memory: one invocation of the service cannot alter its behavior in future.

come using only the information provided via the interface. Two identical invocations of the same version of a Decision Service should always yield the same result.

8.1.6.2   Diagrammatic representation

When a set of decisions is packaged into a Decision Service there is a need to define its content and interface. This can be shown on a Decision Requirements Diagram. DMN is declarative and makes no statement about how these services are implemented. DMN has a Decision Service component for Decision Requirements Diagrams that allows the scope of service provision and the interface to be defined. Specifically, it defines which decisions are offered by the service, the inputs they require and the outcomes they yield.

The Decision Requirements Diagram in Figure 8-8 shows a decision model with three decisions packaged into one decision service. The latter is depicted as a thick round-rectangle with two horizontal sections:

- The upper ('public') section depicts the name of the Decision Service and identifies those decisions that it publicly 'offers' via its interface.

- The lower ('private') section shows those the decisions that are encapsulated by the service in order to support the implementation of the public decisions. These are internal to the service and not directly accessible by users.

- If all the decisions encapsulated by a service are public, the lower section can be omitted.

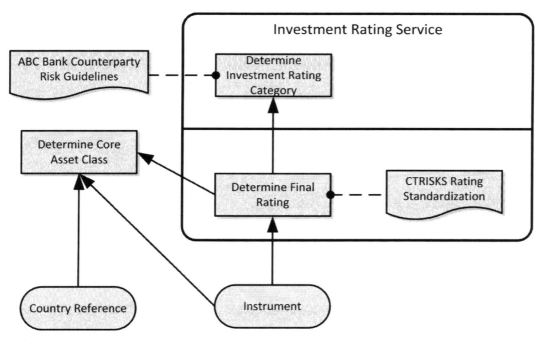

Figure 8-8 Example Decision Requirement Diagram Featuring a Decision Service

The only output decision offered by the *Investment Rating Service* is *Determine Investment Rating Category*. This appears in the upper 'public' interface of the service and the outcome of this decision is the only result this service generates. Because the *Determine Final Rating* sub-decision is required by *Determine Investment Rating Category* decision, it too has been encapsulated in the service[14]. Its representation, in the lower half of the service rectangle, denotes that it is not publicly accessible (it is not included in the interface). The value of the 'private' section is to explicitly document the decision dependencies of the public interface and to drive out all data and sub-decision requirements of the service as a whole. The decision *Determine Core Asset Class* need not be encapsulated by the service as none of the encapsulated services depend on it.

The placement of a decision in the private section of a Decision Service controls its visibility for that service only. This private use is not exclusive, so *Determine Final Rating* could be referenced in the public sections of other Decision Services and be an information requirement (as indeed it is in Figure 8-8) of other decisions. Naturally, *Determine Core Asset Class* cannot satisfy its information requirement for the *Final Rating* using the Decision Service.

The information that must be provided when invoking the service corresponds to all the information requirements that cross the service boundary. This includes any Input Data required by decisions encapsulated by the service and the outcomes of decisions outside the scope of the decision service that are required by encapsulated decisions. The outcomes of the service invocation will be the conclusion(s) of the public decision(s). An inspection of the data dependencies of Figure 8-8 reveals that an invoker of the service must provide *Instrument* Input Data but not *Country Reference*.

In this way, the entire interface of the Decision Service and its requirements are defined in the Decision Requirements Diagram.

Note that although some Knowledge Sources are displayed within the service and some outside, this has no bearing on the definition of the Decision Service which only encapsulates decisions. A single decision model may involve many (even overlapping) Decision Services.

8.1.7 Decision Requirements Diagrams

It is important to understand the difference between Decision Requirements Diagrams and the underlying Decision Requirements Level of the decision model. The relationship between these two could be compared to that between a series of architectural diagrams and a house, or a collection of maps and a city. Each diagram only represents an aspect or partial view of the underlying whole. The underlying information, in this case, is the cumulative network of each decision and the chain of all of the other decisions, Knowledge Sources and Input Data components on which it directly (or indirectly) depends. This is the **Decision Requirements Model**.

Just as a city can be represented by a collection of different maps at different scales and depicting different levels of detail, a Decision Requirements Model can be represented by a series of different (potentially overlapping) Decision Requirements Diagrams. For example, the Decision Requirements Diagrams of Figure 8-1, Figure 8-3, Figure 8-7 and Figure 8-9

---

[14] An alternative, not shown here, is not to embed *Determine Final Rating* and make its outcome available to the invocation of *Investment Rating Service* as a separate input.

are all accurate partial representations of the Decision Requirements Model that is completely visualized by the Decision Requirements Diagram shown in Figure 8-6.

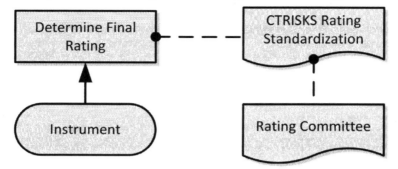

Figure 8-9 Another Decision Requirements Diagram Partially Representing Our Decision Requirements

A decision that is a 'leaf' of one Decision Requirements Diagram may be the top-level component of another. There is no requirement that a single diagram show all the details of a Decision Requirements Model from a subject decision to fundamental, irreducible Input Data. Indeed, it is good practice to split the use and definition of a complex decision between different diagrams, to reflect different concerns or viewpoints, especially where a decision is widely used (14.3.2).

All diagrams must represent a valid subset of the Decision Requirements Model and diagrams may not contradict each other. For example, Figure 8-10 contradicts the Decision Requirements Model above because an authority requirement relationship between two featured components (Knowledge Source *CTRISKS Rating Standardization* and the decision *Determine Final Rating*) is in the opposite direction to that depicted in Figure 8-9. This requirement is potentially legal—it would denote that the Knowledge Source derives its authority from the outcome of the decision (see Section 15.2.5)—but it contradicts Figure 8-9. Both relationships cannot be valid simultaneously.

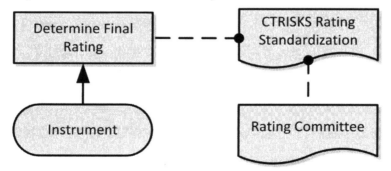

Figure 8-10 Decision Requirements Diagram Inconsistent with the Decision Requirement

In addition, Decision Requirements Diagrams cannot show relationships that would create cyclic dependencies. For instance, no diagram could include requirements that made

Determine Final Rating require *Determine Investment Rating Category* directly or indirectly. This would create a loop that is not permitted in a Decision Requirements Model[15].

8.2 Decision Logic Level

The purpose of the Decision Logic Level is to define the derivation of the outcome of each decision from its inputs. Decision Logic definitions are documented using one or more expressions that 'transform' the decision's inputs to yield an outcome value.

To avoid ambiguity, DMN defines a regimented structure for these transforms: the **Boxed Expression**. Furthermore, it defines a formal language for these expressions (the Friendly Enough Expression Language or **FEEL**, discussed in Section 11.3.2 and Appendix B). It's important to note that these formalisms are not mandated by the standard and informal English statements, analytic models or even examples can be used instead. A complete Decision Logic Level is a set of all of these transforms for all the decisions in the Decision Requirements Model and constitutes a precise and potentially executable model. For reasons explained in Section 13.1, a complete Decision Model does not necessarily require a completely defined Decision Logic Level.

The Decision Logic Level only defines the logic embodied by decisions. The DMN standard also defines how the type and structure of all Input Data and all decision outcomes should be specified. This structure is best managed by a glossary that underlies the decision model and this is addressed further in Chapter 9.

Boxed Expressions can take several standard forms in DMN. The most commonly used is the **Decision Table.** The remainder of this section focusses on Decision Tables and other decision logic representations are discussed in Section 11.3.2 and defined in Appendix B.

8.2.1 Decision Tables

A Decision Table is a tabular representation of decision logic that depicts how the outcome of a decision (consisting of one or more conclusions) is determined by checking specific combinations of values in its inputs. A Decision Table defines a mapping of conditions to conclusions.

The basic elements of a Decision Table are:

- One or more inputs[16], i.e., information that can be tested by the logic in the table to draw a conclusion. These inputs may be simple variables provided by Information Requirements (like *Persons Employment Record*) or an expression calculating a value derived from these (like `Persons Total Debt / Persons Annual Salary`).

- One or more conclusions that can be set when the rules in the table fire.

---

[15] The model is technically a "directed acyclic graph" which means that the direction of relationships matter. No loops can be created by the relationships, no matter how indirect.

[16] In theory, Decision Tables can have no inputs, in which case the conclusion value(s) are unconditional and there is only one rule. This is seldom useful in practice. DMN has other means to represent unconditional structured business constants and functions (see Chapter 9, Section 15.2.5 and appendix B).

- One or more rules consisting of a set of conditions and conclusion values. One condition is specified for each input and one conclusion value is provided for each output.
- A hit policy to determine how the rules in the table should be executed (see Section 8.2.4).

The example Decision Table in Figure 8-11 has two inputs (left most columns), one conclusion and five numbered rules. The rules are laid out in 'rules as rows' format.

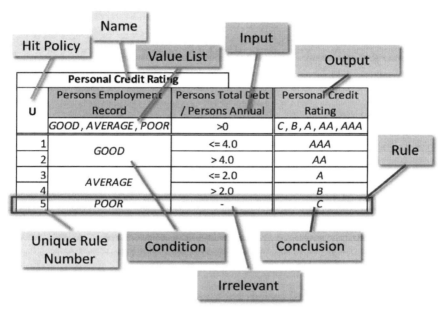

Figure 8-11 Anatomy of a "Rules as Rows" Decision Table

Every rule must specify a condition for each input. The use of a Decision Table representation implies that the same set of inputs will be relevant for most of the rules required to define the decision. It does not mean that every input must be relevant for every rule. The condition '–' is used to show inputs that are irrelevant to a specific rule. Consider rule 5 in Figure 8-11; the second input in this rule is irrelevant and the rule's behavior will be determined entirely by the first condition.

Each rule within a Decision Table can have a unique number to informally[17] identify the rule. This facilitates conversation (e.g., "I expected rule 3 to cover this scenario, but rule 4 was used") and enables traceability (e.g., "During this March, 29% of applicants satisfied rule 2, 18% rule 4,…"). The number has no material impact on the meaning or behavior of rules. By convention, the identity number starts at one and is incremented for each rule.

---

[17] These rule numbers are not preserved when rule insertions and deletions are made and cannot be used as enduring, formal identifiers. They may, however, be useful for quick reference to a rule when reviewing the behavior of decisions.

In this example, some conditions check the equality of the input with a specific value (e.g., the first condition of rule 1 tests 'Persons Employment Record = GOOD'). Notice that explicit use of the equality operator ('=') is omitted. Other cells use an inequality (e.g., '<=' or '>') and in these cases the inequality operator must be explicitly included (e.g., the second condition of rule 1 is equivalent to: '(Persons Total Debt / Persons Annual Salary) > 4.0').

Note that italicized values, such as *GOOD*, *AAA* and *AVERAGE*, are strings. These can also be shown as "GOOD", "AAA" and "AVERAGE" with exactly the same meaning. The book uses the italicized form to emphasize that these values are controlled, enumerated constants, not arbitrary strings.

8.2.2 Decision Table layout

Every Decision Table is named after the outcome it provides and this is, typically, the same as the decision it defines. Decision Tables in DMN have a highly regimented format, as illustrated by the example in Figure 8-11. Note that:

- The name of the table (*Determine Personal Credit Rating*) appears in the tab at the top left. This is the name of the Information Item populated by the logic in the Decision Table. Below this is its header row.

- The header row dictates which inputs are being tested by the table and which conclusions are determined by it. The example shows one conclusion, but DMN allows more than one to be specified. All the conclusions of a table are collectively referred to as the **outcome**.

- Double horizontal lines separate the header row from the rules.

- Double vertical lines separate the conclusion column(s) from the condition(s).

- Each of the input headers can be the name of simple value from the business domain (e.g., the *Instrument Issue Country* or the *Loan Applicant Annual Salary*) or an expression using these values (e.g., the item price minus the discount, or the ratio of debt to salary). These input values are derived from Information Requirements that this decision has on other decision model components (see decision requirements in Section 8.1.5).

- The output header may only contain a simple name (a business term), i.e., the name of the Information Item populated by the Decision Table; hence, it is the same as the Decision Table's name.

- Immediately below each input and output header is an optional value list depicting constraints on the allowed values of inputs and outputs (see Section 8.2.3.6).

- The remainder of the table contains a set of rule rows.

- Every row below the double horizontal line is a single rule, each providing a condition for every input and a conclusion value for every conclusion. Conditions contain a 'test' for the input value that yields a true or false result. A rule is satisfied if and only if every condition it includes is satisfied (i.e., that its test on the condition yields a 'true' value).

- The condition '-' is always satisfied.

- When a rule fires, every conclusion is assigned the value in the corresponding conclusion value cell.

- How many rules are satisfied and how many fire is determined by the hit policy. This is set by the single letter at the top left of the Decision Table. The meaning of this is explored in Section 8.2.4.

Decision Tables do have some style options that impact their visual appearance but not their meaning. For instance, although not dictated by the standard, the input headers are often shown in blue and the conclusion headers in pink. The most notable style option is the orientation.

A table can show rules arranged into rows or columns. For example, the 'rules as rows' Decision Table example in Figure 8-13 can be also be represented by the equivalent 'rules as columns' format as shown in Figure 8-12.

Personal Loan Limit				
Personal Credit Rating	C, B, A, AA, AAA	AAA	not (AAA)	
Branch Lending Limit /Persons Annual Salary		-	> 6.0	<= 6.0
Loan Limit		Branch Lending Limit	Persons Annual Salary * 6	Branch Lending Limit
U		1	2	3

Figure 8-12 Figure 8-13 depicted in 'rules in columns' format

The difference between these two is purely a matter of format, i.e., a simple exchange of columns and rows. Whereas one aligns conditions and conclusions into columns and rules into rows, the other depicts conditions and conclusions as rows and individual rules as columns. This pivot does not give rise to any behavioral differences; Figure 8-12 and Figure 8-13 have the same meaning.

Although the 'rules as rows' format is much more common, there are circumstances in which rules are best arranged into columns. For example, Decision Tables with many inputs and outputs but only a few rules would be more suited to the 'rules as columns' format. See Section 11.2.7 for more detail on Decision Table orientations. Because the rules as rows format is more common, it will be used for the remaining examples in this section and most of the rest of the book. All the statements about Decision Tables in the book work equally well for column oriented tables (see Sections 11.2.7 and 14.4.3.1). From here on, for simplicity, the term rule and row will be used synonymously.

8.2.3   Decision Table Conditions

8.2.3.1   Using expressions in conditions

In rules 1-4 of Figure 8-11, the conditions compare the input value with a literal value that is consistent with its type (i.e., an absolute value like 'GOOD' or '5.5'). DMN also supports comparison with a named input value, which is essentially a variable holding a value (e.g., 'Persons Annual Salary'). This allows, for instance, a condition to compare one input to another. The comparisons permitted in a condition are:

- Checking equality with a value (no operator is shown, e.g., 'AVERAGE', '0', 'true', '"Hello"').
- Checking inequality with a value (e.g., '>Minimum Age', '<=1').

- Checking a value in a range. Both ranges that are exclusive of their extreme values (e.g., '[16..59]'), inclusive of them (e.g., '(15..60)') and mixed ranges (e.g., '[16..60)') are supported.

- A comma-separated list of any of the above, which is satisfied if any one of its conditions are satisfied (e.g., '<15, 20, [29..35]' or '*AAA, AA, A*').

- The logical inverse of any of these (e.g., 'not([16..Minimum Driver Age], >80)'), which is satisfied only if the statement within the braces is not satisfied and vice versa.

If a named value is used in a condition, even if these inputs are not used in the headers of the Decision Table, they count as Information Requirements of the Decision Table and should be derived using an Information Requirement Relationship from either a decision or Input Data on the corresponding Decision Requirements Diagram.

DMN does not permit conditions to contain function calls or arithmetic expressions (see Sections B.3.3 and B.5.4 for more details).

8.2.3.2 Using expressions in conclusions

A conclusion can be a literal value, a named value or a simple arithmetic expression involving either. In Figure 8-13, the *Loan Limit* can be set to an expression of the *Persons* (borrower's) *Annual Salary* (a data input supplied by an Input Data) or the *Branch Lending Limit* (a Data Input determined by a decision). This expression can also include functions, such as max(Minimum Age, Customer Age) or count(product set) (see Section B.3.3 for more details).

Personal Loan Limit			
U	Personal Credit Rating	Branch Lending Limit / Persons Annual Salary	Loan Limit
	C, B, A, AA, AAA		
1	AAA	-	Branch Lending Limit
2	not(AAA)	> 6.0	Persons Annual Salary * 6
3		<= 6.0	Branch Lending Limit

Figure 8-13 Example of Decision Table Using a Conclusion Value Expression

8.2.3.3 The irrelevant condition '-'

If a rule has a condition containing the hyphen symbol, '-', this means that the rule does not depend on the value of this input: any input value will satisfy the condition. For example, rule 1 in Figure 8-13 depicts the fact that if the *Personal Credit Rating* is *AAA*, the *Loan Limit* will be set to the *Branch Lending Limit*, regardless of the ratio of the *Branch Lending Limit* to the *Persons Annual Salary*.

The '-' marker has a different meaning if used as a conclusion value (see Section 8.2.4.1).

Some notations use empty cells to denote irrelevant conditions. DMN uses '-' to ensure that all logic is represented explicitly. This prevents accidental omission (i.e., forgetting to fill in a cell) from being confused with the intention of making a condition irrelevant.

8.2.3.4   The empty cell

An empty cell, whether it is a condition or conclusion value, means the contents of the cell are not yet understood by modelers. A Decision Table with one or more empty cells is not finished and its full behavior is not known. This is an interim condition and completed Decision Tables should not have any empty cells.

This interpretation of empty cell, shared by members of the DMN committee, is not yet explicitly noted in the specification.

8.2.3.5   Merged conditions

Successive rules that have an input column with the same condition (e.g., rules 4 and 5 in Figure 8-14 use the condition 'Asset Category = PREFERRED' and rules 6 and 7 have the same condition 'Instrument is Convertible = FALSE') can have the conditions merged vertically into one condition as shown in Figure 8-15. This explicitly depicts the commonality of conditions and indicates that successive rules are associated. It also prevents accidental inconsistencies from arising and makes the table easier to read. Conclusions cannot be merged in this way.

U	Asset Category	Instrument is Convertible	Issuer Class	Asset Class
1	*OTHER*	-	-	*OTHER*
2	*INDEX*	-	-	*INDEX*
3	*EQUITY*	-	-	*EQUITY*
4	*PREFERRED*	true	-	*CVTPFD*
5	*PREFERRED*	false	-	*OTHER*
6	*DEBT*	false	*SUPRA*	*SUPRA*
7	*DEBT*	false	*not(SUPRA)*	*OTHER*
8	*DEBT*	true	-	*CONVERTIBLE*

Table header: **Asset Class**

Figure 8-14 Unmerged Decision Table

Conditions can only be merged if:

- they are vertically adjacent;
- they contain exactly the same test (including '–'); *and*
- either the conditions to be merged are in the left most column or all of the conditions to their left are already merged. It is illegal to merge conditions if they span unmerged conditions to their left.

Consider the Decision Table of Figure 8-15. The *PREFERRED* condition of rules 4-5 and the *DEBT* condition in rules 6-8 have been merged into one cell each because each set of conditions are the same and in the leftmost column. The *FALSE* Convertibility conditions of rules 6 and 7 have also been merged because they share the *DEBT* condition merged on the left).

In contrast, the merge shown in Figure 8-16 is illegal because the *FALSE* cell merge in the *Instrument is Convertible* column spans different values of the *Asset Category* condition.

Merging is discussed further in Section 15.3.1.

	Asset Class			
U	**Asset Category**	**Instrument is Convertible**	**Issuer Class**	**Asset Class**
1	OTHER	-	-	OTHER
2	INDEX	-	-	INDEX
3	EQUITY	-	-	EQUITY
4	PREFERRED	true	-	CVTPFD
5		false	-	OTHER
6		false	SUPRA	SUPRA
7	DEBT		not(SUPRA)	OTHER
8		true	-	CONVERTIBLE

Figure 8-15 Example of Well-Formed Merges

	Asset Class			
U	**Asset Category**	**Instrument is Convertible**	**Issuer Class**	**Asset Class**
1	OTHER	-	-	OTHER
2	INDEX	-	-	INDEX
3	EQUITY	-	-	EQUITY
4	PREFERRED	true	-	CVTPFD
6			-	OTHER
7		false	SUPRA	SUPRA
8	DEBT		not(SUPRA)	OTHER
9		true	-	CONVERTIBLE

Figure 8-16 Example of Illegal Merge

8.2.3.6   Value lists - inputs and outputs with constrained values

Some inputs and outputs may have their values confined to a set of 'permitted' values. In these circumstances, no other values will be meaningful in any condition or conclusion pertaining to them. This restriction is useful for business terms that have a constrained range of values (e.g., *Customer Age* may not be negative) or even a limited number of discrete, valid values (e.g., *Personal Credit Rating* and *Personal Employment Record*). These are referred to as constrained and enumerated types respectively (see Sections 10.7.2 and 9.7.3). These constrained or permitted values may be documented in a Decision Table by means of a **value list**. Below the column headers in Figure 8-11 there is an optional value list row depicting the permitted values of each Input Data type or a constraint on the value (e.g., '>0'). Note that the use of value lists is entirely optional.

Constrained and enumerated values can also be supported by a glossary and this can be more manageable if the constraints are ubiquitous. Section C.4.1 identifies a more scalable means of representing commonly used data with constrained values that does not require frequent repetition of the constrained values themselves in every Decision Table that uses them. This is especially important for data types that are used in many tables (e.g., currency, country and policy type) and that have very large and volatile sets of values that would be impractical to support with value lists.

The italicized entries in the conditions of *Person Employment Record* and *Personal Credit Rating* also indicate that these (condition and conclusion) values are string literals.

The order of items in the value lists of conclusions has a special significance if the table has a specific hit policy (see Sections 8.2.4 and 11.2.1). Some hit policies will cause the behavior of Decision Tables to be altered if the order of the value list is changed (see Section 8.2.4) and any change to value lists in these circumstances should be carefully controlled.

8.2.3.7   Default values

A value list on a output may also be used to depict the default value of that output. By underlining a <u>single</u> value in the value list, a modeler signifies that the underlined value will be the conclusion if the values of the inputs do not satisfy any rules. The use of value lists to signify defaults can be a useful shorthand that prevents the need for conditions in the table to cover every eventuality. Explicitly covering all possible conditions, although disciplined, can sometimes result in complex and hard to understand tables.

8.2.4   Hit policies

A rule in a Decision Table is often said to 'hit' when all its conditions are satisfied by the data provided *and* it generates an outcome as a consequence. Do not confuse the notion of a rule being satisfied and being 'hit': a rule must be satisfied to be 'hit', but whether a satisfied rule is 'hit' depends on the hit policy.

Usually, for each instance of data to which a Decision Table is applied, only one rule in the table is 'hit' and the table is said to be 'single hit'. A single hit table has a single outcome: it assigns *one* value to each conclusion. In this respect, each rule in such a table is considered to define an alternative outcome (e.g., Figure 8-11). This is, arguably, the easiest Decision Table behavior to understand, the most commonly used and, in most circumstances, the most appropriate (see Section 14.4.3.2). As a consequence, this is the default behavior in DMN Decision Tables. However, some Decision Tables are designed to have multiple rules that are 'hit' for some combinations of data values and these are said to be 'multi-hit' tables.

To support this, DMN allows table modelers to specify the hit and outcome behavior for each table. Each Decision Table has a 'hit policy' or 'hit indicator'. Seven hit policies are defined: Unique (U), Any (A), First (F), Priority (P), Rule (R), Output Order (O) and Collect (C). Hit policy is expressed in a Decision Table, rather tersely, using a single letter (e.g., 'U' for Unique in the example). Hit policy is specified in the top left corner of the Decision Table (see Figure 8-11).

The hit policy of a table defines:

- How many rules may be simultaneously satisfied by a single set of inputs:
  - The Unique hit policy permits at most one rule to be satisfied.
  - All other policies allow multiple rules to be satisfied.
- How many 'hits' can result from these matches:
  - Unique, Any, First and Priority policies all permit at most one hit. These are single hit policies.
  - Rule, Output Order and Collect policies all permit zero, one or many hits. These are multi-hit policies.
- In a single hit table, how to determine which rule is hit if, for given set of inputs, multiple rules are satisfied:
  - The Unique policy asserts that only one rule can be satisfied and hit, resulting in one outcome.

o   The Any policy only permits multiple rules to be satisfied, providing the outcomes of each satisfied rule are the same. It does not matter which rule hits, as the outcome will be the same.

o   The First and Priority policies permit multiple rules to be satisfied and determine what the outcome is from among the satisfied rules. Priority selects the conclusion with the highest priority value in its value list (see Section 8.2.3.6 and First selects the conclusion of the first rule in the table to be satisfied (this is not necessarily the one with the lowest id number).

- In a multi-hit table, how to determine how many outcomes to generate and their order:

   o   The Collect with Aggregation policy combines all the outcomes from the satisfied rules into one outcome using an aggregate function (e.g., sum, max, count) specified by the hit policy (11.2.2.5). If no rules contributed to an aggregate outcome, the result is 0 for a count and null for all other aggregate functions.

   o   The Collect hit policy (without an aggregator) results in a collection of all the hit rule outcomes in which the order is unspecified. This collection is empty if no rules contribute to the outcome.

   o   The Rule hit policy results in a collection of all the hit rule outcomes in which the order is set by the order of the rules that created them in the Decision Table.

   o   The Output Order hit policy results in a collection of all the hit rule outcomes in which the order is set according to the conclusion value priority defined in the value list.

This behavior is summarized in Table 8-2. Most Decision Tables use the Unique or Any hit policy, as these are the easiest to understand and use. Modelers should have a very good reason to use other hit policies and, even then, they should be used sparingly. Hit policies and their uses are described in more detail in Section 11.2.1.

8.2.4.1   The unspecified conclusion '-'

The use of the '–' marker in a conclusion cell has a different meaning to its use in a condition (see Section 8.2.3.3). Its meaning in a conclusion depends in the hit policy of the Decision Table:

- For single hit tables, it denotes that the conclusion is unknown or unspecified. It is often an explicit statement, for documentation purposes, that the combination of circumstances that the rule defines is considered illegal or impossible.

- For tables with multiple hits (i.e., Collect, Output Order, Rule), this rule does not contribute to the outcome collection (or aggregate value).

The use of '-' in the conclusion is not technically supported by the DMN specification at the time of writing. However, this feature is in accordance with the intent of members of the committee[18].

---

[18] Personal communication with Jan Vanthienen, May 2016.

Hit Policy	Rules Satisfied	Hits	Hit rule selection	Outcome (and sort)
Unique (U)	0..1	0..1	The one rule satisfied	That of the only rule hit.
Any (A)	0 or more	0..1	Any rule satisfied providing conclusions are all equal	That of the only rule hit.
First (F)	0 or more	0..1	First rule satisfied in order of table	That of the only rule hit.
Priority (P)	0 or more	0..1	Satisfied rule with highest priority conclusion value	That of the only rule hit.
Collect (C+) with aggregation	0 or more	0 or more	All satisfied rules	Generated from the aggregation of all hit rule outcomes.
Collect (C) no aggregation	0 or more	0 or more	All satisfied rules	All hit rule outcomes are combined into a collection in undefined order.
Rule (R)	0 or more	0 or more	All satisfied rules	All hit rule outcomes are combined into a collection in order of rules in table.
Output Order (O)	0 or more	0 or more	All satisfied rules	All hit rule outcomes are combined into a collection in order of conclusion value priority.

Table 8-2 Summary of Hit Policy Behavior

8.2.4.2   Completeness

A complete table has (at least) one row that is satisfied and yields an outcome for any possible combination of input values. In other words, its covers every possible circumstance.

An incomplete table has no eligible row for some scenarios. Either it is believed that they don't occur in practice or no meaningful conclusion can be yielded if they do.

Default values can be used to make a table complete or to ensure that an incomplete table can be processed. Although the technical behavior is the same in both cases, the intent is worth documenting for a table.[19]

---

[19] The explicit notation of completeness, as part of the hit policy, has been removed from DMN since version 1.1. This does not mean the concept is not useful. You may still see tables with a C denoting Complete or I denoting Incomplete.

8.2.4.3 Side effects

It is important to note that DMN is free from side effects, for example, expressions cannot change the value of inputs. Furthermore, input expressions, conditions and conclusions cannot have any side effects in DMN Decision Tables. The testing of a condition only impacts the eligibility of its rule; it cannot have any other observable impact. Similarly, when a rule is hit, this only impacts its potential outcome (according to its hit policy) and has no other impact. This means:

- Input Data cannot be modified by Decision Tables.
- The expressions in condition headers and conditions cannot alter any variable.
- The evaluation of a conclusion expression cannot change any variables.
- The variable used in an output of a Decision Table is not available for use in an input expression, condition or conclusion in the same table.

8.2.5 Contexts

8.2.5.1 Rationale

All terms used in input expressions, condition and conclusion expressions within Decision Logic must have a clearly defined origin (see Section 8.2.4). Normally, these are values sourced via an Information Requirements from an Input Data or decision. Inputs and conclusions may derive new values using simple arithmetic expressions featuring these values. Occasionally, Decision Tables need to create and use new inputs, specific to them, that are not direct inputs but which are derived from them. These new derived inputs:

1. Provide a synonym or nickname for an existing input, for the purposes of clarity. Perhaps the name for the data input normally requires qualifying adjectives that are unnecessary in this decision (see the example in the following section) or the modeler wants to use a specific synonym in an individual Decision Table to conform to historical norms as a means of boosting ease of comprehension to business users.

2. Hold values mathematically derived from one or more input Information Items. Such expressions cannot appear directly in conditions, as these may, for example, require the use of arithmetic operators or functions and these are forbidden within Decision Table conditions (see Section 8.2.3.2). Although it is legal to use both in input expressions and conclusions, a context may still be preferred to avoid clutter.

3. Represent values that can only be reached by a complex traversal of existing inputs (i.e., a FEEL path expression). Such expressions cannot appear directly in conditions and may be too bulky to fit into input expressions or conclusions.

4. Act to emphasize the importance of a derived value by naming it and allow its consistent reuse without the danger and clutter of repetition.

All of these needs can be met using a **context**: a set of named values which are unique to a single decision definition (contexts can be used by logic representations other than Decision Tables).

Each named value introduced by a context is defined by an expression (a so called **boxed context**, see Section B.4.2) yielding a value which is then associated with that name. The names can only be used within the decision logic with which the context is associated.

Contexts should be used sparingly to introduce derived inputs for use in specific circumstances. The repeated definition of the same derived input across many decisions indicates that it should be a direct input Information Item defined in the Decision Requirements Diagram.

Consider the example of a context used to boost the readability of the Decision Table[20] in Figure 8-17. This context defines five named values with a mix of the rationales defined above. Notice the left hand line binding together the title, context and Decision Table. The gaps between them are for clarity.

Sku Classification Additional Discount

Class Code	Item Store SKU Classification Code
Basket Size	count(Basket.Item)
Channel	Item.customer.conduit.channelType
Cheapest Item	Item.actualPrice = min(Basket.Item.actualPrice)
Applied Discount	Item.actualPrice - Item.normalPrice

U	Cheapest Item	Basket Size	Channel	Class Code	Sku Classification Additional Discount
1	true	-	-	-	0
2	false	>10	INTERNET	-	Applied Discount
3		<=10	INTERNET	-	Applied Discount
4		>5	STORE	not(ELECTRICAL)	Applied Discount *1.5
5		>5	STORE	ELECTRICAL	0
6		<=5	STORE	-	Applied Discount * 1.25

Figure 8-17 Example of Decision Table with Context

The five values defined by the context are:

- *Class Code* is defined as a manageable synonym for an existing attribute of an Input Data. Furthermore, this is the name given to this value by the business experts who manage bonus discounts (reason 1).

- *Basket Size* is mathematically derived from the Basket in which the processed Item is processed using an aggregate function This is placed in the context to avoid clutter and make it available elsewhere (reasons 2 and 4).

- *Channel* is a shortened name given to data that is indirectly related to the data provided. In this case, it refers to the type of sales channel being used to sell this Basket (reasons 1 and 3).

- *Cheapest Item* is another example of a mathematical derivation which that reveals an important relationship between the Item being processed and others in the same Basket. Its definition here both declutters the condition (is this item the cheapest Item in the Basket?) and emphasizes it (reasons 2 and 4).

- *Applied Discount* is an example of a value that is used in many cells. It is defined in the context both to ensure consistency and to emphasize (and clarify) its meaning (reason 4).

Many of the use cases for contexts can be also addressed by the use of a glossary (see Chapter 9), but this is outside the scope of the DMN standard.

---

[20] The use of contexts is permitted for any decision logic, not just Decision Tables (see Section B.4).

8.3 Decision Logic Level and Decision Requirements Level

The Decision Logic Level of a Decision Model is directly related to the Decision Requirement Level and consistency must be maintained between them. Specifically:

- Any decision with defined logic should feature as a decision component in the Decision Requirements Level.

- The name of the defined logic (usually defined in the top tab, see Figure 8-11) should match the name of the decision component in the Decision Requirements Level. It should also define the (set of) conclusions produced.

- All inputs specified in a Decision Table must have an origin; they must be connected by an Information Requirement in the Decision Requirements Level to a source of an information item (i.e., Input Data or sub-decision).

- All names used in Decision Table condition and conclusion expressions must, if not defined as part of a context (see Section 8.2.6), be derived from Information Requirement relationships.

The decision logic and formal conclusions should also match the question and allowed answers defined for the decision (see Section 8.1.1.4). This is a business-level or conceptual check rather than a mechanical one, but it nonetheless important.

A satisfactory Decision Requirements Diagram for the Decision Tables in Figure 8-11 and Figure 8-13 is depicted in Figure 8-18.

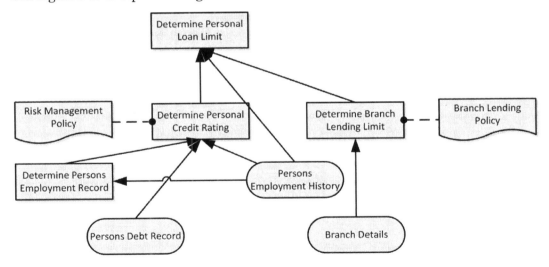

Figure 8-18 Decision Requirements Diagram Consistent with Figure 8-11 and Figure 8-13

Note how each condition and conclusion expression in Figure 8-11 and Figure 8-13 is supported by the decision requirements graph of Figure 8-18. Specifically:

- The condition *Persons Employment Record* used in Figure 8-11 derives from the outcome of the decision *Determine Persons Employment Record* in Figure 8-18. *Persons Employment Record* is an information item provided by the decision of the same name to the *Determine Personal Credit Rating* decision.

- *Persons Total Debt* used in *Determine Personal Credit Rating* derives from one of the attributes of the complex data structure provided by the Input Data *Persons Debt Record*.

- The value *Persons Annual Salary*, used in the expressions of several conditions in Determine Personal Credit Rating and Determine Personal Loan Limit, is one of the attributes of Persons Employment History.

- The value *Branch Lending Limit*, used in the expressions of several conclusion cells in *Determine Personal Loan Limit*, is the outcome of the decision *Determine Branch Lending Limit*.

9 Glossary

Bad terminology is the enemy of good thinking
—Warren Buffett

The DMN standard articulates decision requirements and logic in great detail, but omits any mechanism to describe the business data and terminology that are the foundations of any decision model. This omission is deliberate: standards must be small and have a tight focus to be effective and there are many existing standards for data repositories. To embed another in DMN would be inappropriate. However, a clear understanding of the data glossary and data model underlying a decision model is vital for it to be widely understood. DMN permits the import and definition of user defined data types, but has no means of defining their meaning.

Decision modelers need to understand what a glossary is, why it is needed and specifically how it is used. This section considers what features DMN requires from a business glossary, what glossary entries contain and how they can be used to support decision modeling. The section also includes a description of the data types supported by DMN and how these can be extended for use in decision modeling.

Business data is the most important foundation of decision models. It is referenced in all the data items used by the decision model, including decision inputs, variables and outputs. It gives meaning to the model and plays a central role in the way all elements of the model are named and collaborate. It is essential to understand the content, structure, terminology and, above all, the meaning of the business data involved in a decision model. Furthermore, it is vital to manage this information as it evolves. Without both, a decision model is much less valuable. Therefore, decision models should be underpinned by robust business data models that define and inter-relate the concepts being used (see Section 10.3.4 for more details). These concepts are called *business terms*.

The attributes of corporate data streams (e.g., customer, market and transactional data) and statistics gathered from them are central to the kind of business data model needed in decision modeling. Decision modelers need to base their models on a consistent, unified and easy to understand view of business data. This is often a challenge because organizations frequently have many data sources with overlapping but inconsistent data models. Some of these may be technically oriented. To adequately support decision modeling, there is a need to create a business *glossary* by:

- Consolidating all the required data models into a single coherent view in which all terms have a single meaning.
- Hiding irrelevant technical abstractions that many data models use to improve their efficiency.
- Providing business user friendly translations of relevant business data that have, for whatever reason, been couched in technical jargon, to make them easier for business users to understand when modeling decisions.
- Specifying additional required business terms that do not directly relate to existing

data attributes, but are derived from them.

9.1 Business Terms

Decision models are built from components (e.g., decisions, Knowledge Sources and Input Data) that are named and referenced using natural language phrases (e.g., *the Instrument Asset Class, the Discounted Price*). All the names used within a decision model that are part of the business domain being modeled—rather than words of the notation itself (e.g., not, if, then), everyday language (e.g., *today's date*) or conventional connective language (e.g., 'of', 'the', and 'a')—are made from **business terms**.

Business terms are used to name:

- Decision Requirements Level components: decisions, Decision Services, Input Data, Business Knowledge Models and Knowledge Sources (see underlined items in Figure 9-1).
- Decision Table inputs and outputs (see the underlined items in the headers of in Figure 9-2).
- The individual constants and variables in Decision Tables and the values in value lists (see Figure 9-2).
- The individual constants and variables in textual rules (see Figure 9-3 and Section 11.3.2).

In the last three cases, business terms are used to name variables that contain Information Items, i.e., data used by decisions.

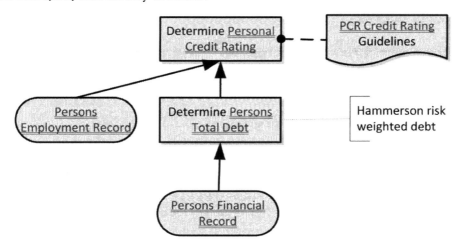

Figure 9-1 Decision Requirements Diagram Showing Business Terms

Note, in Figure 9-1, that annotations at the Decision Requirements (see Section 8.1.4) and Decision Logic Level (see Sections 14.4.4 and C.2.6) are free text. Although it is considered good form to base these on business terms, this is not mandated.

U	Personal Credit Rating		
	Persons Employment Record	Persons Total Debt / Persons Annual Salary	Personal Credit Rating
	GOOD , AVERAGE , POOR	>0	*C , B , A , AA , AAA*
1	*GOOD*	<= 4.0	*AAA*
2		> 4.0	*AA*
3	*AVERAGE*	<= 2.0	*A*
4		> 2.0	*B*
5	*POOR*	-	*C*

Figure 9-2 Example Decision Table Showing Business Terms

Personal Lending Limit
If Personal Credit Rating !=*AAA* and Branch Lending Limit > (Persons Annual Salary * 6) then (Persons Annual Salary * 6) else Branch Lending Limit

Figure 9-3 Example Text Decision Showing Business Terms

To avoid ambiguity, business terms should be explicitly defined in a glossary.

9.2 What is a Glossary

A glossary provides a single, consolidated, conceptual definition of the business terms used by one or more decision models. It acts as a business interface to one or more corporate data models, showing how each business term is supported by them. It explains how each business term used by a decision model maps directly on to a data model attribute or how it is derived from others that do. It manages business terms in an evolving context.

9.3 Why Are They Needed?

It is essential that a decision model is transparent so it can be understood beyond the community that authored it. The transparency of a decision model is a measure of how effectively it communicates the meaning of business decisions to others. Such a model needs to be supported by an agreed definition of all the business terms it uses so that its meaning is explicit and context-free.

Without an explicit glossary, the meaning of a decision model could be ambiguous, misleading or difficult to understand. Consider Figure 9-2: what does *Person's Employment Record*, *AVERAGE* or *Personal Credit Rating* really mean? Where do data inputs like *Person's Employment Record* come from? What authority defines and maintains literal values like *GOOD*? How do the terms relate to each other? Without a deeper documentation of this context, the decision model is disembodied and may not be understood correctly or at all.

It's our experience that the biggest hurdle to understanding a decision model is the use of terminology that falls into one or more of these traps:

- Terms are obscure, industry specific jargon, technical 'buzzwords' or abbreviations, some of which have multiple meanings.

- Terms are specific to the team that created them and hard to understood outside it. Companies, corporate departments and even individual teams often invent their own terms. Worse still, they can take common words, or even industry terms, and overload them with context specific meanings. This can impair the ability of even a business domain expert to understand a decision model they did not author, or give them a false impression.

- Terms many natural language synonyms, some of which are misleading in a business context. For example, the terms *Customer*, *Client*, *Buyer* and *Patron* are dictionary synonyms, but their use within a business context is likely to require that they have different meanings.

- Terms are specific to the time the model was authored and are not easily understood later.

- Terms are related to each other in ways which the decision model cannot articulate.

These issues limit the transparency of decision models, making them hard to understand (or easy to misunderstand) outside the environment in which they are created. Such environments are themselves specific to a time and place: modeling teams disband or change over time; business terms can change meaning or go out of use; and some business terminology is specific to a region. A lack of transparency can be a liability if models need to be used in places or times distant from their creation, for example, if they need to be presented to other business teams for review, provided to IT for implementation or consulted after many months have passed. Lack of glossary literally causes decision models to 'erode' over time and be specific to a locale, imposing a time and location limit on their usefulness by compromising the model's ability to communicate ideas effectively.

Even sharing a decision model on a smaller scale can be hampered without a glossary. While organizations generally have a shared understanding of common business terms, individual modelers may have subtle differences in their understanding and use of terminology. Collaborative, complex decision modeling requires a more structured approach to the definition of these concepts and their on-going management.

In short: without a glossary, decision models are of limited value to others that don't share the terminology of the modelers even if they are very familiar with the business domain.

9.4 Producing a Glossary

Production of a glossary is a vital support activity for non-trivial decision models, especially when they are shared across distributed teams or larger business communities. The set of business terms needed to support non-trivial decision models are often very large and express business concepts that are constantly subject to revision and extension. When building a glossary, it is most effective to reuse one or more existing resources (e.g., corporate data models) and automatically translate them into a glossary, filtering and augmenting their content, as needed, by adding a business centric definition and filtering out exclusively technical terms. This simplifies both their creation and ongoing maintenance. A glossary is best considered as a view to existing enterprise artifacts, rather than a new artifact in its own right.

Although glossaries may be created as purpose-built, stand-alone deliverables to support decision models, this is very expensive and unlikely to be satisfactory as anything other than an interim measure. Stand-alone glossaries are much less likely to consistently reflect an evolving corporate vocabulary over time as the maintenance overhead is too high. It is likely they will rapidly become out of date. Instead, the reuse, consolidation and augmentation of existing sources of glossary information should therefore always be preferred to creation of a new artifact.

Production of a glossary:

- Should *not* be considered a prerequisite to decision model development. Glossary development should proceed alongside decision modeling, each proceeding iteratively.

- Should not become the focus. Building a glossary is a support for decision modeling; it should not become an all-consuming activity.

- Should keep it as small as it can be. Glossaries should only contain the terms needed to disambiguate decision models. Teams should avoid the mentality that demands a 'complete' glossary be developed as a deliverable in its own right. No glossary can ever be complete; instead, they are developed to be 'complete enough' to support decision modeling.

The Semantics of Business Vocabulary and Business Rules (SBVR) is an OMG standard for the declarative representation of business rules in natural language. It includes a component for representing business vocabularies or glossaries. This chapter focuses on the general demands that decision modeling imposes on a glossary, rather than on specific glossary standards. Therefore, SVBR is not examined in any depth here. While a pre-existing SVBR glossary would satisfy many of requirements discussed in this section, the authors would advise against creating a new, stand-alone SVBR glossary to support a decision modeling effort for the reasons discussed above.

9.5 The Responsibilities of a Glossary

9.5.1 Overview

A business glossary supplies a vital context to a decision model that can extend the model's transparency, applicability and shelf life. It provides:

- a strong definition of all business terms;

- traceability to a data model showing how the terms are sourced and related to each other; *and*

- a focus for managing the explicit evolution of this information.

The glossary is a consolidated, business-centric view of data and terminology, generally derived from (and augmenting) one or more corporate data models. It keeps terms consistent with these data models as both change over time. It manages its entries and facilitates the use of a uniform vocabulary across all decision models. It insulates the decision models from the corporate data models, thereby preventing direct dependencies.

9.5.2   Inputs, responsibilities and users

Figure 9-4 shows the inputs (on the left), responsibilities (small rectangles extending from the glossary) and users (large rectangles on the right) of a glossary:

- Attribute, entities and relationships are mapped (potentially from multiple data models) to a unique set of business terms maintained by the glossary. The details of the mapping are preserved for future traceability.

- Not all attributes of the corporate data models are mapped, only those that are of use in decisions models and fulfil the definition of business term in Section 9.1.

- The data types of each attribute, which determine the range of values they can hold and how they are interrelated, are also mapped.

- If attributes may only hold one of a number of permitted values (e.g., currency, credit rating), their permitted values lists are also mapped (see enumerations in Section 9.7.3). Many enumerations' permitted values originate from value lists in the corporate data model, but some are local to the glossary.

Glossaries have two main 'users': decision models and the decision modelers who develop them, as shown on the right of Figure 9-4. To each of these users the responsibilities of the glossary are as follows:

- Modelers need the glossary to manage terms by allowing each to be associated with a definition, imposing some structure on the set of terms (e.g., by classification), controlling term overlaps or synonyms and managing evolution of all glossary items over time.

- Models require access to the term names for use in defining decisions, reference to any derived terms (i.e., new properties, relationships and entities calculated from existing terms) and the ability to use common functions defined for this business domain. They also require definitions of data types and permitted values lists.

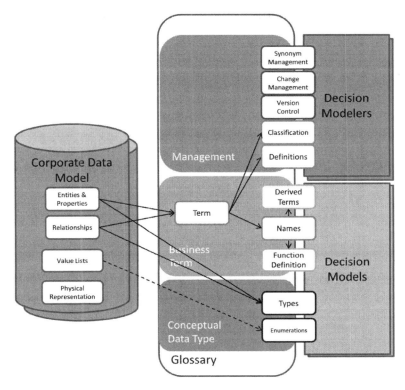

Figure 9-4 The Role of a Glossary

9.5.3 Content

Glossaries contain information derived from the data model:

- business terms;
- complex business data types that are shared by many instances of business terms (e.g., *Customer*); *and*
- business enumerations (e.g., *Credit Rating*) with their permitted values.

They also contain information that augments it:

- business friendly names for terms;
- classifications that connect related terms;
- definitions that describe the meaning of terms using natural language phrases or examples;
- synonyms that denote common names with the same meaning;
- derived terms that are created from existing terms mapped from the data model (and potentially other derived terms), but that don't themselves map directly to business data (e.g., *Current Age* derived from *Birthday* and *Current Date*);
- version metadata that explains how terms evolve through time; *and*

- business functions describing common mathematical derivation of a value from zero or more parameters (e.g., *Net Present Value*).

Typically, derived terms and functions are mathematical derivations that don't benefit from representation as decisions. They only need to be defined in a glossary if their meaning is contested, ambiguous or not uniformly understood by business users. Glossaries should avoid including entries for unambiguous or obvious items. Rapidly changing, complex derived terms or functions should be represented as decisions in the decision model, not within a glossary, so they can be readily changed as needed.

Glossaries never contain implementation or IT oriented information.

9.5.4   Management

The management responsibilities of a glossary include:

- Version control of all artifacts (often derived from the version control of underlying corporate data models).

- Change management, handling the amendments of its content and their consequences, for example, notification of changes to users of a term. Management also includes ensuring only authorized personnel can make changes.

- The definition and amendment of new synonyms, derived terms and functions.

- The ability to search the glossary entries, for example, to select the correct term to use in a specific scenario.

9.6   Glossary Entries

9.6.1   Structure

A business glossary aids transparency by providing the following information for each business term entry:

- **Term Name**. A single name by which the term is known and used in decision models. Within a glossary, the name of each term should be unique.

- **Term Definition**. A clear definition of the business term. These definitions can rely on natural language and terms also defined in the glossary, providing such definitions are not cyclic. Business terms may overload natural language words (e.g., *Transaction*) providing there is no ambiguous mixing of the overloaded and native words.

- **Classification**. Each term can (optionally) be associated with a set of classifying tags (i.e., hash-tags or key value pairs) that label the term with additional, ad-hoc properties. This not only supports an open-ended extension to 'built-in' glossary properties, but it provides additional structure to the glossary itself and each tag can enable a new dimension of search or even represent a sub-glossary. This is especially useful if the glossary is large. Such tags can support additional business classifications (e.g., associations with specific business entities, the names of compliance standards that are relevant), release management information (e.g., whether this term is strategic or tactical, warning of imminent replacement) and governance insight (e.g., who approved this term).

- **Synonyms and Non-Synonyms**. A list of valid synonyms and acronyms for the term and the business contexts with which they are associated. This list should explicitly differentiate between those synonyms that are correct and those commonly, but incorrectly, used (i.e., antiquated, false or deprecated synonyms) to help warn of inadvertent use of the latter. By this means a glossary can actively assist a team in migrating toward a unified and consistent terminology. Ultimately, this is a pragmatic concession to manage synonyms where they are unavoidable in the short term. It should be used to help eradicate the use of synonyms completely in the longer term.

- **Data Type**. Denoting the range of values that can be held by each instance of a term, any constraints on their values and the business meanings of the individual values (see Section 9.7). In addition to data type, this may include validation standards or format 'pictures' (e.g., social security number or telephone number). Glossaries can provide examples where these add clarity.

- **Source**. This (optional) property of a term documents its mapping in the corporate data model; usually, this is done by specifying the names of the data model, entity and even attribute concerned. The mapping denotes:
  - o For a decision model Input Data, the source of the attribute or entity concerned.
  - o For a decision conclusion, the data model attribute in which it may be stored.
  - o For a data type, the name of the entity in the corporate model that defines the type (e.g., Customer).
  - o For an enumeration, the data source controlling its set of permitted values (e.g., database table, XML document or comma separated list) and any standards that define the permitted values (e.g., ISO Currency Code).
  - o Furthermore, it can optionally distinguish between data that is provided to the enterprise (from outside) and that which internal decision models (and other business logic) derive.

- **Comments**. Describing any additional or supporting issues, plans, questions or information about this term.

9.6.2 Example

Consider the example of Figure 8-11 in Section 8.2.1. The glossary might include the information shown in Table 9-1.

Term Name	Person's Employment Record	Person's Annual Salary	Personal Credit Rating
Definition	A classification of how employable an applicant has been in the past five years.	The three-year, average total income from all the employers of a person during a typical twelve month period. It includes pension contribution and the value of salary sacrifice benefits.	The PCR standard classification of personal credit worthiness

Term Name	Person's Employment Record	Person's Annual Salary	Personal Credit Rating
Classification	#PersonalHistory; #ChangeWarning="to be superseded in version 2.11"[6]	#PersonalFinance	#PersonalFinance; #Compliant="FinA 1-09-12"[2]
Synonyms	Employability	PAS, Annual Pay	CB-PCR, PCR
Data Type	Enumeration: GOOD, AVERAGE, POOR[3]	ISO currency code (e.g., "USD", "GBP", etc.) and a non-negative real number with two decimal places of precision[3]. Example: AUD 56500.00	Enumeration: see Credit Bureau PCR-A 50-5661, section 12[2].
Source	Derived: FINBOT::Applicant-EmpRecord[4]	Input: FINBOT::Person-FinancialProfile-AnnualIncome[5]	Derived: FINBOT::Person-CreditRtng
Comments		The average value does not include void periods.	

Table 9-1 Example Glossary Information

Note:

- The contents of the glossary should be searchable, easily accessible to users of the decision model and, if possible, directly supported by or integrated with the decision modeling toolset.

- Any field of a glossary entry can refer to external authorities (e.g., standard documentation or even a corporate data model) to avoid repetition, providing those authorities are also easily obtainable and unequivocal. This reference should be explicitly represented as an Authority Requirement on a Knowledge Source (see Sections 8.1.3 and 8.1.5). Theses Knowledge Sources should be represented within the glossary and within the Decision Requirements Diagram.

- Where an entry has a unique data type, the data type may be defined in the term entry, as shown, for brevity. However, if it is a commonly used type it should be the subject of its own term. Refer to the discussion on reuse of terms in Section 9.6.3.

- The source depicts the origin of an input (denoted 'Input:') or the target of a conclusion (denoted 'Derived:') in terms of the underlying data model. If the term is an enumeration defined by an external data authority, the source can document this fact (see external enumerations, Section 9.7.4).

- The source corporate data model may be conceptual or it may refer to the relational, object, or fact model of a system (see Section 10.3) if any implementation details they contain that might obscure the decision model are hidden. Often, physical (and even logical) data models contain abstractions that, while representing good data modeling practices, are unhelpful for business users (e.g., data versioning, dimensions). These should not be referenced in a glossary.

- The example classification tags support: a business classification (e.g., the tags *PersonalFinance* and *PersonalHistory*), a means of highlighting likely change (e.g., the tag *ChangeWarning*) and references to compliance standards (e.g., the tag *Compliant*). The flexibility of tags allows them to be easily adapted to an organization's needs. Furthermore, tags can be automatically generated to support the 'labeling' of glossary data.

- If a data model attribute and its owning entity are both mapped to terms in a glossary, any classification the entity term has is inherited by all of its attribute terms.

9.6.3   Reuse of terms

Any glossary term can be referenced by name in the definition of another providing this does not lead to a circular definition.

Where the data type of a glossary entry is an internally defined enumeration (i.e., one not defined by an external data source) or a composite data type (see Section 9.7.5), that is only used once in the decision model, its permitted values or attributes can be listed directly in the data type definition of the term, as shown in Table 9-2. This promotes simplicity.

Term Name	Personal Credit Rating
Definition	The PCR standard classification of personal credit worthiness
Classification	#PersonalFinance; Compliant="FinA 1-09-12"
Synonyms	CB-PCR, PCR
Data Type	Enumeration: AAA, AA, A, B, C
Source	Derived: FINBOT::Person-CreditRtng
Comments	

Table 9-2 Type Definition Included in Glossary Entry

If several terms have the *same* complex or enumerated type, the data type field should not repeat the definition; it should refer, instead, to a data type name for ease of maintenance and consistency. A separate glossary definition with that type name would be entered into the glossary that defined the type in detail. Notice that in Table 9-3 the latter two glossary entries both use the type defined in the first.

Term Name	Credit Rating	Applicant Credit Rating	Guarantor Credit Rating
Definition	The PCR standard classification of credit worthiness	The PCR standard classification of an applicant's credit worthiness	The PCR standard classification of a guarantor's credit worthiness
Classification	#PersonalFinance; Compliant="FinA 1-09-12"		
Synonyms	CB-PCR, PCR	APP-PCR	GAR-PCR
Data Type	AAA, AA, A, B, C	Credit Rating	Credit Rating
Source		Derived: FINBOT::Person-CreditRtng	Derived: FINBOT::Gtr-CreditRtng
Comments			

Table 9-3 Type Definition as Separate Glossary Entry

9.7 Data Type

All Information Items manipulated by DMN (e.g., expressions, input data, decision conditions and conclusions), and therefore every glossary entry (and corresponding data model entry), have a data type that determines the range of values it can hold and their meanings. The DMN standard addresses these concepts to a point by defining basic data types and allowing complex ones to be imported. A good glossary is not confined by the standard, though it should be consistent with it. Specifying the data type of a glossary term adds meaning and helps to validate uses of the entry in decisions.

Data types fall into three categories: simple, constrained and complex.

9.7.1 Simple data types

Most simple data types support a single value. Instances of these can be directly created and manipulated in arithmetic expressions, used as the basis of tests in condition cells and used to express conclusion values. The standard DMN simple data types are:

- Number—both decimal and integer values (e.g., 21.7, 9).
- String—a sequence of characters (e.g., `"Steve"`).
- Boolean—a truth value (e.g., `true`, `false` and `null`).
- Time/Date/DateTime—a point in time (e.g., `11:49:09`, `2099-02-21`, `2099-02-21T21:14:09`).
- Duration—a period of time (e.g., `P4DT6H14M33S`, `P4Y5M`).

Some simple types can be extended to support multiple values in standard ways:

- List—a series of values (usually but not always of the same type).
- Context— a set of key value pairs (for example, a set of test scores: `{"Jack": 84, "Jill": 92}`). Each entry has a name by which it can be accessed.

All these types are fully supported by DMN and have built-in functions and operators (e.g., comparisons, handling of literal values, addition and subtraction or construction of new values; see Section B.5).

DMN also supports user defined types, which are imported from an XSD (XML Schema Definition). These include constrained, enumerated and composite types.

9.7.2 Constrained types

Some terms may have a simple data type, but have their values limited to a permitted subset of the simple data types' range. Their type is defined by an underlying simple type and a constraint. These are called constrained types. The constraint may be:

- A condition: the hypothetical[21] type *Integer* could be based on *Number* that has no fractional element. The constrained type *Natural Number* is based on *Integer* and must be non-negative.

---

[21] Note that DMN does not have a built-in Integer type.

- A range: the constrained type *Age* might be constrained by a range [0..130] to prevent the usage of nonsensical values. Ranges may be unbounded (e.g., <17) and others may have gaps (e.g., the *Number* range ([2..5], [10..19]) or the *Time* range ([14:00:00 .. 15:59:59], [18:00:00 .. 20:29:59])).

- A set of permitted values: the constrained type *Marital Status* might be a *String* constrained to one of the values in the set "SINGLE", "MARRIED", "DOMESTIC PARTNER", "DIVORCED". Types constrained in this way are called enumerations.

Constrained types can be imported into DMN, but no built-in constrained types are defined by it[22]. Therefore, it is important that constrained types are captured in the glossary. Decisions and constrained values share the burden of data validation in decision models. Constrained types prevent invalid values system wide, whereas decision models enforce the context specific or rapidly changing value restrictions. For example, the validation of human age in a decision model might use a constrained type and various decisions. An appropriate constrained type for the *CustomerAge* property is Number [0..130] because this prevents gross errors (e.g., an age of 200) across an entire decision model (or group of models). An individual Decision Table that determines the risk posed by a rental car driver might further constrain *CustomerAge* to [18..79] in order to eliminate data entry errors by providing users only the choice of valid values.

9.7.3   Enumerated types

Enumerated types, which are a special kind of constrained type, occur very frequently in decision models. These have a prescribed set of permitted values and cannot meaningfully hold any other. All enumerated types have an underlying type and a permitted value set (which naturally should be consistent with the underlying type). The simplest enumerated type is Boolean, instances of which can hold the values true, false or null. Enumerated types should be used to represent any property of a business object that can occupy only one of a number of limited values, even if these values change often (e.g., *Currency*). The use of an enumerated type, rather than a string, to represent concepts like *Customer Loyalty Class*, *Credit Rating* or *Currency* prevents entry errors and enables a new type of Decision Table validation. If all the possible values of a property are known, the coverage of a table can be tested (see Section 14.5.1); this is not possible for strings which have an infinite number of values. By this means, enumerated types make our decision model safer and less error prone.

9.7.4   Important properties of enumerated types

When considering the definition of enumerated types in a glossary, there is more to consider than the set of allowed values. One should also document:

- Whether the enumeration is stable or unstable. If unstable, document how often it changes.

---

[22] Constrained values are supported by DMN Decision Table value lists (see Section 8.2.3.6), but this is not the same as defining a data type (e.g., mortgage type, credit rating or month) in which the same constraint is integral to every occurrence of every instance of the type. DMN has no means of supporting this, but it can import constrained types.

- Whether the enumeration is inclusive and covers all possible values or it is exclusive and deliberate omits some.

- Whether the enumeration is internally or externally defined and controlled. For an externally defined enumeration, it is also important to know whether change is managed by periodically requesting updates on the enumerations' definition at the initiative of the user or imposed from outside as and when changes occur.

Stable enumerations usually relate to some closed, physical or mathematical quantity. Their allowed values often represent all possibilities and this set is extremely unlikely to change. For example, enumerations representing *Chromosomal Gender*, *Blood Group* and *Hair Color* are likely to be stable (and inclusive). Unstable enumerations, by contrast, are expected to change because they rely on a human imposed classification that is subject to constant revision. The permitted values of enumerations, such as *Mortgage Policy Type*, *Account Type*, *Sales Category* and *Criminal Offense*, are expected to change over time and provision must be made for this.

Internally defined enumerations are either controlled by the organization owning the decision model or are the product of the decision model itself; in both cases their evolution is tied directly to the model: the decision's owners control its evolution and it changes only at their instigation. Externally defined enumerations are subject to external control and their definition may need to be obtained from a Knowledge Source. The evolution of unstable, external enumerations is unpredictable.

Externally defined enumerations may have a 'pull' based change regime which indicates that the decision owner determines when any change in enumeration values is incorporated into the glossary (and decision model). A 'push' model indicates that change can be imposed upon the decision model, with little warning, by external factors.

All of these properties of enumerations are important when devising decision models and planning for their evolution. For example, a Decision Table that has external, unstable and exclusive enumeration inputs would need to be more cautious about handling unexpected (new) value combinations than one handling only stable, internal enumerations. The use of defaults is often more appropriate for Decision Tables processing unstable or exclusive enumerated inputs.

The management of enumeration evolution must be handled carefully (refer to the best practices defined in Section 14.7.1).

9.7.5 Composite types

Often, a business term does not have a single value, but combines multiple values to represent a single business entity. For example, a *MoneyAmount* data item might require both a *Currency* and a *Value*. Composite types are data structures, i.e., single business entities with multiple attributes, often (but not always) reflecting the structure of the underlying corporate data model's entities and attributes. User defined, composite data types can be imported into DMN decision models. Composite types represent compound values that have business integrity, occur frequently together and that may be viewed as a single concept from a business perspective (e.g., *Insurance Applicant*, *Order* and *Accident Report*). The attributes of composite data types may themselves be simple (e.g., an *Accident Report* may have a time and description), constrained (e.g., *EmployeeTitle*) or complex (e.g., a *Trade* may have two instances of *Counterparty*, each of which have attributes of their own). Where a composite type is used, it will be defined in its own glossary entry.

9.7.6 Functions

Glossaries may also document functions. These are mathematical expressions that take zero or more inputs (parameters) and calculate an output value from them. The output is a single simple or complex value, which is the result of the function. Functions can represent domain specific, mathematical calculations or transforms (e.g., the net present value of a list of cashflows or the monthly repayment instalment on a mortgage given the total value and time profile of repayments).

When considering functions, modelers need to consider whether they need to be captured and modeled and, if so, where they should be documented. Modelers should only document a function if any of the following holds:

- The meaning of a function is not commonly understood, not agreed in the organization or not trivial (good examples include: *fractalDimension*, *goodValue* and *isHoliday*; counter-examples include: *sine*, *isPrimeNumber* and *average*).
- The function is part of the organization's proprietary know-how, intellectual property or competitive advantage.
- The function definition changes over time.

A function should be defined in a glossary if it is used across the decisions models of multiple organization departments or it is extremely simple and does not change. However complex or volatile logic, logic describing intellectual property or functions that are subject to product and jurisdictional variation should always be captured in a decision model.

When defining a function within a glossary, the glossary *source* field should contain a reference to the authority that defines this function. The definition of commonly used business functions in the glossary prevents clutter in the decision model without obscuring the function's or the model's meaning. Modelers should be cautious not to overuse functions. Logic that is pertinent to a decision should not be hidden in functions and a decision model riddled with many bespoke functions may be hard to understand.

Glossary functions may be defined using DMN (see an example in Figure 17-40 of Section 17.3.7 and an explanation in Section B.4.7).

9.8 Supporting DMN with a Glossary

The selection of a glossary format to support decision modeling is allied to the selection of a data modeling medium (see Section 10.3.5). Whichever data modeling medium is used, the DMN glossary can either be integrated with it, or separated from it and placed into a documentation tool (or even an Excel spreadsheet). An integrated approach is usually preferred, as it is easier to maintain, but separate sources can sometimes provide richer user access to the glossary's information.

More important than the form of the glossary adopted is the way in which it supports an organization's modeling efforts in DMN. It is important to be clear what decision modeling demands from a glossary:

- The name of each term and its business meaning.

- Any permitted synonyms of the term. From a decision modeling perspective, two artifacts with a name that differs only in that some terms are replaced with their synonyms <u>is the same artifact</u>. It is important, therefore, to explicitly manage and reduce the number of synonyms in use by an enterprise.

- The ability for terms to have the most appropriate data type.

- The separation of data type definition (e.g., the description of a collection of attributes that defines a *Cashflow*, or the permitted values of an enumeration like *Credit Rating*) from specific data instances of this type (e.g., separate attributes like *Settlement Cashflow*, *Fee Cashflow* and *Guarantor Credit Rating*). This allows widely used types (like simple enumerations or complex sets of related attribute terms) to be reused without repeating their definitions.

- Consistency between the decision model and the glossary. The decision model should use only the terms defined in the glossary and the glossary should define only terms used (or to be imminently incorporated into) in the set of decision models. The two evolve together: there is no implication that either must be developed first.

- Traceability between corporate data entities, glossary terms and the decision model.

Although it may be forced by circumstance, multiple glossaries in different formats spread across multiple tools should be avoided. Such distributed schemes invite duplication and overlap. If a split is inevitable (perhaps the decision logic uses data from two sources, one a database and the other an XML stream, each with its own established glossaries), try to establish a clear division of responsibility between them.

An example glossary is presented in Section 17.3.3.4.

10 Integration with Other Models

Wholeness is not achieved by cutting off a portion of one's being, but by integration of the contraries
—Carl Jung

Decision modeling offers a powerful technique for analyzing, understanding and communicating business logic. Chapter 7 described the importance of putting decision models into a business context. This chapter builds on this to describe how existing practices of process, data, and architectural modeling interface with decision modeling.

This chapter's examples show how BPMN, ERD, UML and ArchiMate Business Motivation Extension models relate to DMN and the benefits of combining their use. The boundary between DMN and these other notations is described, as is the division of responsibility between them. The focus is on the value of these additional models, when they should be used, how the information in these models is different from that represented in DMN and how these views interoperate and mutually enrich each other. A basic knowledge of the other modeling standards is assumed of the reader.

10.1 Multi-Model Integration

10.1.1 Introduction

Decision modeling does not function in a vacuum but within a rich, architectural context which must be understood, at least partially, in order for decisions to be fully framed (see also Chapter 7). DMN interoperates with business process, data, architectural and business motivation models. This chapter uses BPMN, ERD/UML, ArchiMate and the business motivation elements of ArchiMate respectively as examples to illustrate model integration. The basics of each of these modeling techniques is discussed briefly before considering in more detail the benefits of using them with DMN, how DMN interfaces with them and how they can be effectively used together. The responsibilities of each of these models, and how they contrast with those of DMN, is discussed—with a focus on how concepts are divided between them and how to avoid inconsistency and duplication.

10.1.2 Using decision modeling with other models

Mature organizations can maximize the value of decision modeling by integrating their use of DMN with business process models (e.g., BPMN), data models (e.g., UML and ERD) and business motivation models (e.g., the business motivation elements of ArchiMate). Each integration offers powerful synergies and mutually enriches the models involved. Each model has specific responsibilities, strengths and points of contact with the others (see the four perspectives represented in Figure 10-1) and the following sub-sections address how DMN integrates with each of these standard notations in turn. Although each section illustrates the interface between DMN and another model, using a specific notation as a vehicle to demonstrate the benefits of model integration, many of the points raised are not notation specific and other notations could be substituted (e.g., Amber for BPMN).

All four perspectives are brought together in an encompassing business architecture. DMN contributes to this by defining Decision Services.

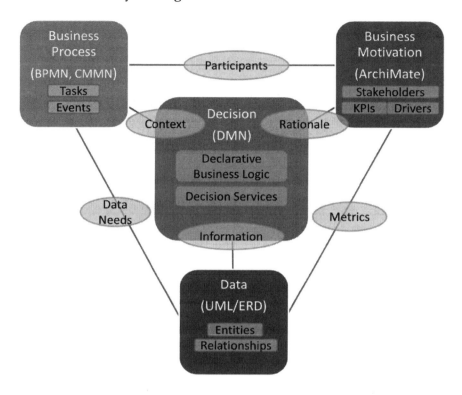

Figure 10-1 Integration of Four Models into Business Architecture

10.1.3 The business case for multi-model integration

Decision Management relies on decision modeling and also benefits from process, data, motivation and architecture modeling techniques. These models allow for early insight into the needs and context of a Decision Management System. They can identify conflicts between these needs early, i.e., before implementation resources are committed. Established notations support effective communication between teams, coordinating team specialists and thereby facilitating the management of requirements in a way that supports effective automation. The models, and the connections between them, are also effective at identifying errors and gaps in requirements and allowing organizations to avoid them or resolve them quickly.

As Figure 10-1 shows, the outer three models each support a facet of business decisions that is important to their definition and not addressed by DMN. Process models show when decisions are made and how their outcomes steer a business process. Data models explain the rich meaning and structure of the data used to make decisions and represent outcomes. Motivation models show why decisions are made, their business rationale, and the ways in which their effectiveness can be measured.

Producing four different models may seem unnecessary and costly. However, the value of the early insight each yields and the foundation they provide for a robust Service Oriented Architecture should not be underestimated. To lessen the up-front cost, organizations should produce models iteratively using agile project delivery so that value is provided earlier, delivered incrementally, associated with executable deliverables and is proportionate to cost. Most projects do not require all models to be developed to the same level of detail; therefore, those less relevant to the effort can be created only at a high level. On no account should modelers be engaged on a 'model to completion' basis as this always results in spiraling costs and compromises value. Furthermore, personnel should not work in silos, producing models of a specific sort. The approach of partitioning teams according to the notation they will use is like dividing a team of collaborating artists and restricting each to use only one color. It is much better to adopt a holistic approach and encourage analysts use all the models needed to express the requirements they are modeling. If teams must be partitioned, use business boundaries to distribute the workload.

Pragmatically a lack of funds, time or skills may mean that all four models cannot be undertaken. In these circumstances, an organization should concentrate on the models that yield insight into the most complex, poorly understood and risky elements of the problem.

10.1.4 Avoiding duplicated efforts

Some care must be given to the overlaps between those different models and potential maintenance issues that might arise as a result. Some short-term duplication may be inevitable, even desirable, to allow a specific modeling effort to proceed quickly. However, flexibility in this regard should not be allowed to result in uncontrolled duplication. Some coordination and supervision is essential to avoid the potential for conflicting or redundant definitions.

An enterprise integrating two or more of these standards is advised to use a common reference for the information that they share, for example:

- **Business Vocabulary**: business terminology from all models must be kept consistent. A business glossary (see Chapter 9) that defines vocabulary and how it is used by models is the most effective approach.
- **Business Actors**: DMN organizations, BPMN participants, UML actors and BME stakeholders should be consolidated into one definitive collection of business entities.
- **Business Events**: BPMN, UML and ArchiMate all define business events; these must be combined and defined in a common list or glossary.
- **Business Data**: BPMN data objects, associations and datastores; DMN Input Data; and UML/ERD classes, entities and attributes should be kept consistent and documented in a business glossary.

10.2 Integrating DMN with Business Process – BPMN

One of the most powerful inter-model synergies available to the decision modeler is that between the decision and business process model. These views strongly complement one another if both are used correctly. The leading business process notation standard is the

Business Process Model and Notation (BPMN) and this is especially effective when used with DMN. There are many good BPMN references (see Appendix A). One of these[23] is a lucid introduction to how process models and decision models can be used together. This section provides a brief overview of business process modeling and BPMN in order to describe in detail the best separation of concerns between BPMN and DMN as well as the details of the interface between them.

10.2.1 What is Business Process Modeling?

Business processes define sequences of activities performed during business operations, many of these will be conditional. A business process model documents how an organization reacts to and resolves business events. It also explains the proactive tasks organizations engage in to support their business. Business Process Models describe how an organization generates business value for its own departments and its clients by characterizing patterns of activity and interactions between them, i.e., sequences of operational business tasks that communicate how an organization reacts to key stimuli and generates benefit from them. It defines how tasks that business personnel (or systems) perform can have outcomes that direct the onward flow of the process, choosing between alternative courses of action. It defines the business entities involved, how activities are orchestrated among them, the hand-offs between them and the automation boundary. It shows how business events, errors and exceptions are detected in the process flow and how these are resolved or escalated. Process models also specify the information that can flow between business entities and tasks: both the documents and datastores that they share and the formal messages that are explicitly exchanged between them (e.g., paper letters or electronic files).

10.2.2 BPMN overview and rationale

10.2.2.1 What is BPMN?

The Business Process Model and Notation (BPMN) is, like DMN, a standard produced and governed by the Object Management Group (OMG). It enjoys wide adoption and broad tool support. The notation is used to precisely document all the aspects described above using a rich, purpose-built set of symbols and conventions.

Like DMN, BPMN is defined precisely enough to support execution. It can model process iteration, token based parallelism, exception detection and propagation, transactions and rollback compensations. However, as with DMN, the main purpose of BPMN is effective communication amongst business personnel, not conveying implementation details. BPMN aims to manifest a company's business processes so that they can be: effectively organized, communicated, reviewed, improved and, above all, so that they become an explicitly managed asset of the company.

10.2.2.2 Example

A business process model, defined in BPMN, is a set of atomic tasks assembled into sequences of activities. Sometimes it includes clearly defined hand-offs between business entities. Each end to end process must generate business value, i.e., its outcome must be of

---

[23]Microguide to Process and Decision Modelling in BPMN/DMN, Debvoise/Taylor, Advanced Component Research, 2014, ISBN 978-1-502-78964-8.

tangible worth to the organization and, often, the end client. BPMN supports a hierarchical definition of business process in which any individual business activity can be broken down into a subprocess of its own.

Figure 10-2 shows a subset of commonly used BPMN symbols that are used in the diagrams in this book. This is not an exhaustive list; many other BPMN symbols exist and an explanation of all of them is beyond the scope of this work. Each symbol has a strongly prescribed meaning:

- Each circle depicts an event. A faint outline denotes a start event that triggers the beginning of a process, a double outline indicates an event that occurs in the middle of a process and a heavy outline signifies an event that ends a process.

- Each rounded rectangle is a business task or activity.

- Each diamond is a gateway symbolizing branching behavior and potential parallelism. The most common of these is the exclusive gateway that takes one input—typically the previous activity's outcome—and has a number of output flows each labelled with a condition. The single condition that is satisfied dictates which alternative output path of the gateway is followed. Other gateways permit multiple outputs (parallelism) or trigger output paths by events rather than conditions.

- Each document icon is an important business data item that is input to or output from a task.

- Each disc symbol is a persistent datastore.

The lines also have strict meanings: arrow lines depict sequence (e.g., a finish to start relationship: the end of one activity, or the occurrence of an event, triggers the following event or activity) and dotted lines depict a data association.

Large rectangles depict business participants (e.g., actors such as individual organizations, departments or systems— 'pools') that perform tasks. Rectangular sections within them represent categories, most often used to denote roles ('lanes'). However, the performer property of a task may contradict its appearance in a pool or lane.

An example BPMN business process for a sub-prime mortgage company is shown in Figure 10-3. This top-level diagram describes the processing of mortgage applications. The overall goal of the process is to provide a customer with a mortgage on the best terms, providing this is consistent with the company's policies.

Figure 10-3 shows all the business tasks between receiving a customer application and either rejecting or accepting it. Rejection can be initiated by the organization (due to an inability to verify a customer's identity or the fact that the mortgage cannot be offered) or by the customer (by rejecting an offer or failing to respond before the offer expires).

The diagram is superficially like a flowchart, but BPMN's symbol set is vastly richer and its meaning is more precise. It is important to note that a fresh instance of this process will be triggered by every mortgage application that is received; therefore, multiple instances can exist simultaneously, each with its own state.

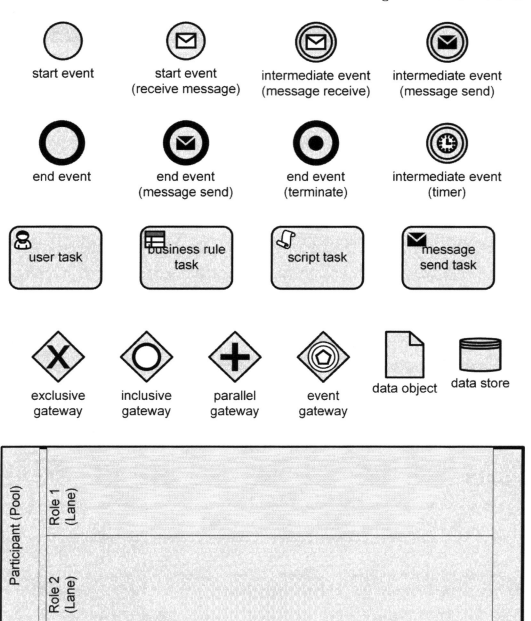

Figure 10-2 Basic BPMN Symbol Set

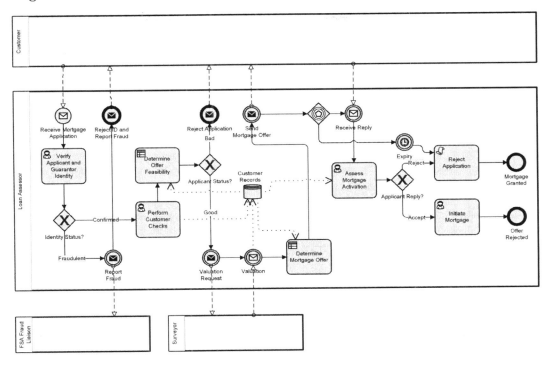

Figure 10-3 Example Business Process in BPMN

10.2.2.3 Responsibilities of a process model

A business process model communicates the following things about every task in a business process:

- **Task context**. How individual tasks fit within the coordinated sequence of a business process. It also depicts how a task's state (i.e., whether it is ready[24], active or complete) defines the progress of the business process as a whole (e.g., *Assess Mortgage Activation, Send Mortgage Offer*).
- **Task Type**. The character of each task. The icons at the top left of the activity boxes show that *Verify Applicant and Guarantor Identity* and *Assess Mortgage Activation* are user tasks (these are coordinated by a process but achieved in part by human effort), whereas *Determine Mortgage Offer* is a business rule driven task, i.e., its outcome is determined by a **decision**. Many other task types exist, including the manual task that represents activity undertaken exclusively by people.
- **Process Automation Boundary**. Task types also help to show the barrier between automated tasks and those performed by users. Notice that, once the identity of the applicant is confirmed, the user task *Perform Customer Checks* is followed immediately

---

[24] A ready task is one that is eligible to proceed but is awaiting some event or data before it can start.

and unconditionally by an automated *Determine Offer Feasibility* task. The automation barrier lies between them and some hand-off is required.

- **Task Data Requirements**. The data with which a task is associated (shown as a dotted line). A process describes activities that prepare data for a task, for example, how data procured during *Perform Customer Checks* is persisted for later use in *Determine Mortgage Offer*.

- **Task Triggers**. When a task is eligible to start and what prevailing circumstances trigger it. For example, *Determine Mortgage Offer* can only occur if a valuation has been received.

- **Task Consequences**. Process flow defines task order and how this is impacted by earlier actions. *Determine Offer Feasibility* yields an estimated feasibility of the mortgage, using local area information and details of the property to determine its value and customer details to infer their ability to service the proposed loan. Only if the *Determine Offer Feasibility* task outcome indicates that the applicant is loan-worthy can a structural survey and valuation be initiated by *Valuation Request* to determine the exact property details. The latter is an expensive action that the company would sooner avoid if the application has obvious issues. The way in which outcomes of a task are used to influence the following business activities is called 'steering'.

More widely, a business process should describe:

- **Actor Responsibilities**. Which business actor performs each task. All of the activities in this diagram are performed by (or on behalf of) a *Loan Assessor*.

- **Process Outcomes**. The possible end results (end events) of this process. In this case, there are four, depicted as heavily bordered circles: *Reject ID and Report Fraud*, *Reject Application*, *Offer Rejected* and *Mortgage Granted*. The process also shows which errors are recognized by each task, whether these interrupt the task and how errors are resolved or escalated.

- **Process Interruption or Delay**. The circumstances in which the process can 'stall' awaiting external events and what events would cause them to continue. For example, once a loan offer is sent to a customer (by message event *Send Mortgage Offer*), the process awaits an external event. It continues when it receives a *Reply* from the customer or the *Expiry* (timeout event) occurs. A similar delay occurs after *Valuation Request* because valuations can take days to perform.

10.2.3 Using DMN and BPMN together
10.2.3.1 How DMN and BPMN connect

Because they were created by the same standards body, BPMN and DMN can work very elegantly together. This is achieved by a single point of interface: the **business rule task** (hereafter referred to as **decision task**). A decision task is a type of business task in BPMN that is associated with one or more DMN business decisions but behaves in all other respects as if it were a normal task. Decision tasks are often automated. Currently BPMN uses the business rules task symbol[25] to represent automated decision tasks (e.g., *Determine Offer Feasibility* in Figure 10-3). However, user tasks can also be associated with decision models when these tasks require complex decision-making and the know-how has been captured in a decision model (for example, *Verify Applicant and Guarantor Identity*).

BPMN and DMN work effectively together through a judicious separation of concerns and it is important to understand this before discussing the details. If an organization already uses BPMN, there is real benefit in extending its use to show the context and process impact of its business decisions. If not, then the organization should consider adopting BPMN to provide clear communication and active management of its business processes. However, BPMN is not required for DMN and process modeling should not be considered a pre-requisite for decision modeling.

10.2.3.2   Responsibilities of the decision model

Most business tasks are straightforward manual or automated actions. Some involve complex logic and are best represented as decision tasks. For each decision task, the DMN decision model will document:

- a detailed definition of all the information required by the decision and how it is used;
- a declarative definition of the logic of the decision and its sub-decisions;
- a description of how logic is distributed across different sub-decisions;
- a detailed definition of the authorities that influence a decision's definition; *and*
- the possible outcomes of the decision.

10.2.3.3   How process and decision models work together

It is possible to summarize the way that BPMN and DMN work together as follows:

- Process models dictate *if* and *when* decisions are made. They specify what events trigger decisions, the order in which decisions are made relative to other tasks and when they must await external events. Events in this case can be simple external stimuli or internally generated events resulting from pattern analysis of simpler events; the latter is referred to as Complex Event Processing (CEP). Decisions may be involved in the detection of complex events, but their detection is choreographed by the business process. Decision models define the meaning and requirements of the decision and the *decision-making approach* used to derive the outcome.

- Process models dictate if the decision is performed by users or automated. They document which business entity makes the decision (if it is a user decision) or on whose behalf it is made (if it is automated). Decision models show the association of the decision with business objectives and who owns the decision-making approach.

- Decision models enumerate the possible outcomes of a decision and the process model describes how each outcome guides the onward flow of the process.

---

[25] Business rule tasks predate DMN. Future releases of BPMN may incorporate specific notation to denote decisions and points of DMN connectivity.

- Decision models define all the data needed to make a decision; process models describe how this is marshalled and provided.

- Process models may explicitly or implicitly define state (e.g., the mortgage vendor is awaiting a property valuation) and reactions to events in a given state. However, decisions are stateless and decoupled from events.

10.2.3.4 Process and decision models should be kept separate

The strict separation of concerns between business process and business decision models is very valuable to the evolution of both, because:

- Process and decision models describe two very different aspects of business behavior: the former is focused on sequence and interactions and the latter on declarative definition of decision-making.

- Decisions and processes evolve at very different rates and for different reasons. Separation into linked decision and process models avoids undue interference between these change processes and allows independent evolution.

- Decisions and process often require the stewardship of different individuals within an organization.

- Process models are not well suited to expressing decision logic mainly because they require the stipulation of sequence and decision models do not. Indeed, a sequence imposed on a decision is often arbitrary, and it needlessly complicates decision-making, hiding more important logical dependencies between sub-decisions and reducing the scalability and reuse potential of a decision model. This can be illustrated by comparing the clarity of representing decision logic directly to a business process as opposed to using a decision (see Section 10.2.3.5).

- Separate models allow decisions and processes to be reused independently of one another. A business process task may elect to use a different definition of specific decision (e.g., an improved version) or reuse a single decision in multiple sub-processes (to promote consistency).

- The management and execution of processes and decisions are also better represented using different media.

10.2.3.5 Process models are poor at representing decisions

To illustrate the problems of combined process and decision models or attempting to represent decision logic in a business process, consider the simple decision logic to determine the discount level to be offered to a customer, as represented in Figure 10-4.

Were the same logic to be represented by a series of gateways within a business process it could[26] appear like Figure 10-5.

Although combining the decision logic with the business process means that the entire behavior is depicted in one place, comparison of these alternative representations reveals

---

[26] This is only one possible representation. Part of the problem of representing decision logic in business processes is that one imposes sequence where it is not required, which yields many alternative representations, all of which are correct.

many drawbacks. Even decision logic requiring only a small Decision Table in DMN is much harder and more cumbersome to represent as gateways in BPMN. These complex process models are much harder to understand and change effectively. They also require considerable repetition of conditions (notice the frequency of *Item Price* and *Date* in Figure 10-5) and pollute business processes with low-level detail.

The separated business process (Figure 10-6) and decision (Figure 10-4) are simpler and better suited to the purpose.

Discount				
U	**Item Category**	**Item Price**	**Date**	**Discount**
				0,[1..100]
1	*PHOTOGRAPHY*	>100	<= *2018-12-31*	2%
2	*DOMESTIC ELECTRICAL*	>500	<= *2018-05-31*	4%
3	*MENS FASHION*	-	<= *2016-06-15*	2%
4	*LADIES FASHION*	>200	<= *2018-06-15*	3%

Figure 10-4 Discount Decision Logic as Decision Table

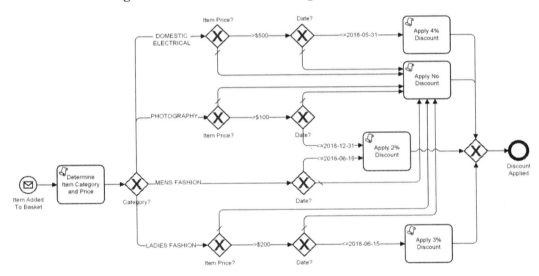

Figure 10-5 Discount Decision Logic as Business Process

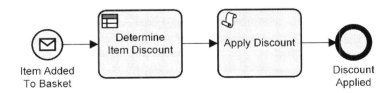

Figure 10-6 Business Process Invoking Discount Decision

10.2.3.6   BPMN Scope and DMN

Because process models 'invoke' decision models, there is a tendency to believe that decision models are sub-ordinate to process models and have a smaller scope (the single task with which they are associated). The misconception is that every decision invoked by a decision task is defined by a separate, complete decision model addressing an isolated decision. This is *not* the case. Process models and decision models often have the *same* business scope: they both concern the delivery of an overall business outcome of tangible worth to the organization (and often the end customer). The process focuses on events, activities and their sequencing and the decision on requirements and the declarative decision logic. We concur with Bruce Silver's alignment of the Decision Requirements Diagram and the 'end-to-end' business process[27]: both should focus on the same tangible business outcome.

Consider the process model of Figure 10-3. An accompanying Decision Requirements Diagram is depicted in Figure 10-7. Note that both have the overall goal of *Determine Mortgage Offer*, i.e., to quantify and provide a customer loan on the best terms, providing this is possible.

---

[27] See DMN Method and Style, Bruce Silver, 2016, ISBN 978-0-9823681-5-2

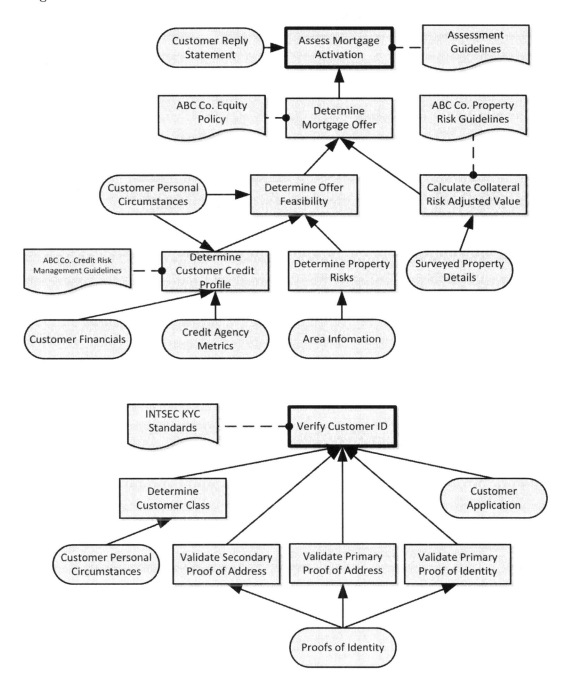

Figure 10-7 Decision Model Representing the Logic of Process in Figure 10-3

Figure 10-8 shows the pattern of connections between decision tasks and decisions. Note that:

- A decision task can invoke a decision at any level in the hierarchy.

- Both user and automated tasks can invoke decisions.

- If a specific instance of a process has invoked a sub-decision to reach an outcome, that outcome will be re-used if a dependent decision is later invoked by the same process. For example, the outcome of *Determine Offer Feasibility*, invoked by the decision task of the same name, will be used by *Determine Mortgage Offer* that is later invoked conditionally by the decision task of that name.

- Not all decisions need to be explicitly invoked by a decision task. If not invoked, they will be used as needed by their dependents. This is often the case when their use is unconditional or of no impact to the business process. Hence *Determine Property Risks* is not explicitly invoked by the business process because it has no direct bearing on the process, but it will be used by dependent decision *Determine Offer Feasibility* as needed.

- The process model sequence can marshal data for, and even reduce the expense of, the decision model without impacting its structure. The use of expensive[28] Input Data or decisions (e.g., *Collateral Risk Adjusted Value*) often needs to be minimized, or at least delayed, until a profitable outcome seems likely in order to justify the expense and therefore improve processing efficiency. Notice the separation of *Determine Offer Feasibility* from *Determine Mortgage Offer* in the process model. This occurs because the latter decision has an expensive data requirement—the sub-decision *Collateral Risk Adjusted Value* that is dependent on the survey report and valuation. The cost of this valuation can be avoided if the outcome of *Determine Offer Feasibility*, which cheaply approximates the feasibility of the loan, means that no offer will be made. This technique ensures that the more expensive operation is used only when essential. The *Approximator* pattern (see Section 16.5) may also be used to defer or avoid the use of expensive decisions.

- Many decision tasks (in the same or different process models) may invoke the same decision. By this means the consistency of behavior is improved.

- The decision model is devoid of detail that the process model covers, e.g., data marshalling issues, interrupts or delays on external events.

- Although they document independent concepts, the process and decision models must be kept consistent.

---

[28] This could represent monetary expense (e.g., paying a credit agency or risk assessor for information) or the consumption of time or other resources where these are critical.

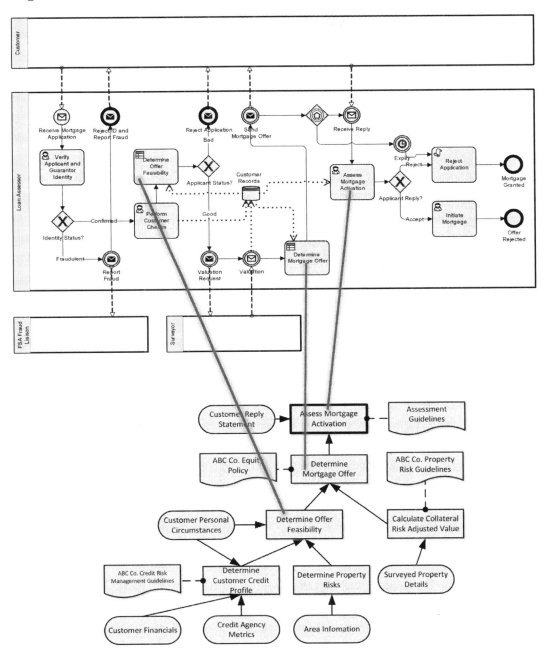

Figure 10-8 Relationship Between Business Process and Decision Model

10.2.3.7 The declarative nature of DMN

DMN is a declarative standard and a good decision model should avoid notions of sequence (see Sections 10.2.3.3 and 13.6). Efficiency is often dependent on execution order.

For example, in the case illustrated in the previous section, an expensive sub-decision was only required under certain circumstances and needed to be deferred to a point where its cost was likely to be recovered by a profitable outcome. If these sequence considerations were added to a decision model, its business meaning would be clouded. It is unnecessary to use sequence in the decision model because:

- Decision information dependencies are 'lazy'. If the logic of a decision does not need the outcome of a sub-decision in a specific case, then the sub-decision will not be used and so incur no expense on this occasion.

- If a decision has several alternative strategies, varying in expenses and accuracy (i.e., a cheap but approximate version and an expensive but accurate version), the *Divide and Conquer* pattern (see Section 16.2) can be used to represent this group and how a specific variation should be selected.

- The business process can specify the optimal sequencing and conditional nature of expensive decisions (as shown above).

10.2.4 DMN's interface with BPMN

10.2.4.1 BPMN decision tasks and DMN

There is no formal interface between BPMN and DMN except for the properties of decisions, defined in the DMN metamodel, which link to BPMN artifacts. These are listed in Section 14.2.5 and summarized in Table 10-1.

DMN Property	Meaning	Links to BPMN
Decision Maker	The organizational units or business roles that make the decision	Pool or lane owning decision[29]
Using Processes	The BPMN processes that require this decision	List of Processes
Using Tasks	The BPMN tasks that make this decision	List of Tasks

Table 10-1 Mapping DMN Properties to BPMN

In this interface, *Decision Maker* holds the name of a business actor that corresponds to a pool or lane within a BPMN process model in which the decision task sits. *Using Tasks* associates a decision with a decision task. The *Using Process* association allows an initial link between processes and decisions when the process is not yet specified to the task level. Once the *Using Tasks* association is specified, then the processes involved can be derived.

10.2.4.2 BPMN input data and DMN

Decisions can 'see' the data that flows into the BPMN decision task that invokes them. Specifically, any of the following data sources that BPMN provides to a decision task are

---

[29] Organization in DMN is not explicitly lined to a Pool or Lane in BPMN, but this is generally an effective way to align the models.

translated to Input Data components in the decision model (with the same name if there is a 1:1 correspondence):

- data inflows from a data object (such as the flow from *Area Risks* into *Determine Offer Feasibility* in Figure 10-3);
- data inflows from data stores (e.g., *Customer Records* to *Determine Mortgage Offer* in Figure 10-3); *and*
- any information attending an event, e.g., a message, time, triggering condition or signal name (for example the *Customer Application* message accompanying the *Receive Mortgage Application* event in Figure 10-3).

All data items, whether input flows in a business process model or Input Data in a decision model, should be defined in the supporting business glossary (see Chapter 9).

Generally, decisions are deployed as a Decision Service that encapsulates all or some of their sub-decisions (see Section 8.1.6); decision tasks effectively invoke Decision Services. All the Input Data required by the decision and its sub-decisions, as well as the information represented by any decisions that are not included in the Decision Service, must be available when the decision task invokes the decision. This information should be defined for each Decision Service. DMN allows the decisions included in the Decision Service, those that can be invoked and those that are required, to be specified along with the necessary Input Data.

10.2.4.3   DMN decision outcomes and BPMN

The (one or more) conclusions that arise from a decision, i.e., its outcome, are available to the business process that invoked it. The business process should use the outcome (or any part of it) in one or more of the following ways:

- Control the path(s) taken by a gateway. The gateway should use the decision outcome to dictate which path (or paths) to follow (e.g., the use of *Credit Rating* in the gateway of Figure 10-9). It must be clear which path is to be taken for every possible value in the decision outcome. In this example, one path leads to a product list offering and the other to a polite decline. It is essential that the decision task and *not* the gateway makes the decision.
- Produce a data outflow (e.g., *Product List* in Figure 10-9) for use later in the process or as an incidental output from the process.
- Populate a datastore (e.g., *Declined Sales Prospects* in Figure 10-9), generally because this information will be persisted and used in another process or by another system. In this case, other processes may benefit from access to a list of declined customers as an anti-fraud measure.

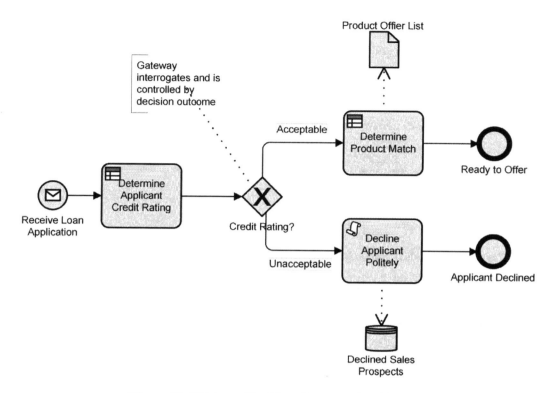

Figure 10-9 Using a Decision Outcome in a Process

When using gateways in this fashion, refer to the outcome (or that part of the outcome that you are using) by its standard glossary name to avoid any ambiguity.

It is important not to make any embedded business decisions in the gateway conditions themselves. Constrain gateway conditions to simple checks on the outcomes of the decision task. The process in Figure 10-10 places complex conditions on the outcome of the decision task *Determine Credit Rating*, but the logic of these is in effect an additional embedded decision about how the combinations of values of *Credit Rating*, *Country* and *Salary* drive eligibility for certain products. This approach injects decision-making logic into the business process, making it more likely that the process definition will have to be changed in the future. This is an inefficient way to represent logic and complicates verification and amendment of the decision-making.

Instead this embedded decision should be the subject of its own decision task, which in turn should drive the selection of products as shown in Figure 10-11. Here, only a single decision task is required

The Decisions Requirements Diagram for this decision is shown in Figure 10-12. Note that the separate sequential steps of the earlier business process model have been correctly depicted here as data dependencies.

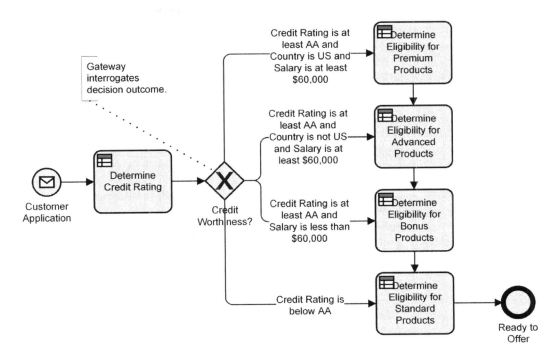

Figure 10-10 Business Process with Embedded Implicit Decision

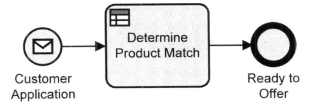

Figure 10-11 Refactored Business Process

It is best practice to use a gateway with a decision outcome condition immediately after the decision task that produced that outcome, as demonstrated in Figure 10-9. However, this is not always feasible. If a gateway using a decision outcome must be placed remotely from the decision, use a dataflow (or a datastore) to link the gateway (or the preceding task if this is more natural) with the outcome on which it is dependent.

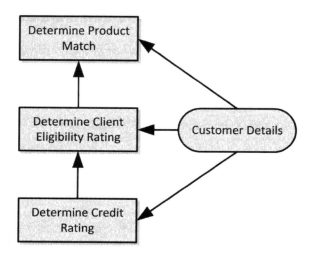

Figure 10-12 Decision Requirement Diagram for Determine Product Match

10.2.4.4   Handling collections in BPMN/DMN

Decisions that produce a collection of outcomes can have these processed as a whole by the following task or individually using a multi-instance subprocess to iterate through them.

Normally, collections of input data are handled by having one instance of the entire business process for each element in the collection. This works well when the processing of any business event is independent of the others (e.g., the receipt of a loan application) and no aggregate information requiring the entire collection is needed. This is typical of processing data, such as sales or website navigation, in which each processing context occurs in isolation from the others.

Occasionally, data needs to be processed as a collection because the handling of each element depends on aggregate properties of the set. For example, when processing a collection of bids for an on-line auction, each bid will be treated according to its relationship with the highest bid.

When entire collections of input data (e.g., a set of applicants for a job) need to be processed as a whole by a single process instance, but need to be individually processed, item-by-item, by a decision task in that process, this can be handled with a BPMN multi-instance subprocess. This allows an invocation of the decision for each item, either in series or in parallel. Figure 10-12 shows an individual parallel invocation of *Pre Filter Candidates* for every *Candidate* in a set. If the decision requires both aggregate knowledge of the collection and individual members, it can operate directly on the collection as a whole and use boxed expressions (see Section 11.3.2.5) to stipulate the level of any collection iteration in the decision-making.

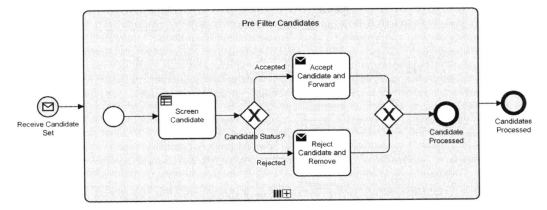

Figure 10-13 Individual Processing of Every Element in a Collection

10.2.4.5 BPMN input events and DMN

BPMN decision tasks can be triggered either by the completion of a preceding task or the triggering of a preceding input or intermediate event. Any of these triggers may be associated with the decision task by an incoming sequence arrow. Decisions are aware of the event that triggered them (technically the entry of a BPMN process token into their decisions task), but only in as much as they have been triggered to start. Decisions do not receive any information about the event itself, the token or the process they are invoked from. They may receive the data payload of an event, a message (see Section 10.2.4.2), as well as the data covered in the previous sections.

To prevent undue dependencies arising between process and decisions, decisions cannot know the state of the process that triggered them. For example, decisions are not aware of the advancement of tasks performed in parallel to the decision task that triggered them or of the events that have occurred. If a decision requires knowledge of this sort, the business process should be reorganized to explicitly provide this as a data input using a datastore or flow.

Decision tasks are instantaneous and are not subject to external interruption. Therefore, once triggered, a given decision task cannot be further influenced by events occurring in the surrounding business process. Data inputs aside, decisions are independent of the state of the business context and this simplifies them and improves their reusability. Reusable decisions are important to ensure a consistent approach to decision-making across multiple processes in an enterprise.

10.2.4.6 BPMN output events and DMN

BPMN offers many types of output events including: those that terminate a process (normally or abnormally), those that synchronously and asynchronously communicate output information, those that indicate the occurrence of a complex condition, those that signify that an error has occurred, those that support transactional behavior and multi events that are complex combinations of the previous types. When these are connected to decision tasks with sequence flows, the behavior is identical to conventional BPMN tasks as the behavior of decision tasks is no different to any other type.

Decision tasks denote the application of logic and are considered 'instantaneous' because they cannot be blocked. It makes little sense to interrupt them as they have no externally observable interim results. As a consequence, they have no state of their own. From the process perspective, a decision has either been made or not; there is no meaningful intermediate position. As decisions are stateless, passive and instantaneous, the only boundary event a decision task can catch is an interrupting error event. This occurs when the decision fails to reach an outcome for any reason. This is often due to one of the decision tables being unable to provide a result (e.g., an incomplete Decision Table being used in a scenario for which it has no applicable rules). Although it is good practice to avoid this wherever possible, it is not practical to avoid it in every case.

10.3 Integrating DMN with Data – ERD/UML

This section does not aim to teach data modeling; there are many good books that serve this purpose[30]. However, it does cover enough of the basics of logical business data modeling to explain why it is important to decision modeling. It describes why one should use business data modeling in conjunction with decision modeling, the best division of labor between DMN and data modeling notations and the details of the interface between them. Integrating decision models with data models is an especially important step in supporting a glossary (see Chapter 9).

10.3.1 What is Data Modeling

Many readers of this book will be familiar with the goals, if not the notation, of logical data modeling. The intent is to depict, graphically and precisely, the individual data items that exist in a business domain, document their properties and capture how they are related to one another.

Logical data modeling is concerned with business information. For example, the concepts of *Customer*, *Address*, *Invoice* and *Item Line* may be important to a business. These can be called business entities or business objects and each has some complexity of its own. From the perspective of a hypothetical business, a *Customer* has properties such as a first name, surname, gender, title, and mobile phone number, while an *Invoice* has properties such as the total amount, the invoice number and the pay-by date. The business will also consider how these items are related in its operations, for example:

- A *Customer* lives at only one *Address* and an *Address* may be associated with many *Customers*.

- A *Customer* may be associated with many *Invoices* but each *Invoice* relates to only one *Customer*.

- An *Invoice* has many *Item Lines*, but each *Item Line* may only be included in one *Invoice*.

---

[30]UML Distilled, Martin Fowler, Addison Wesley. The UML Language Reference Manual, Rumbaugh, Jacobson and Booch, Addison-Wesley. Database Design using Entity Relationship Diagrams, Sikha Bagui and Richard Earp, Auerback Publications.

10.3.2 Rationale for data modeling

The overall rationale for logical data modeling is to capture all of the information of importance to a business, define it and impose sufficient structure to avoid ambiguity, inconsistency and repetition. A good logical data model can become the basis of a company's business vocabulary.

A data model can act as a very compact illustration of the key concepts of a business domain and their interrelationships—something that can be hard to see in many pages of requirements text, across many decisions or in a large glossary. This can be very useful for incoming SMEs who wish to familiarize themselves with the data landscape of the decision model.

10.3.3 Data Modeling notations

The most common notations for representing data structures are the Entity Relationship Diagram (ERD) and Unified Modeling Language (UML). Like DMN and BPMN, UML is a standard produced and governed by the Object Management Group for the analysis and design of object oriented software. One of the principal purposes of UML is the depiction of data and its associated behavior. In contrast to UML, there is no established, standard notation for ERDs. Several variations exist and are used for the representation of conceptual, logical and physical database models.

A logical ERD that describes the business concepts outlined earlier is shown in Figure 10-14. Each of the rectangles represents the entities involved.

The properties, called attributes in ERDs, are shown within the right-hand compartments of each rectangle. Properties in bold are required; the rest are optional. The symbols on the lines joining the entities represent the number of entities that can be involved in each relationship—**the cardinality**—which tells us:

- An *Address* can be home to one or more *Customer* (bar and crow's foot on *Customer* side).
- A *Customer* may have only one home *Address* (double bar on *Address* side).
- Given a *Customer*, one can uniquely identify the *Address* but the converse is not the case.
- A *Customer* may create zero or more invoices (circle and crow's feet on *Invoice* side)

A UML model with the same meaning is shown in Figure 10-15. This imparts the same information, with the minor exceptions that:

- The cardinality of each relation is depicted as numerical ranges (1..*, for example, denotes one to many).
- The model does not visually distinguish between mandatory and optional properties.
- Property data type is depicted, including enumerated types (see Section 9.7.3), although the permitted values are only shown in the glossary.

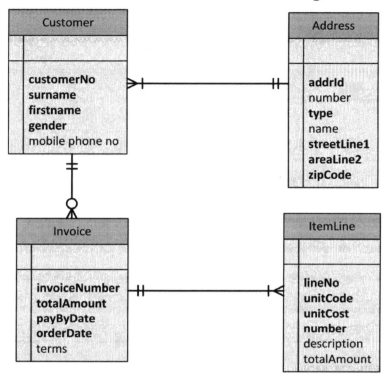

Figure 10-14 Example Logical ERD

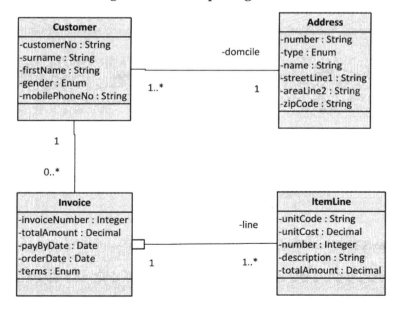

Figure 10-15 Example UML Class Structure Diagram

10.3.4 Data models and decision models

Decisions are highly dependent on the concepts, structure and relationships of business information—input data is literally the foundation of decision models. Logical data models inform many aspects of decision modeling and underpin the business glossary on which a decision model is based. Building a data model is essential when decision modeling unless the business data is extraordinarily simple. A data model:

- catalogs *all* the input data entities and their properties;
- documents the data type of each property and how this constrains its possible values; *and*
- defines entity interrelationships and their cardinality so that a decision may use this information to navigate the data structure.

A data model can be used in as many decision models as needed. Providing that there is no contradiction in content, multiple data models may also be associated to a decision model. Each decision model should explicitly define which data model (or models) are being used to underpin it.

The following associations exist between a data model and any decision model it governs:

- Every Input Data object should be represented by a business entity. Even mundane, non-business-specific objects (e.g., date or address), which may not warrant an appearance in the data model, should at least have a glossary entry to define them.
- Every business entity used in an input, condition, conclusion or outcome should be associated with a single entity or property of an entity (e.g., 'the street line of the *Customer's* address' or 'the *Customer's* latest *Invoice*'); this includes the outcome of the decision.
- If a composite business entity (one with its own properties) is used in a Decision Table condition, it can be checked for equality with another entity of the same type. Otherwise, any composite type used in conditions, conclusions or as part of an expression must be qualified such that it yields a value of the type required. For a property that has a single value, this is achieved by referring to a specific property by name (e.g., 'the *Customer's* surname' or 'the *Item's* value'). For a collection property, this is achieved by using an aggregate function (e.g., 'the number of *Item Lines* in the *Invoice*') unless the type required is a collection in which case it can be used directly.
- Any qualification of an entity must be supported by the relationships between entities. For example, 'the total amount of the first *Item Line* in the *Invoice*' is valid, but 'the area line of the *Address* of the *Invoice*' is not because there is no direct relation between *Invoice* and *Address*.
- Any expression involving properties must be consistent with the type of information they hold. For instance, numbers cannot be compared to dates or strings divided by each other.
- Where an entity is related to a single instance of another entity, it can be unambigu-

ously referred to by this relation (e.g., 'the zip code of the *Address* of the *Customer*').

- Where an entity is related to zero or more instances of another, this type of access must be uniquely qualified (e.g., 'the amount of the first *Item Line* of the *Invoice*').

- Where an entity is related to zero or more instances of another, the existence of the latter can be tested (e.g., 'if the *Customer* has an *Invoice*').

More details about the interface between a decision model and its underlying data models—the business glossary—and how this can be augmented can be found in Chapter 9.

Objects in UML can have their own behavior by defining *methods* (blocks of code that yield a value or make a change). It is important that no business decisions are embedded in these methods.

10.3.5 Supporting DMN with a data model

There are many ways of defining a data model on which a decision model can be built. One can use XML (with a XSD defining the data model), UML object model, an entity relationship diagram/model (ERD), Fact Model[31] or JSON[32]. Which of these is best for a company depends on (in order of priority):

- The previous experience of its personnel. Years of institutional use of UML, ERDs or XML is reason enough to select any of these approaches as a data model definition, providing a standard approach is adopted.

- Existence of (and staff experience of using) data model support tools. The availability and familiarity with infrastructure that maintains these models is a good rationale for adopting them.

- The DMN toolset in use. Although DMN imposes no glossary data model standard, the preferred decision modeling toolset (see Section 18.4) may constrain or impose the choice of data model if it supports the glossary concept. Be aware that DMN can import data types defined in an XSD document.

- The source of the underlying data. For example, if the data is acquired from a relational database, a relational data model is clearly more appropriate than, say, XML, unless an architectural decision has been made to convert the data format before decisions are made. This is not a hard and fast rule, but a matter of pragmatic convenience. Using mismatched models (e.g., a UML model for XML data) is possible but likely to lead to reoccurring discrepancies and an inability to benefit from the idioms of either approach.

---

[31] Business Rule Concepts, Ronald G Ross, Business Rule Solutions LLC, 2013, ISBN 0-941049-14-0.

[32] Javascript and JQuery, Jon Duckett, John Wiley and Sons, 2014, ISBN 978-1118531648.

10.4 Integrating DMN with Architecture – ArchiMate

This book cannot serve as a ArchiMate primer, but there are many good books that fulfil this purpose[33]. This section assumes some knowledge of business architecture modeling and describes the best division of labor between DMN and architecture modeling notations and the details of the interface between them.

10.4.1 The ArchiMate standard

ArchiMate is an open standard for defining enterprise architectures that is maintained by the Open Group, a global consortium of 400 member organizations that strives to define and meet business objectives using IT standards. The primary focus of the standard is to provide a business, application and technical architecture modeling language and framework. An ArchiMate model shows the actors, interfaces, collaborations, objects, processes, functions, events and services of an architecture as well as their mutual dependencies. It shows how the business, application and physical architecture interact to achieve the business goals of the major stakeholders. These descriptions of architectures are designed to support reasoning about: the structural and behavioral properties of architectural components, how data and responsibilities are apportioned between them, how users interact with the architecture, the trade-offs required and how these evolve to meet changing demands. ArchiMate provides a lightweight, scalable and standard visual language to represent these concepts and how they change with time.

Currently the standard offers no explicit definition of business logic, rules or decisions. However, it can be used to show how decisions can be packaged within existing components and used within an architecture.

10.4.2 What is architectural modeling?

An ArchiMate model defines a set of elements that collaborate to achieve business ends. Collectively, these elements and their interrelationships define an architecture. Models are split across three levels:

- The business level denoting the products and services offered to clients of the business being modeled.
- The application level denoting how the business layer is supported with application services and software.
- The technology level showing how this is realized by infrastructure services and hardware.

Architectural models can represent the relationship between specific items across all three views (vertical model) or show one layer in its entirety (horizontal model) or anywhere in between. These views define three classes of elements:

- **Active Structure Elements**: entities capable of behavior such as business actors, business roles, business collaborations, application components, application collaborations, application interfaces, (hardware) devices, networks and nodes.

---

[33]ArchiMate 3.0 Specification, the Open Group, Van Haren Publishing, ISBN 978 94 018 0047 1.

- **Behavioral Elements:** activities such as business functions, business processes, business events, business services, application services, application functions, infrastructure functions and infrastructure services.
- **Passive Structural Elements:** on which this behavior is performed, such as business objects, locations, products, data objects, contracts, meanings and artifacts.

Models describe many relationships between these elements. The types of relations available varies according to the types of elements related. The models document how business functions are realized by application components and how, in turn, these are realized by hardware and software.

The power of ArchiMate is that it manages, with myriad combinations of a few elements and relationships, to express complex concepts elegantly.

10.4.3 Integrating decisions into ArchiMate

Although ArchiMate has no direct means of representing business decisions, or even rules, extensions to include these concepts are being considered by The Open Group[34]. Decisions are best integrated into ArchiMate models by embedding them in Business Services that any other component can use (including application components and business processes). DMN Decision Services are a special type of ArchiMate Business Services and this equivalence links the two models. Much as BPMN gives decisions a process context, ArchiMate can give them an architectural context and show where each decision is supported in the architecture of a system.

10.5 Integrating DMN with Business Motivation – ArchiMate, BMM

This section assumes some knowledge of conceptual business motivation modeling which currently has two, major, competing standards: the business motivation elements of the ArchiMate standard, referenced in the previous section; or the Business Motivation Model[35] (BMM), a standard created by the Business Rules Group (BRG) in 2000 and adopted by the OMG.

All business motivation standards generally aim to structure, communicate and manage business plans by formally defining the goals and objectives of an enterprise. They express how these goals are to be realized, how success can be measured and which business actors are involved. Both standards offer a good integration with decision modeling. This section defines the cooperation of ArchiMate's business motivation elements and DMN. We selected ArchiMate rather than BMM because the former has a motivation notation.

Motivation models document the reasons for, and forces acting on, the initial and evolving design of the enterprise architecture. They also document the sources of the pressures that influence and constrain the design of a system. As decisions are first class citizens

---

[34] As of ArchiMate 3.0 specification, 2016.
[35] The Business Motivation Model, Business Rules Group and the Object Management Group (OMG), http://www.businessrulesgroup.org/bmm.shtml

of the enterprise architecture, they should be integrated into these motivation models. Such integration is an excellent means of documenting the business rationale of decisions.

10.5.1 The business motivation elements of ArchiMate

The business motivation elements of ArchiMate define the business goals, principles, requirements and constraints that govern all views of the architecture. They also model the stakeholders, drivers, assessments and outcomes that initiate these. Motivation models also allow business demands and pressures to be associated with the architectures that satisfy them so that requirements can be traced from source to realization. Furthermore, importantly for decision modeling, they allow quantifiable goals to be attached (directly or indirectly) to any architecture concept, including decisions.

ArchiMate motivation models consist of a number of layers:

- The stakeholder level describes the business communities that have business needs, concerns or interests. These could be individuals or teams, either inside or outside a company (e.g., *Treasury Operations* or *Regulator*). Hierarchical structure and associations between stakeholders can be shown which are a superset of organization charts used by many companies. (e.g., *Operations* is a part of *Treasury*).
- The requirements level defines:
  o Drivers: motivational forces that shape an organization—either concerns from within or pressures from outside. (e.g., *Maintenance Cost*, *Liquidity Risk*).
  o Assessments: analysis reports of how well (or poorly) a driver is currently being met (e.g., *Collateral Burden 20% Under-used in Q4*).
  o Outcomes: statements of the end goals that have been achieved by realization of a goal (e.g., *Compliance Audit Q19 Passed*).
  o Goals: objectives the organization is trying to achieve with respect to a driver or assessment (e.g., *Halve Utilization of Non-Investment Grade in Q1*).
  o Requirements: needs that must be met in order to achieve a goal (e.g., *Perform Daily Test Against MOA Test Set*).
- The influence level defines limitations imposed on achieving a solution, such as:
  o Constraints: limitations on the way a system is implemented (e.g., *Must Use Existing Infrastructure*).
  o Principles: statements of intent about systems or of how they should be realized (e.g., *All Margin Breaches to be Reported Within 24hrs*).

The requirements level permits drivers, assessments, goals and requirements to be associated with each stakeholder. The example in Figure 10-16 shows how a driver (drivers have the ship steering wheel icon on them) has been associated with each stakeholder (shown as a cylinder symbol) representing their concerns. Some concerns are shared. Some drivers have assessments (identified with a magnifying glass icon) regarding noted past performance. Others have goals (with a target icon). Some of the goals are realized by requirements (the oblique rectangles), principles (which have an exclamation mark icon) or constraints (the oblique rectangles with a side bar).

One very useful aspect of motivation modeling is the ability to show how any element in the model reinforces or contradicts another and the strength of this positive or negative influence. Figure 10-17 shows the tension and reinforcements between goals related to certain drivers; note the dotted arrow lines annotated by minus and plus signs. For example, the goal to *Reduce Monthly Misclassification by >=3%* mildly reinforces the goal to *Pass All L1 Stress Tests in First Two Rounds* because the more accurately instruments can be classified the more likely their risk will be successfully mitigated (note the single plus sign). The goal to *Maintain Larger Margin* (a risk mitigation strategy required by compliance regulations) will require more available collateral which will strongly contradict the *Maximize Use of Collateral* goal (note two minus signs). These influences help business analysts to understand the latent tensions between drivers (e.g., *Product Coverage* and *Liquidity Risk*). This helps decision modelers to understand the competing forces influencing the business goals and, therefore, the decisions that are performed to achieve them.

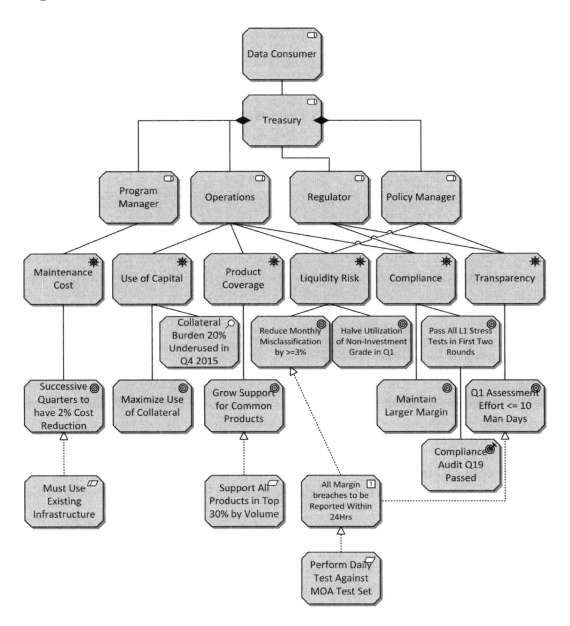

Figure 10-16 Business Motivation Requirements Model

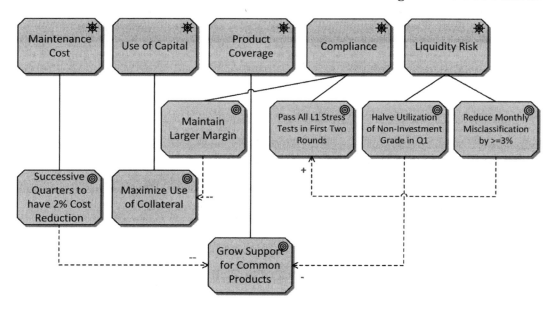

Figure 10-17 Influence Relations in a Business Motivation Model

10.5.2 Integrating decisions into motivation models

Decisions can be usefully associated with many of the concepts in motivation models:

- Decisions can be linked to stakeholders to show the party benefiting from the decision. This may not be the one performing it. As ArchiMate models the structure of an organization, the associations a decision has on this can also be represented.
- Decisions can be associated with drivers and goals to define the motivation for decision-making and to achieve a measurement metric against which their effectiveness can be meaningfully assessed.
- Associating decisions with assessments offers a useful history of the decision's performance.
- Decisions are declarative, goal oriented and not usually associated with requirements. Constraints and principles give valuable insight into the restrictions governing a decision's realization and are best associated with knowledge sources in a decision model.

The first two of these links are also supported by BPMN (see Section 10.2). The advantage of ArchiMate is that, unlike BPMN, it can show the relationships between stakeholders, objectives, drivers and goals.

These relationships are summarized in Table 10-2. A complete list of decision properties can be found in Section 14.2.5.

Motivation Model Artifact	Decision Model Artifact
Stakeholder	Decision owner, maker and interested parties
Driver	Decision supported objective classification
Assessment	The decision assessment
Goal	The decision supported objective
Outcome	Satisfaction of a decision supported objective
Constraint	Knowledge Source that defines it
Principle	Knowledge Source that defines it

Table 10-2 Useful Associations Between Motivation Artifacts and Decisions

The DMN metamodel defines decision properties that can be used to link to motivation models. An appropriate mapping is depicted in Table 10-3.

DMN Property	Meaning	Links to Other Models
(Decision) Supported Objective	The objective supported by the decision	(ArchiMate) Goal
(Decision) Impacted Performance Indicator	The key performance indicator against which the decision can be measured	(ArchiMate) Goal KPI
(Decision) Decision Maker	The actor on whose behalf the decision is made	(BPMN) Participant
(Decision) Decision Owner	The actor responsible for the accuracy and evolution of the decision	(ArchiMate) Stakeholder
(Decision) interested Parties[36]	The actors interested in the decision's performance and evolution	(ArchiMate) Stakeholder

Table 10-3 Mapping DMN Properties to Other Models

---

[36] This is not in the DMN standard but is strongly recommended (see Section 14.2.5).

11 Advanced Business Decision Modeling in DMN

Any sufficiently advanced technology is equivalent to magic
—Arthur C Clarke

The Decision Model and Notation (DMN) standard, like any industry standard, has some advanced and powerful features that require experience to apply effectively. When used judiciously these features can greatly enhance models. However, when misapplied or overused, these features can obstruct communication and undermine the purpose of modeling. Occasionally this impediment is not obvious to those without modeling experience. In this section these advanced features are introduced, the situations in which they yield genuine benefit are explored and the hazards of their use are explained. Modelers should have built three to four non-trivial models before reading this section and using the concepts explained here.

11.1 Advanced Decision Requirements Concepts

11.1.1 Business Knowledge Models

11.1.1.1 Definition

A Business Knowledge Model is an element of reusable business logic, generally a function yielding an outcome from a set of inputs. Business Knowledge Models usually represent an encapsulated fragment of business know-how that is required by multiple decisions. They are a useful means of representing identical logic that is applied in many different circumstances.

Business Knowledge Models behave like a decision and have zero or more inputs and an outcome. However, unlike decisions, they:

- May be applied to different information sources, derived from a different set of Input Data and sub-decision outcomes, in each instance in which they are used.
- Can provide reusable decision logic to one or more decisions (or other Business Knowledge Models) using the Knowledge Requirement Relationship (see definition in Table 11-1 and example in Figure 11-2).
- Cannot act as the subject of an Information Requirement Relationship. Only a decision or Input Data may do this. This is because Business Knowledge Models provides business knowledge, not information.

Business Knowledge Models 'wrap' decision logic so that it can be reused: that is, applied to different inputs in different contexts. As with decision logic modeled directly for a decision, this represents corporate policies, expert knowledge or internalizations of external regulations. A Business Knowledge model may use any logic representation that a decision can, e.g., Decision Tables. It can be considered to be a function that requires a set of parameters. The invoker of a Business Knowledge Model, usually a decision, must provide values for each parameter, either literal values or expressions. Knowledge models represent intentional reuse of decision logic in multiple contexts without needless duplication.

11.1.1.2   Diagrammatic representation

Business Knowledge Models are represented as a rectangle with clipped corners (see Figure 11-1). This should not be confused with the plain rectangle symbol representing decisions (see Section 8.1.1). Business Knowledge Models are labeled with a name depicting the logic being reused.

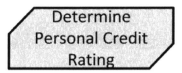

Figure 11-1 Depiction of Business Knowledge Model in Decision Requirements Diagram

11.1.1.3   Dependencies between Business Knowledge Models and decisions

In Figure 11-2, the subject decision *Determine Investment Rating Category* uses the Business Knowledge Model *Categorize Rating* that represents the reusable business logic of the categorization of ratings. The dotted arrow between *Categorize Rating* and *Determine Investment Rating Category* depicts the application of the logic and shows the Knowledge Requirement that the *Determine Investment Rating Category* decision has on this Business Knowledge Model (see Table 11-1). The decision *Determine Final Rating* needs to derive a single rating for each instrument from several ratings sourced from different agencies using different standards. It uses the *Standardize SFM Rating* Business Knowledge Model to standardize each one.

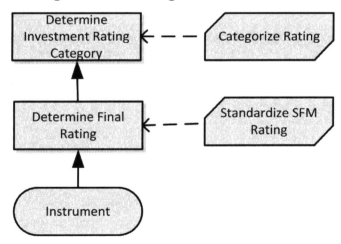

Figure 11-2 Example Business Knowledge Model

Both of these Business Knowledge Models can be reused by other decisions to apply their logic in different contexts, for example to categorize or standardize ratings in other contexts.

The Knowledge Requirement Relation is a dotted line ending in an arrow. The arrow side shows the decision (or Business Knowledge Model) using or requiring the knowledge and the other end depicts the Business Knowledge Source providing it.

Knowledge Requirement Relation	$\cdot - - - - \rightarrow$	A decision or Business Knowledge Model requires (invokes) the knowledge of (another) Business Knowledge Model.

Table 11-1 Knowledge Requirement Relation

In Section 11.3.2.5, there is an example of how the decision logic encapsulated by Business Knowledge Models and the decisions that use this knowledge work together at the Decision Logic Level.

11.1.1.4 Standard properties of Business Knowledge Model components

Additional standard properties of Business Knowledge Models include:

- A description.
- A unique identifier.
- A set of parameters defined in terms of DMN data types to map onto its inputs and capture the value of its outputs.

11.1.1.5 Rationale

At the Decision Logic Level, Business Knowledge Models are similar to decisions. Their logic is usually defined using boxed expressions (most often Decision Tables, see Section 8.2) or analytic models that describe their business behavior. The distinction between a Business Knowledge Model and a decision is that when a decision has an Information Requirement on a sub-decision, it is merely obtaining the value of the subordinate's outcome. However, when a decision (or another Business Knowledge Model) has a Knowledge Requirement on a Business Knowledge Model it is allowed to actively apply the subordinate's knowledge to data of its choosing. This allows the Business Knowledge Model to be used in many different contexts by many invokers as long as each invoker can provide values for the parameters of the Business Knowledge Model and use its outcome.

The logic encapsulated within Business Knowledge Models can be directly associated with ordinary decisions, but the explicit packaging of logic within Business Knowledge Models allows more flexibility. Decisions choose how to apply the logic embodied by a Business Knowledge Model. The decision binds information of its choosing to the Business Knowledge Model's parameters (inputs) and consumes its outcome (outputs) for its own ends.

Business Knowledge Models can be put to many uses. Specifically, supplying logic this way supports:

- reuse of the same logic across multiple decisions, promoting consistency *and*
- avoidance of repetition and ease of maintenance when the same logic is required by many invokers.

For example, if the Business Knowledge Model *Calculate Individual Credit Risk* is a means of determining the credit rating of an entity, then a decision to assess the overall credit rating of a mortgage applicant could apply the same Business Knowledge Model to assess the risk of *both* the applicant and the guarantor (see Figure 11-3). A decision (such as *Determine Guarantor Credit Risk*) applies a Business Knowledge Model by invoking it (see Section 11.3.2.5). The benefit of using this Business Knowledge Model that the calculation logic of credit risk does not have to be repeated in each case and it could easily be applied to other parties without modification.

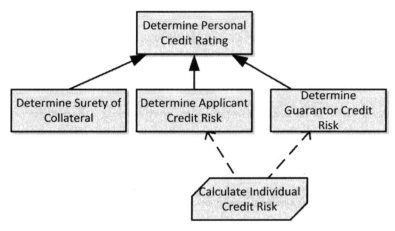

Figure 11-3 Example of Business Knowledge Model Reuse

Business Knowledge Models can even be invoked multiple times by the *same* decision, typically by applying the same logic to each of several parameters. Consider the example above where the decision *Determine Personal Credit Rating* has no sub-decisions and invokes the Business Knowledge Model twice itself to determine the applicant and guarantor risk and derives the overall risk from this. In this case, the Decision Requirements Diagram only depicts one Knowledge Requirement Relationship between *Determine Personal Credit Rating* and the Business Knowledge Model *Calculate Individual Credit Risk* (see Figure 11-4).

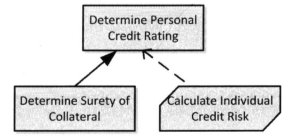

Figure 11-4 Multiple Reuse of a Business Knowledge Model by One Decision

Business Knowledge Models are only needed to avoid duplication. They should not be used if there is no immediate prospect of reuse. If in doubt, use a decision instead and refactor once the need for reuse is established. Do not wrap all business logic in Business Knowledge Models to maximize *potential* reuse. This needlessly increases the size and clutter of your Decision Requirements Diagram by replacing every decision with a decision and

Business Knowledge Model pair. It also obscures genuine cases of reuse. Often it can be a challenge to make Business Knowledge Models sufficiently flexible to allow their reuse in different contexts, this effort should not be expended if there is no immediate prospect of gaining from it.

11.1.2 Input data and decisions as Knowledge Sources

Knowledge Sources (as defined in Section 8.1.3) represent constraints, boundaries and influences on decisions or other Knowledge Sources. These are frequently imposed by authoritative documents or knowledgeable entities. However, Knowledge Sources themselves can be influenced by Input Data or the outcomes of decisions. Consider Figure 11-5, in which the decision *Determine Investment Rating Category* is influenced by the Knowledge Source *ABC Counterparty Risk Guidelines*. In this model, this Knowledge Source is itself influenced by both the Input Data *Counterparty Capital Adequacy Record*—representing historic, capital-adequacy record data—and an analytical decision, *Determine Counterparty Default Likelihood*. These two additional authority requirements of the Knowledge Source show that the risk guidelines themselves are guided by the historical data and the results of the analytic decision. This shows how data can inform decision logic, rather than just be input to it.

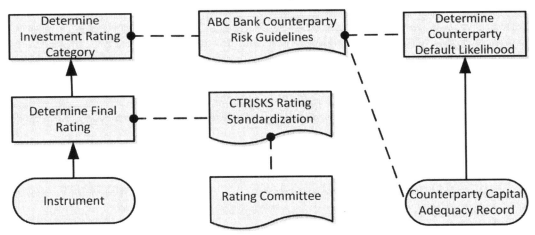

Figure 11-5 Knowledge Sources Authorized by Decisions and Data

If risk guidelines had an authority requirement on their own historical performance they could even be maintained on an ongoing basis with a feedback loop (see Section 15.2.6).

11.2 Decision Table Concepts

11.2.1 What is hit policy?

The hit policy of a Decision Table (see Section 8.2.5) describes its behavior in terms of how many satisfied rules actually contribute to outcomes, how many outcomes are generated and how they are sorted. Be careful about the distinction between outcome and conclusion: A Decision Table generates one outcome for each 'hit' rule, however, if a table has multiple conclusion columns, each single outcome is composed of multiple conclusions (see Section 8.2.2). Also, it is important the reader understand that there is a distinction between a rule being satisfied (i.e., the inputs provided meeting all the conditions it specifies) and it being 'hit' (i.e., being fired and thereby contributing to the outcome, see Section 8.2.5). For a rule to be 'hit' it is necessary, but not sufficient, for it to be satisfied.

Hit policy defines, for a single application of the table to a single data instance, the following:

- How many rules can legally be satisfied simultaneously. Is the logic of rules allowed to overlap such that more than one rule is satisfied by the same set of input values or not?
- Which satisfied rules can contribute to the outcomes of a Decision Table (i.e., be **'hit'**).
- How many outcomes the Decision Table can yield in total.
- If only one outcome is permitted but multiple rules are 'hit', how a single outcome can be derived from the many results.
- If multiple outcomes are generated, the order in which they should be presented.

Hit policies can be broadly separated into two types: those describing tables that yield a single outcome (single outcome policies) and those that yield a collection of zero or more outcomes (multi-outcome policies). Section 11.2.2 explains the meaning of single outcome policies, whereas Section 11.2.3 focuses on multi-outcome policies.

Hit policies apply to all forms of Decision Tables (see Section 11.2.7), whether they represent Decisions or Business Knowledge Models. In this section they are illustrated as the definition of decision logic using 'rules as rows' format.

11.2.2 Single outcome hit policies

DMN defines five hit policies that yield a single outcome and these are summarized in Table 11-2. For a complete table, at least one row must be satisfied under all circumstances.

The Unique, Any, First and Priority policies hit a single rule and yield the single outcome associated with it. They only differ in the means by which they select the hit rule from the available alternatives (i.e., all the satisfied rules). The Collect policy also yields a single outcome if an aggregation function (see below) is specified: it is a multi-hit policy which aggregates all the outcomes of the hit rules into one value.

In some circumstances a Decision Table that is incomplete (see Section 8.2.6) can be presented with inputs that satisfies no rules. In these instances, there are no 'hit' rules and the table will yield the result `null`.

Hit Policy	Rules Satisfied Simultaneously	Rules 'hit' (number and selection)	Determination of Single Outcome
Unique (U)	0..1	0..1, the only one satisfied	That of the only rule hit.
Any (A)	0 or more	0..1, any satisfied rule as all have the same conclusion	That of the only rule hit.
First (F)	0 or more	0..1, first satisfied in order of rules in table	That of the only rule hit.
Priority (P)	0 or more	0..1, satisfied rule with highest priority conclusions	That of the only rule hit.
Collect (C) with aggregation	0 or more	0 or more, all the satisfied rules	Generated from the aggregation of all hit rule outcomes. The aggregation function is specified as part of the hit policy.

Table 11-2 Single Outcome Hit Policies Defined by DMN

11.2.2.1 Unique

Decision Tables using the Unique hit policy have a set of rules that are mutually exclusive—their conditions do not overlap. Any set of inputs can only be satisfied by (at most) one rule. When a rule is hit, the outcome associated with it is the result yielded by the Decision Table. Unique is the one of the most common hit policies and is the default in DMN because it is usually the simplest to understand and the most appropriate.

The policy is single outcome and single hit. It is illegal for multiple rules to overlap (be simultaneously satisfied) in a Unique table. The example in Figure 11-6 decides if a configuration alarm should sound in the cockpit of a jet airliner. Notice how mutually exclusive conditions (e.g., *Cabin Altitude* in rules 1-2 and *Flap Setting* and *Gear Setting* in rules 3-5) have been used to prevent any rule condition overlap.

	Cockpit Alarm Status					
	Barometric Altitude	Radio Altitude	Cabin Altitude	Flap Setting	Gear Setting	Configuration Alarm
U				*UP, 1, 2, 5, 10, 15, 25, 30, 40*	*UP, DOWN*	*SOUND, INTERMITTENT, SILENT*
1	>10000	-	>6000	-	-	*INTERMITTENT*
2			<=6000	-	-	*SILENT*
3	<=10000	<2500	-	*not(25, 30, 40)*	-	*SILENT*
4				*25, 30, 40*	*DOWN*	*SILENT*
5					*UP*	*SOUND*
6		>=2500	-	-	-	*SILENT*

Figure 11-6 Example Unique Hit Policy Decision Table

One benefit of this approach, providing the table is legal, that each rule is independent of all the others and can be understood in isolation. The order of rule placement has no bearing on their individual or collective behavior. This feature makes this hit policy flexible, as the rule author is free to use rule order to maximize ease of understanding and reference (see Section 15.3.1.2).

11.2.2.2 Any

The Any hit policy is a slight variation of Unique and is also commonly used. It permits multiple business rules to be satisfied simultaneously, providing there is no contradiction in the outcome values of overlapping rules. It prevents the need to add conditions just to mutually exclude the conditions of rules that produce the same outcome. Consider the example in Figure 11-7 that determines the status of an engine failure alarm. Note the first four rules have the same conclusion and therefore are allowed to simplify their conditions and overlap. This makes the table easier to read because it draws the eye to the exceptional ranges for each condition (the defining boundary conditions for each specific rule) without cluttering the table with mutual exclusion conditions. Be aware that rules with different conclusions (e.g., rule 5) still require full logical separation from all others.

	Engine Failure Alarm Status				
A	Oil Pressure	Oil Temperature	Fuel Flow	Vibration	Engine Failure Alarm
	[0..100]	[-50..200]	[0..10]	[0..5]	*ON , OFF*
1	<25	-	-	-	*ON*
2	-	>140	-	-	*ON*
3	-	-	<1,5, >4	-	*ON*
4	-	-	-	>4	*ON*
5	>=25	<=140	[1.5..4]	<=4	*OFF*

Figure 11-7 Example Any Hit Policy Decision Table

Use the Any hit policy when there is frequent repetition of some outcome values.

It should be noted that some implementations of Any tables will stop executing as soon as a rule is "hit" on the grounds that any subsequent hit will return the same value. This can impact traceability and, if it is essential to know all the rules that hit, a true multi-hit table should be preferred.

11.2.2.3 First

The First hit policy allows many rules to be satisfied but only one to be hit. It prioritizes the satisfied rules in the order they appear in the decision table (top down in a 'rules as rows' table and left to right in a 'rules as columns' table). As the name suggests, the first satisfied rule is 'hit', provides the outcome and none of the remaining rules are considered, even if their conditions are satisfied.

Typically, this policy is used to describe logic with several specific, high-priority, rarely occurring outcomes, driven by intricate sets of conditions which override a smaller set of more general and more frequent 'fallback' cases which provide default outcomes. Consider Figure 11-8, which embodies the same behavior as Figure 11-6, where the specific rules 1 and 2 override a general 'fallback' of rule 3.

| | Cockpit Alarm Status | | | | | |
	Barometric Altitude	Radio Altitude	Cabin Altitude	Flap Setting	Gear Setting	Configuration Alarm
F				UP, 1, 2, 5, 10, 15, 25, 30, 40	UP, DOWN	SOUND, INTERMITTENT, SILENT
1	>10000	-	>6000	-	-	INTERMITTENT
2	<=10000	<2500	-	25, 30, 40	UP	SOUND
3	-	-	-	-	-	SILENT

Figure 11-8 Example First Hit Policy Decision Table

This policy is only effective for small tables (fifteen or fewer rules) that are very unlikely to grow and that have the logic profile described above (see Section 14.4.3.2 for further details). First can be an elegant hit policy in these specific circumstances. However, it is generally best to avoid it as large tables of this type very quickly become hard to understand and are susceptible to human error (see Section 15.3.3 for a full discussion of the issues).

11.2.2.4 Priority

Like First, the Priority hit policy is a single-hit, single outcome policy that allows many rules to be simultaneously satisfied. Unlike First, it requires that the Decision Table modeler define the relative priority of conclusion values in order to facilitate selection of the hit rule. They must provide a conclusion priority list: a sorted value list of potential conclusion values specified under each conclusion header of the decision table (see Section 8.2.3.6). The order of values in the value list determines the priority of 'hit' selection. If multiple rules are satisfied, the single rule with the conclusion coming earliest in the conclusion priority list is 'hit'.

If a table specifies multiple conclusions with priority lists, any precedence of priority runs left to right for a 'rules as rows' table and top down for a 'rules as columns' table. The example in Figure 11-9 illustrates this.

The Priority hit policy is usually used for decisions that classify a situation (or data) using multiple, independent inputs in which:

- There is a reasonable chance that the inputs will conflict in their indications of which classification is the most appropriate.

- The possible results are not equal in terms of risk, preference or safety and there is a clear order of preference among them.

| | Cockpit Alarms Status | | | | Cockpit Alarm Status | |
	Barometric Altitude	Radio Altitude	Cabin Altitude	Flap Setting	Configuration Alarm	Warning Light
P				UP, 1, 2, 5, 10, 15, 25, 30, 40	SOUND, INTERMITTENT, SILENT	ON, OFF
1	>10000	-	>6000	-	INTERMITTENT	OFF
2			-	not(UP)	SILENT	ON
3	-	<2500	-	-	SOUND	ON
4			-	UP, 1, 2	INTERMITTENT	ON
5	-	-	-	-	SILENT	OFF

Figure 11-9 Example of Multiple Conclusions with Priority Hit Policy

Consider the Priority hit policy Decision Table in Figure 11-9 that determines the status of two different warning indicators in an airliner cockpit. If the barometric altitude of the aircraft is 13,000ft *and* its cabin pressure altitude exceeds 6,000ft (indicating a potential issue with cabin pressurization) *and* the flaps are deployed (i.e., not *UP*) then rules 1, 2 and 5 are all satisfied. In this case rule 1 is 'hit' because the conclusion priority of the *Configuration Alarm* (*INTERMITTENT* versus *SILENT*) takes precedence over the *Warning Light* (*ON* versus *OFF*) because *Configuration Alarm* conclusion occurs to the left of the *Warning Light* conclusion. Were the two conclusion columns exchanged, rule 2 would have the higher priority. The *Warning Light* conclusion can be used to select the 'hit' rule only if the *Configuration Alarm* values for the conflicting rules are the same. For example, deploying flaps at 15,000ft would 'hit' rule 2, as opposed to rule 5 which is also satisfied). This illustrates one of the challenges with the Priority hit policy in that behavior can be changed without changing any of the rules.

11.2.2.5 Collect with aggregation

The Collect with aggregation hit policy is a multi-hit, single-outcome policy. It can only be used for Decision Tables having one conclusion. It permits the simultaneous satisfaction of many rules, each of which is 'hit' and each of which produces one conclusion value. It then yields a single result by applying a function to all the conclusion values to combine them into a single value. This function is called the *aggregation* function. The aggregation function is denoted by a symbol following the 'C' hit policy name. The supported aggregation functions are listed in Table 11-3.

Aggregation Function	Symbol	Meaning	Notes
Sum	+	Yields the arithmetic sum of all conclusions	Requires numeric or duration conclusion type.
Minimum	<	Yields the smallest value of all the conclusions	Requires a magnitude conclusion type that supports comparison (e.g., numeric, duration, string, date, time but not Boolean).
Maximum	>	Yields the largest value of all the conclusions	As Minimum, above.
Count	#	Yields the number of conclusions generated	Works with any conclusion type, always yields a number.

Table 11-3 Collect Hit Policy Supported Aggregation Functions

If no rules are satisfied the count and sum aggregation functions yields zero and the others null (i.e., an undefined result). Each of the aggregation functions has the same meaning as the equivalent FEEL function: sum(), min(), max() and count() (see Appendix B).

The example Decision Table of Figure 11-10 uses the Collect hit policy with a *sum* aggregation function. It calculates a cumulative library fine for the late return of a book. The fine depends on the customer's class of library membership, the number and timing of previous offenses and the type of book involved. No member is fined for their first offence. For instance, a $6 fine would result for a normal library member's second offence within one month, when returning a reference book more than three months late (rules 5, 7, 8 and 9 are satisfied, hit and their penalties aggregated). Notice how DMN supports the specification of literal durations. For example, '*P30DT*' means thirty days (see Section B.5.2).

Total Library Fine						
C+	Previous Offences	Time Since Last	Late Period	Membership Class	Book Class	Library Fine
				STUDENT , MEMBER , *PENSIONER*	*NORM , REF ,* *LTD*	[0..10]
1	0	-	-	-	-	0.00
2		-	-	*MEMBER*	*NORM*	1.00
3		-	-	*STUDENT*	*NORM*	0.50
4		-	-	*PENSIONER*	*NORM , REF*	0.00
5	>0	-	-	*MEMBER , STUDENT*	*REF*	2.00
6		-	-	-	*LTD*	3.00
7		*<=P30DT*	-	*not(PENSIONER)*	-	1.00
8		-	*>P30DT*	*not(PENSIONER)*	-	1.00
9		-	*>P90DT*	*not(PENSIONER)*	-	2.00

Figure 11-10 Example Collect with Aggregation Hit Policy Decision Table

Notice that there is no need to 'initialize' the Penalty to zero, the Decision Table just yields the sum of the conclusions of all the fired rules.

The Collect hit policy with aggregation is frequently used when a decision needs to derive a cumulative measure of something which is determined by many independent factors. The most common application is in scorecard decisions which attempt to derive an overall 'score' to represent a continuous property (e.g., credit worthiness, risk or customer loyalty, see Section 16.1) based on the aggregated contributions of many separate heuristic tests.

Although this hit policy is a quick means of aggregating the outcomes of multiple rules into a single result, it is not very flexible. Firstly, it only supports the four aggregation functions shown in Table 11-3. Regrettably, DMN offers no means of nominating its other aggregate functions with this hit policy (e.g., mean(), concatenate(), and() and or()). Secondly, it does not provide much explanation of the individual outcomes should this be required after the fact. A more flexible approach is to use two decisions:

- One defined as a Decision Table using a Collect hit policy *without* aggregation (see Section 11.2.3.1) that preserves each individual outcome in a collection and allows lots of ancillary details to be stored about each outcome *and*
- A second one, that may not be represented as a table, to perform any aggregation required while preserving any required additional detail.

This is explained further in the Scorecard pattern (see Section 16.1).

11.2.3 Multi-outcome hit policies

Using multi-outcome hit policies, such as those listed in Table 11-4, Decision Tables can yield a collection of outcomes from one set of inputs. All these policies allow zero or more rules to be satisfied simultaneously. Every satisfied rule is hit and contributes their outcome to a collection of outcomes.

Collections of results are often useful outcomes for decisions that:

- Generate itemized lists arising from single instances of inputs (e.g., risk factors, discounts, fines, validation errors) that other decisions can then iterate through or aggregate for their own purposes.
- Filter input collections into an outcome collection that has a subset of its values (e.g., filtering of appropriate products for a client, appropriate taxes to apply).

Hit Policy	Conclusion Order
Collect (C) without aggregation	Undefined
Output (O)	In order of conclusion priority
Rule (R)	In order of table rule placement

Table 11-4 Multi-Outcome Policies Defined by DMN

11.2.3.1   Collect without aggregation

The Collect hit policy, in the absence of an aggregation function, yields an *unsorted* collection of outcomes—one for every satisfied rule. Consider the example overdue book scenario detailed in Section 11.2.2.5. If the Decision Table in Figure 11-10 had specified a Collect without aggregation hit policy it would have yielded a list of four fine values (e.g., [2, 2, 1, 1]) in an **undetermined** order.

11.2.3.2   Rule

The Rule hit policy yields a *sorted* list of outcomes for every satisfied rule. The sort order of this collection is the order of the satisfied rules in the Decision Table (i.e., top down in 'rules as rows' tables and left to right in 'rules as columns' tables). This hit policy is a multi-outcome version of the First hit policy. Consider the example overdue book scenario detailed in Section 11.2.2.5. If the Decision Table in Figure 11-10 had specified a Rule hit policy, it would have yielded a list of four fine values (i.e., [2, 1, 1, 2]), sorted by the order of the rules that generated them.

The generation and use of sorted collections is rare in Decision Modeling and this hit policy is very seldom useful. In fact, the authors have, in their collective experience, yet to come across a compelling use case for this hit policy and do not recommend its use. Instead, the Collect policy should be used to generate an unordered list of outcomes. If necessary, this can include the information needed for other decisions to sequence them.

11.2.3.3   Output Order

The Output Order hit policy is a multi-hit, multi-outcome version of the Priority hit policy. Like the latter, it requires that the table author define the relative priority of conclusion values as a conclusion priority list. The order of values in the value list determines the sort order of the result collection: outcomes coming earliest in the value priority list appear earlier in the collection of outcomes.

If a table specifies multiple conclusions with priority lists, any precedence of priority runs left to right (or top down in 'rules as columns' format) when selecting the sort order of the outcomes.

As with the Rule hit policy, the authors have yet to come across a compelling use case for this hit policy either. It is recommended that modelers use a Collect policy to generate an unordered list of outcomes that can be ordered separately.

11.2.4 Hit policy and order dependency

It is preferable for the order of rules in a Decision Table to have no impact on its behavior. Decision Tables using the First and Rule hit policies exhibit rule order dependent behavior. This requires extreme caution, especially when using the First hit policy: any unintended logical overlap between one rule and another may cause the later rule to be disabled by the earlier one. Order dependency is an idiom that can be very effective in narrowly defined situations. It must be used with care as it can obscure the meaning of even moderately large tables (see Sections 14.4.3.2 and 15.3.3). Remember that effective communication is the main goal of DMN.

11.2.5 Hit policy does not guarantee consistency

Hit policy communicates our intent about the behavior and meaning of a Decision Table, but it is not the sole determinant of such matters. For example, a Unique Decision Table documents the intent that at most one rule can be satisfied for any single set of inputs. However, such a Decision Table may still have rules with logical overlaps. This contradiction indicates that the table is inconsistent and either the hit policy or the conditions must be corrected. This redundancy between the logic expressed in the table and the stated hit policy can reveal contradictions in the table's design and is useful. Many tools will provide automated consistency checks that compare the rules in a Decision Table to its hit policy to detect such contradictions. The hit policy informs this consistency checking.

11.2.6 Selecting the right hit policy

Some of the advanced hit policies can be challenging to understand. Avoid using a complex hit policy when a simpler one could be used to convey the same business meaning. When in doubt use the Unique and Any policies where a single outcome is required and Collect without aggregation when multiple outcomes are required (see Sections 14.4.3.2 and 14.4.3). See Section 15.3.2 for a deeper comparison of hit policies.

11.2.7 Other Decision Table formats

Decision Tables are good representations of business logic when the outcome nearly always depends on the same set of inputs. As discussed earlier (see Section 8.2.2), a Decision Table's familiar layout has a number of variations in style and orientation. These are:

- **'Rules as rows'**—as used in most of the examples with inputs and outputs aligned in columns.
- **'Rules as columns'**—as above but pivoted about the top left so that each input and output has its own row.
- **Crosstab**—a two-dimensional depiction of input conditions, aligned vertically and horizontally with the resulting conclusion value shown in the intersections.
- **Shorthand**—a 'tickbox' style of conclusion value selection.

The following section demonstrates the same logic expressed in each format.

11.2.7.1 Rules as rows

Most of the Decision Table examples considered so far have been of the 'rows as rules' format of which there is an example in Figure 11-11. Conditions and conclusions are arranged into columns, headed with inputs and outputs at the top and rules are numbered rows across these columns indicating possible combinations of conditions and the conclusion values that result if they are hit.

Personal Credit Rating			
U	**Persons Employment Record**	**Persons Total Debt / Persons Annual**	**Personal Credit Rating**
	GOOD , AVERAGE , POOR	>0	*C , B , A , AA , AAA*
1	*GOOD*	<= 4.0	*AAA*
2		> 4.0	*AA*
3	*AVERAGE*	<= 2.0	*A*
4		> 2.0	*B*
5	*POOR*	-	*C*

Figure 11-11 Example 'Rules as Rows' Decision Table

Many Business Rule Management Systems use this layout as their default format.

11.2.7.2 Rules as columns

The logic of Figure 11-11 can also be depicted in the 'rules as columns' format shown in Figure 11-12. In this style conditions and conclusions are arranged into rows, with input and output headers in the left most column. Rules are numbered columns across these rows indicating possible combinations of conditions and the conclusion values that result if they are hit. Note the changed position of the hit policy indicator and rule numbers.

Personal Credit Rating						
Determine Persons Employment Record	*GOOD , AVERAGE , POOR*	*GOOD*		*AVERAGE*		*POOR*
Persons Total Debt / Persons Annual Salary	>0	<= 4.0	> 4.0	<= 2	> 2.0	-
Personal Credit Rating	*C , B , A , AA , AAA*	*AAA*	*AA*	*A*	*B*	*C*
U		1	2	3	4	5

Figure 11-12 Example 'Rules as Columns' Decision Table

11.2.7.3 Crosstab

In the crosstab style the same logic looks like Figure 11-13. Inputs are arranged in a two-dimensional array of rows *and* columns. Each input column and row is split with a sub-header into the appropriate condition classes (e.g., 'Person Total Debt / Persons Annual Salary' is split into two classes: '<= 4.0' and '> 4.0'). Intersections of these columns and rows depict condition combinations which can be assigned a conclusion value: the outcome for this combination of conditions. Additional inputs can be depicted as rows nested inside horizontal conditions or columns nested within vertical conditions, but this requires repetition of the condition classes and does not scale very well.

This type of Decision Table can only have one conclusion that is named in the Decision Table name tab; multiple conclusions are not supported. The hit policy for crosstab tables is not explicitly specified—it is always Unique.

Personal Credit Rating				
Personal Credit Rating		Persons Employment Record		
		GOOD	AVERAGE	POOR
Persons Total Debt	<= 4.0	AAA	A	C
/ Persons Annual Salary	> 4.0	AA	B	C

Figure 11-13 Example of Crosstab Decision Table

11.2.7.4 Shorthand

The shorthand notation is an alternate style that can be combined with 'rules as rows' or 'rules as columns' formats. It can only be applied if the Decision Table has one conclusion with the same name as the Decision Table itself. The shorthand form of Figure 11-11 is shown in Figure 11-14.

	Personal Credit Rating						
U	Persons Employment Record GOOD , AVERAGE , POOR	Persons Total Debt / Persons Annual Salary	AAA	AA	A	B	C
1	GOOD	<= 4	X	-	-	-	-
2	GOOD	> 4.0	-	X	-	-	-
3	AVERAGE	<= 2.0	-	-	X	-	-
4	AVERAGE	> 2.0	-	-	-	X	-
5	POOR	-	-	-	-	-	X

Figure 11-14 Example of Shorthand 'Rules as Rows' Decision Table

Shorthand replaces the output name (*Personal Credit Rating* in this example) with columns (or rows) representing all the possible conclusion values. As there is only one conclusion this introduces no ambiguity. Shorthand eliminates the need to repeat the conclusion values in each rule: when a specific conclusion value is selected, an 'x' is used in the appropriate column. '-' is used for every inappropriate conclusion value.

Providing the decision table has a multi-outcome policy (see Section 11.2.3), multiple 'x's can be depicted in one rule, otherwise only one may be shown.

11.2.7.5 Selecting decision table format

The 'rules as rows' format is usually the most appropriate. Modelers are advised to use this unless a special circumstance favors the selection of another format.

11.3 Representing Logic in DMN

Decision Tables are just one of many ways to represent decision logic within the Decision Logic Level of DMN. Despite the disproportionate attention given to them in the DMN specification and decision modeling literature, they are sometimes not the most appropriate representation. They should not be considered the 'default option' in DMN; good decision models should use the most apt formats for each decision and be prepared to combine techniques as necessary.

All decision definitions determine an outcome from zero or more inputs. This outcome can be derived informally, using an ad-hoc, non-standard representation, or formally, using a strictly defined, standard representation from DMN or another source. Informal techniques are best suited to represent decisions that are poorly understood, less important or where formality might be counterproductive. Formal techniques are better if precision is required or the model ultimately needs to be executed. The following sections outline the major informal and formal techniques.

11.3.1 Informal representation of logic

11.3.1.1 Simple text

Perhaps the simplest, and occasionally the most elegant, representation of logic is that based on free-form text. Decisions defined in this way have a title tab, denoting their name, but in place of a Decision Table there is just a textual expression that has a conditional or unconditional result.

The text of a definition can be informal, such as that in Figure 11-15, and often this is the most agile means of capturing logic that is simple and well understood and not expected to change. Figure 11-15 describes the same logic as Figure 8-13 in Section 8.2.3.2. Informal statements can be less rigorous than this example and assume business knowledge on the part of the reader. Informal text is also a good means of describing cases in which aspects of the decision logic are temporarily unknown.

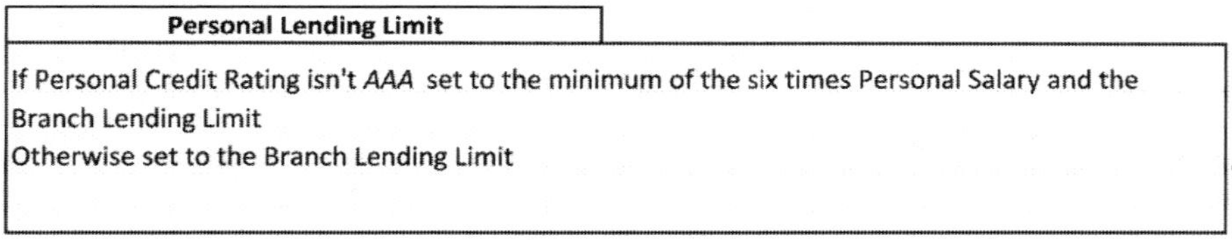

Personal Lending Limit
If Personal Credit Rating isn't *AAA* set to the minimum of the six times Personal Salary and the Branch Lending Limit Otherwise set to the Branch Lending Limit

Figure 11-15 Decision Logic Definition Using Informal Text

Providing the result of a decision is clear and uses defined variables, corresponding to direct sources of data such as Input Data or sub-decisions, there are no rules governing the format of text within the informal definition box. Conveying an accurate understanding is the main objective.

11.3.1.2 Examples and use cases

Decision logic can be defined using examples from existing systems documentation or well-known use cases (see Section 14.4.4.1) that act as exemplars. Providing these have a good coverage and are easily understood they can be a replacement or stand-in for a more formal definition.

Some informal decision representations are appropriate for short-term use, for example: references to existing implementations that are currently undocumented and for which some 'archeology' is required. These systems can act as 'black-box' definitions of legacy requirements or, if interactions with them are captured these can serve as use cases. Less satisfactorily, references to other specification documents or even spreadsheets can be adopted as decision definitions.

11.3.2 Formal representation of logic with FEEL

The Friendly Enough Expression Language (FEEL) is the means by which DMN formally defines the Decision Logic Level of a decision model. All formal Decision Logic Definitions in DMN can use FEEL to express calculations, if/then/else logic statements, functions and complex data structures. FEEL is used to:

- Allow the inputs and conclusions of Decision Tables to contain calculated values (e.g., the second input of Figure 11-11).
- Define the expressions used to define names in contexts (e.g., Section 8.2.6).
- Describe the ultimate results of a decision in the result box (e.g., Figure 11-16).
- Define (and invoke) a function or Business Knowledge Model.

FEEL, as its name implies, is underpinned by the creation and manipulation of expressions to define decisions.

11.3.2.1 All decision definitions are based on expressions

All of DMN's formal logic representations express information in terms of expressions. These expressions are made partly or entirely from:

- **Literal values**: a simple value constant, be it a string, numeric, Boolean, date, time duration or a list thereof (e.g., `"Mary"`, `5.9`, *2099-02-21*, `[1, 4, 3]`) *and*
- **Variables**: a name, corresponding to an input from an Information Requirement Relation or a context entry (see Section 8.2.6), that holds a value (e.g., `Item Price`, `Credit Rating`, `Mortgage Rate`, `Recommended Products`).

Expressions are mathematical constructs that yield values and are used to calculate decision outcomes. The simplest value expressions are just literal values (as above). More complex ones may (in any order):

- Combine literals or variables in mathematical expressions (e.g., `Item Price - 1.15`, `Value * Mortgage Rate`).
- Use functions to derive values (e.g., `max(Worker Salary, Manager Salary)`, `count(Workers)`).
- Use conditional logic (e.g., `if (Cover > Cover Threshold * 2) then "REFER" else "APPROVE"`).

Decisions may use multiple expressions, but must be explicit about how these are combined into a single outcome (e.g., by calculation, aggregation or building a composite type) or how they contribute to a multiple outcome collection. See Section B.5.6 for more information about expressions.

11.3.2.2 Variables hold values

Variables are named quantities that hold a value that are initialized from an Information Requirement relationship or an expression in a context entry. Each of the variables used within a decision must have a unique name to avoid ambiguity. Two Decision Requirement Diagram relationships dictate how variable values are assigned from external sources:

- An Information Requirement requests a variable's value be assigned from a specified Input Data or derived as the outcome of a sub-decision within the model.
- A Knowledge Requirement requires that the input parameters of a Business

Knowledge Model to be bound to values imposed by the invoker. The Business Knowledge Model is then invoked and its outcome is the result of the invocation expression. If it was invoked as the logic of a decision, its result becomes the outcome of that decision. Section 11.3.2.5 explains how this works.

In addition, variables can be created by context entries (see Section 8.2.6) and each one holds the outcome of a decision.

Every variable in the decision must be derived by one of the four means discussed in this section. Aside from the outcome, values assigned to variables in this way are not usually be accessed outside the scope of the decision that uses them.

11.3.2.3 An overview of FEEL constructs

FEEL provides the following set of constructs for defining the logic of a decision or Business Knowledge Model:

- **Boxed expression**. A formal, table-based medium for defining decision logic (see Sections 11.3.2.4 and B.4.2). Decision Tables are a specialist type of boxed expression.

- **Boxed invocation**. A means of using a defined function or Business Knowledge Model to calculate a result from supplied data (see Sections 11.3.2.5 and B.4.3).

- **Boxed context**. A means of establishing a set of variables that can simplify decision logic definition (see Sections 8.2.6 and B.4.4). Also used as a means of defining literal data that can be used to test decision definitions.

- **Relation**. A tabular representation of data that can be referenced by decision logic definitions (see Sections 17.1.6.2 and B.4.6).

- **Boxed function definition**. A means of defining a reusable function, embedding some business know how, that can be reused (see Section B.4.7).

A decision's definition is made from:

- A mandatory **name** tab which identifies the decision and names the variable holding the value of the decision outcome.

- Zero or more boxed contexts or relations which define data needed for the decision.

- One or more boxed expressions or boxed invocations each of which is named and can refer to the results of previous expressions by using their name.

Some examples follow.

11.3.2.4 Boxed Expressions

The DMN boxed expression is a formal means of representing decision logic. Decision Tables are a special type of boxed expression. General boxed expressions are a more flexible, if less readable, means of formally documenting logic in DMN.

For example, the logic of Figure 11-15 can be represented formally using the boxed expression in Figure 11-16. This incorporates a simple name and expression.

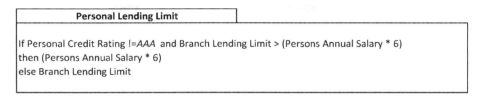

Figure 11-16 Decision Logic Definition Using Formal Text

11.3.2.5   Boxed Invocations

This construct allows a decision (or Business Knowledge Model) to derive its output from the invocation of one or more subordinate Business Knowledge Models or functions. Consider a Business Knowledge Model housing the logic of *Determine Personal Credit Rating* as defined in Figure 11-11.

The decision *Determine Guarantor Credit Rating*, shown in Figure 11-17, uses a boxed invocation of this Business Knowledge Model to determine a guarantor's credit rating. The three parameters (*Employment Record*, *Annual Salary* and *Total Debt*) are bound to the appropriate values for the guarantor. The expressions (on the right) that generate these values are paths that traverse the *Applicant* data structure for nested attributes. The data model of *Applicant* (see Section 10.3) or the glossary (see Chapter 9) informs these expressions, dictating the valid paths that can be used. For instance, the data model of Applicant would show the sub-attributes *Guarantor*, *Employment Record*, *Annual Salary* and *Total Debt*. This is why an underpinning data model is so important.

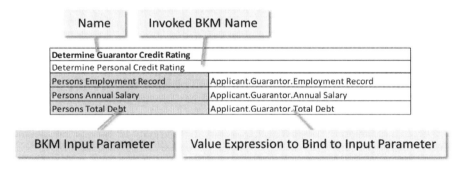

Figure 11-17 Anatomy of a Boxed Invocation

The boxed invocation denotes the name of the decision being defined in the top left tab and the name of the Business Knowledge Model being used in the tab just below this. Note that Business Knowledge Models may be defined in terms of other Business Knowledge Models providing the definition is not circular. Underneath the business knowledge model name is a series of bindings of the input parameters of the model being used to value expressions. This allows the logic of deriving a personal credit rating to be reapplied to determining the credit rating of a guarantor, without repetition of the logic.

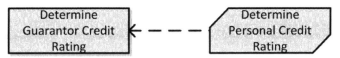

Figure 11-18 Decision Requirements Diagram for Figure 11-17

The Decision Requirements Diagram presentation of Figure 11-17 is depicted in Figure 11-18.

A decision's invocation of multiple Business Knowledge Models, or even the same one invoked multiple times, would require multiple invocations as shown in Figure 11-19. Each invocation has a set of bindings and each is headed by the name of the Business Knowledge Model being used. The result of each invocation is stored in a variable *Applicant Credit Rating* and *Guarantor Credit Rating* shown by the enclosing box to the left. Multiple invocations require a 'result box' (a boxed expression) at the bottom to denote how the multiple results are combined into one outcome for this decision.

Application Credit Rating		
	Personal Credit Rating	
Applicant Credit Rating	Persons Employment Record	Applicant.Employment Record
	Persons Annual Salary	Applicant.Annual Salary
	Persons Total Debt	Applicant.Total Debt
	Personal Credit Rating	
Guarantor Credit Rating	Persons Employment Record	Applicant.Guarantor.Employment Record
	Persons Annual Salary	Applicant.Guarantor.Annual Salary
	Persons Total Debt	Applicant.Guarantor.Total Debt
max(Applicant Credit Rating, Guarantor Credit Rating)		

Figure 11-19 Example of Multiple Business Knowledge Model Invocation

11.3.2.6   Handling collections of inputs with boxed expressions

Boxed expressions may be used to handle decision inputs that are collections by applying the same logic to each member of the collection in turn, e.g., applying some discount decision to every item in a shopping cart. This is called iteration.

Iteration is often needed in decision modeling to apply a Business Knowledge Model or Decision Table to every member of a collection, yielding either another collection of outcomes or a single aggregate value. An example of the latter is shown in Figure 11-20.

Total Price

```
sum(
  for The Item in Cart.items
  return Discount Price(
    The Item.type, The Item.cost, The Item.discount offer))
```

Figure 11-20 Using Iteration to Handle Collection Inputs

In this example, the Business Knowledge Model *Determine Discount Price* is being applied in turn to every *Item* within a *Cart*. The invocation of the Business Knowledge Model is as before, depicting the binding of its arguments. The result box at the bottom performs the iteration and calculates the total price using the FEEL function sum.

The iteration is performed explicitly by the FEEL for .. in .. return expression. The meaning of the FEEL expression "for The Item in Cart.items return Item Discounted Price" is "for each member of Cart.items, which we shall temporarily call *The Item*, invoke the Business Knowledge Model *Determine Discounted Price* and return its result". The collection of results is then aggregated.

11.3.3 Other formal representations

DMN can also incorporate externally defined analytic logic using PMML (see Section 14.4.4.4) and logic defined in other DMN models. External data types may be imported from external XSD definitions. Decisions may even be defined using external Java code blocks and bespoke representations of logic, although these has poor consequences for their broad business transparency. Consequently, they are rarely appropriate unless they represent existing resources. For more information about the value, operator and function syntax of FEEL consult Appendix B.

12 Methodology Overview

Methodology is applied ideology
—Mason Cooley

OMG imposes a number of constraints on standards it adopts. One in particular is that the standard shall define only "what" and not "how"—it must avoid promoting a specific methodology for using the standard. Thus, it is acceptable for a standard to define the notation for a diagram but not to describe how one constructs such a diagram.

In the context of decision modeling this means that the DMN standard offers no specific tasks or steps that can be performed to build a Decision Requirements Model, no definition of what constitutes a "good" model beyond some very basic structural constraints and no suggestions as to how building a decision model might fit into a broader framework.

This chapter is designed to address this, providing an overview of a methodology for decision modeling based on the experience of dozens of decision modeling projects. This chapter could be considered the first 'Best Practice', as applying a consistent and well-defined methodology when building decision models is a key element in successful projects.

12.1 Decision Modeling Overview

As noted in Chapter 5, decision modeling plays a critical role in an overall Decision Management methodology. Decision modeling is a highly iterative approach that may be completely contained within a Decision Discovery and Modeling exercise but is more likely to begin there and continue into a Decision Service Definition and Implementation phase and ultimately influence and scope a Decision Monitoring and Improvement phase. It is also possible, for instance, to use decision modeling in other methodologies by applying these steps as part of a general requirements approach.

The key steps of decision modeling (shown also in Figure 12-1) are:

1. Identify the Decisions that are the focus of the project.
2. Describe the Decisions (with questions and allowed answers) and document their business and operational context including how improving these decisions will impact the business objectives and their metrics.
3. Specify initial requirements in terms of Input Data and Knowledge Sources in particular.
4. Refine and iterate, decomposing these Decisions, identifying additional Decisions, Input Data and Knowledge Sources that need to be described and creating outline decision logic or examples for key decisions.
5. Complete the model. This can include specifying complete decision logic for Decisions, identifying analytic or other implementation details or documenting detailed manual decision-making approaches. It may also involve identifying and adding additional Decisions, Input Data and Knowledge Sources as necessary.

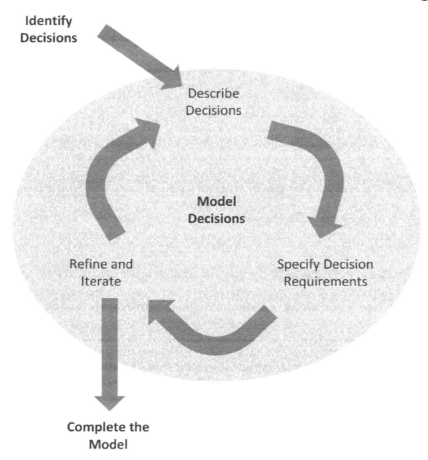

Figure 12-1 Steps in Decision Modeling

This core modeling steps in this process – describing decisions, specifying their requirements, refining and iterating - repeat until the Decisions are specified to a level that is fit for purpose (see Section 12.6.1) and that ensures everyone involved shares a clear sense of how the decisions will be made, how to measure their value and where the automation boundary is. A series of decision discovery workshops are often used to identify an initial set of decisions and create the initial models (see Section 12.6.7).

Each step in this methodology is defined in more detail below.

12.2 Identify Decisions

Decisions may be identified as part of the overall requirements gathering process for a system or process, or as part of a broader, more diffuse effort to improve decision-making and thus business results. When focused on a specific process or system, most organizations will find that a relatively small number of decisions are clearly required and will need to be identified and modeled. Broader efforts will often find that it is worth creating a long list of decisions initially, before focusing attention on specific decisions that have value in addressing the issue at hand. The former frames the latter and prevents confusion between decisions.

Many projects will find that the decisions at issue are clear and unambiguous. When the project is more complex or the business problem novel or broader and more diffuse, additional techniques will be useful in finding decisions. The most commonly used techniques are to brainstorm and examine existing or potential:

- Business Processes
- Performance Measures
- BI Reports
- Legacy Systems
- Regulations and Standards
- Micro Decisions

In many organizations, decision-making appears embedded in business process specifications and in use cases. If this is the case, then these decision definitions need to be extracted and these documents amended to reference external definitions of the decisions identified instead. This allows decisions to evolve independently and makes them available for reuse.

12.2.1 Brainstorm

The decisions involved in a project can often be listed in a straightforward brainstorming session with business owners and SMEs. This is generally a top-down approach that begins with the senior staff in a business area. Groups of three to six people work best as this promotes debate without the tendency to get bogged down in the detail.

The first decisions identified may be those strategic or tactical decisions made by executives or management. These are not generally a good target for decision modeling as they don't repeat often enough. More suitable decisions can be identified in several ways:

- Managers and executives can be asked about the exceptions they handle and the issues that get referred 'up the chain' to them. These are likely to be specific instances of a decision more often made by others lower in the organization.

- Organizations can discuss what people are trained in and consult manuals, guidelines and checklists to see what they are intended to teach people and what guidance they can give. Much of this guidance relates to decision-making.

- Customer-facing organizations can brainstorm around complaints, identifying the decisions that were made that made customers unhappy as well as those that resolved complaints.

- Managers can be asked to compare their "best" staff with underperformers and experienced staff with newcomers. By understanding what do they do differently and where experience and ability show it is often possible to identify the decisions that matter to the role. They should consider what vital skills they would miss most if their senior employees retired.

12.2.2 Examine Business Processes

Many organizations have invested in business process modeling and will have models of their business processes before they begin decision modeling. Business process modeling is not by any means a pre-requisite for decision modeling. If process models do exist, they can be a rich source of decisions and of business context for those decisions. This is because most, if not all, business processes require decisions to be made. For instance, claims must be approved or rejected before a claims process can be completed, cross-sell offers must be selected and product discounts must be calculated before an order to cash process can be completed and so on. Much of the sophistication of a business process may be in its decisions.

Decision models in organizations with a history of developing process models are likely to lag behind process models, at least initially, because teams are already used to beginning with a process model and have an existing inventory of such models. Over time the intent should be to develop decision models and process models in parallel. For those organizations that have invested heavily in process modeling, this is the critical approach and the one most likely to identify suitable decisions.

Many business processes have decision tasks identified in them initially. These decision tasks are each likely to require a specific decision to be made and this decision is the candidate for definition. It should be noted that sometimes a task involves several decisions, though this is unusual. It is also sometimes the case that the decisions required by different steps in the process are related and will be part of the same overall decision model. More on how process and decision models interact is described in Section 10.2 and especially Section 10.2.3.

In addition, "nests" of gateways with few intervening tasks often represent decision-making modeled directly in a business process (consider the example in Section 10.2.3.4). Decision modeling can replace these nests with a single, explicit decision point clarifying the behavior of the process, improving its effectiveness and lowering its maintenance burden. The decision required by such a replacement is a candidate for modeling and the gateways being replaced are a useful input to the modeling exercise.

Organizations that develop detailed use cases or written procedures may find that there is an analogous inclusion of decision-making in these documents. This may also be clear and distinct, with specific steps for decision-making, but the decision-making may also be wrapped up into the rest of the use case and needs to be extracted and externalized as above.

12.2.3 Examine performance measures

Another approach is to look at the Key Performance Indicators (KPIs) and metrics that the business has in the area(s) under consideration. By determining when and where people make choices that move KPIs/metrics up or down, a project team can identify decisions. Each opportunity for choice-making, for selecting an action from a possible set of actions, is a decision that could be usefully described and modeled.

For instance, an organization might be focused on its customer retention metric. Identifying decisions that impact customer retention might begin by considering direct decisions, such as the customer retention offer made when someone threatens to leave. Talking with customers or reviewing customer complaints might reveal that decisions determining which technical problems to escalate or what fee refund decisions were often cited by customers as reasons they cancelled their service. Data analysis may reveal that the initial pricing of a package and the customer's use of package features are strongly correlated with customer retention, leading to the inclusion of pricing and outreach decisions in the list.

It is worth noting that some of these decisions may not lend themselves to automation. It is common to find a set of decisions for a KPI that includes many human decisions. These decisions can be identified and described with questions and allowed answers even if they are not currently worth modeling.

12.2.4 Examine business intelligence outputs

Most business organizations use Business Intelligence (BI) tools to generate a lot of reports, build dashboards, support queries and dump data into spreadsheets for analysis. Most organizations' BI investments are intended to improve decision-making. It is possible therefore to assess each report or dashboard and ask "then what?" to see what action might be taken as a result. Similarly, users of each report or dashboard can be asked when they refer to it and what they are doing when they use it. Both will generate candidate decisions.

For instance, consider the users of a dashboard showing information about software test results, reported software problems and development project status information. These users must decide if they should reassign resources from one project to another or delay a release. They need to decide if work can be reprioritized or the release's scope changed. The value of the dashboard is enabling them to make these decisions and the dashboard can be used as a prompt to identify these decisions.

12.2.5 Examine legacy systems

When legacy systems are being modernized, or enterprise applications extended, decisions suitable for modeling can be found in several ways. Those modules or components that are frequently changing and where change requests are made regularly, or that have a long backlog, are often decision-making components. This is because decision-making is highly volatile: changing regularly in response to external stimuli like new policies, regulations, competitors' pricing changes and much more. In addition, modules that generate many exceptions or referrals or otherwise have a big impact on the business process, especially those for which this effect is more noticeable now than in the past, are also often decision-making modules that have aged to the point where they no longer work correctly.

For instance, sections 4.3.7.2 and 4.3.7.3 describe the benefits of externalizing a specific decision from a legacy system. In this case, it was analysis of the change requests that revealed the pricing decision as a separable component. Almost all the change requests related to changes in fee calculations, with none related to any other aspect of the system.

It is especially important to identify and prioritize decisions in pivotal, rapidly changing legacy systems that encapsulate knowledge that is being, or could be, lost by an organization due to staff churn. This typically manifests itself as a central legacy application that is well understood by very few key personnel.

12.2.6 Examine regulations and standards

Organizations that are subject to new regulations or standards can often use these to derive an initial set of decisions. As discussed in Section 5.2.3.2, there is tremendous value in modeling the decision-making that is described in a regulation or standard. Working systematically through a regulation, looking for questions, generates a candidate list of decisions that are often new to the business and not previously viewed as important to conducting their operations. Some may never have intrinsic value to the business, but may nevertheless be imposed by regulatory bodies. Such analysis helps to identify if and where an organization is already addressing the issues raised[37].

While some decisions under analysis will be one-off, such as the determination of the extent to which an organization must be compliant, most will be the kind of repeatable operational decisions suitable for modeling. Many of these will support controls and risk mitigation decisions that are both new to the organization and have a pervasive impact on their business processes. These decisions should be associated with business objectives and KPIs that measure the burden of the regulations whilst ensuring that the operational performance of the business is not negatively impacted.

12.2.7 Micro decisions

Not all decisions are considered in the current state. Often there are places where everyone or everything is currently treated the same way. For example, parts are moved from the warehouse to the factory floor based on the same logic no matter what the part, all customers see the same information on the website, all orders get the same discount. The organization is doing the same thing every time without considering alternatives.

These can be documented as Micro Decision opportunities. A Micro Decision is one where each transaction or interaction is an opportunity for a decision that results in a specific decision made about that one transaction. When Micro Decisions are being made, the organization focuses on each transaction or interaction as a unique opportunity to improve results.

To find candidates, the team can evaluate each step in a process and consider:

- If they had perfect knowledge (about the future of this customer or order for instance), what could be done more effectively? Could customers at high risk of churn be treated differently, would different supplier choices be made if an order would be delayed by the current choice?

- If a specific transaction was the only transaction that ever had to be handled what would be done? It is unlikely the default behavior would be the right behavior for each transaction considered.

- When customers or suppliers or employees are being processed, it can be worth considering what they would like to have happen. This can lead to the identification of decisions about what that ideal behavior might be and when it might be worth doing.

There are often many such opportunities and it can be hard to tell which ones will have the greatest return. Generating a long list and then considering where complaints and prob-

---

[37] In this way, decision modeling can help in the impact assessment of supporting mandatory regulatory compliance procedures.

lems originate as well as the importance of the metrics impacted to filter the list is recommended.

Generally, it is analytics that provide the insight needed for differentiation and business rules that make it happen. In each case the team can ask why something is always done the same way and in what circumstances might it be done differently?

12.3 Model Decisions

12.3.1 Describe decisions

Once a set of repeatable and non-trivial decisions have been identified, they need to be described at a high level to ensure that everyone involved shares the same understanding of them. Details and best practices for this can be found elsewhere, but a basic set of properties should be captured for each decision in addition to the name and short description documented when the decision was identified (see Section 5.1.3 and Chapter 7):

- Question and Allowed Answers
- Business Context
- Organizational Context
- Operational Context

Figure 12-2 shows the core relationships between a Decision in DMN and various other kinds of object that make up the business, organizational and operational contexts. Some of these are described in Chapter 10 as they relate to other standards. The links to Process and Task (BPMN objects) are part of the Operational Context, the links to Key Performance Indicators and Objectives are part of the Business Context, and the links to Organizational Unit define the Organizational Context. Refer to Chapter 7 for more details.

12.3.2 Specify decision requirements

Identifying and documenting the decisions involved scopes the project. A Decision Requirements Model requires the identification of a number of elements:

- Input Data requirements
- Knowledge about the decision
- Related decisions

All of these elements can be displayed on a Decision Requirements Diagram where they can be associated to form a Decision Requirements Model (see Section 8.1).

An initial set of decision requirements should focus on the context of each Decision being described. An immediate context diagram (see Section 14.3.2) shows a single Decision and its nearest requirements. The information that the Decision most obviously requires is identified, shown as Input Data and linked with information requirements. Later iterations are likely to show that much of this data is required at a lower level in the model—by Decisions that are part of the decomposition—but initially it is more useful to show the information context of the Decision in order that the data requirements be clearly understood as soon as possible.

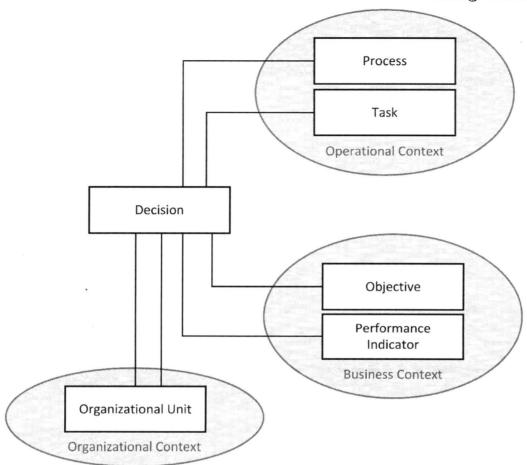

Figure 12-2 The Context of a Decision

Similarly, the most important Knowledge Sources should be identified and linked with authority requirements. Those Knowledge Sources, or *authorities*, representing high level regulatory frameworks and organization-wide policies are likely to dominate with more granular Knowledge Sources not being considered until later. The Knowledge Sources that identify what must be done and what can/cannot be done are critical here, with those that relate to best practices perhaps best left for later iterations.

This initial context diagram (see example in Figure 12-3) can be enhanced with a single layer of decision decomposition. Most non-trivial decisions have at least one layer of sub-decisions and these should be identified early. At this stage, it is enough to describe them as noted above and add the information requirements links from these Decisions to the original Decision. Refinement is likely to identify additional Input Data and Knowledge Sources related to these sub-decisions but this too can be omitted for this iteration.

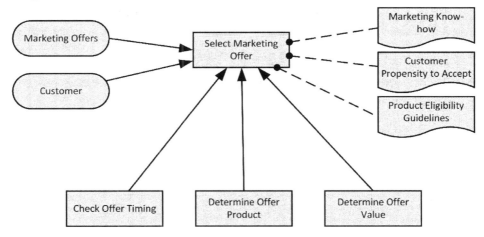

Figure 12-3 Example Early Stage Decision Requirements Diagram

It can also be useful to consider example decision logic at this stage. If existing documentation or specifications contain decision logic, then this can be used to further clarify the behavior of these initial Decisions. Examples should not be created for this purpose and a significant time investment is not appropriate at this early stage. To the extent to which decision logic is already defined, however, it should be referenced and used.

The intent of this initial stage is to allow decisions to be more accurately assessed for complexity and suitability for automation while also identifying the organizations and roles that are central to the decisions. Decisions with many obvious information requirements, onerous externally-defined authorities or complex and inaccessible authorities/information are going to be more complex and difficult to define. These initial models can be reviewed and the organization's appetite for automation, and indeed for modeling, can be assessed before more detail is added.

Initial projects will often discover they have to create all the Input Data and Knowledge Sources needed at this stage but later projects will find that they are reusing Input Data defined in their glossary (see Chapter 9) and that many Knowledge Sources are already in use in other projects. Even at this level it is important to avoid duplication—check for existing objects that can be reused rather than simply creating new ones.

At this stage consider the following checklist:

- Have all agreed sources of decisions been consulted and mined for input (see Section 12.2)?

- Has each decision been associated with question and allowable set of answers (see Section 12.3)?

- Have business SMEs resolved contradictions? If not, have the decisions been labelled as contentious?

- Has a list of poorly understood Knowledge Sources and Input Data been identified along with potential sources of help?

- Has a list of Input Data which has no known sources been identified?

12.3.3 Refine and iterate

The next stage in Decision Requirements modeling is to decompose and refine the model, working until enough detail is included that the project can be successful. The level of detail required is somewhat subjective and depends on the project (see Section 12.6.1). The initial model is not going to be sufficient for any project unless it reveals whether or not the decision is not worth modeling any further.

The process for this step involves a number of techniques that are generally applied in parallel and in a highly iterative fashion:

- Decompose decisions.
- Refine Input Data requirements.
- Refine Knowledge Sources.
- Document critical decision logic.
- Document example decision logic structure.
- Define Input Data for analytic Knowledge Sources.
- Review for completeness.
- Iterate.

This iterative approach can be used as part of a single requirements step to produce a complete requirements model. It can more pragmatically be integrated into an agile development approach. In an agile approach a high-level model is defined in the first iteration. Each subsequent iteration takes part of this model and drills down to a level of completeness that allows design and implementation of that part of the model in the same iteration. In this way, the model is gradually fleshed out in a series of iterations each of which delivers value. There is likely to be some re-work and care must be taken with respect to consistency of data and terminology, but the iterative nature of decision modeling lends itself well to an agile approach.

12.3.3.1 Decompose decisions

The most basic approach to decomposing decisions is to use open-ended questions as a knowledge elicitation technique with those who understand the decision-making. Asking questions like: "How do you go about determining X?", "Is X the only way you can determine Y?" and "How does someone on your team decide Z?" will almost always result in descriptions of elements of decision-making. These will most often be the next level of detail, though they will sometimes capture a large number of smaller pieces that will need to be organized into a model later.

Any decision made manually, defined in a business process or automated in code is made sequentially. As someone describes the Decision they will likely, naturally, describe it in terms of a set of steps or pieces that are made one after another. These steps are likely to be Decisions in their own right, though the sequence will need to be removed when the decision is modeled as noted in Sections 13.6 and 14.8.4.

Many decisions are made differently in different circumstances or perhaps not even made at all if specific conditions are met. Decisions to determine if those circumstances are true or not should be added to the model.

Many decisions appear to rely on Input Data but, on closer examination, the decision does not need the data itself but some derivation or classification of it. In these circumstances a new decision is added to perform this derivation and it is added between the Input Data and the original decision (see the Classifier pattern in Section 16.9).

In all cases, it is important to focus on the current operational requirement and business need and not allow discussions of legacy implementation details such as the processing sequence or specifics of program behavior to dominate.

12.3.3.2 Refine Input Data requirements

Each decision in the model as it stands should be assessed for Input Data requirements:

- Consider the Input Data on which a decision depends and any decisions that, in turn, depend on this decision—its parents. This Input Data may also be required at the parent decision's level. It is not uncommon for decisions to share some information requirements with their parents/children.

- It is also worth considering if the information requirements of the parent should be "moved"—if, in fact, the information requirement is to the child decision and not to the parent decision. This can be because the decision categorizes or derives something from the Input Data and it is the result of this derivation that the parent needs rather than the raw data. For instance, the parent decision may not actually need to know the country of residence of a person (Input Data), it may just need to know if there is an extradition treaty with that country (a classification decision). It is important to distinguish dependencies on raw data versus those facts which can be derived from it (see Section 15.2.5).

- In addition, it is common to move information requirements "down" the model in early iterations where information requirements have been brainstormed but not refined simply because now the model only has the specific decision that requires the relationship.

- Input Data required by other decisions in the model should be considered next to see if any of it is required for this Decision. Most decision models have a core set of Input Data that are used by several Decisions in the model. Be sure that each independent Input Data required is identified and that there are no implicit or amalgamated sources.

- Any additional data that is required by the decision can now be identified and the relevant business entity looked up in the data model or glossary. This should then be added as an Input Data, checking first to see if the Input Data exists in the model repository already to maximize reuse and traceability across models.

12.3.3.3 Refine Knowledge Sources

The authorities documented for each decision need to be similarly assessed. Each decision should have a set of authority requirements to Knowledge Sources that document:

- How the decision must be made.
- How it should generally be made.
- How it may not be made.
- How it might be made better.

Most decisions will have at least one Knowledge Source. Some Decisions are truly based on things "everybody knows" and so don't have one. Others are included in a model to manage the decision-making structure (for instance, seeing which of three defined approaches has resulted in an outcome and then using it) and may not therefore be based on external knowledge. Knowledge Sources should not be created just to ensure that all Decisions have one, but Decisions that lack Knowledge Sources should be double checked to make sure that there is nothing worth documenting.

The authority requirements and Knowledge Sources attached to the parent(s) of the decision can be assessed just as its information requirements can:

- It is not uncommon for a Knowledge Source to be linked to both parent and child Decisions. However, if the parent Decision is linked to a regulation or policy object that consists of multiple distinct chapters or parts and the child Decision is impacted only by part of that policy or regulation it may be worth creating a new Knowledge Source specific to the part. This can be linked back to the parent Knowledge Source (see Section 15.2.1) allowing all the various parts to be coordinated.

- When building a decision model, it is also common to identify a Knowledge Source as an authority for a Decision only to discover that it really impacts only part of the Decision. In these situations, the authority requirement can simply be moved "down" the hierarchy to a more specific sub-decision.

- Anyone who is already identified as an interviewee for knowledge elicitation, or better, the group of experts to which they belong, should be shown as a Knowledge Source.

12.3.3.4 Document critical decision logic

At each stage in the refinement process, Decisions may be identified that are central to the overall decision-making approach. These often act as "traffic cops", coordinating and orchestrating a set of lower-level Decisions to come up with an answer. Alternatively, they may use a small, precisely structured set of Input Data to classify an entity. Understanding exactly how these Decisions work can be important for ongoing refinement of the decision model.

When these decisions are identified, it is worth fully documenting their decision logic as described in Section 12.4. This will ensure that the information requirements identified are correct, will clarify and confirm the allowed answers for both the Decision and the Decisions it requires and will ensure that everyone is clear how this element of the decision model behaves.

This step may identify properties needed by the decision logic that are not properties of the Input Data already linked with information requirements. These must be added so that they are available in the information requirements shown in the model—the decision logic cannot use properties that are not represented by an information requirement. In a new area of the business or one without a well-defined data model it may be that these new properties simply need to be added to one of the business entities already shown as Input Data. More likely it means that there is a Decision or an Input Data that is not yet linked as an information requirement.

12.3.3.5 Document example decision logic structure

In addition to identifying critical decision logic it is often helpful to identify example decision logic for some of the decisions in the model. Writing a few rules or a few rows in a decision table can validate the information requirements in a useful way without the expense of analyzing the logic of entire table. It can:

- Confirm that at least one property is required from each of the Input Data elements linked as information requirements.

- Confirm that the Decisions linked with information requirements are going to be used and that the allowed answers for those Decisions seem reasonable.

- Confirm that there are no properties required in conditions that are not part of one of the information requirements.

- Demonstrate the likelihood that decision logic can be defined that will produce all the allowed answers defined for this Decision.

None of this will be definitive for a complex decision but some initial example rules are often very helpful at this stage. This process may identify new information requirements almost as effectively as documenting the complete decision logic. Indeed, this is one of the best reasons for documenting example decision logic in this way.

12.3.3.6 Define Input Data for analytic Knowledge Sources

While many Knowledge Sources will be policies or regulations, others will be analytical in nature. These may be reports or dashboards, designed to inform decision-making directly. They may be data mining results designed to find patterns of rules in historical datasets. These Knowledge Sources are often added to a model to show what analytic knowledge will help improve the accuracy of a decision.

When analytic Knowledge Sources are identified, it is worth linking them to the data from which they are derived. In a DMN decision model this can be done by taking advantage of the fact that Input Data and Decisions can be authorities for Knowledge Sources (see Section 11.1.2). An analytic Knowledge Source can therefore be linked to the data from which it is derived at a structural level. The information structure of the Input Data, or Decisions, represents the historical data being analyzed. So, for instance, a piece of analytic knowledge about customer retention risk might be based on the customer, usage and subscription data. The model would show this by linking those three Input Data elements to the Knowledge Source as its authorities. This creates a chain of authorities where the data is an authority for the knowledge which is in turn an authority for some decisions. This chain allows for traceability and management over time.

It should be noted that a surprising number of policy documents are actually based on data analysis. Risk policies, life underwriting manuals and many others are presented as though they are policies even though the specific guidance they contain was derived analytically. This should be captured and documented whenever it is observed so that the model shows clearly which Knowledge Sources may need to be revised in the light of new data or even automatically updated on a regular basis (see Section 15.2.6).

12.3.3.7 Review for completeness

After each iteration, it is worth considering if the model is complete enough to be fit for purpose. The degree of detail this involves will vary (see Section 12.6.1). Some models will contain a mix of automated and non-automated decisions, meaning that completeness needs vary across the model. In addition, decision models are often not "balanced" in that one leg of a Decision Requirements Diagram may need to be much deeper and more complex than another. The fact that one leg is only a couple of levels deep while another is 10 levels deep does not necessarily mean that it is less well defined or less complete.

12.3.3.8 Iterate

If all or part of the model is not "complete for purpose" then additional iteration will be required. Decisions that do not seem sufficiently complete can be re-assessed and additional detail added as described above. This process can be repeated as necessary to build a complete model.

At this stage consider the following checklist:

- Do the Knowledge Sources represent everything a brand-new employee would need to make the decision? Is the know-how of all the SMEs who might advise them represented? Are the SME groups identified?

- Are all the dashboards, reports and analytics being used in current state decision-making shown in the model?

- Do the documented Input Data include all the data shown in any current UI as well as any and all forms or examples used? All presented data should be used in the decision.

- Have unstructured data, images, videos, conversations or other sources been considered in addition to the traditional structured data stored in databases?

- Are all Input Data fully defined in terms of underlying data specified in the glossary?

- Are some Input Data required by a significant number of decisions and, if so could the model be simplified by splitting the Input Data into orthogonal pieces (see Section 14.7.5)?

- Have all decisions that have multiple Knowledge Sources been checked to see if there are additional, finer grained Decisions that could be identified? It is not unusual for each Knowledge Source to be linked to a single Decision once the model is complete.

- Patterns and repetition in decision logic are generally a bad idea (see Section 14.4.3.3) so the model should be "normalized" to break these repeating groups out into their own Decisions.

- Check that any leaf decisions that have identical Input Data and Knowledge Sources are truly decisions, not individual rules.

- Has example or outline decision logic been defined for every decision? Has complete decision logic been defined for the most stable and simplest decisions?

12.4 Complete The Model

Iteration continues until the model is fit for purpose at which point it can be said to be completed. What it means for a model to be completed depends its purpose (see Section 12.6.1). DMN was developed for three use cases:

- A model for manual decision-making.
- A model of the requirements for automated decision-making.
- An executable model of decision-making.

As this last one covers two possible approaches—one where all the logic is specified in the model and one in which the logic is specified in one of more external environments and linked to the model—this yields three main scenarios for completion that are covered below and two full implementation approaches that are covered thereafter.

Particularly for 1 and 2 in this list, Decision Requirements Models can be used as the basis for documents. For instance, a model of decision requirements can be used to build part of a formal requirements document. However, the best way to use a complete Decision Requirements Model is as a shared specification of decision-making, its associated knowledge and glossary should be housed in a collaborative environment. Such a collaborative environment is also the best way to develop a complete model. In this way, the requirements will remain "live", shared and updated as part of ongoing operations.

12.4.1 Specifying human decision-making

Human decision-making can sometimes require less than a complete, well defined Decision Requirements Model. The decomposition of decision-making to sub-decisions, the identification of the Input Data required and a robust set of Knowledge Sources as authorities completely define the decision-making. It is often, however, worth completing the model with some additional information:

- Ensure that all Knowledge Sources have links to complete documentation so that those making the decision can use the model to find the right reference to consult.
- Consider using a decomposition of complex Knowledge Sources (see Section 15.2.1) to help decision-makers find the most relevant authority.
- Consider documenting detailed decision logic for well-defined, structured decisions in the model. Using formal but natural language statements, either as a list of "rules" or as a simple natural language Decision Table, can greatly increase the likelihood of consistent, accurate manual decision-making.
- For less well-defined decisions, consider documentation of decisions by example to help novice decision-makers.
- Consider making the model available in the environment where decision-makers work. For instance, including the decision model in the help for a user interface related to the decision or embedding it in a dashboard can make it much more relevant and likely to be used. This should ideally be "live" so that changes in the model are immediately reflected.

12.4.2 Requirements for automated decision-making

A Decision Requirements Model that is a complete and accurate representation of the decision-making involved in a proposed Decision Service can form the basis for specifying the requirements for an implementation project. These requirements should include the following information derived from the Decision Requirements Model:

- KPIs and business objectives being impacted by the decisions included.

- The decisions and their model, including sub-decisions, Input Data, Knowledge Sources and Decision Service definitions.

- Complete sets of decision logic examples, analytic models or optimization models for those decisions to be implemented as well as clearly identified Knowledge Sources for those few rules that have not yet been articulated as decision logic.

- Analytic Knowledge Sources required by the decision-making and the data that should be analyzed to produce them.

- An operational context for the decisions in terms of business processes, tasks, events and systems.

- Nonfunctional requirements (e.g., throughput, latency, security).

- An organizational context in terms of owners, makers and interested parties.

- Example test cases to illustrate function.

All projects will have additional details such as phases and scope, sponsorship and organizational change requirements. These are easier to specify precisely with reference to a Decision Requirements Model. While these will need to be added, this should be done using the Decision Requirements Model as the touchstone of the project's intent.

Ideally these requirements can be delivered as a living repository containing the various decision model elements, related models such as process models or business architecture models (see Chapter 10), publications supporting Knowledge Sources and other associated documents.

If a requirements document needs to be produced, for a formal Request for Proposal process for instance, then the decision model can be used as the basis for such a document. It is worth keeping the underlying models in a repository where they can be shared and kept live and accurate over time: the document should be regarded as a snapshot not as a replacement for the model.

12.4.3 Implementing automated decision-making

A complete and implementable DMN model includes the decision logic needed to constitute an executable model or links to artifacts in implementation environments that represent all the needed executable logic or a mixture of these. In any case, a Decision Model that is associated with an executable representation should also remain "live" and be kept current and representative throughout the life of the decision. These two approaches are discussed and compared in the next section.

Models that are defined at this level can also support a degree of simulation and testing of the decisions involved, either leveraging a linked implementation environment or because the modeling environment itself can use the complete executable definition to support this.

12.5 Approaches to implementing decision models

When decision models are being automated, they can be extended to include decision logic or mapped to an external implementation.

12.5.1 Decision requirements extended to decision logic

One implementation option is to take all the decisions and Input Data required by one or more Decision Services and completely specify the information and decision logic models related to them. The Input Data must be completely defined with an information model suitable for the implementation environment (DMN's default is XML but this can be overridden for a model if desired) and this information should all be managed in a glossary. This last stipulation is not required by DMN but is strongly recommended (see Chapter 9). Decision Logic Modeling should be completed for all the decisions that will be inside the automation boundary and included in the Decision Service.

Decision logic in DMN is predominantly expressed using Decision Tables, although it does define other formats (see Section 11.3 and Appendix B). The standard also acknowledges that there are other representations for business rules or decision logic (see Section 14.4.4) and that some elements of a Decision Requirements Model might be better represented by, for instance, a predictive analytic model rather than business rules. DMN provides some mechanisms for referencing external definitions as functions, for instance, to allow such additional representations to be included.

To be executable, the decisions within the Decision Service must be completely specified and every decision included must be fully specified using decision tables, FEEL expressions, FEEL invocations of Business Knowledge Models or FEEL invocations of external functions that have been imported into the model.

If an alternative expression language is specified for the model as a whole, or for individual elements, then this expression language can be used instead of FEEL. Such an expression language might, in principle, allow the decision logic and related expressions to be specified as decision trees, rule sheets, decision graphs or using other formats (see Section 14.4.4).

12.5.2 Decision Requirements mapped to external implementation

An alternative approach exists for implementing a Decision Requirements Model. Instead of specifying all of the decision logic in the model it is possible to link parts of the model to components developed in an external implementation environment.

For instance, where the decision requirements are best implemented as decision logic or business rules, the model can be linked to items maintained by Business Rules Management Systems. These contain decision logic in well-defined artifacts, not only decision tables but also decision trees and whatever additional representations the BRMS supports. The decision logic for a specific decision can be specified in the BRMS and then linked to the decision model so that a user can easily navigate from one to the other. This allows business users to find the rules they need to manage in their BRMS using the Decision Requirements Model they are already familiar with. It also allows the implementation team to create other artifacts in the BRMS without exposing them to the business users.

The example below shows a decision in a Decision Requirements Model linked to a Decision Table implemented in the open source rule engine JBoss Drools. These implementations may present decision logic in a DMN compliant way, when Decision Tables are being used for instance, or may use their own representation. As DMN becomes established it is expected that more of the BRMS interfaces used to manage decision logic will become compliant.

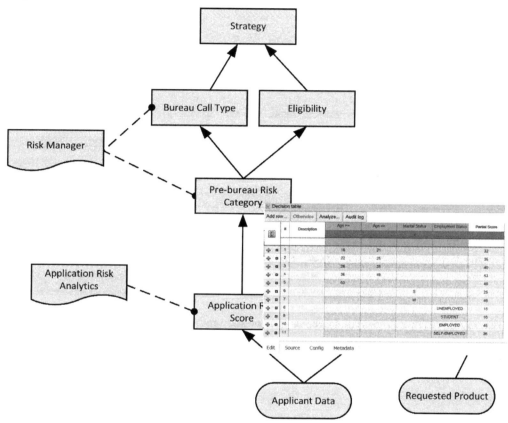

Figure 12-4 Example Linkage of a Decision Requirements Model to a BRMS

Decision Requirements Models can also be linked to the predictive analytic models developed in data mining and other advanced analytic tools. The model shows the information from which the analytic was derived as well as how it is used in decision-making. Linking the Decision Requirements Model directly to the predictive analytic model allows business users to see where analytic models are used and ensures these analytic models are kept consistent with their business context.

Finally, Decision Requirements Models can be linked to other analytic implementations such as visualizations, reports or dashboard components. Where the decision-making being modeled is manual, this ties the BI and analytic components being developed more explicitly to best practice decision-making approaches. It allows those recording and managing these best practices to see what analytic components are available to support them.

12.5.3 Implementation considerations

There are several considerations that need to be balanced when comparing these two approaches. Depending on the specific project environment there are likely to be various advantages and disadvantages for each approach. The approaches can also be mixed and should not be considered mutually exclusive. Remember the following considerations:

- It is important to keep the decision requirements and decision logic implementation consistent. If the model is completely specified, then this requires either that no changes are ever made to the implementation other than through the model or that the environment supports full round-trip editing such that an edit made to the implementation can be reflected back to the model. If the model is linked to external implementations, changes to the model and to the implementation must be synchronized. This may create additional manual tasks or require additional tooling.

- The integration and management of a glossary and information model is much more straightforward when the decision logic is implemented in the model directly. When the model is linked to implementations, especially if there are several implementation environments involved, vocabularies maintained by each must be synchronized. In addition, some of these environments may have an approach to the underlying data and glossary that does not support business user access. Keeping environments consistent between a decision model and external BRMS is a challenge unless the technology integration is very well designed.

- Decision logic management benefits from sophisticated editors to validate, verify, test and simulate decision-making. If the logic is to be added to the model, then the modeling tool must provide this kind of tooling. If the model is linked to existing implementation environments, these should have such capabilities.

- Some organizations may have already implemented significant amounts of decision-making before adopting a decision modeling approach. This needs to be available to the developers of new decision models so that it can be leveraged. When adding logic to the model directly, it should be possible to import existing functions and capabilities so they can be executed by decisions or it should be possible to re-engineer this logic into a fully specified model. Linking models to existing implementations offers this kind of reuse directly as a new model can be built and simply pointed at existing assets. This can be particularly important in organizations with multiple decision-making implementation environments. Elements of a single Decision Requirements Model might be implemented in several BRMSs for instance while also leveraging a predictive analytic model built in an analytic tool and visualizations to assist in the manual elements of the decision.

Both approaches offer some advantages over considering the decision model as requirements for a completely separate implementation effort, however:

- They ensure that business users can find and edit the decision logic or other implementation components directly from a Decision Requirements Model they are familiar with—the one that describes their problem.

- They ensure that only one version of the decision logic is maintained. Either the logic is part of the model or the model is linked directly to the logic executed by the implementation environments. Requirements are not disconnected from the implementation as they can be when business rules are documented independently before being translated into a BRMS.

12.6 Methodological Best Practices

DMN is only a notation and the standard specifically avoids including the kind of methodology detail documented above. Similarly, the best practices documented in Chapters 14 and 15 are additive to the notation itself. Without repeating best practices documented elsewhere in the book, this section covers some best practices associated with this method of decision modeling

12.6.1 Level of detail should be driven by purpose

As noted, decision models can be developed for various purposes and the specific purpose can drive the level of detail required. Decision models can be used to:

- Document manual decision-making for consistency and repeatability.
- Document and illustrate an automation boundary and interface for a Decision Service.
- Identify the potential for analytics in manual decision-making.
- Scope and structure decision logic, managing business rules analysis and design.
- Generate a complete, executable specification of a decision.
- Act as a front-end to an executable decision managed in one or more external environments.
- Frame predictive analytics efforts to ensure the resulting analytic will improve decision-making.
- Design dashboards and other interactive analytic environments designed to support decision-making.
- Integrate and orchestrate business rules, predictive analytic and optimization technology in a decision management system that delivers prescriptive analytics.

Each of these is a valid use case for decision modeling. Decision models fit for each of these purposes can be developed using the approach outlined above. How much detail to add, what kind of details matter and when to stop varies depending on the intended use but the basic approach is the same. For instance, Decisions expected to be completely automated, those on the automation boundary, those that are volatile or those with a contentious or externally imposed definition require a much higher level of completeness than those that are expected to remain manual, are stable and simple, are away from the automation boundary and have an uncontested, internal definition. Similarly, decisions likely to be automated using decision logic, business rules, will need that decision logic specified while those that might be implemented by analytics, machine learning or optimization models will require a different set of definitions (see Section 14.4.4).

12.6.2 Build models incrementally, top down

Incremental, top down generation of decision models is the most effective means of seeing the big picture, avoiding getting mired in the detail, identifying re-factoring opportunities and reuse potential early, and identifying missing logic. This incremental approach is the one described above and it should be followed even if a waterfall approach is being used to develop the complete decision model in a single project phase. The incremental development of decision models helps integrate decision modeling into an agile project management environment, but should be used even when an agile approach is not. A series of workshops can be scheduled to work through this iterative process (see Section 12.6.7).

12.6.3 Make decisions measurable

A common error in decision modeling is to focus on decisions that "everyone knows" are important without considering their measurable value to the business. Decision modeling requires an investment of time and effort. Automating or analytically supporting modeled decisions requires a further investment. Unless there is a clear return on this investment, decision modeling will be perceived as a failure or as unnecessary overhead. This means that there must be a way to measure the improvement in a decision.

Teams modeling decisions can get sucked in to thinking that there is obviously value to better understanding a decision without checking that it will be possible to measure any improvement. This should be resisted. Similarly, just because something can be modeled as a decision does not automatically mean there is value in doing so (see Section 5.2). Teams must keep an eye on the measurability of decisions as they model them.

It should be noted that some decisions are modeled and managed because they must be. Data translation decisions (see Section 14.6.2), for instance, often have no measurement of value but are essential to other decisions that do.

12.6.4 Define release and governance processes

During and especially after the creation of a decision model, organizations will need a workable approach to releasing and governing the models. It is unlikely that an existing release process, designed for a traditional SDLC, will work for decision models so one will need to be developed and evolved as an organization gains experience with decision modeling. Such an approach should have a number of characteristics:

- It should reflect the iterative nature of decision modeling, recognizing that not all parts of a model are at the same level of detail at any given time.

- It should recognize that not all decision models require the same degree of governance. A decision model that is central to a regulatory compliance mandate will need different governance than one related to marketing offers, for example.

- It should not allow inconsistency and unmanaged change. At the same time, it should not impose so much governance that needed agility is sacrificed. Agility and governance are not absolutes and must be traded off against each other intelligently.

- It cannot rely on a hierarchical model where all decisions are "owned" by parent decisions or by specific decision requirements diagrams. The models are interconnected graphs not top-down trees and the level of reuse is often high. The interconnectedness of decision models (see Section 14.3.2) must be adequately reflected in the release and governance process.

- It should be integrated with the release and governance processes of any related implementation technology used. If a model is developed that does not contain all of the decision-making as model artifacts, then changes to the model will need to be coordinated with changes in the implementation environment.

Organizations should resist the temptation to fully define their release and governance process before building decision models. A lack of experience with decision modeling will mean that any governance and release process developed is likely to be a poor match for the approach. As more experience is gained the approach can and should evolve.

12.6.5 Manage models in a repository

The decision models produced by this approach should be managed in a shared repository not as documents. Section 18.5 discusses tooling support and its importance for decision modeling.

12.6.6 Ensure decision is cohesive and concise

A number of best practices defined in Chapter 14 are particularly important in keeping decision models cohesive and concise. Specifically:

- Always define questions and allowed answers for all decisions as this prevents "drift" in the model (see Section 14.2.1)
- Decompose decisions before deciding where to automate, as it's much easier to define a coherent automation boundary with an extra layer of detail in hand (see Section 14.2.6)
- Use multiple views of the decision model to focus different groups of SMEs on the piece of the model they care about so they can validate it more easily (see Section 14.3.2)
- Use Decision Tables to define decision logic where possible as they are easier to validate and cross-check but keep them as simple as possible (see Section 14.4.3.3)
- Use enumerations, not strings, to prevent imprecision in decision-making based on textual data (see Section 14.5.1).
- Reuse Decisions (and Input Data and Knowledge Sources) wherever possible to minimize duplication and increase the return on time spent precisely defining them (see Section 14.6.1).
- Eliminate sequence as it clutters and confuses decision models (see Section 14.6.4).
- Keep decision models self-contained (see Section 14.6.5).

All the documented best practices are worth following, but these are critical to developing a coherent and concise decision model.

12.6.7 Run decision discovery workshops

When working in an area that has not previously been modeled, one of the most effective ways to identify decisions, describe them and specify their decision requirements is using a Decision Discovery Workshop. This is a classic elicitation workshop but one focused specifically on the decisions involved in a project.

A decision discovery can be used to elicit details of an identified decision or to identify an initial set of decisions and then extract details for those decisions. While both approaches work, spending some time identifying candidate decisions before the session generally works better, as it allows the focus of the session to be defined and shared in advance. This makes it easier to identify the right participants and to make sure the team has reviewed the documents most likely to be relevant.

The workshop will generally take several days and the most effective approach is to have half day elicitation sessions with everyone, followed by half day working sessions to clean up and enhance the models produced while identifying questions for the following elicitation session. Each session should be timeboxed and limited to no more than 3 hours. If the model is expected to be complex or contentious, more sessions should be used rather than longer sessions. The first session should focus on breadth—a wide but shallow overview—and depth should be added to this model in subsequent sessions.

The modeling team should plan to have domain experts and decision makers be the majority of attendees. Some IT and analytic resources are often useful but are not a substitute for actual business owners and domain experts, even if they have worked in the relevant area for many years. Firsthand experience with the business domain is essential.

The workshop generally has the following elements:

1. **Introduce the Decision Discovery Workshop, agenda and attendees**. Those attending should introduce themselves, the focus area should be clearly described and the agenda / timeframe outlined. Gather contact information for subject matter experts at this point as their schedule often means they must leave immediately after the session!

2. **Describe and explain the DMN notation.** The material in Sections 6.3 and 8.1 should be presented on the white board. Try and avoid using slides at this stage as it puts the audience into "presentation" mode when they need to be engaged. Walk through the key objects—Decisions, Knowledge Sources and Input Data—and the two main relationships between them—Information Requirements and Authority Requirements. Make sure to spend some time talking about the power of decision modeling to break down even very complex decisions into manageable components.

3. **Before diving into the decision-making, make sure the team understands the context of the decisions involved:** Ask questions about the organizational breakdown and organizational roles of those involved in the decision-making to be modeled; identify and discuss any existing or required measurement approaches and metrics; document existing operational context assets such as assets business processes, events and applications; list and quickly document relevant databases, reports and data-presentation user interfaces that might indicate Input Data. These will be useful during modeling and can be documented on flipcharts or secondary white boards so they are visible during modeling. See Chapter 7 for more details on business context.

4. **The core of the workshop is to model the decisions involved**. Make sure always to clarify the question and allowed answers as decisions are identified to avoid any

ambiguity. The information required for each decision can be identified and whether this is Input Data or the result of a Decision can be decided. Avoid getting into too much detail as to how a decision is made or what the exact information items are for an Input Data, as these can generally be added during the non-workshop sessions. Focus instead on capturing the structure of the model and the Knowledge Sources that determine the decision-making approach to be used.

5. **During the workshop, do not be constrained by what will be automated or by the technologies you expect to use.** Model the decision-making itself regardless of expected approach. If necessary, an automation boundary can be discussed during the workshop to reassure participants that they understand what will be automated and what will be left to human decision-makers. If this is not broadly agreed, then time should be allowed for discussing where the boundary goes towards the end of the workshop once the decision model is largely settled.

In general, it is best to wrap up the workshop by agreeing follow-up procedures as the model is unlikely to be complete at this point. A formal report or presentation should be scheduled for later, once the team has had time to flesh out and complete the model based on the agreed follow-up procedures.

13 Dispelling Some Common Misconceptions

Ignorance cannot lead to evil, misconceptions lead to evil.
—Leo Tolstoy

Even as decision modeling gains traction and support, there remain some persistent misconceptions about it. Ranging from misunderstanding the nature of a decision model, to underestimating its value, to unnecessary limitations on the scope of its application, these misconceptions can needlessly restrict the benefit an organization will get from decision modeling. This chapter identifies and addresses the most common misconceptions, explaining why they are understandable but counterproductive. The best practices and guidance that should replace these misconceptions are discussed in the next few chapters.

13.1 Misconception: Decision Modeling only works for business rules

The differences between business rules and decisions were noted earlier (see Section 4.2.3). Even among those who understand the difference between decisions and business rules, however, there is a tendency to believe that the only reason for building a decision model is to capture business rules or decision logic. While decisions and business rules are different, goes the reasoning, the only value of a decision model is to frame and correctly capture the logic of the decision, i.e., the business rules.

While the chain of reasoning that leads to this mistake is clear, experience with decision modeling has shown it to be misguided. Decision models actually have multiple use cases including: describing the structure of a decision for which the logic is not well defined or need not be completely defined (a manual decision for instance), framing the requirements for an analytic designed to support the decision and 'mining' the structure of an existing implementation of automated decision-making.

13.1.1 Structure only models

When a decision is not being fully automated, i.e., when it is being left in whole or in part to human decision-makers, decision modeling can still play an important role in standardizing and communicating the approach, managing risk and improving training.

A decision model breaks down an otherwise coarse grained and opaque decision into more manageable pieces, each of which can be described more precisely. By describing each such sub-decision in terms of a precise question to be answered and a set of allowed answers (see Section 5.1.3), the model clarifies what must be decided and why. The model also documents the data to be used and the policies or regulations to be referenced and complied with. Even if the decision logic—the set of business rules—is not specified for every decision in the model, the model itself still has value:

- Such a model outlines a standard approach that can be replicated across many decision-makers for consistency.

- Where a decision is partially automated, a decision model improves the definition of the automation boundary, i.e., the interface between manual and automated decisions. This clarifies how the two will interoperate and prevents any inconsistencies or gaps between them.

- Models, based on one or more diagrams, are much easier to use when training new staff. This reduces the time to bring new decision-makers up to speed.

- When decisions must be explained or justified, to a regulator for instance, a model of the decision-making that is shared and understood by all decision-makers is a lot more credible.

- Such a model demonstrates how each part of the decision depends on other parts, on Input Data and on externally defined legal mandates or policies to which they must conform. This ensures that the genuine need for each of these can be clearly understood and the impact of any change to them can be quickly assessed.

- The declarative nature of a decision model avoids imposing a standard sequence on the decision (see Section 14.6.4), allowing for managed flexibility, reuse and consistency in decision-making.

- Finally, an organization concerned about risk can benefit from a well-defined decision-making approach. A decision model ensures that each decision-maker considers all the elements of the decision and follows established best practices. The decision model also ensures consistency in decision-making. These are important especially for risk-centric decisions.

13.1.2 Framing analytic requirements

As noted elsewhere (see Section 4.3.6), a decision model can be used to frame requirements for analytics. Clearly defining the structure of a decision that requires an analytic, or for which an analytic would be beneficial, helps ensure that the analytic will, in fact, improve the decision-making. While defining the decision logic for parts of such a decision is often useful, it is not generally required—the structure of the decision and the questions/allowed answers are often enough.

With a model in hand, the analytics team is able to identify:

- which piece of the decision-making they are trying to improve;
- what answers they are trying to help users discriminate between;
- how this fits in to the overall decision-making;
- which corporate entities are involved; *and*
- what business objective or Key Performance Indicator (KPI) is being influenced.

13.1.3 Revealing an existing decision-making approach

Building a decision model for an existing implementation is often extremely revealing. Whether the decision-making is represented analytically, as a set of business rule artifacts, or simply coded into a traditional programming or scripting language, modeling it reveals its logical structure and its purpose, unobscured by the technical details of its implementation. While other diagramming approaches can also be used for this—UML, for instance, contains several such approaches—a decision model is better at representing business intent and is a more accessible approach for business analysts. It reveals the approach more clearly and can be maintained and, if necessary, re-engineered more easily. Again, the structure is generally sufficient for this purpose and the decision logic need not be modeled, at least not for every decision in the model.

13.1.4 Why this is a misconception

These examples bring up an interesting question: if these scenarios are powerful and clearly supported by the approach, why do people still associate decision models with business rules?

The primary reason is that decision modeling has a longer history with business rules than with these other scenarios so there are more examples, more stories, and more people with experience. Previous decision modeling approaches (such as The Decision Model, see Appendix D) were focused purely on model-centric representations of business rules or decision logic. In addition, business rules practitioners have been seeking ways to identify and analyze business rules more efficiently, having become aware of the costs and time delays inherent in existing approaches that attempt to gather all the business rules first before considering how they will be used in decision-making. In addition, they need a means of managing business rules at scale as large rule repositories have no organizing concept and can become unwieldy. Finally, the standard itself devotes a large number of words to the decision logic level and to the expression language, making this aspect of the decision modeling appear disproportionately important.

Organizations adopting decision modeling should focus on applying the approach to any and all repeatable decisions (see Section 5.4) regardless of how they expect to implement or support the decision-making being modeled.

13.2 Misconception: Decision Models are only complete if you can generate code from them

The most obvious way to tell that a decision model is complete is that it is possible to generate code, an executable, for the decision that is the subject of the model, i.e., the "top" decision (see Section 8.1.1.3). If all the various elements of the model that are required by this decision are completely defined, then it is possible to create code or business rules that will execute the decision-making in production. Because this is definitive, it is easy to see it as the primary (even the only) way to "prove" a model is complete.

As noted above, however, there are scenarios in which decision models do not require decision logic or business rules. If one is building a decision model in one of these other scenarios, then a model may be "complete"—fit for purpose—without it being possible to generate code from the model. For instance, a model being built to describe a manual decision may be considered complete when someone can use the model to make a set of sample decisions without error. DMN is at least as much about precise communication of intent as it is about execution.

In addition, decision models provide an effective tool for mapping and orchestrating implementations being developed in multiple environments. A decision model can be combined with a mix of newly developed and existing artifacts that are being reused, all of which are outside the modeling environment. Linking the model to the artifacts that implement it means that the model is complete once every element is linked to a working implementation—whether or not the implementation has been generated from the model. The model becomes "complete" when it is mapped to a complete implementation. Indeed, a decision model without decision logic but with links to a BRMS and/or analytic engine may be considerably easier to understand than a complete decision model with everything expressed in FEEL or PMML.

In short, decision modeling should not always have the implied goal of expressing the detailed business logic of every last nuance of a company's operations. This is frequently not the best approach and can lead to obscuring, rather than communicating, key ideas.

13.3 Misconception: Decision Tables are what matter in DMN

Related to this discussion of the importance of code generation and decision logic to decision models is the misconception that the only piece of the standard that really matters is the boxed expression—a formal representation of decision logic, the most common variant of which is the Decision Table. The sections of the DMN standard relating to Decision Tables specifically and to boxed expressions in general are much larger than the section on Decision Requirements Diagrams. Add to this the fact that the Decision Logic Level is essential for code generation and it is not surprising that some discussions of the power of DMN relate almost entirely to the value of standard, executable Decision Tables.

This misconception is particularly widely held among Business Process Management System (BPMS) users and those already using the Business Process Model and Notation (BPMN). Among this community, it can lead to the modeling of decision-making as a fine-grain process or rule flow. Often, each element of the decision has already been identified as a business rules task or step in the process and a Decision Table is then written for each task. This allows the decision-making to be automated using the process engine and a Decision Table execution model.

This approach is best considered an anti-pattern—something to be avoided at all costs (see Section 16.8 for a pattern to replace this approach). The proper relationship of BPMN and DMN models is explained in summary in Section 6.4.2 and in detail in Section 10.2. Modeling a decision using BPMN in this way has a number of issues:

- It models sequence rather than dependency (see also Section 13.6).
- It results in over-large Decision Tables because there is resistance to breaking a Decision Table into multiple Decision Tables when those tables must each become a new task in the process.
- It exposes data that should or could be internal to the decision to the process and requires that it be managed by the process and passed on from one Decision Table to the next.
- It implies decision-making might stop after any of the decision tasks, when in prac-

tice it cannot.

Using a process model that has a series of tasks each of which invokes an individual Decision Table is a poor way to model decision-making.

13.4 Misconception: Decision Modeling is just about diagrams

This is almost a corollary of the previous misconception. Just as a decision model is more than just decision logic, so it is also more than just a diagram. This is a common misconception because notation—how a diagram is drawn—is central to the standard. After all, it is the Decision Model and *Notation* standard. This misconception has two main flavors.

The first is that the information represented by the graphical notation is *all* the information required for or contained within a model. This leads to Decision Requirements Diagrams that show the decisions, Input Data and Knowledge Sources involved in a decision with just their names and perhaps descriptions captured. However, the notation does not show all the information *required* by a model. It does not include the rich set of extra metadata, defined by the standard, for decisions and other elements of the model that should be captured. These are listed in Section 14.2.5, which also includes copious additional suggestions beyond the standard. Of course, it is impractical to show all this information on a diagram. However, it must be captured, stored and managed in a repository or document related to the diagram(s) being developed, whether or not decision logic is being captured for the decisions on these diagrams.

The second mistaken belief is that a diagram is a synonym for a model. This leads to teams drawing diagrams that show a particular decision and its decomposition and then treating the diagram like a management framework. The symptoms of this include:

- The entire Decision Requirements Diagram is linked to the process decision task, rather than the decisions within it. This obscures the specifics of the decision-making in the process and makes an implicit assumption that the whole diagram is the only unit of work where experience suggests that multiple entry points are possible.

- The decisions on the diagram are considered "owned" by the diagram. This limits reuse of decisions (as well as Input Data and Knowledge Sources) between diagrams.

- Teams focus on identifying the diagrams that contain a specific Input Data or Knowledge Source when the focus should be on the elements that are related to it. Teams end up knowing, for instance, which diagrams contain a Knowledge Source called *Credit Product Eligibility*, rather than knowing which decisions have an Authority Requirement to this policy and so depend on it.

- Governance and control is imposed at the diagram level even though elements of the model might appear on several diagrams.

This approach seriously compromises reuse and management of the underlying objects and fails to consider that diagrams are all views on the model, on an underlying repository of information (see Sections 6.4.3 and 14.3.2). Diagrams in DMN show the relationships between objects but it is the decision model that contains those objects, their relationships and the rest of the metadata captured about them. This is one of the key strengths of basing decision modeling on DMN.

One of the reasons for this diagram-centric misconception is the simplicity of the core diagram notation. With only a few node types, a few relationship types and some simple rules for how they are used together, it is easy to develop a diagramming tool or template for Decision Requirements Diagrams. This very simplicity can blind people to the richness of the underlying model and to the necessity of managing these non-diagram elements.

13.5 Misconception: Business rules should be captured first, independently of decision models

Many business rules analysis techniques exist and many pre-date effective BRMSs. These approaches focus on the absolute imperative to capture business rules in a technology independent way and use business rule formats that do not match the *If..Then* and Decision Tables formats common in executable business rules. These techniques also tend to focus on capturing all the business rules in a domain before attempting to do anything else and on fine-grained and nuanced differentiation between types of rules. Often, they also require an exhaustive dictionary of business terms to be built specially to support them and specify a detailed set of metadata that must be captured for every rule, whether it results from complex legislation or the whim of the marketing department.

These techniques are expensive, time consuming and wildly inefficient for developing rules-based systems using a BRMS. In particular:

- They tend to omit, more or less completely, any development of an understanding of the *decisions* the rules are intended to make, focusing instead on the specifics of low-level business rules.

- Some approaches have attempted to get around this by layering a decision modeling approach on top of the rule analysis. Analysts are encouraged to first identify, describe and classify all their rules. They are then given techniques that group and assemble these rules into decision models. This is actually a very poor way to build decision models and our experience is that those who attempt it find that they end up with lots of rules they cannot fit into the decision model, even though the decision model is complete and fit for purpose.

- The classifications used for these rules turn out to have no value in a decision model and it is unclear, at the end of the effort, why the attempt was made to classify them.

- The way the rules are written in these approaches is not conducive to their participation in a business decision and they have to be re-expressed as decision logic to fit the action-oriented question and answer approach that drives decision modeling.

For all these reasons, it is essential to *begin* with the decision model itself and apply any useful rule analysis techniques only within the framework of your decision model. There is one exception: if you are trying to rescue a bloated rule repository created using these older techniques, then a decision model can be used to frame and systematically extract/reformulate the rules that matter.

13.6 Misconception: Decision Models need to include sequence

One of the most common errors in a decision model is to include sequence rather than just dependency. Subject matter experts will often describe a decision in a way that implies a sequence, but in fact there is no actual dependency between the sub-decisions identified and, therefore, no need for the sequence to be modeled as part of the decision. However, when this sequence is removed, those building the model may be uncomfortable. They will say things like "it makes no sense to decide A before we decide B" or "it's really inefficient to decide C unless we have decided D already". These are real concerns and need to be captured somewhere, but the decision model is not the place.

Modeling sequence in a decision model embeds current practice, possibly based on an outdated rationale, into what should be a model of requirements. It can complicate decision logic by tying it to a particular sequence, preventing future change and making it hard to scale the model. Decision-making must often be sequenced at implementation time but this can often be automatically inferred from properly modeled dependencies. In those few cases where it cannot, or where performance or cost considerations necessitate a sequence other than the one suggested purely from the dependencies, a decision flow is often used to specify this sequence.

A decision flow depicts the order in which a set of related decisions are made. Decision flows or rule flows are commonly supported by BRMSs and may be required to execute a decision model at run time. Broad support for this concept in BRMSs is a contributing factor to this misconception, especially when decision modeling is being used to specify the requirements for a BRMS implementation.

DMN does not support the decision flow concept, nor is there any particular reason for it to do so. There is no need for the concept of decisions flows at a requirement level and they should not appear in a DMN decision model. The only sequence needed for a decision is that enforced by dependencies (within a decision) and the order of tasks imposed by a business process (between decisions). Even in complex decisions with multi-layer sub-decision hierarchies, in which some decisions serve to generate outcomes for others, there is very rarely a need to specify sequence and many reasons not to. Controlling sequence to address efficiency concerns can be achieved in process and decision models without decision flows.

Eliminating sequence from a decision model to keep sequence and dependencies separate is a best practice described in Section 14.6.4. The dependencies—the requirements of the decision—are the essential details and the decision model should be restricted to these. Such a restriction will allow the model to be validated and will ensure a separation between true business requirements and those that might be temporarily efficient or convenient or merely reflect some arbitrary historical precedent.

13.7 Misconception: Decision Models are created once then handed off to developers

Some organizations that adopt decision modeling regard it as a way to produce a new kind of requirements document. The decision model is developed and reviewed by business analysts and subject matter experts. Once, it is complete from their perspective, it is packaged up as a requirements document, combined with documents describing other elements of the system (e.g., process models, non-functional requirements) and handed over to IT for development. Most of these documents are never consulted again once the system has been developed. If they are, then inconsistencies between the IT view of the (continuously evolving) implemented system and the business view represented in the (static) document often emerge.

Using decision models in this way is better than using traditional prose requirements documents or long lists of rules to describe decision-making, but it fails to maximize the value of decision modeling. Instead, decision models can and should replace a subset of a project's requirements documents with a 'living' repository. This is developed iteratively and maintained as decision-making needs change. It represents a current view of the decision-making requirements as they are understood—a prime record. It should also be developed and maintained by business analysts, subject matter experts and IT working together to create a shared understanding.

The goal is a decision model that is a continuously maintained, ('living') prime record of the requirements that can be simulated and deployed to (or linked with) executable artifacts that can be packaged into Decision Services. This avoids the errors normally associated with the translation of paper specifications to code. Furthermore, by using this approach the current business view of the decision model is always a match for the current implementation view of it. Business experts can then interact directly with the decision model and work with their IT partners to keep the implemented decision-making aligned with current business needs.

In addition, the development of decision models can have some beneficial side effects in the requirements process. For instance:

- A decision model simplifies a process model by externalizing all the decision-making from the process.

- A decision model both consumes a data model (Section 9.5) and helps to validate the content and structure of the data required by the project.

- A decision model can be used to design the user interface for a decision-making task and to drive requirements for reporting and dashboard designs intended to help someone make the decision that has been modeled.

There is a related misconception that projects must create or find complete textual requirements documentation before decision modeling can start. This is neither necessary nor desirable as the intent is to create decision models in place of these documents. If they exist, they can be processed into a decision model, but if they do not exist, then teams should create the decision model directly.

13.8 Misconception: Decision Models are technical assets

Some organizations that have accepted the fact that decision models are living models that should be kept up to date and linked to implementation tend to think of them purely as technical assets that are the exclusive purview of IT. This largely results from a focus on the Decision Logic Level of decision models. The argument goes that an effective definition of the decision logic requires the kind of precise logical thinking in which IT professionals—developers, architects, and programmers for instance—are well versed. To some extent, this misconception grows out of the code generation and decision table misconceptions noted above (see Section 13.2), though it also has an independent existence.

It is a completely understandable misconception because a facility with precise logic is typically a core skill for IT professionals. Many IT professionals find their business partners lacking in precision when it comes to logic and most have prior experience of the difficulty of explaining detailed logic in programs to business owners.

However, decision models should not be primarily a technical asset. This is true even if they are being used to generate code or otherwise completely specify the logic of a decision. It is especially important when the decision model is being used for some other purpose such as specifying manual decision-making or framing analytic requirements (as discussed above). In fact, decision models should always be considered a business asset:

- Decision models are an attempt to communicate a business approach concisely and unambiguously. Only business experts can validate that this has been achieved.

- Decision models are intended to explicitly break down complex decision-making into more manageable and simpler pieces. This increases the degree to which they are understandable by business people relative to traditional code. In some cases, decision models may be the only means the business has of achieving an accurate understanding of the current behavior of its systems. The transparency of a decision model also has value for a SME because it fosters their understanding of the consequences of their decisions and builds a bridge between them and their IT partners. This helps prevent miscommunication but relies on the model being a shared asset and not a technical one.

- SMEs need to interact with the decisions, test them and determine the consequences of the modeled behavior to reveal gaps in thinking. Establishing decision models as technical assets is likely to make this much more difficult. Indeed, the need to test and simulate decisions can be a driver for IT to take over if organizations are not careful. The business impact of changes to decision models and business rules should also be managed by SMEs and this can be done much more readily than other kinds of system changes.

There may be technical implementation details related to a decision model that should be treated as a technical asset, but the core decision model must be a business asset that is truly shared between business and IT professionals.

13.9 Misconception: Decision Models eliminate the need for IT

There is a notion, usually offered by BRMS marketing personnel, that using business rules or decisions would allow business SMEs to maintain, test, change and deploy business logic without ongoing need for any IT support. While it is true that decision modeling and the use of a BRMS can dramatically reduce the burden on the IT department and empower business SMEs, the idea that IT's role can be eliminated is another misconception. This is not generally attainable, nor is it the goal of Decision Management, decision modeling or a BRMS.

In fact, the goal is to build a strong working relationship between SMEs and IT so they can collaborate effectively. A decision model is a shared asset that all can understand. This means that changes are not being 'translated' by IT into code, but are being expressed in a business asset that can generate or be directly associated with business rules in a BRMS.

In some parts of a decision model, SMEs may make and test changes themselves and be able to deploy them directly into production. In others, there is likely to be a more formal release and update process. Some decision models are deployed into complex technical environments, limiting the testing and simulation that is possible to SMEs. Other models are simpler or deployed to more "green field" environments where simulating the impact of changes to a decision is practical. In no case is the role of IT eliminated.

Empowering business SMEs to make some changes themselves and to collaborate directly with others should not be confused with giving them unfettered access to change production systems. Safe agility is the objective and this involves combining decision modeling with an appropriate governance process to ensure that:

- The items that can be changed are controlled appropriately given their importance and any applicable regulatory frameworks.
- The impact of changes is appropriately tested, understood and accepted prior to deployment into production.
- Reviews, approvals and fraud prevention controls that are necessary are applied.
- All changes are audited.

13.10   Misconception: Decision Modeling is Yet More Overhead for Little Gain

The first reaction of some project managers to the suggestion of using decision modeling is concern about the perceived cost. Managers' initial concern is that the technique represents additional modeling overhead and potentially the need for yet another software tool. They see decision modeling as something that might delay "real work", especially if they have defined progress in terms of the number of business rules written (a variation on counting the number of lines of code written and almost as useless).

It's easy to understand why teams may be reluctant to add a new modeling technique to a project but experience shows that the non-obvious benefits of decision modeling more than compensate for its tangible costs. Specifically:

- There is an overall saving of time because decision modeling structures and focuses the specification of decision-making, business rules, far more effectively than other techniques. It is generally quicker to build a decision model and capture the business rules within it than it would be to capture the business rules directly.
- A decision model reduces waste by ensuring that data (fact) models and infrastructure are not developed for information that is not going to have a direct impact on the decision. Many SMEs initially identify data that they "need" but that never shows up in the decision model.

- Decision modeling reduces time to market for a working solution by revealing an initial solution's data gaps and logical 'holes' very quickly. Business SMEs and IT staff can collaborate more effectively because the model prevents misunderstanding.

A fuller analysis of the benefits of Decision Modeling is covered in section 4.4.

13.11   Misconception: Decision Modeling is easy

Experience suggests one final observation. Decision models are easy to read, easy to understand and easy to participate in developing. The notation itself is simple and can be quickly set up in a diagramming tool. Decision modeling's very accessibility can lead to a misconception that it is easy, that it requires neither skill nor practice, that one can simply draw the model and get on with it.

Decision modeling is, indeed, very accessible. Like any modeling approach, however, building good decision models requires modeling skills, some training and time to review, check and confirm that the models are accurate. Some investment in time and effort is going to be required to adopt decision modeling; a pilot project is likely to be a good first step (see Section 5.5.). Be aware: not everyone is going to prove equally able to use the approach.

In many ways, this misconception is the reason for this book. Reading the standard, considering your experience with other standards and modeling approaches and applying the obvious techniques can get you started. Building good decision models takes more than the standard and it's worth learning from the mistakes and successes of others. This is the purpose of the chapters on best practices (see Chapters 14 and 15).

14 Core Best Practices

Without a coach, practice is merely a means of perfecting your mistakes
—Traditional

As DMN is only a notation, it can only provide limited and implicit guidance on modeling technique and style. Seeking knowledge of best practices from the DMN specification itself is rather like looking for tips on literary style from a dictionary. This section describes best practices based on the core set of DMN features and assumes no experience of modeling. It is therefore appropriate for new adopters of decision modeling, in addition to those with more experience. The best practices explained here use DMN's advanced features sparingly, only when absolutely essential, in order to keep models clear. Advanced best practices that that make much more sense to modelers with some experience are deferred to chapter 15.

The specific goal of these best practices is to maximize the effectiveness of decision modeling and make it as successful as it can be. Best practices help modelers to produce and maintain lucid, accurate and complete models of business policy that replace unwieldy paper documents, spreadsheets and other media to become 'living' embodiments of decision-making within an enterprise. 'Living' in the sense that decision models become the prime record for policy documentation within an organization—the first asset to consult in the case of inquiry or change—and are, or are linked to, an executable representation of decision-making.

This is a large chapter designed more for reference than for reading end-to-end. Many readers not seeking an immediate in-depth guide to decision modeling may prefer to browse section headers looking for practices of immediate interest rather than slavishly reading the entire text.

14.1 Introduction

For ease of reference, this chapter partitions best practices for newcomers to decision modeling into five separate areas:

- **Business Context**. These practices address how decision models align to organizations' structure and business objectives.
- **Decision Requirements**. These techniques focus on capturing and maintaining the requirements level structure of the decision model, specifically Decision Requirement Diagrams.
- **Data**. The most effective means of modeling and managing data in decision models is considered in this section.
- **Decision Logic**. The best procedures for modeling decision logic are considered in this section. It includes principles for modeling logic in many formats, not just those specific to Decision Tables and FEEL.

- **General**. These are principles which apply to all aspects of decision modeling or which deal with the relationship between all of its components.

Separate sections consider best practices for advanced users (see Chapter 15), some of the practical issues and limitations with DMN as currently defined (see Appendix C) and decision model patterns (see Chapter 16).

14.2 Business Context Best Practices

14.2.1 When designing decisions, focus on questions and answers

The properties of a decision are described in Sections 8.1.1.4 and 14.2.5. The most important properties of a decision are the question and allowed answers. Strong, specific, context-rich questions help avoid vague or overlapping decisions and illustrate a decision's meaning by defining the 'contract' it upholds with those that use its outcome. A question should specify what the decision provides, what information it needs and how it is typically used. Defining the question and answers of a decision should include:

- The business question that the decision answers in one sentence, using standard vocabulary[38]. This should make the subject of the decision and the context clear.

- The possible answers (outcomes) the decision could have that might influence a business process. These should follow from the question. Every decision should have clearly defined business outcomes.

- Any circumstances in which the decision might fail or be unable to yield a result and how the decision might indicate this.

Two good examples are:
1. Decision 'Select Best Supplier For Order'
    a. Question: Of all known suppliers, which of them fits most of the criteria[39] to fulfil a specific part order?
    b. Answers: Any active and approved supplier from which the part can be sourced.
    c. The answer may be UNKNOWN if no supplier for the part can be found.
2. Decision 'Determine Tax Payable by Taxpayer'
    a. Question: What is the tax payable by a taxpayer given their profit and losses over a financial year?
    b. Answers: An amount of money and a list of IRS[40] approved tax codes representing the rationale for taxes imposed and deductions.
    c. The amount of tax payable is supplied in all cases.

---

[38] Ideally the business vocabulary should be defined in a glossary (see Chapter 9).

[39] Note the deliberate omission of specific qualities (e.g., price, availability quality and supply time) in this question—these factors should be part of the decision and many change with time.

[40] This is just an example of a set of identifiers referenced from a Knowledge Source defining standard tax classes.

A poor example would be one that:

- Uses vague names or undefined terms for the decision name: e.g., 'Process Sourced Data'.

- Refers to unqualified answers: e.g., 'The type of asset', 'How risky is the security'.

- Does not define failure cases where they exist[41].

14.2.2 Specify a main owner for all decisions

A decision may have multiple owners, and this is supported by the DMN standard, but a main owner should be appointed with whom responsibility for the decision ultimately rests. Specifying one ultimate owner in this way helps to resolve conflicts and prevents responsibility being diluted or equivocated. It also identifies cases in which related decisions with different owners have conflicts of interest which might jeopardize accuracy of the outcome. Decision interdependencies that bridge different owners can give rise to a 'responsibility fracture' in which case the hand off of responsibility between the owners must be carefully orchestrated. This can be very dangerous if there are no shared reporting lines between the owners of the decisions involved (see example 17.2.7.1). The two decisions used in 14.2.1 might have owners as follows:

- Decision 'Determine Tax Payable by Taxpayer'
  Taxpayer Services is responsible for this Decision

- Decision 'Select Best Supplier For Order'
  Supply Logistics is responsible for this Decision but Account Management is an interested party

Note that the decision owner is not necessarily the same as the decision maker, the entity which benefits from the decision (see Section 14.2.5).

14.2.3 Align models to business goals and KPIs

Decision definitions should focus on business objectives that are defined exclusively in business terms. Every decision should either have goals defined using quantitative performance metrics, or be part of the dependency network of one that does, long before its logic is even analyzed. This is especially important if the decision sits on the boundary between two different business entities and acts as a vehicle for delivering value from one to the other. For instance, a decision to determine if a proposed trade is ethical, owned by the Trading Ethics Committee, could be a sub-decision required by a decision to approve a trade proposal, owned by Operations. Here the KPI of the sub-decision (to minimize unethical trading) may be distinct from the parent (to maximize trading profit and use of collateral) and this must be explicitly stated.

These goals can be associated with decisions by populating the properties of a decision with the relevant information 14.2.5 (see section 14.2.5). Often this refers to business goals articulated in a motivation mode (see section 10.5 for an example). This information clarifies

---

[41] Naturally it is acceptable for early drafts of a model to lack this detail. However, a complete definition should identify failure cases.

the decision's essential business intent as distinct from details of its current or planned implementation. It defines what a "good" decision outcome looks like.

Aligning decisions with goals and KPIs facilitates the continuous measuring and monitoring of decision performance. Tracking progress towards the defined goals and measuring the KPIs ensures that each decision, and decision management in general, is yielding measurable and meaningful benefit.

Aligning with business goals in this way also allows informed prioritization of resources to modeling efforts such that modeling investment is reasonable given the potential gain.

Any goal associated with a decision should be SMART (Specific, Measurable, assignable, Realistic and Timely) and any KPI should be both measurable and measured. Goals and KPIs mapped to decisions should:

- Be associated with a specific business area (e.g., underwriting of new health insurance policy applications).

- Be assigned as the responsibility of a named business entity, department or role (e.g., underwriting back office).

- Offer an exact means of determining progress or improvement (e.g., percentage of low risk policies referred for manual underwriting per month).

- Be realistically attainable given the time, effort and other costs.

- In the case of a goal, have a specific time period and success boundary (e.g., decrease manual underwriting by 7% over the next two quarters).

- Be truly relevant to the business.

Always cross-check the goals or metrics identified for a decision against the organizations that make the decision. If those making a decision do not share the goals being used to drive the design of the decision they will find its design baffling at best and they may actively undermine it at worst. For instance, a customer retention decision might be designed to balance two metrics—the cost of the retention program and the percentage of customers retained. If the makers of the decision (the call center representatives) are only being measured on retention rate, then they will find the decision-making too passive because it will sometimes make cheaper offers to manage the budget where they would prefer to make the best offer possible at all times.

14.2.4 Use business oriented names for decision model components

All decision model components should be named using a consistent set of terms derived from a glossary. As previously discussed, this set of business terms should be as small as possible and avoid synonyms. Terms should avoid non-specific (weak) words like *Value*, *Type*, *Result* and *Limit* in favor of specific business terms, for example: *Mark-to-market Collateral Value*, *Country Rating Class*, and *Mortgage Value Cap*. Abbreviations should only be used if they are industry or company standard or defined in the glossary. Avoid a profusion of acronyms, even if they are widely understood, as this creates models that are harder to share widely.

Follow the following conventions for each type of decision model component.

14.2.4.1 Naming decisions

Decisions should be named after their outcome. This name may have to be a collective term if there is more than one conclusion attribute. For instance, a decision yielding a loan amount, interest rate and repayment date might have the name *Determine Loan Structure*. The name should be a plural if the decision yields a collection of results (e.g., *Calculate Applicable Fines*).

In decision models featuring decisions of many different types (e.g. calculations, determinations, selections, filters, inferences, verifications, analytics), the name should begin with a strong verb (e.g. 'Calculate', 'Determine', 'Select', 'Filter', 'Infer', 'Verify', 'Analyze') followed by the outcome. If, however, this would result in a model in which almost all of the decision names begin 'Determine' or 'Decide' then the initial verb can be omitted. In all these cases, be led by the needs of the user of the decision model. If a user needs to appreciate the difference between *Estimate Applicant Creditworthiness* versus *Determine Applicant Creditworthiness,* then ensure this is specified.

The name may have to be context specific to distinguish it from others with similar outcomes. For example, if a set of decisions all produce credit ratings, it will be necessary to add adjectives to differentiate them (e.g., *Guarantor Credit Rating, Issuer Credit Rating, Agency Credit Rating*). It may also be necessary to qualify decision names when the decisions categorize inputs rather than deriving them (e.g. *Categorize Credit Score*).

Decision names should not feature literal values that reflect their outcomes (e.g., 'Determine eligibility for 5 days of vacation') or specific thresholds within the decision-making approach. It is better to name them after the business significance of their value (e.g., 'Determine eligibility for long service vacation'). This conveys more information and means the decision names do not need to change if policy (in this case the duration of the vacation) is changed. Use a name selected to express business meaning that will be immune to the most likely dimensions of change.

So far, examples in this book have obeyed the DMN specification's dictate that all Decision Tables are named after the information item that they return (their outcome). In practice this is redundant because this same information item is specified by the output label of the Decision Table. This means that the name (in the top left tag) and output label (the conclusion header) of compliant Decision Tables are always the same. In future examples in this text we abandon this redundancy in favor of a convention we find more useful: the name of a Decision Table is the same as that of the decision it describes. As a consequence, many of the Decision Table names in this and later chapters have verbs at the start of their names.

14.2.4.2 Naming Input Data

Input Data (and simple Decision Table conditions) should be named after the entity (or attribute) they represent (e.g., *Promotion, Instrument Issuer Class, Customer*). Avoid Input Data synonyms.

Input Data names should be singular unless they represent a list or collection of data items. In this case, they should either be pluralized or singular terms like 'Next Best Action List' should be used.

Where multiple instances of a single entity are used for distinct purposes in a decision or play different roles (e.g., the asset classification of *Instruments* can involve two *Counterpar-*

ties: Issuer and *Guarantor)* the Input Data name should be the role followed by the entity name in braces, (e.g., *'Issuer (Counterparty)')*. Therefore, in Figure 14-1, the approach shown on the left is incorrect and the one shown on the right is preferred. See Section 10.3 for more detail on how to associate a decision model with an underlying data model.

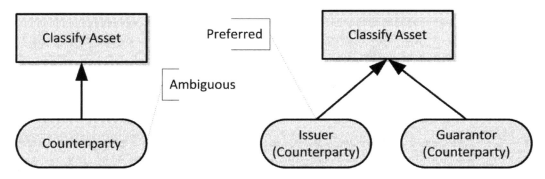

Figure 14-1 Illustration of Input Data with Role Names

14.2.4.3   Naming Knowledge Sources

Knowledge Sources should be named after the policy, constraint, authority or guideline they represent (*e.g., FAA IFR Visibility Minima, ECB Eligibility Constraints, Federal Driving Offense Limits*). Notice how these examples focus on the agency or issuer (e.g., *Federal Aviation Authority, European Central Bank*) and, optionally, the content of the source (e.g., *IFR Visibility Minima, Eligibility Constraints*).

Avoid naming sources after the form of the authority (e.g. by using words like 'database', 'spreadsheet') as this can change and is not substantive. Also include in the name any indication of the level of influence of the Knowledge Source that is apparent from the colloquial name given to them by the organization's business community (e.g., 'Guideline', 'Policy', 'Regulation' or 'Law'). Above all, select a name that will maximize ease of comprehension and traceability to the underlying Knowledge Source.

Knowledge Sources may also be named after roles, departments or groups who have undocumented knowledge. Avoid using an individual's name unless it is genuinely the case that only that named individual can provide the knowledge (a rare case and a situation to be avoided). Personal Knowledge Sources of this kind can be a means of documenting that a company has an undesirable, and hopefully temporary, key person dependency.

14.2.4.4   Naming Business Knowledge Models

Business Knowledge Models should be named after the generic function they embody (e.g., *Calculate Party Credit Limit*). Avoid weak verbs like *Process, Do, Perform*; instead focus on specific verbs like *Calculate, Determine* or *Classify*.

14.2.5 Capture decision properties

When modeling decisions and other decision model artifacts, it is good practice to capture properties—metadata, above and beyond that mandated by the standard itself. These include both those properties discussed in Section 8.1.1.4, that are typically captured during analysis and that document our expectations of the decision, and those that can be obtained from an environment that uses decisions.

14.2.5.1 The properties of decisions

The most important properties of decisions are listed in Table 14-1 and some optional, additional properties are illustrated in Table 14-2. These properties marked with an asterisk (*) are part of the DMN standard.

Name	Description
Business Meaning (specified in discovery)	
Question*	The business question for which the decision provides an answer. Usually this is comprised of free text.
Question - Allowed Answers*	The natural language list of possible outcomes of the decision in answer to the Question. Usually an enumerated value.
Connection with Business Entities (specified in decision discovery)	
Interested Party	Those organization units or business roles that need to be kept informed about the decision.
Decision Maker*	The organizational units or business roles that make the decision.
Decision Owner*	The organizational units or business roles responsible for the decision, its evolution and outcomes. Ideally, only one unit exists, in practice often several do. A main owner should be specified in order to ensure that the ultimate responsibility for the decision's evolution is not lost.
Execution Statistics (specified in decision discovery and monitored in execution)	
Frequency	How often the decision is made. Initially perhaps a qualitative measure, ultimately something more quantitative (e.g., executions per second or a classification of frequency).
Supported Objective*	A list of objectives that represent goals for the decision (e.g., manual referrals to decrease >5% by Q1).
Impacted Performance Indicator*	A list of business key performance indicators by which this decision can be measured (e.g., increase automated processing, increase client retention).
Business Process Context (specified in decision discovery)	
Using Processes*	The business processes which depend on this decision.
Using Tasks*	The process tasks that invoke this decision.
Governance (used to coordinate decision evolution)	
Lifecycle	The stage of evolution of this version of the decision within a governance lifecycle. For instance, one of: New, In Progress, Draft, In Review, Accepted, Rejected, Deployed, Retired.
Business Data Context (specified in decision discovery)	
Type Reference*	The data type of output generated by this decision.

Table 14-1 Decision and Business Knowledge Model Properties (Mandatory)

The optional properties listed here illustrate the real benefit that metadata brings to managing a large repository of decisions, but it is important to stress that these are only used where relevant. Properties should not be captured simply to be complete nor should the assumption be that all decisions identified will require the same set of properties to be documented. Some judgment will be required. Decision modelers may always add their own properties.

Name	Description
Decision Business Properties (specified in decision discovery)	
Complexity	The degree of sophistication of the decision (e.g., the number of boundary conditions).
Confidentiality	The minimum security clearance required to read and edit the decision.
Cost of Failure	The monetary implications of making a mistake with this decision (e.g., a regulatory fine), usually a cost or cost function combining the cost and probability of error.
Cost to Make	The monetary cost of making the decision (e.g., the resource cost).
Cost to Replace	The cost of re-analyzing and re-implementing the decision or Business Knowledge Model if the knowledge is lost, usually a cost or cost function.
Documentation	The URI of any ancillary documents about the purpose, context or history of the decision.
Ease of Valuation	How easy it is to measure operational value (e.g., mechanistic, derived, guess).
Equivocation	The extent to which the decision or model definition is contested (e.g., agreed, has variation, contested) or subject to ambiguity.
Immediacy	The time pressure exerted to get this decision working. Includes the deadline and cost of missing the deadline.
Operational Value	The monetary value of correctly making a decision (e.g., money earned or saved per instance).
Subject to Audit	Whether (or not) the outcome of the decision is subject to audit and if this is internal or external.
Time to Value	The lag between applying the decision and measuring its value. Usually a measure of time.
Value Decay	How quickly the insight provided by a decision loses its value. Usually expressed as a decay function (e.g., exponential with half-life, linear, cutoff) and a length of time.
Decision Performance Statistics (captured in use)	
Performance Assessment	A judgement of how well a decision currently meets its supported objectives. This is an actual performance achievement as measured in selected KPIs or Objectives.
Resource Intensity	The extent to which the decision is resource intensive (CPU or data) to implement. This is a measure of expected execution complexity (e.g., this decision time is proportional to the number of items in a shopping basket) and measured run-time performance.
Change Control (updated continuously as decision evolves)	
Lifetime	The life span of this decision's relevance. The time until the next recertification and revaluation is required. Enforcing this promotes healthy attrition of a decision repository and avoids bloat.
Version Metadata	Version and evolution information.
Volatility	The change frequency, extent of change (e.g., impacted boundary conditions per unit time) and whether change is originated within or from outside the organization.

Table 14-2 Decision and Business Knowledge Model Properties (Optional)

14.2.5.2 Decision model governance properties

A governance process defines the required lifecycle of every decision and decision model component within an enterprise: formalizing the progression of each model from creation to review and from approval to ultimate retirement, constraining the circumstances under which this state can change. A governance process can ensure that models are reviewed as needed and that appropriate sign-off occurs before release. Mature enterprises that require accountability in the management of their decisions will need to use a consistent lifecycle, even if it is dependent on other decision metadata (e.g., it specifies a lifecycle that is more rigorous for confidential or high operation value decisions). Lifecycles are required both to ensure that each decision has undergone the appropriate degree of analysis, review and testing before it is deployed within an automated system (or approved for manual use) and to record the route each decision has taken through this cycle to improve the situational awareness of all decision stakeholders.

14.2.5.3 The properties of Knowledge Sources

The suggested properties of Knowledge Sources are listed in Table 14-3. The properties with an asterisk are part of the DMN standard.

Name	Description
Classification	
Degree of influence	To what extent the Knowledge Source exercises control over logic. For example: dictates, constrains, informs, justifies. For a given Knowledge Source providing authority to many decisions, this may vary by decision but most Knowledge Sources have a general tone that is worth documenting.
Content Type*	The type of source. For instance, law, regulation, policy, standard, know-how, organization (see 8.1.3).
Document URI*	URI to external document embodying the source.
Owner*	The business unit owning this source.
Change Control (updated continuously as decision evolves)	
Volatility	The change frequency and extent of change (e.g., impacted boundary conditions per unit time).

Table 14-3 Properties of Knowledge Sources

14.2.5.4 The properties of Input Data

The standard properties of Input Data components are listed in Table 14-4. The properties with an asterisk are part of the DMN standard.

Name	Description
Classification	
Structure	How structured is the data in this Input Data—is it completely structured data, unstructured data or semi structured data like a document or sensor record?
Dynamism	Where on the spectrum from streaming to static does this data fall?
Source	The origin of this data. For instance, internal data, external or third party data, pooled data collected from multiple organizations.
Owner	The business unit owning this data.
Latency	The sensitivity of this Input Data to time: how 'fresh' should the data be?
Type Reference*	The data type of this Input Data (see Section 9.7)

Table 14-4 Properties of Input Data

14.2.5.5   Universal properties

The properties pertinent to all components of a Decision Requirement Diagram are listed in Table 14-5.

Name	Description
General	
Description*	A business oriented description of the component.
Id*	A unique identifier of the component.
Name*	The name given to the component.

Table 14-5 Properties of All Requirement Components

One optional but useful property of decisions and all other decision model components is classification. This is a means of adding ad-hoc 'tags' to a component that categorizes it in some way. Tags can be simple values (akin to hashtags in social media, for example #Urgent) or key-value pairs (e.g., #NextReviewer='John Smith'). The uses of classification tags include but not limited to categorizing a component's:

- Business meaning (e.g., #DerivativePricing, #Product='Loan', #InheritanceTaxLaw).
- Governance information (e.g., #Tier4Reviewed, #RejectedBy='David Ruthbey', #NextRecertification='04-Aug-2019').
- Geographical or organizational jurisdiction (e.g., #TexasOnly, #State='TX', #Office='FAA').
- Technical evolution (#ForRelease='12-Dec-2016', #Obsolete).

Decision components can use their tags:
- To facilitate query and search.
- To enrich reporting.
- To identify a subset of decision components to undergo a process (e.g., code generation).

- For any other purpose requiring the identification of a subset.

Tags can also be managed in a hierarchy such that, for instance, *#Texas* is below *#US*. If a hierarchy is created in the glossary, then items with subordinate tags are also considered to be tagged with the higher-level tag. For instance, something tagged *#Texas* is also relevant when someone is looking for *#US*. This can be particularly helpful when using tags for projects and repository management but it is only worthwhile if the tooling being used supports this.

14.2.6 Decompose decisions before deciding on automation

Many organizations find the idea of automating decisions intensely uncomfortable. This can result in decisions being pre-emptively added to a "do not automate" list because the organization: wants to keep a manual element to the decision; does not believe it can completely express the logic for the decision or feels that the decision will be too complex to completely express in a reasonable time frame.

Experience shows that rejecting automation too early leaves opportunities unrealized. A best practice therefore is always to model one more layer of requirements below a modeled decision before deciding not to model it fully or automate it. This additional analysis may discover that the need for manual engagement is isolated to one specific aspect of the decision-making or may reveal that there are specific sub decisions that are clear automation opportunities.

For instance, it is common for commercial underwriting decisions to be left unautomated due to their complexity. Modeling them, however, reveals many sub-decisions about locations, companies or individuals. These can and should be fully defined and automated, even if they are part of an overall decision-making approach that also includes significant manual decision-making.

14.3 Decision Requirements Best Practices

14.3.1 Decompose decisions until they rely on separate Input Data and Knowledge Sources

When analyzing decisions for the first time it can be challenging to know when to stop decomposing decision hierarchies into sub-decisions. How much detail is sufficient for a model?

Insufficient decomposition results in complex decisions that fail to expose and resolve concerns and which conceal dependencies on data and Knowledge Sources. They result in hidden detail in Decision Requirement Diagrams and excessive complexity in the underlying Decision Tables or analytic models. Alternatively, over-analysis can yield trite, self-evident decision tables and sprawling decision models. Over specified models are seldom useful to the business and can easily stray from specification to implementation detail. The former documents only what is required from the decision and precisely what this means; the latter describes a specific means of deriving the answer by recourse to an unnecessary sequence of operations and references to implementation technologies. The difference between them is the inclusion of unnecessary detail in the latter (see Section 6.4.2). Both mistakes reduce the value of a model and make comprehension more difficult.

It is generally only worthwhile to further decompose a decision if:

- It is dependent on information that is not provided as Input Data and your enterprise needs to derive this.
- It combines two or more business concerns that evolve independently and that are governed by separate sources of expertise—separate Knowledge Sources.
- The decision can be divided into parts that have different data requirements.

If a decision decomposition yields a set of sub-decisions that share identical Input Data and Knowledge Sources or that have mutual dependencies, this is generally an indication that it is excessive.

The leaves[42] of a Decision Requirements Model, as opposed to a specific Decision Requirements Diagram that shows a subset of it, should be Input Data, not decisions. Only use a decision as a leaf if:

- Its outcome is a constant, perhaps the outcome of a placeholder decision that is expected to be elaborated later;
- Its definition is trivial or unknown *or*
- The decision documents the derivation of data supplied by another party which would be lost if it were an Input Data and which is important to know when using it.

These rules of thumb should be used to 'bottom out' the decision model as a whole.

14.3.2 Represent multiple perspectives using multiple diagrams

A good decision model casts light on a business decision from many angles, but it is not practical to attempt to do this in a single view. Multiple views are required each represented by a different Decision Requirement Diagram.

Consider the documented architecture of a building. All but the most trivial buildings are drafted as a collection of plans, projections, detailed lists and tables. Each of these elements is important but the complete design underlies all the elements and each element must tie into this underlying whole for the architectural design to be consistent. Much of the information is represented visually to promote effective communication to various stakeholders. It would be of limited use (and scarcely possible) to represent an entire architecture on a single diagram. Instead, important aspects of the design are the focus of many individual charts (e.g., projections, elevations, electrical and water subsystems). Some of these have overlapping content but each diagram is designed to present a view of use to specific participants in the project: masons, structural engineers, quantity surveyors, plumbers, electricians and so on.

Similarly, a decision model (the building) should not be confused with a Decision Requirements Diagram (one chart). A decision model contains the detailed properties of many components (e.g., decisions, Input Data, Knowledge Sources) and the web of relationships between them. These relationships form a collection of disjoint decision requirement networks that is much richer than any diagram. Indeed, each Decision Requirements Diagram

---

[42] Those components at the bottom of the tree of dependencies, that are dependent on no other component.

is a visual depiction of **part** of a decision model, just as each architectural chart represents one aspect of a building's design.

There is no need to include the entire model on a single Decision Requirements Diagram and it is nearly always counterproductive to do so—consider the clutter in the example in Figure 14-2.

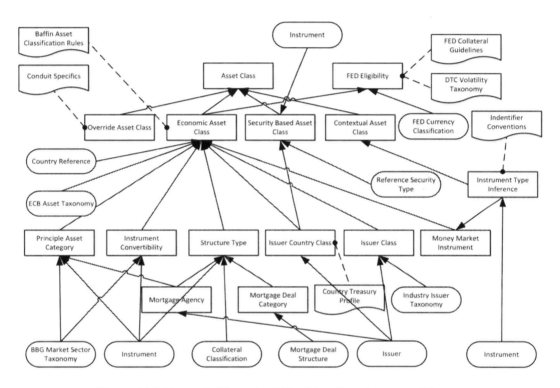

Figure 14-2 Example 'Complete' Decision Requirements Diagram

When building decision models, it is normal to use separate diagrams, each with content potentially overlapping those of others, to show the specifics of a certain viewpoint and meet the needs of stakeholders with a particular perspective.

This need to focus on multiple overlapping views for different purposes makes it hard to produce and maintain these diagrams manually. It means that software tools are important for any non-trivial decision modeling involving multiple stakeholders (see Section 18.5). The best tools can even generate diagrams when requested to depict certain views of specified decisions.

When specific views of a Decision Requirements Model are shown in a Decision Requirements Diagram some information is, by definition, omitted. DMN can represent the fact that information that has been deliberately hidden from a diagram for simplicity (see DMN specification 1.1 section 6.2.4), but has specified no notation to reflect this. For illustration purposes, the Decision Requirements Diagrams that follow in this section use ellipsis markers ('…') to represent elided information. An ellipsis at the bottom of a component indicates that it has hidden requirement relationships with dependents. An ellipsis at the top of a component indicates that other components have requirements on it that are not shown. An alternative would be to use a single ellipsis when any requirements are not shown. This notation is defined and explored further in Section C.1.2.

The following Decision Requirement Diagram views, represented in Figure 14-3 through Figure 14-7, are recommended. Each of them is consistent with the decision model represented by Figure 14-2. Each presents a different perspective of the overall model and together they form a decomposition that is useful for easier presentation and comprehension.

14.3.2.1   Goal oriented view

A goal (or subject) oriented view includes all the components required to support a specific goal decision, but no others (e.g., Figure 14-3) The goal is shaded here for emphasis. This can be a useful means of focusing on a specific end-to-end business decision for specific business experts. By definition these views have only one subject (see Section 8.1.1.3).

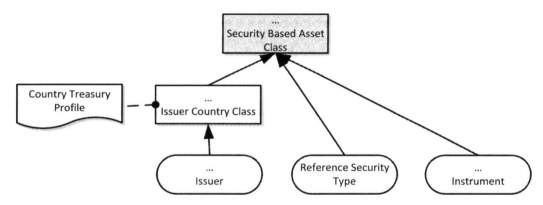

Figure 14-3 Goal Oriented Decision Requirement Diagram

14.3.2.2 Input oriented view

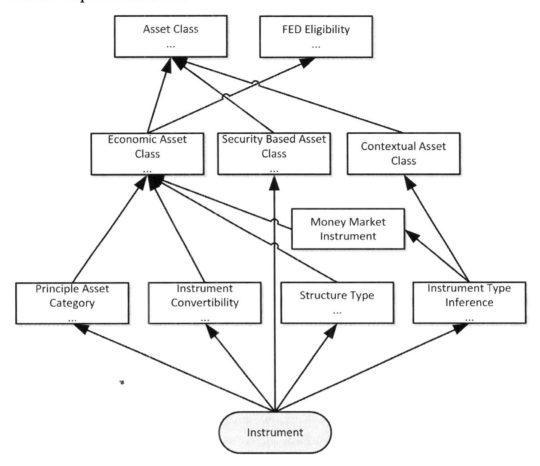

Figure 14-4 Input Oriented Decision Requirement Diagram

An input oriented view includes all the users of a specific Input Data, Knowledge Source or Business Knowledge Model component (e.g., Figure 14-4). Frequently this view is used for data (or knowledge) change impact analysis or to determine the nature of data or knowledge dependencies. If the Input Data is commonly used, these views may have multiple subject decisions as shown in the example.

14.3.2.3 Immediate context view

This view covers all the 'nearest neighbors' of a specific item. (e.g., Figure 14-5). It is used for decision change impact analysis, especially for decisions that are widely reused. Again, as is the case with this example, these views can have multiple subjects.

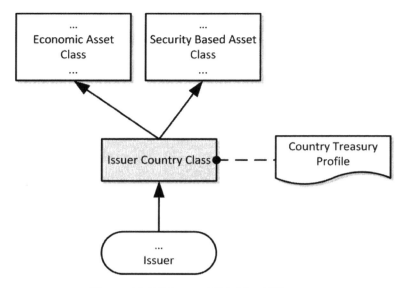

Figure 14-5 'Nearest Neighbor' Diagram

This view is also useful for "top-level" decisions that have no decisions dependent on them—subjects. It is also often a useful development step, where a decision is initially considered as a black box, to start with this view and identify the Input Data and Knowledge Sources it or its sub-decisions will require.

14.3.2.4   Aspect oriented view

This view displays all the items involved in analogous or business related activities or that have some property in common. For instance: all those that are linked to counterparty risk, all those that share a goal of compliance to a mandated regulatory specification or all those that are impacted by a certain change. Aspect oriented diagrams usually depend on decision metadata such as classification, business owners or other properties (e.g., using tags see 14.2.5.5), as a means of filtering what is and is not displayed in the view. The example in Figure 14-6 focuses on instrument type inference decisions. This view is useful to review business activities and facilities consolidation. Although this example only has one, aspect oriented views often have many subjects.

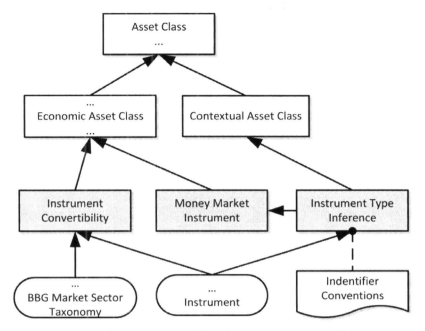

Figure 14-6 Aspect Oriented Decision Requirements Diagram

14.3.2.5   Single leg view

In large decision models, it is often useful to display a part of the model in detail—a decision and its complete set of dependencies—and then to walk "up" the dependencies from this decision to show how it contributes to higher level decisions. An example of this is shown in Figure 14-7. Other branches at these levels are not shown to keep the focus on the particular part of the model being considered.

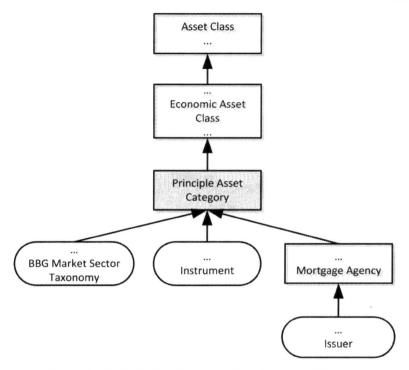

Figure 14-7 Single Leg Decision Requirements Diagram

This technique helps the audience keep track of context without being overwhelmed with detail, particularly when reviewing multiple diagrams.

14.3.3 Document constraints and authorities with Knowledge Sources

Where a decision is constrained or guided by business know how, compliance regulations or legal requirements, the relevant Knowledge Sources must be identified and cited in the model as soon as possible. This is even more important if the Decision Service fulfilling this model is ultimately to be assessed against a body of legislation. This may prevent oversight or infringement of these sources and helps to avoid false paths by grounding the model in the reality of the business context. It may also reveal valuable sources of additional knowledge in the enterprise.

As a decision model is developed, a series of questions can be asked about each to identify possible Knowledge Sources:

- What tells someone what they **must** do when they make the decision? This will identify regulations and policies that direct decision-making.

- What tells someone what they **can** (or cannot) do? This identifies additional regulations and policies that constrain decision-making.

- What tells someone what they **should** do? Best practices, tribal knowledge and expertise will often define practical limits or otherwise direct decision-making.

- What tells someone what they will **probably** do? Historical documents, analytic results or reporting might be available that provides a practical summary of how decisions have been made in the past.

- What would help someone do it **better**? The knowledge of skilled practitioners as well as analytics or data mining results commonly show how a decision-maker might improve their decision-making.

As the model is developed, the Knowledge Sources identified so far will both define the decision logic for decisions identified and will likely also provide insight into the next layer of decisions. These new decisions might be defined using the same Knowledge Sources but may also involve new ones, allowing the Knowledge Sources identified to evolve as the decision model evolves.

Once a model is complete, Knowledge Sources also support the traceability of decision models: both statically—by depicting how each statute of a regulation is supported by the decisions through the use of annotations (see Section 14.5.7)—and dynamically, by allowing Decision Services to persist the annotations associated with selected rules in Decision Tables.

14.3.4 Associate Knowledge Sources with the lowest level decision

As a decision model is developed, and specifically as new levels of decision-making are added, it is important to reconsider existing authority requirements. It is common to find that a Knowledge Source linked as an authority to a 'parent' decision only applies to one or some of the sub-decisions identified when the decision is later decomposed. Similarly, the Knowledge Source may actually have nothing to say about the parent decision it was originally linked to—it may only have knowledge about the sub-decisions. It is important to track this as a model evolves and to reassign requirements at the appropriate level. Developing decision logic will be quicker and more focused if only the most relevant authorities are used and impact analysis will yield more specific results when a Knowledge Source changes and the scope of the impact of this change must be assessed.

An analogous case applies to Information Requirements. An initial model might show that a decision requires an Input Data, but a more detailed analysis might reveal that the decision actually depends only on the results of some sub-decisions, some or all of which require the Input Data. Once again: the more specific the link the better.

14.3.5 Clarify meaning with spatial layout

When creating Decision Requirement Diagrams, the decisions, Input Data and Knowledge Sources and their interconnections convey meaning, but their relative position and orientation do not. The layout of a diagram should therefore always be chosen to maximize ease of comprehension by a viewer without overloading it with meaning. It is often useful to adopt some conventions. For example:

- If the diagram is focused on a specific subject decision, then this subject should be either at the top or the middle of a diagram to emphasize its importance.
- The subject can be further emphasized by: setting its name in bold face, denoting the decision rectangle with a thicker line, making the subject item larger or even by use of a color fill. None of these conventions are part of the standard and such additions should be minimal, consistently applied and as simple as possible. Specific

conventions used by the standard for other purposes should, of course, be reserved for those purposes.

- Avoid the repetition of individual components that connect with many others (e.g., the repetition of *Instrument* in Figure 14-2). It is preferable to draw attention to the importance of this component by fanning connections from a single symbol (see Instrument in Figure 14-4). Complex diagrams (like Figure 14-2) may be forced to repeat items to avoid complex intersections of relationships ('spaghetti'), but this is an indication that the diagram itself requires simplification, perhaps by creating several diagrams each with a more narrowly defined scope (see Section 14.3.2.3).

- The spatial arrangement should be as simple as possible, avoiding 'spaghetti' and information overload. It is almost always more effective to use a larger number of simpler diagrams than one big one.

- Have the 'flow' of dependencies progress in a consistent direction (top to bottom, bottom to top, left or right, inside out) rather than be haphazard or circuitous.

Avoid giving meaning to the relative orientation of items that the standard does not support (e.g., using the left-to-right sequence of sub-decisions to indicate evaluation order in a group of sub-decisions that share an immediate parent). This is only acceptable if used as part of a convention to improve diagram clarity. For instance, using left to right ordering to show a familiar sequence to a reviewer without implying execution ordering.

14.3.6 Clarify Decision Requirement Diagrams with annotations

Model authors should use annotations within Decision Requirement Diagrams, without cluttering them, to denote unusual features or draw the attention of readers to an important part of the diagram. For example:

- When a group of decisions have something in common (the annotation can be used in conjunction with a group box[43], see Figure 14-8).

- When a pattern (see Chapter 16) is applied.

- When some facet of a decision merits special attention.

- When a specific version of a Knowledge Source is required.

- When an imminent change is expected or part of the model is a temporary measure.

- To identify open questions not yet resolved with respect to the model or to document answers only recently added.

Many of these will be removed when the model is complete or finalized, others may be part of the permanent record. Consider the example in Figure 14-8 which uses annotation to show the use of a pattern and to make an observation about the current nature of a decision in the model.

---

[43] Such as that used in BPMN, though this has not been formally adopted in DMN as of 1.1

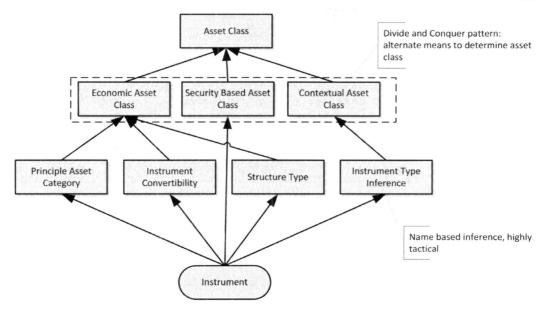

Figure 14-8 Example Decision Requirement Diagram Featuring Annotations

14.4 Decision Logic Best Practices

14.4.1 Remember not all decisions have decision logic

The DMN standard makes it clear that not all decisions have to be described using Decision Tables and that other forms of decision logic, such as decision trees or analytic models, are acceptable (see Section 14.4.4). When using decision modeling, however, it is not always necessary, desirable or even possible to document decision logic for all decisions. A desire to document every decision with decision logic is a common misconception. As noted in Section 13.1, a number of specific scenarios make decision modeling a good choice even if no decision logic is specified.

In addition, the decision might be implemented by an external or otherwise opaque[44] service. The developers of the decision model might have no idea how the decision is made but this need not prevent them knowing its question, allowed answers and information requirements. Documenting this external view of the decision can be extremely helpful, even if the decision logic cannot be specified, as it shows how the outcome of that decision will be consumed as part of a larger decision-making approach. For instance, a third party service might be used to assess whether someone is who they say they are. The strength of likelihood it returns might be a material input to other decisions such as loan approval or check cashing.

---

[44] Perhaps a very old legacy system, the design of which has been lost.

The decision might also be outside the automation boundary and designed to be made manually. There are many examples where the decision logic can and should be completely documented even for a manual decision. However, in some circumstances, it may be neither possible nor desirable to document the decision logic of the decision. The human experts may not be consciously aware of how the decision is made. In these cases, it may make more sense to document suggestions or advice rather than decision logic for the decision. Rarely, the value of a decision lies in the variability of decision-making resulting from having people make the decision. For instance, having investment analysts apply their own logic as part of an investment decision might help ensure a diverse portfolio. In those circumstances being prescriptive about the logic may even be counter to good decision-making.

As a practical matter a decision might also be in development or temporarily unknown. While this is likely to be resolved in the future it may well be necessary to conduct modeling while the decision logic is not specified. In any case, defining the question being answered and the possible answers will allow the decision to be effectively used in modeling in the meantime.

14.4.2 Avoid redundant inputs

Avoid specifying inputs, such as the columns in a Decision Table, that are unnecessary to the logic of the decision. For example, inputs which are always subject to the same test or on which the logic is independent (e.g., Decision Table conditions for that input are populated with '-' throughout or the text of a decision does not refer to the input). Such inputs can appear when sequence is not removed from the model (see Section 14.8.4). If a decision is shown as a requirement for another decision, then its output must be used by that other decision. If the input is a means of transporting data to another stage of decision-making, i.e., it is being used to facilitate sequence, then there will be nothing in the decision-making that depends on it and the input is unnecessary (see Section 16.8 for an example).

Redundant inputs can also occur when subject matter experts have incorrectly assumed that a wide range of data must be available to make a specific decision and this is actually not the case. When these inputs are removed from the logic, be sure to remove the Information Requirement from the Decision Requirements Model also.

14.4.3 Express decision logic in a format inspired by existing business policy statements

Where the logic definition replaces some existing expression of business strategy, perhaps a spreadsheet or policy document, and it is agreed that this existing representation is clear and effective, the logic should emulate the form and terminology of its predecessor as much as possible without contravening other best practices. For instance, the form of a Decision Table can mimic the format of a spreadsheet that analysts have used effectively in the past. The familiarity this engenders improves the ease of logic comprehension and lessens the impact of decision modeling. However, such emulation should not be a parroting of past dogma, historical accident or implementation detail. Any recreation of past formats should only reflect sound, SME-reviewed and approved business practice.

14.4.4 Select an appropriate format for logic

There are a wide variety of formats for representing decision logic only some of which are directly supported by the DMN standard. You should select the representation most suited to purpose. These include:

- Decision Tables of various orientations.
- FEEL Boxed Expressions or invocations (e.g., of a Business Knowledge Model).
- Text (e.g., informal natural language).
- Definition by Example.
- Definition by reference to business rules managed externally (e.g., in a BRMS).
- Decision Trees.
- Analytic Models.
- Optimization Models.

Only the first two of these are currently defined by DMN. All these representations have different pros and cons that can be used to choose between them. Figure 14-9 illustrates an approximate guide to selecting an appropriate representation.

Note that the use of analytic models shown in the mid-left of the diagram need not rule out representation of logic using Decision Tables or Boxed Expressions. The output of some data mining analytics can be expressed as a Decision Table or Decision Tree. A single shot analysis can generate logic in one of these representations which can then be tuned and evolved by subject matter experts as a regular table or tree. Alternatively, a regular data mining exercise can be used to generate periodic updates to a read-only table or tree as analytics are reapplied to new data sets.

14.4.4.1 Use example rules when appropriate

It is often useful to document the decision logic for a decision model using example rules. Developing the decision logic is often very effective at identifying issues in the Decision Requirements Model. If a requirement has been missed, then writing the decision logic for the decision may identify the omission when a condition is clearly required to make a specific rule complete yet that data element is not currently included in the decision's' information requirements. Similarly, writing decision logic can identify requirements that are unnecessary because they represent sequence not requirement. Sometimes it is not necessary to develop all the rules for a decision to check the decision requirements model. Developing a few core example rules is generally sufficient to confirm the basic outlines of the requirements.

Developing only example rules in this way has a number of advantages:

- The rules can be developed in a less rigorous fashion and therefore more rapidly, allowing for a quick check on the Decision Requirements Model early in an iteration.
- If the rules are going to be developed in a different environment from the Decision Requirements Model—for example using: a BRMS, a package's built-in rule engine or some other tool imposed by a supplier—then it saves effort and avoids inconsistency to use example rules in the Decision Logic Level rather than create a complete set of duplicate rules there.

Is the Decision Logic...?

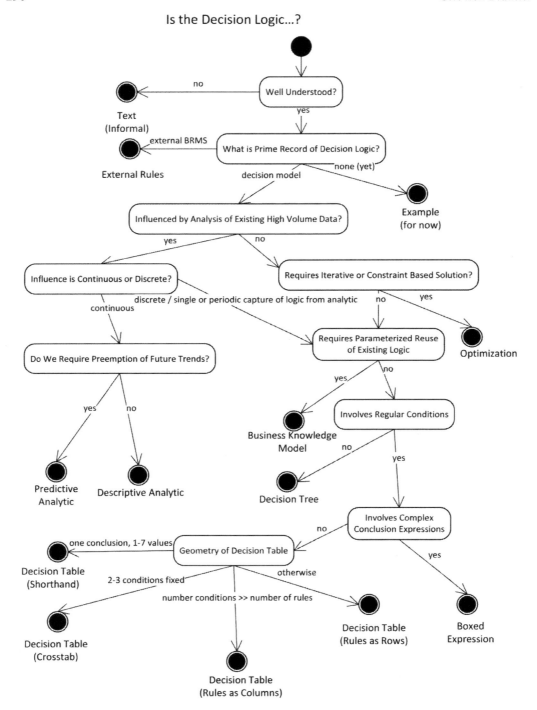

Figure 14-9 Rough Guide to Choosing Logic Representation

- Some rules change continuously—marketing rules or pricing rules might be updated daily for instance. Attempting to capture all these rules as part of as formal model can be futile due to the pace of change. It is often better to use example rules to verify the structure of the logic and then allow the business very direct access to change these rules (within the defined structure) with lighter weight review and governance processes to support the needed agility.

- If the rules are simple, not contentious and yet voluminous, it may be more pragmatic to represent them with examples in early phases of the project to facilitate focus on higher risk areas.

During the iterative development of decision models, it is possible to base informal business logic definitions on examples, that is a series of scenarios for which the inputs and outcome values are documented. This technique is useful if the decision being analyzed is historical, very well understood and presents little risk. This technique is useful when an early, exhaustive definition of a decision would be time consuming and not profitable and in situations where analysts need to prioritize their efforts on poorly understood or risky decisions elsewhere.

If you are documenting a decision using examples, ensure you include enough examples to accurately represent the data requirements of the decision. Example based definitions are very seldom used to represent decision logic in the final state.

14.4.4.2 Use text rules when appropriate

DMN supports decision logic expressed in various textual form: informal if-then-else statements, formal FEEL (boxed) expressions, boxed invocations and the textual equivalent of Decision Tables. Decisions can sometimes benefit from an informal, textual presentation style e.g., when the logic is very simple, when there is uncertainty on the specifics of the logic and a placeholder is required or where a business audience would be alienated by a more formal approach. Such informal statements are seldom recommended as a final state unless the decision is going to remain completely unautomated. Structured and well written natural language—a check list or interview guide for instance—may well be the best way to represent a manual decision or one that is currently partially understood.

There is little benefit in using formal FEEL expressions as opposed to the DMN standard Decision Table representation unless the logic is:

- Very simple (based on two or fewer conditions), making a decision table representation overkill.

- Has a large number of inputs many of which are only used in specific circumstances.

- Is very stable.

- Requires the reuse of a parameterized decision logic (i.e., boxed invocation, see Section B.4.3).

- Requires complex or irregular expressions to generate outcomes (using collection manipulation or function calls).

In all other cases the information presented is identical and the two formats are equally expressive, yet the tabular view is both easier to read because it is more structured, more scalable and easier to modify.

The textual equivalent to a Decision Table should never be used as it is inferior in every way to a tabular representation and is included in the standard only for completeness.

14.4.4.3   Use Decision Trees when appropriate

Decision Trees represent logic as a set of alternate paths diverging from a single starting point. Each path then forks in turn into sub-paths of its own, like branches in a tree. At each fork there is a condition, the answer to which determines which of the many exit paths to take. Ultimately, each path ends with an outcome. DMN does not define a standard format for Decision Trees (yet), but this is a popular means of representing decision logic. Decision Trees are also widely supported in Business Rules Management Systems and are a common result of data mining efforts. For instance, customer segmentation logic is often represented as a Decision Tree.

An example Decision Tree for determining when to sound a cockpit configuration alarm in a jet airliner can be found in Figure 14-10. The purpose of this alarm is to warn pilots if the aircraft is improperly configured for take-off or landing[45]. The tree consists of a set of condition checks on inputs (questions), the answers to which determine either the outcome of the decision or what question to ask next. To read the tree start at the top and work downward. Every possible path ends with an outcome (the tree is complete).

Decision Tables and trees hold the same information: any decision that can be expressed in one form can, more or less effectively, be rendered in the other form. Whereas tables have a grid structure to represent conditions and outcomes, trees use a graph structure. Paths in the tree, like rows in the table, represent sets of conditions which, when satisfied, lead to a specific conclusion.

The key distinction between the two is how well they represent certain types of logic. This depends on the degree of uniformity involved—do most of the rules use the same condition and conclusion headers, or are the conditions used highly varied and dependent on the value of other conditions?

- Tables are preferred when most of the rules in a decision use the same inputs, inputs do not have to be tested in a specific order and each rule yields a conclusion of the same type. Although the actual conditions and conclusion values will vary from row to row the decision logic is *uniform*.

- Trees are preferred when the inputs have to be checked in a certain order because the result of one input condition check determines the next input to be consulted.

- Also, trees work better if there is a wide variation in the inputs used on the different paths—the logic is not uniform.

The equivalent decision table to the tree in Figure 14-10 can be found in Figure 14-11.

---

[45] Naturally this example is considerably more complex on a real aircraft.

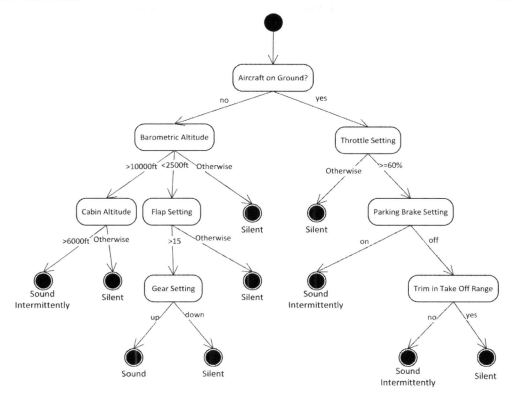

Figure 14-10 Aircraft Configuration Alarm Decision Tree

	Cockpit Config Alarm Status								
U	Aircraft on Ground	Barometric Altitude	Cabin Altitutude	Flap Setting	Gear Setting	Throttle Setting	Parking Brake	Trim in Take Off Range	Configuration Alarm
	YES, NO			UP, 1, 2, 5, 10, 15, 25, 30, 40	UP, DOWN		ON, OFF	YES, NO	SOUND, INTERMITTENT, SILENT
1	NO	>10000	>6000	-	-	-	-	-	INTERMITTENT
2			<=6000	-	-	-	-	-	SILENT
3		<2500	-	<=15	-	-	-	-	SILENT
4			-	>15	DOWN	-	-	-	SILENT
5			-		UP	-	-	-	SOUND
6		[2500..10000]	-	-	-	-	-	-	SILENT
7	YES	-	-	-	-	<60	-	-	SILENT
8		-	-	-	-	>=60	OFF	YES	SILENT
9		-	-	-	-		OFF	NO	INTERMITTENT
10		-	-	-	-		ON	-	INTERMITTENT

Figure 14-11 Aircraft Configuration Alarm Decision Table

Note:

- For any given Decision Tree there is an equivalent Decision Table and vice versa.
- The number of conclusion states at the bottom of the Decision Tree equals the number of rows in the Decision Table.

- A Decision Table representation of non-uniform logic (such as Figure 14-11) has many '-' cells[46]. Many of its inputs are frequently irrelevant to the outcome. It is sparse and therefore a Decision Tree would be a better, more easily understood representation.

- A Decision Tree representation of uniform logic (see Figure 14-13) is often large and repeats conditions; a Decision Table would be more compact.

- One advantage (and drawback) of a decision tree is that it imposes a sequence on the determination of the decision.

Another advantage of Decision Trees is that they can be intuitive and easy to read. It is no coincidence that many publications that need to describe complex logic to professionals outside of IT use Decision Trees as their medium of choice (including this example when presented to real pilots).

For uniform decision logic, in which the same conditions are used in all cases, a decision tree representation is less applicable and suffers from repetition of conditions. Consider the tabular representation of Figure 14-12, designed to determine the discount applicable to a specific item in a shopping cart. Figure 14-13 shows the equivalent Decision Tree representation. Each path has nearly identical conditions so the tree is less compact than the table.

It should also be apparent that trees also do not scale as well as tables. A completely uniform table with five inputs and twenty rows is manageable; the equivalent tree would have 100 question nodes!

Discount				
U	Item Category	Item Price	Date	Discount
				0,[1..100]
1	PHOTOGRAPHY	>100	<= 2018-12-31	2%
2	DOMESTIC ELECTRICAL	>500	<= 2018-05-31	4%
3	MENS FASHION	-	<= 2016-06-15	2%
4	LADIES FASHION	>200	<= 2018-06-15	3%

Figure 14-12 Example Discount Decision Table

---

[46] This example has been simplified, the real logic in this case is much less uniform.

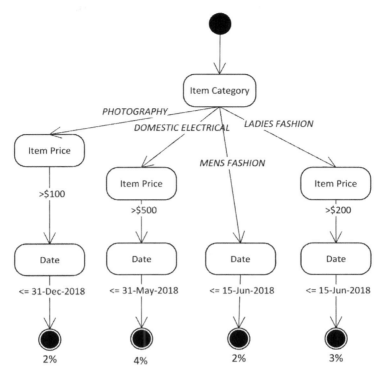

Figure 14-13 Decision Tree with Uniformity of Conditions

Decision Graphs are a somewhat unusual extension of Decision Trees that allow sub-trees to be reused. These are significantly more manageable when the logic is complex but are not commonly supported in BRMSs. Both Decision Trees and Decision Graphs can be more challenging to change and keep consistent than Decision Tables and require sophisticated tool support.

14.4.4.4 Use analytic models when appropriate

Analytic models in decision modeling might be descriptive analytic models or predictive analytic models. Descriptive analytic models classify, categorize or associate existing things based on historical data. They use current and historical data to deduce something about the current state. Predictive analytic models use historical data to infer the likelihood that something will be true in the future. They have been described as turning uncertainty about the future into a usable probability. One cannot always know, for instance, which insurance claims are fraudulent but it is possible to predict how likely it is that a specific claim is fraudulent.

In both cases, mathematical analysis of historical data is used to identify the patterns the data contains that might allow the categorization, classification, prediction or estimation of something of business interest. Rather than interviewing experts or reviewing a document, data is analyzed to see how something can be calculated, derived or decided. Generally, the raw data (Input Data) is first transformed into more analytical data elements and then mathematical algorithms such as clustering, regression, neural networks, tree analysis or forecasting are applied.

In terms of decision modeling:

- An analytic model can be described in terms of a question and allowed answer. For instance: 'what is the probability that this claim is a fraudulent one?': a number between 0 and 1. This means that a decision can be shown in a decision model that is best represented not by explicit decision logic, but by a predictive analytic model—an algorithm.

- Analytic models are often initially represented by Knowledge Sources in a decision model. In this form, they represent knowledge gained from the mathematical analysis of data and can be linked to the data from which they are derived (see Section 15.2.4).

- As a decision model is extended and detailed it is likely that a specific decision will be added to the model that represents the decision made using the analytic model itself. The decision's information requirements will represent the data consumed by the model while the result of the model—its score or classification for instance—will be represented by the data structure of the decision's outcome.

The DMN standard actually defines how an analytic model can be represented within a decision model. For instance, DMN allows the Predictive Model Markup Language (PMML[47]), a standard notation, independent of DMN, to be used to describe a decision based on a predictive analytic model. PMML files are never built by hand but are generated by data mining and predictive analytic development tools and algorithms. A PMML file contains several elements:

- A header describing the file.

- A Data Dictionary that describes the data that needs to be provided to execute the model (`DataField`). Ensure that this is consistent with any data model or glossary supporting the decision model.

- Data transformations that turn the raw data passed to the model into the data fields needed by the analytic model if these are different.

- One or more models. Different models (clustering, neural network, decision trees) have different structures but generally these include the mining schema—the subset of fields used in this model (`TreeModel`).

- Output definitions such as the predictive value, probability, reason codes etc. (`OutputField`).

Figure 14-14 shows a summary example of a PMML model with a single input `DataField` expanded to show the allowed `Values`, the `OutputFields` of the model (the results) and some of the other nodes in the Decision Tree. In this case the model is a Decision Tree built on the Audit dataset provided in the R Rattle package. This is a fictional dataset that is intended to categorize clients based on how likely an audit of their finances is to find errors

---

[47] PMML is supported by the Data Mining Group and information is available at www.dmg.org

in their reporting. The output is the likelihood of a productive or non-productive audit given various client characteristics.

```
<PMML xmlns="http://www.dmg.org/PMML-3_2" xmlns:xsi="http://www.w3.org/2001/XMLSchema-instance" version="3.2"
xsi:schemaLocation="http://www.dmg.org/PMML-3_2 http://www.dmg.org/v3-2/pmml-3-2.xsd">
 <Header copyright="Copyright (c) 2012 DMG" description="RPart Decision Tree
  Model">...</Header>
 <DataDictionary numberOfFields="10">
  <DataField name="as.factor(TARGET_Adjusted)" optype="categorical"
   dataType="string">...</DataField>
  <DataField name="Age" optype="continuous" dataType="double"/>
  <DataField name="Employment" optype="categorical" dataType="string">...</DataField>
  <DataField name="Education" optype="categorical" dataType="string">...</DataField>
  <DataField name="Marital" optype="categorical" dataType="string">...</DataField>
  <DataField name="Occupation" optype="categorical" dataType="string">...</DataField>
  <DataField name="Income" optype="continuous" dataType="double"/>
  <DataField name="Gender" optype="categorical" dataType="string">
   <Value value="Female"/>
   <Value value="Male"/>
  </DataField>
  <DataField name="Deductions" optype="continuous" dataType="double"/>
  <DataField name="Hours" optype="continuous" dataType="double"/>
 </DataDictionary>
 <TreeModel modelName="RPart_Model" functionName="classification"
  algorithmName="rpart" splitCharacteristic="binarySplit"
  missingValueStrategy="defaultChild">
  <MiningSchema>...</MiningSchema>
  <Output>
   <OutputField name="as.factor(TARGET_Adjusted)" optype="categorical"
    dataType="string" feature="predictedValue"/>
   <OutputField name="Probability_0" optype="continuous" dataType="double"
    feature="probability" value="0"/>
   <OutputField name="Probability_1" optype="continuous" dataType="double"
    feature="probability" value="1"/>
  </Output>
  <Node id="1" score="0" recordCount="2000" defaultChild="2">
   <True/>
    <ScoreDistribution value="0" recordCount="1537" confidence="0.7685"/>
    <ScoreDistribution value="1" recordCount="463" confidence="0.2315"/>
    <Node id="2" score="0" recordCount="1083">...</Node>
    <Node id="3" score="0" recordCount="917" defaultChild="6">...</Node>
  </Node>
 </TreeModel>
</PMML>
```

Figure 14-14 Example PMML Decision Tree Model

PMML, like DMN, is a broadly supported standard and many analytic models can be represented in PMML. Most analytic tools and languages that can be used to develop analytic models allow the export of models in PMML, allowing the model to be interchanged with other modeling environments but also allowing the model to be integrated into a Decision Management System and into a decision model. The Data Mining Group continually update and refine PMML to support a broader array of models and add more nuances to models already supported in the standard. This has allowed PMML to become an established interchange format for analytic models.

Literal expressions can invoke the PMML model as can a boxed function (an example of such an invocation can be found in Section B.4.7). The Data Dictionary defined for the model should match the information requirements for the analytic decision or the parameters defined for the analytic Business Knowledge Model. Allowed values defined in the model should match those defined in the glossary for the decision model as a whole. The outputs from the model should match the decision's or Business Knowledge Model's result structure so that they can be effectively consumed by other decisions in the model.

It is also worth noting that some decision logic formats can be used to represent the results of data mining efforts. For instance:

- A Decision Tree might be built not by experts selecting the appropriate branching criteria but by analyzing historical data to see which criteria result in the most clearly delineated branches, e.g. for customer segmentation.

- A multi-hit Decision Table using the Collect or Collect-Sum hit policies can be used to represent an additive scorecard that has been derived from a predictive analytic, as is widely done in credit scoring for instance (see the Scorecard pattern in Section 16.1).

- Rules, written in FEEL or not, might represent the results of data mining for associations such as products sold together.

Even when decision logic appears to be driven by a policy document, it is worth considering how that policy was derived—was data analyzed to develop the policy? If so, it is better thought of as an analytic Knowledge Source that should be periodically reconsidered when the data changes.

14.4.4.5   Use optimization models when appropriate

Occasionally, a decision modeler needs to use a decision that cannot be expressed with analytics or rule based logic—or at least that cannot be reasonably expressed that way. Some decisions need to derive an optimum result (or set of results) given a set of conflicts and limitations. These can be expressed as optimization decisions. In the context of decision modeling, an optimization model refers to a mathematical construct that defines a problem that can be solved using mathematical optimization or constraint programming.

At the core of such a model is an objective function that defines how to calculate the measure that must be optimized. A set of decision variables, representing choices available to this function, is also defined along with a set of constraints on what is allowable. At run time, a constraint-based engine or solver can be used to find the best possible result for the objective functions given a set of values and the constraints. Linear programming and mixed integer programming many also be used. This generally involves maximizing or minimizing the function but can also involve finding possible solutions. Examples include finding the minimum distance for a delivery route, the maximum value of goods that can be produced given various supplies and equipment and finding all possible ways to schedule a group of people to cover certain activities that each require specific skills.

In a decision model the information requirements for an optimization model decision will be its decision variables and constraint values (where these are not fixed) and the result of the decision will be constrained by the objective function.

For example, in deciding on the best layout for a set of equipment in a compact space, a decision model might involve several decisions that result in lists of equipment that must be placed. These are then required by an optimization decision, along with Input Data representing information about the available space. This decision finds all possible combinations of equipment that can be packed into the available space given constraints that might prevent certain kinds of equipment being placed next to each other. The resulting list of possible layouts is the output from the optimization model decision. These can then be consumed by another decision that ranks those layouts using business rules to reflect customer preferences and perhaps an analytic model that predicts how easy each layout will be to maintain and repair by comparison with historical designs.

14.5 Decision Table Best Practices

14.5.1 Adopt a consistent Decision Table format

DMN has three different format classes for decision tables: 'rules as rows', 'rules as columns' and crosstab (see 11.2.7). In addition, there are a number of stylistic variations: for example: merged cells (to reflect repeated conditions) and the DMN shorthand notation. Tables in any of these formats can be translated into any other representation with no loss of meaning but the following constraints exist on their use:

- 'Rules as rows' works best if the number of rules is likely to exceed the sum of the number of inputs and outputs. This occurs in simple decisions that have many combinations of condition values but a small number of inputs.

- 'Rules as columns' works best if there are fewer rules than the total number of inputs and outputs combined. This occurs in very complex decisions with few rules.

- 'Crosstab' works best when there is only a single output and the decision has 2-4 inputs. Each input should have no more than five condition classes of interest and nearly all of the condition combinations should be meaningful.

- The 'Shorthand' variation can be used in 'rules as rows' and 'rules as columns' Decision Tables. It works only when there is one conclusion and, ideally this should be an enumerated type with ten or fewer possible values. This can be a useful format if there is a need to reflect the pattern of conclusion value selection for every condition combination or to ensure that each possible conclusion value is selected by at least one rule. Generally, however, this small advantage is not worth the constraints the format imposes and the overhead of using multiple formats.

These constraints make one of the formats preferable to the others in a given situation. Crosstab is very occasionally useful when every single combination of condition values must be considered, but quickly becomes hard to understand for more than three conditions. It is not a flexible format and required change to the Decision Table over time is likely to invalidate its constraints. Therefore, widespread use should be avoided unless it is currently, and likely to remain, a good fit for requirements as well as one that is familiar and liked by business SMEs.

Rather than use all of these variations and confuse business users with the wealth of different formats, it is better to adopt a single format. If an external BRMS is involved in the solution architecture, this should be a format supported by the BRMS so that users will find its presentation of decision logic familiar. This format should then be used whenever possible, adopting another only when it is necessitated by the considerations discussed above.

As Decision Tables with more than eight rules are common and those with more than eight inputs can be avoided by careful factoring of logic (see the Divide and Conquer pattern in Section 16.2), it is best to adopt 'rules as rows' as the default format. In our experience this is the best format to use as your default representation. In the remainder of this book we assume this format and consider 'rule' to be synonymous with 'row'. References to 'rows' should be read as 'columns' if you wish to apply these concepts to rows as columns tables.

14.5.2 Use only Unique, Any and Collect hit policies

Experience indicates that newcomers to decision modeling should select the hit policy (see Section 11.2) of a Decision Table based on the following guidelines:

- If a single outcome is required use the Unique hit policy. Unless…
  - o you wish to fire multiple results and aggregate the results into a single outcome. In this case consider using the Collect with Aggregation hit policy (see Section 11.2.2.5).
  - o there are more than ten rules that yield the same result and adding rules to disambiguate all of these possibilities is counter-productive. In this case consider using the Any hit policy (see Section 11.2.2.2).
  - o The table has 15 rules or fewer, is certain never to grow and benefits considerably from the simplification of order-based tables (see Section 15.3.3 for full details). In which case consider using the First or Priority hit policies.

- If multiple outcomes are required use the Collect hit policy (see Section 11.2.3.1).

As far as possible, avoid the First hit policy unless the simplification that results is very significant (see Section 15.3.1.2). Order dependent Decision Tables are hard to understand and maintain above seven rules.

Avoid the use of the Priority hit policy unless you explicitly need the ability to have some rules override others according to their conclusion value. This can be a powerful idiom if used sparingly and only on small Decision Tables.

Likewise, do not use the Rule or Output Order hit policy in a Decision Table for generating ordered collections because assigning meaning to the order of items in a collection makes that collection harder to use by other decisions. If a sorted list is required, the Rule and Output Order hit policies are rarely flexible enough to support it. Instead, use a Collect policy Decision Table to produce the list and use another decision to sort it.

Collect is the only multi-hit policy that is frequently useful (see Scorecard pattern 16.1)—either to produce a single result (Collect with Aggregator) or multiple results (Collect without Aggregator).

14.5.3 Do not assign multiple jobs to a single Decision Table

One of the biggest barriers to understanding Decision Tables is excessive complexity. Large Decision Tables are simply challenging to understand. This can frequently arise if a modeler commits to a Decision Table layout before completing decision requirements modeling or attempts to pack too much detail into a table. This can result in:

- A large number of inputs and outputs (more than seven is usually undesirable).
- A large number of rules (more than a few hundred is cumbersome).
- Complex input expressions, conditions or outputs (e.g., lengthy formulae or contexts).
- Repetitive rule logic resulting from incompletely normalized decision-making.

These challenges to comprehension can be often avoided by splitting dense Decision Tables into simpler, separate, cooperating sub-decisions each of which addresses a separate aspects of the requirement or by using contexts (8.2.5) to isolate the definition of complex derived terms from the main body of the table. To avoid or repair complex Decision Tables it is important to understand why the tables are so large initially.

A common mistake in designing Decision Tables is to compress multiple independent decisions into one large table for the sake of 'brevity'. Especially large examples (the authors have seen decision table proposals in excess of 200,000 cells expressing eight combined decisions!) are referred to as 'Swiss Army Knife' tables because they combine so many separate purposes. This is often driven by a misguided desire to see all the logic in one place or a reluctance to refactor an evolving table. Frequently, it is a hangover from the business analysts' tendency to build all-encompassing spreadsheets that express many ideas on one sheet.

Although they may appear to have the advantage of creating a single point of reference for all business behavior, Swiss Army Knife tables are not a good idea because they:

- Obscure individual decisions by mixing them with others.
- Discourage independent evolution of the decisions.
- Make reuse of individual decisions harder.
- Make validation, testing and maintenance of individual decisions harder.
- Needlessly complicate maintenance of Decision Tables by inviting accidental modification of one aspect of their behavior during the intentional alteration of another.
- Cause the table to grow exponentially, easily exceeding the size of the separate Decision Tables when expressed individually.

Tables can usually be refactored to avoid these problems. Some Swiss Army Knife Decision Tables have multiple outputs that are not related. Combing these unrelated outputs results in repetition of conditions and bloat. These can be resolved by splitting tables to address decisions individually (see Section 15.3.4.1).

Other Swiss Army Knife tables arise when there is only one output but multiple unrelated ways of determining that output that use different inputs. These large tables are characterized by non-overlapping clumps of conditions as stylized in Figure 14-15. These 'islands' of dependencies use different subsets of table inputs to determine the output; all other inputs are ignored; hence the tables are often sparse[48]. Because the islands don't overlap they can be separated into distinct tables. (see the *Divide and Conquer* pattern 16.2).

---

[48] Those with large numbers of irrelevant condition cells ('–').

Decision Table									
U	input 1	input 2	input 3	input 4	input 5	input 6	input 7	input 8	conclusion
1	condition 1.1	condition 2.1	condition 3.1	condition 4.1	-	condition 6.1	-	-	conclusion output 1
2	condition 1.2	condition 2.2	condition 3.2	condition 4.2	-	condition 6.2	-	-	conclusion output 2
3	condition 1.3	condition 2.3	condition 3.3	condition 4.3	-	condition 6.3	-	-	conclusion output 3
4	condition 1.4	condition 2.4	condition 3.4	condition 4.4	-	condition 6.4	-	-	conclusion output 4
5	condition 1.5	condition 2.5	condition 3.5	condition 4.5	-	condition 6.5	-	-	conclusion output 5
6	condition 1.6	condition 2.6	condition 3.6	condition 4.6	-	condition 6.6	-	-	conclusion output 6
7	-	-	-	-	condition 5.7	-	-	-	conclusion output 7
8	-	-	-	-	condition 5.8	-	-	-	conclusion output 8
9	-	-	-	-	condition 5.9	-	-	-	conclusion output 9
10	-	-	-	-	condition 5.10	-	-	-	conclusion output 10
11	-	-	-	-	condition 5.11	-	-	-	conclusion output 11
12	-	-	-	-	condition 5.12	-	-	-	conclusion output 12
13	-	-	-	-	condition 5.13	-	-	-	conclusion output 13
14	-	-	-	-	condition 5.14	-	-	-	conclusion output 14
15	-	-	-	-	condition 5.15	-	-	-	conclusion output 15
16	-	-	-	-	condition 5.16	-	-	-	conclusion output 16
17	-	-	-	-	-	condition 6.17	condition 7.17	condition 8.17	conclusion output 17
18	-	-	-	-	-	condition 6.18	condition 7.18	condition 8.18	conclusion output 18
19	-	-	-	-	-	condition 6.19	condition 7.19	condition 8.19	conclusion output 19

Figure 14-15 Stylized Representation of Non-Cohesive Decision Table

Other Swiss Army Knife Decision Tables have large numbers (many hundreds) of rules in which the conclusions are uniformly dependent on the same set of conditions. These can be separated by classifying the rules into distinct business classes and handling these as separate Decision Tables. This requires that the classification scheme used is both meaningful from a business perspective (it presents a useful scheme to partition the logic, for example product, regional or customer type) and that it can yields partitions of approximately equal size—so that the size of the largest partitioned table is significantly smaller than the original.

The best approach of all is to avoid Swiss Army Knife tables. Ensure each decision table is addressing a single issue and rely on decision requirement models to tie decisions together into a coherent whole.

14.5.4 Ensure Decision Tables cover all logical possibilities

Where possible, ensure that the logic of your Decision Tables cover all possible eventualities. This can be achieved by specifying a default value using a conclusion value list, explicitly specifying all possible cases or using catchalls.

Specifying a default outcome by using a conclusion value list (see Section 8.2.3.7) can be an elegant solution. For example, in the (otherwise incomplete) table of Figure 14-16 notice that the default value *DOWN* is underlined. The use of a default makes the table complete. This is a useful approach even if the default is not strictly needed. For instance, in a complete Unique hit policy table.

U	Aircraft Spoiler Position			
	Aircraft on Ground	Spoiler Control	Brakes Applied	Aircraft Spoiler Position
	true, false	DOWN, ARM, UP	true, false	DOWN, UP
1	true	ARM	true	UP
2		UP	-	UP
3	false	UP	-	UP

Figure 14-16 Use of Default in Incomplete Unique Decision Table

Another solution is to express all possible logical cases explicitly in a Unique or Any hit policy Decision Table such as that shown in Figure 14-17. This has the advantage that the behavior is clearer and less easily missed than the underlined default value representation shown previously.

U	Aircraft Spoiler Position			
	Aircraft on Ground	Spoiler Control	Brakes Applied	Aircraft Spoiler Position
	true, false	DOWN, ARM, UP	true, false	DOWN, UP
1	true	DOWN	-	DOWN
2		ARM	true	UP
3			false	DOWN
4		UP	-	UP
5	false	DOWN, ARM	-	DOWN
6		UP	-	UP

Figure 14-17 Explicit Expression of All Logical Cases

However, one disadvantage of this approach is that, for very intricate logic, it can become very large and convoluted.

Finally, a row of '–' conditions can be used to denote a *catchall* (failsafe) condition in a First hit policy Decision Table. A catchall is a rule that succeeds only if all others fail, for example row 3 in Figure 14-18.

F	Aircraft Spoiler Position			
	Aircraft on Ground	Spoiler Control	Brakes Applied	Aircraft Spoiler Position
	true, false	DOWN, ARM, UP	true, false	DOWN, UP
1	true	ARM	true	UP
2	-	UP	-	UP
3	-	-	-	DOWN

Figure 14-18 Example '-' Row Catchall

This application of a '–' row must be the last row on a table and is equivalent to a default result for the table. It is less elegant than a default value because it requires the First hit policy with all of its attendant disadvantages (see Section 15.3.3) and because the row must be the last one so that it does not disable any rules that follow it. However, it has the advantage of being more visually obvious—the default notation of Figure 14-16 is subtle and easy to overlook—and it allows the default value to be an arithmetic expression (a simple expression in DMN parlance, see Section B.5.5) rather than just a literal value specified by the value list. Despite this, it is best practice to use default values rather than a row of '−' unless there is a compelling case to use the First hit policy and the table will remain small.

This use of catchalls to make tables complete should only be used if the table expresses many intricate exceptional cases that have specific conclusions and a need to explicitly define some default conclusion in all *other* cases. In these scenarios, the only alternative solution is the explicit representation of all the *other* cases (i.e., the negation of all the intricate exception cases) which can be complex, error prone and a maintenance hazard. However, for simpler examples like the aircraft spoiler logic, the explicit statement of all possible conditions in Figure 14-17 is preferred to the briefer (but more complex and less scalable) Figure 14-18.

In summary, the best practice here is to use a complete Unique hit policy table to express every logical case. If this is too convoluted or results in maintenance issues, simplify the table to be incomplete and use conclusion value list defaults. The use of First hit policy catchalls should be a last resort.

The use of '−' row as a catchall can be dangerous if conditions are an enumerated type that has a range of permitted values that changes frequently (see Sections 9.7.4 and 14.6.1.5). This is because the occurrence of new enumerated values is not accommodated by the Decision Table and will always exercise the catchall even if this is not appropriate. Tables with defaults or catchalls are complete by definition so validation of a decision model after changing the definition of an enumeration will never reveal any flaws.

14.5.5 Be explicit about failure modes

Some decisions can fail. Under certain circumstances, they are incapable of rendering an outcome. In the case of a multi-hit Decision Table it may be that one or more rules cannot make a contribution to the collection of outcomes. In the case of a single-hit Decision Table there may be no outcome at all. These situations should be documented clearly by using 'failure' rules, rather than handling them by omission. A failure rule uses the '−' marker or null in a conclusion (see 8.2.4.1) to show that a specific rule within a Decision Table yields no outcome.

It is acceptable to use the '−' marker in Collect, Output Order and Rule hit policy tables to indicate that a rule has no contribution to make to the outcome selection or aggregation.

The use of the '−' marker or null in a conclusion should be avoided for Unique, Any, First and Priority hit policy tables because such use is ambiguous—it doesn't tell the reader the meaning of the outcome. The intent of the unspecified conclusion could be to represent:

- An error.
- An empty result, generally in the case of a decision table with multiple conclusion columns.
- An impossible case for the sake of decision table completeness.
- Another special case recognized by the modeler.

Instead, modelers should document precisely what is meant by the conclusion. If the conclusion is an enumeration use special values to explain the outcome (e.g., **UNSPECIFIED**, **UNKNOWN**, see Section 14.6.1.4).

It is best practice for decisions in the public section of a Decision Service to yield an explicit result in all cases. Furthermore, use of the '−' marker in a conclusion should always be annotated (see Section 8.2.4.1).

14.5.6 Refactor Decision Tables to keep them as small as possible

Decision Tables should be written carefully to prevent needless bulk and the repetition of conditions and conclusions. Consider for example the Decision Table of Figure 14-20, designed to determine the *Driver Risk Level* given the driver's age, car type and whether or not the vehicle has customized modifications to enhance its performance (*has Modifications*).

The level of logic repetition in this table is unacceptable because: it needlessly increases the table's size, making it harder to understand; the repetition suggests an inherent policy which should be made explicit (e.g., that certain groups of cars share a higher level of risk than others and that enhancements increase this risk) and the table could easily be inconsistently edited in a manner that breaks this inherent policy. For example, are rules 38-40 deliberately inconsistent with the style of the policy expressed in other rules or was this the result of an error during editing? An explicit policy would make these cases easier to separate.

Just as data can be normalized to reduce repetition and the opportunity for inconsistency, so can Decision Tables. An immediate improvement can be obtained by gathering the car groups that exhibit the same behavior (e.g., *COMPACT, ECO, SMART*) into a single rule to make the group explicit. Applying this 'grouping' to the entire table yields the Decision Table in Figure 14-21.

	Driver Risk Level			
U	Driver Age	Car Type	has Modifications	Driver Risk Level
1	<21	-	-	VERY HIGH
2	[21..29]	COMPACT	false	MEDIUM
3			true	HIGH
4		ECO	false	MEDIUM
5			true	HIGH
6		SMART	false	MEDIUM
7			true	HIGH
8		HATCHBANK	false	HIGH
9			true	VERY HIGH
10		LUXURY	false	VERY HIGH
11			true	VERY HIGH
12		SPORTS	false	VERY HIGH
13			true	VERY HIGH
14		SUPER	false	VERY HIGH
15			true	VERY HIGH
16	[30..65]	COMPACT	false	LOW
17			true	MEDIUM
18		ECO	false	LOW
19			true	MEDIUM
20		SMART	false	LOW
21			true	MEDIUM
22		HATCHBANK	false	MEDIUM
23			true	HIGH
24		LUXURY	false	HIGH
25			true	VERY HIGH
26		SPORTS	false	HIGH
27			true	VERY HIGH
28		SUPER	false	HIGH
29			true	VERY HIGH
30	>65	COMPACT	false	MEDIUM
31			true	HIGH
32		ECO	false	MEDIUM
33			true	HIGH
34		SMART	false	MEDIUM
35			true	HIGH
36		HATCHBANK	false	MEDIUM
37			true	HIGH
38		LUXURY	-	VERY HIGH
39		SPORTS	-	VERY HIGH
40		SUPER	-	VERY HIGH

Figure 14-20 Repetitive Decision Table

Driver Risk Level				
U	Driver Age	Car Type	has Modifications	Driver Risk Level
1	<21	-	-	*VERY HIGH*
2	[21..29]	*COMPACT, ECO, SMART*	false	*MEDIUM*
3			true	*HIGH*
4		*HATCHBACK*	false	*HIGH*
5			true	*VERY HIGH*
6		*LUXURY, SPORTS, SUPER*	false	*VERY HIGH*
7			true	*VERY HIGH*
8	[30..65]	*COMPACT, ECO, SMART*	false	*LOW*
9			true	*MEDIUM*
10		*HATCHBACK*	false	*MEDIUM*
11			true	*HIGH*
12		*LUXURY, SPORTS, SUPER*	false	*HIGH*
13			true	*VERY HIGH*
14	>65	*COMPACT, ECO, SMART, HATCHBACK*	false	*MEDIUM*
15			true	*HIGH*
16		*LUXURY, SPORTS, SUPER*	-	*VERY HIGH*

Figure 14-21 Table with Groups Identified

This is an improvement, being less than half the size, but the table still exhibits a great deal of repetition. Both the *Car Type* groups and the *has Modification* conditions are still repeated. A further improvement can be achieved by *factoring* the table into two: one that determines the risk of a vehicle type (see Figure 14-23) and another which uses age and vehicle class risk to determine the overall *Driver Risk Level* (see Figure 14-24). This change is reflected in the before (left) and after (right) Decisions Requirement Diagrams shown in Figure 14-22.

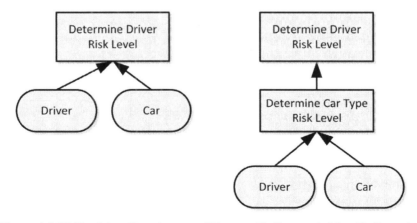

Figure 14-22 Decision Requirement Diagram Before and After Refactoring

Car Type Risk Level			
U	Car Type	has Modifications	Car Type Risk Level
1	ECO, SMART, COMPACT	false	*LOW*
2		true	*MEDIUM*
3	HATCHBACK	false	*MEDIUM*
4		true	*HIGH*
5	*LUXURY, SPORTS, SUPER*	-	*HIGH*

Figure 14-23 Table to Determine Car Type Risk Level

The combination of these last two Decision Tables behaves identically to those of Figure 14-20 and Figure 14-21 but is collectively more compact. These smaller Decision Tables are easier to read, make the vehicle group policy explicit and are less likely to introduce inconsistency when amended.

Driver Risk Level			
U	Driver Age	Car Type Risk Level	Driver Risk Level
1	<21	-	*VERY HIGH*
2	[21..29]	*LOW*	*MEDIUM*
3		*MEDIUM*	*HIGH*
4		*HIGH*	*VERY HIGH*
5	[30..65]	*LOW*	*LOW*
6		*MEDIUM*	*MEDIUM*
7		*HIGH*	*HIGH*
8	>65	*LOW, MEDIUM*	*MEDIUM*
9		*HIGH*	*VERY HIGH*

Figure 14-24 Table to Determine Driver Risk Level

This grouping and factoring is related to (but not the same as) the normal forms of Decision Tables that is well documented in the works of Jan Vanthienen and in TDM (see Section D.2.4).

14.5.7 Use rule level annotation of rationale

The documentation of a Decision Table should include the broad rationale for the policy that the table embodies, as a contextual introduction for a new reader. This should be supported by documentation properties of the decision and its authority requirements (see Section 14.2.5).

In addition, non-trivial tables should use rule-level annotation to explain the purpose of their logic (see Section C.2.6). An annotation is an optional, additional conclusion added to the end of a rule in decision table, beyond all the existing conclusions. It is an optional free-text field, for each rule, that explains the rule's:

- Rationale and logic.
- Satisfaction of specific (named or numbered) business requirements.

- Conformance to specific (named or numbered) Knowledge Sources (see Figure 14-25, below).
- Known business issues, flaws or ongoing problems.
- Unusual, counterintuitive, noteworthy or company specific features.
- Recent changes.
- Explanatory details to be persisted in a run-time execution log.

Decision Tables which have one or more authority requirements should, where possible, use annotations to associate rules with numbered regulations, statutes or sections of the Knowledge Source to which it relates (e.g., Figure 14-25).

U	Issuer Based Asset Class				
	Asset Category	Instrument is Convertible	Issuer Class	Issuer Based Asset Class	Annotation
1	OTHER	-	-	OTHER	"IASIC 5-19-4b rights issues, warrants, misc products"
2	INDEX	-	-	INDEX	"IASIC 2-6-14a-d indexed securities and pseudo-baskets"
3	EQUITY	-	-	EQUITY	"IASIC 3-1-2 equity, stock; Country Class " + Issuer Country Class
4	PREFERRED	true	-	CVTPFD	"IASIC 3-3-2 preferred " + Issuer Class + " convertible instrument"
5	PREFERRED	false	-	OTHER	"ABEICS 4B-2 (p19) non-preferred convertibles"
6	DEBT	true	-	CONVERTIBLE	"IASIC 3-3-3 convertible instrument"
7	DEBT	false	SUPRA	SUPRA	"IASIC 4-4-2 supernational debt"

Figure 14-25 Example Decision Table with Authority Reference Annotations

If an annotation column (or row, depending on the decision table orientation) is added to a Decision Table it does not follow that every row must populate it. Avoid creating annotations that:

- Document rule logic that is readily apparent from visual inspection—redundant annotations are not helpful.
- Are pertinent to the table in general and not to a specific rule—there are other places for table documentation.
- Are verbose—volume is no substitute for clarity.
- Are allowed to get out of date—inaccurate rationale is worse than no rationale.

Annotations can also carry a narrative about which rules have fired and, if persisted by the execution environment, can explain the circumstances and behavior of a rule after the fact. This text, which may include expressions, should be designed with this opportunity in mind.

Be aware that one side effect of annotations is that Decision Tables may need to grow in size to accommodate them. This can occur when a single rule with conditions satisfied by many values needs to be re-written as several related rules with different annotations.

14.6 FEEL Best Practices

14.6.1 Avoid confusion with ranges

FEEL supports three formats of ranges—[a..b], (a..b) and]a..b[(see Section B.5.4). These different bracket types can be used in combination so, for instance, (a..b[is valid and so is]a..b]. These three sets of brackets are used to define inclusive and exclusive ranges:

- [a..b] defines an inclusive range—for example 1 and 4 are both in the range [1..4].

- (a..b) and]a..b[both define exclusive ranges—in the same example 1 is not in the range (1..4) but 1.1 is and 4 is not in the range]1..4[but 3.99999 is.

If you have a background in computer science this may all seem familiar. If you don't then this seems very strange, even arcane—how can 1 not be in (1..4)? The problem is twofold: First, non-computer science practitioners generally consider all ranges to be inclusive—this is how most people think of ranges. Second, most non-programmers regard the choice of (or [to be an issue only of style, not of meaning.

DMN's first job is to communicate requirements effectively. Fortunately, as almost all business logic can be easily written using only inclusive ranges, one can and should avoid confusion by not using () for ranges. Always default to using inclusive ranges with [ ]. To show a range that has to be greater than 1 currency unit and less than 100 units without using the exclusive range one should use [1.01..99.99]. In those rare business cases where an exclusive range is essential or much more obviously compliant then use]1..100[. The reverse square brackets have to be learned, they are not intuitive or easy to read, but at least no-one will assume they know what they mean and be incorrect.

14.6.2 Only use boxed expressions as a last resort

FEEL is a powerful means of expressing complex conditions, but it should be used with caution as complex conditions can be challenging to understand. Conditions or contexts that use FEEL expressions to represent complex condition derivation should be avoided if possible. The goal of DMN is to communicate and complex FEEL expressions can hamper this. For example, the use of the complex condition in Figure 14-26 is better represented by the Decision Table in Figure 14-27, an example of how the Priority hit policy, although generally not recommended, can be very elegant for some problems.

Auto Potential Theft Rating
if (Auto is on High Theft Probability List or Auto is Convertible or Auto Price >45000) then "High" else if not (Auto is on High Theft Probability List) then if (Auto Price <20000) then "Low" else if (Auto Price in [20000..45000]) then "Moderate" else "High"

Figure 14-26 Potential Auto Theft Rating as FEEL Boxed Expression

Define Auto Potential Theft Rating			
P	**Auto is on High Theft Probability List**	**Auto is Convertible**	**Auto Price**	**Auto Potential Theft Rating**
				High, *Moderate*, *Low*
1	false	-	<20000	*Low*
2		-	[20000..45000]	*Moderate*
3	true	-	-	*High*
4	-	true	-	*High*
5	-	-	>45000	*High*

Figure 14-27 Potential Auto Theft Rating as Decision Table

Similarly, the use of a compact path expression, such as that demonstrated in Figure 14-28, might be more accessibly represented as Figure 14-29.

Value of Discountable Goods
sum(Shopping Cart.Item[promoApplied or (category=ELECTRICAL and (standardPrice>=2000 or item.Shopping Cart.buyer.loyaltyClass in [GOLD, PLATINUM])).price

Figure 14-28 Using a Path Expression

Although the latter is larger, it is more expressive and more easily modified.

Value of Discountable Goods				
Promotion Applied	An Item.Promotion Applied			
Item Category	An Item.Category			
Standard Price	An Item.standardPrice			
Customer Loyalty Class	Shopping Cart.buyer.loyaltyClass			

U	Promotion Applied	Item Category	Standard Price	Customer Loyalty Class	Discountable Value
	true, false			SILVER, GOLD, PLATINUM	[0..Standard Price]
1	true	-	-	-	Standard Price
2	false	ELECTRICAL	>=2000	-	Standard Price
3			<2000	GOLD, PLATINUM	Standard Price

sum(for An Item in Shopping Cart.Item return Discountable Value)

Figure 14-29 Equivalent Calculation as Decision Table

On occasion, the use of FEEL expressions is inevitable, for example:

- Yielding aggregate or set-based functions of collection inputs (e.g., Figure 21 in Section 17.1.7.2).
- Producing function and aggregate based calculations that cannot directly be expressed in conclusions (e.g., Figure 22 in Section 17.1.7.2).
- Expressing iteration (e.g., Figure 21 in Section 11.3.2.6).

When used, such expressions should be as simple as possible, correspond to well understood business concepts and be defined either in the context of a Decision Table, if their usefulness is confined to this table, or in the glossary if they are more widely used.

14.7 Decision Data Best Practices

14.7.1 Use enumerations not strings

14.7.1.1 String handling in decision tables

Many businesses encode information in the strings they use. For instance, the letters used at the beginning of a code assigned to a mutual fund may show which country issues it or a supplier code may show which department originally signed up the supplier. This encoded information may be material to decision-making. Trying to encode this kind of string handling, pattern analysis, truncation and splicing into Decision Tables makes them complex and is generally not recommended.

The best practice is to isolate string processing to format translation (see Section 14.8.2) in which string segments are converted to dedicated attributes. At the very least, separate out a decision to derive the information you need (e.g., country of issue, department) from the string and then have other decisions require that decision rather than the string itself. This localizes the extraction of the information and makes it easy to replace if at some point the data format is changed or codes are separated out into a distinct field.

14.7.1.2 When to use enumerations

Whenever inputs or outputs are used that appear to be strings, modelers should consider if this information would be better represented as an enumerated type (see Section 9.7.3). It is rare that a business term can meaningfully hold *any* string value. This is because few business terms are genuinely arbitrary, unconstrained sequences of characters. Only names, identifiers and unprocessed user inputs are common examples and these are very rarely used in decision models. The vast majority of business terms in a decision model that may appear to be strings can, in reality, only have certain permitted values (e.g., currency, country, state) and should therefore be defined as enumerations.

This is particularly important if the term is used as an input or conclusion in a Decision Table. A business condition that tests a string term is very unusual[49]. It is unlikely that an enduring business decision is dependent on the contents of a series of characters. The benefits of using enumerated types are:

- The prevention of possible entry errors (e.g., typos)—if you know the permitted values, they can be validated on entry in to a decision table. They also act as a guide to the Decision Table editor.

- Enhanced consistency, for example, eliminating non-significant spelling or case differences.

- Ease of automated validation. A decision modeling tool that knows all the permitted values of a term can check the completeness of the logic using the term to de-

---

[49] Except perhaps when there is a need to compare two strings for equality.

termine if all possibilities have been addressed.

- Prevention of overlap. The complete freedom of text values and the flexibility of string conditions (see Section B.6.1) makes overlaps in the logic of rules using these conditions impossible to detect. Detecting overlaps with conditions on enumerated values is easy.

- Performance. The use of enumeration instead of strings is more efficient during execution. The difference is not great enough to be of concern on small to moderate models, but can become significant as models scale up in size.

14.7.1.3 Naming of permitted values in enumerations

Ensure that the names of an enumeration's permitted values are meaningful, business oriented and mutually consistent. Permitted value names should be all italicized capitals for emphasis. Avoid symbols or whitespace in names and don't use FEEL reserved words (see Appendix B). All names should reflect their purpose, be free from synonyms and be consistent with other glossary terms. For instance, if the business term for the person who vouches that a mortgage will be repaid is *Mortgage Guarantor* and there is a permitted value of *Counterparty Type* pertaining to this, it should be named ***GUARANTOR*** and not ***BONDSMAN***. Note that all enumerated string constants must appear in italics (or in double quotes) in Decision Tables. The italicized form is preferred when referring to enumerated strings and the quoted form when referring to ad-hoc arbitrary strings.

Occasionally a list of 'business codes' will be a natural first candidate for a set of permitted values, for example, the European Central Bank list of asset type codes (***AT01***, ***AT02***, ***AT03***, ...). These may be cryptic to outsiders but meaningful to business experts familiar with the ECB standards. There is often a case for using a more descriptive set of values (e.g., ***COVERED BOND***, ***ASSET BACKED SECURITY***, ***STRUCTURED***) because decision modeling is about communication and not all of business analysts may be familiar with the codes. Enumerations should only use cryptic business codes if most of the following apply:

- The codes are defined and maintained by widely known external authority (e.g., the Federal Reserve or the European Central Bank).

- The codes represent common industry terms and abbreviations used by many organizations in the industry.

- The codes reflect a long standing set of values within the organization (e.g., trading book name, legal entity, internal broker reference).

- The codes are well understood by business subject matter experts and such an understanding is a reasonable and established prerequisite for any business analyst working in the enterprise.

Sometimes, cryptic codes are used as a substitute for a more comprehensible set of values in the interests of brevity and space saving. Analysts may argue that a four-digit code enables more conditions to be squeezed into a Decision Table than a more readable, but more verbose, plain English value set. Unless most of the conditions above are met, this is usually a false economy as it needlessly obscures their meaning and limits their accessibility.

Occasionally it is possible to benefit from cryptic external standards and the clarity of longer names by using a hybrid approach in which the code and the long name are combined (e.g., **AT10-COVEREDBOND, AT11-ASSETBACKEDSECURITY**).

Whichever standard is adopted permitted value sets should follow the conventions consistently. Avoid special cases and naming anomalies (e.g., mixtures of cryptic and non-cryptic codes or names with radically different formats). Also, avoid giving the same name to permitted values across two or more enumerated types that are commonly used together or where it may cause confusion. Any cryptic codes in use should always be documented in the glossary.

14.7.1.4   Common special permitted values

Enumerated values acquired from external data sources, or even other decisions are often subject to two special circumstances:

- The value of an enumerated term cannot be determined. This can occur if the value supplied by the source was outside the valid range of values or because the means to determine their value, perhaps a decision, failed to do so. Consequently, the value is unknown.

- The value, which is optional in a given context, could not be supplied or was not relevant. Consequently, the value is unspecified.

Standard values of enumerated types (e.g., **UNKNOWN** and **UNSPECIFIED**) should be used to denote these two situations throughout a decision model. These terms should be entered into the glossary.

14.7.1.5   Enumerations and value lists in DMN

Enumerated types are supported with value lists in DMN (see 8.2.3.6). Decision Tables that use conditions or conclusions with enumerated types can specify the permitted values of these types in the Decision Table header. This is of value as a memory aid to readers of the table: it reminds them of the meaning of the term and can be used to check they have covered all eventualities in the logic of the table. It can also be used to prioritize the conclusion value selected in Decision Tables with priority or output hit policy (see Section 11.2) and specify default conclusion values.

However, value lists used in this way have some drawbacks. When the same enumerated type appears in many decision tables, value lists quickly become a maintenance liability—any change in the list of permitted values must be reflected in all these tables and opportunities for inconsistencies abound. Additionally, enumerations with more than five permitted values are hard to display in a value list. Value lists cannot constrain the values of enumerated types used outside of Decision Tables (e.g., in FEEL text, Decision Trees, etc.). Consequently, Decision Table authors should avoid using value lists and instead place the permitted values list with the definition of the enumerated type in the glossary. This is especially appropriate when the enumeration concerned is volatile, large or frequently used (see also Section C.4.1 for a proposed solution).

14.7.1.6   Managing change in enumerations' permitted values

In Section 9.7.4 the concepts of enumeration stability, source and change model were considered. The most challenging scenarios involve the management of widely used, unstable enumerations.

If these are internally managed enumerations, the glossary governance process should define a change procedure for adding or removing permitted values as these changes will materially impact the behavior of dependent tables. Adding permitted values compromises the completeness of tables whereas removing them threatens the possibility of redundant rows. One can sometimes protect against the former by ensuring that tables depending on unstable enumerations have default values (see sections 8.2.3.7 and 14.5.4), though it is sometimes essential that new rules be written to handle the new permitted values.

Externally managed enumerations are even more fraught with danger, especially if instances of the enumeration are used as part of the interface to a decision service (i.e., they are bottom line inputs to or outcomes of the decision model of the service). Such modifications should be managed using a 'pull' model in which the user of the enumeration dictates when updates to its permitted values can be made. This permits a coordinated impact assessment and rigorous testing to be performed before any changes are released. The pull approach allows change development to be scheduled conveniently by the owner of the impacted decision service, rather than foisted upon them.

14.7.2 Don't neglect unstructured Input Data

Many organizations are capturing and retaining more unstructured data today than in the past. Emails, call center notes, call transcripts, contract annotations, legal documents and more are all being stored electronically. It is often said that 80% of the data in an organization is unstructured. Even discounting the value of unstructured data to allow for the high levels of "noise" it contains, it seems reasonable to assume that some of it has an impact on decision-making.

While it is hard(er) to write decision logic for decisions handling unstructured content, it is increasingly practical to handle this content programmatically. While Decision Tables are often a poor vehicle for expressing the kind of string handling needed for processing unstructured data (see 14.7.1), other approaches for defining the Decision Logic Level requirements may be able to handle unstructured text. Analytic techniques can be useful for entity identification or sentiment analysis, for instance. When specifying a decision with text, or other less execution-oriented approaches, there is no particular reason why structured data inputs should be preferred over unstructured data as an input.

Consider both structured and unstructured data when looking for Input Data. Evaluate data stored in traditional databases and data warehouses as well as data in document stores and NoSQL data infrastructure. Any of these may yield potential Input Data entities.

14.7.3 Carefully consider placement of business data constraints

During modeling one must decide the extent to which business operational constraints should be reflected in data models versus decision models of a business. Relationships between business objects may be a fixed law of the domain that must be documented, and enforced, in the data model ('strict') or they may be determined, more dynamically, by business decisions instead ('lazy'). For example, consider the business constraint that every mortgage application must have at least one guarantor. Is it preferable to document this in the data model or should this be part of a validation decision?

Representing such restrictions purely as decisions certainly facilitates agility. This enables SMEs to represent changes to business constraints by changing only a few decisions. It ensures that a data model's integrity constraints will not impede such alterations. It would be easier, for example, using an agile, 'lazy' data model like Figure 14-30, with no integrity constraints, to affect a new business policy of supporting guarantor-free loans under specified conditions. To amend this policy, the SME has merely to change the decision that validates the application/guarantor relation and amend some dependent decisions. No change to the data model is required.

This removal of constraints from the equivalent 'strict' data model (see Figure 14-18) forces these constraints to be represented in explicit validation decisions. In this example, this might ensure:

1. Each *Loan Application* has one *Applicant.*
2. Each *Loan Application* has at least one *Guarantor.*
3. Each *Person* cannot act as *Guarantor* to more than one *Loan.*
4. Each *Person* has a single *Financial Profile* which is unique to them.
5. Every *Asset, Liability* and *Employment* (*Record*) belongs to only one *Financial Profile.*

Once explicitly and precisely documented as decisions, these former restrictions become candidates for rapid change and are more readily perceived as 'degrees of freedom' by SMEs. They can be encouraged to spot new business opportunities by imagining circumstances under which former restrictions could be weakened or lifted for mutual gain.

The drawback of this loss of integrity constraints are:

*   Often a constraint is so fundamental that the flexibility of rendering it as a decision provides no real benefit (e.g., point 5, above).

*   The proliferation of validation decisions adds the demand for additional exception processing to handle cases when they are violated.

*   Representation of integrity constraints in a data model is more elegant and compact than its equivalent representation as a decision.

*   Representation of constraints is now split into two places both of which must be understood by the business and both have to be reconciled for consistency.

*   Other systems using the data model may find it much easier to use integrity constraints that are built in rather than reaching out to the decision model.

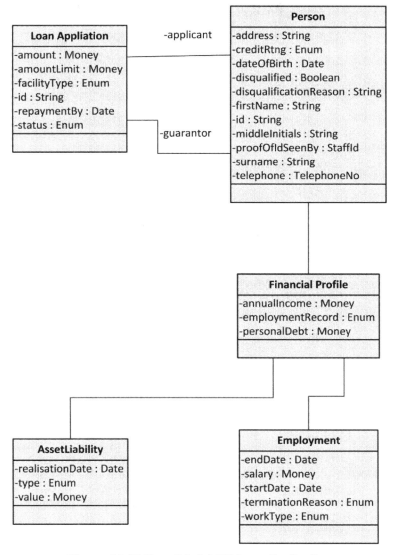

Figure 14-30 Data Model Without Cardinality

A mixed approach seems prudent. Integrity constraints should therefore only be represented as decisions if:

- They represent current business policy and there is a reasonable expectation of change.
- The constraint itself is conditional (it relies on complex data conditions).
- Handling non-compliance does not unduly burden the decision model or automated systems built from it.

14.7.4 Consider the boundary conditions of data

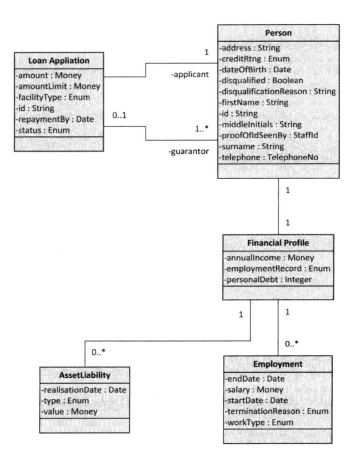

Figure 14-31 Example Data Model

Once early iterations of the data model are established, they can be a useful means of spotting potential weaknesses in business decision definitions. Logical gaps may be exposed when a certain combination of facts (i.e., a specific business data scenario) encounters a business event which changes them—challenging the boundaries of the defined business logic or violating the data model. These events are called 'flash points[50]'. This usually occurs when a relationship changes cardinality. For example, given the data model of Figure 14-31 what would happen if the applicant took on a new liability, the employment record was proven to be fraudulent or the guarantor died? Addressing these gaps will make the decision

---

[50] Chapter 8, "Business Rule Concepts", Ronald G. Ross, Business Rule Solutions LLC, 2013, ISBN 0-941049-14-0.

model and the data model more robust and may open new opportunities for business. At the very least any such shortcomings and assumptions should be documented.

14.7.5 Split up large Input Data objects

The best initial set of Input Data are the logical data entities at the top level of an enterprise or project information model. Using these effectively balances specificity with a reasonable number of Input Data components on each diagram. Each Input Data will represent more than one piece of information but even diagrams involving complex decisions are not likely to require more than a handful of Input Data objects. Furthermore, these Input Data objects are likely to be familiar and supported by a robust set of properties making them easy to integrate into the glossary.

Many organizations have some core entities that are large and complex. For instance, in some organizations an entity like *Customer*, *Account* or *Part* may involve a very large number of attributes. Used as Input Data, such an entity may be linked to all or most of the decisions in a model or on a Decision Requirements Diagram. This significantly degrades both as it increases the visual complexity of diagrams and reduces the model's clarity and specificity, potentially defeating the model's usefulness in change impact assessment. Splitting such an entity into multiple Input Data components, each representing a logical section or subset of its attributes, can help with both of these.

For instance, a large complex *Account* entity might be split into the data captured when an account is opened, a set of data about its current state and a set of data about the trading allowed in the account at the present time. These sets of properties are distinct, change at different rates and may be owned by different groups. Also, they are likely to influence different decisions, making them a reasonable division.

The Input Data created should be named so it is clear they are a set and the glossary should accurately reflect this arrangement. Splitting a large entity into multiple Input Data components in this way will allow the decisions in a model to more obviously show how and where each part of the data entity is being used without the overhead of showing each individual attribute.

14.7.6 Only classify data with property flags when they are independent

Many business domains classify data in order to make decision-making easier and classification decisions are among the most common (see Section 16.9), for example *Determine Financial Product Type*. Such classification can take one of two forms: classification by property flag, in which data is "labelled" with a set of Boolean flags (yes/no values) to denote key properties and classification by enumeration in which each data item is associated with a single value which denotes its class. In the case of financial product classification, classification by property flags might use flags such as *is Derivative*, *transacts an Underlying Asset*, *is Optional* and *is Bond*. However, a classification by enumeration would contain the same information in a single enumerated value (e.g., *SWAP*, *SWAPTION*, *BOND*, *FUTURE*).

To determine which of these approaches is most appropriate consider the following questions:

- Are all the property values entirely (or mostly) independent of each other? Are their values unrelated and free of mutual constraint?
- Are all combinations of properties meaningful (e.g., *is Bond* and *is Derivative*)?

- Are all (or most) of the possible combinations of properties relevant to the decision-making?

If the answer to all of these questions is yes, classification by property flags is most appropriate. This can be a very flexible approach that is excellent for separating different facets of decision-making. If, however, any of the questions are not satisfied, classification by enumeration is the better option.

If in doubt, compose a Decision Table that shows the relationship between the candidate property flags and enumeration values, such as that of Figure 14-32[51].

U	is Derivative	is Swap	Transacts an Underlying Asset	is Optional	is Buy	is Bespoke	is Bond	Product Class
Product Class								
1	true	true	false	false	-	-	-	*SWAP*
2			true	true	-	-	-	*SWAPTION*
3		false	true	false	-	false	-	*FUTURE*
4				false	-	true	-	*FORWARD*
5				true	false	-	-	*PUT OPTION*
6				true	true	-	-	*CALL OPTION*
7	false	-	-	-	-	-	true	*BOND*

Figure 14-32 Product Classification: Properties vs Enumeration

If this Decision Table has many '-' cells or shows many gaps in its coverage (e.g., no rules for *isSwap* and *isBond*) then classification by enumeration is most appropriate.

14.8 General Best Practices

14.8.1 Seek out reuse within and across models

Decision models are generally developed iteratively. With each new iteration, new decisions, Input Data and Knowledge Sources are identified. While these may be genuinely new components, especially when developing the first decision model in a business area, over time the iterations will be identifying new uses for existing components. It is important to remember that every diagram in DMN is considered a view on a shared repository of information. As such a diagram can reuse a decision, an Input Data or a Knowledge Source that already exists in this (real or virtual) repository just by placing a component with the right name. When developing decision models, it is critical that such reuse is actively sought. Modelers should get into the habit of checking that a component they need does not already exist and should reuse those that do as a matter of course.

Experience with many different decision models shows that reuse is very frequent. The most common is reuse of Input Data, where an organization's core data entities are input to many different decisions. It is also common to reuse Knowledge Sources, especially when they relate to core policy documents or industry-standard regulations. Decision reuse is also

---

[51] Note that this table is truncated for brevity.

common and maximizing the benefits of this requires that organizations are more methodical—a more proactive approach is often called for.

Decisions are reused both within a single model and across models. Once a model has several levels of decomposition, it is worth checking that none of the lower level decisions is inadvertently repeated, perhaps under a synonym. Often the same decision may be required by several different decisions further "up" the hierarchy and this may not be immediately apparent. Decisions that classify or categorize someone or something are reused particularly often. For instance, whether a customer lives in a jurisdiction that does or does not have a tax treaty with the organization's country of operation might be relevant to several decisions in an overall model of eligibility. The decision that is modeled to handle this will therefore be required by several other decisions within the same model—creating reuse. Separating this logic into its own decision will also ensure that it can be changed in one place rather than embedding that logic into multiple decision tables, boosting consistency and ease of maintenance. This reuse is also a good means of allowing decision models to scale while retaining their cohesion.

Decisions about the organization's core entities (e.g., customers, suppliers, parts) may well be reused across many models. For instance, a decision as to whether a customer is or is not a 'good' customer may well be something an organization wants to standardize. This means that a decision must be defined that determines customer 'goodness' and this decision will then be required by all decisions that need to differentiate between good customers and bad ones. Because these decisions are likely to be spread across multiple models, this will require more effort and coordination. The organization will need to: tag (e.g., see Section 14.2.5.5) or otherwise identify such decisions to make them easy to find, actively organize teams to discuss potential reuse and aggressively track these decisions in a repository.

14.8.2 Separate preparation, validation and business decisions

Decision models can be used to express logic for many purposes, the most common being:

- **Business decisions**. Drawing conclusions from valid business data and recommending business actions based on these conclusions. These operational decisions are the applications predominantly considered elsewhere in this book.

- **Validation of information**. Ensuring that formatted business data is sufficiently internally consistent, complete and meaningful for its purpose. Taking or suggesting measures to fix or report information that cannot be validated. Notice that data only needs to be sufficient for the proposed application; it is rare that data has to be entirely complete and perfect.

- **Preparation of Information**. This involves transformation of information from its original form to another more suitable for some kind of processing. Sometimes this involves the transformation of unstructured data to structured data. Preparation is often used in data standardization to translate different native representations of the same type of information from multiple sources to a single standard, canonical form so that the information can be consolidated for uniform processing. The value of representing this transformation as a decision model depends on the extent to which it uses business inference to enrich data. It can be argued that purely structural transformations, that do not have any business inference, benefit little from decision modeling.

Each of these purposes involve business know-how and decision modeling is justified in each case. Modelers should avoid mixing these applications in a single decision model as this can:

- Reduce the clarity and simplicity of the model by merging separate concerns.
- Cause the inadvertent repetition of preparation and validation logic within business logic.
- Decrease the stability of the model by coupling preparation, validation and business decision issues unnecessarily, for example by including volatile, source specific preparation details in an otherwise stable business decision model.
- Make it harder to devolve preparation and validation to separate decision services and support their independent reuse.

If a business context requires preparation, validation and business decisions, it is best to layer the model into three independent models. Make the business decision model depend on the outcomes of your validation model which, in turn, depends on the outcomes of the preparation decision model as shown in Figure 14-33.

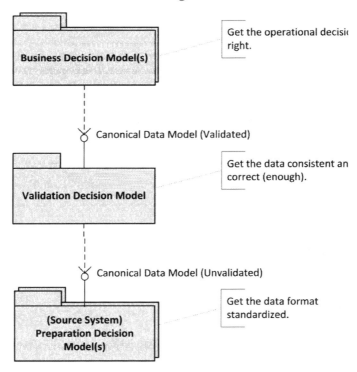

Figure 14-33 Layered Decision Model

The preparation model creates data consistent with a single (unvalidated) canonical data model which is defined in a glossary. There is one decision model for each source system native format of the data that requires translation to the canonical form. This prevents the need to have source system dependent decisions in the validation model thereby simplifying it. The validation model produces data of the required quality in a validated canonical model. There is one model per business domain. The validation decision model simplifies business decision models by removing the need to address source specific format variations or data quality checks. All three decision models should be independent. Never add source system specifics to any layer other than the preparation decision model.

Preparation layers are vital in adapting the form of the data to its application and making value constraints more explicit. For example, much of the business data consumed as string data types actually are, or contain, enumerated types (see Section 14.7.1). A preparation layer can decouple business decisions from messy and obscure string processing by converting all of these implicit enumerations into real enumerations.

The best practices for preparation and validation layers include those in the *Data Preparation* and *Positive Validator* patterns (see Sections 16.11 and 16.7).

14.8.3 Maintain the integrity of Information Requirements

Information Requirement Relationships, like those featured in Figure 14-34 and discussed in Section 8.3) denote a reliance of one decision, the consumer, on information supplied by a provider: either another sub-decision yielding a conclusion or a Data Input yielding data. It is therefore important that the type and range of values produced by the provider matches that handled by the consumer, especially if the consumer is designed to be complete and have an explicit rule for every possible set of input values. More completely: the type and range of an information item which a decision uses as an input must match the type and union of the ranges of all providers.

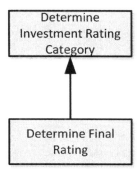

Figure 14-34 Example Information Requirement

Mismatches between the provider and consumer can result in flaws with the decision model:

- If the producer can yield values not handled by the consumer, then the consumer cannot be considered complete. For example, if *Determine Final Rating* yields a value *AA-* and *Determine Investment Rating Category* specifies no rules for this value and is unable to yield any outcome. This is only a problem if the intent is that the consumer is complete and no default is provided.

- If the producer cannot yield values handled in the consumer, then the consumer has redundant rules. For example, if *Determine Investment Rating Category* has rules which check the *Determine Final Rating* is *BB* and *Determine Final Rating* has no means of concluding this value, then these rules are unusable.

The maintenance of producer/consumer consistency is especially important for enumerated types that change frequently (see Section 14.7.1.5) and for cases in which a decision can select from multiple providers to yield the same information item (see the *Divide and Conquer* pattern 16.2). Modelers must ensure that any mismatches are clearly understood and documented and, if permanent, are reflected in the annotations and completeness of both producer and consumer.

14.8.4 Eliminate sequence

One of the most important aspects of a decision model is that requirements are modeled and *not* sequenced. Decision models capture the dependencies between their components not process or execution order. For instance, the fact that someone generally checks that a claim is complete before checking the eligibility of the claim does not mean that the decision *Claim Eligibility* depends on the decision *Claim Completeness*. Unless the answer from *Claim Completeness*—potentially a Complete/Incomplete flag—is used in the logic that determines eligibility then there is no dependency between the two decisions.

A desire to model sequence in a decision model is a common misconception (see Section 13.6) and has a number of negative consequences:

- These sequences are often arbitrary and based on technical rationales that are long since lost. Building this kind of sequence into a decision model simply persists this without challenging and understanding the rationale. This reduces the value of the model in expressing actual *business* requirements.

- It will not scale well as models become more complex. Capturing implementation sequence can become very involved when decisions are complex and including this in a decision model reduces its clarity and usability.

- Because each information requirement is expected to create a column in a decision table, modeling sequence in this way will hard-wire information into decision logic simply because it was output from a previous step[52]. This reduces the ability of a modeler to check the structure of their decision table and ties decision logic to the current implementation sequence. The latter also reduces the reuse potential of decisions by embedding sequence details within their definition that make them context specific. As noted in Section 13.6, this is particularly common when single decision tables are linked directly into a process model.

- Finally, there is no standard notation in DMN for sequence as the standard assumes, correctly, that sequence will be managed in a process defined in BPMN.

Eliminating sequence from a decision model can be difficult as subject matter experts and process modelers are very used to thinking of a decision as a series of steps—it's very

---

[52] The modeling of sequence can also be identified by looking for this problem in Decision Tables. When a Decision Table has a condition that is not used or one that always has the same value for all rules in the table then it is likely that there is a requirement documented where none is needed.

natural to confuse the order in which requirements are stated, or that in which they were historically performed, with a mandate for a specific execution order. It is often possible to identify that sequence has crept into a model when experts start saying things like "it would make no sense to do that before this" or "it will be more efficient to do that before this". These are discussions of sequence and implementation. Decision models are based on requirements and a requirement is just that—required. A true Information Requirement demands at least one situation in which the decision cannot be made without the information.

If a sequence of activity is imposed by the business, it should be reflected in the business process model (see Section 10.2), not the decision model. Reflecting sequence in a decision model is unnecessary because the set of Decision Requirements Diagrams specifies all logical dependencies between decisions and sub-decisions and the necessary sequence of execution can be directly inferred from this.

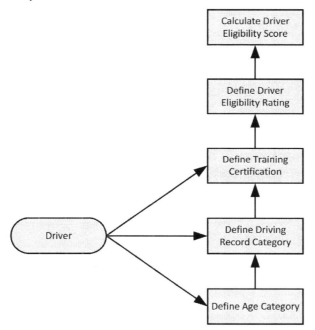

Figure 14-35 A Decision Requirements Model Showing Sequence

For example, Figure 14-35 shows a decision requirements model for determining *Driver Eligibility Score* that contains an unnecessary sequence. This model takes a description provided by a business expert such as "I take the driver, categorize them by age and figure out their driving record. Then I check for certification to get an overall rating and score". The result is a deep and narrow model that implies that the age category is needed to determine the driving record, that the driving record is needed to determine training certification and so on.

While some models really are deep and narrow, it is more often a sign that sequence has been modeled instead of requirements. Once the sequence has been removed and only the requirements are left, the model is wider and shallower as shown in Figure 14-36.

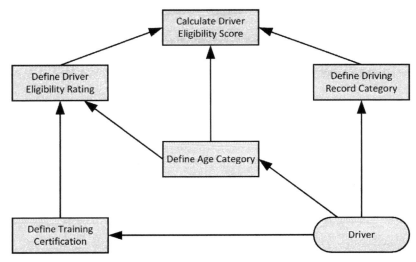

Figure 14-36 A Decision Requirements Model with Sequence Eliminated

This is more accurate as it correctly shows that only *Age Category* and *Training Certification* are required for *Driver Eligibility Rating* while *Driving Record Category*, *Age Category* and *Driver Eligibility Rating* are required for the overall score. It does not imply unnecessary dependency.

Unfortunately, many users are used to thinking of a decision as a sequence and often requirements documents specify them that way. Because DMN does not use the spatial layout of a diagram to mean anything, the layout can be used to show sequence to users (see also Section 14.3.5). For instance, a set of dependent decisions can be ordered from left to right or top to bottom in the familiar order. This does not change the meaning of the model but may make it easier to review with subject matter experts and business users.

For implementation some sequence may be required and can often be automatically inferred from dependencies. In those few cases where it cannot, or where performance or cost considerations necessitate a sequence other than the one suggested purely from the dependencies, a **decision flow** is often used to specify this sequence. A decision flow depicts the order in which a set of related decisions are made. This may include design elements that flow directly from the model—such as beginning by making the lowest level decisions in the model. These are the foundations on which other decisions are built and, as the flow progresses, higher level decisions will be made. At points in this flow there are likely to be multiple possible approaches to ordering sub-decisions that will all work from a decision model perspective. The flow can ensure that more "expensive" decisions (in terms of fees or processing time say) can be made later in the flow once it is clear they will definitely be needed. None of this changes the decision-making, it just flexes it for efficiency (see also the *Approximator* pattern in Section 16.5).

DMN does not support decision flows. If a decision model is being implemented in a BRMS that requires one (decision flows are often called ruleflows in BRMSs), it should either be generated automatically from the decision model or manually derived from the dependencies of the decision model and minimally altered to achieve the required effect. If a decision flow must be maintained in a BRMS, then it should be annotated to show how it was derived from the original decision model and kept synchronized with it.

It may seem harmless to leave these requirements in but they contribute to maintenance work and make verifying and validating decision logic harder. Avoid mixing sequence and requirements in DMN. Use annotations to document implementation concerns and depict sub-decisions in sequence order from left to right in DRDs to aid understanding on the part of Subject Matter Experts (see Section 14.3.5). Refer also to 16.8 for a pattern for eliminating unnecessary sequence.

14.8.5 Make decision models self-contained

Any representation of decision models must communicate business requirements effectively and in a self-contained way that avoids the need to frequently access other documentation. Therefore, modelers must make clear use of business vocabulary and ensure model representations are lucid, free from any personal or team context, self-documenting and as simple as possible. Every business term used in a decision model should be distinct from other terms and term synonyms should be avoided. Modelers should not use technical terms, informal names (unless these are documented and in wide usage) or cryptic data model attribute names. They should restrict terminology to that which is standard (and widely understood) for the business domain or defined in the glossary (discussed fully in Section 9.2). Decision models should side step any requirement for readers to consult other documentation to understand the model by including the necessary information in the model documentation itself (via hyperlinks if the reference is voluminous). Use annotations and comments (in Decision Requirement Diagrams, Decision Tables and FEEL) to explain non-obvious content.

The acid test for lucidity is that a colleague (with a similar business background) can understand your model without explanation. Furthermore, that you can understand your own model after a year.

15 Advanced Best Practices

Practice is the best of all instructors
—Publilius Syrus

This section contains best practices for experienced and advanced decision modelers. Its advice is more meaningful once some experience of decision modeling has been attained. Some of the potential of DMN's flexibility and some of the consequences of its advanced features can only be appreciated when they have been applied to real projects.

Some of these facilities (e.g., hit policies, multiple conclusions, complex Knowledge Sources with their own knowledge or analytical requirements, Business Knowledge Models) are attractive, but can inadvertently encourage bad practice. They can lead to models that scale poorly or are more complex than necessary, confusing those trying to understand them. This section describes guidelines to prevent this. It suggests restrictions and checks to ensure that DMN's primary duty—the effective communication of decision-making—is not overshadowed by those of its features that are more technically oriented. It also suggests techniques for the management of models over time to prevent models degrading with age.

15.1 Introduction

This section introduces best practices that require some experience of decision modeling to apply effectively. It also concentrates on avoiding the misuse of some advanced features. For ease of reference, this chapter considers advanced best practices across two distinct areas:

- **Decision Requirements**. These techniques focus on capturing and maintaining the requirements level structure of the decision model, specifically Decision Requirement Diagrams.
- **Decision Logic**. The best procedures for modeling decision logic are considered in this section. It includes principles for modeling logic in many formats, not just those specific to Decision Tables and FEEL.

Related content can be found in two other chapters. Chapter 14 considers best practices for newcomers to decision modeling and chapter 16 considers decision modeling patterns.

15.2 Decision Requirements Best Practices

15.2.1 Document hierarchical Knowledge Sources

Where a high-level decision is influenced by a single Knowledge Source which itself consists of a hierarchy of sub-sections or component parts and these parts individually provide authority to other (lower level, child) decisions, it is best practice to represent this as a hierarchy of Knowledge Sources. For example, the Federal Reserve Bank regulatory specification controlling the disclosure of liquidity movements ("FED 5G") consists of different sections which address how assets are defined, counterparties are classified and how disclosures are made. The latter is further divided into liquidity inflow, outflow and supplementary reporting sections. This Knowledge Source hierarchy can be represented as shown by the darker components in Figure 15-1.

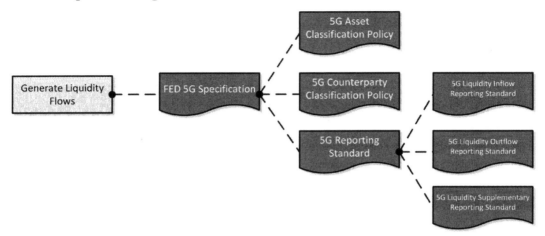

Figure 15-1 Example Single Source Knowledge Source Hierarchy

In Figure 15-1, the entire regulatory specification, the *FED 5G Specification* Knowledge Source, draws its authority from its constituent parts defining the asset classification, counterparty classification and flow reporting guidelines. The last derives authority in turn from the sub-sections describing specific types of liquidity flow, specialist knowledge of which the parent Knowledge Sources are unaware. In general, the larger part of the Knowledge source derives authority from the smaller, more specialist parts. Some modelers' instinct is to perceive this hierarchy inverted: so that a small part of the Knowledge Source derives authority from the larger part. This is an equally good modeling strategy. What matters is that, as a team, you pick one style or the other and <u>apply it consistently across all your models</u>.

Note that this attention to detail is <u>only</u> required when the subordinate Knowledge Sources are individually used as authorities by other decisions. Usually these decisions will be sub-ordinates of those using the top-level Knowledge Source. The Decision Requirements Diagram in Figure 15-2 shows an example of this, although the Knowledge Source hierarchy (the same as Figure 15-1) is harder to see here.

Where a decision is influenced by multiple Knowledge Sources that have *different* origins that overlap in scope or have conflicting guidance, this can also be documented as a hierarchy of Knowledge Sources in the decision model. Figure 15-3 depicts such a hierarchy.

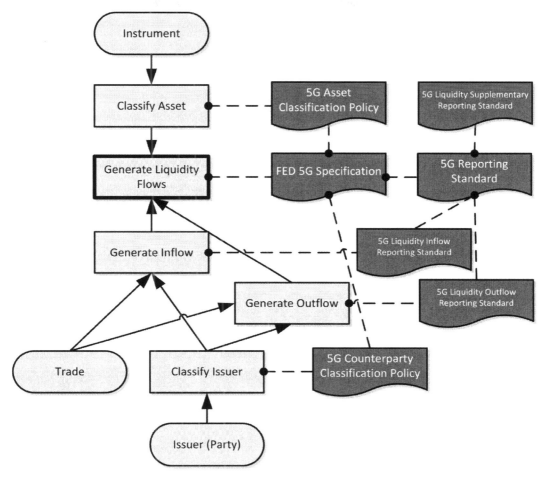

Figure 15-2 Hierarchical Knowledge Source used by Hierarchical Decision

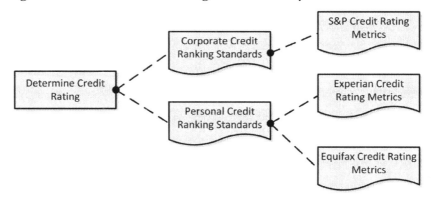

Figure 15-3 Example Multiple-Source Knowledge Source Hierarchy

This example shows that the decision *Determine Credit Rating*, which is made for both personal and corporate entities, is guided by disjoint[53] *Corporate Credit Ranking Standards* and *Personal Credit Ranking Standards*. These have separate scope and do not conflict with each other. The former in turn refers to standards defined by S&P, but it may override these with local knowledge if necessary. The Knowledge Source *Personal Credit Rating Standards* requires authority from standards defined by Experian and Equifax. These have overlapping scope and can conflict. The parent Knowledge Source must mediate and resolve any such conflicts.

Note that sub-ordinate Knowledge Sources cannot provide authority to the decisions for areas that are completely out of scope for its superior. For example, under no circumstances could *S&P Creditor Metrics* provide knowledge concerning personal credit ratings.

When Knowledge Sources are linked in this way, decisions can be associated to the most specific Knowledge Source that constrains or directs them (a best practice) while retaining a sense of the broad impact of the overall Knowledge Source. For instance, the hierarchy in Figure 15-3 could be used to find all decisions dependent on Credit Rating knowledge by identifying the decisions linked to each Knowledge Source and using the relationships between the Knowledge Sources to tie these together.

15.2.2 Use Business Knowledge Models only when necessary

A Business Knowledge Model (see Section 11.1.1) is a means of reusing 'packaged' logic among many decisions (or other Business Knowledge Models). They provide a facility to apply the same parameterized logic in multiple scenarios, even in the same Decision Requirements Diagram (e.g., the figure in Section 11.1.1.5). This flexibility is not required as often as many modelers believe and Business Knowledge Models should only be applied when an actual reuse scenario is imminent. Use a Business Knowledge Model:

- In those circumstances where not to apply them would lead to an actual duplication of logic (e.g., cut and paste between two decisions).

- Where the logic under consideration is genuinely applicable in each reuse scenario. Avoid the temptation to 'shoe-horn' logic into places where it does not fully apply.

- According to the best available knowledge, where the logic applied in each usage will remain consistent in the future and not diverge.

If all of these conditions are not met, then the logic should be housed within decisions.

Logic should *not* be expressed within a Business Knowledge Model in order to anticipate, an as yet unrealized, need for reuse or from a misguided attempt to 'increase the flexibility of the model.' This is a common habit of IT professionals who habitually 'wrap' functions in Business Knowledge Models to support ad-hoc reuse later. The use of Business Knowledge Models has a cost (i.e., model complexity, difficulty of comprehension) and this cost should not be borne by a model without clear and immediate benefits.

Modelers should also be careful not to stop modeling decisions and start using Business Knowledge Models to keep the model "simple". Some modelers worry about exposing

---

[53] The fact that these authorities are disjoint is denoted by mutually exclusive, qualifying adjectives in their names.

the full structure of a decision to business owners and so stop modeling decomposition using decisions and information requirements, using a network of Business Knowledge Models to implement details below a certain level instead. This substitutes the less friendly Business Knowledge Models and their related FEEL invocation logic for Decision Requirements Diagrams, reducing business accessibility. The ability to build multiple Decision Requirements Diagrams as views on an underlying model (ref 14.3.2) allows modelers to build the detail needed to correctly model a decision while building views that are tailored to the technical level of each specific audience. This is generally the preferred approach.

15.2.3 Assess Input Data to see if it is really a decision outcome

Information Requirements expressing a dependency on an Input Data should be assessed to ensure that the Input Data is really raw data and not the outcome of a decision. This situation occurs when a decision output is stored in a database for later use or a decision output is provided by a third party as part of a data packet. Most decision modelers assume that every piece of data stored in a database or in such a data packet should be represented by an Information Item in an Input Data. This generally works well as most data provided to a decision is best considered as input to the decision model and represented as Input Data.

This can obscure decision-making if the data was actually decided (e.g., calculated, determined, selected) and then stored for later use. Similarly, if the means of derivation of an Information Item supplied by a third party becomes known or becomes important within the scope of the decision model, representing it as Input Data conceals this derivation. For instance, a customer record may contain the flag "US Citizen". While this may appear to be Input Data, in fact it is better considered to be the result of a Decision—one that happens to have been stored in a database for later use. Any Decision that needs this flag should be dependent on the Decision that derives it.

Modeling it this way has a number of advantages.

- It allows the modeler to document how that information was created and expose this to other modelers who may need to know if they can use it. That is, if their assumptions or needs are the same as the original creator's intent.

- It allows each user of the result, each decision dependency, to be assessed for suitability (e.g., timeliness, accuracy, regional application). For instance, a piece of data flagging a person as a US citizen may have been set when the person first opened an account. This may be a significant period earlier. It is much clearer for modelers to decide if they want to reuse a decision like *Account Opener is US Citizen* with that suitability documented than rely on a piece of data simply labeled *Is US Citizen* the provenance of which is uncertain.

- It more cleanly differentiates between "raw" Input Data and derived decision outputs, helping modelers differentiate between the data over which they have no control and the data they (or others) are responsible for deriving.

When the decision model is packaged up as a Decision Service, it is semantically equivalent to pass the result of this decision or a piece of Input Data into the Decision Service so that this packaging is not impacted even if the data is redefined as a decision.

One potential complexity arises when defining Decision Services. If a decision is included in one Decision Service but the result of the decision is passed into the other Decision Service as a parameter, it may be tempting to define it as a decision in the one case but as Input Data in the other—i.e., to represent it both ways. For instance, a *Calculated Monthly Payment* is required by an eligibility decision that is deployed in two Decision Services. In one it is calculated from raw data input to the service—the calculated Decision is in the private section of the Decision Service and so encapsulated in the service (See Section 8.1.6). In the other it is calculated and stored before the service is invoked and passed in to the service.

The fact that it is calculated inside one Decision Service (because the calculation decision is inside the execution boundary) and outside of the other (the decision is outside the execution boundary and supplies information for a decision that is inside it) does not change its representation. *Calculate Monthly Payment* should be shown in every diagram as a decision. If it must be decided, then it's always a decision and if it is just input as-is to the decision-making then it's Input Data. The fact that its value is sometimes stored in a database or passed it as an XML structure and then consumed as though it was a piece of data does not change its nature.

A related problem occurs when a first pass assessment of a decision identifies the need for some Input Data but more thorough analysis reveals that the requirement is actually to something derived from that Input Data. For instance, a Decision about tax payments may be modeled as needing to know the country of residence of a party. This information is correctly modeled by Input Data and so the initial model shows the dependency on the Input Data. However in reality the country itself is not important, only its status in terms of tax treaties. An additional Decision should be added to manage the derivation of this status, as discussed in the Classifier pattern (Section 16.9).

DMN allows Information Requirement Relationships to use both Input Data and decisions as the source (see Section 8.1.5)—therefore decisions can depend on either. This allows a decision definition to remain unchanged if a specific Input Data is replaced with a sub-decision that results in the same information item(s). This is a useful feature, allowing models to evolve as discussed above without having to change decision definitions further "up" the model.

15.2.4 Assess decision models for analytic authorities

Many Knowledge Sources are based on formal documents, policies or regulations, or on the expertise and know-how of specific groups or roles. Increasingly, however, organizations are looking to their data for insight. The idea that historical data about what worked (or did not work) can direct and guide more effective decision-making is the basis for the investment organizations are making in analytics. Decision models provide an excellent framework for finding opportunities for analytics to improve decision-making.

As a decision model is developed, it is likely to be dominated by explicit knowledge of how the decision is made today and by current practice. Analytic insight—knowledge derived from data—must generally be added to the model distinctly and systematically. Analytic insight plays one of several roles in a decision model:

- **As an historical check**. The analytic insight might serve as a check on policy or expertise, confirming that a set of proposed rules does what it purports to do. This generally involves comparing the policy or expertise against historical data. For instance, a Knowledge Source such as *Assessment of Fraud Rules Against Historical Patterns* might be included in a model and be an authority to the same components as the policy or expertise being checked (see Figure 15-4). The Knowledge Source shows how well the *Assess Likelihood of Fraud*, guided by the *Current Fraud Detection Policy*, fits past behavior both generally and even specifically against cases like those currently being processed. The same Knowledge Source could even be used as an authority for a decision to check if the fraud assessment decision needs updating (see Figure 15-5). A more sophisticated example of this feedback is shown in Section 15.2.6.

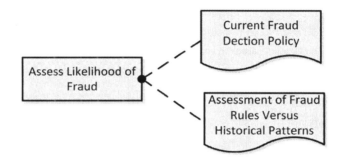

Figure 15-4 Analytic Insight as Knowledge Source

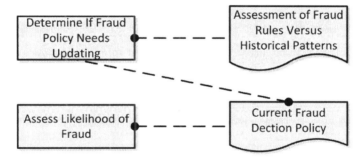

Figure 15-5 Analytic Insight to Trigger Update

- **As a source of new rules**. The analytic insight might be used to derive a set of rules from data directly using data mining. For instance, a customer segmentation might be developed analytically to group customers based on their behavior or to determine the most likely product combinations. A Knowledge Source such as *Customer Behavior Segmentation* would be included and would act as an authority to any decision where this customer knowledge might influence the rules to be defined.

- **As an indicator of new knowledge requirement**. The need for analytic insight that makes predictions might also be identified. This often involves looking for decisions where new knowledge might help make the decision better. One of the best ways to find this is to ask "if only"—"if only we knew x we could make this decision more accurately." Where domain experts or decision-makers wish for additional insight to improve their decision-making there is a clear opportunity for analytic insight. For instance, a Knowledge Source *Predicted likelihood of customer churn* might be identified as influencing a marketing offer decision.

Consider the example in Figure 15-6. The Knowledge Source *Customer Satisfaction Survey Results* represents historical data analysis that might be used to check the rules for *Customer Service Actions* being created based on *Customer Service Expertise*. The *Customer Lifetime Value Model* is an example of an analytic model developed to create the rules necessary for calculating *Customer Value*. *Customer Retention Risk* represents new insight— "if only we knew which customers were a retention risk we could suggest different actions for them". This is likely to evolve into a decision as the model is finalized.

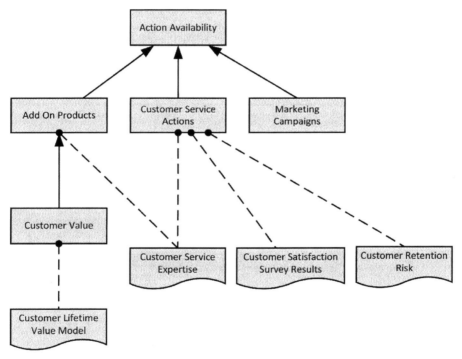

Figure 15-6 Different kinds of analytic insight in a decision model

In each case these can be modeled initially even if it is not clear that it is possible to derive the analytic insight from the available data. The data for which a need is expected can be linked as an authority for the Knowledge Source at this early stage. The practicality of the insight must be determined before the model is finalized and, when this is done, the actual Input Data considered should be linked to the Knowledge Source. It may also be worth considering modeling the feedback loop implied by this data, see Section 15.2.6 .

15.2.5 Consider Knowledge Sources that have Input Data as authorities

One of the less common relationships in DMN allows an Input Data to be an authority for a Knowledge Source (see Section 11.1.2). The Input Data at the plain end of the Authority Requirement relationship, as shown in Figure 15-7, represents information that is analyzed to derive the Knowledge Source at the rounded end. This is used to show Knowledge Sources that represent (or are derived from) structured data constants or mappings (e.g., tax thresholds or property value bands). They are also used to represent policies that are determined through data mining or analysis.

Knowledge Sources based on simple mappings are shown as an authority requirement of the Knowledge Source on an Input Data representing that mapping. Consider the example in Figure 15-7, in which the Knowledge Source *Default Country Credit Rating*, which provides guidance on a default *Credit Rating* associated with a specific *Country*, has an authority requirement on an externally sourced mapping of *Country* to *Default Issuer Credit Rating*, represented by the Input Data *Country Credit Rating Mapping*. There is often confusion as to whether dependency on such a mapping table should be shown as an Information Requirement on Input Data (as in Figure 15-9) or as an Authority Requirement on Knowledge Source (Figure 15-7) as DMN allows both the source data and the knowledge derived from it to be shown and linked. Generally, if the mapping is used directly as data the presentation in Figure 15-9 should be adopted. However, if the mapping informs an active policy, Figure 15-7 is more appropriate. The distinction between a decision having a requirement on simple Input Data versus a Knowledge Source which itself has an authority requirement on Input Data is that the first represents passive information made available to a decision whereas the latter is prescriptive and actively dictates decision behavior.

Figure 15-7 Knowledge Source with Active Data Input Authority

If a mapping acting as an authority for a Knowledge Source is in turn derived using a decision, the Knowledge Source has a decision as its authority, see Figure 15-8.

Figure 15-8 Knowledge Source with Decision Authority

In addition, a surprising number of Knowledge Sources are actually derived from data. Many policy documents are written based on what a particular set of data implied at the time of writing. For instance, a Life Underwriting Manual is a policy document for many projects, and thus a Knowledge Source. However, these policies are generally written based on the analysis of lives, tests performed and outcomes.

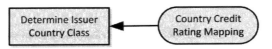

Figure 15-9 Depicting a 'Passive' Mapping as an Input Data

15.2.6 Model decision feedback loops

How organizations make decisions changes over time, often partly in response to the measured effectiveness of the decision-making. Indeed, ensuring such a feedback loop is an essential ingredient in Decision Management (see Section 5.5.3). Most such feedback loops are conditional in that there is a decision made as to the need to update the decision-making approach. This kind of feedback loop can and should be explicitly shown in a decision model.

DMN uses Authority Requirements to model this kind of feedback. Just as Knowledge Sources can be authorities for decisions, so other decisions as well as Input Data can be authorities for Knowledge Sources (see Section 11.1.2). This allows both the data being analyzed and decisions about the need to make a policy change to act as authorities for a policy that itself is an authority for an operational decision.

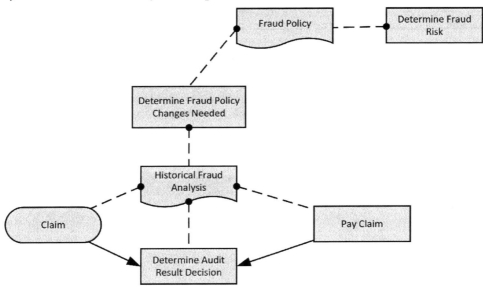

Figure 15-10 Modeled Feedback Loop For Fraud Risk

Consider the model in Figure 15-10. The decision *Determine Claim Fraud Risk* is an operational decision that applies to a specific *Claim*. It answers the question "Does this claim seem at significant risk for fraud?" One of the Knowledge Sources for this Decision is the *Fraud Policy*. This policy is regularly updated by the organization based on its analysis of historical fraud patterns. A decision is made regularly "Does the Fraud Policy need to be updated to better reflect patterns of fraud being detected?". This is modeled as *Determine Fraud Policy Changes Needed* and this decision acts as an authority for the Fraud Policy. *Historical Fraud Analysis* is represented as an analytic Knowledge Source that is an authority for this

Decision. The data that is analyzed is also shown as authorities for this Knowledge Source and consists of *Claim* data, payment data resulting from the *Pay Claim* decision and the outcome of the *Determine Audit Result Decision.*

In the decision *Determine Audit Result Decision* the organization is auditing certain claims and combining the results of these audits with claim and payment data to drive historical fraud analysis. This analysis informs the decision about changing policy and the updated policy then changes the original decision. The assessment of a claim's fraud risk might be manual or automated but the policy change needed decision is almost certain to be manual because this kind of update is still largely beyond the realm of machine learning/automation. The audit decision is likely to be manual as a matter of company policy to in order to provide a manual check even if the original decision was automated.

It is also possible to have decisions that self-learn. Machine learning technologies allow a decision to evaluate its own results and run experiments before revising its own decision-making approach. Modeling this in DMN is harder to represent as the "knowledge" for the decision could be said to be learning from the results of the decision and that would create an illegal cyclic dependency.

To model this kind of learning use an approach like that in Figure 15-11 where the same data that is input to the Decision is shown as authorities for a parallel machine learning Knowledge Source.

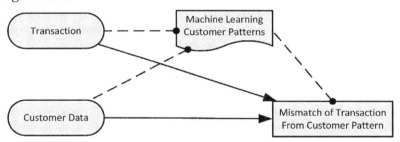

Figure 15-11 Machine Learning Feedback Loop Example

15.3 Decision Table Design Best Practices

15.3.1 Use order to aid readability

Decision Tables should be used as a declarative means of communicating business logic and should not embed implementation concepts. Two areas where such implementation concepts can cause problems are condition ordering and rule ordering. The examples that follow assume a 'rules as rows' layout (see Section 11.2.7.1) which means conditions are arrayed in columns and rules in rows. But these issues are equally applicable to other Decision Table formats.

15.3.1.1 Input column (condition) order

Aside from the convention that condition columns appear on the left of a Decision Table and conclusions on the right, DMN assigns no significance to the order in which inputs appear in a Decision Table. There is no concept of condition evaluation order in Decision Tables (as there is in some BRMSs) and no possibility of optimizing condition evaluation using order[54]. Consider the Decision Table in Figure 15-12, which uses expensive and cheap inputs to reach a conclusion. Whether the expense of these inputs is computational or monetary is immaterial.

Result			
U	**Expensive Input**	**Cheap Input**	**Result**
1	A	X	*Value 1*
2	not(A)	X	*Value 2*
3	-	Y	*Value 3*
4		not(X, Y)	*Value 4*

Figure 15-12 Simple Decision Table, Expensive Condition First

Some analysts and modelers with experience of a BRMS may be tempted to assume that this version is 'less efficient' than the variation of Figure 15-13, in which the evaluation of conditions on the expensive inputs can be avoided if the cheap input does not have value *X*. Such optimization is not the focus of DMN.

Result			
U	**Cheap Input**	**Expensive Input**	**Result**
1	X	A	*Value 1*
2		not(A)	*Value 2*
3	Y	-	*Value 3*
4	not(X, Y)	-	*Value 4*

Figure 15-13 Simple Decision Table, Cheap Condition First

From the standpoint of decision modeling the two Decision Tables of Figure 15-12 and Figure 15-13 are identical. Similarly, inputs should never be ordered because of some assumption that one condition has a side-effect that somehow influences another and must therefore be considered first. Neither conditions nor conclusions can have side-effects and they have no ability to influence each other (see Section 8.2.4.3).

The only consideration for input column ordering is ease of comprehension. Specifically, when ordering inputs, consider:

- **Business significance**. Inputs of vital business import or those that are crucial to the definition of a table or that denote a significant partition of the logic, should be placed to the left of inputs of lesser consequence. A Decision Table that classifies assets by type would be likely to have the input *Asset Type* very close to the left hand edge.

- **Discriminatory power**. The more the conditions of an input divides the table logic

---

[54] That is, there is no suggestion that conditions that are resource intensive should be placed to the right of less demanding tests so that the need for their evaluation in a given rule can be eliminated should the earlier tests yield `false`.

into major, multi-rule sub-sections, as opposed to minor variations, the further to the left it should appear. Inputs with conditions that evenly split the entire logic into large subsets should appear further to the left than those that distinguish minor, single row variant cases. Hence a Decision Table to determine the fine for traffic violation is more likely to have the input *Violation Type* to the left of a less impactful one like *Number of Vehicle Occupants*.

- **Frequency**. The higher the proportion of rules that test an input with a condition (as opposed to marking it irrelevant with '-') to determine the outcome, the further to the left it should appear. Inputs that always have an impact on the action should be placed to the left of those that are only occasionally used or those not used at all (and which appear because the need for them is imminently anticipated).

- **Mutual Association**. Where related inputs are used they should be kept together—side-by-side to reinforce the association between the two inputs. One illustration of this is a hierarchical classification where one category input is a sub-category of another because two or more inputs form multiple layers of a taxonomy, e.g., *Industry Class* and *Industry Sub-class*.

- **Existing Conventions**. Where a company has a well-founded, widely used and long standing convention for ordering the columns in Decision Tables or the Decision Table is emulating an existing document with which policy makers are very familiar, the established format should be honored to improve readability.

However, these indicators are not to be slavishly followed: there are a few exceptional cases that merit deviation from these rules. Use an alternative ordering of a table if it improves business clarity, helps to group related or co-evolving content or makes the rule more expressive and easier to maintain from a business perspective. If there are two or more rival orderings which rate equally on all of the above factors, be guided by visual aesthetics and the consistency of a table in this model with related tables elsewhere.

Consider the proposed Decision Table, in Figure 15-14, for determining the number of points to add to a driver's license based on the nature of a traffic offense[55]. The decision determines the penalty (in terms of points) given the type of driving license held, the nature of the violation, the frequency of previous offenses and whether or not the offender provided out of date documentation (e.g., insurance documents and permits) when challenged by police. The hit policy of this table (see section B.3.2 for a brief overview of hit policies) allows one or more rows to be hit simultaneously; the conclusion of each is summed to reach an overall outcome.

Figure 15-14 is somewhat hard to read, in part because the column order is counterintuitive. Business significance would dictate that, when penalizing drivers, the *Offense Type* is the most significant factor. In terms of discriminatory power, the *Driving License Type* is the next most substantial input. Finally, the frequency of conditions shows that the *Number of* Offenses *in Last Three Years* is more impactful than the *Documentation Up to Date* input because the latter is only significant in one rule. The re-ordering suggested by these metrics

---

[55] This is a trivial example to explore these concepts and bears little resemblance to real traffic law.

leads to the Decision Table of Figure 15-15, which is easier to read (although there is still room for improvement as later sections will show).

C+	Driving Offense Penalty Points				
	Documentation Up to Date	Number of Offenses in Last Three Years	Driving License Type	Offense Type	Driving Offense Penalty Points
	true, false		FULL, PROVISIONAL, LEARNER	DUI, RECKLESS, SPEED	
1	false	-	-	-	3
2		3	FULL	SPEED	6
3		<=2	FULL, PROVISIONAL	RECKLESS	6
4		<=2	PROVISIONAL	SPEED	2
5		-	FULL, PROVISIONAL	DUI	9
6	-	<=2	FULL	SPEED	3
7		>2	PROVISIONAL	SPEED	9
8		>3	FULL	SPEED	9
9		>2	FULL, PROVISIONAL	RECKLESS	9
10		-	LEARNER	-	3

Figure 15-14 Driving Offense Penalty Decision Table, Initial Version

C+	Driving Offense Penalty Points				
	Offense Type	Driving License Type	Number of Offenses in Last Three Years	Documentation Up to Date	Driving Offense Penalty Points
	DUI, RECKLESS, SPEED	FULL, PROVISIONAL, LEARNER		true, false	
1	-	-	-	false	3
2	SPEED	FULL	3	-	6
3	RECKLESS	FULL, PROVISIONAL	<=2	-	6
4	SPEED	PROVISIONAL	<=2	-	2
5	DUI	FULL, PROVISIONAL	-	-	9
6	SPEED	FULL	<=2	-	3
7	SPEED	PROVISIONAL	>2	-	9
8	SPEED	FULL	>3	-	9
9	RECKLESS	FULL, PROVISIONAL	>2	-	9
10	-	LEARNER	-	-	3

Figure 15-15 Driving Penalty Decision Table, Columns Ordered

15.3.1.2   Rule order

With some hit polices (i.e., First, Priority, Output and Rule), the order of rules influences the meaning of a Decision Table. Depending on the hit policy employed, rule order can act as a tie-breaker when multiple rules are satisfied (First, Priority) or determine the order of the results if more than one is generated (Rule). Section 15.3.3 considers the pros and cons of using these hit policies in detail.

For hit policies Unique, Any and Collect, rule order is irrelevant to the behavior of a Decision Table. Once the correct order for a set of condition columns has been established as shown in the previous section, the rules should be sorted to optimize: clarity, the ease with which overlapping rules or gaps can be identified and simplicity of reference. Such sorting should also ensure that related logic is 'bunched' for ease of maintenance. Condition values should be sorted, either by business convention, alphabetically, numerically, or in the case of Boolean conditions, true then false. This assists readers in looking up specific values (e.g., *Offense Type,* or *Driving License Type*). Irrelevant cells can be put first in the search order if they represent the most frequently occurring or important outcome (i.e., they represent a general, common case to which there are known, infrequent exceptions) or last if they are rarely occurring 'catchalls'. Consider the row sorted version of Figure 15-15 shown in Figure 15-16—this is both clearer to read and to reference.

Driving Offense Penalty Points					
C+	**Offense Type**	**Driving License Type**	**Number of Offenses in Last Three Years**	**Documentation Up to Date**	**Driving Offense Penalty Points**
	DUI, RECKLESS, SPEED	*FULL, PROVISIONAL, LEARNER*		*true, false*	
1	*SPEED*	*FULL*	<=2	-	3
2	*SPEED*	*FULL*	3	-	6
3	*SPEED*	*FULL*	>3	-	9
4	*SPEED*	*PROVISIONAL*	<=2	-	2
5	*SPEED*	*PROVISIONAL*	>2	-	9
6	*RECKLESS*	*FULL, PROVISIONAL*	<=2	-	3
7	*RECKLESS*	*FULL, PROVISIONAL*	>2	-	9
8	*DUI*	*FULL, PROVISIONAL*	-	-	9
9	-	*LEARNER*	-	-	3
10	-	-	-	false	3

Figure 15-16 Driving Penalty Decision Table, Rows Ordered

Another benefit of this sorted view is that the completeness of the logic and the absence of any unintended overlap can more easily be gauged. For example, a reader can tell at a glance that every possibility of number of previous offences is taken in account for speeding violations on a full license (rows 1-3) and that such offences will satisfy one and only one of these rows. The close proximity of these lines also helps with maintenance: if the third condition of row 2 were changed to 3, 4 it would be more obvious that an attendant change to the equivalent condition in row 3 was needed (i.e., to >4). Row ordering also helps modelers who are amending a Decision Table to locate the best place to insert new logic and to ensure changes do not introduce new overlaps or gaps.

A final (and related) embellishment is to merge (see Section 8.2.3.5) related condition cells as in Figure 15-17.

Driving Offense Penalty Points					
C+	**Offense Type**	**Driving License Type**	**Number of Offenses in Last Three Years**	**Documentation Up to Date**	**Driving Offense Penalty Points**
	DUI, RECKLESS, SPEED	*FULL, PROVISIONAL, LEARNER*		*true, false*	
1	*SPEED*	*FULL*	<=2	-	3
2			3	-	6
3			>3	-	9
4		*PROVISIONAL*	<=2	-	2
5			>2	-	9
6	*RECKLESS*	*FULL, PROVISIONAL*	<=2	-	3
7			>2	-	9
8	*DUI*	*FULL, PROVISIONAL*	-	-	9
9	-	*LEARNER*	-	-	3
10	-	-	-	false	3

Figure 15-17 Driving Penalty Decision Table, Rows Merged

Merging related conditions has a number of advantages, it:

- Clearly associates rules related by shared conditions and visually highlights important condition groups and logical structure (i.e., the sub-trees of conditions) within them.

- Lowers the likelihood of accidental splitting of related logic.
- Ensures the logical integrity of a group of conditions by preventing inconsistency due to typos. If a set of rules specifies the shared values only once, no inconsistency can arise among them. This can reduce the introduction of errors during maintenance.
- Simplifies the Decision Table (by avoiding the text repetition) making it easier to read and verify.

Remember condition cells may only be merged under certain circumstances (see Section 8.2.3.5). For example, the second condition of rows 6-8 cannot be merged because they do not all share the condition to the left (however 6-7 can be merged). Similarly, the '-' value for the *Documentation Up to Date* conditions in rows 1-9 cannot be merged because they don't share all the other conditions.

For small tables (less than a page in size), an alphabetic sort of enumerated conditions is often not the best approach. A business oriented sort is more effective in many circumstances, especially where the table is small and there is a strong, unambiguous business convention for sorting. For instance, *Offense Type*, is sorted by condition complexity (*SPEEDING* then *RECKLESS* then *DUI*[56]), and *Driving License Type* which is sub-sorted by frequency (*FULL* then *PROVISIONAL* then *LEARNER*). Whichever sort convention is used, be consistent between Decision Tables and maintain the sort order after table amendments. A partial (or inconsistent) sort is worse than no sort.

15.3.2 Keep inputs logically independent

It is good practice to make each input in a Decision Table logically independent of all others. Ensure that:

- The value of one input is not derivative of (calculable from or a by-product of) another.
- Values derived for one input don't impact the possible values of another. This can be the case if two or more inputs represent a multi-stage, hierarchical classification, like *Industry Class* and *Industry Subclass*, where the value set for one impacts the valid values of the other.
- Input meaning is consistent. That is, the interpretation of one condition test is not dependent on the tests made on another.

15.3.2.1 Inputs must not be derivative

For example, having *Candidate Birthday*, *Current Date* and *Candidate Age* in the same Decision Table would violate (1) because the last can be derived from the others. Derivative conditions allow the possibility of expressing paradoxical rules that can never be satisfied and present a maintenance hazard. This is especially dangerous when the dependency be-

---

[56] Driving Under the Influence (of drugs or alcohol).

tween inputs is not obvious or not well understood. Derivative inputs must be removed and the logic re-expressed in terms of the remaining inputs.

15.3.2.2 Inputs values must not be covariant

If two or more inputs in the same table are independently derived, but have related values, such that the value of one constrains the permitted (or actual) values of the others, this violates (2). This flaw can present apparent gaps in the logic of a Decision Table and prevent the table passing completeness verification tests. These gaps correspond to the input value combinations that cannot occur in practice. Worse, this practice can inadvertently lead to the inclusion of rules that cannot be satisfied (i.e., those that appear to satisfy the gaps). Consider the amended *Driving Offense Penalty Points* logic of Figure 15-18.

Driving Offense Penalty Points				
C+	Offense Type	Driving License Type	Number of Offenses in Last Three Years	Penalty Points Due
	DUI, RECKLESS, SPEED, WEIGHT	*FULL, GOODS, PROVISIONAL, LEARNER*		
1			<=2	3
2		*FULL, HGV*	3	6
3	*SPEED*		>3	9
4		*PROVISIONAL*	<=2	2
5			>2	9
6	*RECKLESS*	*FULL, HGV PROVISIONAL*	<=2	3
7			>2	9
8	*DUI*	*FULL, HGV PROVISIONAL*	-	9
9	*SPEED, RECKLESS, DUI*	*LEARNER*	-	3
10	*WEIGHT*	*HGV*	-	2
11	*LICENSE*	*not(HGV)*	-	10

Figure 15-18 Decision Table with Related Conditions

This features two new offences: *WEIGHT* and *LICENSE*. A *WEIGHT* offense is committed if the offender drives an overweight vehicle over a weak structure (e.g., an old bridge). The *LICENSE* offense is committed by anyone who is caught driving a vehicle for which they lack a license or a certified instructor. Two business assumptions are made:

- Conventional road vehicles cannot be overweight; the *WEIGHT* offence is only relevant to holders of a heavy goods vehicle (license type *HGV*)

- The heavy goods vehicle (*HGV*) license conveys the right to drive any vehicle and therefore holders of this license cannot commit the *LICENSE* offence.

For readers unaware of these business assumptions, there are apparent gaps in the logic of this (supposedly complete) table: *WEIGHT* offences by holders of non-*HGV* licenses and *LICENSE* offences by holders of *HGV* licenses. The best ways to handle this undesirable situation are:

- Avoid the dependency between the inputs by redesigning them to be independent. In this case by redefining the *WEIGHT* offence as pertaining to heavy goods vehicles only, eliminating the need to consider *HGV* licenses explicitly. This would simplify the *Driving License Type* condition in rules 10 and 11 to '-'. This option is preferred but is not always possible: decision models must faithfully represent the current practices of the business and provide traceability to requirements documents (Knowledge Sources)—often it is not feasible to change these just to improve Decision Table design.

- Include the missing logic—by adding two new rules covering *WEIGHT* offences for non-*HGV* licenses and *LICENSE* offences for *HGV* licenses—but denote with an annotation that neither rule is expected to be satisfied. This is appropriate if the number of gaps is few and the relationship between inputs it reflects is non-obvious. It has the benefit of documenting the relationship between the conditions and the hidden business assumptions.

- Relegate the heavy goods vehicle and licensing specific logic to subordinate sub-decisions which would yield a combined classification of *Offense Type* and *Driving License Type*. Values of the latter would only include valid combinations, for example *DUI-FULL, SPEED-HGV, LICENSE* and *WEIGHT*. This is a good approach only if the combination classification is meaningful from a business perspective and does not yield too many combinations. This solution does not work well in this example.

The concept of business completeness, which allows tables with logical gaps to be nevertheless considered complete because the omitted logic cannot occur, is covered in Section C.2.7.

15.3.2.3   Inputs must have consistent meaning throughout

If the interpretation of one input varies according to the value of one or more other inputs, then the meaning of input is not consistent and violates (3). Using the example in Figure 15-18, this would occur if the interpretation of *Driving License Type* depended, for example, on *Offense Type*. For instance, if *Driving License Type* referred in most cases to the license *currently* held by the offender, but in the case of *LICENSE* offences referred to the license that *should have been* held.

This flaw is obvious in this example, but subtle problems can occur when an input's term has alternate, context dependent interpretations. To resolve this flaw, modelers should use specific, non-contextual input terms, for example: *Offender's Driving License Type*.

15.3.3 Only use rule order dependent hit policies in appropriate situations

15.3.3.1   Hit policy and rule order

When creating a Decision Table, the concept of hit policy is vitally important (8.2.4 and 11.2.1). For simplicity and clarity, it is best practice to use hit policies for which the order of rules is immaterial (i.e., Unique, Any or Collect, see Section 14.5.2). As discussed above, the hit policies First, Priority and Rule are the only ones to rely on the order of rules in the Decision Table.

The Rule Policy is *mildly* dependent on row order in that shuffling the rows for a given Decision Table would change the order of the outcomes yielded in a given scenario, but not their values or frequencies. This is a minor consideration because very few decisions require a collection in which the order of items conveys meaning.

However, the First policy is crucially dependent on the rule order of a Decision Table. Using this policy, shuffling the rules could yield a different result in a given scenario. A given rule will not even be considered if an earlier one is satisfied. The First hit policy establishes an *order of priority* for each rule based on its position in the table. For this reason, this hit policy prevents use of rule order to aid readability and maintainability (see Section 15.3.1.2) and this detracts from its usefulness.

15.3.3.2 Comparing order independent hit policies

To compare the strengths and weaknesses of hit policies a single Decision Table will be examined. Consider the example of a decision that determines whether a child is eligible to use a 'high G-force' fairground ride. Suppose the child 'applicant' is permitted to use the ride providing: he or she has no disqualifying medical conditions (e.g., a weak heart) *and* they have the consent of a parent or guardian *and* they are at least the minimum age specified by the ride *and* they have at least the minimum height required for the ride (to ensure they fit the safety harness). This Decision Table yields a single conclusion per invocation: the 'eligibility' of a child applicant. Which hit policy is most appropriate?

Figure 15-19 depicts the required logic expressed using the Unique hit policy.

	Child Eligible for 'High G' Fairground Ride				
U	**Child has Disqualifying Medical Condition**	**Parental Consent**	**Child Age**	**Child Height**	**Eligibility**
1	true	-	-	-	false
2	false	false	-	-	false
3	false	true	< Minimum Age	-	false
4	false	true	>= Minimum Age	< Minimum Height	false
5	false	true	>= Minimum Age	>= Minimum Height	true

Figure 15-19 Fairground Decision Table using Unique Hit Policy

The Unique policy dictates that rule order is *not* significant in selecting the outcome and that there may not be any rule conflict in selecting that outcome. There is no set of circumstances in which more than one row can be satisfied simultaneously and there is no 'logical overlap' in the conditions. To achieve this, many conditions need to be added to prevent any such overlap. For every condition with a stipulation in Figure 15-19, negations also need to be provided in other rows to avoid overlap. In all, this table expresses 14 explicit conditions over 5 rules.

The same logic expressed with the Any hit policy (in Figure 15-20) is slightly more concise (8 conditions over 5 rules) because the satisfaction of multiple rows simultaneously is acceptable providing they yield the same conclusion(s).

| **Child Eligible for 'High G' Fairground Ride** | | | | |
A	Child has Disqualifying Medical Condition	Parental Consent	Child Age	Child Height	Eligibility
1	true	-	-	-	false
2	-	false	-	-	false
3	-	-	< Minimum Age	-	false
4	-	-	-	< Minimum Height	false
5	false	true	>= Minimum Age	>= Minimum Height	true

Figure 15-20 Fairground Decision Table using Any Hit Policy

In this version, only those rows with different conclusion values need to be distinguished. The last row, as it yields a different conclusion from the others, must be completely separated from them using negation. Overlap between the first four rows is permissible as they yield the same result. Some find this less satisfying than the Unique policy, but it does reduce maintenance.

Also, when using a BRMS that supports the association of a message with each row, the Any hit policy allows multiple messages to be collected to explain the multiple causes of ineligibility. Even without messages the BRMS using this hit policy can report multiple rows matched to show multiple factors caused an ineligibility.

15.3.3.3   Comparing order dependent hit policies

Compare this to the equivalent table expressed using the First hit policy in Figure 15-21.

| **Child Eligible for 'High G' Fairground Ride** | | | | |
F	Child has Disqualifying Medical Condition	Parental Consent	Child Age	Child Height	Eligibility
1	false	true	>= Minimum Age	>= Minimum Height	true
2	-	-	-	-	false

Figure 15-21 Fairground Ride Decision Table using First Hit Policy

For this hit policy, the first rule to be satisfied, for a given applicant, automatically disqualifies any rules below it, therefore the conditions can be terser. Figure 15-21 uses only 4 conditions and 2 rules—it requires fewer conditions because, due to the 'knock-out' nature of the policy, all rules effectively acquire the negations of all the conditions of the rows above them. For example, the second row of the Decision Table in Figure 15-21 is only considered if the applicant has violated one or more of the eligibility conditions in row 1 (thus disqualifying that first row).

	Child Eligible for 'High G' Fairground Ride				
P	**Child has Disqualifying Medical Condition**	**Parental Consent**	**Child Age**	**Child Height**	**Eligibility**
1	-	-	-	-	false
2	false	true	>= Minimum Age	>= Minimum Height	true

Figure 15-22 Fairground Ride Decision Table using Priority Hit Policy

As shown in Figure 15-22, the same logic expressed with the Priority hit policy is slightly less concise. It needs an extra row to specify the priority order of its conclusions. There is no dependency on row order in this version and we rely on the conclusion priority (expressed in the value list cell just below the conclusion title) to resolve any conflicts. In the case that rules stipulating a `false` and a `true` conclusion are simultaneously indicated for a candidate, the latter value takes precedence. As a result, the order of the rules in Figure 15-22 does not impact its behavior and a reverse order to that of Figure 15-21 has been used to emphasize this.

There is a significant down-side to the First hit and Priority hit policies as shown in the examples in Figure 15-21 and Figure 15-22. Consider a scenario where multiple conditions cause a False eligibility conclusion to be reached. The Decision Tables have no mechanism to detect and report multiple failures. They reach the correct conclusion, but an analysis of the results can never know the reason for ineligibility.

15.3.3.4   The case for First and Priority hit policies

In the preceding examples, the advantages of the First (and Priority) hit policies over policy Unique seem overwhelming:

- **Brevity**. The use of First or Priority considerably simplifies the logic of the table making it smaller and easier to comprehend.

- **Internal Consistency**. The use of First or Priority eliminates the need for consistent mutual exclusion conditions between the logic in certain rules—simplifying maintenance of the table. For example, changing the logic of the last row in Figure 15-19 to reflect a fairground policy change requires corresponding modifications to one or more of the other rows to maintain mutual consistency. However, because of lack of repetition in First and Priority tables, fewer edits would be required.

- **Fewer Condition Variations**. By virtue of having four inputs, the Decision Table columns can be ordered in 24 (i.e., $4!$) alternative ways. The use of First or Priority yields the same conditions for each variation, however the Unique hit policy variants with the same behavior must have different conditions.

U	Child Eligible for 'High G' Fairground Ride				
	Child Height	Child Age	Parental Consent	Child has Disqualifying Medical Condition	Eligibility
1	< Minimum Height	-	-	-	false
2	>= Minimum Height	< Minimum Age	-	-	false
3	>= Minimum Height	>= Minimum Age	false	-	false
4	>= Minimum Height	>= Minimum Age	true	true	false
5	>= Minimum Height	>= Minimum Age	true	false	true

Figure 15-23 Variant Fairground Ride Decision Table using Unique Hit Policy

This last point requires some explanation. Figure 15-23 shows another Unique hit policy variation of the fairground logic. It behaves the same way as Figure 15-19, but discriminates among the same conditions in a different order. Each of the 24 variants of the Unique table differ in condition content (unlike the equivalent cases in the First or Priority tables), but has the same behavior. Having so many different means of representing the same logic could be construed as a disadvantage. Often however, readability and business norms will narrow the viable options (see Section 15.3.1.1).

These advantages of the First policy are accentuated if many conditions have to be jointly satisfied to reach a high priority conclusion. If one of the high priority outcomes has a large set of ANDed condition terms and failure to meet these means other alternatives have to be considered, then the 'knock-out' behavior of the First hit policy can make the logic much more succinct. This is because the complexity of negating these conditions, that the Unique hit policy requires us to add explicitly and that the First hit policy automatically provides, can be considerable.

15.3.3.5 Disadvantages of the First hit policy

In our experience, this brevity in presenting small Decision Tables using the First (or Priority) hit policy can persuade some decision modelers that these policies might be the best choice when designing *any* new Decision Table—therefore, the First hit policy may become the default choice for new tables. This seems especially convenient as many people find that the First hit policy is intuitive and that this 'knock-out' style of logic naturally reflects the way they think: reducing all logic requirements to the consideration of a series of sequenced cases, the satisfaction of any of which eliminates all that follow.

This style of thinking – 'if A then A' *otherwise* if B then B' *otherwise…*' is very appealing. This is exacerbated by the fact that business requirements represented as prose are always listed in some order, if only for clarity. Even though there is rarely a genuine business precedence and this 'presentation order' is usually arbitrary, this can lead to rules with unnecessary sequence which can in turn obscure business logic.

The First hit policy has a number of specific weaknesses of which decision modelers should be very wary, many of which become much more acute when the Decision Tables grow in size:

- **Atomicity (Rule Independence).** The behavior of each Decision Table rule is dependent on those above it in the table—the behavior of the table can therefore only be understood as a whole. Inspection of a subset of the table is rarely useful and considering the behavior of individual rules is extremely hard unless the table is small or the row is near the top. In order to understand the behavior for rule 100 of a First hit policy table, one must first understand the preceding 99 rules.

- **Hard to Comprehend**. Unlike a Unique or Any Decision Table, a First table cannot benefit from any of the ordering techniques used to enhance business clarity of a Decision Table discussed in Section 15.3.1. For example, they cannot be row sorted to ensure that related rows—these that use similar conditions—are close to one another. Such sorting must also be prevented during maintenance to maintain accurate results.

- **Hard to Verify**. Because of these inter-rule order dependencies it is much harder (for humans and software) to verify the correctness of the table. This also makes it harder for business users to justify the behavior of rules after the fact, when reading a traceability report after rule execution for example.

- **Hard to Modify**. The rule preference order makes modifications to the table more challenging. For each addition of a rule you must ensure it is not accidentally eclipsed (i.e., completely logically eliminated or 'knocked-out') by any rule above it, nor must it accidently eclipse any rules beneath. On occasions it may be necessary to shuffle many rules to express the desired behavior. Every amendment threatens to fragment the table logic a little more. This modification becomes harder as the Decision Table gets older and larger and as maintainers of the model become less familiar with its meaning. In practice, we have seen that the effort of properly integrating new logic into the fabric of large, order-dependent tables becomes too challenging for analysts under time-pressure. The temptation is to save time by ignoring existing logic and adding new logic to the top of the table with very specific conditions to avoid eclipsing. This '*Wallpapering over the cracks*' leads to excessively large and specific tables with poorly factored and repeated logic, obscuring their meaning and compounding the maintenance issue.

- **Hard to Scale**. It is easy to split large order independent tables by business partition if their size is unwieldy (see the *Divide and Conquer* pattern in Section 16.2). This is much harder for order dependent tables which can only be split by priority order.

- **Unable to detect multiple causes**. Where there is a business requirement to identify and report every cause that leads to a particular conclusion, such as the ineligibility of a loan application, the First hit policy is an inappropriate choice. It will return the correct conclusion, but will only identify a single cause where multiple causes may exist.

15.3.3.6 Summary

Avoid the use of First, Priority or Rule hit policies unless your tables are small, will stay small and have complex negations. The use of these policies can greatly obscure decision logic and compromise the long-term comprehension of Decision Tables. They rarely yield a sufficient value to offset this risk.

15.3.4 Keep multiple conclusions cohesive but independent

Most Decision Tables will have a single conclusion after which the decision they define will often be named. Although DMN does allow a single Decision Table to express multiple conclusions and this offers the decision modeler great flexibility, it should be employed carefully. Multiple conclusions can lead to *Swiss Army Knife* (see 16.2) Decision Tables into which modelers have tried to combine too many separate concerns causing issues with ease of comprehension and maintenance.

Concise Decision Tables should avoid stipulating multiple conclusions unless there is a strong relationship between them and this is expected to endure. Specifically, multiple conclusions should only be employed if the conclusions:

- are cohesive;
- share dependencies; *and*
- are mutually independent.

Consider the examples that follow below.

15.3.4.1 Ensure the conclusions are cohesive

In a multiple conclusion Decision Table ensure each conclusion is associated with the others and together the set forms a cohesive business entity—the outcome is conceptually one thing. In effect, these related conclusion values are attributes being attached to what otherwise would be a single conclusion of the Decision Table. For example: the account, date, direction and amount of a bank statement entry; the day, month and year of a date or the latitude and longitude of a map coordinate. In these cases, there are situations where it does not make sense to set these attributes in separate Decision tables because the conclusions don't stand alone. To separate such conclusions may cause duplicated logic and maintenance issues. Conversely, avoid Decision Tables with entirely unrelated conclusions.

The Decision Table of Figure 15-24 has two conclusions that might, after casual inspection, appear to be related. In fact, the *Accident Risk Level* and *Illness Risk Level* are largely independent. Although they currently vary based on the same conditions, they are clearly reliant on different sets of (overlapping) values of these conditions.

C+	Risk Factors	Age (Years)	Policy Risk Level	
	Policy Risk Level		Accident Risk Level	Illness Risk Level
1	SPORTS PROFESSIONAL	<20	3	0
2		[20..26]	8	2
3		>26	21	11
4	URBAN DRIVER	-	10	0
5		<20	11	0
6		[55..65]	14	0
7		[66..75]	21	0
8		[76..80]	40	0
9		>80	72	0
10	RURAL DRIVER	-	14	0
11		[55..65]	23	0
12		[66..75]	30	0
13		[76..80]	55	0
14		>80	97	0
15	INDUSTRIAL CHEMIST GROUP A	-	5	19
16	INDUSTRIAL CHEMIST GROUP B	-	7	33
17	URBAN LAW ENFORCEMENT, TRAFFIC	-	12	8
18	NON COMMERICAL PILOT	-	33	2
19		[55..65]	77	6
20		>65	150	16

Figure 15-24 Multiple Conclusion Insurance Risk Decision Table

The only justification for keeping these conclusions in the same table is if the two depended on the same patterns of conditions, making a table split very repetitious, or there was a business need to keep conclusion values correlated. The cost of keeping these two unrelated conclusions in the same table are:

- The logic for determining *Illness Risk Level* is obscured because the granularity of logic is a combination of that needed for both conclusions. Consider the simplicity of this logic when represented alone (Figure 15-25).

- As this table evolves with time it is likely that additional conditions will be added that impact only one of these conclusions (illness risk might be impacted by family history and accident by number of prior claims). This will cause the table to become larger and diverge.

Illness Risk Level			
C+	**Risk Factors**	**Age (Years)**	**Illness Risk Level**
1		<20	0
2	SPORTS PROFESSIONAL	[20..26]	2
3		>26	11
4	INDUSTRIAL CHEMIST GROUP A	-	19
5	INDUSTRIAL CHEMIST GROUP B	-	33
6	URBAN LAW ENFORCEMENT, TRAFFIC	-	8
7		-	2
8	NON COMMERICAL PILOT	[55..65]	6
9		>65	16

Figure 15-25 Illness Risk Level Separated into Separate Decision Table

Coalesce multiple conditions into one table only when they are inseparable properties of the same underlying entity, are likely to be impacted by the same changes and will evolve together.

15.3.4.2 Ensure the conclusions share dependencies

In a multiple conclusion Decision Table each conclusion should be dependent on all (or most) of the conditions of the table. If different conclusions are dependent on small, disjoint subsets of the conditions the table should be split into separate tables; one per conclusion, unless their mutual cohesion is very strong.

In Figure 15-26, it appears that, whereas *Issuer Risk Weight* depends on all conditions in the table, *Guarantor Risk Weight* depends only on *EU Guarantor* and *Risk Rating*. If this were generally true, the table would develop a high degree of repetition in the latter conclusion. This would pose a maintenance issue, making the table larger than it needs to be and offering the possibility of inconsistency. It is acceptable for multiple conclusions to be dependent on different combinations of condition constraints under different circumstances, but not for conclusions to depend on a small, strict subset of the available conditions in all cases.

EU Non-Agency Risk Weight					Non-Agency Risk Weight	
C+	**Treasury Asset Class**	**EU Guarantor**	**Issuer Country**	**Risk Rating**	**Issuer Risk Weight**	**Guarantor Risk Weight**
1		true	-	-	0%	0%
2	GOVT DEV, GOVT EMG			[AAA..AA-]	0%	0%
3		false	-	[A+..A-]	0%	20%
4				<=BBB+	0%	50%
5		true	DE, UK	-	0%	0%
6				[AAA..AA-]	0%	0%
7			DE, UK	[A+..A-]	0%	20%
8	MUNI	false		<=BBB+	0%	50%
9				[AAA..AA-]	20%	0%
10			not(DE, UK)	[A+..A-]	20%	20%
11				<=BBB+	50%	50%

Figure 15-26 Multiple Conclusion Risk Weight Decision Table

Be prepared to separate conclusions into separate tables if they are dependent only on small subsets of the conditions.

15.3.4.3 Ensure the conclusions are mutually independent

In a multiple conclusion Decision Table each conclusion should not be entirely derivative of any other(s). If one of the conclusion values can be derived from the others in every case, then that conclusion should be the subject of another Decision Table which uses the other conclusions as its conditions.

Although they should be coherent, conclusions should be independent of one another. In Figure 15-27 it is apparent that one conclusion, *Rating Category*, is a classification of the other and not varying independently. If the *Rating Category* value can always be determined from the *Rating* value, this Decision Table should be split into two: the first determining *Rating* from *Issuer is Mortgage Backed Security Agency* and *Instrument Class* and the second determining *Rating Category* from *Rating*. The two decisions would be related by an Information Requirement and they are likely to have different Knowledge Sources.

Instrument Risk			Instrument Risk	
U	Issuer is Mortgage Backed Security Agency	Instrument Class	Rating	Rating Category
1	true	-	AAA	AAA
2		US AGENCY	AAA	AAA
3		US TBILL	AAA	AAA
4		CHINESE AGENCY	A	OTHER INVEST
5	false	GOVT EMG	AA	AA+ TO AA-
6		SINGAPORE AGENCY	AA	AA+ To AA-
7		XF SECURITY	B	NON INVEST
8		UNKNOWN	UNKNOWN	UNKNOWN

Figure 15-27 Multiple Conclusion Instrument Risk Decision Table

15.3.4.4 When to use multiple conclusions

Strong indicators that two or more Decision Tables should be merged into one with multiple conclusions are:

- The conclusions can be considered attributes of the same business entity;
- The logic is understood and managed by the same subject matter experts;
- The tables use the same (or nearly the same) conditions;
- The same patterns of condition values occur in each; *and*
- An amendment of one frequently requires a parallel modification of the other(s).

In addition, merged tables that contravene many of the above should be candidates for splitting.

15.3.5 Consider refactoring when you make changes

As with other information assets, unnecessary complexity is the enemy of decision models. Often this complexity is not present at the outset but grows over time as the items within the model are amended inconsistently. Each amendment, if not carefully considered, can add needless complexity undermining a model over time. The authors have encountered cases in which initially well-designed decision models have decayed into chaos only a few years after they were initially created. Largely this was due to a series of hasty amendments, performed by a succession of modelers who, in their haste to meet their deadlines:

- Failed to perform an impact assessment for the proposed change causing a modification to result in model inconsistency.
- Made changes with a narrow focus creating inconsistencies within the model and obscuring its overall ethos or approach. For example 'Wallpapering over the cracks' (see Section 15.3.3.6).
- Made tactical changes to address short-term issues which were not removed when the original motive expired.
- Failed to capitalize on reuse opportunities.
- Failed to restructure the model once existing structures and patterns were clearly no longer suited for purpose.
- Failed to update 'peripheral' dependencies (e.g., to Knowledge Sources) when decisions changed and so lost the opportunity to manage subsequent changes more readily.
- Used ordered hit policies to minimize the number of rules required in the short term, but inappropriately continued to use ordered hit policies that became unsuitable in the medium term.

As a consequence, the changes (or lack of changes) they make:

- Duplicate, obviate or eclipse existing decision dependencies or logic.
- Undermine the benefits of the decision model's current structure and patterns or even make them a liability.
- Make the model harder to understand.
- Make the model incorrect, introducing 'collateral damage'.
- Lead the model to be inconsistent with the real decision.

To avoid this decline, every change to the model should be 'surgical' and do no harm. Every time a model is amended ask:

- How can the goal be achieved most simply?
- How could the required change be made with the least impact to, and most consistently with, the current approach of the model?
- Does a decision model component, or components, already exist to meet the requirements of the change?
- What is the impact of the change on existing model components, is any rework required for them?
- Does the change impact the requirement for any remaining decision component? Could any be simplified or removed?

- In hindsight, could a series of decisions be refactored into a simpler, more generalized or more enduring representation? For example, repeating patterns could be an indication that you need to use the *Kaleidoscope* pattern (see Section 16.4). Some new patterns may be indicated and others may no longer be serving the model well.
- Is the amendment going to add any repetition to the decision model? If so, try to achieve the amendment by reuse or variation of existing content rather than by adding new material.

Like any series of changes made to the fabric of a large structure, a succession of hasty or ill-considered changes can degrade the quality of the whole or even seriously undermine it. To build a durable decision model, business analysts must make changes with minimal extra complexity, which is often not the same as changes of minimal effort. Failure to do will usually result in the need to recreate the model entirely, a much more expensive undertaking.

If this continual effort is not pragmatic, consider instead periodically and systematically reevaluating decision logic to simplify knots of complexity that have grown over time. It is good practice to maintain a list of decision model elements that 'need refurbishment,' perhaps by tagging those elements with something like *#refurbish*.

16 Patterns, Anti-Patterns and Approaches

Meaningful architecture is a living, vibrant process of deliberation, design, & decision, not just documentation.
—Grady Booch

As with any other problem solving endeavor, experienced practitioners notice that certain problem elements appear repeatedly. There are some demanding requirement structures and decision modeling challenges that reoccur across many business domains. These reoccurring problems can be addressed by the application of specific techniques and reusable model structures or templates. The most frequently used model templates are often referred to as *patterns*[57]. Experienced decision modelers are familiar with these patterns, quickly recognize the situations in which they apply and immediately use them without the need for detailed analysis. This is at the heart of why experienced modelers are more productive than inexperienced ones.

Established patterns that have proven useful on a number of occasions can be articulated clearly so that they progress from being useful personal insights to explicitly defined and shared assets. Documented patterns can be shared with less experienced modelers and their application to a specific problem can be debated without ambiguity. They can be refined over time and their use can be combined with other patterns. Patterns become reusable 'packets of experience'.

Ultimately, patterns add to the language used by those engaged in decision modeling and help them to succinctly express complex issues. Using this shorthand, business analysts can cooperate and evaluate rival models more effectively. Ultimately, the best patterns become part of the decision modeler's vocabulary and significantly raise the effectiveness of their communications.

Some patterns are very specific to certain problem contexts and others are widespread and almost commonplace. All of them need to be documented effectively and consistently to facilitate sharing.

This section describes the most useful decision modeling patterns we have encountered. For each pattern this section includes:

- The **name** of the pattern describes (sometimes figuratively) what the pattern does and the problem it addresses.

- A **synopsis** conveys the essence of the pattern and reveals to experienced practitioners if this is a pattern they have encountered before

---

[57] This idea is ubiquitous and not confined to decision modelling, see Gamma Erich, Helm Richard, Johnson Ralph and Vlissides John, *Design Patterns: Elements of Reusable Object-Oriented Software*, Addison-Wesley, 1994, ISBN 0-201-63361-2.

- The **problem** that the pattern addresses—when and why to apply the pattern.

- The **application** explains in general how to apply the pattern.

- The **example** includes a problem, such as a fragment of a decision model, to which the pattern can be applied. It also shows the results of applying the pattern to the example problem to illustrate the practical advantages the pattern has to offer.

- The **consequences** explain the advantages and disadvantages of applying this pattern.

- The **notes** describe any known limitations with the pattern—those circumstances where the approach cannot be used effectively. It also includes any related ideas, including any variations of the pattern and which other patterns are related to it

All of the patterns in this chapter relate to decision models and decision modeling. Three (*Approximator, Process Sequence,* and *Approve, Decline, Refer*) relate to decision models in the context of process models and have implications for both process and decision models. Some represent means to avoid problems (*Scorecard, Change Shield, Kaleidoscope, Approximator, Classifier* and *Data Preparation*), some address existing problems (*Divide and Conquer, Exception Based Logic, Positive Validator* and *Process Sequence*) and some are general approaches to using decision models (*Champion/Challenger* and *Approve Decline, Refer*). Many are full patterns but some fall on the borderline between best practice and patterns.

Each of the sections that follows documents one pattern. Each section is named after the pattern it describes followed by the problem it addresses in brackets.

16.1 Scorecard (So Many Competing Factors)

16.1.1 Synopsis

The scorecard pattern is used to determine a single, continuous measure, from a set of diverse and competing inputs, when a discrete value is not appropriate or possible. Some business decisions cannot easily reach a discrete, enumerated result. Instead a continuum of values signifying the extent of an outcome is more relevant and useful. In these cases, the decision can determine a 'score'.

16.1.2 Problem

Some business decisions don't have simple yes or no answers or even a small number of expected alternative outcomes. Instead their output is a continuous, analog quantity representing a magnitude or propensity. Examples include credit score, IQ, likelihood of tax evasion and skilled worker immigration eligibility score. In some instances, the score will have an established range (e.g. a credit rating of [0..1000]). In other instances, there will be no cap on the value, just the understanding that higher values are always better (or worse) than lower ones. Most often, a score is partially subjective and is not strictly proportional to the property it measures (i.e., twice the score does not literally signify double the value).

These decisions are characterized by certain qualities:

- The outcome of these decisions is influenced by many competing factors of differing importance.

- Few if any of these factors are individually conclusive.

- It is possible that a large number of low weight factors can overrule a small number of high weight ones.

- The outcome needs to express a continuum of results in a single dimension (bad to good).

- Different parent decisions will set their own thresholds or score cut-offs on this quantity.

Instead of weighing each factor individually against the others to arrive at a set conclusion, this pattern calculates an overall numerical score allowing every factor to have a weighted contribution. Usually the score is the cumulative total of the product of factor values and their weights. This is a form of continuous classification (see also Section 16.9).

It should be noted that developing an effective scorecard is almost always an analytic exercise in that data should be assembled and analyzed to see which factors have an impact and how much each contributes. Turning an analytic model, such as a regression model, into a scorecard is a well-established technique in analytics, widely used in the consumer credit and insurance markets. This pattern concerns itself with how to represent the decision in a model, not with the analytics involved defining an effective decision.

16.1.3 Application

Two distinct applications of this pattern are used: a Simple Scorecard and an Instrumented Scorecard.

16.1.3.1 Simple scorecard

Simple scorecards use a Decision Table with a Collect with Aggregation function hit policy (see 11.2.2.5). Most scores are cumulative sums of their contributions. The inputs of the Decision Table are the contributing factors. The conditions of each rule are used to determine if a factor should be applied and to translate enumerated factors into numerical score contributions. Each conclusion holds a numeric literal or formula denoting the contribution to the score.

If a fixed range of scores is desired, the weightings and contributing factor values must be normalized so that the assigned maxima and minima cannot be exceeded under any circumstances. If the desired output range is [0..1000] and there are five contributing factors each with a separate weight, one solution would be to ensure the sum of the weights is 1.0 and the maximum, unweighted factor score is 1000.

Weightings are often derived from an analytic Knowledge Source and are subject to periodic revision.

16.1.3.2 Instrumented scorecard

A slightly more sophisticated version of this pattern is used when the scorecard needs to be accountable for the result it generates. For instance, a scorecard calculating a credit risk will need to produce not only a score but also an explanation that could be presented to a consumer who was declined.

Instead of using the Collect with Sum Aggregation ('C+') hit policy to generate the total score, the scorecard uses the Collect policy to yield a collection of score components and, crucially, an explanation or justification of each component. This justification can be another conclusion or a rule level annotation (see Section 14.5.7) to explain each specific contribution). A decision that has an information requirement on the scorecard may then trivially determine the total score by calculating the sum of the scores, or by using some more sophisticated process.

This solution requires two decisions as opposed to one, but has the benefits of being able to explain score components after the fact and providing more flexible aggregation. Consumers of the score components can process them as they wish; the aggregation function is not limited to the four available to the Collect hit policy. It also allows the decision to be used in circumstances where the list of score components is the critical element not the total score, such as in an advisory situation.

16.1.4 Example

Determining the likelihood that a household will be burgled depends on a number of factors: the inherent risk associated with the zip code, security features installed at the property (window and door security, lighting), daily occupancy patterns, pet ownership and the number of past burglaries. There is a need to build a decision that uses factor weightings derived from past data to build a score that indicates likelihood of burglary. The score has an upper value of 100 but is not a probability. The scores 0 and 100 merely reflect the minimum and maximum likelihoods from our perspective, not the impossibility and certainty of being robbed.

The Decision Requirements Diagram of one example solution is shown in Figure 16-1. The scorecard decision is shown with a thick border for emphasis. Note how it relies on a Knowledge Source for the weightings of the contributing factors and that this Knowledge Source is analytical, itself relying on historical data. The decision also relies on the Input Data *Property Details* for information about the security features of the property (*Security Features*) and *Area Details* for risks associated with the area (*ZIP Inherent Risk*). This scorecard determines a score that is used, among other things, to determine the insurance premium.

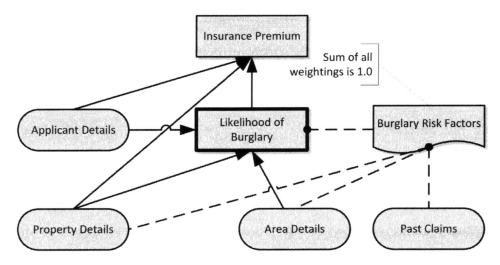

Figure 16-1 Example Scorecard Decision Requirements Diagram

Notice the Decision Table (in Figure 16-2) has the Collect with Aggregation function hit policy to sum the score from multiple contributions. It uses a context to marshal the weightings from the analytic Knowledge Source and to calculate risk factors from them.

Likelihood of Burglary

Security Features	Property Details.Security Features
ZIP Inherent Risk	Area Details.ZIP Inherent Risk
Inherent Weighting	Burglary Risk Factors.Inherent Risk Weighting
Security Weighting	Burglary Risk Factors.Security Risk Weighting
Occupancy Weighting	Burglary Risk Factors.Occupancy Risk Weighting
Dog Weighting	Burglary Risk Factors.Dog Risk Weighting
History Weighting	Burglary Risk Factors.History Risk Weighting
Has Alarm	list contains(Security Features, ALARM)
Has Deadlock	list contains(Security Features, 3P DEAD LOCK)
Has Flood Lights	list contains(Security Features, FLOOD LIGHTS)

C+	ZIP Inherent Risk	Has Alarm	Has Deadlock	Has Flood Lights	Average Occupancy Hr per Dy	Pet	Past Burglaries	Likelihood of Burglary (Score)
	[0..100]	true, false	true, false	true, false	[0..24]	FIERCEDOG, QUIETDOG, NONE	>=0	
1	<90	-	-	-	-	-	-	Inherent Weighting * ZIP Inherent Risk * 2/3
2	[90..100]	-	-	-	-	-	-	Inherent Weighting*((ZIP Inherent Risk-90)*4 + 60)
3	-	false	-	-	-	-	-	Security Weighting * 40
4	-	-	false	-	-	-	-	Security Weighting * 40
5	-	-	-	false	-	-	-	Security Weighting * 20
6	-	-	-	-	<5	-	-	Occupancy Weighting * 100
7	-	-	-	-	[5..9]	-	-	Occupancy Weighting * 60
8	-	-	-	-	(9..18]	-	-	Occupancy Weighting * 20
9	-	-	-	-	-	not(FIERCEDOG)	-	Dog Weighting * 100
10	-	-	-	-	-	-	[1..2]	History Weighting * Past Burglaries * 40
11	-	-	-	-	-	-	>2	History Weighting * Past Burglaries * 100

Figure 16-2 Example Scorecard Decision Table

Some Boolean contributing factors (i.e., the existence or absence of security features) conditionally contribute specific weighted components to the score. Other numerical factors (e.g., *ZIP Inherent Risk*) have calculated contributions.

16.1.5 Consequences

The scorecard decision allows us to succinctly express and control all of the contributing factors and how they accumulate to build a continuous measure of the decision outcome. The contribution weightings can be dynamically updated in the light of new findings arising from analysis of emerging trends, for instance, discovery that occupancy deters burglaries more than was previously believed. Because other decisions depend on the score, they are well insulated from such changes.

16.1.6 Notes

The scores generated by a scorecard can be used by a parent decision that:

- Tests the score against a threshold to determine if the score indicates some eligibility or derived fact.
- Classifies the score into a band of values.
- Uses the score in another calculation to determine other continuous values, for example insurance premium, interest rate and credit card reward points.

A scorecard can become hard to understand if there are more than 6 or so contributing factors or the sparsity of the table is high (greater than 70%). In these cases the individual contributions need to be separately managed or the complexity is otherwise excessive. Such tables can be split using the *Divide and Conquer* pattern (see Section 16.2). If the scorecard is a strict implementation of an analytic model, however, it should be implemented as the analytic model dictates to maintain traceability. It will not be changed except to reflect a refreshed analytic model. This intent should be clearly noted in the decision's description.

16.2 Divide and Conquer (The Swiss Army Knife)

16.2.1 Synopsis

The Divide and Conquer pattern is a means of splitting a single, over complicated decision that violates complexity best practices into several sub-decisions that together perform the same task. Each specialist sub-decision is simpler, smaller and more focused than the original. Once split, the responsibility for maintaining these sub-decisions can be devolved as needed. The pattern adds a parent decision to consolidate all the sub-decisions to achieve the same ends as the original complex decision. This parent replaces the original decision in the model.

16.2.2 Problem

Occasionally decisions are created as, or more commonly evolve into, behemoths—mounds of complexity that are simply trying to accomplish too much in one place. Such 'Swiss Army Knife' decisions (see Section 14.5.3)) are created accidentally, from a desire to keep the logic in one central location, or because there is a historical precedent ("we've always done it this way"). Swiss Army Knife decisions can also arise over time as a succession of inexperienced decision modelers implement change by adding new logic to an existing decision rather than creating a new one.

Regardless of how it came to be, given time, experienced analysts become familiar with the complexity of the Swiss Army Knife decision and grow blind to it. Newcomers are intimidated by the complexity and so make changes in a way that minimizes their need to understand what is already there. Inevitably the Swiss Army Knife becomes ever more bloated and complicated.

Although the modelers of these decisions may accept that a split might aid comprehension and improve accuracy, they are often concerned that it might disperse the whole and make it harder to manage. Actually the opposite is the case.

Symptoms of the Swiss Army Knife include:

- Complex, unwieldy decision logic that is hard to comprehend and maintain. Any logic in which specific rules are very hard to understand in the context of the whole—for instance a large Decision Table with the First hit policy. These often involve complex chains of priority, violating best practice 15.3.3.

- Unmanageable size featuring either 'tall' Decision Tables with hundreds of rows or 'fat' tables with tens of inputs. This violates the best practices in 14.5.3.

- A single decision that actually has multiple, completely independent (*specialist*) parts often under the jurisdiction of different experts. Indicators of this are that the decision has more than seven conditions that are used independently or in small groups, but never all together, or the sparsity of the Decision Table (the density of '–' cells) exceeds 70%. This violates best practice 14.5.3).

- Indications that new logic has been added to the top of a rule-ordered table with no attempt to integrate it with other rules. For example, very specific conditions in a new rule are used to avoid eclipsing existing rules. This '*Wallpapering over the cracks*' is covered more in Section 15.3.3.5.

- Maintenance issues arising from a change in one aspect of a decision's behavior that inadvertently impacts another.

- A set of SMEs that all require jurisdiction over disjoint parts of a single decision.

- They have two or more unrelated conclusions (violating the best practices in 15.3.4).

The motivation for applying the Divide and Conquer pattern is to overcome these symptoms by splitting apart the separate aspects of the logic. These parts are then able to evolve independently, potentially under the control of different SMEs.

16.2.3 Application

Divide and Conquer splits Decision Tables (or decisions) into subordinates of much smaller and more manageable size using a partition—a criterion for performing a split that preserves behavior. The nature of this partition depends on the original table and the motivation for applying the Divide and Conquer pattern.

To determine the partition used to split the tables, consider why the table is being split and refer to Table 16-1. If there is a mixed rationale, multiple partitions can be applied.

The split into sub-tables must *always*:

- have a business justification (splits based on arbitrary or technical rationales should be avoided);

- be reviewed and approved by a subject matter expert;

- divide the Swiss Army Knife into appreciably smaller, evenly-sized sub-tables (a 1%/1%/98% split is clearly not worthwhile);

- split the table into mutually independent sub-tables that are unlikely to require co-ordinated maintenance;

- avoid the need for large scale repetition (e.g., of input sets or conditions) between tables; *and*

- reduce sparsity.

The best splits divide the decision into sub-tables with different expertise jurisdictions that can evolve independently.

The four variants of this pattern ('specialization', 'tall table', 'non-cohesion' and 'order complex') are depicted visually in Figure 16-3, Figure 16-4, Figure 16-5 and Figure 16-6 respectively.

Rationale for Split	How to Split
Specialization: the table represents many different (specialist) techniques of determining the same outputs, each of which: use a disjoint (or nearly disjoint) set of inputs, evolve independently and are governed by different experts. The table has many (>10) conditions and many cells (>70%) use '-', i.e., table is sparse.	Separate out each distinct technique for determining the output into a separate Decision Table. Each sub-table should test a unique set of inputs on which the outputs are exclusively dependent. There may be small, unavoidable overlaps in the inputs of the sub-tables in practice.
'Tall Table': the table has hundreds of rules and all of its inputs are tested in nearly all rules.	Find one or more discriminating inputs, used throughout the tall table. Then identify classes of values of this input that represent a business partition (e.g., product type, state). Split the tall table by this partition, creating a set of small, evenly sized sub-tables.
Non-cohesion: the table has multiple unrelated outputs determined by similar inputs and conditions (see Section 15.3.4.1).	Split the table into sub-tables with cohesive sub-sets of outputs that avoid systematic repetition of the inputs and conditions.
Complex order: the table is complex and order dependent (see Section 15.3.3.3). It has more than 30 rules or irrelevant ('-') conditions that alternate between inputs.	Split into multiple sub-tables using any progressive business classification that cleanly stages the rule order of the original. Re-write to avoid the order dependency if possible (see example).

Table 16-1 Determination of Table Split Criteria Based on Rationale for Split

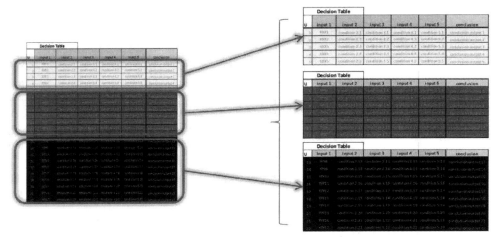

Figure 16-3 Visual Depiction of 'Specialization' Table Split

When Divide and Conquer splits a Decision Table into fragments, a single parent decision is needed to consolidate the results. This parent rule can be one of two types:

- **Active** parents select which outcome from the split tables to use as the overall result.

- **Passive** parents allow the outcomes of the split tables to determine the result, typically by consulting each in priority sequence. Each child uses a special return value to signify "I return no outcome of value" that causes the parent to consult other children.

Generally, this parent decision can be used in place of the original Swiss Army Knife decision without a need to change any Decisions that depended on the original.

16.2.4 Example

The Decision Table of Figure 16-7 is clear enough initially but the latter third is hard to understand because the table is using an order dependent hit policy. A special complexity here is the use of irrelevant ('–'), which alternates from *Issuer Industry* to *Issuer Type* and back in rules 2, 3, 5, 6, 7 and others. This makes comprehension of some rows harder because of the implicit negations of earlier rows. For example, Rule 3 has the unstated condition that *Issuer Industry* is not *GOVT AGENCY* and rule 6 that *Issuer Industry* is not *GOVT_AGENCY or REGIONAL GOVT*. This has a cumulative effect that obscures the meaning of lower priority rules and it gets worse as the reader scans down the table.

F	Issuer is Mortgage Agency	Issuer Industry	Issuer Type	Issuer Country	Issuer Classification
1	true	-	-	-	AGENCY
2		GOVT AGENCY	-	-	AGENCY
3		-	OFFS_ISSUER	-	AGENCY
4		BANK	AGENCY_ISSUER	GB	AGENCY
5		REGIONAL GOVT	-	-	MUNI
6		-	MUNI_ISSUER	-	MUNI
7		NATIONAL GOVT	-	-	GOVT
8			GOVT_ISSUER	-	GOVT
9			AGENCY_ISSUER	-	AGENCY-OTHER
10		-	SPV_ISSUER	-	SPV
11			MBS_ISSUER	-	MBS
12			ABS_ISSUER	-	ABS
13		SPECIAL	CORP_FIN_ISSUER	-	SPV
14		BANK , FINANCIAL	-	-	CORP FIN
15		-	CORP_FIN_ISSUER	-	CORP FIN
16			COR_FIN ISSUE	-	CORP FIN
17		GAS , TELEPHONE , RAIL	-	-	CORP NON-FIN
18		-	NON_FIN_ISSUE	-	CORP NON-FIN
19			-	-	UNKNOWN

Figure 16-7 Decision Table Featuring Complex Priorities

Figure 16-7 is a Swiss Army Knife. The simple decision requirement diagram corresponding to Figure 16-7 is shown in Figure 16-8.

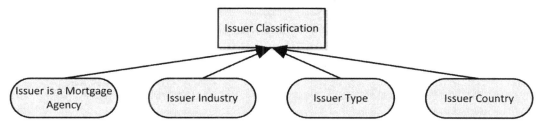

Figure 16-8 Decision Requirement Diagram for Figure 16-7

The problem example of Figure 16-7 requires the application of Divide and Conquer with a complex order split. This requires the use of a partition, a business criterion that changes progressively as the table progresses from high to low priority. In this case it is the class of the conclusion that moves from agency variants in the first set of rules (1-4), to municipal and government asset issuers (5-13) and ends with purely financial issuers (14+). This is a good split strategy as it:

- is a meaningful business distinction;
- results in a three-way split into much smaller sub-decisions with no condition value repetition; *and*
- uses the different input dependencies of each partition (agency, government and financial) to reduce the number of inputs in the second two tables.

The new sub-decisions and a replacement parent decision are shown in the amended Decision Requirements Diagram of Figure 16-9.

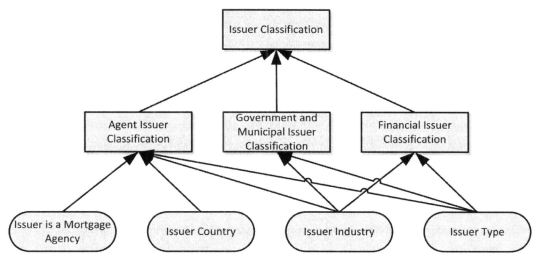

Figure 16-9 Decision Requirements Diagram Post Application of Consolidator

Note the introduction of three split Decision Tables in the second layer of Figure 16-9. The logic of these is depicted in Figure 16-10, Figure 16-11 and Figure 16-12 respectively.

Agent Issuer Classification					
U	Issuer is Mortgage Agency	Issuer Industry	Issuer Type	Issuer Country	Agent Issuer Classification
					AGENCY, *UNKNOWN*
1	true	-	-	-	AGENCY
2		GOVT AGENCY	-	-	AGENCY
3	false	not(GOVT AGENCY)	OFFS_ISSUER	-	AGENCY
4		BANK	AGENCY_ISSUER	GB	AGENCY

Figure 16-10 New Agent Issuer Classification Decision Table

Figure 16-10 corresponds to the first four rules of the original table (Figure 16-7), however it has been translated to a simpler Unique hit policy. It represents the highest priority agent classifications. Unlike the original it is not complete (see Section 8.2.4.2) and it has a default value of *UNKNOWN*, which signifies that its subset of the logic was not applicable in a given case.

Government and Municipal Issuer Classification			
U	Issuer Industry	Issuer Type	Government and Municipal Issuer Classification
			ABS, AGENCY-OTHER, GOVT, MBS, MUNI, SPV, UNKNOWN
1	REGIONAL GOVT	-	MUNI
2	not(REGIONAL GOVT)	MUNI_ISSUER	MUNI
3	NATIONAL GOVT	not(MUNI_ISSUER)	GOVT
4		GOVT_ISSUER	GOVT
5		AGENCY_ISSUER	AGENCY-OTHER
6	not(REGIONAL GOVT , NATIONAL GOVT)	SPV_ISSUER	SPV
7		MBS_ISSUER	MBS
8		ABS_ISSUER	ABS
9	SPECIAL	CORP_FIN_ISSUER	SPV

Figure 16-11 New Government and Municipal Issuer Classification Decision Table

Figure 16-11 depicts the new representation of rows 5-13 of the original table. As with Figure 16-10, this table has also been translated to the simpler Unique hit policy, it is not complete and has a default *UNKNOWN* value.

Financial Issuer Classification		
A	Issuer Industry	Issuer Type	Financial Issuer Classification
			CORP FIN, CORP NON-FIN, *UNKNOWN*
1	BANK , FINANCIAL	-	CORP FIN
2		CORP_FIN_ISSUER	CORP FIN
3	-	COR_FIN ISSUE	CORP FIN
4	GAS , TELEPHONE , RAIL	not(CORP_FIN_ISSUER , COR_FIN_ISSUE)	CORP NON-FIN
5	not(BANK , FINANCIAL)	NON_FIN_ISSUE	CORP NON-FIN

Figure 16-12 New Financial Issuer Classification Decision Table

Figure 16-12 is the final split table: it represents the logic of the final five rules of Figure 16-7. Again it is not complete, has the Any hit policy (which serves to simplify its logic somewhat) and a default of *UNKNOWN*.

	Issuer Classification		
U	Agent Issuer Classification	Government and Muncipal Issuer Classification	Issuer Classification
1	not(*UNKNOWN)*	-	Agent Issuer Classification
2	*UNKNOWN*	not(*UNKNOWN)*	Government and Municipal Issuer Classification
3		*UNKNOWN*	Financial Issuer Classification

Figure 16-13 New Issuer Classification Decision Table

Figure 16-13 replaces the original complex table and serves to use, and prioritize the results of, the three new sub-decisions—selecting the correct sub-decision to use in each case. Notice how this passive, 'consolidating parent' table imposes order on the sub-decisions, but is entirely decoupled from them. The use of *UNKNOWN* to communicate that a specific sub-decision was unable to yield a result in a given case is a good practice for this pattern as it ensures the sub-decisions can evolve independently of the main decision. Other applications of the pattern may use other cues to determine which of the sub-decisions to apply in each given case.

Figure 16-13 also illustrates how non-First hit policy tables can impose priority while remaining scalable and maintainable.

16.2.5 Consequences

Comparing the original versus the split models, it is apparent that the major benefits of the application of Divide and Conquer are two fold:

- The single, complex, First hit policy decision can be translated to four smaller, Unique and Any hit policy equivalents that are easier to understand and can be more easily maintained separately.
- The logic associated with each conclusion category (agencies, municipal and financial issuers) can now evolve independently and be assigned to different subject matter experts.

Less significant benefits worthy of note include:

- Slight size reduction from 53 condition cells to 45.
- '-' cell reduction from 60% to 29%.
- The data item dependencies are reduced: from an average of 4 to 2.

If the original Decision Table is sparse, it is often possible that the sum of the consolidated Decision Tables will be substantially smaller than the original. In other scenarios the sum can be slightly larger than the original but the increase in clarity of the result is still worthwhile.

There are some associated costs to using Divide and Conquer, including:

- The three additional items in the Decision Requirements Diagram may be perceived as additional cognitive load on modelers, though this can be mitigated by making this detail the subject of its own diagram.

- There is a new need to ensure that updates to one new table do not have adverse consequences for the others. This is unlikely in this case because of the business separation of the selected split partition.

16.2.6 Notes

There are rare occasions when a good split partition cannot be found when using this pattern (e.g., tall tables that have no clear business partitions). This can sometimes be solved by devising synthetic criteria to split the logic or using *Exception Based Logic* (see Section 16.6).

Divide and Conquer is equivalent to Decision Table refactoring. When applied to multi-conclusion tables it should not be confused with *Kaleidoscope*. The principle difference is that *Divide and Conquer* devolves independent conclusions, whereas *Kaleidoscope* eliminates condition group repetition.

For the specialist version of this pattern, ensure all newly created 'child' Decision Tables return a result under all circumstances (if necessary by defaulting to UNKNOWN) so that their failure to yield a normal result can be handled properly by the parent Decision Table.

This pattern is considered by some to be two related patterns: one handling wide or non-cohesive Decision Tables and the other handling 'tall' tables. We combine them here because their causes and resolutions have much in common.

16.3 Change Shield (Volatility)

16.3.1 Synopsis

The Change Shield is a decision that shields many others that depend on it from a source of persistent change. It isolates and protects its parents from the consequences of expected alteration and lowers the associated maintenance costs of the entire system.

16.3.2 Problem

One of the largest components of a Decision Management System's running costs is maintenance in the face of perpetual, externally imposed change. Decision Management streamlines change, reducing costs. However, occasionally ubiquitous Input Data and Knowledge Sources can be so prone to change that they are a major disruption to the multiple decisions that depend on them.

Symptoms of this problem include the regular impact to multiple, complex decisions, possibly spanning many decision models, due to:

- A constant stream of changes in the format, structure or meaning of commonly used Input Data components from outside the company.

- High frequency modifications to the range or permitted enumerated values of these Input Data components.

- Periodic changes mandated by an externally managed Knowledge Source, or dependence on an internally managed one with another purpose that causes high-frequency change (e.g., a guideline for claims adjustors used in both specifying automated decisions and provided as a document to contractors).

- High rate of change in an externally provided decision or Business Knowledge Model.

These changes are often driven by the same events, for example the release of a new version of a regulatory specification or feeder system, and require the same kind of change each time. Frequently such changes require quick impact assessment and modifications in some or all of the dependent decisions.

16.3.3 Application

The impact of changes to attribute meaning, permitted values of Input Data properties or of Knowledge Sources on which a decision model is dependent cannot be completely avoided, but they can be lessened.

This is achieved by introducing a new decision or Knowledge Source—a Change Shield or proxy—that breaks the direct dependency of many components on a single volatile Input Data or Knowledge Source. All other components that once depended on the volatile component should now depend on the proxy.

The proxy can further protect its dependents from change by classifying the values of Input Data or using specific Knowledge Sources to isolate consumers from detail that is irrelevant to its purpose. The technique depends on using a proxy sub-decision or Knowledge Source to define a more enduring abstraction of the domain of this decision than the original.

16.3.4 Example

An important trading decision is to determine what margin to leave to allow for unexpected market events—a volatility margin. This margin is a function of several trade attributes and conventions surrounding different credit agencies' means of representing volatility. A candidate Decision Requirements Diagram is shown in Figure 16-14.

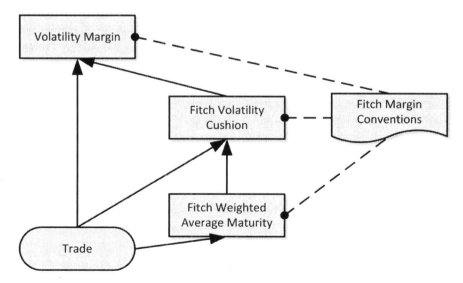

Figure 16-14 Candidate volatility margin Decision Requirements Diagram

One drawback of this approach is that the representation of trade (including attribute format and their interpretation) and the margin conventions used by the agency are subject to constant change. As both components are required by three decisions, the impact of a change could be widespread.

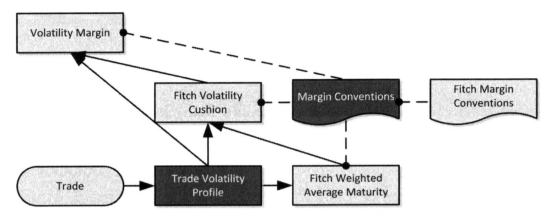

Figure 16-15 Decision Requirements Diagram featuring two isolators

In the example solution of Figure 16-15, two proxies have been introduced (shown with a dark fill): *Trade Volatility Profile* generalizes (and classifies) those aspects of trade data that are needed by its dependents and *Margin Conventions* generalizes the detail provided by the *Fitch Margin Conventions* Knowledge Source, again filtering out irrelevant detail. Many types of change in *Trade* or *Fitch Margin Conventions* will now only require amendments to the proxy components of the model, leaving all of their original dependents unchanged.

The introduction of a new Trade product type, for example, would have directly impacted up to three decisions in the original model. Now, providing *Trade Volatility Profile* can classify the new product type into an existing class, only the proxy is impacted.

Note that the Knowledge Source proxy in Figure 16-15 is only required because the original Knowledge Source had many different independent Authority Requirements. Knowledge Source proxies are much less common than decision proxies because ubiquitous Knowledge Sources can often be 'hidden behind' a single decision proxy. That was not possible in this case.

16.3.5 Consequences

The Change Shield lessens the impact of changes in volatile Input Data and Knowledge Sources on large parts of a decision model by interposing a proxy sub-decision or parent Knowledge Source in front of the original which is internally controlled. This proxy can then absorb much of the change imposed from outside and protect the rest of the decision model.

This pattern adds additional decisions and Knowledge Sources to Decision Requirements Diagrams neither of which represent real business concerns, rather these are abstractions designed to control change. This can complicate the model.

Those changes that occur to Input Data, Knowledge Sources and sub-decisions that cannot be isolated now incur a larger change impact because of the additional proxy decisions and Knowledge Sources introduced. The probability of this can be minimized by judicious design.

16.3.6 Notes

Decision models should *never* be hostage to changes of format in inbound data and this pattern should not be used simply because this is the case. Instead, either all decision models assume a dependency on a defined, canonical standard data format or there is a separate layer of decision-making to produce this (see Section 14.8.2). This initial step avoids any dependency, on the part of business decision models, on any aspect of format.

The Change Shield cannot protect internal components of a decision model from all change. It is always possible for changes in Input Data or knowledge models to 'leak' through a Change Shield.

The Change Shield is not worthwhile if the volatile component has few direct dependents, unless this is expected to increase in the future.

16.4 The Kaleidoscope (Repetition)

16.4.1 Synopsis

A kaleidoscope uses mirrors to create the illusion of complex patterns from a small number of colored beads arranged in simple ways. This pattern achieves an analogous effect in reverse by allowing complex symmetrical logic to be expressed more simply. This is achieved by representing simple logic and a means of 'mirroring' it.

16.4.2 Problem

Occasionally modelers need to represent logic that has a natural symmetry or reoccurring patterns of logic. This can be seen in Decision Tables, trees and text by the need to repeat groups of conditions, but it can exist for all logic forms. Examples of domains featuring this symmetry include accounting, financial product processing and intermediated service provision that require equal and opposite behaviors (e.g., buy and sell transactions, put and call options, etc.).

Symptoms of this problem include:

- Obvious and large scale repetitive patterns involving one or more inputs and one or more outputs.

- Requirements featuring the need for symmetry which are expressed implicitly (i.e., the need for symmetry is observable but not stated), for example, any application where there is a buy/sell symmetry or something similar.

One or both of these can result in needlessly complex decisions and the potential for consistency issues if the symmetry is accidently undermined (e.g., by implementing a change and forgetting to update all of the reflected logic). This pattern is applied both to reduce the size of the logic and to be explicit about the need for symmetry—both of which make the decision easier to understand and maintain.

16.4.3 Application

Many business domains require the application of symmetry in their decision models. For example, in an accounting decision model, the direction of a ledger posting (i.e., whether the posting is a debit or credit) depends on the accounting journal type, whether the position is long or short with respect to the underlying asset and whether the cash flow is a premium or a discount. A considerably simplified sample of this logic is presented in Figure 16-16.

Determine Posting Direction			
	Accounting Journal	Position	Cashflow Type	Direction
U		LONG, SHORT	DISCOUNT, PREMIUM	CR, DR
1	AFS AMORTIZATION	LONG	DISCOUNT	CR
2			PREMIUM	DR
3		SHORT	DISCOUNT	DR
4			PREMIUM	CR
5	SELF BOND AMORTIZATION	LONG	DISCOUNT	DR
6			PREMIUM	CR
7		SHORT	DISCOUNT	CR
8			PREMIUM	DR
9	HGB AMORTIZATION	LONG	DISCOUNT	CR
10			PREMIUM	DR
11		SHORT	DISCOUNT	DR
12			PREMIUM	CR

Figure 16-16 Decision Table Illustrating Condition Symmetry

Inspection of this example demonstrates a symmetry of conclusion about *Position* and *Cashflow Type*. Variations in these values always affect the conclusion in the same manner. This symmetry is implicit—it's unclear if it should be preserved for any new Decision Table entries or whether it is purely coincidental. It is also fragile because an editing oversight could easily break it. It is also a clumsy, oversized means of expressing the logic that would not scale well. To address x accounting journals the table will need $7x$ conditions.

A Decision Requirements Diagram of this logic is provided in Figure 16-17.

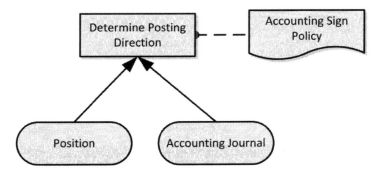

Figure 16-17 Decision Requirements Diagram for Posting Direction

There are two means of applying the Kaleidoscope pattern:

- If the symmetry is moderately consistent throughout, one can split the decision into the base logic and an explicit statement of the symmetry (see Figure 16-18).

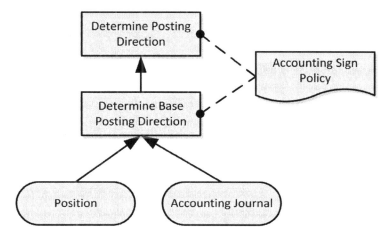

Figure 16-18 Decision Requirements Diagram with Base Logic Split

- If the symmetry is less uniform, one can represent the symmetry as a *strategy outcome*. A strategy outcome is a conclusion reached by a decision that definitively tells the recipient how to obtain an answer without yielding an answer itself (see *Determine Sign Strategy* in Figure 16-19). Another decision (or Business Knowledge Model) can then use this strategy to determine the outcome itself.

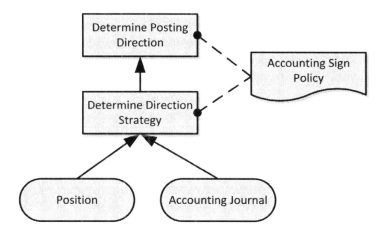

Figure 16-19 Decision Requirements Diagram with Strategy Conclusion

16.4.4 Example

As shown in the Decision Requirements Diagram in Figure 16-18, the example Decision Table can be split to produce the two decisions in Figure 16-20 and Figure 16-21. This approach reduces repetition. To address x accounting journals this solution needs $x + 14$ conditions expressed across two Decision Tables. It's easy to see how this scales better than the original design (that required $7x$ conditions) for large numbers of accounting journals. More importantly, however, we are being explicit about how position and cashflow type influence direction for all journal types because Figure 16-21 states this completely, without any need for changes when new journal types are encountered.

Determine Base Posting Direction		
U	Accounting Journal	Base Direction
		CR, DR
1	AFS AMORTIZATION	CR
2	SELF BOND AMORTIZATION	DR
3	HGB AMORTIZATION	CR

Figure 16-20 Base Logic Decision Table

Determine Posting Direction				
U	Base Direction	Position	Cashflow	Direction
	CR, DR	LONG, SHORT	DISCOUNT, PREMIUM	CR, DR
1	CR	LONG	DISCOUNT	CR
2			PREMIUM	DR
3		SHORT	DISCOUNT	DR
4			PREMIUM	CR
5	DR	LONG	DISCOUNT	DR
6			PREMIUM	CR
7		SHORT	DISCOUNT	CR
8			PREMIUM	DR

Figure 16-21 Symmetry Definition Decision Table

Figure 16-21 has symmetry of its own and could even benefit from a second application of the Kaleidoscope pattern. The larger the original table, the more effective this approach becomes at simplifying the logic.

A strategy outcome solution for the same problem is shown in Figure 16-22. The enumerated values of the outcome represent different strategies to calculate the direction. Another decision can use this, combined with the *Position* and *Accounting Journal* to determine the direction. As these represent a slight sophistication of the logic, they would need to be clearly documented in the glossary, for instance, *IF LONG DISC CR* implies that Long Positions with a Discount Cashflow are credit postings and that Short/Discount or Long/Premiums would therefore be debit postings. Additionally, a double negative implies that Short/Premiums would result in a credit posting. Strategy outcomes are only useful if the business already has this concept. The word "If" that occurs in the strategy name has nothing to do with the FEEL if then else construct; rather, it serves to illustrate the meaning of the strategy.

Determine Direction Strategy		
U	**Accounting Journal**	**Direction Strategy**
		CR, DR
1	*AFS AMORTIZATION*	*IF LONG DISC CR*
2	*SELF BOND AMORTIZATION*	*IF LONG DISC DR*
3	HGB AMORTIZATION	*IF LONG DISC CR*

Figure 16-22 Strategy Conclusion Decision Table

The strategy resulting from this Decision Table can be used, given the *Position* and *Cashflow Type*, to calculate the direction of any posting using a twelve-cell Decision Table.

16.4.5 Consequences

The logic is reduced in size and any required symmetry is made explicit. Ease of comprehension and maintenance are achieved as a result. The symmetry rules or strategies can be reused in other applications.

This pattern increases the number of decisions creating additional complexity at the decision requirements level.

16.4.6 Notes

This pattern is a form of factorization that should not be confused with *Divide and Conquer* (see Section 16.2).

16.5 Approximator (Needless Cost)

16.5.1 Synopsis

Many business processes end with a complex and expensive decision that unconditionally requires all the information gathered by the process. Often it would be useful to be able to decide what the outcome will be, at least approximately, earlier in the process. This might allow other actions to be taken or costs avoided. This pattern analyzes a large, complex and expensive decision to identify a way to provide an early approximate outcome.

16.5.2 Problem

All business processes aim to deliver value, both to clients and the organizations that perform them. In many cases whether or not this value can be delivered successfully is contingent on prevailing circumstances that become known during the process. The difficulty is that often the activities and decisions made during this process have associated costs such as the monetary cost of services provided by third parties (e.g., using a credit rating agency to assess a mortgage applicants credit worthiness), the time spent by personnel in supporting manual tasks such as inspections and the paperwork burden to clients[58]. Clearly there is a

---

[58] This is an intangible cost to the company: clients who are rejected for a mortgage loan after spending several hours filling forms are unlikely to recommend that company to their friends.

need to minimize this cost, especially when the likelihood of deriving additional value from these costs is low. This is a challenge for some processes in which the value outcome is only determined by a complex decision at the end of the process, after all the costs have already been incurred.

Symptoms of this problem include:

- a long process with unconditional tasks that are costly;

- complex decisions at or near the end of a business process that have a substantial chance of yielding a 'no-value' scenario (e.g., failed mortgage application) and little apparent opportunity to avoid this scenario or mitigate its cost; *or*

- decisions at or near the end of the process that have possible outcomes that make previously completed tasks "worthless".

16.5.3 Application

Approximator is applied in three stages:

- **Cost Analysis**. Analyzing the process to determine the cost of each activity.

- **Identification of Mitigation Opportunities**. The most expensive activities are examined to see if they could be avoided or deferred under any circumstances.

- **Creation of Approximators**. For each mitigation opportunity define decisions that could reliably identify these circumstances.

Cost analysis involves the classification of how expensive a task or decision is. When considering cost, include:

- the labor costs of manual activities;

- the purchase cost of Input Data for a decision (providing the Input Data is not already available as a consequence of another activity);

- the requirement that a task or decision might have for an expensive or contentious resource (e.g., SME time, powerful or specialist hardware); *and*

- in time critical processes, the time taken to perform the task.

This cost should be documented as a metadata field on process tasks and decisions. The goal is to classify cost against a single three-point (high, medium, low) or five-point scale. Accuracy is the goal, not precision. The modeler must be able to reliably determine those process tasks or decisions that are most likely to compromise the return on investment of the process. Cost should be weighted by probability: so unconditional tasks should have a higher weighting that one that is only applicable in a tiny fraction of cases.

Identification of Mitigation Opportunities involves analyzing, for the most expensive tasks and decisions, circumstances under which the organization may, or definitely should, avoid incurring the expense of the decision or task. Avoidance can occur if the process is aborted, a cheaper alternative is pursued or if the expensive task or decision can be delayed until such time that the return on the investment might increase.

The final stage involves the creation of approximator decisions which cheaply deduce if a mitigation should be exercised in each case. These decisions should be used by the process to control gateways that avoid the expensive tasks or decisions. Often, but not always, the Approximator will base this decision on an estimate of the value that the process's final decision is based on, for example *Applicant Creditworthiness*. Very often, Approximators will use analytics.

16.5.4 Example

The claims payment process for an auto insurer involves a series of tasks to gather data about the accident and damage done to an insured auto. The vehicle is towed to an inspection site and an initial inspection is done. It is then taken to a suitable repair facility where a repair quote will be drawn up. A valuation inspection determines the value of the vehicle immediately before the accident. Additional costs such as replacement rental cars and towing are accumulated as this process continues. Eventually, all the data has been gathered and the decision—to repair the vehicle or to declare it a total loss and pay the owner its pre-accident value—is made.

The problem is that improvements to this decision, such as using predictive analytics to predict the likelihood of hidden repair costs, do not affect the core costs of the process. Given that the decision is made so late in the process, all the costs of the process have been incurred before the decision is made.

The approximator pattern adds a new decision to this process, *First Notice of Loss*, that approximates this decision: is it *likely* that this vehicle will be declared a total loss? This decision relies heavily on a predictive model derived from historical data and on third party information as to the characteristics of vehicles likely to be badly damaged in accidents.

Because this decision is made early in the process, it can be used to short-circuit the process, reducing the expenses incurred by not performing certain tasks. For instance, if the approximate decision is to declare the car a total loss, then there is no need to estimate its cost to repair or to tow it to and from a repair shop.

In this case the process is only short-circuited if the approximator decision has a reasonably high confidence; otherwise the process proceeds as normal.

16.5.5 Consequences

The approximator should increase the average return on investment of the process. The best ones will also reduce the mean cost. Note, however, that the cost of successful process outcomes may be slightly increased by the use of this pattern and the process will necessarily be more complex.

16.5.6 Notes

The behavior of approximators should be carefully monitored—one that is never exercised or that is exercised by every case is clearly a cause for concern. Trends in approximator use should also be heeded carefully.

The use of Approximator occasionally demands that a decision selects a means of determining its outcome from a set of alternative sub-decisions, each with a different expense profile. This decision must choose based on an accuracy versus expense trade-off. It may use the *Divide and Conquer* pattern (see Section 16.2) to do this.

16.6 Exception Based Logic (1000 Special Cases)

16.6.1 Synopsis

Some decisions present fairly simple logic for 98% of the data cases presented to them, but 98% of the effort of analyzing and expressing the decision is taken up with the remaining 2% of cases. This pattern allows us to separate these two so that the former is not obscured by the latter and so it may be independently reused.

16.6.2 Problem

Special cases, even if rare, can account for much of the work of a decision modeler. Many business domains have regional, jurisdictional or product based variations which are very specific, often low frequency and yet have a disproportionate impact on the model. The chief symptoms of this problem is 'death by 1000 special cases'—in other words, the structure of Decision Requirements Models (and often the associated Decision Logic Models) is dominated by special cases that only occur in a tiny fraction of the presented data and which keep changing.

Symptoms of this problem include:

- There are a significant number of specific Input Data components required that are only used in a very small proportion of data cases and yet feed into many decisions. Often these have specific names (e.g., *Cayman Islands Withholding Tax Thresholds*) that mention places, products or some other signifier of a special case.

- Individual decisions have many (more than seven) Input Data components that are shared with others.

- An analogous symptom involves many decisions with an authority requirement on the same, very specific Knowledge Source. Alternatively, there are individual decisions with authority requirements on many specific Knowledge Sources.

- Occasionally even multiple disjoint sets of coordinated Input Data are encountered in a model—one for each class of special case—on which a large number of decisions depend.

- Even mainstream decision logic is dominated by special conditions that occupy a lot of 'real estate' in the logic, but which are very rarely used. There may be disjoint sets of inputs that have many '-' conditions. This results in wide Decision Tables[59].

- Even the very rare and specific special cases exercise many of the decisions in the model.

- Specialist subject matter experts (responsible for specific subsets of your business, be it the specifics of a particular state, product or legal mandate) cannot focus on specific parts of the decision model but must apply their expertise throughout and review the whole model.

- Changes in special cases have a broad impact throughout the decision model.

- It is estimated (or discovered by profiling) that there are a significant number of

---

[59] The authors have encountered examples in excess of fifty inputs.

rules, or even decisions, that are no longer used.

Pervasive special cases should be treated with suspicion. Because of the rarity of expertise pertaining to these special cases, they can evolve into 'magic' decisions that are so convoluted and poorly understood that modelers fear to change them. This in turn leads to issues with comprehension and maintenance—decision models become hard to understand and accumulate stale rules.

16.6.3 Application

The Exception Based logic pattern requires that the decision model be dominated by decisions (and decision logic) of the mainstream cases and that exceptional cases be specified and handled *separately* with a purpose built, localized decision and then re-integrated with the overall outcome. This can be achieved in two ways depending on the structure of the decision model:

- **Mainstream plus low frequency exceptional cases**: if the exceptional case(s) account for a very low volume of outcomes and everything else results in one of a reasonable number of mainstream outcomes, the exceptional cases should be factored out and made the focus of their own decisions within the same Decision Requirements Diagram. This is *separation*.

- **No mainstream, just a diverse set of similar frequency special cases**: if the decision model consists of no mainstream cases and is entirely composed of a set of special cases, each of which accounts for a similar fraction of the data and has unique logic, then the model should be *partitioned* into entirely different decisions. A separate decision determines which partition (e.g., state, product type) should cater for each set of inputs.

Separation involves isolating the dependencies on Input Data and Knowledge Sources that are unique to a special case, to a single decision or a small network of decisions. The original, top-level decision should then have an information requirement directly to the top-level special case decision to allow the latter to "exercise its veto".

Partitioning involves designing entirely separate Decision Requirements Diagrams for each of the special cases. These can pursue entirely different decision structures. If some of the special cases are similar to one another, a partition can feature more than one and use separation (see above) to isolate the special variations.

16.6.4 Example

A decision to determine if an *Instrument* can be used as collateral— *Determine ECB Collateral Eligibility*—is modeled in Figure 16-23. In this decision it is important to handle the rare case in which a proposal to use an *Instrument* as collateral must be vetoed because it is associated with the organization requiring collateral (a company cannot use its own stock as collateral). In the decision model this exceptional veto influences the treatment of instruments of particular types (*Product Based Eligibility*), intermediaries (*Institution Based Eligibility*) and countries (*Country Based Eligibility*).

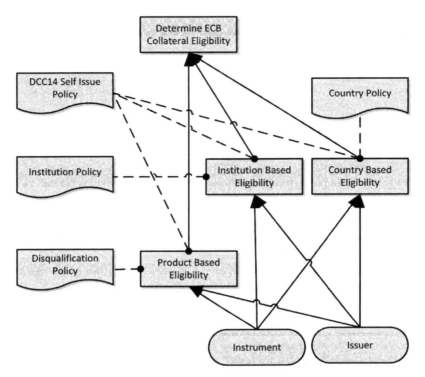

Figure 16-23 Decision Requirements Diagram with Widespread Exception

Immediately, it is obvious that the self-issue exceptional case (as supported by the Knowledge Source *DCC14 Self Issue Policy* and *Issuer* Data Input) has many incoming dependencies. However, in this scenario, self-issue only accounts for 0.9% of Instruments. Clearly, this special case has far too much impact on the entire decision and it has not been sufficiently localized.

A much better Decision Requirements Model with the same behavior is shown in Figure 16-24. Here, the self-issue special case has been assigned to an explicit decision and this alone has a dependency on *Issuer* and *DCC14 Self Issue Policy*. This special case has been effectively isolated to the left of the diagram.

Once this factoring is achieved, maintenance of the self-issue decision is easier and the other decisions are simplified.

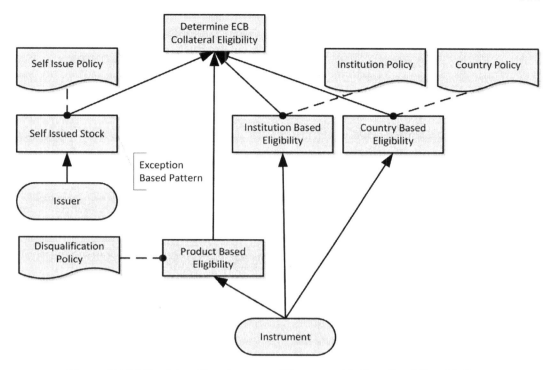

Figure 16-24 Decision Requirements Diagram with Localized Special Case

16.6.5 Consequences

Application of the Exception Based Logic pattern adds decisions to your decision model. However, the overall complexity (both in the dependency relationships within Decision Requirements Diagrams and the logic of any Decision Tables defined) will be reduced. Specialized expertise can be focused on smaller sub-parts of the decision model and changes are likely to have a more localized effect.

16.6.6 Notes

In the example, the situation was known to apply to only a small percentage of instances of a given Input Data. Sometimes, this case frequency information is common knowledge among SMEs. On other occasions, it is necessary to analyze the results of a decision to see how outcomes are distributed as well as Input Data to determine how many special cases are involved and their relative frequency.

Special cases are prone to change and obsolescence without warning. Ensure that special case decisions are regularly reviewed and ruthlessly pruned of redundant content.

This pattern is a variation of *Divide and Conquer* (see Section 16.2) that takes into account the frequency of use of specific cases and is Decision Requirements Diagram rather than Decision Table oriented.

16.7 Positive Validator (Bad Data)

16.7.1 Synopsis

Data quality and data validation are big issues in decision modeling; the higher the relevant[60] data quality, the simpler and more reliably a decision can be made based on that data. This pattern is used to validate data in a compact way that separates this concern from the rest of the decision model (see best practice in 14.8.2) and acts as documentation for the data quality constraints in a way that traditional (negative) validation logic cannot.

16.7.2 Problem

A data structure must be checked for intra and inter-field validity in a compact manner that does not yield a wide Decision Table and also serves to document the data validation and make it as transparent as possible. A decision is required that identifies relevant flaws with inbound data. A parent decision may then reject data with serious flaws, protecting 'pure' business decisions that consume this data from the need to do this, isolating them from the change in validation procedures and allowing them to focus on business issues.

Data validation frequently presents three challenges:

- **Validation logic becomes mixed with business decisions**. This can cause decision models to become as much concerned with finding inconsistencies in the Input Data as they are with business logic. There is sometimes a tendency to embed validation within a business decision simply because it has all the required information—something that can be difficult to create just for stand-alone validation. This can lead to a 'check data as and where you need it' philosophy. Keeping data validation logic decoupled from business decisions is important for clarity, maintenance, preventing repetition, controlling change impact and reuse.

- **Validation logic is 'fat'**. Validation logic has many different conditions by virtue of the fact that many fields will typically require checking. Achieving a compact yet readable representation of logic that has many conditions is challenging.

- **Validation decisions are often a poor documentation of data validation**. Often the business community looks to validation decisions not only to check its data but to act as documentation for data standards, i.e., self-documenting validation. This is rarely as successful as experts hope. Validation rules typically look for and report faults—an ideal data input should therefore cause no validation rules to be satisfied. This means that validation rules are negative and express the inverse logic of 'good' data. Paradoxically this can make them hard to read.

16.7.3 Application

The Positive Validator pattern assumes that all attributes of an Input Data are individually available in a DMN context (see 8.2.5) and that a context variable *Attributes* contains a

---

[60] The extent to which data validation is performed must be led by the decision requirement. Few exercises are as wasteful as performing unnecessary data validation to get 'perfect data'. Only perform validation that decisions need.

list of their names. The approach also requires that a set of functions are defined in DMN that are described below. The variable along with a purpose built set of DMN functions can be used to:

- Test for the provision of a specific attribute: `exists("name")` is true if the attribute *name* is provided. `has("name")` is true only if the attribute name is provided and has a value other than `null`. The less friendly `Attributes[name="name"]!=null` can be used but is not recommended.

- Obtain the value of an attribute: the expression `name` yields the value of the attribute *name*.

- Note that each attribute may itself have attributes and therefore a hierarchical structure can be validated. For example, `Issuer.name` yields the value of the *name* attribute of the complex attribute *Issuer*.

- Ensure that an attribute contains a valid instance of a specific data type. For example, `is date(name)` is `true` only if *name* contains a valid date.

- Ensure that certain conditions are satisfied, reporting an error if they are not. For example:

```
If Issue Type=GLT
then ensure(Issuer Type=GOVT,
    "EIT-017 invalid issuer type for gilt")
```

ensures that all gilts are issued by governments and issues an error message (that is appended to the collection of errors for the datum concerned) if the data violates this.

Using this context variable allows DMN text rules to replace Decision Tables in which many columns would be needed if each were dedicated to specific attributes.

16.7.4 Example

Consider a data input with five attributes A..E that needs to be checked for adherence to the following validation conditions:

1. The attribute A must exist and have some valid data content.
2. The attribute B is optional but if it exists its value must be greater than zero.
3. If D exists, C must exist, otherwise C and D are optional. Both C and D must be valid dates if they exist.
4. If both C and D are specified, then D must be later than C.
5. Attribute E is mandatory: if B exists it must have values E1, E2 or E3; otherwise it must have value E4 or E5.

c	A	B	C	C is Valid Date	D	D is Valid Date	E	Validation Issues	Annotation
	Validation Issues								
				true, false		true, false			
1	UNSPECIFIED, EMPTY	-	-	-	-	-	-	V-001	A absent or has no content
2	-	not(null, >0)	-	-	-	-	-	V-002	B exists and is zero or less
3	-	-	null	-	not(null)	-	-	V-003	D exists without C
4	-	-	not(null)	false	-	-	-	V-003	C is not a valid date
5	-	-	-	-	not(null)	false	-	V-003	D is not a valid date
6	-	-	>=D	true	-	true	-	V-004	D is not later than C
7	-	-	-	-	-	-	null	V-005	E absent
8	-	not(null)	-	-	-	-	not($E1, E2, E3$)	V-005	B supplied, E value out of range
9	-	null	-	-	-	-	not($E4, E5$)	V-005	B absent, E value out of range

Figure 16-25 Validation Decision Table

This simple, five attribute validation requirement expressed in conventional DMN yields a sparse, seven column Decision Table shown in Figure 16-25. This Decision Table builds a list of validation errors for each set of inputs presented to it. Note the best practice of using a row annotation (see Section 14.5.7) to clarify each validation failure and a Collect hit policy to build a list of error codes. The plural decision name is a best practice naming convention when yielding a collection of results.

It is easy to see flaws with this approach:

- It will not scale: ten or fifteen attribute validation using the same principles would yield a very fat table.

- The logic is negative and hard to read. For example, rule eight does not obviously align with the second clause of requirement 5 that it represents. Although the logic is satisfactory, the negatives mean it is not a clear reflection of the requirement.

This requirement needs a more compact representation based on positive logic. Using the Positive Validator pattern, validation logic satisfying the specification is shown in the text rule of Figure 16-26.

Note that rules V-003-2 and V-003-3 use the is date() function to build a date from the contents of attributes c and d. If this fails, the expression yields false, reporting the error. Notice also the analogy between the text representation in Figure 16-26 and the original specification and how this is aided by the use of comments.

```
                    ┌─────────────────────────────────┐
                    │        Validation Issues        │
        ┌───────────┴─────────────────────────────────┴──────────────────────────────────┐
        │ // validation rule V-001                                                         │
        │   ensure (has(A) and not(A in [UNSPECIFIED, EMPTY]), "V-001 A absent or has no content)│
        │ // validation rule V-002                                                         │
        │   if has(B) then ensure(B>0, "V-002 B has a sub-zero value")                      │
        │ // validation rule V-003-1                                                       │
        │   if has(D) then ensure (has(C), "V-003-1 D exists without C")                    │
        │ // validation rule V-003-2                                                       │
        │   if has(D) then ensure(is date(D), "V-003-2 D is not a valid date")              │
        │ // validation rule V-003-3                                                       │
        │   if has(D) and has(C) then ensure(is date(C), "V-003-3 C is not a valid date")   │
        │ // validation rule V-004                                                         │
        │   if has(D) and has(C)                                                            │
        │     then ensure(and(is date (C), is date(D), D>C), "V-004 D is not later than C") │
        │ // validation rule V-005-1                                                       │
        │   ensure(has(E), "V005-1 E absent")                                               │
        │ // validation rule V-005-2                                                       │
        │   if has(E) and has(B)  then ensure (E in [E1, E2, E3], "V-005-2 E value not consistent with provision of B")│
        │ // validation rule V-005-3                                                       │
        │   is has(E) and not(has(B)) then ensure (E in [E4, E5], "V-005-3 E value not consistent with absence of B")│
        └──────────────────────────────────────────────────────────────────────────────────┘
```

Figure 16-26 Validation using Positive Validator Pattern

16.7.5 Consequences

Positive Validator ensures that validation conditions are both compact and expressed as assertions of the data quality requirements, rather than negatives.

A knowledge of FEEL, or some other language, is required to provide the flexibility and power needed to express the validation constraints. Be careful to ensure that the conditions do not become too complex such that they threaten the ease of comprehension of the logic.

16.7.6 Notes

Complex validation logic may challenge the ease of comprehension of decisions using this pattern.

The `ensure` conditions use negative logic and are contrary to the conventions of DMN. This pattern should not be used by newcomers to DMN.

16.8 Process Sequence (Salami Decision)

16.8.1 Synopsis

Because BPMN and DMN have been designed to be used together, modelers can sometimes misuse BPMN to manage the steps in a decision, mapping each business task to a Decision Table to express the logic of those steps. This is an anti-pattern and should be replaced with a higher-level, end-to-end decision and decision requirements (see Section 10.2.3.6 for an example).

16.8.2 Problem

Modelers are often working with subject matter experts who are used to making a decision in a particular way. In particular, they will describe the decision in terms of a sequence of steps (see Section 13.6). This sequence is very important to them and feels very much part of the definition of the decision. Eliminating unnecessary sequence from decision models is a best practice (see Section 14.6.4) but this relies on the sequence being captured in the decision model itself. If the sequence is captured in a process model, however, then multiple decision models, none containing any problematic sequence, may be defined.

The key symptom for this problem is that a process model will contain a series of tasks each of which is linked to a decision that is expressed as a single Decision Table with no sub-decisions. Process models often exhibit long, unconditional chains of these tasks.

There is also a tendency to use fields that are not required in decision logic/business rules simply because they were output from a previous step to transfer 'state' between steps. As a consequence, the Decision Tables are very context specific to the process in which they are used and have little reuse potential.

16.8.3 Application

The first step is to identify the beginning of the higher level decision in the process model. This is likely to be the first decision-making task in the sequence. To ensure that the highest level decision possible is modeled coherently, the next step is to find the "end" of the sequence. The end will be represented either by a final gateway or, more likely, by a set of tasks that do not involve decision-making and only one of which is selected for execution each time through the process. These final tasks can and should be mapped to the actions the overall decision is choosing between.

It is also possible that there is a second decision that follows immediately after that being extracted—i.e., that the sequence contains more than one top-level decision—in this case, the "end" of the sequence is the last task before the break. Here, it can be difficult to spot the end of one decision and the beginning of the next. Be guided by any change of business focus in the process (e.g., change of lane or pool) or the start of a completely separate business activity.

Everything between the beginning and the end of decision-making is a candidate for inclusion in the decision model. Each task in the identified section of the process model should be identified as an independent decision in the new model. The questions and allowed answers for each should be defined and clarified. It is very common for these decisions to involve large, complex Decision Tables because they have been overloaded to avoid adding additional tasks or sub-decisions. Such decisions should be simplified using patterns and best practices, especially *Divide and Conquer* 16.2 above. This may create more decisions in the model while also reducing the complexity of each decision.

The pool of decisions can be analyzed both bottom-up and top-down. The simplest, most granular decisions can be analyzed to see which other decisions require their answers. This will start to accrete decisions into sub-models. The most significant decisions, the ones most obviously related to the final process outcome, can also be identified and the dependencies between these decisions and the overall decision identified. In both cases only dependency should be modeled—if a decision is made differently depending on the value of another decision's outcome then it depends on it and has an information requirement on it. One way to spot unnecessary requirements is that there is no pair of rows in the Decision Table with different conclusions where the value produced by the sub-decision is the only difference between those rows. Often when sequence is modeled, the Decision Table contains the sub-decision as a condition column but this column only checks to see if the decision has a value or always checks for the same value. This condition is being used to enforce the sequence, nothing more. For instance, considering the example in 14.8.4, a Decision Table for *Define Driving Record Category*, may contain a column for the driver's *Age Category* that checks only to see if this is one of the allowed values (*Young, Standard, Senior*). This check is repeated for every rule. This column has been forced into the table due because *Age Category* is historically determined first, before *Driving Record*, and this sequence has been modeled by making *Define Driving Record Category* dependent on *Define Age Category*.

As these top-down and bottom-up approaches are followed the model will come together in the middle and a complete model can be developed, cleaned and finalized.

The process can now be simplified to use the higher level decision, with the Input Data in the new decision model mapped to process data objects. If there are costs or delays associated with specific process data objects, then it may be necessary to have process tasks that invoke sub-decisions directly before a final task invokes the overall decision. This is acceptable as it imposes a process sequence onto the declarative decision model without implying that the sequence is material to the decision-making (see also Section 10.2.3.6).

16.8.4 Example

Consider part of the UServ example (discussed in Section 17.3). Determining the *Driver Eligibility Score* for a *Driver* could be modeled as a process as shown in Figure 16-27

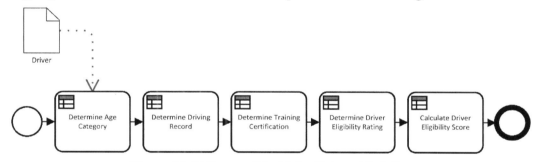

Figure 16-27 Process Model for Driver Eligibility

Driver data is input and then a series of tasks derive additional information about the *Driver*—their *Age, Category, Driving Record* and *Training Certification*. The data created in each task must be passed to the next in an updated *Driver* record.

In fact, only the *Driver Eligibility Score* has any impact— drivers whose eligibility score is too low will be dropped out of the process— and the remaining tasks are elements of decision-making presented as process tasks.

This should be replaced with a simpler process and an associated decision model as shown in Figure 16-28 and Figure 16-29 below.

Figure 16-28 Simplified Process

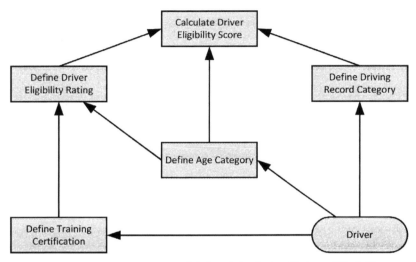

Figure 16-29 Decision Model for Calculating Driver Eligibility

The decision model shows the dependencies, reflecting the need to know the *Training Certification* before determining *Driver Eligibility Rating*, for instance, while not implying that the *Age Category* is needed to decide on *Driving Record*.

16.8.5 Consequences

Applying the pattern eliminates a great deal of complexity from process models. In the authors' experience, processes often only seem complex or even noteworthy because decision-making has been wrapped up in the process. The process is often completely straightforward once the decision-making is separated out into a decision model.

A single decision task also avoids exposing data to the process that should or could be internal to the decision. This prevents data that has no meaning once the decision is complete—an interim result, say—cluttering the process.

Representing end-to-end decisions in full with a decision model, rather than in disjointed pieces, allows the full richness of decision modeling to be exploited.

Decision Tables that are clearer, easier to maintain and more accurately modeled are the other main benefit of applying the pattern. When Decision Tables are chained together in a process model, they can be polluted with state information as noted above in Section 16.8.2.

This problem is made worse because modelers can become reluctant to add a new Decision Table if doing so means adding a new decision step in a process model. This makes modelers resist breaking an over-large Decision Table into multiple collaborating Decision Tables (as required by some of the patterns in this chapter). Encapsulating the whole decision as a single task frees the modeling team to develop the most effective decision model possible.

The main disadvantage is that the process model no longer stands alone—the decision model is linked to it and must be considered at the same time for a complete understanding. While this can be initially troublesome for some reviewers and modelers, the overall simplification is worth it and will be rapidly recognized as such.

16.8.6 Notes

Sometimes the sequence has been modeled in a decision model rather than a process model. A similar approach can be followed. The lowest level decision is likely to be the "first" step in the dependency chain and the "end" is the highest level decision, the one at the top of the dependency chain.

If the implementation platform for the decision is limited to executing single Decision Tables, each time the logic engine is invoked, as some older and more limited business rules environments are, this may result in a single business decision requiring many service invocations. However, this is a problem with the implementation technology not the pattern.

The DMN standard explicitly allows one or more decisions to be invoked by a specific task in a process (see Section 14.2.5). These decisions can each have requirements of (dependencies on) other decisions and Decision Tables can be written for any or all of them. This richness is deliberate and using a process model that has a series of tasks each of which invokes an individual Decision Table is a poor way to model decision-making. See Section 10.2 for more details on the relationship between a business process model and a business decision model.

16.9 Classifier (Reused Data)

16.9.1 Synopsis

A set of decisions as originally specified requires a common piece of Input Data. Each decision is checking the data to see if it occupies certain value ranges or deriving something from the data. Rather than restating this logic in every decision this pattern aims to separate out a single, reusable classification decision to avoid repetition, ensure consistency and improve maintainability.

16.9.2 Problem

Business scenarios often involve many decisions that share Input Data. This shared Input Data is generally ancillary information about a customer or a transaction. Each decision is considering the Input Data to see if something is true or not about the customer or transaction that is the focus of the decision-making. In scenarios addressed by this pattern the logic in these different decisions is similar, at least as it relates to this particular piece of Input Data; generally it pertains to how to classify or categorize a transaction. This repetition of logic makes for more complex and expensive maintenance if the categorization approach changes while also increasing the risk of inconsistency in how this particular Input Data is handled.

16.9.3 Application

All the decisions that use the same property (or set of properties) of the reused Input Data should be reviewed. Each time the property is used in a Decision Table it will be compared with a specific set of values. This list might be defined explicitly through the use of a comma separated list of values (e.g., 'AAA, AA+, AA, AA-') in the Decision Table to see if the value is in a specific list or implicitly by having a set of rules that are identical apart from the value of the specific property. An example of implicit versus explicit classification can be found in Section 14.5.6. Either way, if many Decision Tables are checking the same Input Data against the same or overlapping sets of values, this pattern is indicated. In that eventuality, all the various lists should be assembled in one place.

These lists represent the categorization of the property concerned. The lists should be examined for errors and inconsistency and each one should be investigated and corrected before further analysis. Where one list of values is a subset of another, it might reflect a hierarchical classification or a decision in which only certain values are relevant and so only those values were checked.

Once the lists are clean, consistent and verified, a classification label should be developed for each list. Ideally this is a single value but it may be necessary to produce a multipart classification. This enumeration of values should be properly defined in the glossary.

A decision is created that takes the original Input Data as an input, outputs one of the allowed classification values as an answer and has a Decision Table that describes the classification logic.

All the original decisions can now be refactored. If the classification property was the only reason for an Information Requirement to the Input Data, then the requirement should be removed. A new requirement should be added to the classification decision. Within each Decision Table the classification property column should be removed and replaced with one that uses the output of the new decision instead with simple equality checks.

16.9.4 Example

Many decisions about trades rely on the country of residence of the originating party. Each decision considers the country as part of its decision logic. Setting tax rates or restricting eligibility, for instance, is in part based on the country code stored for the party linked to the trade. Each of these decisions needs to know the country because the tax arrangements with that country are material to the outcome of the decision. Typically, each decision uses a list of countries as one of the conditions in each row of is logic. In each case, the countries are being checked against the *same* sets of values according to existing tax treaties, not differently for each decision in turn. The tax treaty classification is implicit in each of these Decision Tables.

A decision *Party Tax Treaty Type* is developed that has an information requirement to *Party*. A Decision Table for this decision uses the Party's country code to categorize the party based on the kind of tax treaty that exists between the country in which decisions are being made and the country of the party involved. The result of this decision is one of an enumerated list of *Tax Treaty Types—RECIPROCAL, EXEMPT, NONE*. All the decisions that previously used the country Input Data are changed to use this new decision instead, replacing explicit lists of countries with *Tax Treaty Type* checks such as not(EXEMPT) or RECIPROCAL,NONE.

16.9.5 Consequences

This pattern reduces the complexity of a significant number of decisions by isolating a commonly used classification into its own decision. This drives consistency across the business by ensuring that the classification is always made the same way and is not vulnerable to misunderstanding by a modeler. It also eliminates the repetition inherent in having the same classification logic in multiple Decision Tables and ensures that it can be changed in one place when circumstances change.

This pattern also makes these Decision Tables much easier to read. To someone unfamiliar with the classification, the table may appear to contain an apparently random list of values in their conditions. The classification decision makes the purpose of these lists much clearer and so improves readability.

By making the classification explicit rather than implicit, the pattern also reveals and documents an important business concept. In the example, the concept that it is important to know if a country has a tax treaty or not is revealed and documented.

Finally, by isolating the classification decision the pattern buffers the decisions that use it from changes. If a country moves from one tax treaty status to another, for example, the classification decision must be changed but not those that depend on it.

16.9.6 Notes

In some ways this pattern is a form of the *Change Shield* pattern described in Section 16.3.

16.10 Champion/Challenger (Experimentation)

16.10.1 Synopsis

The ability to conduct experiments is a critical part of an analytical or data-driven approach to business. One of the most important aspects to experiment on is decision-making. Continuous improvement of a decision requires that the approach be compared with other approaches and found to be superior. Conducting experiments to see which approach to decision-making works best—should the marketing offer be selected using this logic or that logic, should this approach be used to flag fraudulent claims or that one—requires that decisions support experimentation.

16.10.2 Problem

When engaged in a program of continuous improvement by experimentation, decisions often contain elements that cannot be varied. This may be because they are based on regulations, or that organizations are reluctant to vary them, perhaps due to overlapping areas of responsibility with another part of the organization involved with the decision. In addition, organizations may want to run multiple experiments at the same time and need a reliable way to track which experiments were conducted for a specific customer or transaction. Consequently, treating the whole business decision as the unit of experimentation is not generally satisfactory. Therefore, a finer grain approach to experimentation is required in which decisions that need a degree of freedom to support experimentation are separated from those that cannot vary.

16.10.3 Application

The first step is to build a decision model including the decision to be experimented on. Generally, it is best to build a model that represents current practice or planned default decision-making first, without introducing the experimental concepts.

This model can then be reviewed to identify those decisions within the model that could be varied as part of the experiment. All the decisions in the model should be listed along with some discussion of why it might be valuable to experiment or why no experimentation is possible (due to regulatory constraint, for instance).

If any of these decisions is partially regulated, consider partitioning it with *Divide and Conquer* (ref ch.16.2) to separate the regulated from the non-regulated parts.

Experimental design is beyond the scope of this book, however the next step is to consider: what kinds of experiments will be helpful, how many experiments can be conducted at the same time and what will be measured to evaluate the experiment. Once the experiments are designed, the decision model will need to be updated to reflect the proposed experiments.

For each decision in the experiment, consider if the decision logic is the only thing varying. If so, create Business Knowledge Models for each distinct approach to the logic and write a Boxed Expression (see Sections 11.3.2.4 and B.4.2) to assign transactions randomly to one of the associated Business Knowledge Models.

If the requirements of the decision also vary, or if you prefer to model the whole experiment consistently without Business Knowledge Models, duplicate each decision that will be different in the experiment. Create one duplicate for each approach to that decision included in the experimental design and name it after the original decision and the specific variation to be included in that version.

Build a new decision model that completely defines the new decision, including its experiments, using a mix of decisions reused from the original (you may continue to use a classification decision for instance that is not being varied in the experiment) and the duplicated experimental ones.

Each decision that has more than one variation will also need a distribution decision that assigns transactions to the original or an experimental approach and that is dependent on the original and experimental subject decisions. This generally uses a random number generator to assign a certain percentage of transactions to each experiment and to the default. These may be evenly distributed where no one approach is expected to be superior (a/b testing) or weighted toward an established approach (champion/challenger testing)

The result is likely to be a single network with some duplicated decisions in the middle. The top layer of the decision is often stable; then there will be a layer that includes the distribution decisions and then a mix of experimental and original decisions. The lowest level decisions are often the same across both default and experiments as they relate to standard classifications and calculations.

Ensure that the distribution decisions record which approach— which of the decision options—is used in each transaction. It is essential that the approach used is captured along with the decision made so that results can be analyzed later.

16.10.4 Example

A claims approval decision is developed that includes some decision-making related to complete documentation – *Additional Claim Information Needed*. The company does not want to pay claims before the complete documentation has been received. The high level model is shown below in Figure 16-30.

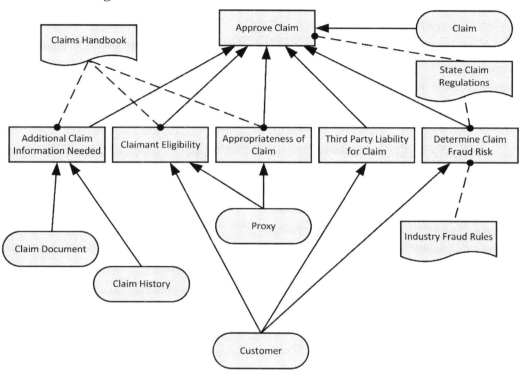

Figure 16-30 High Level Claim Approval DRD

There is disagreement about what counts as complete, however, with certain kinds of documentation only being required in certain circumstances and some flexibility in what those circumstances might be. Other kinds of documentation, however, are required by law. The company would like to know when specific pieces of documentation are useful and when they are not so they can design a best practice decision that reflects this.

A decision model is developed that contains decisions for each area of documentation that might be required for a claim. Where these are set by law no experimentation is designed. In other areas, two approaches are defined—the current approach that requires complete documentation at all times and two lighter-weight approaches that require less documentation. The revised decision model distributes 95% of the transactions to the decisions checking for complete documentation and distributes the other 5% randomly among the alternative approaches. The overall decision now returns the original Yes/No flag for additional documentation being required for this claim and a string describing the approach(es) used.

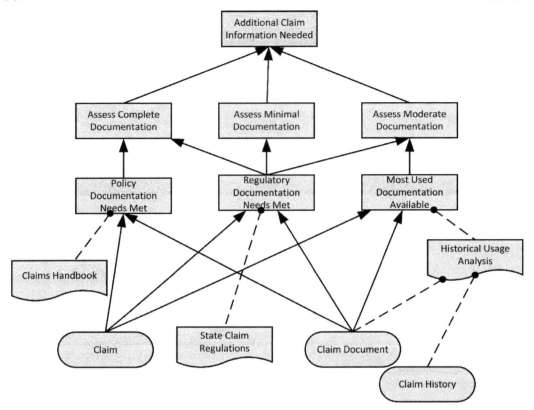

Figure 16-31 Champion Challenger Documentation Requirement

Figure 16-31 shows how this might be modeled. Three approaches are defined – *Assess Complete Documentation*, *Assess Minimal Documentation* and *Assess Moderate Documentation*. A decision *Regulatory Documentation Needs Met*, based on *State Claims Regulations*, is shared between all three approaches to ensure all meet the regulatory requirement. The current approach is modeled using *Policy Documentation Needs Met*, based on the *Claims Handbook*. This combines with the regulatory framework to form the current, complete documentation approach. A final decision to determine the *Most Used Documentation Available* is based on historical analysis of *Claims* and is designed to check only for the most widely referenced material. Each of these decisions could and likely would have its own sub-decisions and some of these might also be shared.

Once the decision has run for a while the organization will have a set of data to see if the number of claims that were paid when they should not have been or that required manual follow-up are different between the various approaches.

16.10.5   Consequences

The key advantage of this approach is transparency. Because decision models are visible and understood by everyone involved, the experimentation is likewise visible and clear. This reduces the challenge of building support for experimentation and reassures compliance and audit groups, among others, that regulations will not be breached by the experiments.

The models can become quite complex, however, especially if a significant number of experiments are being run at the same time. Compared with the original decision model, one extended to include experimentation would be significantly more complex. Multiple views (see Section 14.3.2) can and should be used to minimize this impact, focusing each group of reviewers on the experiments or decisions they care about.

16.10.6   Notes

Rarely have business decision-makers conducted this kind of comparison of experimental approaches explicitly. Persuading them to do so is often very difficult. They are often reluctant because they don't see how the experiment might affect their customers or whom it might affect and they worry about compliance issues. A clear decision model and well thought out experimental design can mitigate this but getting a group of business owners to agree to their first experiment can be difficult.

Decision Management involves a continuous and rigorous assessment stage: Decision Measurement and Improvement (See section 5.5.3). Managing experiments as part of an overall decision design is an important element in this continuous improvement mindset.

16.11   Data Preparation (Messy Data)

16.11.1   Synopsis

Rather than feeding incomplete, mismatched data into business decisions or supplying them with data formatted in a source system dependent manner, a set of decisions is defined to prepare or transform the data to make it more uniform and suitable for use in business decision-making. These decisions consume the incomplete or mismatched data inputs available, apply some business or transformation logic and output the data required by the actual business decision under consideration.

16.11.2   Problem

There is a disconnect between a business decision's information requirement and available data inputs. Typically, the available data is incomplete, mismatched or too technically structured for use in business decision-making. Sometimes the same Input Data are sourced from many systems, each with its own format. If the business decisions are designed to handle the data in its native state, then they will be tied to a current (flawed) implementation of that data, need to cope with format variations and will contain unnecessary and confusing complexity. Business decisions must be isolated from these issues to maintain clarity (see best practice 14.8.2).

16.11.3   Application

Decision modeling often involves a mix of top-down decision decomposition and bottom-up data analysis. If the available data is not a good fit for the decisions being identified, then it will be necessary to create a data preparation layer to present the data to the business decisions.

When a decision is identified that has potential data issues then a data preparation decision should be created. Potential issues include:

- Input Data with variations of structure between instances originating from different data stores or where the available properties are highly varied between different groups of instances.

- Multiple Input Data need to be correlated by the logic but the relationship between these Input Data is either poorly defined (partial string matches are used for instance) or known to be incomplete or problematic. In this case the data needs to be reconstructed.

- Multiple approaches have been used to define allowed values or enumerations in an Input Data (e.g., M/F is used in some instances, Male/Female in others and even multiple languages have been used to express enumerated values).

Working with the glossary, the team should define the clean data structure that business decision-makers would like to have (the Decision Canonical Data Model see Section 18.2.4) and then specify decisions to create that structure from the available Input Data.

16.11.4   Example

Consider an organization that has grown by acquisition. It may keep customer information in several distinct databases. While there is a clear overlap between the designs of these customer databases, they are not the same. If the information structure of each is used to create Input Data, then any decision that relies on customer data will need to have requirements to all the various Input Data and will have to include logic to handle customers who may be in any of the databases and so presented in any format.

Instead, a Customer data preparation decision is designed. This is a technical decision and is not intended to be reviewed by business owners. This decision has information requirements to all the various kinds of Input Data and produces a standard customer record.

Once this decision is defined, any business decision that needs information about a customer has a requirement on the data preparation decision instead of on the original Input Data.

16.11.5   Consequences

The biggest advantage of this approach is that it isolates potentially complex data transformation and problem resolution logic into a decision that can be managed and owned by those most responsible for the data in all its complexity. For all others involved in decision modeling, there is simply a decision that "gets" a standard customer record. This keeps business decision-making from being polluted with data preparation logic.

This approach also allows an incremental approach to improving data quality and integration. As technical teams eliminate redundant data stores, improve data consistency or otherwise improve the data environment, there is no impact on the business decisions. Because the business decisions are already isolated from the data using the data preparation decisions, changes to the data do not ripple through the model.

16.11.6 Notes

The data preparation decisions do not appear on the first cut of decision requirements; nor will they generally be found during top-down decision modeling. They will generally become apparent as detailed data requirements are being added and decision logic is being developed. In this sense, they may be considered a form of refactoring. In general, don't apply this pattern to pure format translations. These should be kept separate from validation (see 14.8.2).

See also the *Change Shield* pattern in section 16.3 and the *Classifier* pattern in section 16.9.

16.12   Approve, Decline, Refer (Only the paranoid survive)

16.12.1   Synopsis

It is common to find a 3-value decision that gives either a clear positive or negative response (where knowledge and data clearly support it) but where for every other case the default indicates a need for human review. Every referral can potentially result in new knowledge being gained and automated, so that over time there will be fewer and fewer referrals. This pattern addresses how to incrementally automate such a 3-value decision as insight and client confidence improves.

16.12.2   Problem

Many organizations have a degree of irrational fear that makes them reluctant to automate decisions, preferring to keep their manual checks and balances. Others are reluctant to automate a decision because it is not currently clear how the decision is really made in many circumstances due to poor documentation and opaque or limited record keeping. Neither circumstance is easy to change in the abstract and so, generally, the problem persists indefinitely. A means of gradual automation is required that can progress at a pace that matches the organization's confidence and the key facts learned from boundary cases that are processed manually but illustrate something about how they might be automated.

16.12.3   Application

Organizations applying this pattern begin with a process that pushes every transaction to a manual approval task that is in turn followed by a gateway for accept or reject, approve or decline.

The first step is to amend this process so that it has a task to make an automated decision that has a three-way gateway after the task—one for the positive outcome (approve, accept), one for the negative outcome (decline, reject) and one that leads to the manual review. Downstream tasks should be the same for the automated and manual tasks—there should be a single set of positive outcome processing tasks and a single set of negative outcome processing tasks. The process should capture and record the outcome of the automated task distinctly from the overall outcome for future analysis.

A decision model is then defined for this automated decision task that has a decision with a single line of decision logic—one that assigns every transaction unconditionally to the deferred or manual decision-making category.

This model can be deployed as a decision service, as can the new process, with the automated decision task using the decision service as usual in the prevailing technical environment.

At this point all transactions are being processed manually as this is the only possible outcome from the decision service but the infrastructure is in place to add more sophistication over time.

A series of iterative development efforts should now begin. The first should be to identify the absolutely archetypal positive and negative transactions. The decision model and decision logic can then be developed to assign these transactions directly to positive or negative processing. A new version of the decision service can then be deployed. The process does not change but fewer transactions will now be referred to the manual tasks.

Subsequent iterations can gradually add decisions and decision logic to refine the model within the decision service to handle more transactions.

A regular review should be conducted to identify transactions that were manually referred but where the outcome could be determined automatically and to review automated decisions to see if they match expectations. Each review will likely result in changes to the decision model and decision logic, further increasing the degree of automation. Each case will identify boundaries between the accept, refer and decline cases that can be used as test cases for the decision.

16.12.4   Example

It is common for organizations to define approval thresholds and conditions for important transactions. For instance, trades above a certain value or involving specific clients might be referred for a manual review before being finalized. Many organizations find it much easier to add new reasons to have a manual review than to retire old ones. In addition, this "kick-out" logic may be running in a legacy application that is designed to allow many such kick out rules but that is both high performance and hard to modify or analyze.

Over time, the number being kicked out climbs to the point where not all can be truly reviewed. The team doing the manual review therefore has a series of quick checks that can be applied to accept or reject most of the trades and spends most of its time working on the small number of genuine corner cases. To handle the number of approvals and to ensure that none are missed, the organization applies a business process that is initiated each time a transaction is kicked out, assigns the transaction to someone who can review it in a timely fashion and then handles all the necessary clean up/post-processing implied by an accept or reject decision.

This problem could, in theory, be addressed by changing the legacy application and replacing the flawed kick-out logic with a decision service. In practice this is unacceptable and the Accept, Reject, Refer pattern can be applied to the process to allow a clean-up decision to be developed.

Once the basic framework described is in place, the first rules relate to out of date kick-out rules that should be removed from the legacy application but cannot be. Those doing approvals are interviewed for the criteria they apply for rapid rejection or approval, especially those that allow multiple transactions to the accepted or rejected at the same time such as "I select all the ones less than $XX from US clients and approve them all". Historical analysis is used to confirm that these criteria don't categorize any transactions incorrectly and that the relevant rules and decisions are added.

16.12.5   Consequences

This pattern allows a very incremental approach to automating approvals, which is an essential ingredient in most organizations. By establishing the process and service infrastructure first, subsequent changes require only new versions of the decision service and therefore meet with less resistance. This is generally easy to manage with a commercial BRMS.

Initial iterations may not handle many transactions automatically. Even if they do, these are likely to be the simplest and quickest to review manually. It can be easy at this point to ask "why bother" with the automation. It is worth noting, however, that even removing the obvious transactions helps manual reviewers as it de-clutters their inbox and focuses them on the transactions they need to actually read. This will increase their accuracy even if the time saving is quite modest.

This approach will generally work best in organizations that have some commitment to continuous process improvement.

16.12.6   Notes

Given the incremental nature of decision development in this pattern, there is likely to be a need to revisit and refactor the decision once it reaches a mature level. The other patterns in this chapter, as well as the best practices discussed previously, should be applied periodically.

17 Examples

You can't do a fine thing without having seen fine examples
—William Morris Hunt

Like any complex endeavor, once the essentials of decision modeling are understood, one of the most effective ways to learn more is by means of representative examples. This section contains several worked examples illustrating not only how DMN works at scale and the range of ways in which it can be applied, but also giving an insight into the modeling process and its benefits.

17.1 Example One: Instrument Credit Rating

17.1.1 Purpose

The intent of this example is to illustrate a typical incremental build of a simple decision model. The intent is to demonstrate the use of key best practices, method and patterns to evolve a decision model. In particular, this example demonstrates the value of the following best practices: the separation of validation from business logic, spatial layout, group annotation, reuse, modeling with appropriate detail, assessing Input Data to see if they are decisions, using multiple perspectives and splitting large Input Data. It also highlights the correct use of *Change Shield, Classifier* and *Divide and Conquer* patterns.

Unlike the other examples in this section, it will be presented as a succession of figures. Each figure represents an iteration that builds on the previous ones given the findings of continued business analysis. Each figure will highlight the change from the last by featuring dark shapes with bold, italicized text depicting the model components or logic that have been amended or added since the last iteration.

The business background and context below would normally be captured in the decision metadata (see Section 14.2.5) and glossary (see Chapter 9). Not all decision metadata and the glossary are depicted here for brevity.

17.1.2 Background

This example builds on the financial scenario explained in Section 8.1 and reiterated in the sidebar that follows. It was modeled, as part of a much larger decision model, as part of a regulatory compliance initiative for a major investment bank. It concerned the determination of an Instrument's *Credit Rating Category*, a decision used to guide many business processes for determining investment, collateral, hedging and charging behavior.

Investment banks trade in a diverse set of **assets** each with a changing value. Some of these assets represent tangible products with inherent value, for example: commodities (e.g., gold, oil); debt issued by a government, corporation or municipal body or shares issued by a corporation. Others are more abstract and derive their value from some underlying asset, for example: an option to buy or sell something at a set price or a share in an index like the Dow Jones. **Instrument** is a collective term for these assets. Instruments are provided or issued by a company, known as the **issuer**. Some instruments are secured (underwritten) by a third party: the **guarantor**.

When an organization trades in instruments, it is interested not only in the current and potential value, but in the **risks** of trading (e.g., the chances that the trade may default for any reason). Risk can come from a number of factors including: the country issuing the instrument (it may be politically unstable); the currency being traded (it may have a volatile exchange rate); the issuer (it may be financially unsound or have a poor credit history) and the risk of the asset itself (it may have a volatile value). To offset the risk, the organization must understand the net short-term exposure of every trading portfolio and ensure it is covered by **collateral**—underlying, high quality liquid assets that address the risk of a deleterious events.

Deciding the inherent risk of every instrument traded is therefore a key decision for any financial organization. The risk level is needed to determine: whether or not to trade, how much margin to charge to offset the risk and what collateral will be required. Risk classification usually occurs in at least three stages:

- Inferring the type of asset represented by the instrument—the **asset class.**
- Finding the standard credit risk rating of an instrument by using external rating agencies that rank the risk using a standard scale (the CTRISKS scale in our example).
- Determining the company's own view of the investment rating category, which is informed by its own policies and attitudes to risk (e.g. *ABC Bank Counterparty Risk Guidelines*).

From this a categorizations of risk (the *Instrument Rating Category*) can be determined.

17.1.3 Business context

17.1.3.1 Decision definition

Adhering to best practice 14.2.1, a Q&A style definition of the decision was created. This decision answered the question: *"What is the credit rating category of the supplied Instrument?"* This is an important consideration when choosing, collateralizing, managing the risk of or recommending investments. The possible answers to this question were a series of alternative rating categories that dictated the organization's attitude towards a certain asset. The decision had to yield a valid category for each instrument *under all circumstances*.

The possible investment categories were: *Prime Investment Grade, AA Investment Grade, Other Investment Grade* and *Non-Investment Grade*. The decision was owned by Risk Management and made on behalf of Operations. The compliance departments were an interested party (see Section 14.2.5).

17.1.3.2 Decision selection

There was a strong motivation to model this decision. It is required for every instrument the organization traded, intermediated or issued—therefore it was high frequency. Consistency was vital to prevent anomalies in trading behavior between departments that would have caused a loss of client credibility or created an opportunity on which competitors could arbitrage. The outcome had high business value. Inaccuracy could have resulted in reduced profits, liquidity shortfalls, loss of trading reputation and missed opportunities. it was also a vital part of the company's risk management strategy. Finally, this was a heavily scrutinized decision and business transparency was important.

In short, this decision met all of the criteria listed in Section 5.4 for identifying good decision modeling candidates.

17.1.3.3 Business motivation

The primary business motivation to perform this decision was the need for Accuracy—the rating category had to be an accurate predictor of the ultimate corporate default rate within the following year. Each rating category was associated with a target band of ultimate default rates. For instance, the *Prime Investment Grade* was not allowed to be associated with Instruments which exceeded an ultimate default rate of 0.18%. The other business motivations for this decision are listed in Table 17-1 (best practice 14.2.3).

Driver	KPI Impacted Performance Indicator	Goal Supported Objective
Accuracy of rating category	Default frequency for each investment category.	Prime investment grades cannot exceed a default rate of 0.18%.
Latency	Age of investment category determination.	Value must take into account all events over twenty minutes old at time of use
Compliance	Traceability to specification.	Must meet and demonstrate >99% of auditor's test scenarios A2 and >90% of the test scenarios in A1.

Table 17-1 Decision Business Motivations

Table 17-2 shows the impact of the key decisions, identified in the first stage of the modeling process, on the accuracy KPI.

KPI: Accuracy of Rating Category		
The more accurate our determination of rating category the more cost effective our risk management will be.		
Decision	Impact	Contribution
Determine Lowest External Rating	Medium	This is the most frequently used means of determining external rating and the one over which the organization has the least control.
Determine Country Rating	Low	This means of determining external rating is infrequently used and linked to safe government products with low inherent risk.
Determine Instrument Rating	High	The selection of the external rating strategy directly determines the result.
Determine Instrument Rating Category	Medium	This is a rating classification and the value ultimately used by business processes.

Table 17-2 Impact of Key Rating Decisions on a KPI

17.1.3.4 Data

The (grossly simplified) data model linking the Information Items on which these decisions will be acting is shown in Figure 17-1.

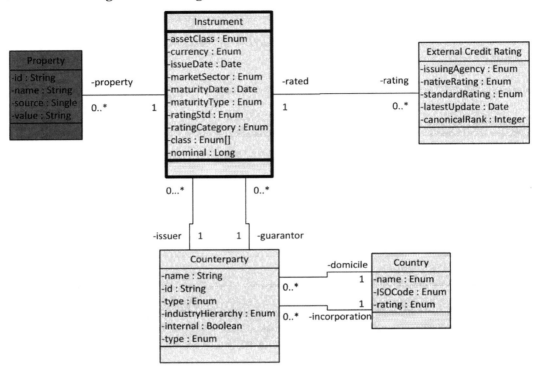

Figure 17-1 Instrument Data Model

The classes with a light background concern structured data: The *Instrument*, its *External Credit Ratings*, its *Issuer* and *Country* of issue. The darker object refers to unstructured text records that accompany some instruments and are referred to as *Properties*. The contents of the latter are unpredictable. This data model was a draft, a 'strawman' to provoke discussion during the modeling processes. The idea was to use decision modeling to confirm this model and to embellish it to the minimum extent required, not to spend a great deal of time perfecting a data model up-front. Decision modeling is an iterative activity with a side goal of creating a data model that is just good enough to support the decision model.

When writing a book it is necessary to place sections in a particular order, but do not infer from the placement of this section ahead of decision modeling that a fully-fledged data model is the prerequisite of decision modeling. The exact opposite is the case: decision models and data models co-evolve with decisions leading the need for data. The reason this data model is defined here is to allow the following sections to concentrate on the development of the decision model that is the subject of this chapter.

For brevity we do not provide a full glossary for this example. A full glossary example can be seen in Section 17.3.3.4.

17.1.3.5 Process context

This decision was used by the business processes and owners shown in Table 17-3 (in accordance with best practice 14.2.3).

Using (Business) Process	Purpose	Decision Maker
Client Product Selection	Make appropriate investment recommendations to fit client risk profile.	Client Advisor
Liquidity Risk Management	Determine if we should increase collateral used to managing the risk this holding.	Risk Manager
Pricing	Determine margin on depot services charged for this instrument.	Bid Officer
Product Innovation	Support design of new structured products.	Product Designer

Table 17-3 Decision Process Context

The risk management business process that used this decision is described by the BPMN model in Figure 17-2. When a set of Instruments underwent a momentous event (e.g., a significant price change, an update of its rating by an external agency, a corporate merger or demerger or an amendment of one of its core properties), an automated process determined which Instruments are impacted.

For each impacted Instrument (note the parallel multi-instance process), the grey decision task *Determine Instrument Rating Category* determined if the category has changed as result of the event and, if so, their liquidity flow was updated accordingly. Relevant changes were then communicated so that to the collateral burden for this holding could be adjusted.

17.1.3.6 Organizational context

This decision was primarily the concern of the Liquidity Risk Management function as it assists with safe burdening of collateral and liquidity balance and with satisfactory demonstration of compliance to the relevant agencies. However, as shown in Table 17-3, the accurate risk assessment of Instruments is essential to private banking, pricing and product innovation all of which are the concern of separate entities. The possibilities for organization fracture (see Section 14.2.2) is high.

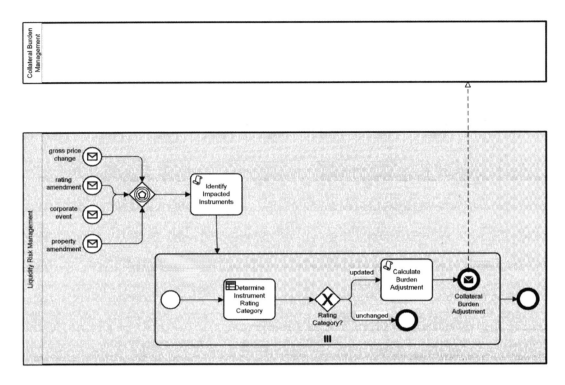

Figure 17-2 Liquidity Risk Management Business Process

17.1.4 Initial pass

17.1.4.1 Requirements Level

Initial analysis revealed that, as its name implies, the *Instrument Rating Category* subject decision is a classification of the finer grain *Instrument Rating* Decision. The modeler suspected that the latter will be reused in many other decisions. Coarse grain classification of *Rating* into a *Rating Category* provided a simpler view of the rating that is less likely to change should the rating scheme itself be altered (this is an instance of the *Classifier* pattern, see Section 16.9). The sub-decision *Determine Instrument Rating* asks *"What CTRISKS standard credit rating is most appropriate for this instrument?"* The answer is any one of the standard CTRISKS levels or a value indicating that no rating could be determined.

This level of credit risk was itself determined by the sub-decision *Determine Country Rating*, a decision that asks *"What is the CTRISKS standard rating appropriate for the issuer's country of incorporation of this instrument?"* However, if this were not available for a given *Instrument*, the *Determine Lowest External Rating decision* could be used instead. This asks *"what is the most pessimistic CTRISKS credit rating assigned to the Instrument by an external agency?"* Both of these sub-decisions required *Instrument* information. Both yielded one possible answer in the same set of possible answers—the CTRISKS values. The first iteration of the Requirements Level, in Figure 17-3, shows all of this. Notice the graphical convention of increasing the weight of the line enclosing the subject decision. This decision is focused exclusively on the business determinations—consideration of data validation and transformation issues is completely absent.

Figure 17-3 First Iteration Requirements Level

Because latency was one of the KPIs of the subject decision and it was (in this version) dependent on one Input Data, the decision model suggested the latency of the *Instrument* Input Data would have to be very low to satisfy this goal. Because *Instrument* information could change unexpectedly for many reasons (see the range of events in Figure 17-2) and the outcome was sensitive to it, the metadata for the *Instrument* Input Data reflected this low latency requirement. The organization could have lost money or reputation if it acted on outdated information.

17.1.4.2 Logic Level

The first draft of the *Determine Instrument Rating Category* Decision Table is shown in Figure 17-4. It classified the (CTRISKS standard) *Instrument Rating* into an *Instrument Rating Category*. Note that the value lists for both the input and output refer to enumerated types defined in the glossary. The value lists are not defined inline because of the maintenance issue this would create *Rating*s and *rating categories* were very commonly used and large scale repetition would have been onerous[61]. The angled brace notation in the value list section is our own convention and not part of the DMN standard (see Section C.4.1).

---

[61] Tooling that allowed value lists to be displayed inline but be managed across multiple Decision Tables would, of course, mitigate this.

	Determine Instrument Rating Category	
U	**Instrument Rating**	**Instrument Rating Category**
	<Instrument Credit Rating>	<Instrument Rating Category>
1	AAA	PRIME INVESTMENT GRADE
2	AA+ , AA , AA-	AA INVESTMENT GRADE
3	A+ , A , A- , BBB+ , BBB , BBB-	OTHER INVESTMENT GRADE
4	BB+ , BB , BB- , B+ , B , B- , CCC+ , CCC , CCC- , CC+ , CC , CC- , C+ , C , C- , D	NON-INVESTMENT GRADE

Figure 17-4 Instrument Rating Category Decision Table

For government issued *Instruments*, the *Instrument Rating* was determined to be the same as the *Country Rating* (if this was known) and is the *Lowest External Rating* for non-government issues or cases when *Country Rating* was unknown. *Instrument Asset Class* determines whether or not the stock is government issue (or equivalent for the organization's purposes). This was informally captured as the text rule of Figure 17-5. The DMN standard uses the special value *null* to indicate that the value of a specific variable is not provided or undefined. We prefer to use the enumerated value *UNKNOWN* as business analysts frequently see null as indicative of programming and *UNKNOWN* is more precise.

Determine Instrument Rating
If Country Rating not(*UNKNOWN*) and the Instrument Asset Class is *GOVERNMENT* then Country Rating else Lowest External Rating

Figure 17-5 Determine Instrument Rating Text Rule

The new dependence of *Determine Instrument Rating* on *Instrument Asset Class* had to be reflected at the Requirements Level, necessitating the update shown in Figure 17-6.

The *Determine Country Rating* sub-decision had a range of different derivations within the organization. This version of the model included a favored one as an example and a note, in the decision metadata and the diagram in Figure 17-3, was made that this sub-decision has a high *Equivocation* (the property of a decision that means that its definition is contested, not fully understood or ambiguous, see Section 14.2.5). Consequently, no separate logic definition for *Determine Country Rating* was required at that moment, but an investigation was started to identify the correct definition. The definition of *Lowest External Rating* was sufficiently ambiguous and contested that analysis could not supply a logic definition at this stage. This changed later.

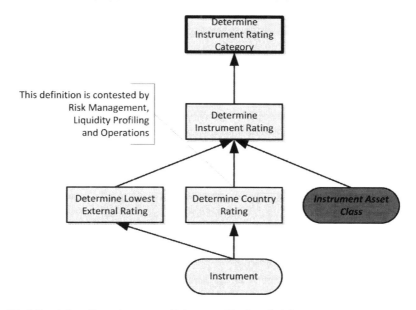

Figure 17-6 Decision Requirements Diagram Updated After New Logic Dependency

17.1.4.3 Best practices and patterns applied

- Start simple (to act as a focus for new ideas).
- Classification *Instrument Rating Category* is an instance of the *Classifier* pattern (see Section 16.9).
- Identify likely reuse candidates such as *Determine Instrument Rating* (see Section 14.8.1).
- Decision Requirements Level free from validation or data transformation issues (see Best Practice 14.8.2).
- Definition of large, volatile enumerations in a glossary (see Chapter 9 and Section C.4.1).
- Not all decisions need decision logic (see Section 14.4.1).
- Keep Decision Requirements Level consistent with the Decision Logic Level (see Section 8.3).
- Use of enumerated values as opposed to strings, use of *UNKNOWN* in enumerated values (see Section 14.7.1).

17.1.5 Second pass - substantiate

17.1.5.1 Requirements Level

The second iteration focused on refining and substantiating the initial model.

Further analysis confirmed that *Determine Instrument Rating* could be achieved in one of many alternate ways depending on the business scenario; *Determine Country Rating, Determine Lowest External Rating* were two strategies of which we are already aware. Analysts reported that, under exceptional circumstances, an externally imposed rating must take priority over any value determined internally. Therefore, a new sub-decision *Determine Imposed Rating* was needed to represent this third possibility. These alternative strategies for determining the rating were mutually independent and therefore *Determine Instrument Rating* constituted an instance of the *Divide and Conquer* pattern (see Section 16.2). This pattern is typified by a decision that selects one from a set of mutually-independent, alternate sub-decisions to provide its outcome, as opposed to those that combine the outcomes of their sub-decisions. To emphasize this, the next iteration Decision Requirements Diagram (Figure 17-7) used horizontal alignment of the alternate sub-decisions and a group annotation to enclose them. Notice that although the convention is to place the alternates in priority order, left to right, this is not a reflection of strict sequence—Decision Requirement Diagrams do not indicate sequence or procedure, they focus on dependency. Note that Input Data, Knowledge Sources and other uninvolved sub-decisions were moved out of the group annotation to accentuate this pattern instance.

Faced with a series of alternative sub-decisions, the question *"what business scenarios are not covered by any of these sub-decisions?"* arose. In this case, this question exposed examples in which no currently defined strategy applied, notably for non-government *Instruments* without an *Issuer Country* or *External Rating*. This decision was missing a failsafe—a means of determining a rating from the properties of an *Instrument* if all the other strategies failed or were not appropriate. The sub-decision *Infer Failsafe Rating* is added as a failsafe. This sub-decision used unstructured *Instrument* data, as a last resort, to infer a rating—hence its name.

Substantiating a model means looking for local expertise, externally imposed standards or mandates to support and influence the definition of their decisions. *Infer Failsafe Rating* was driven by internal policy on the inference of *Instrument* classification from unstructured instrument data (the Knowledge Source *Internal Instrument Class Policy*). Similarly, the decision *Determine Lowest External Rating* was influenced by the CTRISKS ratings standard which ranks the relative value of ratings from different external agencies—this was represented by the new Knowledge Source *CTRISKS Ratings Standard*. The standard policy for selecting a rating determination technique, embodied by *Determine Instrument Rating*, was guided by a Knowledge Source *Instrument Rating Policy (IR)*. The short name in parenthesis allowed rule level annotations to quote sections from this policy (see Figure 17-8). By this stage of the analysis, the earlier uncertainty on the definition of *Determine Country Rating* was resolved: it was driven by the externally-defined Knowledge Source *Country Rating Standards*.

Analysis of the Instrument data confirmed that it did not include *External Credit Ratings* and these had to be sourced independently. Therefore, an Input Data *External Credit Ratings* was added. It was plural because, as the data model of Figure 17-1 shows, an individual Instrument has many external ratings.

The resulting Requirements Level now looked like Figure 17-7.

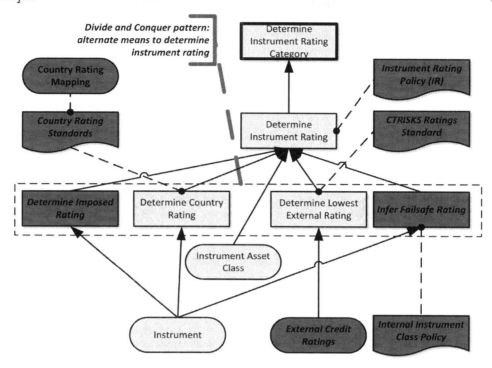

Figure 17-7 Second Iteration Requirements Level

17.1.5.2 Logic Level

The means by which *Determine Instrument Rating* selected a strategy to provide the *Instrument Rating* was refined as shown in Figure 17-8. Note that nearly all the conclusion values are input variables, this is typical for the *Divide and Conquer* pattern. It was assumed that any strategy that fails to determine a rating yields *UNKNOWN*. This Decision Table uses the First hit policy to avoid repetition of the last three rows for the case in which the *Country Rating* is *UNKNOWN* and the case that it is known but the *Instrument Asset Class* is not *GOVT ISSUE*. The logic for both cases is identical to rules 3-5. Despite the dangers of using this hit policy, this Decision Table was small, its growth options were limited and it was therefore a rare example that met the requirements for using the First hit policy. Notice how every rule annotation refers to a specific section of the authority *Instrument Rating Policy*, guiding this Decision Table, in order to substantiate the rule (see Figure 17-7).

Determine Instrument Rating						
F Imposed Rating	Country Rating	Instrument Asset Class	Lowest External Rating	Failsafe Rating	Instrument Rating	Annotation
<Instrument Rating>	<Instrument Rating>	<Instrument Asset Class>	<Instrument Rating>	<Instrument Rating>	<Instrument Rating>	
1	not(*UNKNOWN*)	-	-	-	-	Imposed Rating	IR A.2.2-19 exceptional circumstances
2		not(*UNKNOWN*)	*GOVT ISSUE*	-	-	Country Rating	IR 3.1-17 government issued stock
3	-		not(*UNKNOWN*)	-	Lowest External Rating	IR 2.2-4, 2.7 externally rated private stock
4	-	-		not(*UNKNOWN*)	Failsafe Rating	IR 2.5-6 'private stock, intrinsic rating
5				UNKNOWN	*UNKNOWN*	IR B.1 private stock, no rating

Figure 17-8 Instrument Rating Decision Table

A straw man logic definition for *Determine Imposed Rating* is provided in Figure 17-9. It depicts two exceptional criteria for rating imposition known at this point: the instrument was issued by one of the organization's own entities or a trusted rating was provided that supplanted all others. The table uses a context entry to simplify the determination that an *Instrument* is an *Own Issue*. If the *Instrument Issuer* was one of *Our Issuers*, the organization considered this an Instrument issued by itself, thus affording it special status. The Input Data *Our Issuers* needed to be added to the Requirements Level to reflect this (shown in the next iteration, Figure 17-13). Notice how Decision Table's readability is improved when they are explicit about their failure modes (i.e., the use of the UNKNOWN conclusion in Figure 17-9 and elsewhere).

Determine Imposed Rating		
Owner Issue	list contains(Our Issuers, Instrument.Issuer.Id)	

U	Owner Issue	Trusted Rating	Imposed Rating
	true, false	<Instrument Rating>	<Instrument Rating>
1	true	-	AAA
2	false	not(*UNKNOWN*)	Trusted Rating
3		*UNKNOWN*	*UNKNOWN*

Figure 17-9 Exceptional Rating Decision Table

The Knowledge Source *Internal Instrument Class Policy* advised a rating based on the *Instrument Class* which is shown in the definition of *Infer Failsafe Rating* in Figure 17-10.

Infer Failsafe Rating		
U	Issuer Type	Instrument Class	Failsafe Rating
	<Issuer Type>	<Instrument Class>	<Instrument Rating>
1	*US MORTGAGE SECURITIES*	-	*AAA*
2	not(*US MORTGAGE SECURITIES*)	*US AGENCY, US TBILL*	*AAA*
3		*AP AGENCY*	*AA*
4		*FAR EAST AGENCY*	*A*
5		*GOVT EMERGING*	*AA-*
6		*UNKNOWN*	*UNKNOWN*

Figure 17-10 Failsafe Rating Decision Table

Determine Country Rating had a provisional logic definition shown in Figure 17-11. This was a sample for illustration—the means of making this determination was due to be automated from the mapping underlying the Knowledge Source *Country Rating Standards* because it dictated a mandatory standard (as denoted in its *Influence* metadata). This underlying mapping was represented as an Input Data authority for the Knowledge Source—*Country Rating Mapping*. Large but simple Decision Tables of this sort are generally not good candidates for explicit maintenance in a decision model. They are volatile and don't represent the organization's expertise because they have been externally imposed. Instead, modelers should reference the underlying Knowledge Source (and possibly the Input Data that provides it). Note also the use of row level annotation to improve the readability of the sample in Figure 17-11.

Determine Country Rating		
U	**Issuer Country Id**	**Country Rating**
	<Country>	<Instrument Rating>
1	AD	A-
2	AE	AA
3	AL	B+
4	AN	BB-

Figure 17-11 Country Rating Decision Table (Excerpt)

Finally, the original logic definition of the subject decision, *Determine Instrument Rating Category* (shown in Figure 17-4), omitted the possibility that the *Instrument Rating* is not one of these explicitly addressed. This decision must produce a result under all circumstances, therefore an additional rule was added to the logic definition, see Figure 17-12. The Decision Table is now complete.

Determine Instrument Rating Category		
U	**Instrument Rating**	**Instrument Rating Category**
	<Instrument Rating>	<Instrument Rating Category>
1	AAA	PRIME INVESTMENT GRADE
2	AA+ , AA , AA-	AA INVESTMENT GRADE
3	A+ , A , A- , BBB+ , BBB , BBB-	OTHER INVESTMENT GRADE
4	BB+ , BB , BB- , B+ , B , B- , CCC+ , CCC , CCC- , CC+ , CC , CC- , C+ , C , C- , D	NON-INVESTMENT GRADE
5	UNKNOWN	UNKNOWN

Figure 17-12 Refined Instrument Rating Category Decision Table

17.1.5.3 Best practices and patterns used

- *Divide and Conquer* pattern (see Section 16.2).
- Diagram does not model sequence (see Best Practice 14.8.4).
- Layout Conventions: horizontal alignment of the alternates (see Best Practice 14.3.5).
- Use of group annotation to show pattern (see Best Practice 14.3.6).
- Use of First hit policy (see Best Practice 14.5.2 and Section 15.3.3.5).
- Use of Context (see Section 8.2.5).
- Naming of decisions and Knowledge Sources to show inference versus determination and to distinguish policies from standards (see Best Practice 14.2.4).
- Use of metadata for Knowledge Source influence level (see Section 14.2.5).
- Avoid string handling in Decision Tables and use enumerations instead (see Best Practice 14.7.1).
- Be explicit about decision failure modes (see Best Practice 14.5.5).
- Use rule level annotations in conjunction with Knowledge Sources (see Best Practice 14.5.7).
- Split up large Input Data (see Best Practice 14.7.5).
- Consider Knowledge Sources that have Input Data as authorities (see Best Practice

15.2.5).

17.1.6 Third pass - realization of dependencies

17.1.6.1 Requirement Level

This pass examined the extent to which the current decisions needed to be further decomposed. The usual rationale for descending another level when analyzing decision models (i.e., dividing an existing decision into sub-decisions) is the suspicion that: subordinate decisions have different Input Data or Knowledge Sources, that their definitions are unknown or have issues or that there is repetition in the decision logic due to insufficient normalization. In addition, Input Data components are analyzed to determine those which are really disguised sub-decisions.

Instrument Asset Class was previously considered a Data Input because its data was provided by a database. However, this obscured the fact that it must have been derived by the organization during an earlier business process and was itself the subject of another decision model. Reuse of this form must always be expressed as a sub-decision—even if the sub-decision is not the responsibility of the project for which a decision model is being created. This is because its definition, and its evolution, are important to the organization and because sub-decision reuse should be managed explicitly. Therefore, *Instrument Asset Class* changed from an Input Data to a decision *Determine Instrument Asset Class* (see Figure 17-13). The full dependencies and definition of this sub-decision are not shown here for brevity and to avoid clutter, it was the subject of its own Decision Requirements Diagram. This is an example of representing multiple perspectives using multiple diagrams (see Section 14.3.2).

The dependencies of *Infer Failsafe Rating* needed to be determined in more detail. Analysis revealed that this decision relied on *Instrument* classification by type (*Infer Instrument Classes*) and the type of *Issuer* (*Determine Issuer Type*). These were independent and had different Knowledge Sources and Input Data. Only the former relied on inference so the parent decision could be renamed *Determine Failsafe Rating* as its prior inference had been delegated. The Knowledge Source *Internal Instrument Class Policy* was refactored into two new independent Knowledge Sources: *Internal Classification Policy* which influenced *Infer Instrument Classes* and *Default Rating Policy* which influenced how *Determine Failsafe Rating* established a default rating given *Instrument* class, type and other information. Whenever Knowledge Sources with disparate sources, influences and governing bodies are involved they should be separately represented.

Similarly, and following the same best practice, the *Country Rating Standards* Knowledge Source was decomposed into two separate sources that were maintained by different authorities. One was internal and the other was an external one provided by Standard and Poor's. These were consolidated and resolved into local authority: *Country Rating Standards*.

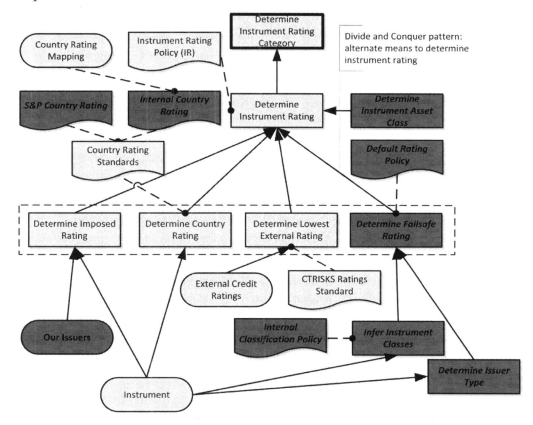

Figure 17-13 Third Iteration Requirements Level

17.1.6.2 Logic Level

The requirements and logic definition of the *Determine Instrument Asset Class* decision was discovered in another decision model and its decision component was referenced in this model after it was reviewed and found to be fit for purpose. As a result, it is not defined here.

The logic definition of *Infer Instrument Classes* relied on naming and numbering conventions in unstructured *Instrument* identifiers and used string matching to infer the class of instrument from these. It was therefore highly tactical and this was noted as part of the decision's metadata: it's *Lifetime* property was set to twelve months to reflect the fact that it required recertification. This signified that, in order to safely meet business needs, a more substantial approach would be needed ultimately. The organization planned to replace this with better up-front data capture in future. The (illustrative) definition of the sub-decision can be found in Figure 17-14. This used a literal relation to express patterns of text (`idPattern`) found in specific Instrument identifiers (`identifier`) and to dictate which *Instrument Classes* to assign to an *Instrument* if these patterns were discovered. The result box (at the bottom) searched for these patterns and assigned the classes if they were found. Duplicate values and the results of unsuccessful searches were removed from the output. Although this boxed expression avoided embedding the logic exclusively within FEEL, keeping it as a relation that could be separately understood, this definition was on the borderline of readability for business SMEs. Comments were added to improve readability.

Infer Instrument Classes			
	identifer	idPattern	class
	ISIN	^US313	US AGENCY
	CUSIP	^313	US AGENCY
	ISIN	^US912[89]	US TBILL
patterns	CUSIP	^912[89]	USTBILL
	NAME	^SDBCR	AP AGENCY
	NAME	^[HJ]SDBSP	FAR EAST AGENCY
	NAME	^CBC	GOVT EMG
	NAME	*COMMERCIAL*	COMMERCIAL PAPER

```
// build a list of unique Instrument Classes indicated for this Instrument
// each class is detected by the occurance of a string matching idPattern
// occuring in the specified identifier
distinct values (
 ( for pattern in patterns  return
  if some property in Instrument.properties satisfies
    ( property.name=pattern.identifier and matches(property.value, pattern.idPattern) )
  then pattern.class
  else null
 )[item!=null] )
```

Figure 17-14 Instrument Class Boxed Expression

Because it could have multiple identifiers, each indicating a different source of issue, an Instrument could have *multiple* classes, something that was not appreciated before this point. Therefore, the definition of *Determine Failsafe Rating* had to be amended, as shown in Figure 17-15, to handle a collection of *Instrument Classes*. Notice the use of a context to detect various classifications and to represent each as a Boolean flag (e.g., *US Issue* and *AP Issue*). Note also the cascade of conditions in rules 2-6 that prevent a condition overlap in the case that a single *Instrument* has multiple classes. This enforces a precedence between the classes in determining the *Failsafe Rating*.

Determine Failsafe Rating	
EMG Issue	list contains(Instrument Classes, *GOVT EMERGING*)
FE Issue	list contains(Instrument Classes, *FAR EAST AGENCY*)
AP Issue	list contains(Instrument Classes, *AP AGENCY*)
US Issue	list contains(Instrument Classes, *US AGENCY*) or list contains(Instrument Classes, *US TBILL*)

U	Issuer Type	EMG Issue	FE Issue	AP Issue	US Issue	Failsafe Rating
	<Issuer Type>	true, false	true, false	true, false	true, false	<Instrument Rating>
1	*US MORTGAGE SECURITIES*	-	-	-	-	*AAA*
2	not (*US MORTGAGE SECURITIES*)	true	-	-	-	*AA-*
3		false	true	-	-	*A*
4		false	false	true	-	*AA*
5		false	false	false	true	*AAA*
6		false	false	false	false	*UNKNOWN*

Figure 17-15 New Failsafe Rating Decision Table

The need to have a context in Figure 17-15 is enforced by the fact that neither inputs nor conditions can use functions in DMN (see Sections 8.2.3.1 and B.3.2). This style of Decision Table scales very badly if the number of Instrument Classes were to increase sharply because every class requires its own input flag. However, were DMN to support full expressions (with functions, see Section C.2.1) then the much more scalable representation shown in Figure 17-16 could be adopted. Because `list contains()` can cause overlap in rules 2-6, it is necessary to support the precedence of classes using the Priority hit policy. This requires that the value list explicitly establish the priority.

Determine Failsafe Rating		
P	Issuer Type	Instrument Classes	Failsafe Rating
	<Issuer Type>	<Instrument Class>	*AA-, A, AA, AAA, UNKNOWN*
1	*US MORTGAGE SECURITIES*	-	*AAA*
2	not(*US MORTGAGE SECURITIES*)	list contains(*US AGENCY*)	*AAA*
3		list contains(*US TBILL*)	*AA*
4		list contains(*AP AGENCY*)	*A*
5		list contains(*FAR EAST AGENCY*)	*AA-*
6		list contains(*GOVT EMERGING*)	*UNKNOWN*

Figure 17-16 Failsafe Rating Decision Table with Expression Conditions (Not Currently Supported)

No fan-in or -out interpretation of multiple cardinality (see Section C.1.1) needs to be depicted in the Decision Requirements Diagram because Infer *Instrument Classes* generates a single collection which is consumed by *Determine Failsafe Rating* as a single data item.

The logic definition of *Determine Issuer Type* is similar to *Instrument Asset Class*, above. It is already defined as the subject of its own decision model and has been assessed for reuse, no further elaboration is appropriate here.

17.1.6.3 Best practices and patterns used

- Model to appropriate level of detail (see Best Practice 14.3.1).
- Assess Input Data to see it is really a decision outcome (see Best Practice 15.2.3).
- Seek out reuse opportunities (see Best Practice 14.8.1).
- Assign Knowledge Source requirements to the lowest level possible (see Best Practice 14.3.4).
- Don't show everything in one Decision Requirements Diagram, represent multiple perspectives using multiple diagrams (see Best Practice 14.3.2).
- Name Knowledge Sources according to their origin (see Best Practice 14.2.4.3).
- Use of metadata for decision recertification (see Section 14.2.5).
- Compact and normalize Decision Tables (see Section 14.5.6).
- Use comments in FEEL expressions (see Best Practice 14.8.5.).
- Model hierarchical Knowledge Sources (see Best Practice 15.2.1).

17.1.7 Fourth pass – migration and detail

17.1.7.1 Knowledge Level

In this iteration the model's Input Data nodes were migrated, split and refactored as needed for greater clarity as the true data dependencies of leaf decisions were analyzed in greater depth. In addition, the handling of *External Credit Ratings* was decomposed further.

The Input Data *Issuer* was a sufficiently large entity (having many attributes of its own and different sources) to be referenced separately from *Instrument*. These were then depicted as discrete Data Inputs, the interrelationship between *Issuer* and *Instrument* is documented in the underlying data model. It is this data model (see Figure 17-1) that describes how many instances of other objects are related to a single *Instrument* (e.g., one *Issuer*, many *Properties*, many *External Credit Ratings*, two *Counterparties*—one *Issuer* and one *Guarantor*). Note that where multiple Input Data instances could occur (e.g. *External Credit Rating*) the name of the Input Data is pluralized to indicate a collection. The DMN committee are currently considering introducing a new notation to formalize this[62].

There was now a need to formally distinguish the uses of structured and unstructured sources of instruments suggested by the last increment's definition of *Infer Instrument Classes*. An additional Input Data was added to explicitly refer to the unstructured *Instrument Properties* required for this inference.

The *External Credit Ratings* attributed to an *Instrument* needed to be individually standardized before they could be compared by *Determine Lowest External Rating*. This is because different agencies have different rating scales. Only when standardized and ranked can the worst (lowest) rating be selected from the set. It is this standardization that was influenced by the existing Knowledge Source *CTRISKS Ratings standard*. Therefore, a new decision *Determine Standard Ranked Ratings* was needed to represent this ranking and the Knowledge Source had to migrate downwards to act as an authority for the new child. Naturally the standardization and selection of the lowest rating could have been performed by decision,

---

[62] Personal communication between James Taylor and the OMG DMN committee.

but the split is both easier to understand and yielded more reusable sub-decisions. Make the readability of the Decision Requirements Diagram the main aim when making this type of choice.

The results of these changes are shown in Figure 17-17.

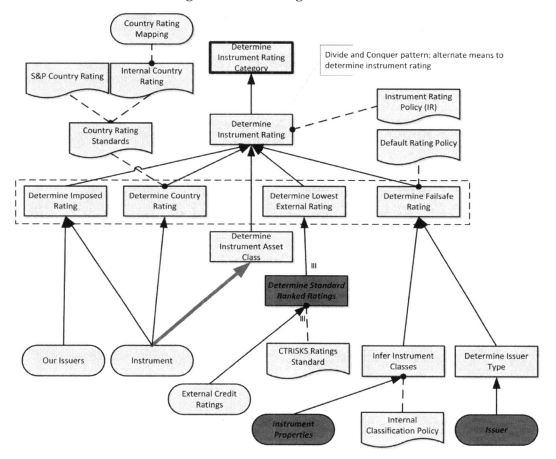

Figure 17-17 Fourth Iteration Requirements Level

The collection of ratings pertaining to an *Instrument, External Credit Ratings*, is standardized and ranked by *Determine Standard Ranked Ratings*. As the Input Data is a collection and is consumed as an entire collection by a single instance of *Determine Standard Ranked Ratings* there was no need for fan in (see Section C.1.1). However, *Determine Lowest External Rating* effectively aggregates this collection into a single rating and therefore fan-in was shown.

Note the horizontal alignment of Input Data components and the positioning of the subject at the top of the diagram to enhance clarity. Ideally Decision Requirement Diagrams should not become much more cluttered than this.

Determine Standard Ranked Ratings had to both standardize and rank a collection of ratings. These were different areas of expertise depicted by the invocation of two different Business Knowledge Models by *Determine Standard Ranked Ratings* in Figure 17-18. The Business Knowledge Models act as functions: the first standardized each rating, accounting for the differences between the various agencies. The second then ranked each standard rating. These two Business Knowledge Models share a single Knowledge Source which influences them both. How this invocation works is covered in the description of the logic in the next section.

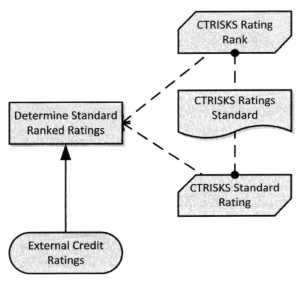

Figure 17-18 Detailed Analysis of Determine Standard Rating

17.1.7.2 Logic Level

The logic definition of *Determine Standard Ranked Ratings* was composed of three parts as shown in Figure 17-18: the standardization Business Knowledge Model (*CTRISKS Standard Rating*), the ranking Business Knowledge Model (*CTRISKS Rating Rank*) and the application of these to a collection of *External Ratings* to yield a collection of standard, ranked ratings (*Determine Standard Ranked Rating*). A fragment of the first of these is depicted in Figure 17-19.

U	Agency <Agency>	Native Rating <Any Rating>	Standard Rating <Std Rating>
1		AAA	AAA
2		A-1+	AAA
3	SP	AA+	AA+
4		AA	AA
5		AA-	AA-
6		Aaa	AAA
7		P-1	AAA
8	MOODY	Aa1	AA+
9		Aa2	AA
10		Aa3	AA-
11		AAA	AAA
12		F-1+	AAA
13	FITCH	AA+	AA+
14		AA	AA
15		AA-	AA-

CTRISKS Standard Rating

Figure 17-19 CTRISKS Standard Rating Business Knowledge Model (Excerpt)

This Business Knowledge Model was defined as a Decision Table that maps agency specific ratings to a CTRISKS standard rating. The sample shown here is for illustration and is not exhaustive. The inputs shown are Business Knowledge Model parameters that are initialized in the invocation of the model (shown later), they are not Decision Table inputs from Information Requirements. One drawback of this approach was that the ratings scales of each agency use different values. Therefore, the *Native Rating* enumeration *Any Rating* had to be the union of all rating values expected from any agency and it was not possible to avoid expressing an invalid condition combination such as Agency=*FITCH* and Native Rating=*P-1*. One way to avoid this was to re-express the logic as a series of agency specific Decision Tables as in Figure 17-20. This entailed extra work, makes the model larger (and safer) and introduces a direct dependency of the Decision Requirements Model on the number of agencies ratings are sourced from. If this number changed in future, the model would require refactoring. Selection of the correct approach in cases like this should depend on the likelihood of new agencies being introduced. In this example this was considered very likely, so the approach of Figure 17-19 was adopted.

Once a standard rating is known it could be ranked using the Business Knowledge Model *CTRISKS Rating Rank*. An excerpt from the logic of this is shown in Figure 17-21. This Business Knowledge Model yielded a numerical value for each value of the standard rating scale, the higher the number the better the rating. The separation of this logic from standardization allowed independent reuse and avoided repetition.

Standard Moody Rating

U	Native Moody Rating	Standard Rating
	<Moody Rating>	<Std Rating>
1	Aaa	AAA
2	P-1	AAA
3	Aa1	AA+
4	Aa2	AA
5	Aa3	AA-
6	A1	A+
7	A2	A+
8	A3	A
9	P-2	A-
10	Baa1	BBB+

Standard Fitch Rating

U	Native Fitch Rating	Standard Rating
	<Fitch Rating>	<Std Rating>
1	AAA	AAA
2	F-1+	AAA
3	AA+	AA+
4	AA	AA
5	AA-	AA-
6	A+	A+
7	F-1	A+
8	A	A
9	A-	A-
10	F-2	BBB+

Figure 17-20 Agency Specific Rating Standards Decision Tables (Excerpts)

CTRISKS Rating Rank

U	Standard Rating	Standard Rank
	<Std Rating>	[0..22]
1	AAA	22
2	AA+	21
3	AA	20
4	AA-	19
5	A+	18
6	A	17
7	A-	16
8	BBB+	15
9	BBB	14
10	BBB-	13

Figure 17-21 CTRISKS Rating Rank Decision Table (Excerpt)

These Business Knowledge Models were invoked in combination by *Determine Standard Ranked Ratings* using a boxed expression to achieve the ranking of a set of external ratings as shown in Figure 17-22. This expression iterates over all the *External Ratings* for each *Instrument* invoking both Business Knowledge Models already defined and yielding a collection of standard and ranked ratings. Its plural name reinforces the fact it yields a collection.

Determine Standard Ranked Ratings

```
// iterate through each rating adding its standard value and rank to a collection
for rating in Instrument.External Credit Ratings
  stdRating = CTRISKS Standard Rating(rating.issuingAgency, rating.nativeRating)
  return {rating: stdRating, rank: CTRISKS Rating Rank(stdRating)}
```

Figure 17-22 Standard Ranked Rating Boxed Expression

Examining this in more detail:

- The result box shows the iteration though each one of the *External Credit Ratings* for this *Instrument*. The whole decision is executed once per Instrument.

- Each rating associated with the Instrument yields a context with two keyed members: *rating* (the CTRISKS standard rating equivalent for this rating) and *rank* (the CTRISKS rank of that rating).

- Each of these values is determined by the invocation of the respective Business Knowledge Model: *CTRISKS Standard Rating* and *CTRISKS Rating Rank*. These invocations argument bindings are depicted in the two subsections above the result box. *CTRISKS Standard Rating* is invoked with the native rating of the agency and the agency name and *CTRISKS Rating Rank* is invoked with the standard rating just determined.

Finally, *Determine Lowest External Rating* selects the ratings code of one of these ratings with the lowest valued (most pessimistic) rank. The examples illustrate two of the many purposes for which FEEL uses square braces: the first braced expression selects those items in the collection that share the minimum rank and the next selects which occurs first.

Figure 17-23 Lowest External Rating Boxed Expression

The use of FEEL in these examples was minimized as much as possible to prevent the logic definition acquiring 'the air of programming'. Comments were used to provide clarification of meaning.

17.1.7.3   Best practices and patterns used

- Use of Input Data naming conventions to show a collection input using a plural (see Section 14.2.4.2).
- Model to an appropriate level of detail (see Best Practice 14.3.1).
- Split up large data objects (see Best Practice 14.7.5).
- Don't neglect unstructured data sources (see Best Practice 14.7.2).
- Clarify meaning with spatial layout (see Best Practice 14.3.5).
- Seek out reuse opportunities (see Best Practice 14.8.1).

17.1.8 Conclusion

This example focused on the fine detail of decision modeling technique as applied to a specific part of a financial decision model. It illustrated to clients how modeling can help to consolidate a team's understanding of important business decisions and provide a precise definition of these to aid communication. This was particularly useful here because the teams were geographically distributed across three continents. These decisions involved many different strategies requiring the expertise of different departments and the decision model helped to bring together the experts concerned, articulate their knowledge and capture the vital Knowledge Sources.

The decision model also helped to identify inconsistencies and errors and to thrash out requirements misunderstandings early. These early corrections helped to avoid wasted effort later in the project. Modeling also helped clients to pinpoint existing resources (decisions and Business Knowledge Models) for reuse and to create reusable assets of their own.

As a result of this modeling, clients were able to define better strategies for asset classification and resolve inconsistencies long before a BRMS became available to facilitate testing.

The example is a good illustration of just how far a decision modeler should use FEEL. Naturally the extent to which an organization uses FEEL will depend on their culture. However, business analysts were left to judge how much FEEL was used, to be sufficiently expressive while at the same time avoiding obfuscation of their requirements, without undue influence from IT who would naturally go further.

17.2 Example Two: Customer Next Best Action

17.2.1 Purpose

The intent of this example is to illustrate a higher level, more conceptual decision model. This model is presented in its final form, which did not include or require detailed decision logic. The intent is to show the value of a conceptual decision model in creating a shared understanding of the decision-making required. This model clarified requirements for a package selection and implementation while also revealing some critical organizational issues and framing the need for some specific analytic efforts.

As with other examples in this chapter, the additional data captured here on the business background and context would normally be captured in the decision metadata (14.2.5).

Because most of the decision names in this example would begin 'Determine', the leading verb has been removed in accordance with the best practice discussed in Section 14.2.4.1.

17.2.2 Background

This example relates to an effort by a retail bank to develop an understanding of how it would approach its customers as part of a Customer Next Best Action (CNBA) initiative (see sidebar for explanation). The bank had several specific objectives for this program:

- Replace its existing product-centric approach with a more customer-centric one.
- Ensure consistency and customer development across multiple channels.
- Replace a focus on marketing offers with a more holistic customer action mindset.

The bank was investigating several packages and platforms at the time and this model was developed in parallel with a technology architecture and a series of more general recommendations about the best overall approach to the program.

> Every interaction with a customer is an opportunity to build or improve a relationship. It could be a personalized marketing offer or proactive customer service. To make sure this interaction maximizes the value of a customer relationship, many organizations are developing Customer Next Best Action (CNBA) programs. A Next Best Action program considers all possible actions, from marketing offers to customer service actions, and selects the one most likely to build long term value in the client relationship. No matter what the context or channel, Next Best Action allows organizations to optimize each and every decision across the customer lifecycle—customer acquisition. cross and up-sell, retention, customer service and more. Next Best Action optimizes every customer interaction in an increasingly complex business environment made challenging by ever-increasing volatility in customer relationships. It effectively responds to increasing customer expectations, promoting the use of more product lines and channels.
>
> Next Best Action programs are cross-channel, focus equally on inbound and outbound, are customer-centric and deliver more than mere marketing offers. Specifically, they are:
>
> - Cross-Channel because businesses have multiple channels for interacting with their customers. Customers and potential customers, however, don't view a company differently channel by channel and increasingly expect the same service no matter which channel they use.
> - Focused on both inbound and outbound customer interactions. Next Best Action means ensuring customers get a response to their question or issue that reflects their relationship with the company as well as meaningful, relevant, personalized outreach.
> - Cross-Product and customer-centric, cutting across products and considering all possible products and services as part of each interaction. Next Best Action focuses on responding to the changing needs and behaviors of customers, rather than internal drivers.
>
> Next Best Action is not narrowly focused on the "promotion of the week" but rather asks "What is the Next Best Action to maximize the long term value of this particular customer?" This may mean correcting bad data, capturing life events or improving service rather than just finding the next offer to push.

17.2.3 Business context

17.2.3.1 Decision definition

The program's initial focus was two-fold—how to deliver consistency across channels and how to integrate marketing offers with other kinds of possible customer actions. This led to an initial high-level decision model shown in Figure 17-24. This used three channels as examples—the call center, the branch and outbound marketing. In each case the processes and systems in these channels would require a decision to be made and that decision needed to be consistent, customer-centric and workable in the channel context.

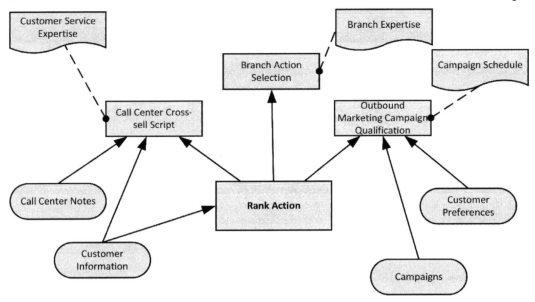

Figure 17-24 High level model of Next Best Action approach

The *Rank Actions* decision became the focus of the project and its question was initially defined as *"What are the best actions for this customer at this time, in priority order?"*

17.2.3.2 Decision selection

The bank had done some initial research and had identified that it had 140 million customer interactions each month. While the volumes of decisions varied significantly between channels, it was clear that the *Rank Actions* decision would need to execute in very high volumes for the CNBA initiative to work. Because the decision value decay (see Section 5.4.7) for this decision was steep, the decision would also have to be made more or less instantaneously or it would often have little or no value. In addition, many of the channel specific decisions had to be made interactively and therefore in real-time. This meant that any decisions on which the *Rank Actions* decision relied would also need to be made in real-time and be based on very current data.

17.2.3.3 Business motivation

The motivation for the program cut across all of these decisions and focused on developing multi-product customers (those with more than one banking product). The impact of these decisions on the KPI *Multi-product Customers* is shown in Table 17-4.

Later, in the modeling, it was identified that these decisions also had an impact on *Product Profitability* that would need to be considered as the decisions were designed.

KPI: Multi-product Customers		
Customers with more products are more loyal and profitable so we track how many customers have multiple products. #cnba		
Decision	Impact	Contribution
Branch Action Selection	Medium	Branch interactions are effective at increasing product count
Call Center Cross-sell Script	Medium	Customers who call regularly are most likely to become multi-product customers when cross-sold
Outbound Marketing Campaign Qualification	Low	Marketing campaigns are better at initial acquisition than development
Rank Actions	High	Core decision driving all others

Table 17-4 Next Best Action Motivation KPI

17.2.3.4   Data

The bank had an enormous number of systems and databases identified as relevant to its customers and to decisions about those customers. Rather than attempt to model this data upfront, the project chose to build a decision model and flesh out the data required for the decision as the model was built. This would allow only the data required for decision-making to be considered for integration, prevent unnecessary work and avoid the modeling becoming mired in depth-first analysis.

17.2.3.5   Process context

It was clear that these decisions would need to be made in the context of a wide range of business processes—from customer onboarding to loan processing, from call center interactions to online banking operations. At this stage in the project, however, this was deliberately left undefined so as to focus purely on the decision-making.

17.2.3.6   Organizational context

The project was being conducted by the Retail Delivery organization within the bank. This was the customer-facing portion of the Retail Bank and handled call centers, ATMs, branches and online banking for retail customers. The Retail Bank was one of several units of the overall Bank Group along with commercial, private, international and business banking units. These units were all supported by some corporate teams at the group level such as IT and Risk Management.

17.2.4 Initial decisions

The model began with four decisions, described in Table 17-5. While all the customer-facing decisions, the channel-specific ones, relied on the same rank-ordered list of actions it was also clear that each required additional decision-making to effectively consume this list of actions. This additional decision-making was not defined in detail at this time but was illustrated through the use of Input Data and Knowledge Source objects. Note that the specific questions and allowed answers are central to explaining why this is the case and note also the use of a tag (#cnba, see classification in Section 14.2.5.5) to group these decisions in a repository that was going to contain many overlapping projects.

Decision	Description	Question	Allowed Answers
Call Center Cross-sell Script	The critical decision in the call center is to decide what, if any, cross sell script to display for a call center representative. Such a script needs to be clear and usable as well as based on the highest ranking action that makes sense. #cnba	What script for cross-sell should be generated for this customer call?	A single custom script.
Branch Action Selection	Select the top 3 actions for a branch worker to see when interacting with a customer. #cnba	What three actions should be presented to a branch worker when working with a customer?	Ordered list of currently valid actions.
Outbound Marketing Campaign Qualification	What offer, if any, matches this customer for an outbound campaign at this time. #cnba	What offer should be proactively made to this customer at this time, if any?	Single currently active offer with approved creative (images etc.).
Rank Actions	This decision orders the available actions from best to worst. #cnba	What are the best actions for this customer at this time, in priority order?	Ordered list of currently active, approved and fully defined actions.

Table 17-5 Initial Customer Next Best Action Decisions

17.2.5 Core decision model

At this point the key was to understand how the core *Rank Actions* decision would be made. A second Decision Requirements Diagram was developed, shown in Figure 17-25 with *Rank Actions* as the subject. This took advantage of DMN's concept of using multiple requirements diagrams as different perspectives to develop a diagram focused only on ranking actions that shared decisions, Input Data and Knowledge Sources with the original diagram. The use of multiple perspectives is common in decision modeling and the use of multiple diagrams with shared objects allows these perspectives to be developed and discussed without losing a sense of the underlying model.

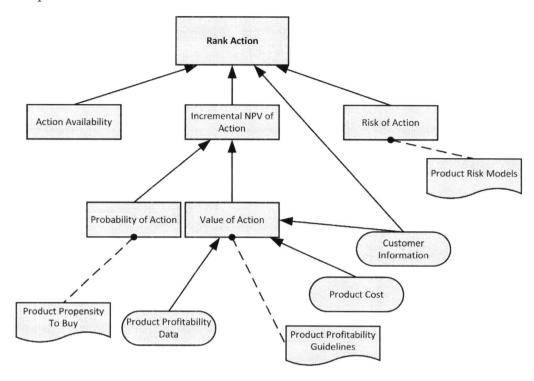

Figure 17-25 Rank Actions Decision Requirements Diagram

In the diagram, for instance, there is no implication that *Rank Actions* does not have any decisions that require it, they are simply not shown. In fact, the Rank Actions Immediate Context diagram (see Section 14.3.2.3) shown in Figure 17-26 can be generated from these two diagrams.

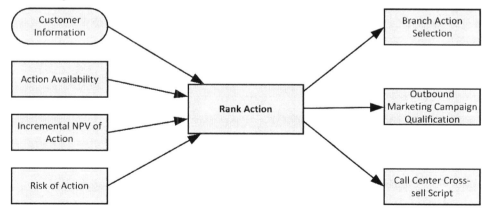

Figure 17-26 Rank Actions Immediate Context

Additional analysis of the *Rank Actions* decision identified that three factors—three sub-decisions—needed to go into producing the rank ordered list of actions:

- Not every action was available for every interaction with a customer, so the list of available actions would need to be decided for each interaction.

- For each action, the incremental net present value (NPV) of the action would need to be calculated so that very different actions could be compared. As a practical matter, this would need to be made for each available action, but an action does not need to be available to have a NPV so the two Decisions are peers in the model.

- Because many of the actions are related to credit products, it might be necessary to assess the credit risk of the action. Again, this would need to be made for each action identified as available but there is no need for an action to be available before this can be determined so the model shows no dependency between *Risk of Action* and *Action Availability*.

Incremental NPV was to be determined using a relatively simple formula that combined the probability of the action being taken by the customer (e.g., accepting the offer, providing the requested data, setting up an automatic deposit in their savings account) and the profitability of the action if it was taken. The profitability was a complicated decision in its own right, but as this research had been completed the decision could be left lightly defined at this point. While this profitability calculation included elements of credit risk, it was determined that the risk of a specific action might cause it to be excluded completely. Hence the inclusion of the decision *Risk of Action* in the model.

As this model was developed some obvious Input Data elements such as *Customer Information* and *Product Cost* data were identified and linked. A conceptual model such as this may or may not be linked to a well-defined glossary or data model and, in this case, the glossary was left as an exercise for the future because the team consuming the decision model was small enough to permit an informal, implicit terminology. Similarly, only a very cursory set of Knowledge Sources were developed. The focus here was on a number of analytic Knowledge Sources—*Product Propensity To Buy* and *Product Risk Models*—that would need to be developed and integrated.

17.2.6 Extending the model

Many organization units and departments were going to have to collaborate to determine the available actions so the next focus was on the availability of specific actions. The *Action Availability* decision was decomposed as shown in Figure 17-27. Specifically, the three main sources of available actions were identified—customer service, marketing campaigns and add-on product offers:

- Customer *Service Actions* might be available to a customer based on the products they own, their location, status of customer data and other service-related considerations. Not all *Customer Service Actions* are relevant to all customers.

- The Marketing department have specific offers that are made available at certain times to specific types of customers. These offers are a particular kind of action and have time and other constraints on when they can be presented.

- Many actions relate specifically to cross-selling or up-selling add-on products. These actions depend on the specific products a customer has—the add-ons all require specific base products to which they care added. As a result, not all customers can be offered all add-ons.

These decisions, and an assessment of their customer value, are described in Table 17-6.

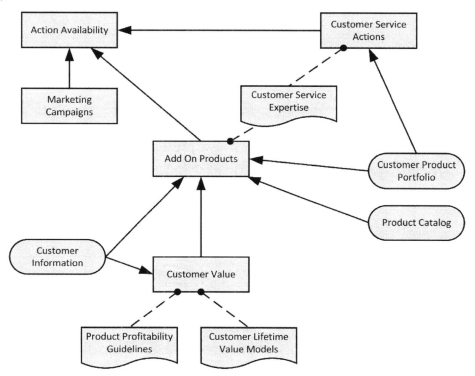

Figure 17-27 Action Availability model

Decision	Description	Question	Allowed Answers
Action Availability	Determine which actions are pertinent to the current medium of interaction and the customer status. #cnba	What actions are available to this customer at this time?	0+ currently active, approved and defined actions.
Add On Products	Determine possible add-on product actions. #cnba	Which product offers are available as add-on offers for this customer at this time?	0+ active, approved and defined actions promoting add-on products.
Customer Service Actions	Actions available to a customer, based on their current products, that are customer service oriented. #cnba	Which customer service actions are available for this customer at this time?	0+ active, approved and defined actions related to customer service.
Marketing Campaigns	Actions available due to marketing campaigns that are running. #cnba	Which marketing actions are applicable for this customer at this time?	0+ active, approved and defined actions available due to ongoing marketing campaigns.
Customer Value	Determination of the value tier of this customer. #cnba	Which value tier is appropriate for this customer at this time given their products, behavior and future potential?	Not Profitable; Marginally Profitable; Typical; Superior; Top-tier.

Table 17-6 Action Availability Decisions

17.2.7 Organizational impact

While additional decision-modeling was done to further describe the model, enough had been done at this point to identify some key organizational issues that would have to be resolved before the project could succeed. These related to risk, marketing and the branch organization.

17.2.7.1 Risk organization issue

Figure 17-25 shows the structure of the *Rank Actions* decision. As described in Sections 14.2.2, ch.14.2.4, each decision in this model was mapped to the organizations that owned the approach and to other organizations that were impacted. Because these decisions are all intended to be automated there was no mapping to "makers" (though the channel-specific decisions did have some makers involved as noted below).

As the model's organizational impact was being reviewed a critical issue was identified with respect to risk. All the decisions in the model with the exception of the *Risk of Action* decision were owned by the Retail Delivery organization or by a subdivision of it. The *Risk of Action* decision itself, however, was owned by the Credit Risk Management group who were also responsible for the risk models that were going to drive this decision. This created a serious organizational issue as the Credit Risk Management group did not report into the Retail Delivery organization nor to the Retail Bank as a whole. Instead, the Credit Risk Management group reported to the overall bank group. This represented an organizational "fracture" (see section 14.2.2) in the decision model and such fissures have many associated risks such as conflict of interest, lack of coordination and potential maintenance issues.

The *Risk of Action* decision was clearly going to be central to the *Rank Action* decision for those customers whose list of actions included actions related to credit products, which was likely to be almost all of them. Any changes to the bank's risk approach would be reflected in changes to this decision and would ripple through the decision-making that depended on the *Risk of Action* decision as shown in the risk decision impact analysis model (a single leg view, see section 14.3.2.5) in Figure 17-28. Because the groups had essentially no organizational structure in common, this model made an immediate case for a governance committee and review process to ensure that the overall *Next Best Action* decision remained coherent as the risk management strategy evolved.

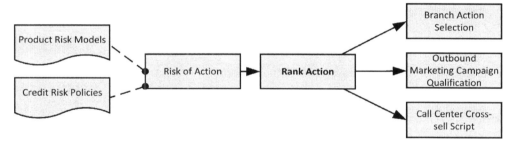

Figure 17-28 Risk Decision Impact Analysis

17.2.7.2 Marketing issues

The second set of issues related to how marketing saw the Next Best Action initiative. The model highlighted the difference between an outbound marketing action, selected as a Next Best Action (see Figure 17-25), and a marketing campaign that fed additional actions (lower fees for an account for the first year for instance, see Figure 17-27) into the mix. The marketing department had originally supposed that, even though the whole organization was moving to Next Best Action, they would still be able to guarantee to get a specific campaign in front of everyone. Of course this was not going to be the case given the customer-centric focus of a Next Best Action program. The clear distinction between deciding what outbound action to assign to a customer and deciding which additional campaign-actions to add to the mix made this clear. This prompted a discussion of how the marketing department might be able to over-weight, or give extra emphasis to, their actions when they really needed to drive the same offer to a large segment of the customer base at the same time. For instance, to coordinate with a TV campaign.

17.2.7.3 Branch data issue

The model (Figure 17-24) clearly shows that branch staff would be making the final decision about Next Best Actions for customers in the branch. Realistically there was no way to change this as only the branch staff would be able to see the customer, hear what they were saying, judge their mood, etc. To provide both direction and flexibility the design was to select a set of top-ranked actions for each customer and present them to the branch staff, allowing the staff the final choice.

While this is a perfectly sound design approach, it created an issue when the team was thinking through its feedback and learning approach for the program. Its data collection from the branch was very poor at the time and the team realized it would have no idea which of the top-ranked offers, if any, were actually discussed with the customer. It would know what actions were accepted, if any, but it would have no context information. As this was considered an important vehicle for learning, an initiative was begun to see how this information might be effectively captured without disrupting the branch experience for customers or burdening the branch staff too heavily.

17.2.7.4 Analytic deployment issue

The final issue revealed by the model was one related to analytic technology. The bank had historically pushed the results of predictive analytic models, scores, into its systems using a batch process. This used overnight data to recalculate the scores and then transferred these scores into the various databases and the data warehouse that contained customer data—a batch enrichment of customer data including various predictions such as credit risk.

Reviewing the model, it became clear that the program was going to include some decisions being made in real-time based on data that might have been updated that day, even that minute. This meant that scores created using a batch process would be potentially out of date. This discussion prompted a re-evaluation of the technology architecture, being developed in parallel, to establish an analytic deployment approach that would allow models to be scored against current customer data on demand rather than only in batch.

17.2.8 Framing analytics

The final element of this model to emphasize is its use as a vehicle for framing predictive analytics. In the decision model the need for two specific kinds of analytic insight, analytic knowledge, were identified—*Product Risk Models* and *Product Propensity To Buy* models. The decision model in Figure 17-25 clearly shows how these models will be used: to assess the risk of an action that involves a credit risk product and to determine the probability that an action will be accepted by a customer. The model therefore frames the analytic development that will be required to develop this insight as noted in Section 13.1.2. At the same time DMN can be used to think through the data analysis that might be required to develop these models and Figure 17-29 shows how the key types of Input Data to be considered in each case are authorities for the Knowledge Sources themselves (see Section 11.1.2). This shows how the data feeds the analytics which in turn support decision-making.

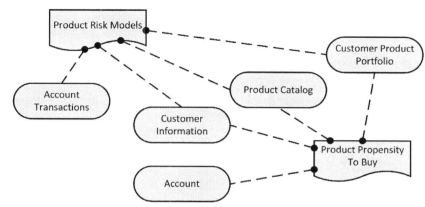

Figure 17-29 Analytic Requirements

17.2.9 Conclusion

The bank had several next steps that were informed by this decision model. Firstly, a build versus buy decision had to be made regarding the core Next Best Action system. Regardless of which approach was taken, the initial decision model could be extended to provide detailed requirements. For a build project this could include detailed decision logic but for a buy project it might not—the structure of the decision and the elements involved could instead be mapped to functionality in the package. In parallel, the marketing department was upgrading some of its email management capabilities and the model also informed those choices to ensure that any campaign-centric technology purchased in the short term would be compatible with the longer term customer-centric approach.

Secondly, there was an ongoing effort to revise and update the data and analytic infrastructure designed to support these decisions. The requirements for this infrastructure in terms of volume, response and the degree to which batch versus real-time analytics needed to be supported were driven by the evolving decision model.

Finally, various organizational change efforts were initiated, primarily to ensure that all the groups identified as being involved in an integrated Next Best Action approach would be able to manage and resolve issues as they integrated their needs into a single customer-centric whole.

17.3 Example Three: UServ Insurance Example

17.3.1 Purpose

The intent of this example is to illustrate a decision model that is based on a publicly available set of requirements, specifically the UServ Product Derby. In the early 2000s, Business Rules Management Systems demonstrated their product capabilities at what was then called the Business Rules Forum (now the Building Business Capability conference) by implementing a business requirement known as the "UServ Product Derby". This requirement deals with vehicle insurance problems including eligibility, pricing and cancellation policies for a hypothetical insurance company. This was re-published as the Decision Management Community Challenge in late 2014[63]. The idea of this challenge was to see how this requirement might be addressed using modern modeling and technology approaches. This example lays out a (partial) solution to the problem, based on work done jointly by Decision Management Solutions and OpenRules.

As with previous examples, the additional data captured here on the business background and context would normally be captured in the decision metadata (14.2.5).

17.3.2 Background

The UServ product derby requirement focuses on the vehicle insurance products and contains information on:

- Client Segmentation Business Rules
- Eligibility Business Rules
- Pricing Business Rules
- Example Scenarios
- Business Concepts (Fact) Model
- Business Process Models

The UServ Product Derby lacks much of the typical business context but a reasonable amount can be inferred (see sidebar). In addition, no Knowledge Sources were specified. Generally, Decision Requirements Models should include Knowledge Sources to show where the decision logic can be found or what authorities can be used to refine it.

UServ Financial Services provides a full portfolio of financial products across insurance and banking including: property and casualty insurance, vehicle insurance, life and health insurance, demand deposit, savings, money market, retirement and loans. UServ's objective is to satisfy the complete financial services of its clients. With this focus on complete relationship services, clients are rewarded for their loyalty as they deepen their relationship with UServ by increasing their financial portfolio.

UServ plays a balancing act between rewarding their best **clients** and managing the risk inherent in providing on-going service to clients whose portfolios are profitable, but violate the eligibility rules of individual products. UServ's business rules are an essential component for managing this risk. The business rules address eligibility, pricing and cancellation policies at both the individual product and portfolio level. This case study focuses on UServ's vehicle insurance products, but differentiates the basic business rules from those that apply to preferred and elite clients. The base business rules are dependent on the type of **vehicle** being insured and the characteristics of the **drivers** covered by the policy.

17.3.3 Business context

It should be noted that the business context for this example is fairly lightweight as it was not documented in the Product Derby specification.

---

[63] The challenge was posted to the dmcommunity.org site https://dmcommunity.wordpress.com/challenge/challenge-dec-2014/ and the original case study document was available at the time from http://ai.ia.agh.edu.pl/wiki/_media/hekate:2005_product_derby.pdf

17.3.3.1 Decision definition

The specification includes several decisions and the focus for this example is the auto premium pricing decision *Calculate Auto Premium,* a critical part of *Calculate Client Premium* decision.

17.3.3.2 Decision selection

No details were provided for the decision in terms of volume or usage. However, premium pricing is generally a high volume, repeatable, regulated and precise decision that is extremely suitable for both decision modeling and for automation using a BRMS. In addition, such a decision is likely to require channel consistency (see Section 5.2.2.3) and be subject to rapid change as UServ adapts to the market and its competitors' activities.

17.3.3.3 Business motivation

The Product Derby specification provides little guidance for the motivation of UServ beyond the general statement about balancing rewarding good customers with managing risk at the individual product level. From this one might infer some KPIs that would be impacted by decisions as shown in Table 17-7.

Decision	KPI Impacted
Calculate Client Premium	Manage risk effectively
	Number of unprofitable insurance policies
	Customer retention percentage

Table 17-7 Decision Business Motivations

17.3.3.4 Data

The example requires a simple glossary, the used subset of which is shown in Table 17-8. Many unused attributes have been elided from this table.

Term Name	Definition	Classification	Data Type	Source	Comments
Auto Model Name	Marketing label for the car's model	#label #manufacturer	String	auto. model_ name	Not used in processing
Auto Year	Year of manufacture associated with VIN	#manufacturer	Number [1900..2050]	auto.year	
Auto Price	The dollar amount for which this car is currently insured		Number >0	auto. price	
Auto is Convertible	Flag showing if the car is convertible or not	#risk #manufacturer	Yes/No	auto. isConvertible	
Auto is on High Theft Probability List	Flag showing that car is considered a high theft risk	#risk	Yes/No	auto. high Theft Risk	Based on matching against published list of high theft autos
Auto Potential Theft Rating	Determination of overall theft risk	#risk	LOW, MEDIUM, HIGH		Outcome of decision
Auto is New	Flag showing that car is still considered "New" by dealer		Yes/No	auto.isNew	Cars can be less than 1 year old but still not new

Term Name	Definition	Classification	Data Type	Source	Comments
Auto Age	Number of years since car's manufacturer, rounded up		Number >0	auto.age	
Auto Features	Enumerated list of 0,1, or many features installed in car	#manufacturer	List from DRIVER AIR BAG, FRONT PASSENGER AIR BAG, SIDE PANEL AIR BAG, ROLL BAR	auto. featureList	
Auto Uninsured motorist coverage is included	Policy includes uninsured motorist coverage for this car	#rider	Yes/No	auto. unisured Motorist	
Auto Medical coverage is included	Policy includes medical coverage for those riding in this car	#rider	Yes/No	auto. medical Coverage	
AutoPotential Occupant Injury Rating	Determination of overall likelihood that occupants of this car can be injured in a crash		EXTREMELY HIGH, HIGH, MEDIUM, LOW	auto. potential- TheftRating	Output of a decision
Auto Base Premium	Minimum premium assigned to car		Number >0	auto. basePremium	
Auto Discount Percentage	Percentage discount, if any, resulting from safety features		Number [0..100]	auto.discount	Determined by decision
Auto Premium	Final calculated premium to insure this car		Number >0	au-to.premium	Result of pricing decision
Auto Combined Premium	Final calculated premium with discount applied		Number>0	Auto. combine Premium	Result of combined premium decision
AutoType	Categorization of car size and type by manufacturer	#manufacturer	COMPACT SUDAN, LUXURY	auto.type	
Client's Drivers	All drivers associated with the client		List of Drivers	client.drivers	
Client's Cars	All cars associated with the client		List of Cars	client.autos	
Client's Client Segment	Segment to which the client is allocated based on overall relationship		...	cli-ent.segment	

Table 17-8 UServ Glossary

17.3.3.5 Process context

The example is focused on calculating the auto policy eligibility and premium. This is part of the *Process Vehicle Insurance Application* business process shown in Figure 17-30. Specifically, it is by the *Determine Policy Eligibility and Premium* decision task.

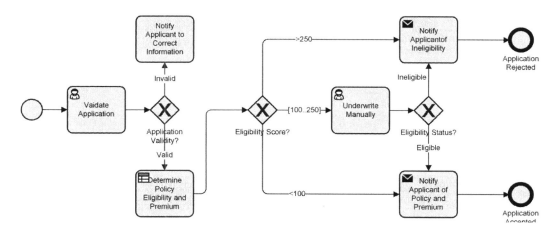

Figure 17-30 Process Vehicle Insurance Application

17.3.4 High level overview model

First, summary models were developed to show the high level specification of the problem. Core decisions and Input Data were identified and linked. DMN allows for an underlying shared repository so these objects can be on multiple diagrams without duplication (see Section 8.1.7 and 14.3.2)—they are reused between the diagrams. Each business area can be focused on individually, creating a model for that one area and taking advantage of the repository to manage reuse. Figure 17-31 shows the highest level: how eligibility and premium calculation are both involved and Figure 17-32 shows a focused, detailed model showing how the *Client Premium* is calculated. A complete model can be developed iteratively in this way, repeating the iteration to the level required at each step.

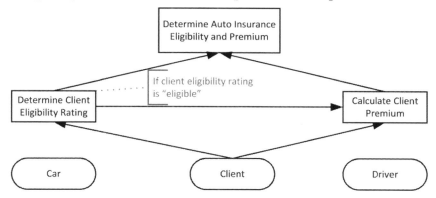

Figure 17-31 High Level UServ Decision Requirements Diagram Overview

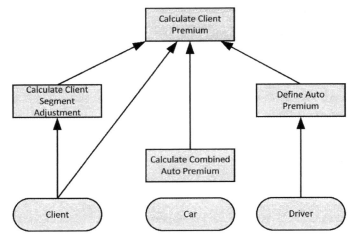

Figure 17-32 Calculate Client Premium Model

17.3.5 Calculate Combined Auto Premium model

In this example, the next stage was to model the *Calculate Combined Auto Premium* decision so that the logic could be specified for this part of the model. Figure 17-33 shows the decision requirements for this iteration. The premium is calculated from two sub-decisions, one to *Define Auto Premium* and one to *Define Auto Discount Percentage*. The premium is calculated from a series of decisions made about the Car as well as some of the data for the Car itself. The *Calculate Combined Auto Premium* decision is made for each Car on the policy application. Figure 17-34 shows the immediate context diagram (see Section 14.3.2.3) for *Define Auto Premium* which focuses only on the requirements involving this decision. In this case, this diagram contains only links also shown on the main diagram but in many situations an immediate context diagram usefully pulls together requirements from many other diagrams

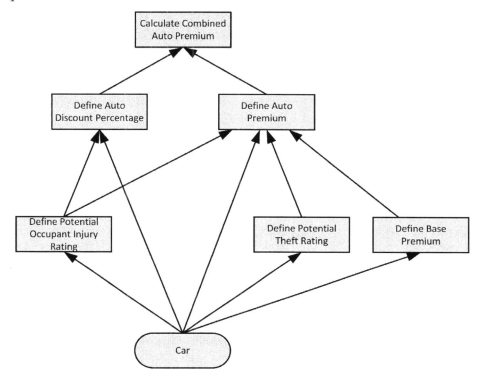

Figure 17-33 Calculate Auto Premium Model

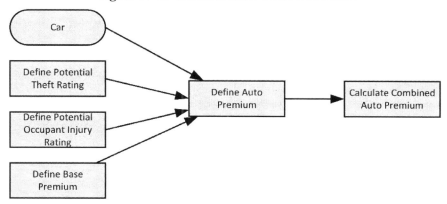

Figure 17-34 Define Auto Premium Nearest Neighbor

17.3.6 Auto Premium details

The details for these decisions emerged as the model was developed. The questions and allowed answers are shown in Table 17-9. The specification did not provide enough business context to define additional properties such as organizational ownership.

Decision	Description	Question	Allowed Answers
Define Potential Theft Rating	Determine how likely the car is to be stolen, given price, convertibility, and whether this model is on the theft list.	What is the potential theft rating for the automobile?	High, Moderate, Low
Define Potential Occupant Injury Rating	Determine the potential for occupant injury with this car based on power and safety features.	What is the potential occupant injury rating for the car?	Extremely High, High, Moderate, Low
Define Auto Premium	Calculate the auto premium. This includes base premium plus adjustments.	What is the premium for the auto (includes base and adjustments)?	Number ($)
Define Auto Discount	Determine the discount percentage for the auto premium.	What is the premium discount percentage for this car?	Percentage
Define Base Premium	Determine the base premium to apply to a vehicle with no adjustments.	What is the base premium for this auto?	Number ($)
Calculate Combined Auto Premium	Calculate the combined auto premium by applying discount and premium	What is the discounted auto premium for this car?	Number ($)

Table 17-9 Auto Premium Decision Details

With this information defined, the decision logic was created for each decision.

17.3.7 Auto Premium decision logic

The decision logic was defined for each decision in turn. Figure 17-35 shows the logic for *Define Base Premium* that simply takes the type of car and sets a base premium amount based on it.

Define Base Premium		
U	Auto Type	Base Premium
	COMPACT SEDAN, LUXURY	[0..500]
1	COMPACT	250
2	SEDAN	400
3	LUXURY	500

Figure 17-35 Define Base Premium

Figure 17-36 and Figure 17-37 show the *Define Potential Theft Rating* and *Define Potential Occupant Potential Injury Rating*. These use characteristics of the car to categorize the car in terms of theft risk and occupant injury risk. Notice the former uses the Any hit policy in order to avoid the need to totally disambiguate the conditions for rules 3-5 in Figure 17-36 which share the same conclusion value.

Define Potential Theft Rating			
A	Auto is on High Theft Probability List	Auto is Convertible	Auto Price	Auto Potential Theft Rating *HIGH, MODERATE, LOW*
1	false	false	<20000	*LOW*
2	false	false	[20000..45000]	*MODERATE*
3	true	-	-	*HIGH*
4	-	true	-	*HIGH*
5	-	-	>45000	*HIGH*

Figure 17-36 Define Auto Theft Rating

Define Potential Occupant Injury Rating	
Auto has Driver Air Bag	list contains(Auto Features, *DRIVER'S AIG BAG*)
Auto has Passenger Air Bag	list contains(Auto Features, *FRONT PASSENGER AIR BAG*)
Auto has Side Panel Air Bag	list contains(Auto Features, *SIDE PANEL AIR BAG*)
Auto has Roll Bar	list contains(Auto Features, *ROLL BAR*)

P	Auto has Driver Air Bag	Auto has Front Passenger Air Bag	Auto has Side Panel Air Bag	Auto has Roll Bar	Auto is Convertible	Auto Potential Occupant Injury Rating
	true, false	true, false	true, false	true, false	true, false	*EXTREMELY HIGH, HIGH, MODERATE, LOW*
1	true	true	true	-	-	*LOW*
2	true	true	false	-	-	*MODERATE*
3	true	false	-	-	-	*HIGH*
4	-	-	-	false	true	*EXTREMELY HIGH*

Figure 17-37 Define Potential Occupant Injury Rating

Define Potential Occupant Injury Rating uses the Priority hit policy because: it has some special cases which must have precedence over all other conditions (e.g., the absence of a roll bar on a convertible), to express these conditions using the Unique hit policy would entail many repeated rules in the table and the table is now and likely to remain small.

Note that DMN inputs can include expressions (e.g., Chapter 8, Figure 11) but may not include function invocations (see Section 8.2.3.1). Therefore, we need to use a context to determine which features a car has and use these as inputs.

With these two *Classifier* decisions (see Section 16.9) made and some additional properties of a Car, the auto premium can be calculated using a *Scorecard* approach (see Section 16.1) as shown in Figure 17-38.

Define Auto Premium

C+	Auto is New	Auto Age	Auto Uninsured Motorist Coverage is Included	Auto Medical Coverage is Included	Auto Potential Occupant Injury Rating	Auto Potential Theft Rating	Auto Premium
	true, false	>=0	true, false	true, false	*EXTREMELY HIGH, HIGH, MEDIUM, LOW*	*HIGH, MODERATE, LOW*	>=0
1	-	-	-	-	-	-	Base Premium
2	true	-	-	-	-	-	400
3	false	<5	-	-	-	-	300
4		[5..10]	-	-	-	-	250
5	-	-	true	-	-	-	300
6	-	-	-	true	-	-	600
7	-	-	-	-	*EXTREMELY HIGH*	-	1000
8	-	-	-	-	*HIGH*	-	500
9	-	-	-	-	-	*HIGH*	500

Figure 17-38 Define Auto Premium

The other "leg" of the Decision Requirements Diagram in Figure 17-33 requires a calculation of the discount based on the potential theft rating, which is reused, and car features as shown in Figure 17-39. Finally, a formula is defined to calculate the overall price as shown in Figure 17-40. This is the top level (subject) decision of the model.

Define Auto Discount Percentage

Auto has Driver Air Bag	list contains(Auto Features, *DRIVER'S AIG BAG*)
Auto has Passenger Air Bag	list contains(Auto Features, *FRONT PASSENGER AIR BAG*)
Auto has Side Panel Air Bag	list contains(Auto Features, *SIDE PANEL AIR BAG*)
Auto has Alarm System	list contains(Auto Features, *ALARM SYSTEM*)

C+	Auto has Driver Air Bag	Auto has Front Passenger Air Bag	Auto has Side Panel Air Bag	Auto has Alarm System	Auto Potential Theft Rating	Auto Discount Percentage
	true, false	true, false	true, false	true, false	*HIGH, MODERATE, LOW*	[0..100]
1	true	-	-	-	-	12
2	true	true	-	-	-	3
3	true	true	true	-	-	3
4	-	-	-	true	*HIGH*	10

Figure 17-39 Define Auto Discount

Calculate Combined Auto Premium

Auto Premium * (100 - Define Auto Discount Percentage) / 100

Figure 17-40 Calculate Combined Auto Premium

17.3.8 Conclusion

This example is included as a simple illustration of the use of both a set of Decision Requirements Diagrams and Decision Table logic to represent a business scenario. The model shows several strengths of decision modeling as an approach:

- The use of different data in each part of the overall model shows how the Input Data flows into the final decision.

- The cardinality of the data involved— that a client may have many autos and many drivers for instance—can be easily overlain on the model to show the matching decision cardinality.

- The model can be developed incrementally and iteratively, adding detail at each level. This supports an agile approach.

- The Decision Requirements Diagram plus the questions and allowed answers gives a remarkably complete view of the decision-making even before the decision logic is written.

- Each Decision Table is simple, clear and unambiguous.

- The reuse of the *Potential Theft Rating* is clear.

- The impact of changes to decisions can be seen clearly in the model, e.g., that a change to how theft ratings are determined affects both premium and discounts.

18 Establishing a Decision Modeling Practice

The world hates change, yet it is the only thing that has brought progress
— Charles Kettering

Decision modeling is a powerful technique that yields considerable benefits to individual projects that use it and still more to the companies that coordinate its adoption across their enterprises. This chapter considers the prerequisites of systematically introducing decision modeling to an organization—what needs to be in place before you can obtain the full benefit of the method. It considers the factors that increase effectiveness of decision modeling and how to build teams within an organization. Finally, it discusses the tools required, why they are needed and how to survive without them.

18.1 Preparing For Corporate Adoption

Companies that plan to implement a decision modeling program should be aware that adopting the technique in a consistent and lasting manner requires certain pre-requisites to be satisfied. Specifically, value should have been demonstrated in a pilot project and there should be strong business backing. Specific infrastructural support is also required.

The institutionalization of decision modeling should not even be considered unless the enterprise has established that it can benefit from the approach (see Chapter 4.) and that it has suitable decisions (see Section 5.2). Most enterprises that find it worthwhile to adopt decision modeling will also be organizations that can benefit more broadly from Decision Management (see Section 4.2).

Although the technique does bring value when applied to individual projects, wide adoption is considerably more beneficial (see Section 18.2).

18.1.1 Demonstrate value with a pilot project

Some organizations, especially those with a strong history of adopting and using modeling approaches, may feel that they can move directly to an organization-wide adoption of decision modeling. Building perhaps on infrastructure and teams dedicated to process or data modeling, decision modeling may seem like such an obvious fit that it can be broadly adopted immediately.

This is generally a high risk strategy. Adopting decision modeling without reference to successful projects runs a serious risk that it will be a technical approach and remain in the hands of technologists and architects. This tends to exclude the business owners and subject matter experts that are critical to success. Broad, effective adoption of decision modeling requires the active engagement of business people and an architectural match between decision modeling and other modeling approaches is unlikely to be compelling enough that they will actively engage with the new technique. The best way to engage these groups is through an effective, high value pilot project that demonstrates the value of the technique.

A means of selecting the best pilot project is discussed in Section 18.2. A pilot minimizes risks while still offering enough potential value for the technique to demonstrate benefit. A visible pilot establishes that decision modeling works and that it delivers value to the organization in a realistic scenario. It generates both management and business support. Regardless of how often and how effectively the organization has adopted previous modeling approaches, a pilot project is a critical prerequisite for broad decision modeling adoption.

18.1.2 Build business backing

A successful pilot builds an initial level of business support for decision modeling. Firsthand experience with the approach usually builds a strong community of advocates. It also engages an initial group of business experts in decision modeling, beginning the process of building business expertise in the technique. These initial steps are critical because the business expertise and backing needed for a broad decision modeling practice cannot be delivered solely by IT departments. Such an IT-centric approach has been tried, but experience with these efforts suggests strongly that a broader impetus is needed for several reasons including:

- A lack of business backing often translates into a lack of business engagement in modeling from the start, reducing the accuracy of models because business domain expertise is not applied effectively. This initial undermining of the initiative's credibility and lack of model accuracy is hard to overcome and threatens its long-term success.

- IT-centric efforts tend to narrowly focus on deployable decision models (see Section 13.2) and so miss opportunities to improve manual decision-making, apply analytics and think more broadly about the value of decision modeling.

- IT will prioritize decision modeling efforts based on current technology adoption—where a BRMS is already planned for instance—and not where the business value might be greatest.

- Without the business commitment to a permanent adoption of decision modeling, many business units perceive it as a one-off 'special project'. An investment in decision modeling underpinned solely by IT, even if it can capture models accurately at the outset, risks becoming stale quickly as the business reverts to its earlier process and innovates without reflecting this in the model. Many of the advantages of decision modeling require the model to be the on-going, prime record of business decision requirements.

Broad adoption of decision modeling involves more than the adoption of a new notation by business analysts and architects. Adopting decision modeling requires the wholesale involvement of business experts to ratify, own and design operational decisions. A pilot project will create an initial set of business backers but organization-wide adoption will require broad and deep business backing for the approach. The benefits to agility and integrity of key business decisions are considerable but these require cultural commitment within an organization.

18.1.3 Invest in specific infrastructural support

Decision modeling is a technique with a strong application, business and technical context (see Chapter 7). The full power of decision modeling is most easily exploited when it is adopted and used in an environment that supports this broad context and allows decision models to be connected to the rest of the business environment. These connections are easier to make when the following are already established:

- **Data modeling practices** (see Chapter 9 and Section 10.3). Decision modeling benefits from a widely shared, consistent understanding of both source data for decisions and reference data are important. Their meanings and properties—for instance, latency and data quality—must be understood and shared. Decisions will act on this data and modeling decisions broadly will require a solid foundational understanding of this data.

- **Formalized reference data access**. Much of an organization's decision modeling effort will be focused on decisions that are expected to be automated. Well defined structured or unstructured data sources containing reference and operational data with well-defined interfaces will make broad decision automation practical.

- **Shared document repository**. A collaborative document creation, sharing and version control system to manage Knowledge Sources. Some organizations find they must gather and review their policies and best practices more effectively to support their decision modeling efforts while others just need to invest generally in better document management. Accessing and referencing these materials is critical to the decision modeling process and broad adoption will be difficult if teams are creating this infrastructure as they go.

- **Integrated modeling approach (optional)**. Decision modeling can yield many benefits when used in isolation and many organizations have benefited from this targeted approach. However, it is even more powerful when integrated with other modeling disciplines that establish a context for the decisions being made. Investing in process and architecture modeling, for instance, will compound the value of decision modeling, especially as an organization moves to broad adoption (see Chapters 7 and 11). This is an optional step and one that requires significant investment. It should not be attempted all at once, rather it can be adopted at any time and grown, incrementally, as needed. Some organizations have an existing investment to data or process modeling to which their decision modeling approach can be allied.

18.2 Select A Pilot Project

Broad adoption of decision modeling requires the identification of a suitable first project. Such a project needs to be focused in an area that will contain decisions that are suitable for decision modeling. It also needs to be a suitable pilot project in that it: has a reasonable scope, is moderately visible, is important to the business but not business-critical, and has a timeframe that allows for some training and learning to be included.

18.2.1 Determine if decision modeling applies to your business area

Most organizations will use decision modeling in a specific business area in which other activities are already planned or underway. The business area may be one that is being modeled extensively using BPMN process models or one in which there is a heavy focus on automation. The criteria outlined in Section 5.2: (value, scale and transparency) can be applied to any business area to see if it is likely to contain decisions that will show a return on decision modeling.

18.2.2 Develop an initial decision inventory

Assuming that the business area seems suitable the next step is to develop an initial decision inventory. This is discussed in detail in Section 12.2. It is not essential or even desirable that all possible decisions are inventoried before any are modeled, but a robust initial set will allow a suitable decision or two to be identified for the pilot.

18.2.3 Rank available decisions

Often the initial decision inventory will contain many potentially suitable decisions. It is possible to estimate the value of decision modeling for these decisions using the criteria outlined in Section 5.4. A scorecard can be developed as follows:
- Identify the characteristics, such as those listed in Section 5.4, which will be used to rank the decisions.
- Decide if any characteristics should be over- or under-weighted. For instance, a strict audit regime may result in over-weighting the degree to which a specific decision is audited.
- Score each decision against each characteristic, at least approximately.
- Score each decision based on the sum of characteristic scores, each of which has been multiplied by any assigned weights.

This is not generally a very scientific assessment so it should not be used to differentiate between two decisions that score very similarly. It does, however, broadly differentiate between better and worse candidates.

18.2.4 Scope a first project

Once a small number of candidate decisions are identified as suitable then a small cohesive set should be selected for an initial project. As with any pilot the decisions should be selected such that they have reasonable visibility within the organization and are examples that will broadly resonate. High risk projects should be avoided initially as adopting a new modeling technique will have new demands on project management, estimating and other elements of the project.

18.2.5 Example

One of the authors recently provided consultancy to an international project to support and coordinate multiple, new regulatory compliance initiatives across a global investment bank. Regulatory compliance is a significant logistical challenge for the majority of financial institutions and an area to which Decision Management is especially well suited. The high business value, volume and need for transparency of these decisions were undisputable. The value of regulatory decisions is that they help to avoid punitive fines and mitigate the risk of liquidity crises. Volumes were high because the vast majority of the bank's positions required processing (a population in the hundreds of millions). Transparency was essential because external audits required that all decisions could be both justified after-the-fact and associated with a specific section of the regulatory specification.

Although the project was not associated with a large process modeling effort, automation of regulatory compliance was already underway—to save on the significant costs of manual processing, to forestall the increased complexity of new regulations and to address the reduced latency demanded by the new reporting requirements.

An inventory of twenty five key decisions was drawn up covering a range of regulatory mandates: from guarding the reuse of high-quality collateral in fund transfers, to reporting liquidity flows and from volatility buffer calculations to institutional (e.g., Bank of England) collateral eligibility determinations. SMEs and architects were tasked with rating these decisions according to: frequency, consistency, business value, ease of measuring benefit, rate of change, value decay, current cost, likelihood of external audit and combined risk of failure. Of these factors rate of change, likelihood of audit, consistency and risk cost of failure were over-weighted because these characteristics were internally assessed as posing the biggest challenges and were already objectives of the program.

On this basis the determination of the asset class and institutional eligibility of instruments were the highest ranked decisions because of the rapid pace of change and the impact of these determinations on the use of instruments by many of the bank's departments. These decisions were well understood by SMEs and highly visible because of the many systems that would use them. However, the risk was mitigated by the team's familiarity with the business area, the existence of an existing legacy solution based on business rules technology which could be mined for requirements and agile development practices.

The pilot was a marked success: the decision model was able to simplify the existing business rules by a factor of two-thirds, make complex compliance logic accessible to more personnel, identify many inconsistencies in both the internal and regulatory specifications and detect two missing data requirements. The consistency of the new asset classification led to the elimination of many downstream reporting anomalies. The transparency helped consumers of classification to fully understand the data on which they were dependent and made the monthly update cycle of the eligibility rules faster and more assured.

18.3 Planning for Broad Adoption

Decision modeling and even Decision Management can be achieved in a piecemeal fashion but much greater benefits accrue when it is scaled across an enterprise. In particular, enterprise wide adoption increases the potential for reuse of decisions and ensures enhanced consistency of performance measurement. Many decisions also need to be managed across departmental boundaries, something only a broad adoption can really support. Broad adoption requires a strong focus on staff development and team building.

Some organizations have attempted to avoid the cost of formally adopting decision modeling by distributing books and training business analysts and SMEs informally. This is not an effective means of building any lasting organizational competency for two reasons.

Firstly, such initiatives lack credibility and betray a lack of real commitment. Those involved will immediately classify such an effort as something they can "wait out". Secondly, in the absence of scheduled, 'ring-fenced' time for training, efforts to learn these new techniques will always be subservient to the constant barrage of low value, 'urgent', everyday tasks.

18.3.1 Establish expertise from within

Organizations driving broad adoption should begin by identifying a small group, a *practice*, of experienced and enthusiastic SMEs and business analysts within their organization. These should be people with established business knowledge, a capacity for analytical thought and a talent for communication and engaging others. Some of these should have detailed experience of process or data modeling. Prior knowledge of BRMS or analytics is also very advantageous. Those who worked on the pilot project(s) are obvious candidates initially.

This group should be provided with formal Decision Management and decision modeling training and mentoring first. Thereafter, training should be provided to all analysts, SMEs and developers according to project priorities. Practice members should retain their line duties and responsibilities, but be seeded into projects with external mentors to hone their experience of the practical application of decision modeling.

Broad adoption requires that every project has the backing of experienced decision modeling and management mentors. While these will likely be external consultants initially, organizations should develop home-grown experts as soon as this is practical.

18.3.2 Organizing for growth

Several different approaches can be taken in terms of organization.

- The decision modeling practice can be established as an integral part of the company's process modeling practice. This offers some synergies but runs a risk that decision modeling and management will be considered subservient to process modeling and management, especially if the process practice is already well established.

- A centralized group or center of excellence can be established specifically for decision modeling and management. This is effective in some organizations, especially those with a history of driving change from a central point. Other organizations find such groups become "ivory towers", disconnected from front line projects.

- An informally managed community of practice that cuts across organizational boundaries is sometimes more effective. This allows those involved in decision modeling and Decision Management to meet, share experiences and develop best practices without requiring them to form a new organization. These can be harder to manage as there will be multiple calls on everyone's time but they allow each department to process at its own pace and avoid over-centralization. If centralization becomes necessary or desirable later, this group can provide the core people to form the new organization.

18.3.3 Team building

Following this organization for growth, the key enterprise roles of a Decision Management practice and their responsibilities are as follows. Note that these are roles not necessarily unique to people – one person can cover multiple roles:

- **Practice Manager.** Establishes the vision and goals of the practice as a whole. Wins and maintains business sponsorship. Coordinates the team's personnel, assigning them to projects that will benefit from decision modeling and ensuring that they balance: delivery of value to each project, nurturing and mentoring its less experienced decision and process modelers and growing their own business knowledge. This should be a business facing role, not part of IT.

- **Decision Management/Modeling Champion.** Mentors and teaches Decision Management, governance and modeling across projects. Advocates the use of these techniques and makes others aware of their value. Defines and refines the approach of the practice and ensures it remains up to date with new developments and best practices. Initially, this is likely to be the Practice Manager.

- **Decision Modeler.** Embedded into project teams to perform, mentor and teach decision modeling to team members. Some may be deployed to mine decisions from existing manual or automated systems to prevent loss of business know-how (decision archaeology).

- **Decision Librarian.** Ensures a level of consistency and cross-fertilization between projects' decision models. Identifies, catalogs and raises awareness of common decisions. However, someone performing this role does not obviate the need for everyone to consider and actively manage reuse.

- **Glossary Manager.** Mines, identifies, defines and promotes a consistent vocabulary of business terms and underlying data model between related projects.

- **Infrastructure Architect.** Ensures the infrastructure requirements of Decision Management and modeling (covered in Section 18.1.3) are met, as far as it is practically possible, initially within projects and ultimately within entire organization departments. Defines approach to decision model tool support (see Section 18.4). Integrates decision modeling initiatives with deployment tools (e.g. BRMS, BPMS).

Keep in mind when assigning team roles that decision modelers should be business analysts first and foremost—decision modeling should be an important competence, not the role itself. As with process and data modeling, it is essential that decision modeling mentors have and retain a deep expertise in their own business areas and an ability to communicate this. Modeling of any sort is a means to an end, not an end in itself. Mentors must be practicing business analysts and not 'generic' modeling experts with shallow business expertise. They should be able to draw on their own business expertise to illustrate example solutions not become 'ivory tower' modelers, focusing exclusively on the minutiae of modeling methods and pontificating on the specifics of notations. The latter tend to alienate business subject matter experts. If mentors are perceived as idealists, imposing a standard rather than providing a solution to a genuine problem, they will impede the effectiveness of the practice.

18.4 Optimize Data For Decision Modeling

Decision Management can bring considerable benefits to both manual and automated decision-making processes and can help companies to find the right balance between the two. Data is central to decision-making in both automated and manual scenarios. As a result, there are some key data foundations that can maximize the benefits of decision modeling and Decision Management.

18.4.1 Reduce data quality issues

Meaningful, reliable, integrated reference data is a pivotal requirement for effective Decision Management. Organizations should do their best to ensure that they are free from endemic and acute reference data quality issues when adopting decision modeling and Decision Management approaches. Data inconsistencies are expensive to handle and can:

- Require that decision models are more complex than they need to be, in order to 'protect' decisions from data anomalies.

- Conflate business know-how with data idiosyncrasies making the resulting decision models less clear and much less reusable.

- Obscure or prevent accurate measurement of business value.

Organizations should avoid the temptation to defer all attempts to model decisions until the data is "right", however. Without an understanding of the uses of data in decision-making it can be hard to say how good or integrated the data needs to be. Improving the data quality is thus a parallel (and reinforcing) activity to be carried out as decision models are being developed.

If poor quality data is unavoidable, a decision service for cleansing data should be created from a separate decision model (see Section 14.8.2) to keep data quality issues separate from the business decision model.

18.4.2 Build a shared understanding of business data

All business data should be defined and managed as consistently as possible, preferably by use of a glossary (see Chapter 9). Although this is important to decision modeling, the technique does not require a glossary to yield benefit and it can work in their absence. Plans to adopt decision modeling should on no account be deferred awaiting the painstaking creation of a new, purpose-built glossary.

Once in place, however, a consistent glossary considerably increases the portability and reuse potential of decisions (see 9.2). A glossary is especially useful in cases where the projects have overlapping business scope. The purpose of a Decision Canonical Data Model (hereafter canonical model) is to act as a single common, or federated, business glossary and data model for a business. This should be based on an existing set of data sources or even an existing data standard if one exists. It has the following aims:

- To ensure the common use of business terms and enumerations across a set of projects to avoid ambiguity.

- To accurately reflect available data in order to draw attention to any gaps between requirement and provision.

- To represent the organization's data structures in a business oriented manner, free from implementation concepts such as: abstractions that business SMEs would not recognize, technically motivated data normalizations and exclusively technical attributes.

Decision modeling practices do not need to create a canonical model for a set of projects that are disjoint and unconnected. A canonical model is a platform for inter-project consistency. If a canonical model is required, it should not be produced manually. Instead it should be generated from data definitions that reflect the content of the organization's data stores. This reduces the costs of producing and maintaining the canonical model. When such a model is required, a member of the decision modeling practice should be made responsible for it.

18.5 Provide Tool Support

18.5.1 Why decision modeling requires tool support

There are an increasing number of software packages that support DMN (see the first item in A.2). Although many organizations that elect to use decision modeling will select and use one of these DMN toolsets, other, more conservative organizations will struggle to justify the cost and administrative burden of yet another modeling product. While the basic mechanics of DMN are quite straightforward and seem not to require tool support to be managed effectively, several aspects of DMN emphasize the value of a modeling tool. Initial forays into decision modeling, in which small, simple models are developed, are deceptively simple. They tend to hide the need for specialized tools and encourage the belief that simple document editing and diagramming tools are sufficient. However, when an organization scales up its activity and models decisions of real complexity that change periodically, it will quickly realize this economy is a mistake.

18.5.2 DMN diagrams are not as simple as they seem

A superficial analysis of DMN, especially of the Decision Requirements level, leads some to believe that the notation is trivially straightforward and so can be supported by a simple drawing or presentation tool. In fact, the visual language of DMN's Decision Requirement Diagrams and its representations of decision logic are rich and highly controlled by the standard. The requirements relationships that can exist between decisions, Knowledge Sources, Business Knowledge Models and Input Data are constrained and have very specific meanings. The values permitted for many decision model component properties are restricted. The format of decision logic and the grammar of expressions used in it is strictly defined. Decisions must be kept consistent with their uses in overlapping Decision Requirements Diagrams and with their logic definitions.

All of this makes the standard hard to use consistently in a general purpose drawing or office productivity tool. Although general purpose editing tool templates exist for DMN, they generally capture only a small fraction of the standard's expressive power. Using these templates, the tools may make effective learning and demonstration aids but they are of limited use when using the standard in real situations. By analogy: it is possible to produce the architectural plan of an office building in PowerPoint, but many architectural drafters would consider this an unwise approach.

The main reasons that purpose built tools are required for decision modeling are:

18.5.2.1   Maintaining intra and inter model consistency

DMN expects strong consistency between the Decision Requirements and Decision Logic Levels of a decision model (see Chapter 8.3). This ranges from simple rules governing the selection of names to more complex consistency between elements of the two levels. For instance:

- A decision within the Requirements Level must match the name of its corresponding definition in the Logic Level.

- An input column can only appear in a Decision Table if there is a corresponding Information Item in the Input Data or sub-decisions depicted in the Decision Requirements Level.

- Multiple overlapping views of the Decision Requirements Level (see 14.3.2) must be consistent with each other.

There are also "softer" consistency issues, such as a desire that the Allowed Answer (see 14.2.1) text for a decision matches the more formal outcome Information Items defined for the decision.

One must also consider the consistency between DMN models and other models. Chapter 10 describes how DMN models are linked to process, data and architecture models (in BPMN, UML and ArchiMate respectively). These models refer to many of the same underlying objects and the references to these objects must be kept consistent (if not necessarily identical) between models, for example:

- The name of an Input Data in a Decision Requirements Diagram and the corresponding business object in a data model.

- The name of a decision in a Decision Requirements Diagram and that of a Decision Task in a Business Process Model.

This consistency has to be constantly maintained to ensure the internal integrity of the decision model and its relationships with other models. For example, if the name of a decision is changed on one Decision Requirements Diagram, this should be reflected in related model artifacts. This is done in specialized modeling tools by using an underlying repository model that directly supports the decision model's internal relationships and ensures that there is an explicit association between model components and underlying objects on which they depend.

In some cases, users need to be warned when proposed changes in one view may have negative consequences in another. For example, alteration of the permitted values of an enumeration in a data model might impact a Decision Table that uses it. An alteration to one view frequently requires corresponding alterations, and possible remedial actions, in others. Maintaining these correspondences manually is user intensive and error prone. Software products that are aware of these links can remove much of the drudgery and opportunities for mistakes from consistency maintenance.

18.5.2.2   Navigation and impact analysis

The associations between different parts of a decision model have to be traversed and managed by those developing models. Modelers and readers of a model need to be able to freely navigate within and between models and follow the paths of dependency. For example, a modeler might want to navigate:

- From a Decision Task in a Business Process Model *to*
- The linked decision in a Decision Requirements Model *to*
- The Decision Table that defines the logic of this decision *to*
- The data definition of one of the inputs within this table.

Although navigation can be achieved entirely manually, this is arduous and error prone for users. Pragmatically, only specialized tool support makes this viable given the likely scope of models and the number of times users will need to traverse these links. This does not mean that every model has to be stored in the same tool, only that all the tools involved have to be aware of, and support, the navigation users need.

Related to navigation is the need for impact analysis. A modeler might want to explore a model and navigate to other, related models. Sometimes, however, they are just trying to assess the impact of a proposed change. When making a change to a decision, for instance, they might want to understand all the metrics that might be impacted by the change. These metrics may be associated directly with the decision but, more likely, they are associated with decisions that depend, directly or indirectly, on the decision being changed. Modelers need to be able to quickly and effectively see the impact of a change without having to manually navigate to and inspect every model component involved. An impact assessment is required that can answer questions like: *"which decisions are impacted if I introduce a new loyalty level?"*, *"which metrics would show the impact of a change to this Decision Table?"* or *"which decisions would be impacted if the Counterparty Input Data were split?"*

Impact analysis uses the same underlying linkages as navigation but generally requires more "packaging" of the links and a focus on the end points. This too is easier for a tool to do, especially as models become deeper and more complex.

18.5.2.3 Managing metadata

Decision modeling with DMN involves the capture and management of important metadata for many components. For example:

- Properties of decision model components (see Section 14.2.5).
- Links from Knowledge Sources to the documents or personnel that support them.
- The governance status of decision models.
- The Key Performance Indicators that can be used to measure performance of certain components.
- URIs to external documentation.

The core of this data is mandated by the standard while best practices involve capturing a richer superset of properties. A general purpose document editor will rarely support metadata of this complexity. Given the number of discrete components in a decision model, linking a separate document to each component is impractical. Add the likelihood that a component can be involved in many diagrams and relationships, requiring access to this metadata to be consistent across all of them, and the need for tool support becomes clear. Realistically DMN requires a repository or database of metadata linked to the objects in the model.

18.5.2.4 Referencing DMN models as source information

Decision models will rapidly become a critical point of reference, often replacing the documentation from which they were originally developed. SMEs and others will need to use the information stored within them in several ways:

- To search a model for answers to specific questions.
- To use the dependencies expressed in a model to determine the impact assessment of changing business logic, data structures or Knowledge Sources.
- To make large impact, systematic changes to a model quickly (e.g., supporting a name change in an enumeration's permitted value, the wholesale alteration of boundary conditions, changing a Decision Table from one hit policy to another).
- To generate views from the model to communicate specific aspects of models for stakeholders.
- To cross check the performance of model components against their targets.
- To verify that the logic of a decision is internally consistent.
- The simulate the decision logic of a model to test it.
- To generate an executable implementation of the decision logic.

For tools that represent decision models as drawings or box and line diagrams, each of these requirements is more difficult to meet than the last.

18.5.2.5 Real time collaboration

The business assets that decision modelers document are pivotal to their organization. The models developed are likely to:

- Be the responsibility of geographically distributed teams of experts.
- Be of varying interest to many stakeholders.
- Be reused in many contexts and therefore be subject to simultaneous and even conflicting change pressures.
- Change regularly.

Changes to decision models must be managed and communicated effectively between all responsible parties. Any conflicts that emerge must be detected early, communicated and resolved. The situational awareness of every team member and stakeholder must be heightened with model governance and collaborative modeling functionality according to their own needs. The key areas of tool functionality here are:

- Supporting collaboration by allowing users to make coordinated changes together, even if they are doing so from different locations.
- Communicating change (e.g. visual differencing of successive versions) of a model and its rationale.
- Detecting and communicating conflict.
- Enforcement of organizational change policy.

Some general purpose document editing tools offer support for real time collaboration and governance. Because these tools have no awareness of the meaning of decision models their effectiveness is limited when applied to managing these models. For instance, what constitutes a change conflict in a shared spreadsheet is considerably different to conflicts in a Decision Table, despite the visual similarities. Likewise, communicating a visual difference between two versions of a decision model requires some knowledge of decision modeling.

18.5.2.6 Relationship with glossary

Decision models rely heavily on a set of business terms, a glossary, for all aspects of their definition. While it is preferable that this glossary be an existing artifact (or, less ideally, multiple artifacts) managed by the organization, it is sometimes necessary, in less mature organizations, that it is created for the purposes of decision modeling. Either way, decision models need to be created from, and kept consistent with, a standard terminology and data representation; otherwise they lose their ability to communicate ideas. This is onerous in manually maintained models. If multiple sources of business vocabulary are at hand, any overlapping items will require consolidation into a canonical model. Separate glossary terms will each need to map consistently to the Decision Model. Although the first is beyond the scope of Decision Modeling tools, the latter is essential.

18.5.3 Features to Look for in a DMN Tool

Different teams will find different DMN tools work for them. The authors have maintained decision models using a wide range of tools with very varied results, including different results from using the same tools. The criteria below are not intended to identify the "best" tool but to provide a set of questions that any decision modeling tool evaluation should consider. Different teams will value them differently but all should be considered. Generally, the more important functionality is discussed first with later features being less likely to be critical to success.

18.5.3.1 Organization-wide knowledge sharing

Decision modeling requires wide-scale, ad-hoc and low-fuss sharing of models. Anything that impedes this is a problem. Tool selectors should avoid 'fat client' products—software that requires local installation to user's PC—as these often provide barriers to knowledge sharing such as software, operating system or hardware incompatibilities. In addition, they are expensive to install and maintain. A browser-based, on premise or cloud-based solution is usually better, with private cloud/on premise often offering a compromise between easy access and security.

It is also important that models can be shared with those who are not active in their development—for instance, stakeholders. If only those who can justify the purchase of a modeling tool license have access to a decision model, then real value can be lost.

18.5.3.2 Notation support

Supporting the DMN specification involves supporting Decision Requirement Diagrams with all their components, relationships, constraints (see Chapters 8 and 12) and the mandatory metadata properties described in Section 14.2.5. It also involves supporting Decision Logic Models defined: in terms of formal or informal expressions in English, in external languages such as Java or PMML or in FEEL. FEEL (see Appendix B) can be supported only within Decision Tables or more fully in boxed expressions. Organizations should be clear how they are going to define decision logic, in particular, and ensure their tool choice supports it.

18.5.3.3   Search, query and extraction

Real decision models require considerable time and investment to create and often get large over time. Consequently, accessing large scale models without some search facility will seriously impair its value.   Similarly, a lack of a powerful query, reporting and data extraction facility will undermine the entry investment. It should be possible to search, query and report on decision models based on the value of any property or tag (see Section 14.2.5.5) of any component.

18.5.3.4   Knowledge Source traceability

The ability to establish links between Knowledge Sources and the external documents that define them is a vital function for any decision model that is constrained by, or must adhere to, defined standards or mandates (e.g., regulatory compliance). This function helps clients to achieve—and to demonstrate compliance with—authorities. When evaluating tools consider the granularity of reference you require. For most, the ability to associate a Knowledge Source with a document and open that document directly from the Knowledge Source is enough. Some compliance applications benefit from a finer grain association. For example, the ability to associate individual rules in a Decision Table with specific sections of a document (see Section 14.4).

18.5.3.5   Familiarity

Any product of which a significant fraction of the targeted user population already has a favorable experience should have an advantage in the selection process. For example, a tool already widely used in a different context, such as Business Process Modeling, that is now applied to decision modeling, should have a significant advantage over rival products that are entirely new to an organization. Familiarity can remove many barriers to use and help establish a decision modeling community on the back of another.

Familiarity can also come from using common metaphors, such as browser capabilities and standard diagram manipulation gestures. This is less definite but still valuable.

18.5.3.6   Connection with other models

The ability to link decision models with business process, data and motivation models (see Section 10.1) is part of making decisions a first-class citizen of a business architecture. Other models not only add considerable richness to the decision definition but scope each decision and define its context. This connection could involve a single tool platform that manages and integrates all the various models or multiple products each of which take advantage of APIs and deep linking to coordinate and integrate with other products.

18.5.3.7   Decision model simulation

The ability to simulate and thereby test the execution of fully specified decision models is of vital importance. It permits business users to submit real business data to a decision model, or more pragmatically part of a decision model, examine the outcomes and compare them to expected results. This facility grants business experts some independence from IT and allows them to devise, experiment and hone business decisions on their own terms, isolated from their environment's implementation details. The combination of strong impact analysis with simulation is one of the most effective ways of: encouraging SMEs to 'own' their decision models, improving SME autonomy and exposing logical flaws in their own analysis when exposed to real data. This autonomous approach allows misconceptions to be discovered more quickly than might otherwise be the case and dispels the myth that discovery of business logic flaws is the sole preserve of developers.

This is not to say that all decision models should be developed to a level of detail that supports simulation. Quite the opposite is true: developing all models to simulation ready detail is profligate and unnecessary for simple or uncontested logic. However, where decisions are poorly understood or a focus of disagreement or risk, simulation is an important technique. Simulation can also assist impact analysis.

18.5.3.8   Inter-decision integrity

The integrity of a decision model relies on the relationship between possible values yielded by a sub-decision and those consumed by a parent with an Information Requirement on it (see Section 14.8.3). Tools should support the checking and evolution of such dependencies. In particular, the assurance that all values produced by the sub-decision can be handled by the parent and all cases handled by the parent can be produced by the sub-decision. This is especially relevant for decisions that yield enumerated outcomes with a volatile range of permitted values (see Section 14.7.1.6).

18.5.3.9   Real time collaboration and situation awareness

The ability for every team member to be informed of the activities of all others, either because they have registered an interest in a specific artifact in advance or because the system detects a potential for a conflict of interest between multiple users' activities, is of pragmatic importance in supporting any large scale decision modeling.

Of equal importance is the visualization of changes over time, either to demonstrate compliance with an externally mandated change or document, a proposed improvement ahead of performance monitoring.

18.5.3.10 Glossary support

All decision models express business logic using a business vocabulary. Glossary support is the ability to support a defined vocabulary that can be shared. This is achieved either by reference to an external corporate glossary or, less preferably, by a local lexicon of terms directly supported by the tool. This defines: a set of defined data types both simple and complex[64], business terms, permitted values of enumerated types and a data or fact model that depicts relationships between business concepts (e.g., that each trade as multiple cashflows). Tool based glossary support is important to establish consistency between models in wide-scale decision modeling. Without this, all but the simplest decision models are likely to be parochial and develop inconsistencies in term usage over time.

18.5.3.11 View generation

The ability to derive and display Decision Requirements Diagrams views that are filtered, composited or otherwise generated from the Decision Requirements Model embodied by the hand-entered diagrams is of significant importance both as a means of promoting understanding and to remove the need to create consistent 'summary views' by hand. This facility aids the maintenance and sharing of widely reused decisions and is thereby important to leverage decision modeling at scale. In addition, the ability to create immediate context or

---

[64] A complex data type has multiple properties each with its own value.

input oriented sub-views (see Section 14.3.2) automatically is of practical value to communicate decision models to more remote stakeholders.

18.5.3.12 Hit policy sensitive logic verification

The ability of a tool to statically analyze a Decision Table and report gaps or overlaps in the logic is very useful. Not only does it save time lost to human error but it also builds an understanding of logical integrity within a decision modeling team.

18.5.3.13 User definable metadata

Many useful properties of decision models and their components are not defined in the standard (see Section 14.2.5) and projects often establish their own norms. User defined metadata is an easy concession to this need and allows organizations to adorn decision models with additional data which can then be searched and used to provide new viewpoints. The authors have found tagging of decision model components (see Section 14.2.5.5) to be especially useful in associating decision model artifacts with specific software releases, laws and geographic variations for example.

18.5.3.14 Governance process support

A controlled, coordinated process for model creation and change in highly collaborative environments can, if well designed, speed up the development of models and contribute to their quality. For instance, a 'four-eye' process[65] can ensure appropriate review and sign off of decision models by an authorized expert. Support for this process, typically by communication of the governance state of a model (e.g., drafted, submitted, approved, rejected) or even enforcement of it is valuable in some environments.

18.5.4 In the absence of specialized tools

Although the adoption of a specialized decision modeling toolset is considered a best practice it is, sadly, not always possible. Some organizations elect not to adopt a modeling toolset. Instead, they use decision agnostic software that they have already widely installed—saving on acquisition, installation, familiarization and training costs. This section discusses best practices for decision modeling when specialized tools are not available.

Any argument for the deferred adoption, or non-adoption, of specialized decision modeling tools should take the latent workload of maintaining inter-artifact consistency (see Section 18.5.2.1) into account in any cost comparison. Consider the example of changing the name of a ubiquitous Input Data component: this could result in the hand editing of tens of Decision Requirements Diagrams with no assurance that the resulting decision model is consistent. The savings in specialized software acquisition, installation and maintenance should be weighed against the ongoing drain in terms of effort, time, morale and model quality caused by this method.

Sharing large decision models widely without specialized software support is hard. The choice of software is limited to the lowest common denominator: office productivity applications like Microsoft Office (or OpenOffice) that are most likely to be ubiquitously available across an organization. As glossaries and Decision Tables are tabular in nature, decision

---

[65] A workflow that enforces work products to be reviewed independently by two persons before they are ready for release.

requirement diagrams are graphs with a small selection of nodes and arcs, data models are UML or ERD diagrams and business contexts can be expressed in BPMN, this suggests the following tool selection:

- Requirement diagrams should be supported in a drawing tool (e.g. Visio).
- Logic definitions, including Decision Tables, should be supported in a spreadsheet (e.g., Excel).
- Glossaries should be supported by a spreadsheet or document application (e.g. Excel or Word).
- Data and process models are optional and expressed using tools like Visio that support object modeling and BPMN.

Templates can be defined for some of these tools to ensure some basic consistency of shapes and links, just as they have been for other notations.

In addition, a shared documentation platform (e.g. Sharepoint, Git, SVN or even CVS) will be needed to support collaboration of parallel users, version control and authentication.

Organizations that chose not to use specialized tools will face several challenges:

18.5.4.1 Creating DMN compliant models

This requirement can be partially addressed with templates, stencils and data constraints. Using these templates, office tools support the layout of Decision Requirements Diagrams, Decision Tables and glossaries. They can also constrain data entry to some extent. For example, Excel data validation can enforce the correct use of hit policy in Decision Tables and cell protection can impose the structure of the Decision Tables. The templates for all artifacts can be laden with helpful tool tips to prompt the newcomer to decision modeling. The same tools can enforce the correct use of associated models such as BPMN if the right stencil is selected.

However, none of these products is capable of preventing user 'additions' to the standard or subversion of its strictures. A high level of user education, some discipline and a strong spirit of cooperation, is therefore required.

18.5.4.2 Navigating between model components

This need can be partially met by inserting hyperlinks into documents to allow one-click navigation between artifacts based on a common key. For example, a decision in a Decision Requirements Diagram could be linked to its logic definition and a Decision Table condition to its glossary definition. It is hard to automate this without customization and it requires a lot of additional work for document creators. In most real projects this work will not be done reliably or maintained over time.

The use of naming conventions and ensuring that one document contains only one artifact, for example one Decision Requirements Diagram or one Decision Table, can help. Navigation and sharing are facilitated by laying out the models in individual files in a file hierarchy that is analogous to the decision hierarchy. Hence:

- Commonly needed or broad-reach components such as the business glossary, widely reused decisions or Knowledge Sources, business processes and overarching data models should be near or at the top of the file hierarchy.
- More specific elements such as individual Decision Requirements Diagrams, local Knowledge Sources and Decision Tables can be in specific sub-directories, each of

which represents a decision. File links can be used to represent the reuse of Decision Tables in multiple decisions while avoiding file copying.

Each document should be given a unique identifier in addition to its business name in order to support easy location. Furthermore, each document name should indicate its project and content in a standardized manner, for example, *CHG-071 DT Calculate Personal Loan Limit* or *CHG-019 DRD Asset Category*.

18.5.4.3 Sharing, collaboration and version control

All of the software tools mentioned support document differencing, that is the ability to display the alterations between one version of a document and another. Often this is supported by internal functions of the software (e.g., Excel's 'Compare Documents' feature).

Note that every model diagram is stored in a separate file in this regime. This may at first appear rather profligate. It can make decision models with hundreds of decisions tables rather hard to manage and share. Nevertheless, one file per artifact has many advantages:

- It allows all artifacts to be independently version controlled and locked for editing by different analysts or SMEs—maximizing development parallelism within teams.

- It allows multiple Decision Requirements Diagrams or Decision Tables to be opened on screen at the same time allowing easy comparison and cut and paste between them.

- It allows the Windows' search capability to reflect each artifact that matches the search criteria separately. This is useful for dependency queries designed to determine which decisions depend on which Input Data.

- Each Decision Table may have separate and individual metadata.

- Each Decision Table may be reused between decisions via Windows short cuts (or Linux file links).

- It scales up better than multiple tabs in a single document.

18.5.4.4 Maintenance of model integrity

The effort of manually maintaining a decision model, with widely shared glossaries and reused components increases geometrically with their size (as measured by the number of decision and terms). Therefore, there is an upper bound to the size of a decision model that can be economically supported using decision agnostic tools. Above this size, either the model will become inconsistent or a disproportionate manual effort will be needed to maintain its consistency.

An organization that intends to use decision modeling on a large project, or a set of smaller but related projects, and also requires change agility, should be very wary of the hidden efforts a decision agnostic toolset will demand of it. The requirement for model integrity cannot be met with most office tools without considerable customization. A decision model with internal inconsistencies is a liability. As each DMN artifact is strongly linked to others, inconsistencies can easily arise if they are edited with tools ignorant of decision modeling.

When no specialized modeling tool is being used, the manual maintenance of consistency between decision model artifacts has to be encouraged with a combination of user training and compliance checking (e.g., quality gate reviews). Although often rather tedious, model creators and maintainers must be encouraged to uphold the integrity of their work as it changes. It is important that the various artifacts of decision models are not allowed to become seriously inconsistent (or indeed, out of date) as this undermines their value. Some scripting and customization can help with this.

18.5.4.5 Avoid becoming tool developers

One trap of this approach is that what seems initially like a considerable saving of time and money—the avoidance of supplying specialized tools—actually costs more time ultimately. This can happen if decision modeling teams become absorbed in customizing decision agnostic products to make their jobs easier. This activity can start in a virtuous effort to save time, but in our experience it can lead to cycles of polishing Visual Basic and other scripts until the level of automation is wholly disproportionate to the need.

Appendix A. Glossary and Resources

A.1 Terms Used in this Book

The DMN specification is a technical document aimed at tool vendors. As a consequence, it uses technical jargon (e.g., Input Expression, Value Expression, Decision Requirements Graph) which is ill suited to business analysts. To communicate effectively to this audience, we have used our own terms which are defined here, mapped to the equivalent terms in the standard and defined using terms from the standard. This appendix also includes standard DMN definitions for terms we have not altered. Those terms related to technical aspects of the Friendly Enough Expression Language (FEEL) can be found in Appendix B.

Term	Description	Alias for DMN Term
Annotation	A text comment in a Decision Requirements Diagram. They have no formal meaning, but allow the diagram to be adorned with additional text blocks to explain or embellish some aspect of the model or to document the use of patterns. Section 8.1.4.	
Authority	A role played by a Knowledge Source to another Knowledge Source or decision that it influences or constrains. Input Data may also act as authorities to a Knowledge Source. Section 8.1.3.	
Authority Requirement	A dependency that a decision has on knowledge from a Knowledge Source (authority). Alternatively, it also represents an authority that a Knowledge Source needs from a decision or Input Data. Section 8.1.5.	
Boxed Expression	A formal, text-based medium for defining decision logic. Sections 11.3.2.3 and B.4.2.	
Boxed Invocation	A means of invoking a Business Knowledge Model or function as part of the definition of a decision (or higher level Business Knowledge Model). Sections 11.3.2.5 and B.4.3.	

Term	Description	Alias for DMN Term
Business Knowledge Model	An element of reusable business logic, usually a function yielding an outcome from a set of inputs. Business Knowledge Models usually represent some encapsulated fragment of business know-how that is required by multiple decisions and are a useful means of representing identical logic that is applied in many different circumstances. Section 11.1.1.	
Complete	A Decision Table is said to be complete if it produces an outcome for every possible set of inputs. The table always yields a result. Section 8.2.4.2.	
Component	A shape in a Decision Requirements Diagram such as a decision, Knowledge Source or Input Data. Section 8.1.	(not defined by DMN)
Condition	Within a logic definition, for example a Decision Table, a test applied to an input as part of the determination that a given rule is satisfied. Section 8.2.1.	Input Entry
Condition, Irrelevant	In a Decision Table, a condition on a specific input, represented by the symbol '-', which signifies that the input value is immaterial to this rule and that the test always succeeds. Section 8.2.3.3.	
Conclusion	Within a logic definition, an expression that defines (one of) the outcome(s) of that decision. In a Decision Table, the cells that define the outcome of a rule. Section 8.2.1.	Output Entry
Context	A boxed expression that associates a set of variables with values. Most often used to provide a Decision Table with a set of useful variables to extend its function or improve readability. Section 8.2.5.	
Data Type	A classification of the values that an information item can hold. For example, strings can only hold sequences of characters and Booleans the values true, false or null. Section 9.7.1.	Item Definition
Decision	A determination that businesses make on a regular basis, a selection or a calculation of an outcome that depends on a number of prevailing circumstances (inputs) and which, ultimately, has an observable impact on the behavior of the organization Section 4.1.1.	

Term	Description	Alias for DMN Term
Decision Canonical Data Model (Canonical Model)	A data model and glossary developed to promote the consistency of a set of decision models which use a business vocabulary based exclusively on its content. This acts as a single common, or federated, vocabulary for a business. Section 18.4.2.	(not defined by DMN)
Decision Service	An executable, architectural component; a means of packaging the logic of one or more decisions and delivering it as part of a service oriented architecture (SOA) that can be invoked via a well-defined interface. Section 8.1.6.	
Decision Table	A tabular representation of decision logic that depicts how the outcome of a decision (consisting of one or more conclusions) is determined by checking specific combinations of values in its inputs. Sections 6.4.4, Section and 8.2.1.	
Dependency	A relationship that one component of a decision model has on another, be it a requirement for data, authority or business knowledge. Sections 8.1.5 and 11.1.1.3.	
Decision (Logic) Definition	An explanation of the decision-making approach that details how a decision derives its outcome given a set of input variables. This can be expressed in many ways. Section 8.2.	Value Expression
Decision Logic (Level, Model)	A specification of how an entire decision model's outcome is determined from its inputs. This can take the form of a Decision Table, analytic model, text rule or even examples. The sum total of all logic definitions for a decision model. Sections 6.4.4 and 8.2.	
Decision Requirements (Level, Model)	The total underlying set of relationships between decision components that interconnects all decisions in a decision model. Sections 6.4.3 and 8.1.7.	Decision Requirements Graph
Decision Requirement Diagram	A visual representation of part of a Decision Requirement showing decisions and their dependencies on other decisions, Input Data, Knowledge Sources and Business Knowledge Models. Sections 6.4.3 and 8.1.7.	
Decision Task	A task in a business process that is associated with the use of one or more decisions, the outcome of which can then control the path of the business process. Section 10.2.3.1.	

Term	Description	Alias for DMN Term
Default Value	The value returned by a decision in the absence of a defined explicit alternative, for example, the value returned by a Decision Table if no rule is hit.	
Hit	A rule is said to be hit when it is both satisfied and contributes an outcome to the decision it is defined within. Section 11.2.1.1.	
Hit Policy	The policy a Decision Table uses to determine: how many rules can be simultaneously satisfied in a given instance, how many rules are 'hit', how these are selected and how the results are aggregated or sorted. Section 8.2.5.	
Information Requirement	The dependency (or requirement) that a decision has for data from an Input Data or another decision. Sections 8.1.5 and 11.2.1.	
Information Item	An instance of typed data used by a decision as an input or output; the contents of a named input variable that is sourced via an Information Requirement from a Input Data or subordinate decision; the contents of a variable holding the outcome of a decision. All items have a prescribed data type. Sections 8.1.1.3 and 8.3.	
Input	A variable holding information used to make a decision. The column header in a Decision Table that names the input variable (or expression) being tested in that column Section 8.2.1.	Input Expression
Input Data	Input Data represent specific information that is required by, and supplied to, the decision-making process that is not itself the outcome of a decision. Instead, Input Data comes from outside the model: from users, source systems and datastores. Section 8.1.2.2.	
Knowledge Requirement (Relationship)	See Authority Requirement.	
Knowledge Source	A reference to knowledge or a controlling entity outside the decision model that influences or controls some aspects of how a decision is made. They are sometimes called 'authorities'. Section 8.1.3.	

Term	Description	Alias for DMN Term
Listed Input Data	A compact representation of decisions with a data requirement on an Input Data in which the Input Data is represented in a list box within the decision component. This is an alternative to the more conventional representation of two components joined by a relationship. Section 8.1.2.2.	
Outcome	The set of one or more outputs of a decision. In a Decision Table, the single result generated by the satisfaction of the conditions of a single rule. This might be a simple or composite conclusion. Section 8.2.2.	(not defined by DMN)
Outcome, Composite	An output from a decision that consists of an instance of complex data type with individually addressable attributes. Composite conclusions arise from Decision Tables with multiple conclusion headers or boxed expressions that construct data structures. Section 8.2.2.	(not defined by DMN)
Outcome, Simple	A conclusion consisting of a single value of a simple type. Section 8.2.2.	(not defined by DMN)
Output	Part of the result of a decision. In a Decision Table, the column header that names the output variable being determined by the Decision Table in that column. Section 8.2.1.	
Satisfied	A rule is satisfied if all of its conditions are individually satisfied. Section 11.2.1.	
Sparse (Sparsity)	The extent to which a Decision Table's conditions use the irrelevant ('-') marker. A sparse table has a high proportion (greater than 25%) of '-' entries. Section 14.4.2.3.	(not defined by DMN)
Subject	The decision that is the root of a decision requirement diagram or graph, i.e., the node which, in the context of that diagram, only has inflowing requirement flows and which has no other visible components dependent on it. Section 6.4.3.	(not defined by DMN)
Rule	A set of conditions expressed against every input and a value to be set for each output should this conjunction of conditions be satisfied. A rule corresponds to a single row (or column) of conditions and conclusions in a Decision Table (see Section 8.2.1). A rule can also be represented as text (see Section 11.3.1).	

Term	Description	Alias for DMN Term
Rule Overlap	Two rules overlap if both can be simultaneously satisfied by the same set of inputs. Section 11.2.1.	
Type, Composite	Composite types are user defined types representing data structures with multiple attributes, each of which has a type of its own that may be simple or composite. Composite types may also represent lists of other types. Section 9.7.5.	Complex Type
Type, Constrained	A user defined data type that may only hold values in a confined range. Constrained types are defined in terms of a simple underlying type and a constraint on the values it may hold. Section 9.7.2.	
Type, Enumerated	A constrained string type that may only hold a small, permitted set of values. Section 9.7.3.	
Type, Simple	A data type with a single data value corresponding to the data types built into DMN (e.g., a number, string or date). Section 9.7.1, Section B.2.	Base Type
Value List	A list of values, ranges or constraints provided for a condition or conclusion. This constrains the values that can be used in a condition or specifies the priority order and default for a conclusion. Section 8.2.3.6.	
Variable	Named quantities that hold a value that are initialized from a Requirement Relationship, a context or as the result of a decision. Variables can be used to make a condition or conclusion expression. Variables can also be used to bind a value to an invocation of a Business Knowledge Model. Section 11.3.2.1.2.	

Table A-1 Book Terms and DMN Standard Equivalents

A.2 Resources and References

This work benefits considerably from the work of many others. In some cases, these have been directly referenced in the text, but most of them have contributions that have guided our thinking for many years and have had a profound general impact on this book. For convenience, the list has been divided into sections about Decision Management, Decision Modeling, Business Rules and other topics, such as enterprise architecture. References are alphabetical within these sections.

A.2.1 Decision Management

Taylor James, *Decision Management Systems*, IBM Press, 2011, ISBN 978-0132884389.
Taylor James, *Smart (Enough) Systems*, Prentice Hall, 2007, ISBN 978-0-13-234796-9.

Taylor, James, *The Decision Management Manifesto*, Decision Management Solutions 2013 http://decisionmanagementsolutions.com/decision-management-manifesto.

Taylor, James and Purchase, Jan, *Rapid and Cost Effective Financial Compliance with Decision Modeling*, 2015, http://www.decisionmanagementsolutions.com/whitepaper/rapid-and-cost-effective-financial-compliance/.

A.2.2 Decision Modeling

The DMN Tools Catalog, http://openjvm.jvmhost.net/DMNtools/.

Debvoise Tom and Taylor James, *Microguide to Process and Decision Modelling in BPMN/DMN*, Advanced Component Research, 2014, ISBN 978-1-502-78964-8.

Fish, Alan, *Knowledge Automation*, John Wiley and Sons, 2012, ISBN 978-1118-09476-1

von Halle Barbara and Goldberg Larry, *The Decision Model*, CRC Press, 2010, ISBN 978-1-4200-8281-4.

von Halle Barbara and Goldberg Larry, *TDM White Paper: BDMS Glossary*, Knowledge Partners International LLC, 2010.

Knowledge Partners International LLC, *TDM White Paper: Decision Model Messages version 1.0.00* (with addenda), 2010.

Knowledge Partners International LLC, *TDM White Paper: Decision Model Views: Notation*, 2010.

Knowledge Partners International LLC, *TDM White Paper: List Fact Types: Multiple Values for a Single Business Object version 3.0.00*, 2012.

Knowledge Partners International LLC, *TDM White Paper: Communities in Decision Management*, 2012.

The Object Management Group, *Decision Modeling and Notation (DMN) V1.1*, 2016.

Sapiens Inc., *Navigating Current and Emerging Decision Modeling Methods and Standards*, http://www.sapiens.com, 2016.

Silver Bruce, *DMN Method and Style*, Cody-Cassidy Press, 2016, ISBN 978-0-9823681-5-2.

Vanthienen Jan, *Less rules, more rules? Better rules!*, 2006, Business Rules Journal, vol. 7, no. 8 (Aug.), pp. 1 – 3. http://www.brcommunity.com/b303.php

Vanthienen Jan and Wijsen Jef, On the Decomposition of Tabular Knowledge Systems, Katholieke Universiteit Leuven, 1996, https://lirias.kuleuven.be/bitstream/123456789/102046/1/OR_9604.pdf).

Vanthienen Jan, *Rules as Data: Decision Tables and Relational Databases*, Business Rules Journal, Vol. 11, No. 1, Jan. 2010, http://www.BRCommunity.com/a2010/b516.html

Vanthienen Jan, *Simplifying and Optimizing Tabular Decision Models*, Business Rules Journal, Vol. 12, No. 10 Oct. 2011, http://www.BRCommunity.com/a2011/b618.html

Worsham Steven and von Halle Kenneth, *Data Quality and the Decision Model: Advice from Practitioners*, Modern Analyst, Jan 2014.

A.2.3 Business Rules

Boyer Jérôme and Mili Hafedh, *Agile Business Rule Development*, Springer, 1998, ISBN 978-3-642-19040-7 von Halle Barbara and Goldberg Larry (eds), *The Business Rule Revolution*, Happy About, 2006, ISBN 1-60005-013-1.

Ross Ronald G and Lam Gladys, *Building Business Solutions*, Business Rule Solutions LLC, 2011, ISBN 978-0-941049-10-8.

Ross Ronald G., *Business Rule Concepts*, Business Rule Solutions LLC, 2013, ISBN 0-941049-14-0.

A.2.4 Other

Abbott, Dean. *Applied Predictive Analytics*, John Wiley and Sons, 2014, ISBN 978-1-118-72796-6

Bass Len, Clements Paul and Kazman Rick, *Software Architecture in Practice*, Addison-Wesley, 2007, ISBN 0321154959.

Brady Chris, *The Boeing 737 Technical Guide*, Tech Pilot Services, 2006, ISBN 978-1-291-77318-7.

Cadle James, Paul Debra and Turner Paul, *Business Analysis Techniques*, British Computer Society, 2011, ISBN 978-1-906124-23-6.

Duckett Jon, *Javascript and JQuery*, John Wiley and Sons, 2014, ISBN 978-1118531648.

Fowler Martin, *UML Distilled*, Addison-Wesley, 1997, ISBN 0-201-32563-2.

Gamma Erich, Helm Richard, Johnson Ralph and Vlissides John, *Design Patterns: Elements of Reusable Object-Oriented Software*, Addison-Wesley, 1994, ISBN 0-201-63361-2

Paul Harmon and Roger Tregear, *Questioning BPM?*, Meghan-Kiffer, 2016, ISBN 978-0-929652-54-2

The Open Group, *ArchiMate 3.0 Specification*, Van Haren Publishing, ISBN 978 94 018 0047 1.

Provost Foster and Fawcett Tom, *Data Science for Business*, O'Reilly Media, 2013, ISBN 978-1-449-36132-7.

Rumbaugh James, Jacobson Ivar and Booch Grady, *The Unified Modeling Language Reference Manual*, Addison-Wesley, 1999, ISBN 0-201-30998-X.

Steiner Robert, *Mastering Financial Calculations*, Pearson Education, 1998, ISBN 0 273 62587 X.

Appendix B. FEEL Reference

B.1 Introduction

The Friendly Enough Expression Language (FEEL) is a formal syntax and grammar for describing business logic that is the basis of the DMN Decision Logic Definition. The purpose of this section is to act as a reference for DMN users who need to understand the detailed syntax of Decision Tables or to supplement their decision model with more flexible representations of logic. It summarizes the definition of FEEL in the DMN specification, providing a simplified overview of:

- **Types**. The kinds of values FEEL can express and manipulate.
- **Constructs**. The kinds of logic definitions FEEL can build.
- **Expressions**. The kinds of terms that can generate values.

This reference is designed for ease of use by modelers when they need to augment their Decision Logic Definitions with FEEL constructs. It defines the most commonly used FEEL features and presents examples of their use. While this appendix should resolve most of the questions that might arise from field use of DMN, it is not a formal or complete definition. Therefore, this section is not a substitute for the detailed FEEL reference in the DMN specification for modelers or vendors with questions about the formal FEEL grammar or metamodel. Readers should be aware that this appendix is consistent with version 1.1 of the DMN specification.

B.2 FEEL Types

Feel expressions and values have a simple type corresponding to one of the following:

- **Number**—both decimal[66] and integer values (e.g., `21.7`, `9`).
- **String**—a sequence of characters (e.g., `"Steve"`).
- **Boolean**—a truth value (e.g., `true`, `false` and `null`).
- **Date, Time, Date and Time**—a point in time combining one or more of Date and Time (e.g., `11:49:09`, `2099-02-21`, `2099-02-21T21:14:09`).
- **Duration**—a period of time in days, hours and minutes or years and months (e.g., `P4DT6H14M33S`, `P4Y5M`).
- **Range**—a continuous range of values specified by an exclusive or inclusive start and end point, e.g., `[2..9]` or `[16-Dec-2016..25-Jul-2019)`).

DMN also supports user defined types that allow users to create complex data structures, these include:

- **List**—an ordered series of values, usually but not always, of the same type (e.g. `[1, 2, 4]` or `["Alpha", "Beta", "Gamma"]`). Lists may contain duplicate values and

---

[66] based on IEEE 754-2008 Decimal128 format

members that are themselves lists.

- **Context**—a map of key value pairs (e.g., a set of test scores {"Jack": 84, "Jill": 92}). Each entry has a name by which it can be accessed.

- **Composite**—a hierarchical data type (potentially imported from an XSD) representing entities with their own attributes (e.g., *Cashflow, ComplexNumber, EuclideanCoordinate*). Each attribute may be a simple type or an entity in turn, allowing the definition of a data structure.

It is worth emphasizing the three value logic values used by DMN's Boolean type for representing truth values. Instances of Boolean variables or expressions may yield true or false, but they may also yield null if the result of a truth test cannot be determined or is not meaningful (e.g., an attempt is made to test the equality of two expressions of a different type and to yield true or false would be misleading).

B.3 FEEL Decision Tables Constructs

B.3.1 Decision Tables

The Decision Table is a construct for representing tabular logic that is introduced and defined in Sections 8.2.1 and 11.2. The Decision Table yields one or more outcomes depending on its hit policy (see Section 11.2.1) and the number of rules with satisfied conditions. The general form of a Decision Table is shown in Figure B-1 and its elements (e.g. Name, Input) are labeled.

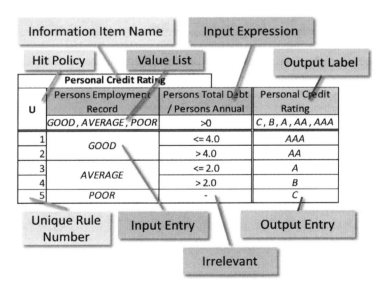

Figure B-1 Example Decision Table

B.3.2 Hit Policy

This is a summary of hit policy codes. More details about hit policy behavior can be found in Section 8.2.4 and 11.2.1.

A rule in a Decision Table is often said to 'hit' when all its conditions are satisfied by the data provided *and* it generates an outcome as a consequence. Each Decision Table has a 'hit policy' that defines: how many rules may be simultaneously satisfied by a single set of inputs; how many 'hits' can result from these matches and, if applicable, the order in which the output is generated. This behavior is summarized in Table B-1. Most Decision Tables use the Unique or Any hit policy as these are the easiest to understand and use.

Hit Policy	Rules Satisfied	Hits	Hit rule selection	Outcome (and sort)
Unique (U)	0..1	0..1	The one rule satisfied	That of the only rule hit.
Any (A)	0 or more	0..1	Any rule satisfied providing conclusions are all equal	That of the only rule hit.
First (F)	0 or more	0..1	First rule satisfied in order of table	That of the only rule hit.
Priority (P)	0 or more	0..1	Satisfied rule with highest priority conclusion value	That of the only rule hit.
Collect (C+) with aggregation	0 or more	0 or more	All satisfied rules	Generated from the aggregation of all hit rule outcomes.
Collect (C) no aggregation	0 or more	0 or more	All satisfied rules	All hit rule outcomes are combined into a collection in undefined order.
Rule (R)	0 or more	0 or more	All satisfied rules	All hit rule outcomes are combined into a collection in order of rules in table.
Output Order (O)	0 or more	0 or more	All satisfied rules	All hit rule outcomes are combined into a collection in order of conclusion value priority.

Table B-1 Summary of Hit Policy Behavior

B.3.3 Structure of Decision Table defined in FEEL

FEEL defines the permitted content and structure of each element of the Decision Table. The composition of FEEL Decision Table elements is shown in Figure B-2. Each element is shown in dark gray and a line depicts which FEEL expression type (in light gray) defines its content. See Section B.4 for a list of FEEL Constructs and Section B.5 for a list of FEEL Expressions.

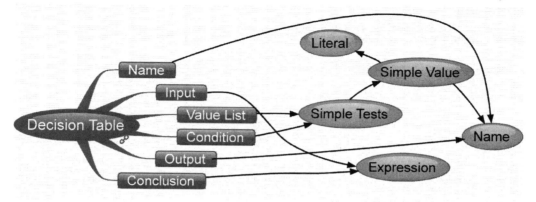

Figure B-2 FEEL Decision Table Constructs

Decision Tables have six elements each of which has a FEEL expression type:

- The name of the Decision Table is an instance of the FEEL expression type *Name*.
- Tables have one or more inputs (more correctly input expressions), which are *Expressions*.
- Each input may define an optional value list, which is a *Simple Test*.
- Tables have one or more outputs, each of which is a *Name* used to label the output.
- Each rule in a table has a condition for each input, expressed as a *Simple Test*.
- Each rule in a table has a conclusion for each output, expressed as a *Expression*.

As Figure B-2 shows, different expressions types may be built from more primitive ones. For example *Simple Tests* consists of a number of operators that use one or more *Simple Values*. In turn, a *Simple Value* may be a *Literal* value or refer to a named valued (*Name*).

B.4 FEEL Constructs

B.4.1 Introduction

Occasionally decision modelers need to express more complex decision logic than Decision Tables. A range of FEEL constructs exists to support this need as shown in Figure B-3. These are less often used by modelers and can express formal, non-tabular text rules like that of Section 11.3.2.3 (*Boxed Expression*), invocation of a Business Knowledge Model (*Boxed Invocation*) or definition of a context like that used in Section 8.2.5 (*Boxed Context*).

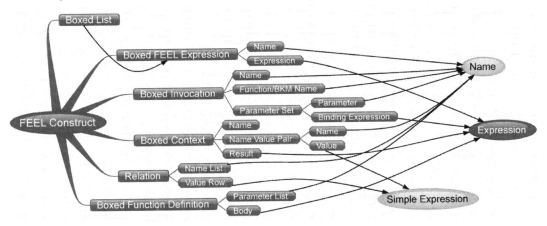

Figure B-3 FEEL Constructs and Their Use of Expressions

Modelers should only use FEEL if their intent cannot be expressed more simply (see Section 14.6.2). FEEL constructs should be used sparingly to prevent obscuring your business logic and to ensure the meaning and intent are conveyed effectively.

B.4.2 Boxed FEEL Expression

A Boxed Expression (see Figure B-4) is the simplest, non-tabular decision format supported by FEEL. It consists of an optional name (*Name*) and an *Expression* in a box. If used to define a decision, the name is mandatory and must match the decision name. The outcome is the value of the expression.

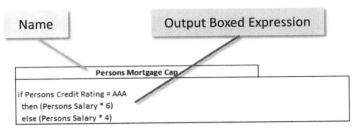

Figure B-4 Example Boxed Expression

B.4.3 Boxed Invocation

A Boxed Invocation is a means of invoking a named Business Knowledge Model (a parameterized decision, see Section 11.1.1) or function and is the main mechanism for decision logic reuse in DMN. Decisions themselves can only be reused if their information requirements exactly match the reuse opportunity. Business Knowledge Models can be invoked with user provided values bound to their inputs, so they are easy to reuse in many contexts. An example is shown in Figure B-5.

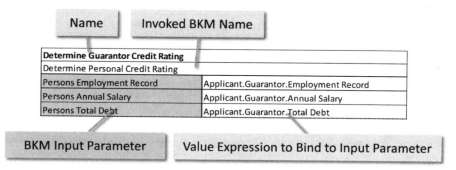

Figure B-5 Example Function Invocation

The invocation has the following components:

- The *Name* by which the invocation (and its results) can be accessed.
- The *Name* of the Business Knowledge Model or function being invoked.
- A set of parameter bindings each of which contains.
- The *Name* of the parameter.
- An *Expression* defining the value bound to this parameter.

The outcome of this construct is that produced by the function or Business Knowledge Model invoked given the values mapped to its parameters.

B.4.4 Boxed Context

A Boxed Context is a set of variables that introduce named values to be used by other constructs (e.g. a Decision Table or Boxed Expression) that follow. An example is shown in Figure B-6.

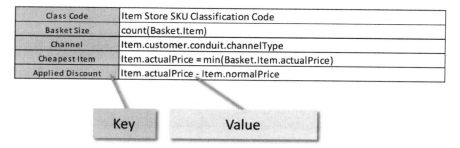

Figure B-6 Example Boxed Context

The keys of each Boxed Context are *Names* and the values are *Expressions*. Each Expression may itself be a Boxed Context; therefore this construct is hierarchical. Boxed Contexts yield no decision outcome but establish an environment in which a Decision Table or Boxed Expression (i.e., a result box) may do so. Contexts allow modelers to extend the flexibility of Decision Tables by introducing new variables that could not be calculated in the table itself. They can also make these other constructs easier to understand (see Section 8.2.5) and prevent repetition.

Contexts can also be used to define sets of sample or test data that can be used by other contructs. A hierarchical sample of test data is shown in Figure B-7.

Leg ID	1	
Start Date	*2018-10-18*	
End Date	*2019-03-18*	
Leg Type	*FEE*	
Cashflow	Currency	*USD*
	Date	*2017-11-19*
	Amount	12350.00

Figure B-7 Example Test Data Context

Again each named attribute in the context is associated with a value of an appropriate type. The attribute Cashflow is complex as it has attributes of its own.

B.4.5 Boxed List

A Boxed List is a list of *Expressions* arranged in a vertical array of boxes or horizontally in a comma separated list (see Figure B-8). The value of a Boxed List is the collection of values yielded by all the members.

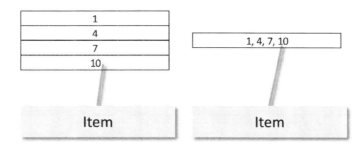

Figure B-8 Example Vertical and Horizontal Lists

Although a decision could yield an outcome from this (a collection), it is more likely that this would form a context entry that would be used by a Boxed Expression or Decision Table.

B.4.6 Relation

A Relation denotes a relationship between a set of values. It is like a literal, relational table of data. Like a Context, Relations do not yield a value, but instead introduce a structured, named set of value mappings, that can be used by other constructs (e.g. a Decision Table or Boxed Expression) that follow. In the example in Section 17.1.6.2, Figure 14 the relation of Figure B-9 is used to define a relationship between:

- the name of an identifier that labels an instrument (ISIN, CUSIP, etc.);
- a (regular expression) pattern of text that can occur within that identifier (e.g., "^313" means 'starts with "313"'); *and*

- the class to assign to that instrument if the pattern is found in the specified identifier.

The decision uses this relationship to check objects for identifiers of the right type, determine whether or not they match the pattern and assign the relevant class if they do.

patterns	identifer	idPattern	class
	ISIN	^US313	US AGENCY
	CUSIP	^313	US AGENCY
	ISIN	^US912[89]	US TBILL
	CUSIP	^912[89]	USTBILL
	NAME	^SDBCR	AP AGENCY
	NAME	^[HJ]SDBSP	FAR EAST AGENCY
	NAME	^CBC	GOVT EMG
	NAME	*COMMERCIAL*	COMMERCIAL PAPER

| Relation Name | Column Name | Row Value |

Figure B-9 Example Relation

Relations are a good means of embedding reference data specific to a decision within a context.

The relation name and column headers are *Names*. The row values are *Expressions*.

B.4.7 Boxed Function Definition

A Boxed Function definition defines a function to be reused (invoked, see Section B.4.3) elsewhere in a decision model. See the example invocation and definition of a function in Figure B-10.

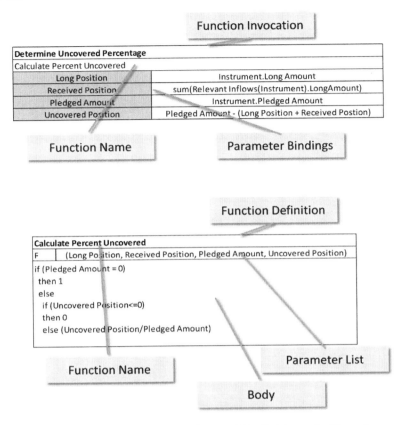

Figure B-10 Example Invocation and Definition of a Function

In the Boxed Function Definition, the function has a *Name* and a list of parameters (each of which is a *Name*). The body of a function can be a FEEL *Expression*, but functions can also be defined using Java or PMML. Functions are usually used to define business specific calculations (see Section 9.7.6).

An analytic can be defined in an analogous matter as shown in Figure B-11 (see also Section 14.4.2.4).

Figure B-11 Example of PMML Analytic Definition

B.4.8 Business Knowledge Model

A Business Knowledge Model is very similar in format to a decision except that the inputs are parameter *Names* not *Simple Expressions*. It can be represented by a Decision Table or by a FEEL construct such as a Boxed Expression (see Sections B.4.2 and 11.1.1).

B.5 FEEL Expressions

This section defines the types of expressions that are used in FEEL constructs.

B.5.1 Name

A name is a sequence of characters intended to make a unique identifier or refer to an existing one. It is used to define the unique identity of something (e.g. the name of an output in a Decision Table, a function in a Boxed Function Definition, the key in a Context entry or a parameter in a Function Invocation) to be used elsewhere or to refer to something by name that was previously defined (e.g., the name of a function in an Boxed Invocation or an input variable in a Decision Table).

Where a name is used to refer to an existing variable, such as the name of an input to a Decision, it can have a simple name (e.g., *Persons Employement Record* in Figure B-1) or a dot delimited path which navigates to a variable in a hierarchical structure (e.g. `Instrument.issuer.type` using the underlying data model in Chapter 17, Figure 1). This is referred to as a *Path Expression* (see Section B.5.7).

Names may contain spaces and symbols although, for legibility, it is best not to use these excessively. Names should not contain FEEL reserved words or function names.

B.5.2 Literal

FEEL literal values can be defined using any of the value constructors shown in Table B-1. Notice that many of the functions used to create time or date literals (e.g. `time("15:12:19")`) can be omitted if the italicized literal form is used. This abbreviated form is shown in all applicable examples in Table B-1 using italics.

Example	Meaning
`18` `-1`	Literal integer numeric value.
`2.7182818`	Literal decimal numeric value with proscribed precision.
`NY` `USD`	Enumerated literal value (e.g., state, currency). Note that enumerated literals must be italicized to differentiate them from Names.
`"My Name"`	String literal.
`true`	Boolean literal.
`time("15:12:19")` *15:12:19*	Time literal.

`date("2015-11-20")`
`date(2015, 11, 20)`
2015-11-20
	Date literal.

`date and time("2015-11-20T15:37:54")` *2015-11-20T15:37:54*	Datetime literal.
`duration("P2DT20H15M")` *P2DT20H15M*	Duration literal (in days, hours, minutes and seocnds).
`years and months duration("P1Y4M")` *P1Y4M*	Long duration literal (in years and months).
`[1,2,3]`	List literal. List values may include names (of variables) and literals, including other lists. A list contains items of the same type. It may contain duplicates.
`[{"Water": 7}, {"Vinegar": 1}, {"Lye": 14}]`	Context literal. Contexts are lists with values that have names.

Table B-1 Literal Values in FEEL

B.5.3 Simple Values

Simple values in FEEL are obtained either using a literal value (see Section B.5.2) or by referring to the name of a variable that holds a value (see Section B.5.1). Therefore, `[1,2,5,10,20,50]` and `Annual Salary` are simple values.

B.5.4 Simple Tests

Simple tests are used in the conditions of Decision Tables and as value lists. They combine an operator with a Simple Value (see Section B.5.3). The operators are shown in Table B-2.

Operator	Example	Meaning

(None) Implicit Equality	`18`
	`Premium Amount`
	`[1,2,3]`
		A simple value in a condition cell with no explicit operator tests the equality of the input with that value.

Inequality <, <=, >, >=	`>7`
	`<=AA`
	`>=Start Date`
		Comparison, applicable to magnitude types (date, duration, time, string and numbers) and enumerations with sort order.

Range (Interval)	`[1..6]`
	`(10:45:01..11:03:00]`
	`(2016-12-31..Today)`
	`[Minimum Age..70]`
		Test a magnitude type for inclusion within a range defined by minimum and maximum limits. '[' and ']' denote a range inclusive of the limits whereas '(' and ')' (or ']' and '[') are exclusive. The two can be mixed.

Unknown	`null`	The value of this input is not known. This is used only in Decision Table conditions.
Irrelevant	`-`	The value of this input is irrelevant. This 'test' always passes. This is used in Decision Table conditions and conclusions (see Sections 8.2.3.3 and 8.2.4.1).

Disjunction	`AUD, GBP, USD`
	`<3.141, [1.0..2.0]`
	`<=16, <Minimum Age`
		A comma separated list of any of the tests above that is satisfied if any member is satisfied.

Negation	`not(AUD, GBP, USD)`
	`not([1..6])`
	`not("Robert")`
	`not(null)`
		An operator that inverts the meaning of any test above such that it is satisfied only when the original test is not and vice versa.

Table B-2 Simple Tests in FEEL

The only distinction between the use of Simple Tests in a value list as opposed to their use in a Decision Table condition is that a value list may not use the '-' and `null` forms. Conditions serve to test the values of inputs whereas value lists represent a constraint on the values of conditions and conclusions.

B.5.5 Simple Expression

These extend the notion of Simple Value with basic arithmetic operations, allowing basic derivation of new values (see Table B-3).

Operator	Example	Meaning

Unary minus	`-12`
	`-60.7`
	`-P2Y6M`
		Supports the negation of numerical and duration amounts.

Addition	`24719+24`
	`2016-01-10 + Minimum Policy Duration`
	`Expiry Date + P30DT`
		Addition of numbers to numbers, strings to strings (concatenation), durations to durations and durations to dates/times.

Subtraction	`19-25`
	`100.1 - 0.1`
	`2015-11-05 - Start Date`
	`23:17:00 - 21:19:30`
	`Birthday - P5DT`
		Subtraction of numbers from number, date times from date times, durations from durations and durations from dates/times.

Multiplication	`365 * 24 * 60 * 60` `P1M * No Months`	Multiplication of numbers by numbers and durations by numbers.
Division	`24 / 6.0` `Policy Duration / P1M`	Division of numbers by numbers and durations by numbers.
Exponentiation	`10 ** 6` `E ** Pi`	Raising numbers to powers.

Table B-3 Simple Expressions in FEEL

B.5.6 Expression

Expressions extend Simple Expressions. They allow for advanced manipulation of all FEEL types (see Table B-4) and include the basic looping constructs of the language. They permit the use of complex functions (see Section B.6) and generation of collections and hierarchical values. Furthermore, they allow the use of path expressions to navigate to specific attributes within hierarchical data structures.

Operator	Example	Meaning

Comparison	`Date>Expiry`
	`Risk Level=`*AA+*
	`Age<=18`
	`Cover!=null`
	`Age in ([6..18])`
	`Position in (1, 2, 3)`
	`IQ in (<100, >150)`
	`Expiry between Today and`
	`Today+`*P30DT*
		Equality and Inequality tests, value set membership tests and range comparisons using intervals and lists. Reserved words shown in bold.

Conjunction	`Age>18 and Height>1.6`	Logical 'and' of two or more Boolean expressions
Disjunction	`Date>Expiry or Value>Insured` `Value`	Logical 'or' of two or more Boolean expressions. This is a simple OR, not an exclusive OR.

Filter Expression	`Item[price>100.00]`
	`[1,2,3][item>2]`
	`Candidate[1]`
	`Special Offer[-1]`
	`Scores[name="Patrick"]`
		Filters items from a collection yielding a smaller collection of items that satisfy the filter condition. Filters are expressed as tests on the attributes of the list entries or on the entries as a whole ('item'). Numerical conditions correspond to the position of the item so it is possible to yield the first (1) or last (-1) element of a collection.

For Expression	`for Item in Shopping Cart`
	`return (Item.price * (100 -`
	`Item.discount))`
		Iterates through one or more collections building a list of results from each member

Function Expression	`Mortgage Payment(Term, Value, Frequency)`	Invokes built-in and user defined functions and Business Knowledge Models.
If Expression	`if (Date > Expiry) then 0` `else Cover Amount`	Yields a value depending on a condition.

Quantified Expression	`some Item in ShoppingCart`
	`satisfies Item.discount>0`
	`every Item in Shopping Cart`
	`satisfies not(Item.sku=null)`
		Yields true if some (or all) items in a collection satisfy a specified condition.

Table B-4 FEEL Expressions

B.5.7 Path Expressions

FEEL expressions support the useful concept of Path Expressions. These allow modelers, given a variable holding a value with a hierarchical data structure, to navigate within the value and return individual attributes or collections. The hierarchical data in Figure B-7 and the relation in Figure B-9 would support the following path expressions in Table B-5.

Operator	Example	Meaning
Simple path	```Start Date → 19-Oct-18 Cashflow.Currency → USD```	Yields the named attribute value.
Filtered path	```Patterns[identifier="ISIN"].class → [US AGENCY, US TBILL] Patterns.idPattern [contains(item, "CR")] → ^SDBCR```	Yields a collection of items satisfying the filter. The filter is expressed in terms of one or more attributes of the items to be filtered or the word 'item' representing the value of the attribute being filtered.

Table B-5 Use of Path Expressions

B.6 FEEL Functions

FEEL supports the following functions for number values (see Table B-6), Strings (see Table B-7) and Lists (see Table B-8).

Function	Example	Meaning
ceiling(number)	```ceiling(-2.3) → -2```	Yields the largest integer that is not smaller than the argument.
floor(number)	```floor(-2.3) → -3```	Yields the smallest integer that is not greater than the argument.

Table B-6 FEEL Number Functions

Function	Example	Meaning
contains(string, match)	`contains("sh1re", "1r")` ➔ `true`	Yields true only if the string contains the match.
ends with(string, match)	`ends with("sh0re", "0re")` ➔ `true`	Yields true only if the string ends with the match.
lower case(string)	`lower case("Mr S.")` ➔ `"mr.s"`	Yields a copy of the string with all characters replaced with upper case equivalents.
matches(input, pattern)	`matches("hello", "e*o$")` ➔ `true`	Yields true only if the input matches the regular expression (regexp) in pattern.
replace(input, pattern, replacement)	`replace("hello", "e*o$", "-$1-")` ➔ `"-ll-"`	Yields a new string where the part satisfying the regular expression is replaced with the regular expression in replacement.
starts with(string, match)	`starts with("sh0re", "0r")` ➔ `false`	Yields true only if the string starts with the match.
string length(string)	`string length("shore")` ➔ `5`	Yields the length of the string.
substring(string, start position, length)	`substring("shore", 3, 2)` ➔ `"or"`	Yields a substring from the original, starting at a position[2] and continuing for a specified number of characters.
substring after(string, position)	`substring after("shore", 3)` ➔ `"ore"`	Yields a substring of all the characters at or following position[2].
substring before(string, position)	`substring before("shore", 3)` ➔ `"sho"`	Yields a substring of all the characters at or before position[2].
upper case(string	`upper case("Mr S.")` ➔ `"MR.S"`	Yields a copy of the string with all characters replaced with upper case equivalents.

Table B-7 FEEL String Functions

Function	Example	Meaning
and(list)	`and(6<7, true)` ➔ `false`	Yields true if all members of the list are true, false otherwise; Boolean lists only.
append(list, item)	`append([5, -2, 1],0)` ➔ `[5, -2, 1, 0]`	Appends the item to the end of the list.
concatenate(list...)	`concatenate([A, D, C], [A, D])` ➔ `[A, D, C, A, D]`	Makes a new list from all of the items of the lists provided joined together.
count(list)	`count([NY, DE, FL])` ➔ `3`	Yields the number of elements in the list.
distinct values(list)	`distinct values([A, D, C, A, D])` ➔ `[A, D, C]`	Yields a copy of list with all duplicate values removed.
flatten(list)	`flatten([1,2,[a,b]])` ➔ `[1, 2, a, b]`	Yields a single level list from the contents of a hierarchical list.
insert before(list, position, new item)	`insert before([5, -2, 1],2,0)` ➔ `[5, 0, -2, 1]`	Yields a new copy of list with the new item inserted at the position[67].
index of(list, match)	`Index of([5,-2,1], >0)` ➔ `[1, 3]`	Yields a list of positions[2] of list items that satisfy the match constraint.
list contains(list, element)	`list contains([NY, DE, FL], DE)` ➔ `true`	Yields true if the list contains the element value provided.
max(list)	`max([5,-2,1])` ➔ `5`	Yields the smallest value in the list; magnitudes only.
mean(list)	`mean([5, -2, 1])` ➔ `1.3333333333`	Yields the average of all items in the list.
min(list)	`min([5,-2,1])` ➔ `-2`	Yields the smallest value in the list; magnitudes only.
or(list)	`or(6<7, true)` ➔ `true`	Yields true if any member of the list is true, false otherwise; Boolean lists only.
remove(list)	`remove([3,5,7], 1)` ➔ `[5, 7]`	Yields a list with the item at the specified position[68] removed.
reverse(list)	`reverse([3,5,7])` ➔ `[7, 5, 3]`	Yields a list with the contents of the original list reversed.
sublist(list, start positon, length)	`sublist([5, -2, 1,40],2,2)` ➔ `[-2, 1]`	Yields the sub-list from the original, starting at a specified position[68] and containing a specified number of consecutive entries.

---

[67] A position may have any value between −L and L, where L is the length of the list. A positive position refers to any index from the start (beginning at 1); a negative position refers to characters from the end (hence -1 is the last character position).

Function	Example	Meaning
sum(list)	sum([5, -2, 1]) ➔ 4	Yields the sum of all items in the list; works for numerics and durations only.
union(list…)	union([A, C], [A, D]) ➔ [A, C, D]	Yields a union of all distinct values in all the lists provided.

Table B-8 FEEL List Functions

Appendix C. Proposals for Enhancements to DMN

Building a good decision model involves more than slavishly applying the DMN standard. Modelers can benefit from considering some additional details, currently beyond the standard, especially when analyzing more complex business decisions. These considerations can be used informally to clarify understanding of issues "on the boundary" of a decision model and to enhance communication with colleagues. Where appropriate, these details also make effective formal supplements to DMN, enriching decision models that include them and overcoming some limitations of the current version of the standard.

This chapter includes a selection of DMN extensions that more advanced modelers should consider using when relevant. The authors have proposed these extensions for future releases of DMN. Given the subject matter, this appendix is more technical than other chapters and newcomers to decision modeling may wish to omit it on their first reading.

DMN is a powerful and broadly applicable standard but it omits some useful concepts. Some of the most useful are presented here to broaden the perspective of decision modelers. These concepts have been of practical benefit on many decision modeling projects and should be considered alongside the "official" elements of the DMN standard. These additional considerations are all established, some featuring in other decision modeling approaches (like TDM, see Appendix D) or having equivalents in adjoining standards such as BPMN.

These omissions should not be viewed as flaws or oversights in the specification. Effective notations need to be small to maximize their clarity and ease of adoption. DMN should be a viewed as a notational and modeling core that these additional concepts can supplement as necessary. The need for some of these extra details is context dependent while others imply a particular approach and so are hard to include in a general standard. If DMN tried to do everything it would risk becoming overly complex. As DMN evolves, it is possible that some of these considerations will be addressed in future versions.

If decision modelers choose to adopt some of these extensions, they should apply them consistently and with the broad agreement of their colleagues to avoid diluting the benefits of a standard through the excessive use of ad-hoc and context specific additions.

Extensions are proposed for the Decision Requirements Level, Decision Logic Level and glossary integration.

C.1 Decision Requirements Extensions

C.1.1 Decision Cardinality

C.1.1.1 Handling collections of data in decision models

The majority of DMN examples in this book have focused on decision inputs and outputs with *single* values, for example, an instrument's asset class or a person's annual salary. However, a decision's data model sometimes contains information items with lists or collections of values (see Section 9.7.1). Typically, this is reflected in the decision data model as a

1:n association between the two objects involved. For example, a *Shopping Cart* can contain a set of *Items* (see Figure C-1). This is an explicit collection.

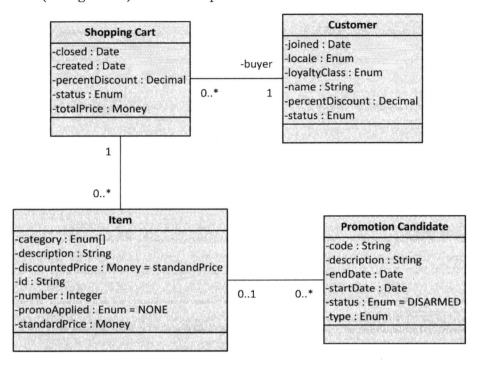

Figure C-1 Decision Data Model for Simple On-Line Shopping System

Some data models have 'nested' collections in which one item contains a collection of others, each of which itself contains a collection of values. If a *Customer* is being processed by a decision then, as in Figure C-1, there is a nested collection with multiple shopping carts each containing multiple *Items*.

C.1.1.2 How many times is a decision made?

These collection Information Items are made available to a decision via an Information Requirement Relationship either with an Input Data that is a list or a sub-decision that yields a list outcome. In a decision model featuring such a relationship, it must be possible to determine how many times a decision is made. Is it made once for the entire collection or once per item? How many separate instances of the decision's logic definition are invoked?

Consider a decision model, based on the data model of Figure C-1, in which there is a decision with logic defined by the table in Figure C-2.

Discount				
U	**Item Category**	**Loyalty Class**	**Item Price**	**Date**	**Discount**
					0,[1..100]
1	PHOTOGRAPHY	GOLD	>50	<= 2018-12-31	4%
2		not(GOLD)	>150	<= 2018-12-31	2%
3	DOMESTIC ELECTRICAL	SILVER, GOLD	>500	<= 2018-05-31	4%
4	MENS FASHION	SILVER, GOLD	-	<= 2016-06-15	2%
5	LADIES FASHION	GOLD	>200	<= 2018-06-15	3%

Figure C-2 Discount Policy Decision Table

This Decision Table has inputs that refer to both properties of an *Item* (e.g., *category*), a *Shopping Cart* (e.g., *date*) and a *Customer* (e.g., *loyalty class*). As a result, to readers with no pre-conceptions of how carts work, there are several possible interpretations of how many times the decision should be evaluated. The Decision Table may be used:

- Once for each *Item;*
- Once for each *Cart*, *or*
- Once for each *Customer*, covering all their *Carts*.

When considering this question further uncertainties arise:

- If the table is invoked once per Item, which Cart should be consulted to check the date? Is it safe to assume the Cart will be the one containing the Item? Is the discount that results applied to the Item that triggered the discount, the Cart that contains it or to all the Customer's Carts? Does the date refer to the Cart or the Customer?

- If the Decision Table is used once per Cart, then each evaluation will have multiple Items to handle—all the Items in the current Cart. Should the Item attribute conditions (category and price) be aggregated and, if so, how? Should the discount of the first rule be applied if the sum of the Item Prices of photography products exceeds $50, or must the maximum individual Item Price exceed this figure?

Without additional information, such as defined decision logic, it is not clear to the reader of a Decision Table at what level of granularity it is 'driven' by the data provided to it. The logic lacks a definition of the '**decision cardinality**'.

C.1.1.3 Collections in information dependencies

A related ambiguity can arise in Decision Requirements Diagrams. For example, in Figure C-3, decisions have Information Requirements on other decisions, and Input Data, potentially involving data collections. This example Decision Requirement Diagram determines the price of all *Items* in a *Shopping Cart*. This has three Information Requirement Relationships. With only the standard DMN notation, it is not clear that data is always consumed with the same level of granularity as it is produced.

Figure C-3 Decision Requirements Diagram with Ambiguous Information Requirements

There are three possible ways that these Information Requirement Relationships can be interpreted. A fan analogy can be used in the sense that the relationship "fans out" based on the cardinality:

- **Fan-Neutral:** for <u>every</u> data Information Item[68] there is <u>one</u> decision. For instance, for every *Item* there is a separate instance of the decision *Discounted Item Price*. This is the most common situation.

- **Fan-In:** for <u>many</u> data items there is <u>one</u> decision instance. For example, a set of *Discounted Item Price* decisions feed their results into a single instance of the decision *Cart Price*.

- **Fan-Out:** for <u>one</u> data Information Item produced that is a collection of sub-items, there are <u>many</u> decision instances. Each decision instance processes one sub-item. For example, in Figure C-4, the *Eligible Products* decision yields a collection of products, each member of which is independently priced by a separate instance of the *Cost Product* decision.

Figure C-4 An Example Decision Requirement Diagram with Implicit Fan Out

C.1.1.4 Why worry about these issues?

If these concepts are ignored, as they are in the standard currently, the decision model leaves some important distinctions unresolved:

- How many times a decision is invoked for a data collection.

- How collections of data are handled by decisions that consume them and whether they handle items independently of one another or as a list.

In simple or very intuitive examples, one may be able to safely infer the meaning from the decision model. For instance, in this example, one could look at the Decision Table and use the name of its inputs and knowledge of how shopping carts normally behave to infer that:

---

[68] Which is itself either a single value or a collection that is processed as one.

- The Decision Table is evaluated once per *Item*.
- The *price* condition therefore pertains to each individual *Item* price.
- The discount is applied to each single *Item*.
- The date condition refers to the closure date of the *Cart* in which the item appears.

Similarly, the inputs and outputs of related Decision Tables could be used to determine if fan-in or fan-out has occurred.

However, decision models must communicate complex, real-world business logic effectively and unambiguously. They must convey their meaning explicitly, so relying on this kind of inference and prior knowledge is inherently unsatisfactory.

In more complex domains, each of the scenario interpretations listed in Sections C.1.1.2 and C.1.1.3 might be equally meaningful and even equally useful. In addition, it might be important to be clear about how these ambiguities will be resolved without any decision logic being specified. The scenarios must be distinguished so that a decision modeler may be completely unequivocal using only a Decision Requirements Diagram. This requires a new concept to be introduced to DMN to capture the cardinality and fan of the decision model.

C.1.1.5 Documenting decision Cardinality and Fan in Decision Requirements Diagrams

This is a proposal to document cardinality and fan using an extension that is small, consistent with DMN and unambiguous.

The least impactful way to document fan in a Decision Requirements Diagram is to indicate visually, using a set of three vertical lines[69], where the end or ends of an Information Requirement Relationship are multi-instance. Specifically:

- Where fan-in occurs, indicate that there are multiple instances data which are fed into a single instance of the decision that consumes them.
- Where fan-out occurs because an Input Data is a collection or a sub-decision, creates a collection, indicate visually that the consuming decision will be invoked multiple times: once per item in the collection.

---

[69] This symbol is used to be consistent with BPMN, where it is used to denote a multi-instance process. We use it to denote the cardinality of a requirements relationship.

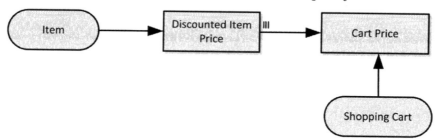

Figure C-5 Decision Requirement Diagram Depicting Explicit Fan-In

Figure C-5 shows how Figure C-3 could be amended to include this idea. Multiple *Items* are each processed by their own instance of the *Discounted Item Price* decision (fan neutral). This produces a collection of item prices that 'fans-in' to a single *Cart Price* decision. The Decision Table definition holds the detail of how the fan-in works (e.g., the mechanics of any required aggregation such as the calculation of a total discount). Similarly, Figure C-6 explicitly depicts the (implicit) fan-out of Figure C-4: for a single customer there will be a collection of *Eligible Products* and each of these will need its own instance of *Cost Product*.

Figure C-6 Decision Requirements Diagram Depicting Explicit Fan-Out

For information dependencies involving data collections, the modeler should:

- Assume fan-neutral is the default.
- For fan-in, the consuming Decision Table must stipulate an aggregate function or be explicit about how it uses the whole collection as an input.
- For fan-out, the consuming decision must be explicit about how it uses each item (in inputs and outputs) and if any filtering or constraints to item selection are applied.

Notice that multi-instance symbols are *not* placed *inside* the symbol of a decision or Input Data that involves data collections. They are a feature of the Information Requirements Relationship between these components, not the components themselves. Marking a data collection Input Data or decision component with a multi-instance symbol makes little sense because the component may have relationships with many other components each of which consume the data it provides in different ways. Some consumers may exhibit fan-in (consumer aggregates multiple sources), some may be fan neutral (consumer uses entire collection as a whole) and others may have fan-out (the consumer iterates).

Cardinality is a property of the Information Requirement Relationship between one component and another, rather than an isolated property of any component—just as cardinality of an inter-class association in UML is seen as a property of the relationship rather than a property of either of the classes involved.

Although fan-in suggests aggregation and fan-out suggests iteration, it is best to leave the specific mechanism to the Decision Logic Level.

The convention (shown in Figure C-6) that any decision that produces a collection uses a plural name also clarifies matters.

C.1.1.6 Documenting decision Cardinality and Fan in Decision Tables

Unambiguous use of Decision Tables with data collection inputs can be achieved in the decision logic level by:

- Phrasing conditions unambiguously. For example, avoid specifying an input 'Date' if there are multiple possible interpretations of the term. Instead, a specific input should be specified: e.g., *Cart closure date.*

- Where necessary, documenting a Decision Table's **decision cardinality** by nominating a data class in its context or result box. When a Decision Table nominates a decision cardinality, it is separately invoked for each available instance of the specified data class. This can be implicit if the class is defined in the context (see Section C.1.1.7) or explicit if iteration is specified in the result box (see examples in Figure 11-22 of Section 17.1.7.2 and Section 11.3.2.6).

- Where a decision has inputs (or outputs) using the properties of two or more data classes (e.g., *Item* and *Cart*), denoting how these data instances should be related to one another. In this case, insisting that each instance of the decision operates on a *Cart* and the *Items* it contains.

An explicit statement of a cardinality is not required if it can be unambiguously inferred from Input Data, which is the case in most situations. This is always the case if:

- A decision only has one non-collection input.
- A decision has multiple non-collection inputs that are related by a 1:1 relationship in the decision data model.

Note the importance of the decision data model in making this determination and resolving ambiguity of this kind.

If there is any chance of ambiguity, the cardinality should be documented by the Decision Table consuming the data. The next section demonstrates how this is done using Decision Table contexts (see Section 8.2.5).

C.1.1.7 Example decision model with Cardinality and Fan

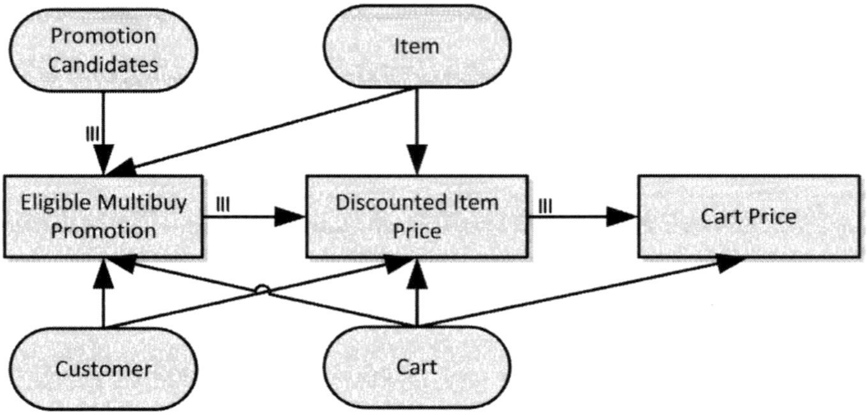

Figure C-7 Example Decision Requirements Diagram with Complex Fans

Consider an example shopping cart Decision Requirements Diagram in Figure C-7 with the underlying business data model shown in Figure C-1. The *Eligible Multibuy Promotion* decision takes a mixed set of *Promotion Candidates* that might apply to an *Item* and determines which of them are active multi-buys[70]. These *Promotions* are then used to determine the *Discounted Item Price*. Each of these is then used to determine an overall *Cart Price*.

The cardinalities in the Decision Requirements Diagram can be explained as follows:

- A collection of *Promotion Candidates* is associated with each *Item* (see Figure C-8). Each *Promotion Candidate* feeds its own instance of the decision *Eligible Multibuy Promotion*. Fan-out is needed to show this. This decision determines if a *Promotion* can be applied.

- As there are multiple *Promotions* per *Item*, each instance of *Discounted Item Price* is dependent on multiple results from *Eligible Multibuy Promotion*. Therefore, fan-in is required.

- *Discounted Item Price* is made once for each *Item* in the context of a *Cart* (to see if other *Items* are included that might trigger a multibuy *Promotion*). Therefore, this relationship is fan-neutral.

- *Cart Price* is dependent on the results from multiple instances of *Discounted Item Price* to form an aggregate price for the *Cart*; hence, fan-in is appropriate.

- Cart and Customer are non-collections and, therefore, their relationships are all fan neutral.

At the Decision Logic Level, contexts are needed to clarify all but the subject decision (*Cart Price*). *Eligible Multibuy Promotion* and its context can be seen in Figure C-8.

---

[70] A multi-buy is a discount for one item that applies only when it is brought with certain others.

Eligible Multibuy Promotion

Promotion	**for** Promotion **in** Item.Promotion Candidates
Customer	Promotion.Item.Shopping Cart.Customer
Current Date	SystemInterface.getCurrentDate()

U	Promotion Type	Promotion Locale	End Date	Current Date	Promotion Status
1	MULTIBUY	Customer Locale	not(*UNKNOWN*)	[Start Date .. End Date]	*ENABLED*
2				not([Start Date .. End Date])	*DISABLED*
3			*UNKNOWN*		*ENABLED*
4		not(Customer Locale)			*DISABLED*
5	not(*MULTIBUY*)				*DISABLED*

Figure C-8 Eligible Multibuy Promotions Decision Table

Notice the context defines three terms used in the Decision Table—*Promotion, Customer* and *Current Date*. The first of these is the cardinality of the table (shown with the FEEL iteration for..in) and indicates that this Decision Table should be applied to every *Promotion* separately. This cardinality stipulates '*Item.Promotion Candidate*', that is all *Promotions* associated with the current *Item. Promotion Candidates* unassociated with the current *Item* are therefore ignored for this decision. Other context entries define how the value of *Customer Locale* is determined (from the customer of the cart containing the item). As the Decision Requirements Diagram shows fan-out to this decision, iteration is required as seen in the context definition of *Promotion*. Decision Tables requiring fan-in are likely to use aggregation of some form.

C.1.2 Supplementary information marker (ellipsis)

Each Decision Requirement Diagram (DRD) shows a subset of the components and dependencies of the complete decision model's Decision Requirements Graph (DRG)—it is a visual view of part of the graph (see Sections 8.1.7 and 14.3.2). Given this, it would be useful to depict visually that a component shown in a DRD is involved in other dependencies that are not shown on this DRD. Consider an example of four separate DRDs in Figure C-9. DRD 'A' represents the entire DRG, whereas DRDs 'B', 'C' and 'D' are subsets of the DRG and the ellipses signify the hidden child and parent nodes respectively. The DMN standard refers to this concept of 'hiding detail' on DRDs but does not nominate a specific visual representation. Because it is important for a model consumer to be able to look at a DRD and correctly interpret its completeness, we propose a notation for this purpose such as that shown here.

An example of this notation in use can be found in Section 14.3.2.

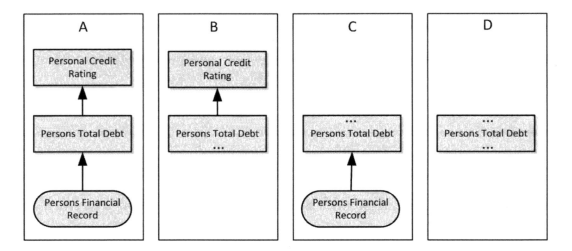

Figure C-9 Decision Component Ellipsis to Denote Missing Content

An even simpler alternative is not to distinguish between missing parent and child components and to show a single ellipsis marker if *any* attached nodes are elided from the DRD in question. This simpler version seems likely to be adopted in DMN 1.2.

C.1.3 Decisions and Business Knowledge Models

A Business Knowledge Model (BKM, see Section 11.1.1) is a reusable element of business logic invoked by a decision or another BKM. BKMs support the parametrized reuse of decision logic. They have their own symbol, dependency relationship and invocation rules but are very close to decisions in many other respects. However, in the interest of supporting potential reuse, many decision models become a sea of decision/BKM pairs. This effectively doubles the size of the DRD. In addition, the current distinction between decision and BKM is too fine to be useful.

An alternative would be to combine the concepts of decision and BKM. The resulting decision component would then be represented as a single symbol in a DRD and would be capable of deriving inputs from the binding of parameters or from Information Requirements Relationships or any mixture. Any decision could then be subject to parameterized invocation if required. The decision symbol could be used to represent both concepts and the standard could retain the knowledge requirement relation to denote invocation only when needed. This would lessen the rework required when unexpected reuse of a decision is required without increasing the complexity of the DRD unduly.

This combination would be a useful way to "hide" BKMs on DRDs while still highlighting decisions that use them. Marking each decision with its current implementation, if any, would be one way to do this. For instance, a decision using a Business Knowledge Model would be represented with one symbol, one with its own Decision Table by another and one defined using PMML with a third.

C.2 Decision Logic Extensions

Many of these proposed extensions refer to parts of DMN grammar (in italics) or structural elements (capitalized). A full definition of these is included in Sections B.5 and B.4 respectively.

C.2.1 Support expressions in Decision Table Input Entries

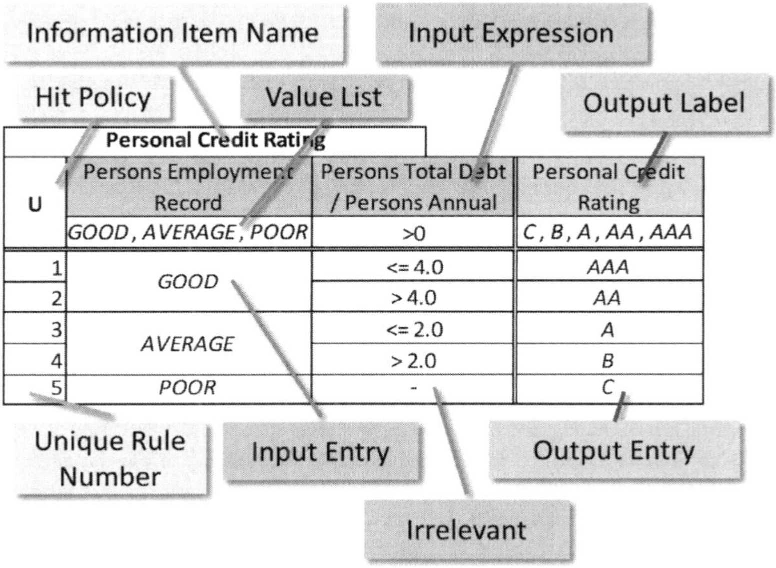

Figure C-10 Typical Decision Table

Currently, Decision Table conditions (formally an Input Entry in DMN, see Figure C-10) are defined in the FEEL grammar as *unary tests* (see *simple tests* in Section B.5.4). This allows Input Entries to perform a number of simple tests on Input Expression values, comparing them with literal values or the values of named variables (e.g., equality, inequality and range inclusion; see Section 8.2.3.1).

However, conditions cannot perform comparisons using fully featured arithmetic expressions (e.g., '<=Salary * 4.0') or use FEEL functions (see Section B.6). In practice, these restrictions mean that many Decision Tables have to resort to contexts or other FEEL-heavy means to use calculated amounts in condition tests. There is a great deal of demand for this kind of condition from business users of DMN in the field. It would be valuable to extend Input Entries. They could be changed to support *simple expression* or even a new type combining FEEL's existing *unary tests* with *arithmetic expression*, *simple value* and *function invocation* types to allow conditions like:

- '>=(Expiry Date + Grace Period)' (*simple expression*).

- '>max(Applicant Credit Limit, Guarantor Credit Limit)' (*function invocation*).

Decision Table Input Entries could also be extended to support all FEEL functions directly. This would allow a great deal of flexibility in Decision Table conditions. For instance, in the case of a Decision Table with a string input, the FEEL function for testing if a string contains a substring (e.g., `contains("shire","ir")`) could be used directly in an Input Entry by:

- using a reserved word or symbol to represent the value of Input Expression being tested (e.g., '`contains(_,"ir")`'); *or*

- using a simplified version of the function (e.g., '`contains("ir")`') where the first argument of any function is always the Input Expression value by convention. This is more compact that the first option but presents some ambiguities that would need to be addressed.

This would allow Decision Tables like Figure C-11 that are currently not possible in the current version of the standard. Such freedom is vital when using DMN to handled unstructured data (see section 14.7.2).

	Instrument Classes		
C	Identifier	Value	Instrument Classes
1	*ISIN , CUSIP*	matches("(US)?519")	*US AGENCY*
2	*ISIN*	starts with("TB")	*US TBILL*
3	*ISIN*	contains("AA")	*AUS GOVT*

Figure C-11 Decision Table Using Function Input Entries

This flexibility requires some discipline to use effectively without over-complicating Decision Tables. Undisciplined use of complex conditions runs the risk of making the Decision Table incomprehensible and hard to validate. FEEL contexts are the only realistic alternative, however. These are far more complex and more likely to alienate business users.

C.2.2 Decision Tables supporting collection Input Expressions

Currently, DMN Decision Table Input Entries can handle only conditions on single values, not collections. This means that if a Decision Table's input is a collection, then there are only three ways to process it:

- test it for equality or inequality with a literal list or list variable; this is seldom needed in practice;

- use FEEL's '`for .. in .. return`' construct to iterate through every member of the collection (e.g., Figure 21 of 11.3.2.6); *or*

- specify an Input Expression that uses an aggregate function to obtain a single value from the collection; this value may then be tested using conventional conditions.

The biggest constraint when using collection inputs is that Input Entries cannot have any set-based operators (e.g., `list contains()`, `sublist()`, `union()`). Simple conditions, such as checking an input collection to see if it contains one of a number of specific values, requires a specific Input Expression for each value being tested which needs to be defined using FEEL context (e.g., Figure 17-37 of Section 17.3.7). This is because Input Expressions are *simple expressions* which do not support functions in FEEL.

This use of a context should not be necessary. Input Entries should be extended to support conditions on collections, perhaps based on the simplified functions idea in Section C.2.1. This would support condition tests like:

- checking collection membership (e.g., 'list contains(*USD*)');
- checking collection size (e.g., 'count()>5'); *and*
- checking aggregate properties (e.g., 'min()<4.5').

C.2.3 Missing FEEL functions

FEEL incorporates a useful set of built-in functions for manipulating and aggregating collections of values. This is excellent as far as it goes, but many of the included functions lack mathematically related counterparts. This is especially true for list functions:

- union() is supported but not intersect(), is superset of(), **or** is subset of().
- sum() is supported but not product().
- there is flatten() but no zip().
- mean() is supported but not median(), mode() or stddev().

There is an interface to add new functions as needed and it is true that the standard should not be encumbered with too many functions. Nevertheless, a more inclusive and mathematically balanced set of built-in functions would be better.

The functions we would particularly like to see are listed in Table C-1.

Function	Example	Meaning
intersect (list...)	`intersect([4,5,6],[5,7,9]` ➔ `[5]`	Returns a list of all the elements that feature in every list.
product (list)	`product([5, -2, 1])` ➔ `-10`	Yields the product of all items in the list; works for numerics only.
stddev (list)	`std([5, -2, 1]))` ➔ `2.867441755681`	Yields the standard deviation of all items in the list; works for any magnitude type.
median (list)	`median([5, -2, 1]))` ➔ `1`	Yields the median of all items in the list; works for any magnitude type.
mode (list)	`mode([1, 5, -2, 1]))` ➔ `[1]`	Yields a list of the modes of all items in the list; works for any type.
range (list)	`range([1, 5, -2, 1]))` ➔ `7`	Yields the range of all items in the list; works for any magnitude type.
Is subset of (list, list)	`subset([5, -2],[5, -2, 1])` ➔ `true`	Yields true if the first list is a strict subset of the second.
Is superset of (list, list)	`superset([5, -2],[-2])` ➔ `true`	Yields true if the first list is a strict superset of the second.
zip (list ...)	`zip([a,b,c],[1,2],[A, B]]` ➔ `[[a,1,A],[b,2,B],[c]]`	Interleaves the values of many lists into one list of lists.

Table C-1 Missing FEEL Functions

C.2.4 Representations of Decision Logic as Decision Trees

Decision Trees (see Section 14.4.2.3) represent logic as a set of alternate paths diverging from a single starting point; each path then forks in turn into sub-paths of its own, like branches in a tree. At each fork, there is a condition, the answer to which determines which of the many exit paths to take. Ultimately, each path ends with an outcome. Decision Trees may not contain cycles (circular paths), but multiple paths can converge on one node if required.

As of release 1.1, DMN does not define a standard format for Decision Trees. Decision Trees are a popular means of representing decision logic and are very appropriate for certain styles of logic such as customer segmentation. Decision Trees are also widely supported in Business Rules Management Systems and are a common result of data mining efforts.

An example decision tree for determining when to sound a cockpit configuration alarm in a jet airliner can be found in Figure C-12. The purpose of this alarm is to warn pilots if the aircraft is improperly configured for take-off or landing[71]. The tree consists of a set of condition checks (questions), the answers to which determine either the outcome of the decision or what question to ask next. To read the tree start at the top and work downward. Every possible path ends with an outcome (the tree is complete).

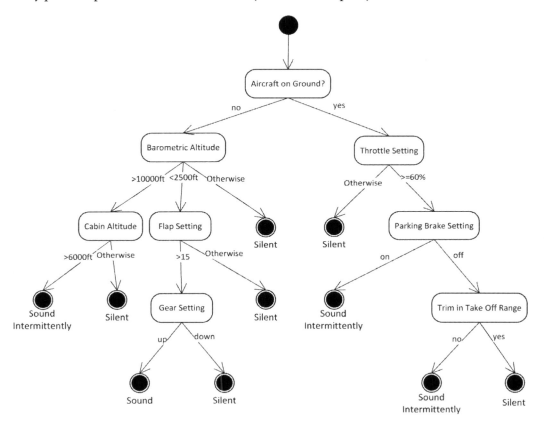

Figure C-12 Aircraft Configuration Alarm Decision Tree

Decision Tables and trees hold the same information: any decision that can be expressed in one can (more or less effectively) be rendered in the other form. Nevertheless, a Decision Tree representation would be a useful addition to DMN as it would allow a standard presentation of the format and allow modelers to pick the most appropriate logic representation without stepping outside the logic styles defined in DMN.

C.2.5 Annotated Decision Tables

Use of DMN Decision Tables on many real projects suggests several practical improvements that could be made beyond the current standard without undermining it.

---

[71] Naturally this example is considerably more complex on a real aircraft.

C.2.5.1 Rule level annotation

Variations of the DMN standard Decision Table have been proposed by some vendors[72] that augment the core definition with comments. One of the most useful variants is the rule-level annotation. This is an optional, additional conclusion that documents the intent of each rule in the table (as opposed the whole table). The Decision Model (TDM, see Appendix D) has a similar concept—the *Message*.

Arbitrated Asset Class			
U	Reference Security Type	Issuer Country Class	Arbritrated Asset Class	Annotation
1	A1	-	ABS	Arbitor: Securitisation - Investor
2	A6	-	ABS	Arbitor: Securitisation - Originator
3	B1	-	COVERED	Arbitor: Covered Bonds SA
4	C7	-	CORP FIN	Arbitor: Corporates SA - FIN (pessimistic)
5	E1	-	EQUITY	Arbitor: Equity
6	F1	-	CORP FIN	Arbitor: Bank (BNK)
7	S7	DEV	GOVT DEV	Arbitor: Central developed governments SA
8	S7	EMG	GOVT EMG	Arbitor: Central emerging governments SA
9	S8	-	MUNICPAL	Arbitor: Regional governments SA

Figure C-13 Example Decision Table with Rule Level Annotations

Using this extension, as illustrated in Figure C-13, table authors may optionally document each rule with an annotation: a comment that aids ease of comprehension of an individual rule. The annotation does not change the behavior of the table or its role in making a decision; it is an optionally populated, free text field. By convention the annotation column is the right most column in the table. The comment may be used to document the rule's:

- rationale (if this is not obvious);
- intent (if a single rule or group achieve a specific effect);
- justification; *or*
- known problems.

Note that the annotation can be different for different rules that reach the same conclusion value. Some tools also allow the text of the annotation to be persisted when the table is executed, supporting run time explain and traceability of decision behavior.

Something similar can be achieved by defining a second conclusion column for every Decision Table but this is a lot of overhead and obscures those cases where a genuine second conclusion is being defined, thereby reducing clarity.

When using a Decision Table as a classifier (see Section 16.9), as in the example above, it can be helpful to use annotations to define each classification value. However, be careful not to repeat these annotations across many Decision Tables. Where multiple Decision Tables use the same classification scheme, the classification enumeration should have its values defined once in a glossary.

---

[72] The authors have seen proposals from Signavio and Sapiens.

C.2.5.2 Propagation of annotation

The TDM concept of Message allows the annotation of one rule to 'propagate' to a dependent rule, higher in the Decision Requirement Diagram hierarchy, where its contents can be further augmented or amended. Consequently, as rule execution traverses up this hierarchy, an explanatory annotation of rule behavior can be 'built up' from the bottom-up to the subject decision. This is a powerful means of supporting explanation as the resulting annotation can contain contributions from all of the sub-decisions. Again, this could be managed in the current approach but only with significant additional work.

C.2.5.3 Rule level annotation with Knowledge Source

One extension that we propose is that rule level annotations can also be used to depict the influence or constraint, on a specific rule, from subsections of a Knowledge Source document. This is a powerful technique as it allows the consumer of the decision model to:

- Examine the traceability and justification for every rule in terms of legal and regulatory mandates contained in Knowledge Sources.
- Determine the extent to which such a mandate is satisfied by a decision model—the model's coverage.

In the latter case, when annotations are used to reference Knowledge Sources, a more formal representation is needed. Users should be sure to unambiguously denote the Knowledge Source reference and a specific section of it, if available.

Consider the example Decision Requirements Diagram in Figure C-14 that depicts a decision with two complementary Knowledge Sources with formal names *IASIC* and *ABEICS*. The latter are denoted in braces after the informal name.

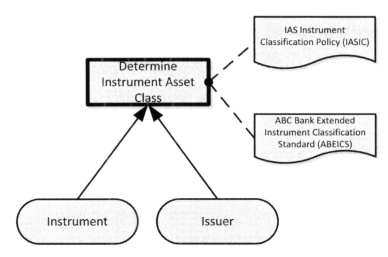

Figure C-14 Decision governed by two Knowledge Sources

These Knowledge Sources can be referred to from the rule level annotations depicted in Figure C-15. Note the use of formal names for brevity and the reference of specific subsections of the Knowledge Source that give high-resolution traceability.

| U | Issuer Based Asset Class | | | | |
	Asset Category	Instrument is Convertible	Issuer Class	Issuer Based Asset Class	Annotation
1	OTHER	-	-	OTHER	"**IASIC 5-19-4b** rights issues, warrants, misc products"
2	INDEX	-	-	INDEX	"**IASIC 2-6-14a-d** indexed securities and pseudo-baskets"
3	EQUITY	-	-	EQUITY	"**IASIC 3-1-2** equity, stock; Country Class " + Issuer Country Class
4	PREFERRED	true	-	CVTPFD	"**IASIC 3-3-2** preferred " + Issuer Class + " convertible instrument"
5		false	-	OTHER	"**ABEICS 4B-2 (p19)** non-preferred convertibles"
6	DEBT	true	-	CONVERTIBLE	"**IASIC 3-3-3** convertible instrument"
7	DEBT	false	SUPRA	SUPRA	"**IASIC 4-4-2** supernational debt"

Figure C-15 Decision Table with Knowledge Source References

C.2.6 Completeness

C.2.6.1 DMN definition

A decision is said to be complete if there is at least one rule that can address every situation; in other words there is no situation in which a decision cannot yield a result because there is no logic to address it. Whether or not a decision is complete is a function of the number and type of its data inputs and its conditions—its completeness can be derived from these factors.

This definition of complete used to be part of the DMN hit policy. However, recent versions of the standard have removed it for a variety of reasons. Chief among these is the Decision Table's ability to specify a default value (see Section 8.2.3.7) that guarantees they will return a result.

However, it is useful to document completeness because there is significant value in differentiating between decisions that are *meant* to be explicitly complete (there is a rule for every combination of input data values) and those that are not.

C.2.6.2 Logical versus business completeness

In practice, there are different levels of completeness which, like hit policy, benefit from being documented clearly. Specifically, there is a distinction between **logical** versus **business** completeness.

- **Logical completeness** is identical to the definition in the previous section: it documents the intent of the author that every possible combination of input values is explicitly covered. In this case, the presence of any scenarios that satisfy no rules indicates an oversight on the part of the modeler since the decision was intended to cover every eventuality.

- **Business completeness** signifies the modeler's intent that a decision covers all combinations of input values that can occur *in practice*, but *not* all the combinations that are theoretically possible given their types. This suggests that certain combinations of input values cannot occur or are meaningless from a business perspective.

- **Incompleteness** is when there are combinations of input values, which can occur in practice, that are deliberately omitted from the decision, i.e., the decision has deliberate 'gaps' in coverage that the author intended.

Business completeness is common in Decision Tables with many enumerated conditions that are interrelated, such that a given value of one constrains the range of the others. In this case, some combinations of values, although permitted by the types of the inputs, are meaningless from a business perspective and are not included in the table. The author stipulating that a table is business complete wishes to document that all the combinations of inputs that are expected in practice are covered. Furthermore, they are asserting that any omitted combinations are nonsensical.

C.2.6.3 Proposed extension

When defining a Decision Table, its completeness must be explicitly described using the definitions above. A Decision Table may be:

- **Logically complete**: having an explicit rule for every possible combination of values;

- **Business complete**: having an explicit rule for every combination of values that is meaningful in practice *or*

- **Incomplete**: neither of the above.

The counter-argument has been made that documenting completeness is not required because Decision Tables should always be logically complete. The suggestion is that, for tables with combinations of inputs values that cannot occur in practice, each of these impossible input combinations should be supported by a rule with a null conclusion to deliberately document 'impossible cases'. We have some sympathy with this argument. However, in practice, there are many 'real-world' Decision Tables with enumerated inputs that have many nonsensical combinations. Listing them all would 'bloat' the table and obscure its business intent. Decision modelers need a means of documenting only the valid combinations—a way of saying: *"this set of rules covers all business valid combinations; all others either cannot happen or are not addressed here."*

C.2.7 Use of text attributes and position to convey meaning

The way that DMN uses text attributes—such as underlining (to denote defaults) and italicization (to represent string literals)—is precarious and easily overlooked. The only difference between a conclusion that yields a string constant versus one that yields the value held by a variable is whether the text is italicized or not. These minute distinctions should be removed in our opinion. More robust ways of representing these concepts should be used, for instance, explicit default rules and enumerated constants.

Similarly, the use of double lines to separate inputs from outputs in Decision Tables is easily misread when there are multiple outputs. It is arguably better to use explicit 'Input' and 'Output' headers.

Finally, the depiction of hit policy as a single letter is somewhat obscure and does not aid comprehension.

C.3 Decision Logic Simplifications

C.3.1 Hit policies

The hit policies 'R' (Rule Order) and 'O' (Output Order) (see Section 11.2.3) are virtually useless—it is very rare to see a useful application for them—and can lead to some spectacularly obscure logic. They should be removed from the standard.

C.4 Glossary Integration Extensions

C.4.1 Reference to named enumerated types in Decision Tables

Chapter 9 recommends the use of a glossary to underpin decision models. Among other benefits, this defines a set of reusable business terms and data types that promote the transparency and consistency of models. One of the most commonly repeated elements in a decision model with lots of Decision Tables is the value lists of frequently used enumerated types (see Section 8.2.3.6), for instance, types such as *Country, Customer Class, Currency, Product Type* which are used throughout a decision model.

We propose a more scalable approach: modelers should define the enumerated type and its permitted values *once* in a glossary and refer to this type by name when a value list is needed. This avoids the maintenance overhead and danger of inconsistency created by repeating the permitted values in value lists every time they are used. Note that, in the example in Figure C-17, in place of the permitted values of *Issuer Type, Instrument Class* and *Instrument Rating* in the value list row, there is instead a reference to the enumerated type in angled braces. This avoids undue repetition, but adequate tool support could easily display and enforce the value list constraint as needed.

Infer Failsafe Rating			
U	Issuer Type	Instrument Class	Failsafe Rating
	<Issuer Type>	<Instrument Class>	<Instrument Rating>
1	*US MORTGAGE SECURITIES*	-	*AAA*
2		*US AGENCY, US TBILL*	*AAA*
3	not(*US MORTGAGE SECURITIES*)	*AP AGENCY*	*AA*
4		*FAR EAST AGENCY*	*A*
5		*GOVT EMERGING*	*AA-*
6		*UNKNOWN*	*UNKNOWN*

Figure C-17 Example Enumerated Type Reference in Value List

Appendix D. The Decision Model (TDM)

The Decision Model (TDM), established in 2009 and documented in *The Decision Model* by Barbara von Halle and Larry Goldberg, is an influential precursor to DMN. It is a decision modeling notation and method that is still practiced and still evolving. This chapter outlines the similarities and differences between the last publicly released version of TDM and the current version of DMN. It offers advice for TDM practitioners who need to transition to DMN and demonstrates how TDM experience can be leveraged to learn DMN quickly. The purpose is not to define TDM, but rather to illustrate how DMN practitioners can benefit from its best principles and to highlight some pitfalls of which experienced users of TDM should be wary. None of the comparisons listed here should be construed as value judgements; there is no single 'right way' to model decisions.

D.1 The Decision Model (TDM)

The Decision Model (TDM) is a closed, vendor-specific decision modeling notation and approach owned by Sapiens Inc. It was originally developed in 2009 by Barbara von Halle and Larry Goldberg and documented in their book *The Decision Model*. Between 2009 and 2012 a number of white paper extensions were produced. It is this public version of TDM that is the focus of this section. TDM has continued to evolve[73] as part of the Sapiens' DECISION tool but this extended approach is not yet a matter of public record and is only addressed fleetingly here[74]. TDM was a pivotal milestone in the development of decision modeling and has had an enormous influence on DMN.

Just as data modeling and the relational model can be applied to improve the structure of business data, TDM's aim is to formalize the structure of business logic. It is an analog of relational calculus for rule based logic that represents decisions as sets of inter-dependent Decision Tables (or *Rule Family Views* in TDM parlance). The approach fuses: a visual depiction of how a decision is defined in terms of cooperating Decision Tables linked by inferential dependencies; Decision Table structure and best practices (strongly influenced by the research of Jan Vanthienen); normal forms of logic by analogy to relational modeling and Decision Management best practices. This fusion yielded a notation, a set of principles and a method for decision modeling.

As Figure D-1 shows, the DMN notation is broadly a superset of that provided by TDM. Because DMN is just a notation not an approach, it lacks TDM's method and best practices. There is no doubt that many of these methodological elements are of huge benefit

---

[73] Some of the features added to TDM in the years since the last public version have been influenced by DMN (as evidenced by communication on the LinkedIn DMN group) and others, in turn, are unique to TDM and inspire change proposals to the DMN committee.

[74] Our thanks to Sapiens International Corporation Decision N.V. for providing information about TDM's recent evolution in private correspondence.

to decision modelers. Although DMN does not define a methodology for decision modeling, as the position of the text in Figure D-1 shows, it does offer some support for the structural, declarative and integrity principles of TDM.

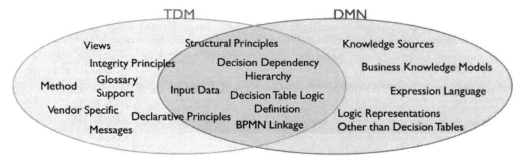

Figure D-1 Feature Comparison of TDM and DMN

D.2 Comparing TDM to DMN

Where TDM and DMN overlap they have broadly similar aims and the vast majority of differences between the two are cosmetic. Both are based on an underlying decision repository (a Decision Requirements Model), views of which are represented in a series of diagrams (see Section 8.1.7). Both offer a decision requirements notation depicting how decisions are decomposed into sub-decisions (TDM terms this *the Decision Model*) and both offer a tabular medium for decision logic definition (TDM calls this a *Rule Family View*). It's apparent that TDM has directly influenced DMN and the two have common notational roots. Furthermore, Sapiens have indicated that TDM's notation will acquire many of DMN features in future. Although DMN is a notation and does not (and cannot) address method or best practice, it is clear that much of TDM's methodological wisdom can be applied using DMN.

D.2.1 Decision Requirements Level

TDM Concept	DMN Concept	See
-	Annotation	8.1.4
Decision Repository	Decision Requirements Model—DRM	8.1.7
Community (a hierarchical subset of a decision repository)	-	-
Context Diagram	Decision Requirements Diagram—DRD	8.1
Context Diagram	Decision Requirement Diagram View	14.3.2
Decision Rule Family	Top level decision (Subject)	6.3.3
Decision View (Octagon and Rule Family View hierarchy)	Decision Service	8.1.6
Glossary	-	9
Fact Type	Information Item	8.1.2

Inferential Relationship	Information Requirement	8.1.5
Iteration (Repeating Groups)	-	-
Rule Family	Decision	8.1.1
View	-	-
-	Authority Requirement	8.1.5
-	Business Knowledge Model	11.1.1
-	Knowledge Source	8.1.3
-	Knowledge Requirement	11.1.1.3

Table D-1 Comparison of TDM and DMN Requirements Level Terms

A comparison of key TDM and DMN terms is listed in Table D-1. Where one notation has a concept that the other lacks a '-' mark is shown in the column of the former notation. A TDM Decision View and its equivalent DMN Decision Requirements Diagram are shown in Figure D-2 and Figure D-3 respectively.

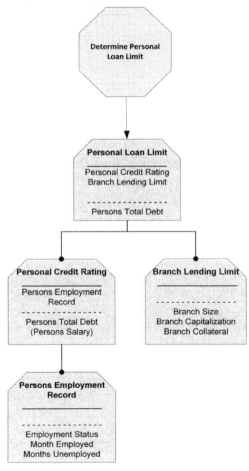

Figure D-2 TDM Personal Loan Limit Decision View

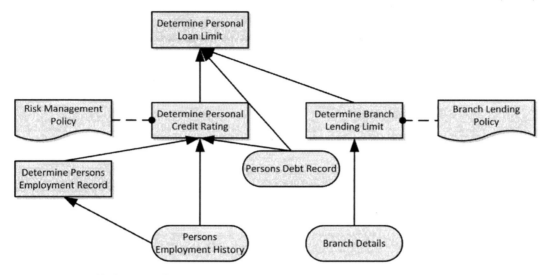

Figure D-3 Equivalent DMN Decision Requirements Diagram to Figure D-2

Notice how both notations:

- Denote a hierarchy of Information Requirements (inferential relationships) between decisions (Rule Families), showing graphically how subject decisions (Decision Rule Families) rely on sub-decisions and how each can be broken down into ever smaller components of decision-making.

- Show the data on which decisions depend. The TDM Decision View shows the Information Items (fact types) which each decision requires in the bottom compartments of the Rule Family 'tablets'. DMN can do the same (see Listed Mode in Section 8.1.2.2.). Dependencies on data needed to express conditions and those needed to calculate conclusions are shown explicitly by both notations.

- Allow decisions to be invoked from a business process model in BPMN (see Section D.2.2).

- Distinguish between a diagram and the underlying decision model repository. Every diagram depicts a view or subset of a model (see Section 8.1.7). Rule Families, like decisions, may appear in many diagrams providing the relationships they participate in are consistent (see Section 14.3.2).

The key differences are:

- DMN introduces the concept of Business Knowledge Model to support the parameterized reuse of decision logic. This is vitally important in promoting the consistent and flexible reapplication of sub-decisions across a decision model and in permitting the same logic to be applied to every member of a collection (iteration, see section 11.3.2.6). Parameterized reuse of Rule Families cannot currently be represented in TDM. However, TDM is capable of representing repeating groups (iteration) in its Rule Family Views and a variation of this useful feature is still being debated for DMN.

- DMN introduces the concept of Knowledge Sources to denote business authorities within the Decision Requirements Diagram and provide requirements traceability for decision models. These have no counterpart in TDM[75]. Although TDM tools often overcome this omission by using decision properties to hyperlink decisions to authorities and thereby provide traceability, this workaround does not permit the more advanced uses of Knowledge Models (see Section 15.2).

- DMN does not distinguish the subject decision in a Decision Requirements Diagram from others—either notationally or semantically—whereas TDM labels the top level Rule Family View of a Decision View with a special blue octagonal symbol. This special notation defines the equivalent of a DMN decision service and impacts TDM's relationship with the business process model (as shown in Section D.2.2). In TDM, only a Decision View, annotated by a blue octagon, can be associated with a decision task, while in DMN any decision can be associated with any decision task (see Section 10.2.3).

- DMN has a graphically richer version of the Decision Service construct supported by TDM. Whereas TDM defines all details of the interface using a Decision View, DMN allows the full interface of the Decision Service, including public and private sections, to be shown graphically.

- DMN has no concept of 'View' of a Decision Model or Rule Family. TDM uses views to show an alternative, context-specific definitions of the logic hierarchy (e.g., flavors of the decision logic to address jurisdictional, product or customer oriented specifics). This is useful for compactly representing a set of logical variations of a single decision.

- DMN lacks the concept of 'Community'. In TDM, this represents a federated and hierarchical subset of a decision repository aligned to a specific purpose or audience. This is used to support larger team collaboration in decision modeling.

- DMN has much less explicit support for the TDM glossary concept (see chapter 9). In TDM, the provision of a glossary is essential for all decision models.

- DMN does not explicitly list decisions' conditions within the top compartment of the decision symbol on a Decision Requirement Diagram. The conditions appear only in associated decision logic definitions.

- DMN can represent required data as a relationship between decisions and Input Data components on the Decision Requirement Diagram. This is useful because it gives a visual indication of the pattern of dependencies on Input Data. TDM is unable to do this.

- Whereas DMN decisions can be associated with Decision Tables, analytic models, optimization models, text, examples or even left unspecified; TDM Rule Families can currently be associated only with a Decision Table logic definition.

---

[75] Sapiens has indicated us, in private communication, that there are plans to introduce this feature to TDM.

- DMN Decision Requirements Diagrams can associate decisions with text annotations. TDM does not currently support this facility[76].

There are also cosmetic differences of less importance:
- In TDM, the subordinate decision logic is depicted as a hierarchy of 'tablet' Rule Families; in DMN, all decisions are shown as rectangles.
- Although the relationships between Rule Families in TDM are equivalent to Information Requirement Relationships in DMN, the lines have different end shapes. Furthermore, these shapes are on the end associated with the Rule Family being depended on, which is the opposite polarity to DMN's arrows.

D.2.2 Relationship with Process Model

Both TDM and DMN allow a decision to be 'invoked' by a decision task in a BPMN business process. However, DMN and TDM have a different relationship with BPMN. TDM subordinates decision models to the business process; DMN does not.

In TDM, the business process represents an overall context in which individual decision tasks can be associated with specific *Decision Views*. An example relationship between a BPMN business process and a set of TDM decision views is shown in Figure D-4. The processes and decisions involved are explained in more detail in Sections 10.2.2.2 and 10.2.3. Each decision view is subordinate to the task in the business process model that invokes it. The decision view has a subset of the overall process scope defined by the task and each decision view must complete before the task is complete. As a result, a TDM decision model is a collection of many small decision views, each invoked by a decision task. These are integrated by the flow of a business process. A DMN decision model can support this approach but also allows a finer grain association of decision tasks and decisions (compare Figure D-4 with the DMN process integration in Figure D-5).

In DMN, a business process model and a business decision model may represent two views with the *same*, end-to-end scope: delivery of an ultimate business outcome (see Section 10.2.3), in this case the grant or denial of a mortgage. The DMN decision model shows the information and knowledge dependencies of decisions, the hierarchy of their structure and definition of declarative logic. The process model shows the sequence of activity, marshalling of data, the choreography of the entities involved and the automation boundary. The whole end-to-end business scope is the same, but individual decision tasks in a process model can be associated with decisions *at any level* in the same DMN DRD hierarchy, without having to denote them as decision services or subjects (see Figure D-5). A decision may be associated with any type of task, even user tasks, allowing DMN to reflect automated and non-automated decision logic.

---

[76] Sapiens has indicated to us, in private communication, that there are plans to introduce this feature to TDM.

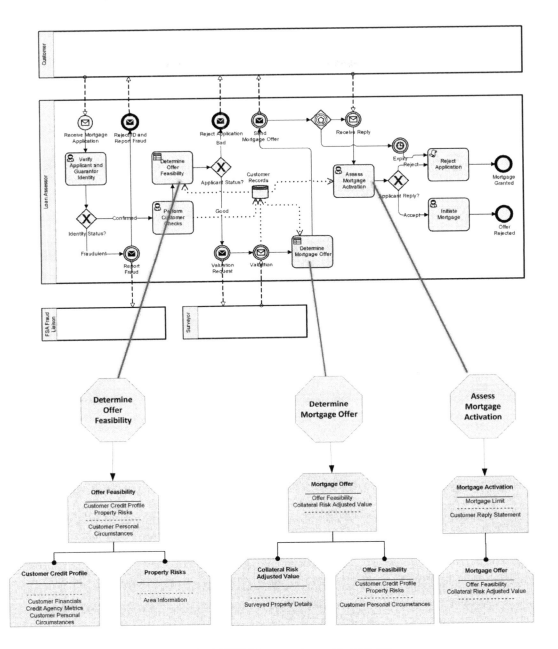

Figure D-4 TDM Integration with BPMN

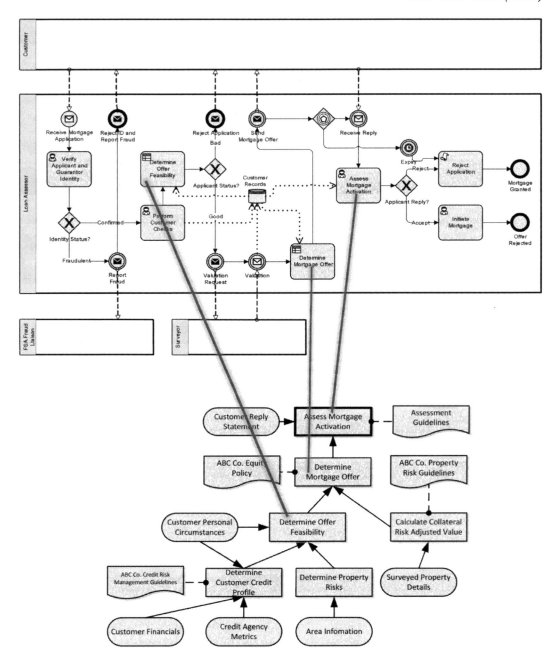

Figure D-5 DMN Integration with BPMN

D.2.3 Decision Logic Definition

TDM and DMN share many concepts in the definition of decision logic using Decision Tables. A list of equivalent terms can be found in Table D-2:

TDM Concept	DMN Concept	Reference
Conclusion	Output entry	8.2.1, B.3.3
Conclusion Fact Type	Output	8.2.1, B.3.3
Condition	Input entry	8.2.1, B.3.3
Condition Fact Type	Input expression (Input)	8.2.1, B.3.3
Empty condition	Irrelevant condition '-'	8.2.3.3
Fact Type	Information Item (Business Terms)	9.1
Iteration (Repeating Groups)	FEEL Iteration	11.3.2.6
Message	- (see Rule Level Annotation[77])	14.5.7, C.2.6.1
Operator	FEEL expression operator	8.2.3.1
Set Based Condition	-	C.2.1, C.2.2
Rule Family View	Decision Table	8.2.1
Rule Pattern	-	-
-	Default	8.2.3.7
-	Empty condition	8.2.3.4
- (determined by condition operator)	Hit Policy	8.2.4
'No Action' Conclusion	Irrelevant conclusion	8.2.4.1
-	Merged conditions	8.2.3.5
-	Value list	8.2.3.6

Table D-2 Comparison of TDM and DMN Logic Level Terms

A TDM Rule Family and its equivalent Decision Table are shown in Figure D-6 and Figure D-7 respectively. The similarity of these expressions is evident. Although there are minor cosmetic differences, both notations:

- Support a logic definition notation in which decision logic can be represented as Decision Tables in a 'rules as rows' format.
- Specify a set of structural principles (see Section B.3.3) that regulates how Decision Tables are used (although TDM is much more explicit about their definition).

---

[77] DMN has no formal support for the Message concept. Rule level annotation is an addition we propose to the DMN standard.

Personal Credit Rating (View: Base)

		Conditions				Conclusion		Messages	
Row ID	Rule Pattern	Personal Employment Record		Persons Total Debt		Personal Credit Rating		Message	
1	1	is	GOOD	<=	Persons Salary * 4	is	AAA	**PCR 2.1.1** all investments grade	
2	1	is	GOOD	>	Persons Salary * 4	is	AA	**PCR 2.1.2** minimal control grade, employed egress	
3	1	is	AVERAGE	<=	Persons Salary * 2	is	A	**PCR 3.1** controlled debt grade; save egress	
4	1	is	AVERAGE	>	Persons Salary * 2	is	B	**PCR 3.2** moderate control; additional safeguard needed	
5	2	is	POOR			is	C	**PCR 4.1** and **5.5** refuse direct dealing	

Figure D-6 TDM Personal Credit Rating Rule Family View

Personal Credit Rating			
U	**Persons Employment Record**	**Persons Total Debt / Persons Annual**	**Personal Credit Rating**
	GOOD , AVERAGE , POOR	*>0*	*C , B , A , AA , AAA*
1	*GOOD*	<= 4.0	*AAA*
2		> 4.0	*AA*
3	*AVERAGE*	<= 2.0	*A*
4		> 2.0	*B*
5	*POOR*	-	*C*

Figure D-7 DMN Equivalent of Figure D-6

Key differences include:

- DMN supports representations of logic other than Decision Tables such as textual rules, examples, analytic models and boxed expressions (See Sections 11.3 and 14.4.4). It can also support other representations outside the standard.

- DMN supports a wider variety of Decision Table formats (see Section 11.2.7) whereas TDM supports only the 'rules as rows' format.

- DMN's Decision Table notation introduces new concepts such as defaults and merging (see items in Table D-2 beginning '-').

- DMN has no equivalent of the TDM 'Message' concept; these are additional conclusion columns that allow metadata to be associated with outcomes. TDM uses messages to adorn rules with explanatory comments, to provide analytic metadata and to hierarchically construct a data structure that explains the outcome of a Decision View.

- DMN requires the hit policy of a Decision Table to be specified explicitly[78] and supports several different hit policies to control the behavior of Decision Tables. TDM asserts an implicit hit policy of *Any* or *Collect with Aggregation* for single outcomes or *Collect* for multiple outcomes. TDM's conclusion operator ('is', 'is incremented by' and 'is appended with' respectively) reflects which of these hit policies is being used in each table. Currently the only aggregation TDM supports is

---

[78] Albeit using a somewhat cryptic letter code.

summation, which is broadly equivalent to DMN's 'C+' hit policy.

- DMN does not support conditions using set based operators (e.g., it has no equivalent of the TDM operator 'contains any') (see Section C.2.1 and C.2.2).

- DMN does not support the TDM notion of rule pattern.

- TDM and DMN conditions are different in content. A TDM condition header is an Information Item and each (non-blank) condition holds an operator (equality, inequality, set membership, string match and other operators are supported) and an operand expression. In DMN the condition header can be an expression, but conditions are simple equalities or inequalities with literal values or variables; expressions are not allowed (see Section C.2.1). The examples in Figure D-6 and Figure D-7 show the consequences of these differences.

- DMN requires that every cell of a Decision Table is explicitly filled with a condition. A blank entry indicates the table is not yet complete. In TDM, a blank entry indicates an irrelevant condition; DMN uses the explicit notation '-' to represent this.

- DMN introduces the notation of value lists to constrain the values of inputs and outputs within a Decision Table and to support the Priority hit policy. This permits constraints to be specific to a given Decision Table. TDM defines enumerated fact types with constrained values in a glossary forcing the constraint to be consistent across all Rule Families using a given fact type (which can be an advantage). Furthermore, it does not use the Priority hit policy.

- Although TDM defines a set of operators for use in Decision Table conditions, it does not define the cell contents rigorously. Unlike TDM, DMN is underpinned by a precisely defined expression language: FEEL (see Sections B.4-6). This provides a more formal basis for expressions in Decision Tables and a precise textual medium for defining logic.

Again, there are minor cosmetic differences between the two notations, for example, the clear text column demarcation between conditions and conclusions in the TDM representation versus the (less clear) use of double lines in the DMN equivalent. Furthermore, TDM separates operator and operands in all table cells but DMN does not.

D.2.4 Using TDM Principles in DMN

TDM defines a set of 15 principles for decision modeling, many of which can be applied using DMN. TDM's declarative and integrity principles represent an approach to modeling which exceeds the scope of a notation definition like DMN, but which can still be very useful when applying DMN.

D.2.4.1 Structural principles

TDM's structural principles (1-7) concern the representation of tabular logic and all except principle 5 are preserved in DMN. Principles 1 ('tabular') and 4 ('row') establish a means of using Decision Tables to express logic; this is compatible with DMN. Principle 7 ('connection') establishes dependency relationships between decisions so that the outcomes of one decision can be used as the inputs of dependents—this is directly applicable to Information Requirement Relationships in DMN. The other structural principles have some differences:

- Principle 2 ('heading') defines the meaning of table headers. DMN allows Decision Table condition headings to be expressions, not just Information Items (Fact Types) as they are in TDM.

- Principle 3 ('cell') defines the contents of table condition cells. DMN allows only equalities and inequalities with literals or variables in its condition cells (*unary tests*, see Section B.5.4)—not operators and operand expressions as TDM does. The condition '< `Persons Salary *4.0`' is legal in TDM but not in DMN. The example in Figure D-6 works around this limitation by deriving the ratio in the Input Expression and testing the value of this.

- TDM's first normal form is part of principle 4 that demands that no row in a Decision Table should be capable of being refactored into more than one row. This is hard to violate in DMN, because the standard does not support 'or' conditions. One can break first normal form in DMN by using the First hit policy to implement 'else' and 'otherwise' (see Section 14.5.4). First normal form should be upheld in DMN by avoiding these practices, except when clarity of expression demands it.

- Principle 5 ('conclusion') allows TDM Decision Tables to have only one conclusion. This constraint is relaxed in DMN although there are many good reasons for upholding TDM's restriction and using this freedom of DMN sparingly (see Section 15.3.4). TDM allows one or more messages to be specified as auxiliary outputs of a Rule Family, but these are for debugging, explanation, conclusion metadata and traceability purposes and are not meant as additional conclusions.

- Principle 6 ('conditions') requires that all the conditions in a rule need to be satisfied in order to yield the accompanying outcome and stipulates how rule patterns are used. DMN mostly supports this but does not explicitly support rule patterns.

- TDM's second normal form, part of principle 6 that ensures that all conditions are relevant to the conclusion, should be a best practice when using DMN but is not mandated by the notation. Conditions in a DMN Decision Table that are redundant and have no role in determining the conclusion should be removed (see Section 14.5.3).

D.2.4.2 Declarative Principles

DMN does <u>not</u> explicitly address TDM's declarative principles (8-10). Principles 8 ('declarative heading') and 9 ('declarative body') forbid any implied meaning for the ordering of condition columns and rule rows in a Rule Family. Similarly, principle 10 ('declarative inferential relationship') forbids any implicit semantics for the top-to-bottom or left-to-right ordering of decisions in decision views They all dictate that shuffling the order of Decision Table inputs, Decision Table rules and Decision placement should have no impact on the meaning of a decision model. Principles 8 and 10 should be adopted as best practices (see Sections 15.3.1.1 and 14.8.4 respectively). These are neither explicitly mentioned nor contradicted by DMN's definition of Decision Requirements or Decision Tables; however, DMN's absence of side effects (see Section 8.2.4.3) partially supports these principles. Furthermore, principle 9 is upheld by the DMN Decision Table definition when using the *Unique*, *Any* or *Collect* hit policy (see Section 15.3.1.2). This is one of the reasons these hit policies are generally preferred. The *First* hit policy violates this principle which is why its use should be avoided.

D.2.4.3 Integrity Principles

DMN does <u>not</u> explicitly address the TDM integrity principles (11-14). Principle 15 ('business alignment') is directly supported in DMN because decisions can be linked to Objectives, Tasks and Processes (see Section 14.2.3 and 14.2.5). The remaining TDM integrity principles, discussed below, should remain best practices when using DMN:

- Principle 11 ('rule pattern transitive conditions') ensures that no condition in a Rule Family depends on any other. It includes the third normal form which forbids the appearance of conditions that can clearly be derived from others. The derivation of these derived conclusions should be addressed explicitly in another Decision Table.

- Principle 12 ('Rule Family consistency') demands that there are no overlaps in the logic of the rules in a Rule Family. This is the best practice for Unique and Any hit policies. It also asserts that at least one conclusion value must result for any set of valid input values. This is the equivalent of the DMN concept of completeness (see Section 8.2.4.2)—there must be no gaps in the logic of a Rule Family.

- Principle 14 ('inferential integrity') enforces the following restrictions on any sub-decision that provides an outcome that is used as a condition in a dependent decision: that the values of the outcome are consistent with the conditions imposed and the range of possible values the outcome can hold are all handled by the dependent decision (see Section 14.8.3).

TDM's principles convey a wealth of best practices that are mostly directly applicable to DMN decision models. Principle 13 ('Rule Family transitive') is an exception. This states that two direct sub-decisions of a specified decision should have no dependencies between them as illustrated in Figure D-8. This is good practice; however, unconditionally adhering to this restriction is often impractical in real engagements. Correcting it requires considerable refactoring of the model and the results of this exercise are often less intuitive for business experts. The consequences of transitive dependencies are seldom serious so this principle should be upheld as an ideal but **not as a best practice**.

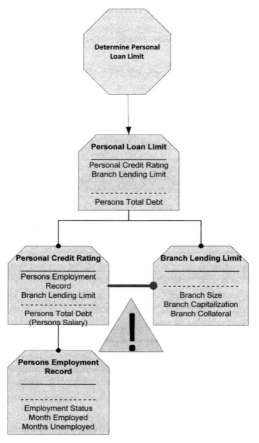

Figure D-8 Example of Transitive Rule Family Dependency Forbidden by TDM Principle 13

D.3 Pitfalls For TDM Users Moving to DMN

Experience with TDM is a strong advantage for any modeler building DMN decision models. The differences between the two are sometimes more significant than they might appear and should not be underestimated. Consequently, experienced TDM practitioners must avoid certain pitfalls when migrating to DMN.

D.3.1 Forgetting to use new DMN concepts where appropriate

Be careful not to omit Knowledge Sources just because they are not related to implementation. They document the origin of local expertise, policies or externally enforced constraints imposed by laws, regulations and mandates. They are a useful means of making models more traceable. TDM focuses solely on executable models of decision logic and so has no equivalent concept.

Also be aware of using Business Knowledge Models to represent reuse as there is no equivalent implementation concept in TDM. When transferring TDM decision models to

DMN, any workarounds used to achieve parameterized reuse of decisions or functions will need to be converted to Business Knowledge Models.

D.3.2 Producing many narrowly scoped decision models

DMN and TDM have a slightly different relationship with BPMN (see Section D.2.2). New users of DMN, familiar with TDM, may make the mistake of perpetuating TDM's concept that decision models are subordinate to business processes and therefore have a narrower scope. This misunderstanding will manifest itself as a set of narrow decision models with outcomes that serve the specific needs of a decision task rather than significant outcomes that are directly visible to business operations or the client. It is important with DMN to ensure the decision model's scope often equals that of the entire process model and that both explain a path to an ultimate outcome (see Section 10.2.3.5).

D.3.3 Failing to consider logic representations other than Decision Tables

Unlike TDM, DMN decision logic can be described using text, example rules, analytic models, optimization models, Java callouts or even left undefined. Although it is not mandatory, TDM is disposed to define every decision using a Decision Table. Newcomers to DMN sometime feel compelled to define every decision with a table (see misconception in Section 13.1) or to remove decisions that will not be inside the automation boundary (an approach TDM tends to favor).

D.3.4 Overwhelming decision models with Data Inputs

TDM depicts the data dependencies of decisions by listing them within the Rule Family 'tablet' symbol. The top compartment denotes fact types outcomes of sub-decisions and the bottom compartment shows fact types of raw input data. The latter consists of Information Items that correspond to individual data attributes required to reach a decision.

In DMN, data dependencies of decisions are denoted as Information Requirements Relationships linking Input Data symbols (rounded rectangles) to Decisions. Although Input Data can represent individual data attributes, they more commonly represent data entities that each have many attributes. The association of entities and attributes is defined in the glossary or data model supporting the decision model. Representing each individual data attribute as an Input Data and linking it to Decisions with Information Requirements Relationships quickly overloads real Decision Requirement Diagrams and compromises their clarity. Therefore, in DMN, it is best practice to show Information Requirements Relationships on composite entities to prevent this when a decision has an existing data dependency on many attributes from the same entity (however see Section 14.7.5).

D.4 In Conclusion

Prior experience with TDM is a huge benefit for any decision modeler. The best practices and principles that TDM provides are effective pre-requisites for rigorous and accomplished decision modeling and, providing they heed the warnings above, TDM will provide modelers with a solid foundation for building valuable decision models.

About The Authors

JAMES TAYLOR has been focused on Decision Management for the last 14 years – since he first came up with the phrase – and he is almost certainly the best known proponent of the approach. While working at FICO he wrote a book on the topic with Neil Raden. Since then he has written Decision Management Systems: A Practical Guide to Using Business Rules and Predictive Analytics (IBM Press, 2012), dozens of articles and white papers and several book chapters expanding and developing the core concepts. One of the original submitters of the Decision Model and Notation standard, he has been using decision modeling on client projects since 2011. He has designed and written effective development methodologies and developed several modeling tools, including one based on DMN - DecisionsFirst Modeler. As the founder and CEO of Decision Management Solutions, he works with clients to help them implement Decision Management and Decision Modeling as well with vendors who are adopting Decision Management as an approach that maximizes the value of their products.

JAN PURCHASE has been working in investment banking for 19 years, the last 13 of which he has focused exclusively on the use of business decisions, decision modeling (TDM and DMN), business rules, business rule management systems (BRMS) and business process modeling. He is a founder of Lux Magi Financial Rules (LMFR), a company specializing in delivering the benefits of all of these concepts to financial organizations, as well as providing training and mentoring in their use. All of LMFR's clients have benefited from the adoption of decision modeling; one international initiative included a set of fourteen separate decision modeling projects trained and mentored by LMFR. Jan has maintained a blog 'Decision Management for Finance' since 2010 highlighting the practical lessons learned from applying decision modeling and BRMS at scale and providing useful feedback to LMFR's clients and vendor partners. He has published many white papers, hosted multiple webinars and chaired several public coaching sessions on the application of decision modeling and BRMS to problems in finance. Lux Magi has been applying TDM and, more recently DMN, to finance and regulatory compliance projects since 2011.

Companion Books from Meghan-Kiffer Press

The Business Transformation Field Guide

Digital Transformation
Innovate ... or Die Slowly

Cognitive Computing
A Brief Guide for Game Changers

Business Architecture
The Art and Practice of Business Transformation

Dot Cloud
The 21st Century business Platform Built on Cloud Computing

Business Innovation in the Cloud
Strategies for Executing on Innovation with Cloud Computing

Serious Games for Business
Using Gamification to Fully Engage Customers, Employees and Partners

Value Networks
And the True Nature of Collaboration

Smart Process Apps
The Next Breakout Business Advantage

Human Interactions
The Heart and Soul of Business Process Management

Enterprise Cloud Computing
A Strategy Guide for Business and Technology Leaders

Extreme Competition
Innovation and the Great 21st Century Business Reformation

Business Process Management
The Third Wave (The Classic BPM book!)

Business Process Management
The Next Wave

Mastering the Unpredictable
How Adaptive Case Management Will Revolutionize
the Way That Knowledge Workers Get Things Done

See more at...

www.mkpress.com

Innovation at the Intersection of Business and Technology